P9-CJK-972

Hands-On Machine Learning with Scikit-Learn and TensorFlow

Concepts, Tools, and Techniques to Build Intelligent Systems

Aurélien Géron

Beijing · Boston · Farnham · Sebastopol · Tokyo

Hands-On Machine Learning with Scikit-Learn and TensorFlow

by Aurélien Géron

Copyright © 2017 Aurélien Géron. All rights reserved.

Printed in the United States of America.

Published by O'Reilly Media, Inc., 1005 Gravenstein Highway North, Sebastopol, CA 95472.

O'Reilly books may be purchased for educational, business, or sales promotional use. Online editions are also available for most titles (*http://oreilly.com/safari*). For more information, contact our corporate/institutional sales department: 800-998-9938 or *corporate@oreilly.com*.

Editor: Nicole Tache	**Indexer:** Wendy Catalano
Production Editor: Nicholas Adams	**Interior Designer:** David Futato
Copyeditor: Rachel Monaghan	**Cover Designer:** Randy Comer
Proofreader: Charles Roumeliotis	**Illustrator:** Rebecca Demarest

March 2017:   First Edition

Revision History for the First Edition

2017-03-10:	First Release
2017-06-09:	Second Release
2017-08-18:	Third Release
2017-11-03:	Fourth Release
2018-01-19:	Fifth Release
2018-06-22:	Sixth Release
2018-07-20:	Seventh Release
2018-08-24:	Eighth Release
2018-10-12:	Ninth Release

See *http://oreilly.com/catalog/errata.csp?isbn=9781491962299* for release details.

The O'Reilly logo is a registered trademark of O'Reilly Media, Inc. *Hands-On Machine Learning with Scikit-Learn and TensorFlow*, the cover image, and related trade dress are trademarks of O'Reilly Media, Inc.

While the publisher and the author have used good faith efforts to ensure that the information and instructions contained in this work are accurate, the publisher and the author disclaim all responsibility for errors or omissions, including without limitation responsibility for damages resulting from the use of or reliance on this work. Use of the information and instructions contained in this work is at your own risk. If any code samples or other technology this work contains or describes is subject to open source licenses or the intellectual property rights of others, it is your responsibility to ensure that your use thereof complies with such licenses and/or rights.

978-1-491-96229-9

[GP]

Table of Contents

Part II. Neural Networks and Deep Learning

Preface

The Machine Learning Tsunami

In 2006, Geoffrey Hinton et al. published a paper[1] showing how to train a deep neural network capable of recognizing handwritten digits with state-of-the-art precision (>98%). They branded this technique "Deep Learning." Training a deep neural net was widely considered impossible at the time,[2] and most researchers had abandoned the idea since the 1990s. This paper revived the interest of the scientific community and before long many new papers demonstrated that Deep Learning was not only possible, but capable of mind-blowing achievements that no other Machine Learning (ML) technique could hope to match (with the help of tremendous computing power and great amounts of data). This enthusiasm soon extended to many other areas of Machine Learning.

Fast-forward 10 years and Machine Learning has conquered the industry: it is now at the heart of much of the magic in today's high-tech products, ranking your web search results, powering your smartphone's speech recognition, recommending videos, and beating the world champion at the game of Go. Before you know it, it will be driving your car.

Machine Learning in Your Projects

So naturally you are excited about Machine Learning and you would love to join the party!

Perhaps you would like to give your homemade robot a brain of its own? Make it recognize faces? Or learn to walk around?

---

1 Available on Hinton's home page at *http://www.cs.toronto.edu/~hinton/*.

2 Despite the fact that Yann Lecun's deep convolutional neural networks had worked well for image recognition since the 1990s, although they were not as general purpose.

Or maybe your company has tons of data (user logs, financial data, production data, machine sensor data, hotline stats, HR reports, etc.), and more than likely you could unearth some hidden gems if you just knew where to look; for example:

- Segment customers and find the best marketing strategy for each group
- Recommend products for each client based on what similar clients bought
- Detect which transactions are likely to be fraudulent
- Predict next year's revenue
- And more (*https://www.kaggle.com/wiki/DataScienceUseCases*)

Whatever the reason, you have decided to learn Machine Learning and implement it in your projects. Great idea!

Objective and Approach

This book assumes that you know close to nothing about Machine Learning. Its goal is to give you the concepts, the intuitions, and the tools you need to actually implement programs capable of *learning from data*.

We will cover a large number of techniques, from the simplest and most commonly used (such as linear regression) to some of the Deep Learning techniques that regularly win competitions.

Rather than implementing our own toy versions of each algorithm, we will be using actual production-ready Python frameworks:

- Scikit-Learn (*http://scikit-learn.org/*) is very easy to use, yet it implements many Machine Learning algorithms efficiently, so it makes for a great entry point to learn Machine Learning.
- TensorFlow (*http://tensorflow.org/*) is a more complex library for distributed numerical computation using data flow graphs. It makes it possible to train and run very large neural networks efficiently by distributing the computations across potentially thousands of multi-GPU servers. TensorFlow was created at Google and supports many of their large-scale Machine Learning applications. It was open-sourced in November 2015.

The book favors a hands-on approach, growing an intuitive understanding of Machine Learning through concrete working examples and just a little bit of theory. While you can read this book without picking up your laptop, we highly recommend you experiment with the code examples available online as Jupyter notebooks at *https://github.com/ageron/handson-ml*.

Prerequisites

This book assumes that you have some Python programming experience and that you are familiar with Python's main scientific libraries, in particular NumPy (*http://numpy.org/*), Pandas (*http://pandas.pydata.org/*), and Matplotlib (*http://matplotlib.org/*).

Also, if you care about what's under the hood you should have a reasonable understanding of college-level math as well (calculus, linear algebra, probabilities, and statistics).

If you don't know Python yet, *http://learnpython.org/* is a great place to start. The official tutorial on python.org (*https://docs.python.org/3/tutorial/*) is also quite good.

If you have never used Jupyter, Chapter 2 will guide you through installation and the basics: it is a great tool to have in your toolbox.

If you are not familiar with Python's scientific libraries, the provided Jupyter notebooks include a few tutorials. There is also a quick math tutorial for linear algebra.

Roadmap

This book is organized in two parts. Part I, *The Fundamentals of Machine Learning*, covers the following topics:

- What is Machine Learning? What problems does it try to solve? What are the main categories and fundamental concepts of Machine Learning systems?
- The main steps in a typical Machine Learning project.
- Learning by fitting a model to data.
- Optimizing a cost function.
- Handling, cleaning, and preparing data.
- Selecting and engineering features.
- Selecting a model and tuning hyperparameters using cross-validation.
- The main challenges of Machine Learning, in particular underfitting and overfitting (the bias/variance tradeoff).
- Reducing the dimensionality of the training data to fight the curse of dimensionality.
- The most common learning algorithms: Linear and Polynomial Regression, Logistic Regression, k-Nearest Neighbors, Support Vector Machines, Decision Trees, Random Forests, and Ensemble methods.

Part II, *Neural Networks and Deep Learning*, covers the following topics:

- What are neural nets? What are they good for?
- Building and training neural nets using TensorFlow.
- The most important neural net architectures: feedforward neural nets, convolutional nets, recurrent nets, long short-term memory (LSTM) nets, and autoencoders.
- Techniques for training deep neural nets.
- Scaling neural networks for huge datasets.
- Reinforcement learning.

The first part is based mostly on Scikit-Learn while the second part uses TensorFlow.

 Don't jump into deep waters too hastily: while Deep Learning is no doubt one of the most exciting areas in Machine Learning, you should master the fundamentals first. Moreover, most problems can be solved quite well using simpler techniques such as Random Forests and Ensemble methods (discussed in Part I). Deep Learning is best suited for complex problems such as image recognition, speech recognition, or natural language processing, provided you have enough data, computing power, and patience.

Other Resources

Many resources are available to learn about Machine Learning. Andrew Ng's ML course on Coursera (*https://www.coursera.org/learn/machine-learning/*) and Geoffrey Hinton's course on neural networks and Deep Learning (*https://www.coursera.org/course/neuralnets*) are amazing, although they both require a significant time investment (think months).

There are also many interesting websites about Machine Learning, including of course Scikit-Learn's exceptional User Guide (*http://scikit-learn.org/stable/user_guide.html*). You may also enjoy Dataquest (*https://www.dataquest.io/*), which provides very nice interactive tutorials, and ML blogs such as those listed on Quora (*http://homl.info/1*). Finally, the Deep Learning website (*http://deeplearning.net/*) has a good list of resources to learn more.

Of course there are also many other introductory books about Machine Learning, in particular:

- Joel Grus, *Data Science from Scratch* (O'Reilly). This book presents the fundamentals of Machine Learning, and implements some of the main algorithms in pure Python (from scratch, as the name suggests).

- Stephen Marsland, *Machine Learning: An Algorithmic Perspective* (Chapman and Hall). This book is a great introduction to Machine Learning, covering a wide range of topics in depth, with code examples in Python (also from scratch, but using NumPy).

- Sebastian Raschka, *Python Machine Learning* (Packt Publishing). Also a great introduction to Machine Learning, this book leverages Python open source libraries (Pylearn 2 and Theano).

- Yaser S. Abu-Mostafa, Malik Magdon-Ismail, and Hsuan-Tien Lin, *Learning from Data* (AMLBook). A rather theoretical approach to ML, this book provides deep insights, in particular on the bias/variance tradeoff (see Chapter 4).

- Stuart Russell and Peter Norvig, *Artificial Intelligence: A Modern Approach, 3rd Edition* (Pearson). This is a great (and huge) book covering an incredible amount of topics, including Machine Learning. It helps put ML into perspective.

Finally, a great way to learn is to join ML competition websites such as Kaggle.com this will allow you to practice your skills on real-world problems, with help and insights from some of the best ML professionals out there.

Conventions Used in This Book

The following typographical conventions are used in this book:

Italic
Indicates new terms, URLs, email addresses, filenames, and file extensions.

`Constant width`
Used for program listings, as well as within paragraphs to refer to program elements such as variable or function names, databases, data types, environment variables, statements and keywords.

`Constant width bold`
Shows commands or other text that should be typed literally by the user.

`Constant width italic`
Shows text that should be replaced with user-supplied values or by values determined by context.

 This element signifies a tip or suggestion.

This element signifies a general note.

 This element indicates a warning or caution.

Using Code Examples

Supplemental material (code examples, exercises, etc.) is available for download at *https://github.com/ageron/handson-ml*.

This book is here to help you get your job done. In general, if example code is offered with this book, you may use it in your programs and documentation. You do not need to contact us for permission unless you're reproducing a significant portion of the code. For example, writing a program that uses several chunks of code from this book does not require permission. Selling or distributing a CD-ROM of examples from O'Reilly books does require permission. Answering a question by citing this book and quoting example code does not require permission. Incorporating a significant amount of example code from this book into your product's documentation does require permission.

We appreciate, but do not require, attribution. An attribution usually includes the title, author, publisher, and ISBN. For example: *"Hands-On Machine Learning with Scikit-Learn and TensorFlow* by Aurélien Géron (O'Reilly). Copyright 2017 Aurélien Géron, 978-1-491-96229-9."

If you feel your use of code examples falls outside fair use or the permission given above, feel free to contact us at *permissions@oreilly.com*.

O'Reilly Safari

 *Safari* (formerly Safari Books Online) is a membership-based training and reference platform for enterprise, government, educators, and individuals.

Members have access to thousands of books, training videos, Learning Paths, interactive tutorials, and curated playlists from over 250 publishers, including O'Reilly Media, Harvard Business Review, Prentice Hall Professional, Addison-Wesley Professional, Microsoft Press, Sams, Que, Peachpit Press, Adobe, Focal Press, Cisco Press,

John Wiley & Sons, Syngress, Morgan Kaufmann, IBM Redbooks, Packt, Adobe Press, FT Press, Apress, Manning, New Riders, McGraw-Hill, Jones & Bartlett, and Course Technology, among others.

For more information, please visit *http://oreilly.com/safari*.

How to Contact Us

Please address comments and questions concerning this book to the publisher:

O'Reilly Media, Inc.
1005 Gravenstein Highway North
Sebastopol, CA 95472
800-998-9938 (in the United States or Canada)
707-829-0515 (international or local)
707-829-0104 (fax)

We have a web page for this book, where we list errata, examples, and any additional information. You can access this page at *http://bit.ly/hands-on-machine-learning-with-scikit-learn-and-tensorflow*.

To comment or ask technical questions about this book, send email to *bookquestions@oreilly.com*.

For more information about our books, courses, conferences, and news, see our website at *http://www.oreilly.com*.

Find us on Facebook: *http://facebook.com/oreilly*

Follow us on Twitter: *http://twitter.com/oreillymedia*

Watch us on YouTube: *http://www.youtube.com/oreillymedia*

Acknowledgments

I would like to thank my Google colleagues, in particular the YouTube video classification team, for teaching me so much about Machine Learning. I could never have started this project without them. Special thanks to my personal ML gurus: Clément Courbet, Julien Dubois, Mathias Kende, Daniel Kitachewsky, James Pack, Alexander Pak, Anosh Raj, Vitor Sessak, Wiktor Tomczak, Ingrid von Glehn, Rich Washington, and everyone at YouTube Paris.

I am incredibly grateful to all the amazing people who took time out of their busy lives to review my book in so much detail. Thanks to Pete Warden for answering all my TensorFlow questions, reviewing Part II, providing many interesting insights, and of course for being part of the core TensorFlow team. You should definitely check out his blog (*https://petewarden.com/*)! Many thanks to Lukas Biewald for his very thorough review of Part II: he left no stone unturned, tested all the code (and caught a few errors), made many great suggestions, and his enthusiasm was contagious. You should check out his blog (*https://lukasbiewald.com/*) and his cool robots (*http://homl.info/2*)! Thanks to Justin Francis, who also reviewed Part II very thoroughly, catching errors and providing great insights, in particular in Chapter 16. Check out his posts (*http://homl.info/3*) on TensorFlow!

Huge thanks as well to David Andrzejewski, who reviewed Part I and provided incredibly useful feedback, identifying unclear sections and suggesting how to improve them. Check out his website (*http://www.david-andrzejewski.com/*)! Thanks to Grégoire Mesnil, who reviewed Part II and contributed very interesting practical advice on training neural networks. Thanks as well to Eddy Hung, Salim Sémaoune, Karim Matrah, Ingrid von Glehn, Iain Smears, and Vincent Guilbeau for reviewing Part I and making many useful suggestions. And I also wish to thank my father-in-law, Michel Tessier, former mathematics teacher and now a great translator of Anton Chekhov, for helping me iron out some of the mathematics and notations in this book and reviewing the linear algebra Jupyter notebook.

And of course, a gigantic "thank you" to my dear brother Sylvain, who reviewed every single chapter, tested every line of code, provided feedback on virtually every section, and encouraged me from the first line to the last. Love you, bro!

Many thanks as well to O'Reilly's fantastic staff, in particular Nicole Tache, who gave me insightful feedback, always cheerful, encouraging, and helpful. Thanks as well to Marie Beaugureau, Ben Lorica, Mike Loukides, and Laurel Ruma for believing in this project and helping me define its scope. Thanks to Matt Hacker and all of the Atlas team for answering all my technical questions regarding formatting, asciidoc, and LaTeX, and thanks to Rachel Monaghan, Nick Adams, and all of the production team for their final review and their hundreds of corrections.

Last but not least, I am infinitely grateful to my beloved wife, Emmanuelle, and to our three wonderful kids, Alexandre, Rémi, and Gabrielle, for encouraging me to work hard on this book, asking many questions (who said you can't teach neural networks to a seven-year-old?), and even bringing me cookies and coffee. What more can one dream of?

## PART I

The Fundamentals of Machine Learning

CHAPTER 1
The Machine Learning Landscape

When most people hear "Machine Learning," they picture a robot: a dependable butler or a deadly Terminator depending on who you ask. But Machine Learning is not just a futuristic fantasy, it's already here. In fact, it has been around for decades in some specialized applications, such as *Optical Character Recognition* (OCR). But the first ML application that really became mainstream, improving the lives of hundreds of millions of people, took over the world back in the 1990s: it was the *spam filter*. Not exactly a self-aware Skynet, but it does technically qualify as Machine Learning (it has actually learned so well that you seldom need to flag an email as spam anymore). It was followed by hundreds of ML applications that now quietly power hundreds of products and features that you use regularly, from better recommendations to voice search.

Where does Machine Learning start and where does it end? What exactly does it mean for a machine to *learn* something? If I download a copy of Wikipedia, has my computer really "learned" something? Is it suddenly smarter? In this chapter we will start by clarifying what Machine Learning is and why you may want to use it.

Then, before we set out to explore the Machine Learning continent, we will take a look at the map and learn about the main regions and the most notable landmarks: supervised versus unsupervised learning, online versus batch learning, instance-based versus model-based learning. Then we will look at the workflow of a typical ML project, discuss the main challenges you may face, and cover how to evaluate and fine-tune a Machine Learning system.

This chapter introduces a lot of fundamental concepts (and jargon) that every data scientist should know by heart. It will be a high-level overview (the only chapter without much code), all rather simple, but you should make sure everything is crystal-clear to you before continuing to the rest of the book. So grab a coffee and let's get started!

If you already know all the Machine Learning basics, you may want to skip directly to Chapter 2. If you are not sure, try to answer all the questions listed at the end of the chapter before moving on.

What Is Machine Learning?

Machine Learning is the science (and art) of programming computers so they can *learn from data*.

Here is a slightly more general definition:

> [Machine Learning is the] field of study that gives computers the ability to learn without being explicitly programmed.
>
> —Arthur Samuel, *1959*

And a more engineering-oriented one:

> A computer program is said to learn from experience E with respect to some task T and some performance measure P, if its performance on T, as measured by P, improves with experience E.
>
> —Tom Mitchell, *1997*

For example, your spam filter is a Machine Learning program that can learn to flag spam given examples of spam emails (e.g., flagged by users) and examples of regular (nonspam, also called "ham") emails. The examples that the system uses to learn are called the *training set*. Each training example is called a *training instance* (or *sample*). In this case, the task T is to flag spam for new emails, the experience E is the *training data*, and the performance measure P needs to be defined; for example, you can use the ratio of correctly classified emails. This particular performance measure is called *accuracy* and it is often used in classification tasks.

If you just download a copy of Wikipedia, your computer has a lot more data, but it is not suddenly better at any task. Thus, it is not Machine Learning.

Why Use Machine Learning?

Consider how you would write a spam filter using traditional programming techniques (Figure 1-1):

1. First you would look at what spam typically looks like. You might notice that some words or phrases (such as "4U," "credit card," "free," and "amazing") tend to come up a lot in the subject. Perhaps you would also notice a few other patterns in the sender's name, the email's body, and so on.

2. You would write a detection algorithm for each of the patterns that you noticed, and your program would flag emails as spam if a number of these patterns are detected.

3. You would test your program, and repeat steps 1 and 2 until it is good enough.

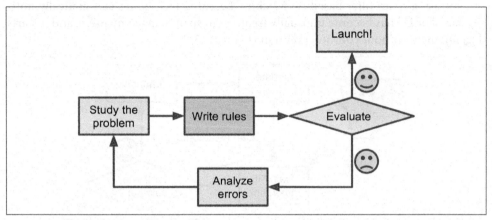

Figure 1-1. The traditional approach

Since the problem is not trivial, your program will likely become a long list of complex rules—pretty hard to maintain.

In contrast, a spam filter based on Machine Learning techniques automatically learns which words and phrases are good predictors of spam by detecting unusually frequent patterns of words in the spam examples compared to the ham examples (Figure 1-2). The program is much shorter, easier to maintain, and most likely more accurate.

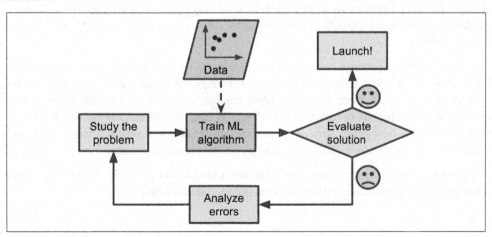

Figure 1-2. Machine Learning approach

Moreover, if spammers notice that all their emails containing "4U" are blocked, they might start writing "For U" instead. A spam filter using traditional programming techniques would need to be updated to flag "For U" emails. If spammers keep working around your spam filter, you will need to keep writing new rules forever.

In contrast, a spam filter based on Machine Learning techniques automatically notices that "For U" has become unusually frequent in spam flagged by users, and it starts flagging them without your intervention (Figure 1-3).

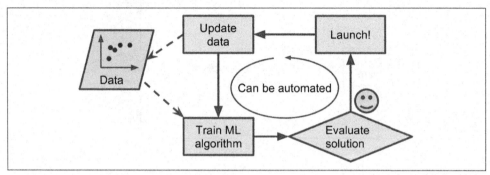

Figure 1-3. Automatically adapting to change

Another area where Machine Learning shines is for problems that either are too complex for traditional approaches or have no known algorithm. For example, consider speech recognition: say you want to start simple and write a program capable of distinguishing the words "one" and "two." You might notice that the word "two" starts with a high-pitch sound ("T"), so you could hardcode an algorithm that measures high-pitch sound intensity and use that to distinguish ones and twos. Obviously this technique will not scale to thousands of words spoken by millions of very different people in noisy environments and in dozens of languages. The best solution (at least today) is to write an algorithm that learns by itself, given many example recordings for each word.

Finally, Machine Learning can help humans learn (Figure 1-4): ML algorithms can be inspected to see what they have learned (although for some algorithms this can be tricky). For instance, once the spam filter has been trained on enough spam, it can easily be inspected to reveal the list of words and combinations of words that it believes are the best predictors of spam. Sometimes this will reveal unsuspected correlations or new trends, and thereby lead to a better understanding of the problem.

Applying ML techniques to dig into large amounts of data can help discover patterns that were not immediately apparent. This is called *data mining*.

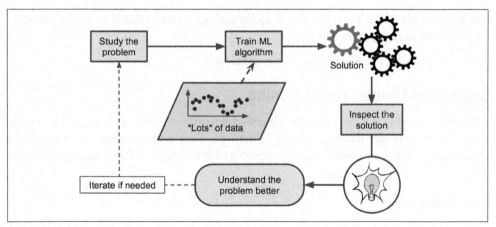

Figure 1-4. Machine Learning can help humans learn

To summarize, Machine Learning is great for:

- Problems for which existing solutions require a lot of hand-tuning or long lists of rules: one Machine Learning algorithm can often simplify code and perform better.
- Complex problems for which there is no good solution at all using a traditional approach: the best Machine Learning techniques can find a solution.
- Fluctuating environments: a Machine Learning system can adapt to new data.
- Getting insights about complex problems and large amounts of data.

Types of Machine Learning Systems

There are so many different types of Machine Learning systems that it is useful to classify them in broad categories based on:

- Whether or not they are trained with human supervision (supervised, unsupervised, semisupervised, and Reinforcement Learning)
- Whether or not they can learn incrementally on the fly (online versus batch learning)
- Whether they work by simply comparing new data points to known data points, or instead detect patterns in the training data and build a predictive model, much like scientists do (instance-based versus model-based learning)

These criteria are not exclusive; you can combine them in any way you like. For example, a state-of-the-art spam filter may learn on the fly using a deep neural network model trained using examples of spam and ham; this makes it an online, model-based, supervised learning system.

Let's look at each of these criteria a bit more closely.

Supervised/Unsupervised Learning

Machine Learning systems can be classified according to the amount and type of supervision they get during training. There are four major categories: supervised learning, unsupervised learning, semisupervised learning, and Reinforcement Learning.

Supervised learning

In *supervised learning*, the training data you feed to the algorithm includes the desired solutions, called *labels* (Figure 1-5).

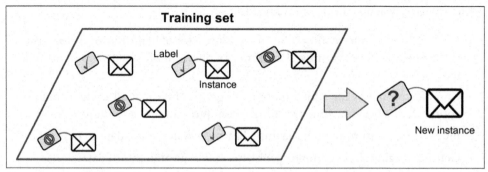

Figure 1-5. A labeled training set for supervised learning (e.g., spam classification)

A typical supervised learning task is *classification*. The spam filter is a good example of this: it is trained with many example emails along with their *class* (spam or ham), and it must learn how to classify new emails.

Another typical task is to predict a *target* numeric value, such as the price of a car, given a set of *features* (mileage, age, brand, etc.) called *predictors*. This sort of task is called *regression* (Figure 1-6).[1] To train the system, you need to give it many examples of cars, including both their predictors and their labels (i.e., their prices).

---

[1] Fun fact: this odd-sounding name is a statistics term introduced by Francis Galton while he was studying the fact that the children of tall people tend to be shorter than their parents. Since children were shorter, he called this *regression to the mean*. This name was then applied to the methods he used to analyze correlations between variables.

In Machine Learning an *attribute* is a data type (e.g., "Mileage"), while a *feature* has several meanings depending on the context, but generally means an attribute plus its value (e.g., "Mileage = 15,000"). Many people use the words *attribute* and *feature* interchangeably, though.

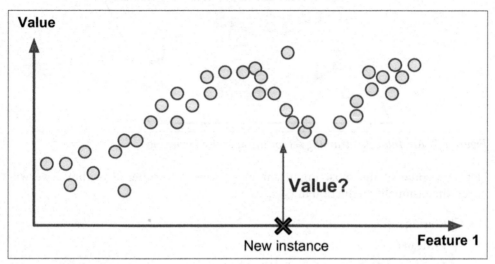

Figure 1-6. Regression

Note that some regression algorithms can be used for classification as well, and vice versa. For example, *Logistic Regression* is commonly used for classification, as it can output a value that corresponds to the probability of belonging to a given class (e.g., 20% chance of being spam).

Here are some of the most important supervised learning algorithms (covered in this book):

- k-Nearest Neighbors
- Linear Regression
- Logistic Regression
- Support Vector Machines (SVMs)
- Decision Trees and Random Forests
- Neural networks[2]

---

2 Some neural network architectures can be unsupervised, such as autoencoders and restricted Boltzmann machines. They can also be semisupervised, such as in deep belief networks and unsupervised pretraining.

Unsupervised learning

In *unsupervised learning*, as you might guess, the training data is unlabeled (Figure 1-7). The system tries to learn without a teacher.

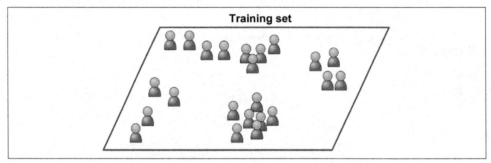

Figure 1-7. An unlabeled training set for unsupervised learning

Here are some of the most important unsupervised learning algorithms (we will cover dimensionality reduction in Chapter 8):

- Clustering
  - k-Means
  - Hierarchical Cluster Analysis (HCA)
  - Expectation Maximization
- Visualization and dimensionality reduction
  - Principal Component Analysis (PCA)
  - Kernel PCA
  - Locally-Linear Embedding (LLE)
  - t-distributed Stochastic Neighbor Embedding (t-SNE)
- Association rule learning
  - Apriori
  - Eclat

For example, say you have a lot of data about your blog's visitors. You may want to run a *clustering* algorithm to try to detect groups of similar visitors (Figure 1-8). At no point do you tell the algorithm which group a visitor belongs to: it finds those connections without your help. For example, it might notice that 40% of your visitors are males who love comic books and generally read your blog in the evening, while 20% are young sci-fi lovers who visit during the weekends, and so on. If you use a *hierarchical clustering* algorithm, it may also subdivide each group into smaller groups. This may help you target your posts for each group.

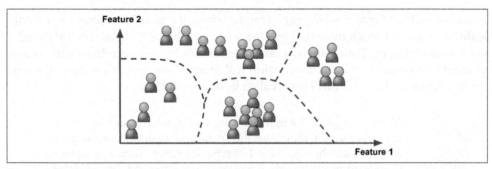

Figure 1-8. Clustering

Visualization algorithms are also good examples of unsupervised learning algorithms: you feed them a lot of complex and unlabeled data, and they output a 2D or 3D representation of your data that can easily be plotted (Figure 1-9). These algorithms try to preserve as much structure as they can (e.g., trying to keep separate clusters in the input space from overlapping in the visualization), so you can understand how the data is organized and perhaps identify unsuspected patterns.

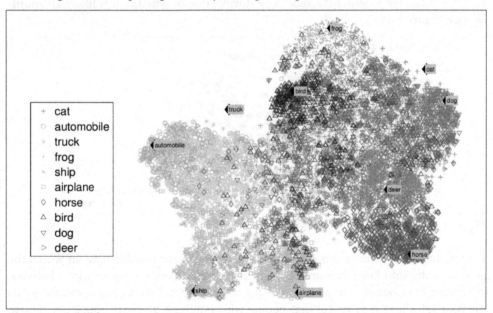

Figure 1-9. Example of a t-SNE visualization highlighting semantic clusters[3]

---

3 Notice how animals are rather well separated from vehicles, how horses are close to deer but far from birds, and so on. Figure reproduced with permission from Socher, Ganjoo, Manning, and Ng (2013), "T-SNE visualization of the semantic word space."

A related task is *dimensionality reduction*, in which the goal is to simplify the data without losing too much information. One way to do this is to merge several correlated features into one. For example, a car's mileage may be very correlated with its age, so the dimensionality reduction algorithm will merge them into one feature that represents the car's wear and tear. This is called *feature extraction*.

 It is often a good idea to try to reduce the dimension of your training data using a dimensionality reduction algorithm before you feed it to another Machine Learning algorithm (such as a supervised learning algorithm). It will run much faster, the data will take up less disk and memory space, and in some cases it may also perform better.

Yet another important unsupervised task is *anomaly detection*—for example, detecting unusual credit card transactions to prevent fraud, catching manufacturing defects, or automatically removing outliers from a dataset before feeding it to another learning algorithm. The system is trained with normal instances, and when it sees a new instance it can tell whether it looks like a normal one or whether it is likely an anomaly (see Figure 1-10).

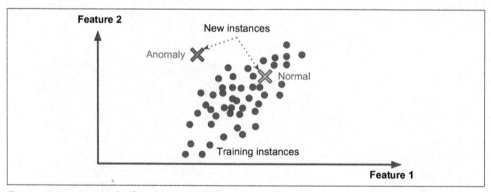

Figure 1-10. Anomaly detection

Finally, another common unsupervised task is *association rule learning*, in which the goal is to dig into large amounts of data and discover interesting relations between attributes. For example, suppose you own a supermarket. Running an association rule on your sales logs may reveal that people who purchase barbecue sauce and potato chips also tend to buy steak. Thus, you may want to place these items close to each other.

Semisupervised learning

Some algorithms can deal with partially labeled training data, usually a lot of unlabeled data and a little bit of labeled data. This is called *semisupervised learning* (Figure 1-11).

Some photo-hosting services, such as Google Photos, are good examples of this. Once you upload all your family photos to the service, it automatically recognizes that the same person A shows up in photos 1, 5, and 11, while another person B shows up in photos 2, 5, and 7. This is the unsupervised part of the algorithm (clustering). Now all the system needs is for you to tell it who these people are. Just one label per person,[4] and it is able to name everyone in every photo, which is useful for searching photos.

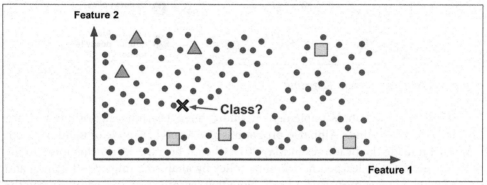

Figure 1-11. Semisupervised learning

Most semisupervised learning algorithms are combinations of unsupervised and supervised algorithms. For example, *deep belief networks* (DBNs) are based on unsupervised components called *restricted Boltzmann machines* (RBMs) stacked on top of one another. RBMs are trained sequentially in an unsupervised manner, and then the whole system is fine-tuned using supervised learning techniques.

Reinforcement Learning

Reinforcement Learning is a very different beast. The learning system, called an *agent* in this context, can observe the environment, select and perform actions, and get *rewards* in return (or *penalties* in the form of negative rewards, as in Figure 1-12). It must then learn by itself what is the best strategy, called a *policy*, to get the most reward over time. A policy defines what action the agent should choose when it is in a given situation.

---

4 That's when the system works perfectly. In practice it often creates a few clusters per person, and sometimes mixes up two people who look alike, so you need to provide a few labels per person and manually clean up some clusters.

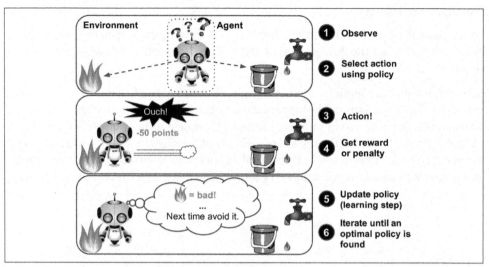

Figure 1-12. Reinforcement Learning

For example, many robots implement Reinforcement Learning algorithms to learn how to walk. DeepMind's AlphaGo program is also a good example of Reinforcement Learning: it made the headlines in May 2017 when it beat the world champion Ke Jie at the game of *Go*. It learned its winning policy by analyzing millions of games, and then playing many games against itself. Note that learning was turned off during the games against the champion; AlphaGo was just applying the policy it had learned.

Batch and Online Learning

Another criterion used to classify Machine Learning systems is whether or not the system can learn incrementally from a stream of incoming data.

Batch learning

In *batch learning*, the system is incapable of learning incrementally: it must be trained using all the available data. This will generally take a lot of time and computing resources, so it is typically done offline. First the system is trained, and then it is launched into production and runs without learning anymore; it just applies what it has learned. This is called *offline learning*.

If you want a batch learning system to know about new data (such as a new type of spam), you need to train a new version of the system from scratch on the full dataset (not just the new data, but also the old data), then stop the old system and replace it with the new one.

Fortunately, the whole process of training, evaluating, and launching a Machine Learning system can be automated fairly easily (as shown in Figure 1-3), so even a batch learning system can adapt to change. Simply update the data and train a new version of the system from scratch as often as needed.

This solution is simple and often works fine, but training using the full set of data can take many hours, so you would typically train a new system only every 24 hours or even just weekly. If your system needs to adapt to rapidly changing data (e.g., to predict stock prices), then you need a more reactive solution.

Also, training on the full set of data requires a lot of computing resources (CPU, memory space, disk space, disk I/O, network I/O, etc.). If you have a lot of data and you automate your system to train from scratch every day, it will end up costing you a lot of money. If the amount of data is huge, it may even be impossible to use a batch learning algorithm.

Finally, if your system needs to be able to learn autonomously and it has limited resources (e.g., a smartphone application or a rover on Mars), then carrying around large amounts of training data and taking up a lot of resources to train for hours every day is a showstopper.

Fortunately, a better option in all these cases is to use algorithms that are capable of learning incrementally.

Online learning

In *online learning*, you train the system incrementally by feeding it data instances sequentially, either individually or by small groups called *mini-batches*. Each learning step is fast and cheap, so the system can learn about new data on the fly, as it arrives (see Figure 1-13).

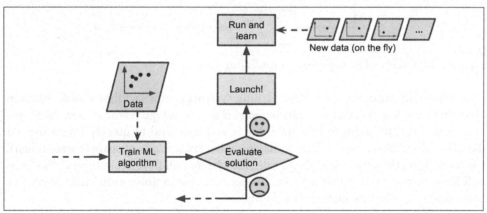

Figure 1-13. Online learning

Online learning is great for systems that receive data as a continuous flow (e.g., stock prices) and need to adapt to change rapidly or autonomously. It is also a good option if you have limited computing resources: once an online learning system has learned about new data instances, it does not need them anymore, so you can discard them (unless you want to be able to roll back to a previous state and "replay" the data). This can save a huge amount of space.

Online learning algorithms can also be used to train systems on huge datasets that cannot fit in one machine's main memory (this is called *out-of-core* learning). The algorithm loads part of the data, runs a training step on that data, and repeats the process until it has run on all of the data (see Figure 1-14).

 This whole process is usually done offline (i.e., not on the live system), so *online learning* can be a confusing name. Think of it as *incremental learning*.

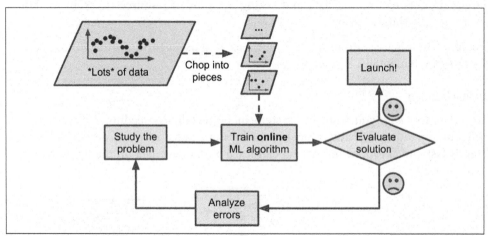

Figure 1-14. Using online learning to handle huge datasets

One important parameter of online learning systems is how fast they should adapt to changing data: this is called the *learning rate*. If you set a high learning rate, then your system will rapidly adapt to new data, but it will also tend to quickly forget the old data (you don't want a spam filter to flag only the latest kinds of spam it was shown). Conversely, if you set a low learning rate, the system will have more inertia; that is, it will learn more slowly, but it will also be less sensitive to noise in the new data or to sequences of nonrepresentative data points.

A big challenge with online learning is that if bad data is fed to the system, the system's performance will gradually decline. If we are talking about a live system, your clients will notice. For example, bad data could come from a malfunctioning sensor on a robot, or from someone spamming a search engine to try to rank high in search results. To reduce this risk, you need to monitor your system closely and promptly switch learning off (and possibly revert to a previously working state) if you detect a drop in performance. You may also want to monitor the input data and react to abnormal data (e.g., using an anomaly detection algorithm).

Instance-Based Versus Model-Based Learning

One more way to categorize Machine Learning systems is by how they *generalize*. Most Machine Learning tasks are about making predictions. This means that given a number of training examples, the system needs to be able to generalize to examples it has never seen before. Having a good performance measure on the training data is good, but insufficient; the true goal is to perform well on new instances.

There are two main approaches to generalization: instance-based learning and model-based learning.

Instance-based learning

Possibly the most trivial form of learning is simply to learn by heart. If you were to create a spam filter this way, it would just flag all emails that are identical to emails that have already been flagged by users—not the worst solution, but certainly not the best.

Instead of just flagging emails that are identical to known spam emails, your spam filter could be programmed to also flag emails that are very similar to known spam emails. This requires a *measure of similarity* between two emails. A (very basic) similarity measure between two emails could be to count the number of words they have in common. The system would flag an email as spam if it has many words in common with a known spam email.

This is called *instance-based learning*: the system learns the examples by heart, then generalizes to new cases using a similarity measure (Figure 1-15).

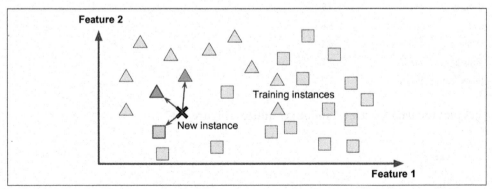

Figure 1-15. Instance-based learning

Model-based learning

Another way to generalize from a set of examples is to build a model of these examples, then use that model to make *predictions*. This is called *model-based learning* (Figure 1-16).

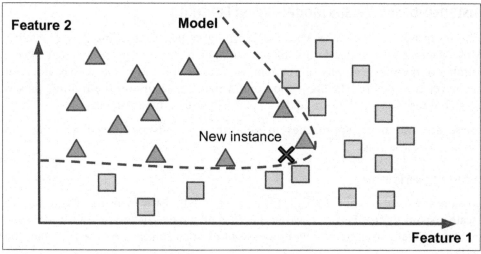

Figure 1-16. Model-based learning

For example, suppose you want to know if money makes people happy, so you download the *Better Life Index* data from the OECD's website (*http://homl.info/4*) as well as stats about GDP per capita from the IMF's website (*http://homl.info/5*). Then you join the tables and sort by GDP per capita. Table 1-1 shows an excerpt of what you get.

Table 1-1. Does money make people happier?

Country	GDP per capita (USD)	Life satisfaction
Hungary	12,240	4.9
Korea	27,195	5.8
France	37,675	6.5
Australia	50,962	7.3
United States	55,805	7.2

Let's plot the data for a few random countries (Figure 1-17).

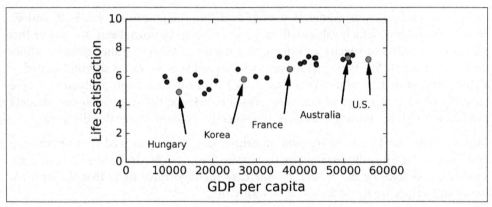

Figure 1-17. Do you see a trend here?

There does seem to be a trend here! Although the data is *noisy* (i.e., partly random), it looks like life satisfaction goes up more or less linearly as the country's GDP per capita increases. So you decide to model life satisfaction as a linear function of GDP per capita. This step is called *model selection*: you selected a *linear model* of life satisfaction with just one attribute, GDP per capita (Equation 1-1).

Equation 1-1. A simple linear model

$$\text{life\_satisfaction} = \theta_0 + \theta_1 \times \text{GDP\_per\_capita}$$

This model has two *model parameters*, θ_0 and θ_1.[5] By tweaking these parameters, you can make your model represent any linear function, as shown in Figure 1-18.

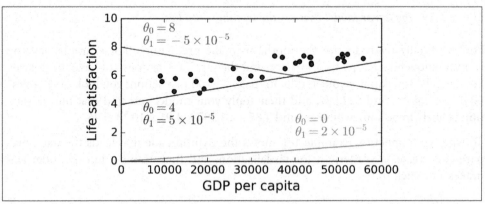

Figure 1-18. A few possible linear models

---

5 By convention, the Greek letter θ (theta) is frequently used to represent model parameters.

Before you can use your model, you need to define the parameter values θ_0 and θ_1. How can you know which values will make your model perform best? To answer this question, you need to specify a performance measure. You can either define a *utility function* (or *fitness function*) that measures how *good* your model is, or you can define a *cost function* that measures how *bad* it is. For linear regression problems, people typically use a cost function that measures the distance between the linear model's predictions and the training examples; the objective is to minimize this distance.

This is where the Linear Regression algorithm comes in: you feed it your training examples and it finds the parameters that make the linear model fit best to your data. This is called *training* the model. In our case the algorithm finds that the optimal parameter values are $\theta_0 = 4.85$ and $\theta_1 = 4.91 \times 10^{-5}$.

Now the model fits the training data as closely as possible (for a linear model), as you can see in Figure 1-19.

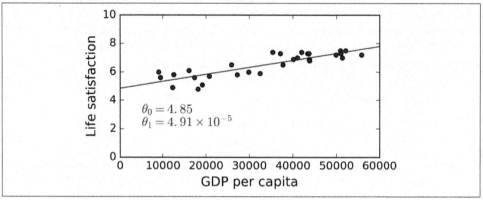

Figure 1-19. The linear model that fits the training data best

You are finally ready to run the model to make predictions. For example, say you want to know how happy Cypriots are, and the OECD data does not have the answer. Fortunately, you can use your model to make a good prediction: you look up Cyprus's GDP per capita, find $22,587, and then apply your model and find that life satisfaction is likely to be somewhere around $4.85 + 22,587 \times 4.91 \times 10^{-5} = 5.96$.

To whet your appetite, Example 1-1 shows the Python code that loads the data, prepares it,[6] creates a scatterplot for visualization, and then trains a linear model and makes a prediction.[7]

---

6 The `prepare_country_stats()` function's definition is not shown here (see this chapter's Jupyter notebook if you want all the gory details). It's just boring Pandas code that joins the life satisfaction data from the OECD with the GDP per capita data from the IMF.

7 It's okay if you don't understand all the code yet; we will present Scikit-Learn in the following chapters.

Example 1-1. Training and running a linear model using Scikit-Learn

```python
import matplotlib
import matplotlib.pyplot as plt
import numpy as np
import pandas as pd
import sklearn.linear_model

# Load the data
oecd_bli = pd.read_csv("oecd_bli_2015.csv", thousands=',')
gdp_per_capita = pd.read_csv("gdp_per_capita.csv",thousands=',',delimiter='\t',
                            encoding='latin1', na_values="n/a")

# Prepare the data
country_stats = prepare_country_stats(oecd_bli, gdp_per_capita)
X = np.c_[country_stats["GDP per capita"]]
y = np.c_[country_stats["Life satisfaction"]]

# Visualize the data
country_stats.plot(kind='scatter', x="GDP per capita", y='Life satisfaction')
plt.show()

# Select a linear model
model = sklearn.linear_model.LinearRegression()

# Train the model
model.fit(X, y)

# Make a prediction for Cyprus
X_new = [[22587]]  # Cyprus' GDP per capita
print(model.predict(X_new)) # outputs [[ 5.96242338]]
```

 If you had used an instance-based learning algorithm instead, you would have found that Slovenia has the closest GDP per capita to that of Cyprus ($20,732), and since the OECD data tells us that Slovenians' life satisfaction is 5.7, you would have predicted a life satisfaction of 5.7 for Cyprus. If you zoom out a bit and look at the two next closest countries, you will find Portugal and Spain with life satisfactions of 5.1 and 6.5, respectively. Averaging these three values, you get 5.77, which is pretty close to your model-based prediction. This simple algorithm is called *k-Nearest Neighbors* regression (in this example, *k* = 3).

Replacing the Linear Regression model with k-Nearest Neighbors regression in the previous code is as simple as replacing this line:

```python
model = sklearn.linear_model.LinearRegression()
```

with this one:

```python
model = sklearn.neighbors.KNeighborsRegressor(n_neighbors=3)
```

If all went well, your model will make good predictions. If not, you may need to use more attributes (employment rate, health, air pollution, etc.), get more or better quality training data, or perhaps select a more powerful model (e.g., a Polynomial Regression model).

In summary:

- You studied the data.
- You selected a model.
- You trained it on the training data (i.e., the learning algorithm searched for the model parameter values that minimize a cost function).
- Finally, you applied the model to make predictions on new cases (this is called *inference*), hoping that this model will generalize well.

This is what a typical Machine Learning project looks like. In Chapter 2 you will experience this first-hand by going through an end-to-end project.

We have covered a lot of ground so far: you now know what Machine Learning is really about, why it is useful, what some of the most common categories of ML systems are, and what a typical project workflow looks like. Now let's look at what can go wrong in learning and prevent you from making accurate predictions.

Main Challenges of Machine Learning

In short, since your main task is to select a learning algorithm and train it on some data, the two things that can go wrong are "bad algorithm" and "bad data." Let's start with examples of bad data.

Insufficient Quantity of Training Data

For a toddler to learn what an apple is, all it takes is for you to point to an apple and say "apple" (possibly repeating this procedure a few times). Now the child is able to recognize apples in all sorts of colors and shapes. Genius.

Machine Learning is not quite there yet; it takes a lot of data for most Machine Learning algorithms to work properly. Even for very simple problems you typically need thousands of examples, and for complex problems such as image or speech recognition you may need millions of examples (unless you can reuse parts of an existing model).

The Unreasonable Effectiveness of Data

In a famous paper (*http://homl.info/6*) published in 2001, Microsoft researchers Michele Banko and Eric Brill showed that very different Machine Learning algorithms, including fairly simple ones, performed almost identically well on a complex problem of natural language disambiguation[8] once they were given enough data (as you can see in Figure 1-20).

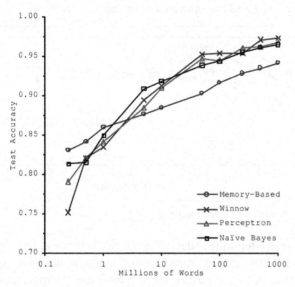

Figure 1-20. The importance of data versus algorithms[9]

As the authors put it: "these results suggest that we may want to reconsider the trade-off between spending time and money on algorithm development versus spending it on corpus development."

The idea that data matters more than algorithms for complex problems was further popularized by Peter Norvig et al. in a paper titled "The Unreasonable Effectiveness of Data" (*http://homl.info/7*) published in 2009.[10] It should be noted, however, that small- and medium-sized datasets are still very common, and it is not always easy or cheap to get extra training data, so don't abandon algorithms just yet.

---

8 For example, knowing whether to write "to," "two," or "too" depending on the context.

9 Figure reproduced with permission from Banko and Brill (2001), "Learning Curves for Confusion Set Disambiguation."

10 "The Unreasonable Effectiveness of Data," Peter Norvig et al. (2009).

Nonrepresentative Training Data

In order to generalize well, it is crucial that your training data be representative of the new cases you want to generalize to. This is true whether you use instance-based learning or model-based learning.

For example, the set of countries we used earlier for training the linear model was not perfectly representative; a few countries were missing. Figure 1-21 shows what the data looks like when you add the missing countries.

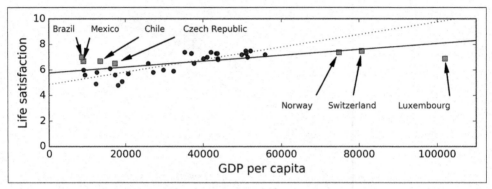

Figure 1-21. A more representative training sample

If you train a linear model on this data, you get the solid line, while the old model is represented by the dotted line. As you can see, not only does adding a few missing countries significantly alter the model, but it makes it clear that such a simple linear model is probably never going to work well. It seems that very rich countries are not happier than moderately rich countries (in fact they seem unhappier), and conversely some poor countries seem happier than many rich countries.

By using a nonrepresentative training set, we trained a model that is unlikely to make accurate predictions, especially for very poor and very rich countries.

It is crucial to use a training set that is representative of the cases you want to generalize to. This is often harder than it sounds: if the sample is too small, you will have *sampling noise* (i.e., nonrepresentative data as a result of chance), but even very large samples can be nonrepresentative if the sampling method is flawed. This is called *sampling bias*.

A Famous Example of Sampling Bias

Perhaps the most famous example of sampling bias happened during the US presidential election in 1936, which pitted Landon against Roosevelt: the *Literary Digest* conducted a very large poll, sending mail to about 10 million people. It got 2.4 million answers, and predicted with high confidence that Landon would get 57% of the votes.

Instead, Roosevelt won with 62% of the votes. The flaw was in the *Literary Digest*'s sampling method:

- First, to obtain the addresses to send the polls to, the *Literary Digest* used telephone directories, lists of magazine subscribers, club membership lists, and the like. All of these lists tend to favor wealthier people, who are more likely to vote Republican (hence Landon).
- Second, less than 25% of the people who received the poll answered. Again, this introduces a sampling bias, by ruling out people who don't care much about politics, people who don't like the *Literary Digest*, and other key groups. This is a special type of sampling bias called *nonresponse bias*.

Here is another example: say you want to build a system to recognize funk music videos. One way to build your training set is to search "funk music" on YouTube and use the resulting videos. But this assumes that YouTube's search engine returns a set of videos that are representative of all the funk music videos on YouTube. In reality, the search results are likely to be biased toward popular artists (and if you live in Brazil you will get a lot of "funk carioca" videos, which sound nothing like James Brown). On the other hand, how else can you get a large training set?

Poor-Quality Data

Obviously, if your training data is full of errors, outliers, and noise (e.g., due to poor-quality measurements), it will make it harder for the system to detect the underlying patterns, so your system is less likely to perform well. It is often well worth the effort to spend time cleaning up your training data. The truth is, most data scientists spend a significant part of their time doing just that. For example:

- If some instances are clearly outliers, it may help to simply discard them or try to fix the errors manually.
- If some instances are missing a few features (e.g., 5% of your customers did not specify their age), you must decide whether you want to ignore this attribute altogether, ignore these instances, fill in the missing values (e.g., with the median age), or train one model with the feature and one model without it, and so on.

Irrelevant Features

As the saying goes: garbage in, garbage out. Your system will only be capable of learning if the training data contains enough relevant features and not too many irrelevant ones. A critical part of the success of a Machine Learning project is coming up with a good set of features to train on. This process, called *feature engineering*, involves:

- *Feature selection*: selecting the most useful features to train on among existing features.

- *Feature extraction*: combining existing features to produce a more useful one (as we saw earlier, dimensionality reduction algorithms can help).

- Creating new features by gathering new data.

Now that we have looked at many examples of bad data, let's look at a couple of examples of bad algorithms.

Overfitting the Training Data

Say you are visiting a foreign country and the taxi driver rips you off. You might be tempted to say that *all* taxi drivers in that country are thieves. Overgeneralizing is something that we humans do all too often, and unfortunately machines can fall into the same trap if we are not careful. In Machine Learning this is called *overfitting*: it means that the model performs well on the training data, but it does not generalize well.

Figure 1-22 shows an example of a high-degree polynomial life satisfaction model that strongly overfits the training data. Even though it performs much better on the training data than the simple linear model, would you really trust its predictions?

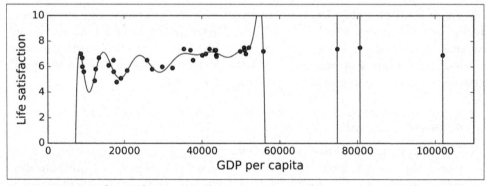

Figure 1-22. Overfitting the training data

Complex models such as deep neural networks can detect subtle patterns in the data, but if the training set is noisy, or if it is too small (which introduces sampling noise), then the model is likely to detect patterns in the noise itself. Obviously these patterns will not generalize to new instances. For example, say you feed your life satisfaction model many more attributes, including uninformative ones such as the country's name. In that case, a complex model may detect patterns like the fact that all countries in the training data with a *w* in their name have a life satisfaction greater than 7: New Zealand (7.3), Norway (7.4), Sweden (7.2), and Switzerland (7.5). How confident are you that the W-satisfaction rule generalizes to Rwanda or Zimbabwe? Obviously this pattern occurred in the training data by pure chance, but the model has no way to tell whether a pattern is real or simply the result of noise in the data.

 Overfitting happens when the model is too complex relative to the amount and noisiness of the training data. The possible solutions are:

- To simplify the model by selecting one with fewer parameters (e.g., a linear model rather than a high-degree polynomial model), by reducing the number of attributes in the training data or by constraining the model

- To gather more training data

- To reduce the noise in the training data (e.g., fix data errors and remove outliers)

Constraining a model to make it simpler and reduce the risk of overfitting is called *regularization*. For example, the linear model we defined earlier has two parameters, θ_0 and θ_1. This gives the learning algorithm two *degrees of freedom* to adapt the model to the training data: it can tweak both the height (θ_0) and the slope (θ_1) of the line. If we forced $\theta_1 = 0$, the algorithm would have only one degree of freedom and would have a much harder time fitting the data properly: all it could do is move the line up or down to get as close as possible to the training instances, so it would end up around the mean. A very simple model indeed! If we allow the algorithm to modify θ_1 but we force it to keep it small, then the learning algorithm will effectively have somewhere in between one and two degrees of freedom. It will produce a simpler model than with two degrees of freedom, but more complex than with just one. You want to find the right balance between fitting the data perfectly and keeping the model simple enough to ensure that it will generalize well.

Figure 1-23 shows three models: the dotted line represents the original model that was trained with a few countries missing, the dashed line is our second model trained with all countries, and the solid line is a linear model trained with the same data as the first model but with a regularization constraint. You can see that regularization forced the model to have a smaller slope, which fits a bit less the training data that the model was trained on, but actually allows it to generalize better to new examples.

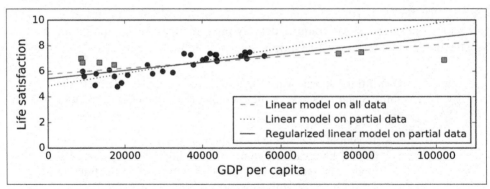

Figure 1-23. Regularization reduces the risk of overfitting

The amount of regularization to apply during learning can be controlled by a *hyperparameter*. A hyperparameter is a parameter of a learning algorithm (not of the model). As such, it is not affected by the learning algorithm itself; it must be set prior to training and remains constant during training. If you set the regularization hyperparameter to a very large value, you will get an almost flat model (a slope close to zero); the learning algorithm will almost certainly not overfit the training data, but it will be less likely to find a good solution. Tuning hyperparameters is an important part of building a Machine Learning system (you will see a detailed example in the next chapter).

Underfitting the Training Data

As you might guess, *underfitting* is the opposite of overfitting: it occurs when your model is too simple to learn the underlying structure of the data. For example, a linear model of life satisfaction is prone to underfit; reality is just more complex than the model, so its predictions are bound to be inaccurate, even on the training examples.

The main options to fix this problem are:

- Selecting a more powerful model, with more parameters
- Feeding better features to the learning algorithm (feature engineering)
- Reducing the constraints on the model (e.g., reducing the regularization hyperparameter)

Stepping Back

By now you already know a lot about Machine Learning. However, we went through so many concepts that you may be feeling a little lost, so let's step back and look at the big picture:

- Machine Learning is about making machines get better at some task by learning from data, instead of having to explicitly code rules.

- There are many different types of ML systems: supervised or not, batch or online, instance-based or model-based, and so on.

- In a ML project you gather data in a training set, and you feed the training set to a learning algorithm. If the algorithm is model-based it tunes some parameters to fit the model to the training set (i.e., to make good predictions on the training set itself), and then hopefully it will be able to make good predictions on new cases as well. If the algorithm is instance-based, it just learns the examples by heart and uses a similarity measure to generalize to new instances.

- The system will not perform well if your training set is too small, or if the data is not representative, noisy, or polluted with irrelevant features (garbage in, garbage out). Lastly, your model needs to be neither too simple (in which case it will underfit) nor too complex (in which case it will overfit).

There's just one last important topic to cover: once you have trained a model, you don't want to just "hope" it generalizes to new cases. You want to evaluate it, and fine-tune it if necessary. Let's see how.

Testing and Validating

The only way to know how well a model will generalize to new cases is to actually try it out on new cases. One way to do that is to put your model in production and monitor how well it performs. This works well, but if your model is horribly bad, your users will complain—not the best idea.

A better option is to split your data into two sets: the *training set* and the *test set*. As these names imply, you train your model using the training set, and you test it using the test set. The error rate on new cases is called the *generalization error* (or *out-of-sample error*), and by evaluating your model on the test set, you get an estimation of this error. This value tells you how well your model will perform on instances it has never seen before.

If the training error is low (i.e., your model makes few mistakes on the training set) but the generalization error is high, it means that your model is overfitting the training data.

It is common to use 80% of the data for training and *hold out* 20% for testing.

So evaluating a model is simple enough: just use a test set. Now suppose you are hesitating between two models (say a linear model and a polynomial model): how can you decide? One option is to train both and compare how well they generalize using the test set.

Now suppose that the linear model generalizes better, but you want to apply some regularization to avoid overfitting. The question is: how do you choose the value of the regularization hyperparameter? One option is to train 100 different models using 100 different values for this hyperparameter. Suppose you find the best hyperparameter value that produces a model with the lowest generalization error, say just 5% error.

So you launch this model into production, but unfortunately it does not perform as well as expected and produces 15% errors. What just happened?

The problem is that you measured the generalization error multiple times on the test set, and you adapted the model and hyperparameters to produce the best model *for that set*. This means that the model is unlikely to perform as well on new data.

A common solution to this problem is to have a second holdout set called the *validation set*. You train multiple models with various hyperparameters using the training set, you select the model and hyperparameters that perform best on the validation set, and when you're happy with your model you run a single final test against the test set to get an estimate of the generalization error.

To avoid "wasting" too much training data in validation sets, a common technique is to use *cross-validation*: the training set is split into complementary subsets, and each model is trained against a different combination of these subsets and validated against the remaining parts. Once the model type and hyperparameters have been selected, a final model is trained using these hyperparameters on the full training set, and the generalized error is measured on the test set.

No Free Lunch Theorem

A model is a simplified version of the observations. The simplifications are meant to discard the superfluous details that are unlikely to generalize to new instances. However, to decide what data to discard and what data to keep, you must make *assumptions*. For example, a linear model makes the assumption that the data is fundamentally linear and that the distance between the instances and the straight line is just noise, which can safely be ignored.

In a famous 1996 paper (*http://homl.info/8*),[11] David Wolpert demonstrated that if you make absolutely no assumption about the data, then there is no reason to prefer one model over any other. This is called the *No Free Lunch* (NFL) theorem. For some

---

11 "The Lack of A Priori Distinctions Between Learning Algorithms," D. Wolpert (1996).

datasets the best model is a linear model, while for other datasets it is a neural network. There is no model that is *a priori* guaranteed to work better (hence the name of the theorem). The only way to know for sure which model is best is to evaluate them all. Since this is not possible, in practice you make some reasonable assumptions about the data and you evaluate only a few reasonable models. For example, for simple tasks you may evaluate linear models with various levels of regularization, and for a complex problem you may evaluate various neural networks.

Exercises

In this chapter we have covered some of the most important concepts in Machine Learning. In the next chapters we will dive deeper and write more code, but before we do, make sure you know how to answer the following questions:

1. How would you define Machine Learning?
2. Can you name four types of problems where it shines?
3. What is a labeled training set?
4. What are the two most common supervised tasks?
5. Can you name four common unsupervised tasks?
6. What type of Machine Learning algorithm would you use to allow a robot to walk in various unknown terrains?
7. What type of algorithm would you use to segment your customers into multiple groups?
8. Would you frame the problem of spam detection as a supervised learning problem or an unsupervised learning problem?
9. What is an online learning system?
10. What is out-of-core learning?
11. What type of learning algorithm relies on a similarity measure to make predictions?
12. What is the difference between a model parameter and a learning algorithm's hyperparameter?
13. What do model-based learning algorithms search for? What is the most common strategy they use to succeed? How do they make predictions?
14. Can you name four of the main challenges in Machine Learning?
15. If your model performs great on the training data but generalizes poorly to new instances, what is happening? Can you name three possible solutions?
16. What is a test set and why would you want to use it?

17. What is the purpose of a validation set?

18. What can go wrong if you tune hyperparameters using the test set?

19. What is cross-validation and why would you prefer it to a validation set?

Solutions to these exercises are available in Appendix A.

## CHAPTER 2

End-to-End Machine Learning Project

In this chapter, you will go through an example project end to end, pretending to be a recently hired data scientist in a real estate company.[1] Here are the main steps you will go through:

1. Look at the big picture.
2. Get the data.
3. Discover and visualize the data to gain insights.
4. Prepare the data for Machine Learning algorithms.
5. Select a model and train it.
6. Fine-tune your model.
7. Present your solution.
8. Launch, monitor, and maintain your system.

Working with Real Data

When you are learning about Machine Learning it is best to actually experiment with real-world data, not just artificial datasets. Fortunately, there are thousands of open datasets to choose from, ranging across all sorts of domains. Here are a few places you can look to get data:

- Popular open data repositories:

---

[1] The example project is completely fictitious; the goal is just to illustrate the main steps of a Machine Learning project, not to learn anything about the real estate business.

— UC Irvine Machine Learning Repository (*http://archive.ics.uci.edu/ml/*)

— Kaggle datasets (*https://www.kaggle.com/datasets*)

— Amazon's AWS datasets (*https://registry.opendata.aws/*)

- Meta portals (they list open data repositories):

— *http://dataportals.org/*

— *http://opendatamonitor.eu/*

— *http://quandl.com/*

- Other pages listing many popular open data repositories:

— Wikipedia's list of Machine Learning datasets (*http://homl.info/9*)

— Quora.com question (*http://homl.info/10*)

— Datasets subreddit (*https://www.reddit.com/r/datasets*)

In this chapter we chose the California Housing Prices dataset from the StatLib repository[2] (see Figure 2-1). This dataset was based on data from the 1990 California census. It is not exactly recent (you could still afford a nice house in the Bay Area at the time), but it has many qualities for learning, so we will pretend it is recent data. We also added a categorical attribute and removed a few features for teaching purposes.

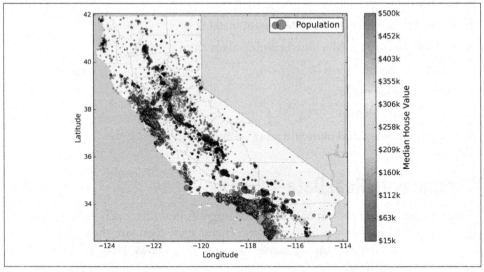

Figure 2-1. California housing prices

---

2 The original dataset appeared in R. Kelley Pace and Ronald Barry, "Sparse Spatial Autoregressions," *Statistics & Probability Letters* 33, no. 3 (1997): 291–297.

Look at the Big Picture

Welcome to Machine Learning Housing Corporation! The first task you are asked to perform is to build a model of housing prices in California using the California census data. This data has metrics such as the population, median income, median housing price, and so on for each block group in California. Block groups are the smallest geographical unit for which the US Census Bureau publishes sample data (a block group typically has a population of 600 to 3,000 people). We will just call them "districts" for short.

Your model should learn from this data and be able to predict the median housing price in any district, given all the other metrics.

Since you are a well-organized data scientist, the first thing you do is to pull out your Machine Learning project checklist. You can start with the one in Appendix B; it should work reasonably well for most Machine Learning projects but make sure to adapt it to your needs. In this chapter we will go through many checklist items, but we will also skip a few, either because they are self-explanatory or because they will be discussed in later chapters.

Frame the Problem

The first question to ask your boss is what exactly is the business objective; building a model is probably not the end goal. How does the company expect to use and benefit from this model? This is important because it will determine how you frame the problem, what algorithms you will select, what performance measure you will use to evaluate your model, and how much effort you should spend tweaking it.

Your boss answers that your model's output (a prediction of a district's median housing price) will be fed to another Machine Learning system (see Figure 2-2), along with many other *signals*.[3] This downstream system will determine whether it is worth investing in a given area or not. Getting this right is critical, as it directly affects revenue.

---

3 A piece of information fed to a Machine Learning system is often called a *signal* in reference to Shannon's information theory: you want a high signal/noise ratio.

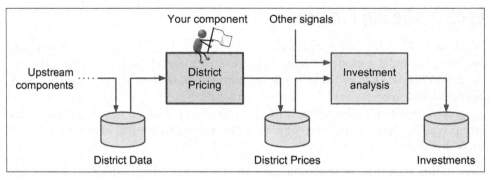

Figure 2-2. A Machine Learning pipeline for real estate investments

Pipelines

A sequence of data processing *components* is called a data *pipeline*. Pipelines are very common in Machine Learning systems, since there is a lot of data to manipulate and many data transformations to apply.

Components typically run asynchronously. Each component pulls in a large amount of data, processes it, and spits out the result in another data store, and then some time later the next component in the pipeline pulls this data and spits out its own output, and so on. Each component is fairly self-contained: the interface between components is simply the data store. This makes the system quite simple to grasp (with the help of a data flow graph), and different teams can focus on different components. Moreover, if a component breaks down, the downstream components can often continue to run normally (at least for a while) by just using the last output from the broken component. This makes the architecture quite robust.

On the other hand, a broken component can go unnoticed for some time if proper monitoring is not implemented. The data gets stale and the overall system's performance drops.

The next question to ask is what the current solution looks like (if any). It will often give you a reference performance, as well as insights on how to solve the problem. Your boss answers that the district housing prices are currently estimated manually by experts: a team gathers up-to-date information about a district, and when they cannot get the median housing price, they estimate it using complex rules.

This is costly and time-consuming, and their estimates are not great; in cases where they manage to find out the actual median housing price, they often realize that their estimates were off by more than 10%. This is why the company thinks that it would be useful to train a model to predict a district's median housing price given other data about that district. The census data looks like a great dataset to exploit for this purpose, since it includes the median housing prices of thousands of districts, as well as other data.

Okay, with all this information you are now ready to start designing your system. First, you need to frame the problem: is it supervised, unsupervised, or Reinforcement Learning? Is it a classification task, a regression task, or something else? Should you use batch learning or online learning techniques? Before you read on, pause and try to answer these questions for yourself.

Have you found the answers? Let's see: it is clearly a typical supervised learning task since you are given *labeled* training examples (each instance comes with the expected output, i.e., the district's median housing price). Moreover, it is also a typical regression task, since you are asked to predict a value. More specifically, this is a *multivariate regression* problem since the system will use multiple features to make a prediction (it will use the district's population, the median income, etc.). In the first chapter, you predicted life satisfaction based on just one feature, the GDP per capita, so it was a *univariate regression* problem. Finally, there is no continuous flow of data coming in the system, there is no particular need to adjust to changing data rapidly, and the data is small enough to fit in memory, so plain batch learning should do just fine.

 If the data was huge, you could either split your batch learning work across multiple servers (using the *MapReduce* technique), or you could use an online learning technique instead.

Select a Performance Measure

Your next step is to select a performance measure. A typical performance measure for regression problems is the Root Mean Square Error (RMSE). It gives an idea of how much error the system typically makes in its predictions, with a higher weight for large errors. Equation 2-1 shows the mathematical formula to compute the RMSE.

Equation 2-1. Root Mean Square Error (RMSE)

$$\text{RMSE}(\mathbf{X}, h) = \sqrt{\frac{1}{m} \sum_{i=1}^{m} \left(h\left(\mathbf{x}^{(i)}\right) - y^{(i)} \right)^2}$$

Notations

This equation introduces several very common Machine Learning notations that we will use throughout this book:

- m is the number of instances in the dataset you are measuring the RMSE on.
  - For example, if you are evaluating the RMSE on a validation set of 2,000 districts, then m = 2,000.
- $\mathbf{x}^{(i)}$ is a vector of all the feature values (excluding the label) of the ith instance in the dataset, and $y^{(i)}$ is its label (the desired output value for that instance).
  - For example, if the first district in the dataset is located at longitude −118.29°, latitude 33.91°, and it has 1,416 inhabitants with a median income of $38,372, and the median house value is $156,400 (ignoring the other features for now), then:

$$\mathbf{x}^{(1)} = \begin{pmatrix} -118.29 \\ 33.91 \\ 1,416 \\ 38,372 \end{pmatrix}$$

and:

$$y^{(1)} = 156,400$$

- $\mathbf{X}$ is a matrix containing all the feature values (excluding labels) of all instances in the dataset. There is one row per instance and the ith row is equal to the transpose of $\mathbf{x}^{(i)}$, noted $(\mathbf{x}^{(i)})^{T}$.[4]
  - For example, if the first district is as just described, then the matrix $\mathbf{X}$ looks like this:

$$\mathbf{X} = \begin{pmatrix} \left(\mathbf{x}^{(1)}\right)^{T} \\ \left(\mathbf{x}^{(2)}\right)^{T} \\ \vdots \\ \left(\mathbf{x}^{(1999)}\right)^{T} \\ \left(\mathbf{x}^{(2000)}\right)^{T} \end{pmatrix} = \begin{pmatrix} -118.29 & 33.91 & 1,416 & 38,372 \\ \vdots & \vdots & \vdots & \vdots \end{pmatrix}$$

---

[4] Recall that the transpose operator flips a column vector into a row vector (and vice versa).

- *h* is your system's prediction function, also called a *hypothesis*. When your system is given an instance's feature vector $\mathbf{x}^{(i)}$, it outputs a predicted value $\hat{y}^{(i)} = h(\mathbf{x}^{(i)})$ for that instance ($\hat{y}$ is pronounced "y-hat").

  — For example, if your system predicts that the median housing price in the first district is \$158,400, then $\hat{y}^{(1)} = h(\mathbf{x}^{(1)}) = 158,400$. The prediction error for this district is $\hat{y}^{(1)} - y^{(1)} = 2,000$.

- RMSE(**X**,*h*) is the cost function measured on the set of examples using your hypothesis *h*.

We use lowercase italic font for scalar values (such as *m* or $y^{(i)}$) and function names (such as *h*), lowercase bold font for vectors (such as $\mathbf{x}^{(i)}$), and uppercase bold font for matrices (such as **X**).

Even though the RMSE is generally the preferred performance measure for regression tasks, in some contexts you may prefer to use another function. For example, suppose that there are many outlier districts. In that case, you may consider using the *Mean Absolute Error* (also called the Average Absolute Deviation; see Equation 2-2):

Equation 2-2. Mean Absolute Error

$$\text{MAE}(\mathbf{X}, h) = \frac{1}{m} \sum_{i=1}^{m} \left| h(\mathbf{x}^{(i)}) - y^{(i)} \right|$$

Both the RMSE and the MAE are ways to measure the distance between two vectors: the vector of predictions and the vector of target values. Various distance measures, or *norms*, are possible:

- Computing the root of a sum of squares (RMSE) corresponds to the *Euclidean norm*: it is the notion of distance you are familiar with. It is also called the ℓ_2 *norm*, noted $\| \cdot \|_2$ (or just $\| \cdot \|$).

- Computing the sum of absolutes (MAE) corresponds to the ℓ_1 *norm*, noted $\| \cdot \|_1$. It is sometimes called the *Manhattan norm* because it measures the distance between two points in a city if you can only travel along orthogonal city blocks.

- More generally, the ℓ_k *norm* of a vector **v** containing *n* elements is defined as $\| \mathbf{v} \|_k = \left(|v_0|^k + |v_1|^k + \cdots + |v_n|^k \right)^{\frac{1}{k}}$. ℓ_0 just gives the number of non-zero elements in the vector, and ℓ_∞ gives the maximum absolute value in the vector.

- The higher the norm index, the more it focuses on large values and neglects small ones. This is why the RMSE is more sensitive to outliers than the MAE. But when outliers are exponentially rare (like in a bell-shaped curve), the RMSE performs very well and is generally preferred.

Check the Assumptions

Lastly, it is good practice to list and verify the assumptions that were made so far (by you or others); this can catch serious issues early on. For example, the district prices that your system outputs are going to be fed into a downstream Machine Learning system, and we assume that these prices are going to be used as such. But what if the downstream system actually converts the prices into categories (e.g., "cheap," "medium," or "expensive") and then uses those categories instead of the prices themselves? In this case, getting the price perfectly right is not important at all; your system just needs to get the category right. If that's so, then the problem should have been framed as a classification task, not a regression task. You don't want to find this out after working on a regression system for months.

Fortunately, after talking with the team in charge of the downstream system, you are confident that they do indeed need the actual prices, not just categories. Great! You're all set, the lights are green, and you can start coding now!

Get the Data

It's time to get your hands dirty. Don't hesitate to pick up your laptop and walk through the following code examples in a Jupyter notebook. The full Jupyter notebook is available at *https://github.com/ageron/handson-ml*.

Create the Workspace

First you will need to have Python installed. It is probably already installed on your system. If not, you can get it at *https://www.python.org/*.[5]

Next you need to create a workspace directory for your Machine Learning code and datasets. Open a terminal and type the following commands (after the $ prompts):

```
$ export ML_PATH="$HOME/ml"      # You can change the path if you prefer
$ mkdir -p $ML_PATH
```

You will need a number of Python modules: Jupyter, NumPy, Pandas, Matplotlib, and Scikit-Learn. If you already have Jupyter running with all these modules installed, you can safely skip to "Download the Data" on page 43. If you don't have them yet,

---

5 The latest version of Python 3 is recommended. Python 2.7+ should work fine too, but it is deprecated. If you use Python 2, you must add from __future__ import division, print_function, unicode_literals at the beginning of your code.

there are many ways to install them (and their dependencies). You can use your system's packaging system (e.g., apt-get on Ubuntu, or MacPorts or HomeBrew on macOS), install a Scientific Python distribution such as Anaconda and use its packaging system, or just use Python's own packaging system, pip, which is included by default with the Python binary installers (since Python 2.7.9).[6] You can check to see if pip is installed by typing the following command:

```
$ pip3 --version
pip 9.0.1 from [...]/lib/python3.5/site-packages (python 3.5)
```

You should make sure you have a recent version of pip installed, at the very least >1.4 to support binary module installation (a.k.a. wheels). To upgrade the pip module, type:[7]

```
$ pip3 install --upgrade pip
Collecting pip
[...]
Successfully installed pip-9.0.1
```

Creating an Isolated Environment

If you would like to work in an isolated environment (which is strongly recommended so you can work on different projects without having conflicting library versions), install virtualenv by running the following pip command:

```
$ pip3 install --user --upgrade virtualenv
Collecting virtualenv
[...]
Successfully installed virtualenv
```

Now you can create an isolated Python environment by typing:

```
$ cd $ML_PATH
$ virtualenv env
Using base prefix '[...]'
New python executable in [...]/ml/env/bin/python3.5
Also creating executable in [...]/ml/env/bin/python
Installing setuptools, pip, wheel...done.
```

Now every time you want to activate this environment, just open a terminal and type:

```
$ cd $ML_PATH
$ source env/bin/activate
```

While the environment is active, any package you install using pip will be installed in this isolated environment, and Python will only have access to these packages (if you

---

6 We will show the installation steps using pip in a bash shell on a Linux or macOS system. You may need to adapt these commands to your own system. On Windows, we recommend installing Anaconda instead.

7 You may need to have administrator rights to run this command; if so, try prefixing it with sudo.

also want access to the system's site packages, you should create the environment using virtualenv's `--system-site-packages` option). Check out virtualenv's documentation for more information.

Now you can install all the required modules and their dependencies using this simple pip command (if you are not using a virtualenv, you will need administrator rights, or to add the `--user` option):

```
$ pip3 install --upgrade jupyter matplotlib numpy pandas scipy scikit-learn
Collecting jupyter
  Downloading jupyter-1.0.0-py2.py3-none-any.whl
Collecting matplotlib
  [...]
```

To check your installation, try to import every module like this:

```
$ python3 -c "import jupyter, matplotlib, numpy, pandas, scipy, sklearn"
```

There should be no output and no error. Now you can fire up Jupyter by typing:

```
$ jupyter notebook
[I 15:24 NotebookApp] Serving notebooks from local directory: [...]/ml
[I 15:24 NotebookApp] 0 active kernels
[I 15:24 NotebookApp] The Jupyter Notebook is running at: http://localhost:8888/
[I 15:24 NotebookApp] Use Control-C to stop this server and shut down all
kernels (twice to skip confirmation).
```

A Jupyter server is now running in your terminal, listening to port 8888. You can visit this server by opening your web browser to *http://localhost:8888/* (this usually happens automatically when the server starts). You should see your empty workspace directory (containing only the *env* directory if you followed the preceding virtualenv instructions).

Now create a new Python notebook by clicking on the New button and selecting the appropriate Python version[8] (see Figure 2-3).

This does three things: first, it creates a new notebook file called *Untitled.ipynb* in your workspace; second, it starts a Jupyter Python kernel to run this notebook; and third, it opens this notebook in a new tab. You should start by renaming this notebook to "Housing" (this will automatically rename the file to *Housing.ipynb*) by clicking Untitled and typing the new name.

---

8 Note that Jupyter can handle multiple versions of Python, and even many other languages such as R or Octave.

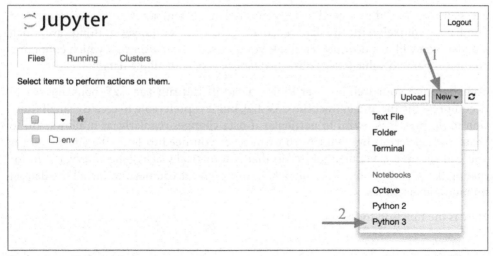

Figure 2-3. Your workspace in Jupyter

A notebook contains a list of cells. Each cell can contain executable code or formatted text. Right now the notebook contains only one empty code cell, labeled "In [1]:". Try typing **print("Hello world!")** in the cell, and click on the play button (see Figure 2-4) or press Shift-Enter. This sends the current cell to this notebook's Python kernel, which runs it and returns the output. The result is displayed below the cell, and since we reached the end of the notebook, a new cell is automatically created. Go through the User Interface Tour from Jupyter's Help menu to learn the basics.

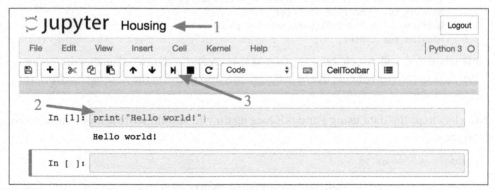

Figure 2-4. Hello world Python notebook

Download the Data

In typical environments your data would be available in a relational database (or some other common datastore) and spread across multiple tables/documents/files. To access it, you would first need to get your credentials and access authorizations,[9] and familiarize yourself with the data schema. In this project, however, things are much simpler: you will just download a single compressed file, *housing.tgz*, which contains a comma-separated value (CSV) file called *housing.csv* with all the data.

You could use your web browser to download it, and run `tar xzf housing.tgz` to decompress the file and extract the CSV file, but it is preferable to create a small function to do that. It is useful in particular if data changes regularly, as it allows you to write a small script that you can run whenever you need to fetch the latest data (or you can set up a scheduled job to do that automatically at regular intervals). Automating the process of fetching the data is also useful if you need to install the dataset on multiple machines.

Here is the function to fetch the data:[10]

```
import os
import tarfile
from six.moves import urllib

DOWNLOAD_ROOT = "https://raw.githubusercontent.com/ageron/handson-ml/master/"
HOUSING_PATH = os.path.join("datasets", "housing")
HOUSING_URL = DOWNLOAD_ROOT + "datasets/housing/housing.tgz"

def fetch_housing_data(housing_url=HOUSING_URL, housing_path=HOUSING_PATH):
    if not os.path.isdir(housing_path):
        os.makedirs(housing_path)
    tgz_path = os.path.join(housing_path, "housing.tgz")
    urllib.request.urlretrieve(housing_url, tgz_path)
    housing_tgz = tarfile.open(tgz_path)
    housing_tgz.extractall(path=housing_path)
    housing_tgz.close()
```

Now when you call `fetch_housing_data()`, it creates a *datasets/housing* directory in your workspace, downloads the *housing.tgz* file, and extracts the *housing.csv* from it in this directory.

Now let's load the data using Pandas. Once again you should write a small function to load the data:

```
import pandas as pd

def load_housing_data(housing_path=HOUSING_PATH):
    csv_path = os.path.join(housing_path, "housing.csv")
    return pd.read_csv(csv_path)
```

---

9 You might also need to check legal constraints, such as private fields that should never be copied to unsafe datastores.

10 In a real project you would save this code in a Python file, but for now you can just write it in your Jupyter notebook.

This function returns a Pandas DataFrame object containing all the data.

Take a Quick Look at the Data Structure

Let's take a look at the top five rows using the DataFrame's head() method (see Figure 2-5).

```
In [5]:  housing = load_housing_data()
         housing.head()
Out[5]:
```

	longitude	latitude	housing_median_age	total_rooms	total_bedrooms	populatiol
0	-122.23	37.88	41.0	880.0	129.0	322.0
1	-122.22	37.86	21.0	7099.0	1106.0	2401.0
2	-122.24	37.85	52.0	1467.0	190.0	496.0
3	-122.25	37.85	52.0	1274.0	235.0	558.0
4	-122.25	37.85	52.0	1627.0	280.0	565.0

Figure 2-5. Top five rows in the dataset

Each row represents one district. There are 10 attributes (you can see the first 6 in the screenshot): longitude, latitude, housing_median_age, total_rooms, total_bed rooms, population, households, median_income, median_house_value, and ocean_proximity.

The info() method is useful to get a quick description of the data, in particular the total number of rows, and each attribute's type and number of non-null values (see Figure 2-6).

```
In [6]:  housing.info()

         <class 'pandas.core.frame.DataFrame'>
         RangeIndex: 20640 entries, 0 to 20639
         Data columns (total 10 columns):
         longitude             20640 non-null float64
         latitude              20640 non-null float64
         housing_median_age    20640 non-null float64
         total_rooms           20640 non-null float64
         total_bedrooms        20433 non-null float64
         population            20640 non-null float64
         households            20640 non-null float64
         median_income         20640 non-null float64
         median_house_value    20640 non-null float64
         ocean_proximity       20640 non-null object
         dtypes: float64(9), object(1)
         memory usage: 1.6+ MB
```

Figure 2-6. Housing info

There are 20,640 instances in the dataset, which means that it is fairly small by Machine Learning standards, but it's perfect to get started. Notice that the total_bed rooms attribute has only 20,433 non-null values, meaning that 207 districts are missing this feature. We will need to take care of this later.

All attributes are numerical, except the ocean_proximity field. Its type is object, so it could hold any kind of Python object, but since you loaded this data from a CSV file you know that it must be a text attribute. When you looked at the top five rows, you probably noticed that the values in the ocean_proximity column were repetitive, which means that it is probably a categorical attribute. You can find out what categories exist and how many districts belong to each category by using the value_counts() method:

```
>>> housing["ocean_proximity"].value_counts()
<1H OCEAN     9136
INLAND        6551
NEAR OCEAN    2658
NEAR BAY      2290
ISLAND           5
Name: ocean_proximity, dtype: int64
```

Let's look at the other fields. The describe() method shows a summary of the numerical attributes (Figure 2-7).

In [8]:	housing.describe()				
Out[8]:		longitude	latitude	housing_median_age	total_rooms	total_bedr(
	count	20640.000000	20640.000000	20640.000000	20640.000000	20433.0000
	mean	-119.569704	35.631861	28.639486	2635.763081	537.870553
	std	2.003532	2.135952	12.585558	2181.615252	421.38507(
	min	-124.350000	32.540000	1.000000	2.000000	1.000000
	25%	-121.800000	33.930000	18.000000	1447.750000	296.00000(
	50%	-118.490000	34.260000	29.000000	2127.000000	435.00000(
	75%	-118.010000	37.710000	37.000000	3148.000000	647.00000(
	max	-114.310000	41.950000	52.000000	39320.000000	6445.0000(

Figure 2-7. Summary of each numerical attribute

The count, mean, min, and max rows are self-explanatory. Note that the null values are ignored (so, for example, count of total_bedrooms is 20,433, not 20,640). The std row shows the *standard deviation*, which measures how dispersed the values are.[11] The 25%, 50%, and 75% rows show the corresponding *percentiles*: a percentile indicates the value below which a given percentage of observations in a group of observations falls. For example, 25% of the districts have a housing_median_age lower than 18, while 50% are lower than 29 and 75% are lower than 37. These are often called the 25th percentile (or 1st *quartile*), the median, and the 75th percentile (or 3rd *quartile*).

Another quick way to get a feel of the type of data you are dealing with is to plot a histogram for each numerical attribute. A histogram shows the number of instances (on the vertical axis) that have a given value range (on the horizontal axis). You can either plot this one attribute at a time, or you can call the hist() method on the whole dataset, and it will plot a histogram for each numerical attribute (see Figure 2-8). For example, you can see that slightly over 800 districts have a median_house_value equal to about $100,000.

```
%matplotlib inline    # only in a Jupyter notebook
import matplotlib.pyplot as plt
housing.hist(bins=50, figsize=(20,15))
plt.show()
```

 The hist() method relies on Matplotlib, which in turn relies on a user-specified graphical backend to draw on your screen. So before you can plot anything, you need to specify which backend Matplotlib should use. The simplest option is to use Jupyter's magic command %matplotlib inline. This tells Jupyter to set up Matplotlib so it uses Jupyter's own backend. Plots are then rendered within the notebook itself. Note that calling show() is optional in a Jupyter notebook, as Jupyter will automatically display plots when a cell is executed.

---

11 The standard deviation is generally denoted σ (the Greek letter sigma), and it is the square root of the *variance*, which is the average of the squared deviation from the mean. When a feature has a bell-shaped *normal distribution* (also called a *Gaussian distribution*), which is very common, the "68-95-99.7" rule applies: about 68% of the values fall within 1σ of the mean, 95% within 2σ, and 99.7% within 3σ.

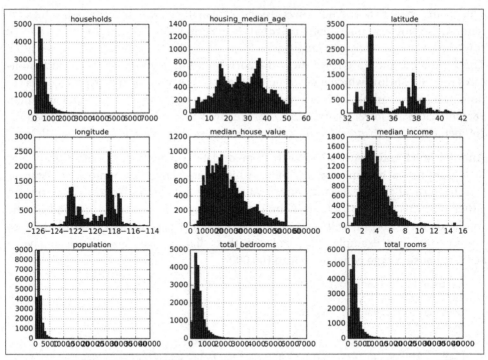

Figure 2-8. A histogram for each numerical attribute

Notice a few things in these histograms:

1. First, the median income attribute does not look like it is expressed in US dollars (USD). After checking with the team that collected the data, you are told that the data has been scaled and capped at 15 (actually 15.0001) for higher median incomes, and at 0.5 (actually 0.4999) for lower median incomes. The numbers represent roughly tens of thousands of dollars (e.g., 3 actually means about $30,000). Working with preprocessed attributes is common in Machine Learning, and it is not necessarily a problem, but you should try to understand how the data was computed.

2. The housing median age and the median house value were also capped. The latter may be a serious problem since it is your target attribute (your labels). Your Machine Learning algorithms may learn that prices never go beyond that limit. You need to check with your client team (the team that will use your system's output) to see if this is a problem or not. If they tell you that they need precise predictions even beyond $500,000, then you have mainly two options:

   a. Collect proper labels for the districts whose labels were capped.

b. Remove those districts from the training set (and also from the test set, since your system should not be evaluated poorly if it predicts values beyond $500,000).

3. These attributes have very different scales. We will discuss this later in this chapter when we explore feature scaling.

4. Finally, many histograms are *tail heavy*: they extend much farther to the right of the median than to the left. This may make it a bit harder for some Machine Learning algorithms to detect patterns. We will try transforming these attributes later on to have more bell-shaped distributions.

Hopefully you now have a better understanding of the kind of data you are dealing with.

Wait! Before you look at the data any further, you need to create a test set, put it aside, and never look at it.

Create a Test Set

It may sound strange to voluntarily set aside part of the data at this stage. After all, you have only taken a quick glance at the data, and surely you should learn a whole lot more about it before you decide what algorithms to use, right? This is true, but your brain is an amazing pattern detection system, which means that it is highly prone to overfitting: if you look at the test set, you may stumble upon some seemingly interesting pattern in the test data that leads you to select a particular kind of Machine Learning model. When you estimate the generalization error using the test set, your estimate will be too optimistic and you will launch a system that will not perform as well as expected. This is called *data snooping* bias.

Creating a test set is theoretically quite simple: just pick some instances randomly, typically 20% of the dataset, and set them aside:

```python
import numpy as np

def split_train_test(data, test_ratio):
    shuffled_indices = np.random.permutation(len(data))
    test_set_size = int(len(data) * test_ratio)
    test_indices = shuffled_indices[:test_set_size]
    train_indices = shuffled_indices[test_set_size:]
    return data.iloc[train_indices], data.iloc[test_indices]
```

You can then use this function like this:[12]

```
>>> train_set, test_set = split_train_test(housing, 0.2)
>>> len(train_set)
16512
>>> len(test_set)
4128
```

Well, this works, but it is not perfect: if you run the program again, it will generate a different test set! Over time, you (or your Machine Learning algorithms) will get to see the whole dataset, which is what you want to avoid.

One solution is to save the test set on the first run and then load it in subsequent runs. Another option is to set the random number generator's seed (e.g., `np.ran dom.seed(42)`)[13] before calling `np.random.permutation()`, so that it always generates the same shuffled indices.

But both these solutions will break next time you fetch an updated dataset. A common solution is to use each instance's identifier to decide whether or not it should go in the test set (assuming instances have a unique and immutable identifier). For example, you could compute a hash of each instance's identifier and put that instance in the test set if the hash is lower or equal to 20% of the maximum hash value. This ensures that the test set will remain consistent across multiple runs, even if you refresh the dataset. The new test set will contain 20% of the new instances, but it will not contain any instance that was previously in the training set. Here is a possible implementation:

```
from zlib import crc32

def test_set_check(identifier, test_ratio):
    return crc32(np.int64(identifier)) & 0xffffffff < test_ratio * 2**32

def split_train_test_by_id(data, test_ratio, id_column):
    ids = data[id_column]
    in_test_set = ids.apply(lambda id_: test_set_check(id_, test_ratio))
    return data.loc[~in_test_set], data.loc[in_test_set]
```

Unfortunately, the housing dataset does not have an identifier column. The simplest solution is to use the row index as the ID:

```
housing_with_id = housing.reset_index()   # adds an `index` column
train_set, test_set = split_train_test_by_id(housing_with_id, 0.2, "index")
```

---

12 In this book, when a code example contains a mix of code and outputs, as is the case here, it is formatted like in the Python interpreter, for better readability: the code lines are prefixed with >>> (or ... for indented blocks), and the outputs have no prefix.

13 You will often see people set the random seed to 42. This number has no special property, other than to be The Answer to the Ultimate Question of Life, the Universe, and Everything.

If you use the row index as a unique identifier, you need to make sure that new data gets appended to the end of the dataset, and no row ever gets deleted. If this is not possible, then you can try to use the most stable features to build a unique identifier. For example, a district's latitude and longitude are guaranteed to be stable for a few million years, so you could combine them into an ID like so:[14]

```
housing_with_id["id"] = housing["longitude"] * 1000 + housing["latitude"]
train_set, test_set = split_train_test_by_id(housing_with_id, 0.2, "id")
```

Scikit-Learn provides a few functions to split datasets into multiple subsets in various ways. The simplest function is `train_test_split`, which does pretty much the same thing as the function `split_train_test` defined earlier, with a couple of additional features. First there is a `random_state` parameter that allows you to set the random generator seed as explained previously, and second you can pass it multiple datasets with an identical number of rows, and it will split them on the same indices (this is very useful, for example, if you have a separate DataFrame for labels):

```
from sklearn.model_selection import train_test_split

train_set, test_set = train_test_split(housing, test_size=0.2, random_state=42)
```

So far we have considered purely random sampling methods. This is generally fine if your dataset is large enough (especially relative to the number of attributes), but if it is not, you run the risk of introducing a significant sampling bias. When a survey company decides to call 1,000 people to ask them a few questions, they don't just pick 1,000 people randomly in a phone book. They try to ensure that these 1,000 people are representative of the whole population. For example, the US population is composed of 51.3% female and 48.7% male, so a well-conducted survey in the US would try to maintain this ratio in the sample: 513 female and 487 male. This is called *stratified sampling*: the population is divided into homogeneous subgroups called *strata*, and the right number of instances is sampled from each stratum to guarantee that the test set is representative of the overall population. If they used purely random sampling, there would be about 12% chance of sampling a skewed test set with either less than 49% female or more than 54% female. Either way, the survey results would be significantly biased.

Suppose you chatted with experts who told you that the median income is a very important attribute to predict median housing prices. You may want to ensure that the test set is representative of the various categories of incomes in the whole dataset. Since the median income is a continuous numerical attribute, you first need to create an income category attribute. Let's look at the median income histogram more closely (back in Figure 2-8): most median income values are clustered around 2 to 5 (i.e.,

---

14 The location information is actually quite coarse, and as a result many districts will have the exact same ID, so they will end up in the same set (test or train). This introduces some unfortunate sampling bias.

$20,000–$50,000), but some median incomes go far beyond 6 (i.e., $60,000). It is important to have a sufficient number of instances in your dataset for each stratum, or else the estimate of the stratum's importance may be biased. This means that you should not have too many strata, and each stratum should be large enough. The following code creates an income category attribute by dividing the median income by 1.5 (to limit the number of income categories), and rounding up using ceil (to have discrete categories), and then keeping only the categories lower than 5 and merging the other categories into category 5:

```
housing["income_cat"] = np.ceil(housing["median_income"] / 1.5)
housing["income_cat"].where(housing["income_cat"] < 5, 5.0, inplace=True)
```

These income categories are represented in Figure 2-9:

```
housing["income_cat"].hist()
```

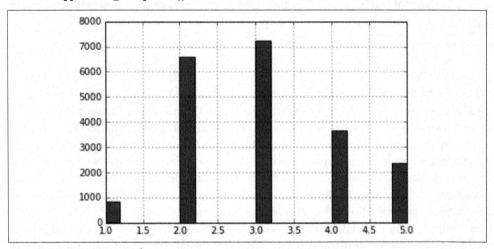

Figure 2-9. Histogram of income categories

Now you are ready to do stratified sampling based on the income category. For this you can use Scikit-Learn's StratifiedShuffleSplit class:

```
from sklearn.model_selection import StratifiedShuffleSplit

split = StratifiedShuffleSplit(n_splits=1, test_size=0.2, random_state=42)
for train_index, test_index in split.split(housing, housing["income_cat"]):
    strat_train_set = housing.loc[train_index]
    strat_test_set = housing.loc[test_index]
```

Let's see if this worked as expected. You can start by looking at the income category proportions in the test set:

```
>>> strat_test_set["income_cat"].value_counts() / len(strat_test_set)
3.0    0.350533
2.0    0.318798
```

```
4.0    0.176357
5.0    0.114583
1.0    0.039729
Name: income_cat, dtype: float64
```

With similar code you can measure the income category proportions in the full data-set. Figure 2-10 compares the income category proportions in the overall dataset, in the test set generated with stratified sampling, and in a test set generated using purely random sampling. As you can see, the test set generated using stratified sampling has income category proportions almost identical to those in the full dataset, whereas the test set generated using purely random sampling is quite skewed.

	Overall	Random	Stratified	Rand. %error	Strat. %error
1.0	0.039826	0.040213	0.039738	0.973236	-0.219137
2.0	0.318847	0.324370	0.318876	1.732260	0.009032
3.0	0.350581	0.358527	0.350618	2.266446	0.010408
4.0	0.176308	0.167393	0.176399	-5.056334	0.051717
5.0	0.114438	0.109496	0.114369	-4.318374	-0.060464

Figure 2-10. Sampling bias comparison of stratified versus purely random sampling

Now you should remove the income_cat attribute so the data is back to its original state:

```
for set_ in (strat_train_set, strat_test_set):
    set_.drop("income_cat", axis=1, inplace=True)
```

We spent quite a bit of time on test set generation for a good reason: this is an often neglected but critical part of a Machine Learning project. Moreover, many of these ideas will be useful later when we discuss cross-validation. Now it's time to move on to the next stage: exploring the data.

Discover and Visualize the Data to Gain Insights

So far you have only taken a quick glance at the data to get a general understanding of the kind of data you are manipulating. Now the goal is to go a little bit more in depth.

First, make sure you have put the test set aside and you are only exploring the training set. Also, if the training set is very large, you may want to sample an exploration set, to make manipulations easy and fast. In our case, the set is quite small so you can just work directly on the full set. Let's create a copy so you can play with it without harming the training set:

```
housing = strat_train_set.copy()
```

Visualizing Geographical Data

Since there is geographical information (latitude and longitude), it is a good idea to create a scatterplot of all districts to visualize the data (Figure 2-11):

```
housing.plot(kind="scatter", x="longitude", y="latitude")
```

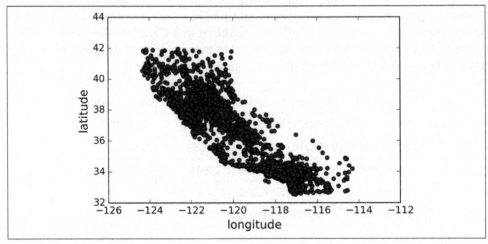

Figure 2-11. A geographical scatterplot of the data

This looks like California all right, but other than that it is hard to see any particular pattern. Setting the `alpha` option to `0.1` makes it much easier to visualize the places where there is a high density of data points (Figure 2-12):

```
housing.plot(kind="scatter", x="longitude", y="latitude", alpha=0.1)
```

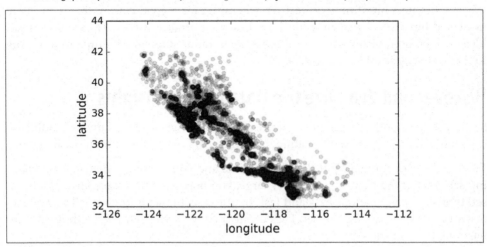

Figure 2-12. A better visualization highlighting high-density areas

Now that's much better: you can clearly see the high-density areas, namely the Bay Area and around Los Angeles and San Diego, plus a long line of fairly high density in the Central Valley, in particular around Sacramento and Fresno.

More generally, our brains are very good at spotting patterns on pictures, but you may need to play around with visualization parameters to make the patterns stand out.

Now let's look at the housing prices (Figure 2-13). The radius of each circle represents the district's population (option s), and the color represents the price (option c). We will use a predefined color map (option cmap) called jet, which ranges from blue (low values) to red (high prices):[15]

```
housing.plot(kind="scatter", x="longitude", y="latitude", alpha=0.4,
    s=housing["population"]/100, label="population", figsize=(10,7),
    c="median_house_value", cmap=plt.get_cmap("jet"), colorbar=True,
)
plt.legend()
```

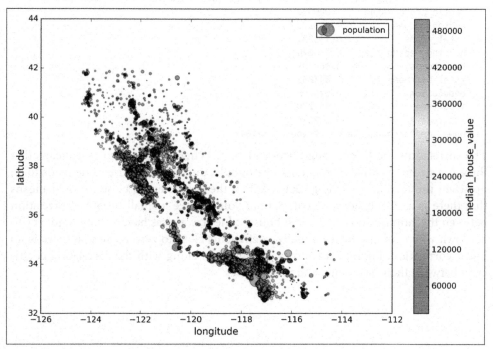

Figure 2-13. California housing prices

---

15 If you are reading this in grayscale, grab a red pen and scribble over most of the coastline from the Bay Area down to San Diego (as you might expect). You can add a patch of yellow around Sacramento as well.

This image tells you that the housing prices are very much related to the location (e.g., close to the ocean) and to the population density, as you probably knew already. It will probably be useful to use a clustering algorithm to detect the main clusters, and add new features that measure the proximity to the cluster centers. The ocean proximity attribute may be useful as well, although in Northern California the housing prices in coastal districts are not too high, so it is not a simple rule.

Looking for Correlations

Since the dataset is not too large, you can easily compute the *standard correlation coefficient* (also called *Pearson's r*) between every pair of attributes using the corr() method:

```
corr_matrix = housing.corr()
```

Now let's look at how much each attribute correlates with the median house value:

```
>>> corr_matrix["median_house_value"].sort_values(ascending=False)
median_house_value    1.000000
median_income         0.687170
total_rooms           0.135231
housing_median_age    0.114220
households            0.064702
total_bedrooms        0.047865
population            -0.026699
longitude             -0.047279
latitude              -0.142826
Name: median_house_value, dtype: float64
```

The correlation coefficient ranges from –1 to 1. When it is close to 1, it means that there is a strong positive correlation; for example, the median house value tends to go up when the median income goes up. When the coefficient is close to –1, it means that there is a strong negative correlation; you can see a small negative correlation between the latitude and the median house value (i.e., prices have a slight tendency to go down when you go north). Finally, coefficients close to zero mean that there is no linear correlation. Figure 2-14 shows various plots along with the correlation coefficient between their horizontal and vertical axes.

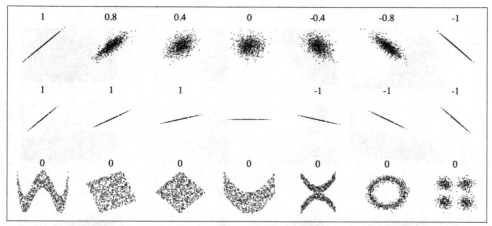

Figure 2-14. Standard correlation coefficient of various datasets (source: Wikipedia; public domain image)

The correlation coefficient only measures linear correlations ("if x goes up, then y generally goes up/down"). It may completely miss out on nonlinear relationships (e.g., "if x is close to zero then y generally goes up"). Note how all the plots of the bottom row have a correlation coefficient equal to zero despite the fact that their axes are clearly not independent: these are examples of nonlinear relationships. Also, the second row shows examples where the correlation coefficient is equal to 1 or –1; notice that this has nothing to do with the slope. For example, your height in inches has a correlation coefficient of 1 with your height in feet or in nanometers.

Another way to check for correlation between attributes is to use Pandas' `scatter_matrix` function, which plots every numerical attribute against every other numerical attribute. Since there are now 11 numerical attributes, you would get $11^2 =$ 121 plots, which would not fit on a page, so let's just focus on a few promising attributes that seem most correlated with the median housing value (Figure 2-15):

```
from pandas.plotting import scatter_matrix

attributes = ["median_house_value", "median_income", "total_rooms",
              "housing_median_age"]
scatter_matrix(housing[attributes], figsize=(12, 8))
```

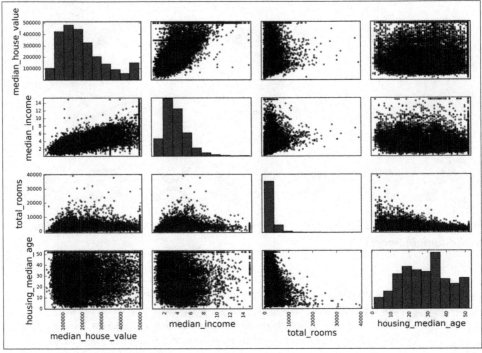

Figure 2-15. Scatter matrix

The main diagonal (top left to bottom right) would be full of straight lines if Pandas plotted each variable against itself, which would not be very useful. So instead Pandas displays a histogram of each attribute (other options are available; see Pandas' documentation for more details).

The most promising attribute to predict the median house value is the median income, so let's zoom in on their correlation scatterplot (Figure 2-16):

```
housing.plot(kind="scatter", x="median_income", y="median_house_value",
             alpha=0.1)
```

This plot reveals a few things. First, the correlation is indeed very strong; you can clearly see the upward trend and the points are not too dispersed. Second, the price cap that we noticed earlier is clearly visible as a horizontal line at $500,000. But this plot reveals other less obvious straight lines: a horizontal line around $450,000, another around $350,000, perhaps one around $280,000, and a few more below that. You may want to try removing the corresponding districts to prevent your algorithms from learning to reproduce these data quirks.

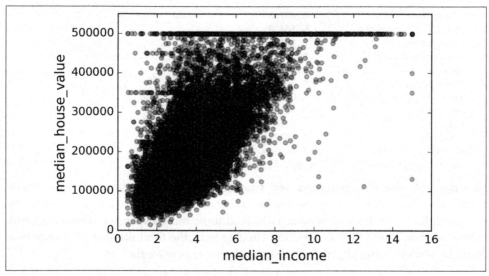

Figure 2-16. Median income versus median house value

Experimenting with Attribute Combinations

Hopefully the previous sections gave you an idea of a few ways you can explore the data and gain insights. You identified a few data quirks that you may want to clean up before feeding the data to a Machine Learning algorithm, and you found interesting correlations between attributes, in particular with the target attribute. You also noticed that some attributes have a tail-heavy distribution, so you may want to transform them (e.g., by computing their logarithm). Of course, your mileage will vary considerably with each project, but the general ideas are similar.

One last thing you may want to do before actually preparing the data for Machine Learning algorithms is to try out various attribute combinations. For example, the total number of rooms in a district is not very useful if you don't know how many households there are. What you really want is the number of rooms per household. Similarly, the total number of bedrooms by itself is not very useful: you probably want to compare it to the number of rooms. And the population per household also seems like an interesting attribute combination to look at. Let's create these new attributes:

```
housing["rooms_per_household"] = housing["total_rooms"]/housing["households"]
housing["bedrooms_per_room"] = housing["total_bedrooms"]/housing["total_rooms"]
housing["population_per_household"]=housing["population"]/housing["households"]
```

And now let's look at the correlation matrix again:

```
>>> corr_matrix = housing.corr()
>>> corr_matrix["median_house_value"].sort_values(ascending=False)
median_house_value          1.000000
```

```
median_income              0.687160
rooms_per_household        0.146285
total_rooms                0.135097
housing_median_age         0.114110
households                 0.064506
total_bedrooms             0.047689
population_per_household   -0.021985
population                 -0.026920
longitude                  -0.047432
latitude                   -0.142724
bedrooms_per_room          -0.259984
Name: median_house_value, dtype: float64
```

Hey, not bad! The new `bedrooms_per_room` attribute is much more correlated with the median house value than the total number of rooms or bedrooms. Apparently houses with a lower bedroom/room ratio tend to be more expensive. The number of rooms per household is also more informative than the total number of rooms in a district—obviously the larger the houses, the more expensive they are.

This round of exploration does not have to be absolutely thorough; the point is to start off on the right foot and quickly gain insights that will help you get a first reasonably good prototype. But this is an iterative process: once you get a prototype up and running, you can analyze its output to gain more insights and come back to this exploration step.

Prepare the Data for Machine Learning Algorithms

It's time to prepare the data for your Machine Learning algorithms. Instead of just doing this manually, you should write functions to do that, for several good reasons:

- This will allow you to reproduce these transformations easily on any dataset (e.g., the next time you get a fresh dataset).
- You will gradually build a library of transformation functions that you can reuse in future projects.
- You can use these functions in your live system to transform the new data before feeding it to your algorithms.
- This will make it possible for you to easily try various transformations and see which combination of transformations works best.

But first let's revert to a clean training set (by copying `strat_train_set` once again), and let's separate the predictors and the labels since we don't necessarily want to apply the same transformations to the predictors and the target values (note that `drop()` creates a copy of the data and does not affect `strat_train_set`):

```
housing = strat_train_set.drop("median_house_value", axis=1)
housing_labels = strat_train_set["median_house_value"].copy()
```

Data Cleaning

Most Machine Learning algorithms cannot work with missing features, so let's create a few functions to take care of them. You noticed earlier that the total_bedrooms attribute has some missing values, so let's fix this. You have three options:

- Get rid of the corresponding districts.
- Get rid of the whole attribute.
- Set the values to some value (zero, the mean, the median, etc.).

You can accomplish these easily using DataFrame's dropna(), drop(), and fillna() methods:

```
housing.dropna(subset=["total_bedrooms"])    # option 1
housing.drop("total_bedrooms", axis=1)       # option 2
median = housing["total_bedrooms"].median()  # option 3
housing["total_bedrooms"].fillna(median, inplace=True)
```

If you choose option 3, you should compute the median value on the training set, and use it to fill the missing values in the training set, but also don't forget to save the median value that you have computed. You will need it later to replace missing values in the test set when you want to evaluate your system, and also once the system goes live to replace missing values in new data.

Scikit-Learn provides a handy class to take care of missing values: Imputer. Here is how to use it. First, you need to create an Imputer instance, specifying that you want to replace each attribute's missing values with the median of that attribute:

```
from sklearn.preprocessing import Imputer

imputer = Imputer(strategy="median")
```

Since the median can only be computed on numerical attributes, we need to create a copy of the data without the text attribute ocean_proximity:

```
housing_num = housing.drop("ocean_proximity", axis=1)
```

Now you can fit the imputer instance to the training data using the fit() method:

```
imputer.fit(housing_num)
```

The imputer has simply computed the median of each attribute and stored the result in its statistics_ instance variable. Only the total_bedrooms attribute had missing values, but we cannot be sure that there won't be any missing values in new data after the system goes live, so it is safer to apply the imputer to all the numerical attributes:

```
>>> imputer.statistics_
array([ -118.51 , 34.26 , 29. , 2119.5 , 433. , 1164. , 408. , 3.5409])
>>> housing_num.median().values
array([ -118.51 , 34.26 , 29. , 2119.5 , 433. , 1164. , 408. , 3.5409])
```

Now you can use this "trained" imputer to transform the training set by replacing missing values by the learned medians:

```
X = imputer.transform(housing_num)
```

The result is a plain NumPy array containing the transformed features. If you want to put it back into a Pandas DataFrame, it's simple:

```
housing_tr = pd.DataFrame(X, columns=housing_num.columns)
```

Scikit-Learn Design

Scikit-Learn's API is remarkably well designed. The main design principles (*http://homl.info/11*) are:[16]

- **Consistency**. All objects share a consistent and simple interface:

  — *Estimators*. Any object that can estimate some parameters based on a dataset is called an *estimator* (e.g., an imputer is an estimator). The estimation itself is performed by the fit() method, and it takes only a dataset as a parameter (or two for supervised learning algorithms; the second dataset contains the labels). Any other parameter needed to guide the estimation process is considered a hyperparameter (such as an imputer's strategy), and it must be set as an instance variable (generally via a constructor parameter).

  — *Transformers*. Some estimators (such as an imputer) can also transform a dataset; these are called *transformers*. Once again, the API is quite simple: the transformation is performed by the transform() method with the dataset to transform as a parameter. It returns the transformed dataset. This transformation generally relies on the learned parameters, as is the case for an imputer. All transformers also have a convenience method called fit_transform() that is equivalent to calling fit() and then transform() (but sometimes fit_transform() is optimized and runs much faster).

  — *Predictors*. Finally, some estimators are capable of making predictions given a dataset; they are called *predictors*. For example, the LinearRegression model in the previous chapter was a predictor: it predicted life satisfaction given a country's GDP per capita. A predictor has a predict() method that takes a dataset of new instances and returns a dataset of corresponding predictions. It also has a score() method that measures the quality of the predictions given a test set (and the corresponding labels in the case of supervised learning algorithms).[17]

---

16 For more details on the design principles, see "API design for machine learning software: experiences from the scikit-learn project," L. Buitinck, G. Louppe, M. Blondel, F. Pedregosa, A. Müller, et al. (2013).

17 Some predictors also provide methods to measure the confidence of their predictions.

- **Inspection**. All the estimator's hyperparameters are accessible directly via public instance variables (e.g., `imputer.strategy`), and all the estimator's learned parameters are also accessible via public instance variables with an underscore suffix (e.g., `imputer.statistics_`).

- **Nonproliferation of classes**. Datasets are represented as NumPy arrays or SciPy sparse matrices, instead of homemade classes. Hyperparameters are just regular Python strings or numbers.

- **Composition**. Existing building blocks are reused as much as possible. For example, it is easy to create a `Pipeline` estimator from an arbitrary sequence of transformers followed by a final estimator, as we will see.

- **Sensible defaults**. Scikit-Learn provides reasonable default values for most parameters, making it easy to create a baseline working system quickly.

Handling Text and Categorical Attributes

Earlier we left out the categorical attribute `ocean_proximity` because it is a text attribute so we cannot compute its median:

```
>>> housing_cat = housing["ocean_proximity"]
>>> housing_cat.head(10)
17606     <1H OCEAN
18632     <1H OCEAN
14650    NEAR OCEAN
3230        INLAND
3555      <1H OCEAN
19480        INLAND
8879      <1H OCEAN
13685        INLAND
4937      <1H OCEAN
4861      <1H OCEAN
Name: ocean_proximity, dtype: object
```

Most Machine Learning algorithms prefer to work with numbers anyway, so let's convert these categories from text to numbers. For this, we can use Pandas' `factorize()` method which maps each category to a different integer:

```
>>> housing_cat_encoded, housing_categories = housing_cat.factorize()
>>> housing_cat_encoded[:10]
array([0, 0, 1, 2, 0, 2, 0, 2, 0, 0])
```

This is better: `housing_cat_encoded` is now purely numerical. The `factorize()` method also returns the list of categories ("<1H OCEAN" was mapped to 0, "NEAR OCEAN" was mapped to 1, etc.):

```
>>> housing_categories
Index(['<1H OCEAN', 'NEAR OCEAN', 'INLAND', 'NEAR BAY', 'ISLAND'], dtype='object')
```

One issue with this representation is that ML algorithms will assume that two nearby values are more similar than two distant values. Obviously this is not the case (for example, categories 0 and 4 are more similar than categories 0 and 2). To fix this issue, a common solution is to create one binary attribute per category: one attribute equal to 1 when the category is "<1H OCEAN" (and 0 otherwise), another attribute equal to 1 when the category is "NEAR OCEAN" (and 0 otherwise), and so on. This is called *one-hot encoding*, because only one attribute will be equal to 1 (hot), while the others will be 0 (cold).

Scikit-Learn provides a `OneHotEncoder` encoder to convert integer categorical values into one-hot vectors. Let's encode the categories as one-hot vectors:

```
>>> from sklearn.preprocessing import OneHotEncoder
>>> encoder = OneHotEncoder()
>>> housing_cat_1hot = encoder.fit_transform(housing_cat_encoded.reshape(-1,1))
>>> housing_cat_1hot
<16512x5 sparse matrix of type '<class 'numpy.float64'>'
        with 16512 stored elements in Compressed Sparse Row format>
```

Note that `fit_transform()` expects a 2D array, but `housing_cat_encoded` is a 1D array, so we need to reshape it[18]. Also, notice that the output is a SciPy *sparse matrix*, instead of a NumPy array. This is very useful when you have categorical attributes with thousands of categories. After one-hot encoding we get a matrix with thousands of columns, and the matrix is full of zeros except for a single 1 per row. Using up tons of memory mostly to store zeros would be very wasteful, so instead a sparse matrix only stores the location of the nonzero elements. You can use it mostly like a normal 2D array,[19] but if you really want to convert it to a (dense) NumPy array, just call the `toarray()` method:

```
>>> housing_cat_1hot.toarray()
array([[ 1.,  0.,  0.,  0.,  0.],
       [ 1.,  0.,  0.,  0.,  0.],
       [ 0.,  1.,  0.,  0.,  0.],
       ...,
       [ 0.,  0.,  1.,  0.,  0.],
       [ 1.,  0.,  0.,  0.,  0.],
       [ 0.,  0.,  0.,  1.,  0.]])
```

You can apply both transformations (from text categories to integer categories, then from integer categories to one-hot vectors) in one shot using the `CategoricalEn coder` class. It is not part of Scikit-Learn 0.19.0 and earlier, but it will be added shortly, so it may already be available by the time you read this. If it is not, you can

---

18 NumPy's `reshape()` function allows one dimension to be –1, which means "unspecified": the value is inferred from the length of the array and the remaining dimensions.

19 See SciPy's documentation for more details.

simply get it from the Jupyter notebook for this chapter (the code was copied from Pull Request #9151). Here is how to use it:

```
>>> from sklearn.preprocessing import CategoricalEncoder # or get from notebook
>>> cat_encoder = CategoricalEncoder()
>>> housing_cat_reshaped = housing_cat.values.reshape(-1, 1)
>>> housing_cat_1hot = cat_encoder.fit_transform(housing_cat_reshaped)
>>> housing_cat_1hot
<16512x5 sparse matrix of type '<class 'numpy.float64'>'
    with 16512 stored elements in Compressed Sparse Row format>
```

By default, the CategoricalEncoder outputs a sparse matrix, but you can set the encoding to "onehot-dense" if you prefer a dense matrix:

```
>>> cat_encoder = CategoricalEncoder(encoding="onehot-dense")
>>> housing_cat_1hot = cat_encoder.fit_transform(housing_cat_reshaped)
>>> housing_cat_1hot
array([[ 1.,  0.,  0.,  0.,  0.],
       [ 1.,  0.,  0.,  0.,  0.],
       [ 0.,  0.,  0.,  0.,  1.],
       ...,
       [ 0.,  1.,  0.,  0.,  0.],
       [ 1.,  0.,  0.,  0.,  0.],
       [ 0.,  0.,  0.,  1.,  0.]])
```

You can get the list of categories using the encoder's categories_ instance variable. It is a list containing a 1D array of categories for each categorical attribute (in this case, a list containing a single array since there is a just one categorical attribute):

```
>>> cat_encoder.categories_
[array(['<1H OCEAN', 'INLAND', 'ISLAND', 'NEAR BAY', 'NEAR OCEAN'], dtype=object)]
```

 If a categorical attribute has a large number of possible categories (e.g., country code, profession, species, etc.), then one-hot encoding will result in a large number of input features. This may slow down training and degrade performance. If this happens, you will want to produce denser representations called *embeddings*, but this requires a good understanding of neural networks (see Chapter 14 for more details).

Custom Transformers

Although Scikit-Learn provides many useful transformers, you will need to write your own for tasks such as custom cleanup operations or combining specific attributes. You will want your transformer to work seamlessly with Scikit-Learn functionalities (such as pipelines), and since Scikit-Learn relies on duck typing (not inheritance), all you need is to create a class and implement three methods: fit() (returning self), transform(), and fit_transform(). You can get the last one for free by simply adding TransformerMixin as a base class. Also, if you add BaseEstima tor as a base class (and avoid *args and **kargs in your constructor) you will get two extra methods (get_params() and set_params()) that will be useful for automatic hyperparameter tuning. For example, here is a small transformer class that adds the combined attributes we discussed earlier:

```
from sklearn.base import BaseEstimator, TransformerMixin

rooms_ix, bedrooms_ix, population_ix, household_ix = 3, 4, 5, 6

class CombinedAttributesAdder(BaseEstimator, TransformerMixin):
    def __init__(self, add_bedrooms_per_room = True): # no *args or **kargs
        self.add_bedrooms_per_room = add_bedrooms_per_room
    def fit(self, X, y=None):
        return self  # nothing else to do
    def transform(self, X, y=None):
        rooms_per_household = X[:, rooms_ix] / X[:, household_ix]
        population_per_household = X[:, population_ix] / X[:, household_ix]
        if self.add_bedrooms_per_room:
            bedrooms_per_room = X[:, bedrooms_ix] / X[:, rooms_ix]
            return np.c_[X, rooms_per_household, population_per_household,
                         bedrooms_per_room]
        else:
            return np.c_[X, rooms_per_household, population_per_household]

attr_adder = CombinedAttributesAdder(add_bedrooms_per_room=False)
housing_extra_attribs = attr_adder.transform(housing.values)
```

In this example the transformer has one hyperparameter, add_bedrooms_per_room, set to True by default (it is often helpful to provide sensible defaults). This hyperparameter will allow you to easily find out whether adding this attribute helps the Machine Learning algorithms or not. More generally, you can add a hyperparameter to gate any data preparation step that you are not 100% sure about. The more you automate these data preparation steps, the more combinations you can automatically try out, making it much more likely that you will find a great combination (and saving you a lot of time).

Feature Scaling

One of the most important transformations you need to apply to your data is *feature scaling*. With few exceptions, Machine Learning algorithms don't perform well when the input numerical attributes have very different scales. This is the case for the housing data: the total number of rooms ranges from about 6 to 39,320, while the median incomes only range from 0 to 15. Note that scaling the target values is generally not required.

There are two common ways to get all attributes to have the same scale: *min-max scaling* and *standardization*.

Min-max scaling (many people call this *normalization*) is quite simple: values are shifted and rescaled so that they end up ranging from 0 to 1. We do this by subtracting the min value and dividing by the max minus the min. Scikit-Learn provides a transformer called MinMaxScaler for this. It has a feature_range hyperparameter that lets you change the range if you don't want 0–1 for some reason.

Standardization is quite different: first it subtracts the mean value (so standardized values always have a zero mean), and then it divides by the standard deviation so that the resulting distribution has unit variance. Unlike min-max scaling, standardization does not bound values to a specific range, which may be a problem for some algorithms (e.g., neural networks often expect an input value ranging from 0 to 1). However, standardization is much less affected by outliers. For example, suppose a district had a median income equal to 100 (by mistake). Min-max scaling would then crush all the other values from 0–15 down to 0–0.15, whereas standardization would not be much affected. Scikit-Learn provides a transformer called StandardScaler for standardization.

 As with all the transformations, it is important to fit the scalers to the training data only, not to the full dataset (including the test set). Only then can you use them to transform the training set and the test set (and new data).

Transformation Pipelines

As you can see, there are many data transformation steps that need to be executed in the right order. Fortunately, Scikit-Learn provides the Pipeline class to help with such sequences of transformations. Here is a small pipeline for the numerical attributes:

```
from sklearn.pipeline import Pipeline
from sklearn.preprocessing import StandardScaler

num_pipeline = Pipeline([
        ('imputer', Imputer(strategy="median")),
        ('attribs_adder', CombinedAttributesAdder()),
        ('std_scaler', StandardScaler()),
    ])

housing_num_tr = num_pipeline.fit_transform(housing_num)
```

The Pipeline constructor takes a list of name/estimator pairs defining a sequence of steps. All but the last estimator must be transformers (i.e., they must have a fit_transform() method). The names can be anything you like (as long as they don't contain double underscores "__").

When you call the pipeline's `fit()` method, it calls `fit_transform()` sequentially on all transformers, passing the output of each call as the parameter to the next call, until it reaches the final estimator, for which it just calls the `fit()` method.

The pipeline exposes the same methods as the final estimator. In this example, the last estimator is a `StandardScaler`, which is a transformer, so the pipeline has a `trans form()` method that applies all the transforms to the data in sequence (it also has a `fit_transform` method that we could have used instead of calling `fit()` and then `transform()`).

Now it would be nice if we could feed a Pandas DataFrame containing non-numerical columns directly into our pipeline, instead of having to first manually extract the numerical columns into a NumPy array. There is nothing in Scikit-Learn to handle Pandas DataFrames,[20] but we can write a custom transformer for this task:

```
from sklearn.base import BaseEstimator, TransformerMixin

class DataFrameSelector(BaseEstimator, TransformerMixin):
    def __init__(self, attribute_names):
        self.attribute_names = attribute_names
    def fit(self, X, y=None):
        return self
    def transform(self, X):
        return X[self.attribute_names].values
```

Our `DataFrameSelector` will transform the data by selecting the desired attributes, dropping the rest, and converting the resulting DataFrame to a NumPy array. With this, you can easily write a pipeline that will take a Pandas DataFrame and handle only the numerical values: the pipeline would just start with a `DataFrameSelector` to pick only the numerical attributes, followed by the other preprocessing steps we discussed earlier. And you can just as easily write another pipeline for the categorical attributes as well by simply selecting the categorical attributes using a `DataFrameSe lector` and then applying a `CategoricalEncoder` .

```
num_attribs = list(housing_num)
cat_attribs = ["ocean_proximity"]

num_pipeline = Pipeline([
        ('selector', DataFrameSelector(num_attribs)),
        ('imputer', Imputer(strategy="median")),
        ('attribs_adder', CombinedAttributesAdder()),
        ('std_scaler', StandardScaler()),
    ])
```

---

20 But check out Pull Request #3886, which may introduce a `ColumnTransformer` class making attribute-specific transformations easy. You could also run `pip3 install sklearn-pandas` to get a `DataFrameMapper` class with a similar objective.

```
cat_pipeline = Pipeline([
        ('selector', DataFrameSelector(cat_attribs)),
        ('cat_encoder', CategoricalEncoder(encoding="onehot-dense")),
    ])
```

But how can you join these two pipelines into a single pipeline? The answer is to use Scikit-Learn's `FeatureUnion` class. You give it a list of transformers (which can be entire transformer pipelines); when its `transform()` method is called, it runs each transformer's `transform()` method in parallel, waits for their output, and then concatenates them and returns the result (and of course calling its `fit()` method calls each transformer's `fit()` method). A full pipeline handling both numerical and categorical attributes may look like this:

```
from sklearn.pipeline import FeatureUnion

full_pipeline = FeatureUnion(transformer_list=[
        ("num_pipeline", num_pipeline),
        ("cat_pipeline", cat_pipeline),
    ])
```

And you can run the whole pipeline simply:

```
>>> housing_prepared = full_pipeline.fit_transform(housing)
>>> housing_prepared
array([[-1.15604281,  0.77194962,  0.74333089, ...,  0.        ,
         0.        ,  0.        ],
       [-1.17602483,  0.6596948 , -1.1653172 , ...,  0.        ,
         0.        ,  0.        ],
       [...]
>>> housing_prepared.shape
(16512, 16)
```

Select and Train a Model

At last! You framed the problem, you got the data and explored it, you sampled a training set and a test set, and you wrote transformation pipelines to clean up and prepare your data for Machine Learning algorithms automatically. You are now ready to select and train a Machine Learning model.

Training and Evaluating on the Training Set

The good news is that thanks to all these previous steps, things are now going to be much simpler than you might think. Let's first train a Linear Regression model, like we did in the previous chapter:

```
from sklearn.linear_model import LinearRegression

lin_reg = LinearRegression()
lin_reg.fit(housing_prepared, housing_labels)
```

Done! You now have a working Linear Regression model. Let's try it out on a few instances from the training set:

```
>>> some_data = housing.iloc[:5]
>>> some_labels = housing_labels.iloc[:5]
>>> some_data_prepared = full_pipeline.transform(some_data)
>>> print("Predictions:", lin_reg.predict(some_data_prepared))
Predictions: [ 210644.6045  317768.8069  210956.4333  59218.9888  189747.5584]
>>> print("Labels:", list(some_labels))
Labels: [286600.0, 340600.0, 196900.0, 46300.0, 254500.0]
```

It works, although the predictions are not exactly accurate (e.g., the first prediction is off by close to 40%!). Let's measure this regression model's RMSE on the whole training set using Scikit-Learn's `mean_squared_error` function:

```
>>> from sklearn.metrics import mean_squared_error
>>> housing_predictions = lin_reg.predict(housing_prepared)
>>> lin_mse = mean_squared_error(housing_labels, housing_predictions)
>>> lin_rmse = np.sqrt(lin_mse)
>>> lin_rmse
68628.198198489219
```

Okay, this is better than nothing but clearly not a great score: most districts' `median_housing_values` range between $120,000 and $265,000, so a typical prediction error of $68,628 is not very satisfying. This is an example of a model underfitting the training data. When this happens it can mean that the features do not provide enough information to make good predictions, or that the model is not powerful enough. As we saw in the previous chapter, the main ways to fix underfitting are to select a more powerful model, to feed the training algorithm with better features, or to reduce the constraints on the model. This model is not regularized, so this rules out the last option. You could try to add more features (e.g., the log of the population), but first let's try a more complex model to see how it does.

Let's train a `DecisionTreeRegressor`. This is a powerful model, capable of finding complex nonlinear relationships in the data (Decision Trees are presented in more detail in Chapter 6). The code should look familiar by now:

```
from sklearn.tree import DecisionTreeRegressor

tree_reg = DecisionTreeRegressor()
tree_reg.fit(housing_prepared, housing_labels)
```

Now that the model is trained, let's evaluate it on the training set:

```
>>> housing_predictions = tree_reg.predict(housing_prepared)
>>> tree_mse = mean_squared_error(housing_labels, housing_predictions)
>>> tree_rmse = np.sqrt(tree_mse)
>>> tree_rmse
0.0
```

Wait, what!? No error at all? Could this model really be absolutely perfect? Of course, it is much more likely that the model has badly overfit the data. How can you be sure? As we saw earlier, you don't want to touch the test set until you are ready to launch a model you are confident about, so you need to use part of the training set for training, and part for model validation.

Better Evaluation Using Cross-Validation

One way to evaluate the Decision Tree model would be to use the `train_test_split` function to split the training set into a smaller training set and a validation set, then train your models against the smaller training set and evaluate them against the validation set. It's a bit of work, but nothing too difficult and it would work fairly well.

A great alternative is to use Scikit-Learn's *cross-validation* feature. The following code performs *K-fold cross-validation*: it randomly splits the training set into 10 distinct subsets called *folds*, then it trains and evaluates the Decision Tree model 10 times, picking a different fold for evaluation every time and training on the other 9 folds. The result is an array containing the 10 evaluation scores:

```
from sklearn.model_selection import cross_val_score
scores = cross_val_score(tree_reg, housing_prepared, housing_labels,
                         scoring="neg_mean_squared_error", cv=10)
tree_rmse_scores = np.sqrt(-scores)
```

 Scikit-Learn cross-validation features expect a utility function (greater is better) rather than a cost function (lower is better), so the scoring function is actually the opposite of the MSE (i.e., a negative value), which is why the preceding code computes `-scores` before calculating the square root.

Let's look at the results:

```
>>> def display_scores(scores):
...     print("Scores:", scores)
...     print("Mean:", scores.mean())
...     print("Standard deviation:", scores.std())
...
>>> display_scores(tree_rmse_scores)
Scores: [ 70232.0136482    66828.46839892  72444.08721003  70761.50186201
  71125.52697653  75581.29319857  70169.59286164  70055.37863456
  75370.49116773  71222.39081244]
Mean: 71379.0744771
Standard deviation: 2458.31882043
```

Now the Decision Tree doesn't look as good as it did earlier. In fact, it seems to perform worse than the Linear Regression model! Notice that cross-validation allows you to get not only an estimate of the performance of your model, but also a measure of how precise this estimate is (i.e., its standard deviation). The Decision Tree has a score of approximately 71,379, generally ±2,458. You would not have this information if you just used one validation set. But cross-validation comes at the cost of training the model several times, so it is not always possible.

Let's compute the same scores for the Linear Regression model just to be sure:

```
>>> lin_scores = cross_val_score(lin_reg, housing_prepared, housing_labels,
...                              scoring="neg_mean_squared_error", cv=10)
...
>>> lin_rmse_scores = np.sqrt(-lin_scores)
>>> display_scores(lin_rmse_scores)
Scores: [ 66782.73843989  66960.118071    70347.95244419  74739.57052552
  68031.13388938  71193.84183426  64969.63056405  68281.61137997
  71552.91566558  67665.10082067]
Mean: 69052.4613635
Standard deviation: 2731.6740018
```

That's right: the Decision Tree model is overfitting so badly that it performs worse than the Linear Regression model.

Let's try one last model now: the RandomForestRegressor. As we will see in Chapter 7, Random Forests work by training many Decision Trees on random subsets of the features, then averaging out their predictions. Building a model on top of many other models is called *Ensemble Learning*, and it is often a great way to push ML algorithms even further. We will skip most of the code since it is essentially the same as for the other models:

```
>>> from sklearn.ensemble import RandomForestRegressor
>>> forest_reg = RandomForestRegressor()
>>> forest_reg.fit(housing_prepared, housing_labels)
>>> [...]
>>> forest_rmse
21941.911027380233
>>> display_scores(forest_rmse_scores)
Scores: [ 51650.94405471  48920.80645498  52979.16096752  54412.74042021
  50861.29381163  56488.55699727  51866.90120786  49752.24599537
  55399.50713191  53309.74548294]
Mean: 52564.1902524
Standard deviation: 2301.87380392
```

Wow, this is much better: Random Forests look very promising. However, note that the score on the training set is still much lower than on the validation sets, meaning that the model is still overfitting the training set. Possible solutions for overfitting are to simplify the model, constrain it (i.e., regularize it), or get a lot more training data. However, before you dive much deeper in Random Forests, you should try out many other models from various categories of Machine Learning algorithms (several Support Vector Machines with different kernels, possibly a neural network, etc.), without spending too much time tweaking the hyperparameters. The goal is to shortlist a few (two to five) promising models.

You should save every model you experiment with, so you can come back easily to any model you want. Make sure you save both the hyperparameters and the trained parameters, as well as the cross-validation scores and perhaps the actual predictions as well. This will allow you to easily compare scores across model types, and compare the types of errors they make. You can easily save Scikit-Learn models by using Python's pickle module, or using sklearn.externals.joblib, which is more efficient at serializing large NumPy arrays:

```
from sklearn.externals import joblib

joblib.dump(my_model, "my_model.pkl")
# and later...
my_model_loaded = joblib.load("my_model.pkl")
```

Fine-Tune Your Model

Let's assume that you now have a shortlist of promising models. You now need to fine-tune them. Let's look at a few ways you can do that.

Grid Search

One way to do that would be to fiddle with the hyperparameters manually, until you find a great combination of hyperparameter values. This would be very tedious work, and you may not have time to explore many combinations.

Instead you should get Scikit-Learn's GridSearchCV to search for you. All you need to do is tell it which hyperparameters you want it to experiment with, and what values to try out, and it will evaluate all the possible combinations of hyperparameter values, using cross-validation. For example, the following code searches for the best combination of hyperparameter values for the RandomForestRegressor:

```
from sklearn.model_selection import GridSearchCV

param_grid = [
    {'n_estimators': [3, 10, 30], 'max_features': [2, 4, 6, 8]},
    {'bootstrap': [False], 'n_estimators': [3, 10], 'max_features': [2, 3, 4]},
  ]

forest_reg = RandomForestRegressor()

grid_search = GridSearchCV(forest_reg, param_grid, cv=5,
                           scoring='neg_mean_squared_error')

grid_search.fit(housing_prepared, housing_labels)
```

When you have no idea what value a hyperparameter should have, a simple approach is to try out consecutive powers of 10 (or a smaller number if you want a more fine-grained search, as shown in this example with the n_estimators hyperparameter).

This param_grid tells Scikit-Learn to first evaluate all $3 \times 4 = 12$ combinations of n_estimators and max_features hyperparameter values specified in the first dict (don't worry about what these hyperparameters mean for now; they will be explained in Chapter 7), then try all $2 \times 3 = 6$ combinations of hyperparameter values in the second dict, but this time with the bootstrap hyperparameter set to False instead of True (which is the default value for this hyperparameter).

All in all, the grid search will explore $12 + 6 = 18$ combinations of RandomForestRe gressor hyperparameter values, and it will train each model five times (since we are using five-fold cross validation). In other words, all in all, there will be $18 \times 5 = 90$ rounds of training! It may take quite a long time, but when it is done you can get the best combination of parameters like this:

```
>>> grid_search.best_params_
{'max_features': 8, 'n_estimators': 30}
```

Since 8 and 30 are the maximum values that were evaluated, you should probably try searching again with higher values, since the score may continue to improve.

You can also get the best estimator directly:

```
>>> grid_search.best_estimator_
RandomForestRegressor(bootstrap=True, criterion='mse', max_depth=None,
          max_features=8, max_leaf_nodes=None, min_impurity_decrease=0.0,
          min_impurity_split=None, min_samples_leaf=1,
          min_samples_split=2, min_weight_fraction_leaf=0.0,
          n_estimators=30, n_jobs=1, oob_score=False, random_state=42,
          verbose=0, warm_start=False)
```

If GridSearchCV is initialized with refit=True (which is the default), then once it finds the best estimator using cross-validation, it retrains it on the whole training set. This is usually a good idea since feeding it more data will likely improve its performance.

And of course the evaluation scores are also available:

```
>>> cvres = grid_search.cv_results_
>>> for mean_score, params in zip(cvres["mean_test_score"], cvres["params"]):
```

```
...      print(np.sqrt(-mean_score), params)
...
63647.854446 {'n_estimators': 3, 'max_features': 2}
55611.5015988 {'n_estimators': 10, 'max_features': 2}
53370.0640736 {'n_estimators': 30, 'max_features': 2}
60959.1388585 {'n_estimators': 3, 'max_features': 4}
52740.5841667 {'n_estimators': 10, 'max_features': 4}
50374.1421461 {'n_estimators': 30, 'max_features': 4}
58661.2866462 {'n_estimators': 3, 'max_features': 6}
52009.9739798 {'n_estimators': 10, 'max_features': 6}
50154.1177737 {'n_estimators': 30, 'max_features': 6}
57865.3616801 {'n_estimators': 3, 'max_features': 8}
51730.0755087 {'n_estimators': 10, 'max_features': 8}
49694.8514333 {'n_estimators': 30, 'max_features': 8}
62874.4073931 {'n_estimators': 3, 'bootstrap': False, 'max_features': 2}
54643.4998083 {'n_estimators': 10, 'bootstrap': False, 'max_features': 2}
59437.8922859 {'n_estimators': 3, 'bootstrap': False, 'max_features': 3}
52735.3582936 {'n_estimators': 10, 'bootstrap': False, 'max_features': 3}
57490.0168279 {'n_estimators': 3, 'bootstrap': False, 'max_features': 4}
51008.2615672 {'n_estimators': 10, 'bootstrap': False, 'max_features': 4}
```

In this example, we obtain the best solution by setting the `max_features` hyperparameter to 8, and the `n_estimators` hyperparameter to 30. The RMSE score for this combination is 49,694, which is slightly better than the score you got earlier using the default hyperparameter values (which was 52,564). Congratulations, you have successfully fine-tuned your best model!

> Don't forget that you can treat some of the data preparation steps as hyperparameters. For example, the grid search will automatically find out whether or not to add a feature you were not sure about (e.g., using the `add_bedrooms_per_room` hyperparameter of your `CombinedAttributesAdder` transformer). It may similarly be used to automatically find the best way to handle outliers, missing features, feature selection, and more.

Randomized Search

The grid search approach is fine when you are exploring relatively few combinations, like in the previous example, but when the hyperparameter *search space* is large, it is often preferable to use `RandomizedSearchCV` instead. This class can be used in much the same way as the `GridSearchCV` class, but instead of trying out all possible combinations, it evaluates a given number of random combinations by selecting a random value for each hyperparameter at every iteration. This approach has two main benefits:

- If you let the randomized search run for, say, 1,000 iterations, this approach will explore 1,000 different values for each hyperparameter (instead of just a few values per hyperparameter with the grid search approach).

- You have more control over the computing budget you want to allocate to hyperparameter search, simply by setting the number of iterations.

Ensemble Methods

Another way to fine-tune your system is to try to combine the models that perform best. The group (or "ensemble") will often perform better than the best individual model (just like Random Forests perform better than the individual Decision Trees they rely on), especially if the individual models make very different types of errors. We will cover this topic in more detail in Chapter 7.

Analyze the Best Models and Their Errors

You will often gain good insights on the problem by inspecting the best models. For example, the RandomForestRegressor can indicate the relative importance of each attribute for making accurate predictions:

```
>>> feature_importances = grid_search.best_estimator_.feature_importances_
>>> feature_importances
array([  7.33442355e-02,    6.29090705e-02,    4.11437985e-02,
         1.46726854e-02,    1.41064835e-02,    1.48742809e-02,
         1.42575993e-02,    3.66158981e-01,    5.64191792e-02,
         1.08792957e-01,    5.33510773e-02,    1.03114883e-02,
         1.64780994e-01,    6.02803867e-05,    1.96041560e-03,
         2.85647464e-03])
```

Let's display these importance scores next to their corresponding attribute names:

```
>>> extra_attribs = ["rooms_per_hhold", "pop_per_hhold", "bedrooms_per_room"]
>>> cat_encoder = cat_pipeline.named_steps["cat_encoder"]
>>> cat_one_hot_attribs = list(cat_encoder.categories_[0])
>>> attributes = num_attribs + extra_attribs + cat_one_hot_attribs
>>> sorted(zip(feature_importances, attributes), reverse=True)
[(0.36615898061813418, 'median_income'),
 (0.16478099356159051, 'INLAND'),
 (0.10879295677551573, 'pop_per_hhold'),
 (0.073344235516012421, 'longitude'),
 (0.062909070482620302, 'latitude'),
 (0.056419179181954007, 'rooms_per_hhold'),
 (0.053351077347675809, 'bedrooms_per_room'),
 (0.041143798478729635, 'housing_median_age'),
 (0.014874280890402767, 'population'),
 (0.014672685420543237, 'total_rooms'),
 (0.014257599323407807, 'households'),
 (0.014106483453584102, 'total_bedrooms'),
```

```
(0.010311488326303787, '<1H OCEAN'),
(0.0028564746373201579, 'NEAR OCEAN'),
(0.0019604155994780701, 'NEAR BAY'),
(6.0280386727365991e-05, 'ISLAND')]
```

With this information, you may want to try dropping some of the less useful features (e.g., apparently only one ocean_proximity category is really useful, so you could try dropping the others).

You should also look at the specific errors that your system makes, then try to understand why it makes them and what could fix the problem (adding extra features or, on the contrary, getting rid of uninformative ones, cleaning up outliers, etc.).

Evaluate Your System on the Test Set

After tweaking your models for a while, you eventually have a system that performs sufficiently well. Now is the time to evaluate the final model on the test set. There is nothing special about this process; just get the predictors and the labels from your test set, run your full_pipeline to transform the data (call transform(), *not* fit_transform()!), and evaluate the final model on the test set:

```
final_model = grid_search.best_estimator_

X_test = strat_test_set.drop("median_house_value", axis=1)
y_test = strat_test_set["median_house_value"].copy()

X_test_prepared = full_pipeline.transform(X_test)

final_predictions = final_model.predict(X_test_prepared)

final_mse = mean_squared_error(y_test, final_predictions)
final_rmse = np.sqrt(final_mse)   # => evaluates to 47,766.0
```

The performance will usually be slightly worse than what you measured using cross-validation if you did a lot of hyperparameter tuning (because your system ends up fine-tuned to perform well on the validation data, and will likely not perform as well on unknown datasets). It is not the case in this example, but when this happens you must resist the temptation to tweak the hyperparameters to make the numbers look good on the test set; the improvements would be unlikely to generalize to new data.

Now comes the project prelaunch phase: you need to present your solution (highlighting what you have learned, what worked and what did not, what assumptions were made, and what your system's limitations are), document everything, and create nice presentations with clear visualizations and easy-to-remember statements (e.g., "the median income is the number one predictor of housing prices").

Launch, Monitor, and Maintain Your System

Perfect, you got approval to launch! You need to get your solution ready for production, in particular by plugging the production input data sources into your system and writing tests.

You also need to write monitoring code to check your system's live performance at regular intervals and trigger alerts when it drops. This is important to catch not only sudden breakage, but also performance degradation. This is quite common because models tend to "rot" as data evolves over time, unless the models are regularly trained on fresh data.

Evaluating your system's performance will require sampling the system's predictions and evaluating them. This will generally require a human analysis. These analysts may be field experts, or workers on a crowdsourcing platform (such as Amazon Mechanical Turk or CrowdFlower). Either way, you need to plug the human evaluation pipeline into your system.

You should also make sure you evaluate the system's input data quality. Sometimes performance will degrade slightly because of a poor quality signal (e.g., a malfunctioning sensor sending random values, or another team's output becoming stale), but it may take a while before your system's performance degrades enough to trigger an alert. If you monitor your system's inputs, you may catch this earlier. Monitoring the inputs is particularly important for online learning systems.

Finally, you will generally want to train your models on a regular basis using fresh data. You should automate this process as much as possible. If you don't, you are very likely to refresh your model only every six months (at best), and your system's performance may fluctuate severely over time. If your system is an online learning system, you should make sure you save snapshots of its state at regular intervals so you can easily roll back to a previously working state.

Try It Out!

Hopefully this chapter gave you a good idea of what a Machine Learning project looks like, and showed you some of the tools you can use to train a great system. As you can see, much of the work is in the data preparation step, building monitoring tools, setting up human evaluation pipelines, and automating regular model training. The Machine Learning algorithms are also important, of course, but it is probably preferable to be comfortable with the overall process and know three or four algorithms well rather than to spend all your time exploring advanced algorithms and not enough time on the overall process.

So, if you have not already done so, now is a good time to pick up a laptop, select a dataset that you are interested in, and try to go through the whole process from A to

Z. A good place to start is on a competition website such as *http://kaggle.com/*: you will have a dataset to play with, a clear goal, and people to share the experience with.

Exercises

Using this chapter's housing dataset:

1. Try a Support Vector Machine regressor (`sklearn.svm.SVR`), with various hyperparameters such as `kernel="linear"` (with various values for the `C` hyperparameter) or `kernel="rbf"` (with various values for the `C` and `gamma` hyperparameters). Don't worry about what these hyperparameters mean for now. How does the best SVR predictor perform?

2. Try replacing `GridSearchCV` with `RandomizedSearchCV`.

3. Try adding a transformer in the preparation pipeline to select only the most important attributes.

4. Try creating a single pipeline that does the full data preparation plus the final prediction.

5. Automatically explore some preparation options using `GridSearchCV`.

Solutions to these exercises are available in the online Jupyter notebooks at *https://github.com/ageron/handson-ml*.

## CHAPTER 3

Classification

In Chapter 1 we mentioned that the most common supervised learning tasks are regression (predicting values) and classification (predicting classes). In Chapter 2 we explored a regression task, predicting housing values, using various algorithms such as Linear Regression, Decision Trees, and Random Forests (which will be explained in further detail in later chapters). Now we will turn our attention to classification systems.

MNIST

In this chapter, we will be using the MNIST dataset, which is a set of 70,000 small images of digits handwritten by high school students and employees of the US Census Bureau. Each image is labeled with the digit it represents. This set has been studied so much that it is often called the "Hello World" of Machine Learning: whenever people come up with a new classification algorithm, they are curious to see how it will perform on MNIST. Whenever someone learns Machine Learning, sooner or later they tackle MNIST.

Scikit-Learn provides many helper functions to download popular datasets. MNIST is one of them. The following code fetches the MNIST dataset:[1]

```
>>> from sklearn.datasets import fetch_mldata
>>> mnist = fetch_mldata('MNIST original')
>>> mnist
{'COL_NAMES': ['label', 'data'],
 'DESCR': 'mldata.org dataset: mnist-original',
 'data': array([[0, 0, 0, ..., 0, 0, 0],
        [0, 0, 0, ..., 0, 0, 0],
```

---

[1] By default Scikit-Learn caches downloaded datasets in a directory called *$HOME/scikit_learn_data*.

```
        [0, 0, 0, ..., 0, 0, 0],
        ...,
        [0, 0, 0, ..., 0, 0, 0],
        [0, 0, 0, ..., 0, 0, 0],
        [0, 0, 0, ..., 0, 0, 0]], dtype=uint8),
 'target': array([ 0., 0., 0., ..., 9., 9., 9.])}
```

Datasets loaded by Scikit-Learn generally have a similar dictionary structure including:

- A DESCR key describing the dataset
- A data key containing an array with one row per instance and one column per feature
- A target key containing an array with the labels

Let's look at these arrays:

```
>>> X, y = mnist["data"], mnist["target"]
>>> X.shape
(70000, 784)
>>> y.shape
(70000,)
```

There are 70,000 images, and each image has 784 features. This is because each image is 28×28 pixels, and each feature simply represents one pixel's intensity, from 0 (white) to 255 (black). Let's take a peek at one digit from the dataset. All you need to do is grab an instance's feature vector, reshape it to a 28×28 array, and display it using Matplotlib's imshow() function:

```
%matplotlib inline
import matplotlib
import matplotlib.pyplot as plt

some_digit = X[36000]
some_digit_image = some_digit.reshape(28, 28)

plt.imshow(some_digit_image, cmap = matplotlib.cm.binary,
           interpolation="nearest")
plt.axis("off")
plt.show()
```

This looks like a 5, and indeed that's what the label tells us:

```
>>> y[36000]
5.0
```

Figure 3-1 shows a few more images from the MNIST dataset to give you a feel for the complexity of the classification task.

Figure 3-1. A few digits from the MNIST dataset

But wait! You should always create a test set and set it aside before inspecting the data closely. The MNIST dataset is actually already split into a training set (the first 60,000 images) and a test set (the last 10,000 images):

```
X_train, X_test, y_train, y_test = X[:60000], X[60000:], y[:60000], y[60000:]
```

Let's also shuffle the training set; this will guarantee that all cross-validation folds will be similar (you don't want one fold to be missing some digits). Moreover, some learning algorithms are sensitive to the order of the training instances, and they perform poorly if they get many similar instances in a row. Shuffling the dataset ensures that this won't happen:[2]

---

2 Shuffling may be a bad idea in some contexts—for example, if you are working on time series data (such as stock market prices or weather conditions). We will explore this in the next chapters.

```
import numpy as np

shuffle_index = np.random.permutation(60000)
X_train, y_train = X_train[shuffle_index], y_train[shuffle_index]
```

Training a Binary Classifier

Let's simplify the problem for now and only try to identify one digit—for example, the number 5. This "5-detector" will be an example of a *binary classifier*, capable of distinguishing between just two classes, 5 and not-5. Let's create the target vectors for this classification task:

```
y_train_5 = (y_train == 5)   # True for all 5s, False for all other digits.
y_test_5 = (y_test == 5)
```

Okay, now let's pick a classifier and train it. A good place to start is with a *Stochastic Gradient Descent* (SGD) classifier, using Scikit-Learn's SGDClassifier class. This classifier has the advantage of being capable of handling very large datasets efficiently. This is in part because SGD deals with training instances independently, one at a time (which also makes SGD well suited for *online learning*), as we will see later. Let's create an SGDClassifier and train it on the whole training set:

```
from sklearn.linear_model import SGDClassifier

sgd_clf = SGDClassifier(random_state=42)
sgd_clf.fit(X_train, y_train_5)
```

> The SGDClassifier relies on randomness during training (hence the name "stochastic"). If you want reproducible results, you should set the random_state parameter.

Now you can use it to detect images of the number 5:

```
>>> sgd_clf.predict([some_digit])
array([ True], dtype=bool)
```

The classifier guesses that this image represents a 5 (True). Looks like it guessed right in this particular case! Now, let's evaluate this model's performance.

Performance Measures

Evaluating a classifier is often significantly trickier than evaluating a regressor, so we will spend a large part of this chapter on this topic. There are many performance measures available, so grab another coffee and get ready to learn many new concepts and acronyms!

Measuring Accuracy Using Cross-Validation

A good way to evaluate a model is to use cross-validation, just as you did in Chapter 2.

Implementing Cross-Validation

Occasionally you will need more control over the cross-validation process than what Scikit-Learn provides off-the-shelf. In these cases, you can implement cross-validation yourself; it is actually fairly straightforward. The following code does roughly the same thing as Scikit-Learn's `cross_val_score()` function, and prints the same result:

```
from sklearn.model_selection import StratifiedKFold
from sklearn.base import clone

skfolds = StratifiedKFold(n_splits=3, random_state=42)

for train_index, test_index in skfolds.split(X_train, y_train_5):
    clone_clf = clone(sgd_clf)
    X_train_folds = X_train[train_index]
    y_train_folds = y_train_5[train_index]
    X_test_fold = X_train[test_index]
    y_test_fold = y_train_5[test_index]

    clone_clf.fit(X_train_folds, y_train_folds)
    y_pred = clone_clf.predict(X_test_fold)
    n_correct = sum(y_pred == y_test_fold)
    print(n_correct / len(y_pred))  # prints 0.9502, 0.96565 and 0.96495
```

The `StratifiedKFold` class performs stratified sampling (as explained in Chapter 2) to produce folds that contain a representative ratio of each class. At each iteration the code creates a clone of the classifier, trains that clone on the training folds, and makes predictions on the test fold. Then it counts the number of correct predictions and outputs the ratio of correct predictions.

Let's use the `cross_val_score()` function to evaluate your `SGDClassifier` model using K-fold cross-validation, with three folds. Remember that K-fold cross-validation means splitting the training set into K-folds (in this case, three), then making predictions and evaluating them on each fold using a model trained on the remaining folds (see Chapter 2):

```
>>> from sklearn.model_selection import cross_val_score
>>> cross_val_score(sgd_clf, X_train, y_train_5, cv=3, scoring="accuracy")
array([ 0.9502 ,  0.96565,  0.96495])
```

Wow! Above 95% *accuracy* (ratio of correct predictions) on all cross-validation folds? This looks amazing, doesn't it? Well, before you get too excited, let's look at a very dumb classifier that just classifies every single image in the "not-5" class:

```
from sklearn.base import BaseEstimator

class Never5Classifier(BaseEstimator):
    def fit(self, X, y=None):
        pass
    def predict(self, X):
        return np.zeros((len(X), 1), dtype=bool)
```

Can you guess this model's accuracy? Let's find out:

```
>>> never_5_clf = Never5Classifier()
>>> cross_val_score(never_5_clf, X_train, y_train_5, cv=3, scoring="accuracy")
array([ 0.909  ,  0.90715,  0.9128 ])
```

That's right, it has over 90% accuracy! This is simply because only about 10% of the images are 5s, so if you always guess that an image is *not* a 5, you will be right about 90% of the time. Beats Nostradamus.

This demonstrates why accuracy is generally not the preferred performance measure for classifiers, especially when you are dealing with *skewed datasets* (i.e., when some classes are much more frequent than others).

Confusion Matrix

A much better way to evaluate the performance of a classifier is to look at the *confusion matrix*. The general idea is to count the number of times instances of class A are classified as class B. For example, to know the number of times the classifier confused images of 5s with 3s, you would look in the 5th row and 3rd column of the confusion matrix.

To compute the confusion matrix, you first need to have a set of predictions, so they can be compared to the actual targets. You could make predictions on the test set, but let's keep it untouched for now (remember that you want to use the test set only at the very end of your project, once you have a classifier that you are ready to launch). Instead, you can use the cross_val_predict() function:

```
from sklearn.model_selection import cross_val_predict

y_train_pred = cross_val_predict(sgd_clf, X_train, y_train_5, cv=3)
```

Just like the cross_val_score() function, cross_val_predict() performs K-fold cross-validation, but instead of returning the evaluation scores, it returns the predictions made on each test fold. This means that you get a clean prediction for each instance in the training set ("clean" meaning that the prediction is made by a model that never saw the data during training).

Now you are ready to get the confusion matrix using the confusion_matrix() function. Just pass it the target classes (y_train_5) and the predicted classes (y_train_pred):

```
>>> from sklearn.metrics import confusion_matrix
>>> confusion_matrix(y_train_5, y_train_pred)
array([[53272,  1307],
       [ 1077,  4344]])
```

Each row in a confusion matrix represents an *actual class*, while each column represents a *predicted class*. The first row of this matrix considers non-5 images (the *negative class*): 53,272 of them were correctly classified as non-5s (they are called *true negatives*), while the remaining 1,307 were wrongly classified as 5s (*false positives*). The second row considers the images of 5s (the *positive class*): 1,077 were wrongly classified as non-5s (*false negatives*), while the remaining 4,344 were correctly classified as 5s (*true positives*). A perfect classifier would have only true positives and true negatives, so its confusion matrix would have nonzero values only on its main diagonal (top left to bottom right):

```
>>> confusion_matrix(y_train_5, y_train_perfect_predictions)
array([[54579,     0],
       [    0, 5421]])
```

The confusion matrix gives you a lot of information, but sometimes you may prefer a more concise metric. An interesting one to look at is the accuracy of the positive predictions; this is called the *precision* of the classifier (Equation 3-1).

Equation 3-1. Precision

$$\text{precision} = \frac{TP}{TP + FP}$$

TP is the number of true positives, and FP is the number of false positives.

A trivial way to have perfect precision is to make one single positive prediction and ensure it is correct (precision = 1/1 = 100%). This would not be very useful since the classifier would ignore all but one positive instance. So precision is typically used along with another metric named *recall*, also called *sensitivity* or *true positive rate* (*TPR*): this is the ratio of positive instances that are correctly detected by the classifier (Equation 3-2).

Equation 3-2. Recall

$$\text{recall} = \frac{TP}{TP + FN}$$

FN is of course the number of false negatives.

If you are confused about the confusion matrix, Figure 3-2 may help.

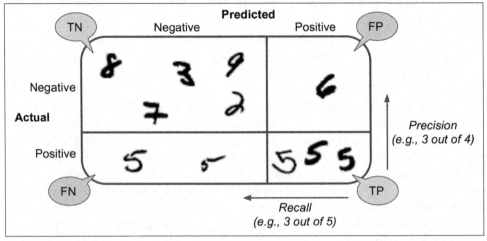

Figure 3-2. An illustrated confusion matrix

Precision and Recall

Scikit-Learn provides several functions to compute classifier metrics, including precision and recall:

```
>>> from sklearn.metrics import precision_score, recall_score
>>> precision_score(y_train_5, y_train_pred) # == 4344 / (4344 + 1307)
0.76871350203503808
>>> recall_score(y_train_5, y_train_pred) # == 4344 / (4344 + 1077)
0.80132816823464303
```

Now your 5-detector does not look as shiny as it did when you looked at its accuracy. When it claims an image represents a 5, it is correct only 77% of the time. Moreover, it only detects 80% of the 5s.

It is often convenient to combine precision and recall into a single metric called the F_1 *score*, in particular if you need a simple way to compare two classifiers. The F_1 score is the *harmonic mean* of precision and recall (Equation 3-3). Whereas the regular mean treats all values equally, the harmonic mean gives much more weight to low values. As a result, the classifier will only get a high F_1 score if both recall and precision are high.

Equation 3-3. F_1 score

$$F_1 = \frac{2}{\dfrac{1}{precision} + \dfrac{1}{recall}} = 2 \times \frac{precision \times recall}{precision + recall} = \frac{TP}{TP + \dfrac{FN + FP}{2}}$$

To compute the F_1 score, simply call the `f1_score()` function:

```
>>> from sklearn.metrics import f1_score
>>> f1_score(y_train_5, y_train_pred)
0.78468208092485547
```

The F_1 score favors classifiers that have similar precision and recall. This is not always what you want: in some contexts you mostly care about precision, and in other contexts you really care about recall. For example, if you trained a classifier to detect videos that are safe for kids, you would probably prefer a classifier that rejects many good videos (low recall) but keeps only safe ones (high precision), rather than a classifier that has a much higher recall but lets a few really bad videos show up in your product (in such cases, you may even want to add a human pipeline to check the classifier's video selection). On the other hand, suppose you train a classifier to detect shoplifters on surveillance images: it is probably fine if your classifier has only 30% precision as long as it has 99% recall (sure, the security guards will get a few false alerts, but almost all shoplifters will get caught).

Unfortunately, you can't have it both ways: increasing precision reduces recall, and vice versa. This is called the *precision/recall tradeoff*.

Precision/Recall Tradeoff

To understand this tradeoff, let's look at how the `SGDClassifier` makes its classification decisions. For each instance, it computes a score based on a *decision function*, and if that score is greater than a threshold, it assigns the instance to the positive class, or else it assigns it to the negative class. Figure 3-3 shows a few digits positioned from the lowest score on the left to the highest score on the right. Suppose the *decision threshold* is positioned at the central arrow (between the two 5s): you will find 4 true positives (actual 5s) on the right of that threshold, and one false positive (actually a 6). Therefore, with that threshold, the precision is 80% (4 out of 5). But out of 6 actual 5s, the classifier only detects 4, so the recall is 67% (4 out of 6). Now if you raise the threshold (move it to the arrow on the right), the false positive (the 6) becomes a true negative, thereby increasing precision (up to 100% in this case), but one true positive becomes a false negative, decreasing recall down to 50%. Conversely, lowering the threshold increases recall and reduces precision.

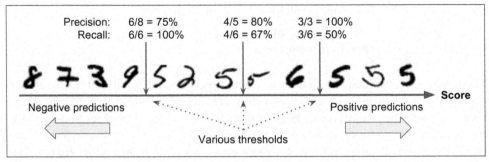

Precision: 6/8 = 75%   4/5 = 80%   3/3 = 100%
Recall: 6/6 = 100%   4/6 = 67%   3/6 = 50%

Negative predictions   Positive predictions

Various thresholds

Score

Figure 3-3. Decision threshold and precision/recall tradeoff

Scikit-Learn does not let you set the threshold directly, but it does give you access to the decision scores that it uses to make predictions. Instead of calling the classifier's `predict()` method, you can call its `decision_function()` method, which returns a score for each instance, and then make predictions based on those scores using any threshold you want:

```
>>> y_scores = sgd_clf.decision_function([some_digit])
>>> y_scores
array([ 161855.74572176])
>>> threshold = 0
>>> y_some_digit_pred = (y_scores > threshold)
array([ True], dtype=bool)
```

The `SGDClassifier` uses a threshold equal to 0, so the previous code returns the same result as the `predict()` method (i.e., `True`). Let's raise the threshold:

```
>>> threshold = 200000
>>> y_some_digit_pred = (y_scores > threshold)
>>> y_some_digit_pred
array([False], dtype=bool)
```

This confirms that raising the threshold decreases recall. The image actually represents a 5, and the classifier detects it when the threshold is 0, but it misses it when the threshold is increased to 200,000.

So how can you decide which threshold to use? For this you will first need to get the scores of all instances in the training set using the `cross_val_predict()` function again, but this time specifying that you want it to return decision scores instead of predictions:

```
y_scores = cross_val_predict(sgd_clf, X_train, y_train_5, cv=3,
                             method="decision_function")
```

Now with these scores you can compute precision and recall for all possible thresholds using the `precision_recall_curve()` function:

```
from sklearn.metrics import precision_recall_curve

precisions, recalls, thresholds = precision_recall_curve(y_train_5, y_scores)
```

Finally, you can plot precision and recall as functions of the threshold value using Matplotlib (Figure 3-4):

```
def plot_precision_recall_vs_threshold(precisions, recalls, thresholds):
    plt.plot(thresholds, precisions[:-1], "b--", label="Precision")
    plt.plot(thresholds, recalls[:-1], "g-", label="Recall")
    plt.xlabel("Threshold")
    plt.legend(loc="center left")
    plt.ylim([0, 1])

plot_precision_recall_vs_threshold(precisions, recalls, thresholds)
plt.show()
```

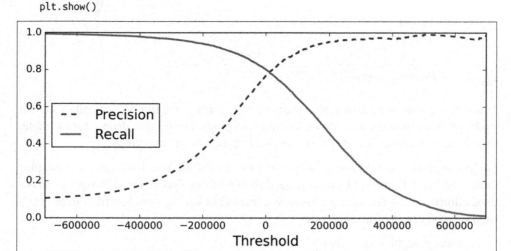

Figure 3-4. Precision and recall versus the decision threshold

You may wonder why the precision curve is bumpier than the recall curve in Figure 3-4. The reason is that precision may sometimes go down when you raise the threshold (although in general it will go up). To understand why, look back at Figure 3-3 and notice what happens when you start from the central threshold and move it just one digit to the right: precision goes from 4/5 (80%) down to 3/4 (75%). On the other hand, recall can only go down when the threshold is increased, which explains why its curve looks smooth.

Now you can simply select the threshold value that gives you the best precision/recall tradeoff for your task. Another way to select a good precision/recall tradeoff is to plot precision directly against recall, as shown in Figure 3-5.

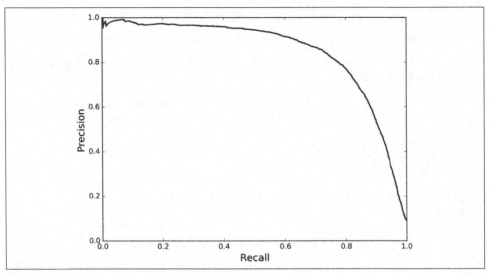

Figure 3-5. Precision versus recall

You can see that precision really starts to fall sharply around 80% recall. You will probably want to select a precision/recall tradeoff just before that drop—for example, at around 60% recall. But of course the choice depends on your project.

So let's suppose you decide to aim for 90% precision. You look up the first plot (zooming in a bit) and find that you need to use a threshold of about 70,000. To make predictions (on the training set for now), instead of calling the classifier's `predict()` method, you can just run this code:

```
y_train_pred_90 = (y_scores > 70000)
```

Let's check these predictions' precision and recall:

```
>>> precision_score(y_train_5, y_train_pred_90)
0.86592051164915484
>>> recall_score(y_train_5, y_train_pred_90)
0.69931746910164172
```

Great, you have a 90% precision classifier (or close enough)! As you can see, it is fairly easy to create a classifier with virtually any precision you want: just set a high enough threshold, and you're done. Hmm, not so fast. A high-precision classifier is not very useful if its recall is too low!

 If someone says "let's reach 99% precision," you should ask, "at what recall?"

The ROC Curve

The *receiver operating characteristic* (ROC) curve is another common tool used with binary classifiers. It is very similar to the precision/recall curve, but instead of plotting precision versus recall, the ROC curve plots the *true positive rate* (another name for recall) against the *false positive rate*. The FPR is the ratio of negative instances that are incorrectly classified as positive. It is equal to one minus the *true negative rate*, which is the ratio of negative instances that are correctly classified as negative. The TNR is also called *specificity*. Hence the ROC curve plots *sensitivity* (recall) versus 1 – *specificity*.

To plot the ROC curve, you first need to compute the TPR and FPR for various threshold values, using the `roc_curve()` function:

```
from sklearn.metrics import roc_curve

fpr, tpr, thresholds = roc_curve(y_train_5, y_scores)
```

Then you can plot the FPR against the TPR using Matplotlib. This code produces the plot in Figure 3-6:

```
def plot_roc_curve(fpr, tpr, label=None):
    plt.plot(fpr, tpr, linewidth=2, label=label)
    plt.plot([0, 1], [0, 1], 'k--')
    plt.axis([0, 1, 0, 1])
    plt.xlabel('False Positive Rate')
    plt.ylabel('True Positive Rate')

plot_roc_curve(fpr, tpr)
plt.show()
```

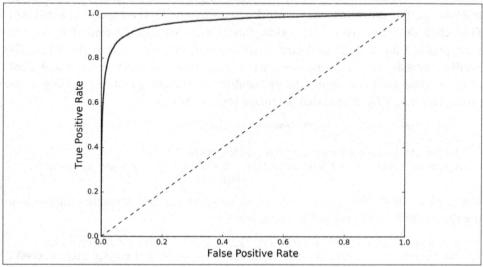

Figure 3-6. ROC curve

Once again there is a tradeoff: the higher the recall (TPR), the more false positives (FPR) the classifier produces. The dotted line represents the ROC curve of a purely random classifier; a good classifier stays as far away from that line as possible (toward the top-left corner).

One way to compare classifiers is to measure the *area under the curve* (AUC). A perfect classifier will have a *ROC AUC* equal to 1, whereas a purely random classifier will have a ROC AUC equal to 0.5. Scikit-Learn provides a function to compute the ROC AUC:

```
>>> from sklearn.metrics import roc_auc_score
>>> roc_auc_score(y_train_5, y_scores)
0.96244965559671547
```

 Since the ROC curve is so similar to the precision/recall (or PR) curve, you may wonder how to decide which one to use. As a rule of thumb, you should prefer the PR curve whenever the positive class is rare or when you care more about the false positives than the false negatives, and the ROC curve otherwise. For example, looking at the previous ROC curve (and the ROC AUC score), you may think that the classifier is really good. But this is mostly because there are few positives (5s) compared to the negatives (non-5s). In contrast, the PR curve makes it clear that the classifier has room for improvement (the curve could be closer to the top-right corner).

Let's train a `RandomForestClassifier` and compare its ROC curve and ROC AUC score to the `SGDClassifier`. First, you need to get scores for each instance in the training set. But due to the way it works (see Chapter 7), the `RandomForestClassifier` class does not have a `decision_function()` method. Instead it has a `predict_proba()` method. Scikit-Learn classifiers generally have one or the other. The `predict_proba()` method returns an array containing a row per instance and a column per class, each containing the probability that the given instance belongs to the given class (e.g., 70% chance that the image represents a 5):

```
from sklearn.ensemble import RandomForestClassifier

forest_clf = RandomForestClassifier(random_state=42)
y_probas_forest = cross_val_predict(forest_clf, X_train, y_train_5, cv=3,
                                    method="predict_proba")
```

But to plot a ROC curve, you need scores, not probabilities. A simple solution is to use the positive class's probability as the score:

```
y_scores_forest = y_probas_forest[:, 1]  # score = proba of positive class
fpr_forest, tpr_forest, thresholds_forest = roc_curve(y_train_5,y_scores_forest)
```

Now you are ready to plot the ROC curve. It is useful to plot the first ROC curve as well to see how they compare (Figure 3-7):

```
plt.plot(fpr, tpr, "b:", label="SGD")
plot_roc_curve(fpr_forest, tpr_forest, "Random Forest")
plt.legend(loc="lower right")
plt.show()
```

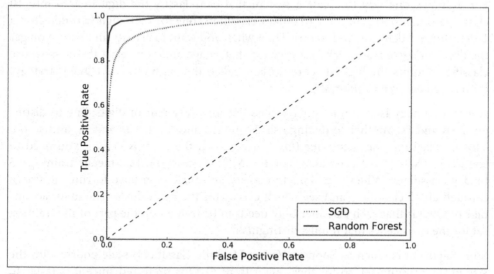

Figure 3-7. Comparing ROC curves

As you can see in Figure 3-7, the RandomForestClassifier's ROC curve looks much better than the SGDClassifier's: it comes much closer to the top-left corner. As a result, its ROC AUC score is also significantly better:

```
>>> roc_auc_score(y_train_5, y_scores_forest)
0.99312433660038291
```

Try measuring the precision and recall scores: you should find 98.5% precision and 82.8% recall. Not too bad!

Hopefully you now know how to train binary classifiers, choose the appropriate metric for your task, evaluate your classifiers using cross-validation, select the precision/recall tradeoff that fits your needs, and compare various models using ROC curves and ROC AUC scores. Now let's try to detect more than just the 5s.

Multiclass Classification

Whereas binary classifiers distinguish between two classes, *multiclass classifiers* (also called *multinomial classifiers*) can distinguish between more than two classes.

Some algorithms (such as Random Forest classifiers or naive Bayes classifiers) are capable of handling multiple classes directly. Others (such as Support Vector Machine classifiers or Linear classifiers) are strictly binary classifiers. However, there are various strategies that you can use to perform multiclass classification using multiple binary classifiers.

For example, one way to create a system that can classify the digit images into 10 classes (from 0 to 9) is to train 10 binary classifiers, one for each digit (a 0-detector, a 1-detector, a 2-detector, and so on). Then when you want to classify an image, you get the decision score from each classifier for that image and you select the class whose classifier outputs the highest score. This is called the *one-versus-all* (OvA) strategy (also called *one-versus-the-rest*).

Another strategy is to train a binary classifier for every pair of digits: one to distinguish 0s and 1s, another to distinguish 0s and 2s, another for 1s and 2s, and so on. This is called the *one-versus-one* (OvO) strategy. If there are N classes, you need to train $N \times (N - 1) / 2$ classifiers. For the MNIST problem, this means training 45 binary classifiers! When you want to classify an image, you have to run the image through all 45 classifiers and see which class wins the most duels. The main advantage of OvO is that each classifier only needs to be trained on the part of the training set for the two classes that it must distinguish.

Some algorithms (such as Support Vector Machine classifiers) scale poorly with the size of the training set, so for these algorithms OvO is preferred since it is faster to train many classifiers on small training sets than training few classifiers on large training sets. For most binary classification algorithms, however, OvA is preferred.

Scikit-Learn detects when you try to use a binary classification algorithm for a multiclass classification task, and it automatically runs OvA (except for SVM classifiers for which it uses OvO). Let's try this with the SGDClassifier:

```
>>> sgd_clf.fit(X_train, y_train)  # y_train, not y_train_5
>>> sgd_clf.predict([some_digit])
array([ 5.])
```

That was easy! This code trains the SGDClassifier on the training set using the original target classes from 0 to 9 (y_train), instead of the 5-versus-all target classes (y_train_5). Then it makes a prediction (a correct one in this case). Under the hood, Scikit-Learn actually trained 10 binary classifiers, got their decision scores for the image, and selected the class with the highest score.

To see that this is indeed the case, you can call the decision_function() method. Instead of returning just one score per instance, it now returns 10 scores, one per class:

```
>>> some_digit_scores = sgd_clf.decision_function([some_digit])
>>> some_digit_scores
```

```
array([[-311402.62954431, -363517.28355739, -446449.5306454 ,
        -183226.61023518, -414337.15339485,  161855.74572176,
        -452576.39616343, -471957.14962573, -518542.33997148,
        -536774.63961222]])
```

The highest score is indeed the one corresponding to class 5:

```
>>> np.argmax(some_digit_scores)
5
>>> sgd_clf.classes_
array([ 0.,  1.,  2.,  3.,  4.,  5.,  6.,  7.,  8.,  9.])
>>> sgd_clf.classes_[5]
5.0
```

 When a classifier is trained, it stores the list of target classes in its classes_ attribute, ordered by value. In this case, the index of each class in the classes_ array conveniently matches the class itself (e.g., the class at index 5 happens to be class 5), but in general you won't be so lucky.

If you want to force ScikitLearn to use one-versus-one or one-versus-all, you can use the OneVsOneClassifier or OneVsRestClassifier classes. Simply create an instance and pass a binary classifier to its constructor. For example, this code creates a multiclass classifier using the OvO strategy, based on a SGDClassifier:

```
>>> from sklearn.multiclass import OneVsOneClassifier
>>> ovo_clf = OneVsOneClassifier(SGDClassifier(random_state=42))
>>> ovo_clf.fit(X_train, y_train)
>>> ovo_clf.predict([some_digit])
array([ 5.])
>>> len(ovo_clf.estimators_)
45
```

Training a RandomForestClassifier is just as easy:

```
>>> forest_clf.fit(X_train, y_train)
>>> forest_clf.predict([some_digit])
array([ 5.])
```

This time Scikit-Learn did not have to run OvA or OvO because Random Forest classifiers can directly classify instances into multiple classes. You can call predict_proba() to get the list of probabilities that the classifier assigned to each instance for each class:

```
>>> forest_clf.predict_proba([some_digit])
array([[ 0.1, 0. , 0. , 0.1, 0. , 0.8, 0. , 0. , 0. , 0. ]])
```

You can see that the classifier is fairly confident about its prediction: the 0.8 at the 5th index in the array means that the model estimates an 80% probability that the image represents a 5. It also thinks that the image could instead be a 0 or a 3 (10% chance each).

Now of course you want to evaluate these classifiers. As usual, you want to use cross-validation. Let's evaluate the SGDClassifier's accuracy using the cross_val_score() function:

```
>>> cross_val_score(sgd_clf, X_train, y_train, cv=3, scoring="accuracy")
array([ 0.84063187, 0.84899245, 0.86652998])
```

It gets over 84% on all test folds. If you used a random classifier, you would get 10% accuracy, so this is not such a bad score, but you can still do much better. For example, simply scaling the inputs (as discussed in Chapter 2) increases accuracy above 90%:

```
>>> from sklearn.preprocessing import StandardScaler
>>> scaler = StandardScaler()
>>> X_train_scaled = scaler.fit_transform(X_train.astype(np.float64))
>>> cross_val_score(sgd_clf, X_train_scaled, y_train, cv=3, scoring="accuracy")
array([ 0.91011798, 0.90874544, 0.906636  ])
```

Error Analysis

Of course, if this were a real project, you would follow the steps in your Machine Learning project checklist (see Appendix B): exploring data preparation options, trying out multiple models, shortlisting the best ones and fine-tuning their hyperparameters using GridSearchCV, and automating as much as possible, as you did in the previous chapter. Here, we will assume that you have found a promising model and you want to find ways to improve it. One way to do this is to analyze the types of errors it makes.

First, you can look at the confusion matrix. You need to make predictions using the cross_val_predict() function, then call the confusion_matrix() function, just like you did earlier:

```
>>> y_train_pred = cross_val_predict(sgd_clf, X_train_scaled, y_train, cv=3)
>>> conf_mx = confusion_matrix(y_train, y_train_pred)
>>> conf_mx
array([[5725,    3,   24,    9,   10,   49,   50,   10,   39,    4],
       [   2, 6493,   43,   25,    7,   40,    5,   10,  109,    8],
       [  51,   41, 5321,  104,   89,   26,   87,   60,  166,   13],
       [  47,   46,  141, 5342,    1,  231,   40,   50,  141,   92],
       [  19,   29,   41,   10, 5366,    9,   56,   37,   86,  189],
       [  73,   45,   36,  193,   64, 4582,  111,   30,  193,   94],
       [  29,   34,   44,    2,   42,   85, 5627,   10,   45,    0],
       [  25,   24,   74,   32,   54,   12,    6, 5787,   15,  236],
       [  52,  161,   73,  156,   10,  163,   61,   25, 5027,  123],
       [  43,   35,   26,   92,  178,   28,    2,  223,   82, 5240]])
```

That's a lot of numbers. It's often more convenient to look at an image representation of the confusion matrix, using Matplotlib's `matshow()` function:

```
plt.matshow(conf_mx, cmap=plt.cm.gray)
plt.show()
```

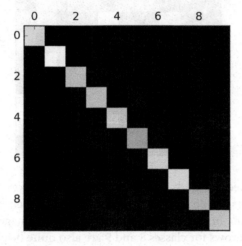

This confusion matrix looks fairly good, since most images are on the main diagonal, which means that they were classified correctly. The 5s look slightly darker than the other digits, which could mean that there are fewer images of 5s in the dataset or that the classifier does not perform as well on 5s as on other digits. In fact, you can verify that both are the case.

Let's focus the plot on the errors. First, you need to divide each value in the confusion matrix by the number of images in the corresponding class, so you can compare error rates instead of absolute number of errors (which would make abundant classes look unfairly bad):

```
row_sums = conf_mx.sum(axis=1, keepdims=True)
norm_conf_mx = conf_mx / row_sums
```

Now let's fill the diagonal with zeros to keep only the errors, and let's plot the result:

```
np.fill_diagonal(norm_conf_mx, 0)
plt.matshow(norm_conf_mx, cmap=plt.cm.gray)
plt.show()
```

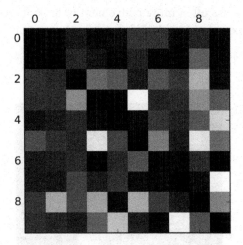

Now you can clearly see the kinds of errors the classifier makes. Remember that rows represent actual classes, while columns represent predicted classes. The columns for classes 8 and 9 are quite bright, which tells you that many images get misclassified as 8s or 9s. Similarly, the rows for classes 8 and 9 are also quite bright, telling you that 8s and 9s are often confused with other digits. Conversely, some rows are pretty dark, such as row 1: this means that most 1s are classified correctly (a few are confused with 8s, but that's about it). Notice that the errors are not perfectly symmetrical; for example, there are more 5s misclassified as 8s than the reverse.

Analyzing the confusion matrix can often give you insights on ways to improve your classifier. Looking at this plot, it seems that your efforts should be spent on improving classification of 8s and 9s, as well as fixing the specific 3/5 confusion. For example, you could try to gather more training data for these digits. Or you could engineer new features that would help the classifier—for example, writing an algorithm to count the number of closed loops (e.g., 8 has two, 6 has one, 5 has none). Or you could preprocess the images (e.g., using Scikit-Image, Pillow, or OpenCV) to make some patterns stand out more, such as closed loops.

Analyzing individual errors can also be a good way to gain insights on what your classifier is doing and why it is failing, but it is more difficult and time-consuming. For example, let's plot examples of 3s and 5s (the `plot_digits()` function just uses Matplotlib's `imshow()` function; see this chapter's Jupyter notebook for details):

```
cl_a, cl_b = 3, 5
X_aa = X_train[(y_train == cl_a) & (y_train_pred == cl_a)]
X_ab = X_train[(y_train == cl_a) & (y_train_pred == cl_b)]
X_ba = X_train[(y_train == cl_b) & (y_train_pred == cl_a)]
X_bb = X_train[(y_train == cl_b) & (y_train_pred == cl_b)]

plt.figure(figsize=(8,8))
```

```
plt.subplot(221); plot_digits(X_aa[:25], images_per_row=5)
plt.subplot(222); plot_digits(X_ab[:25], images_per_row=5)
plt.subplot(223); plot_digits(X_ba[:25], images_per_row=5)
plt.subplot(224); plot_digits(X_bb[:25], images_per_row=5)
plt.show()
```

The two 5×5 blocks on the left show digits classified as 3s, and the two 5×5 blocks on the right show images classified as 5s. Some of the digits that the classifier gets wrong (i.e., in the bottom-left and top-right blocks) are so badly written that even a human would have trouble classifying them (e.g., the 5 on the 8th row and 1st column truly looks like a 3). However, most misclassified images seem like obvious errors to us, and it's hard to understand why the classifier made the mistakes it did.[3] The reason is that we used a simple SGDClassifier, which is a linear model. All it does is assign a weight per class to each pixel, and when it sees a new image it just sums up the weighted pixel intensities to get a score for each class. So since 3s and 5s differ only by a few pixels, this model will easily confuse them.

The main difference between 3s and 5s is the position of the small line that joins the top line to the bottom arc. If you draw a 3 with the junction slightly shifted to the left, the classifier might classify it as a 5, and vice versa. In other words, this classifier is quite sensitive to image shifting and rotation. So one way to reduce the 3/5 confusion would be to preprocess the images to ensure that they are well centered and not too rotated. This will probably help reduce other errors as well.

---

3 But remember that our brain is a fantastic pattern recognition system, and our visual system does a lot of complex preprocessing before any information reaches our consciousness, so the fact that it feels simple does not mean that it is.

Multilabel Classification

Until now each instance has always been assigned to just one class. In some cases you may want your classifier to output multiple classes for each instance. For example, consider a face-recognition classifier: what should it do if it recognizes several people on the same picture? Of course it should attach one label per person it recognizes. Say the classifier has been trained to recognize three faces, Alice, Bob, and Charlie; then when it is shown a picture of Alice and Charlie, it should output [1, 0, 1] (meaning "Alice yes, Bob no, Charlie yes"). Such a classification system that outputs multiple binary labels is called a *multilabel classification* system.

We won't go into face recognition just yet, but let's look at a simpler example, just for illustration purposes:

```
from sklearn.neighbors import KNeighborsClassifier

y_train_large = (y_train >= 7)
y_train_odd = (y_train % 2 == 1)
y_multilabel = np.c_[y_train_large, y_train_odd]

knn_clf = KNeighborsClassifier()
knn_clf.fit(X_train, y_multilabel)
```

This code creates a `y_multilabel` array containing two target labels for each digit image: the first indicates whether or not the digit is large (7, 8, or 9) and the second indicates whether or not it is odd. The next lines create a `KNeighborsClassifier` instance (which supports multilabel classification, but not all classifiers do) and we train it using the multiple targets array. Now you can make a prediction, and notice that it outputs two labels:

```
>>> knn_clf.predict([some_digit])
array([[False,  True]], dtype=bool)
```

And it gets it right! The digit 5 is indeed not large (`False`) and odd (`True`).

There are many ways to evaluate a multilabel classifier, and selecting the right metric really depends on your project. For example, one approach is to measure the F_1 score for each individual label (or any other binary classifier metric discussed earlier), then simply compute the average score. This code computes the average F_1 score across all labels:

```
>>> y_train_knn_pred = cross_val_predict(knn_clf, X_train, y_multilabel, cv=3)
>>> f1_score(y_multilabel, y_train_knn_pred, average="macro")
0.97709078477525002
```

This assumes that all labels are equally important, which may not be the case. In particular, if you have many more pictures of Alice than of Bob or Charlie, you may want to give more weight to the classifier's score on pictures of Alice. One simple option is to give each label a weight equal to its *support* (i.e., the number of instances with that target label). To do this, simply set `average="weighted"` in the preceding code.[4]

Multioutput Classification

The last type of classification task we are going to discuss here is called *multioutput-multiclass classification* (or simply *multioutput classification*). It is simply a generalization of multilabel classification where each label can be multiclass (i.e., it can have more than two possible values).

To illustrate this, let's build a system that removes noise from images. It will take as input a noisy digit image, and it will (hopefully) output a clean digit image, represented as an array of pixel intensities, just like the MNIST images. Notice that the classifier's output is multilabel (one label per pixel) and each label can have multiple values (pixel intensity ranges from 0 to 255). It is thus an example of a multioutput classification system.

> The line between classification and regression is sometimes blurry, such as in this example. Arguably, predicting pixel intensity is more akin to regression than to classification. Moreover, multioutput systems are not limited to classification tasks; you could even have a system that outputs multiple labels per instance, including both class labels and value labels.

Let's start by creating the training and test sets by taking the MNIST images and adding noise to their pixel intensities using NumPy's `randint()` function. The target images will be the original images:

```
noise = np.random.randint(0, 100, (len(X_train), 784))
X_train_mod = X_train + noise
noise = np.random.randint(0, 100, (len(X_test), 784))
X_test_mod = X_test + noise
y_train_mod = X_train
y_test_mod = X_test
```

Let's take a peek at an image from the test set (yes, we're snooping on the test data, so you should be frowning right now):

---

4 Scikit-Learn offers a few other averaging options and multilabel classifier metrics; see the documentation for more details.

On the left is the noisy input image, and on the right is the clean target image. Now let's train the classifier and make it clean this image:

```
knn_clf.fit(X_train_mod, y_train_mod)
clean_digit = knn_clf.predict([X_test_mod[some_index]])
plot_digit(clean_digit)
```

Looks close enough to the target! This concludes our tour of classification. Hopefully you should now know how to select good metrics for classification tasks, pick the appropriate precision/recall tradeoff, compare classifiers, and more generally build good classification systems for a variety of tasks.

Exercises

1. Try to build a classifier for the MNIST dataset that achieves over 97% accuracy on the test set. Hint: the KNeighborsClassifier works quite well for this task; you just need to find good hyperparameter values (try a grid search on the weights and n_neighbors hyperparameters).

2. Write a function that can shift an MNIST image in any direction (left, right, up, or down) by one pixel.[5] Then, for each image in the training set, create four shifted copies (one per direction) and add them to the training set. Finally, train your best model on this expanded training set and measure its accuracy on the test set. You should observe that your model performs even better now! This technique of

---

5 You can use the shift() function from the scipy.ndimage.interpolation module. For example, shift(image, [2, 1], cval=0) shifts the image 2 pixels down and 1 pixel to the right.

artificially growing the training set is called *data augmentation* or *training set expansion*.

3. Tackle the *Titanic* dataset. A great place to start is on Kaggle (*https://www.kaggle.com/c/titanic*).

4. Build a spam classifier (a more challenging exercise):

   - Download examples of spam and ham from Apache SpamAssassin's public datasets (*https://spamassassin.apache.org/old/publiccorpus/*).

   - Unzip the datasets and familiarize yourself with the data format.

   - Split the datasets into a training set and a test set.

   - Write a data preparation pipeline to convert each email into a feature vector. Your preparation pipeline should transform an email into a (sparse) vector indicating the presence or absence of each possible word. For example, if all emails only ever contain four words, "Hello," "how," "are," "you," then the email "Hello you Hello Hello you" would be converted into a vector [1, 0, 0, 1] (meaning ["Hello" is present, "how" is absent, "are" is absent, "you" is present]), or [3, 0, 0, 2] if you prefer to count the number of occurrences of each word.

   - You may want to add hyperparameters to your preparation pipeline to control whether or not to strip off email headers, convert each email to lowercase, remove punctuation, replace all URLs with "URL," replace all numbers with "NUMBER," or even perform *stemming* (i.e., trim off word endings; there are Python libraries available to do this).

   - Then try out several classifiers and see if you can build a great spam classifier, with both high recall and high precision.

Solutions to these exercises are available in the online Jupyter notebooks at *https://github.com/ageron/handson-ml*.

## CHAPTER 4

Training Models

So far we have treated Machine Learning models and their training algorithms mostly like black boxes. If you went through some of the exercises in the previous chapters, you may have been surprised by how much you can get done without knowing anything about what's under the hood: you optimized a regression system, you improved a digit image classifier, and you even built a spam classifier from scratch—all this without knowing how they actually work. Indeed, in many situations you don't really need to know the implementation details.

However, having a good understanding of how things work can help you quickly home in on the appropriate model, the right training algorithm to use, and a good set of hyperparameters for your task. Understanding what's under the hood will also help you debug issues and perform error analysis more efficiently. Lastly, most of the topics discussed in this chapter will be essential in understanding, building, and training neural networks (discussed in Part II of this book).

In this chapter, we will start by looking at the Linear Regression model, one of the simplest models there is. We will discuss two very different ways to train it:

- Using a direct "closed-form" equation that directly computes the model parameters that best fit the model to the training set (i.e., the model parameters that minimize the cost function over the training set).

- Using an iterative optimization approach, called Gradient Descent (GD), that gradually tweaks the model parameters to minimize the cost function over the training set, eventually converging to the same set of parameters as the first method. We will look at a few variants of Gradient Descent that we will use again and again when we study neural networks in Part II: Batch GD, Mini-batch GD, and Stochastic GD.

Next we will look at Polynomial Regression, a more complex model that can fit non-linear datasets. Since this model has more parameters than Linear Regression, it is more prone to overfitting the training data, so we will look at how to detect whether or not this is the case, using learning curves, and then we will look at several regularization techniques that can reduce the risk of overfitting the training set.

Finally, we will look at two more models that are commonly used for classification tasks: Logistic Regression and Softmax Regression.

 There will be quite a few math equations in this chapter, using basic notions of linear algebra and calculus. To understand these equations, you will need to know what vectors and matrices are, how to transpose them, multiply them, and inverse them, and what partial derivatives are. If you are unfamiliar with these concepts, please go through the linear algebra and calculus introductory tutorials available as Jupyter notebooks in the online supplemental material. For those who are truly allergic to mathematics, you should still go through this chapter and simply skip the equations; hopefully, the text will be sufficient to help you understand most of the concepts.

Linear Regression

In Chapter 1, we looked at a simple regression model of life satisfaction: *life_satisfaction* = θ_0 + θ_1 × *GDP_per_capita*.

This model is just a linear function of the input feature GDP_per_capita. θ_0 and θ_1 are the model's parameters.

More generally, a linear model makes a prediction by simply computing a weighted sum of the input features, plus a constant called the *bias term* (also called the *intercept term*), as shown in Equation 4-1.

Equation 4-1. Linear Regression model prediction

$$\hat{y} = \theta_0 + \theta_1 x_1 + \theta_2 x_2 + \cdots + \theta_n x_n$$

- $\hat{y}$ is the predicted value.
- n is the number of features.
- x_i is the ith feature value.
- θ_j is the jth model parameter (including the bias term θ_0 and the feature weights $\theta_1, \theta_2, \cdots, \theta_n$).

This can be written much more concisely using a vectorized form, as shown in Equation 4-2.

Equation 4-2. Linear Regression model prediction (vectorized form)

$$\hat{y} = h_{\theta}(\mathbf{x}) = \theta \cdot \mathbf{x}$$

- θ is the model's *parameter vector*, containing the bias term θ_0 and the feature weights θ_1 to θ_n.
- $\mathbf{x}$ is the instance's *feature vector*, containing x_0 to x_n, with x_0 always equal to 1.
- $\theta \cdot \mathbf{x}$ is the dot product of the vectors θ and $\mathbf{x}$, which is of course equal to $\theta_0 x_0 + \theta_1 x_1 + \theta_2 x_2 + \cdots + \theta_n x_n$.
- h_{θ} is the hypothesis function, using the model parameters θ.

> In Machine Learning, vectors are often represented as *column vectors*, which are 2D arrays with a single column. If θ and $\mathbf{x}$ are column vectors, then the prediction is: $\hat{y} = \theta^{\mathrm{T}}\mathbf{x}$, where θ^{T} is the *transpose* of θ (a row vector instead of a column vector) and $\theta^{\mathrm{T}}\mathbf{x}$ is the matrix multiplication of θ^{T} and $\mathbf{x}$. It is of course the same prediction, except it is now represented as a single cell matrix rather than a scalar value. In this book we will use this notation to avoid switching between dot products and matrix multiplications.

Okay, that's the Linear Regression model, so now how do we train it? Well, recall that training a model means setting its parameters so that the model best fits the training set. For this purpose, we first need a measure of how well (or poorly) the model fits the training data. In Chapter 2 we saw that the most common performance measure of a regression model is the Root Mean Square Error (RMSE) (Equation 2-1). Therefore, to train a Linear Regression model, you need to find the value of θ that minimizes the RMSE. In practice, it is simpler to minimize the Mean Square Error (MSE) than the RMSE, and it leads to the same result (because the value that minimizes a function also minimizes its square root).[1]

---

[1] It is often the case that a learning algorithm will try to optimize a different function than the performance measure used to evaluate the final model. This is generally because that function is easier to compute, because it has useful differentiation properties that the performance measure lacks, or because we want to constrain the model during training, as we will see when we discuss regularization.

The MSE of a Linear Regression hypothesis h_θ on a training set $\mathbf{X}$ is calculated using Equation 4-3.

Equation 4-3. MSE cost function for a Linear Regression model

$$\text{MSE}(\mathbf{X}, h_\theta) = \frac{1}{m} \sum_{i=1}^{m} \left(\theta^T \mathbf{x}^{(i)} - y^{(i)} \right)^2$$

Most of these notations were presented in Chapter 2 (see "Notations" on page 38). The only difference is that we write h_θ instead of just h in order to make it clear that the model is parametrized by the vector θ. To simplify notations, we will just write $\text{MSE}(\theta)$ instead of $\text{MSE}(\mathbf{X}, h_\theta)$.

The Normal Equation

To find the value of θ that minimizes the cost function, there is a *closed-form solution* —in other words, a mathematical equation that gives the result directly. This is called the *Normal Equation* (Equation 4-4).[2]

Equation 4-4. Normal Equation

$$\hat{\theta} = \left(\mathbf{X}^T \mathbf{X} \right)^{-1} \mathbf{X}^T \mathbf{y}$$

- $\hat{\theta}$ is the value of θ that minimizes the cost function.
- $\mathbf{y}$ is the vector of target values containing $y^{(1)}$ to $y^{(m)}$.

Let's generate some linear-looking data to test this equation on (Figure 4-1):

```
import numpy as np

X = 2 * np.random.rand(100, 1)
y = 4 + 3 * X + np.random.randn(100, 1)
```

---

2 The demonstration that this returns the value of θ that minimizes the cost function is outside the scope of this book.

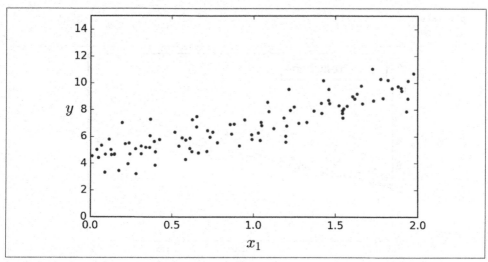

Figure 4-1. Randomly generated linear dataset

Now let's compute $\hat{\theta}$ using the Normal Equation. We will use the inv() function from NumPy's Linear Algebra module (np.linalg) to compute the inverse of a matrix, and the dot() method for matrix multiplication:

```
X_b = np.c_[np.ones((100, 1)), X]  # add x0 = 1 to each instance
theta_best = np.linalg.inv(X_b.T.dot(X_b)).dot(X_b.T).dot(y)
```

The actual function that we used to generate the data is $y = 4 + 3x_1 +$ Gaussian noise. Let's see what the equation found:

```
>>> theta_best
array([[ 4.21509616],
       [ 2.77011339]])
```

We would have hoped for $\theta_0 = 4$ and $\theta_1 = 3$ instead of $\theta_0 = 4.215$ and $\theta_1 = 2.770$. Close enough, but the noise made it impossible to recover the exact parameters of the original function.

Now you can make predictions using $\hat{\theta}$:

```
>>> X_new = np.array([[0], [2]])
>>> X_new_b = np.c_[np.ones((2, 1)), X_new] # add x0 = 1 to each instance
>>> y_predict = X_new_b.dot(theta_best)
>>> y_predict
array([[ 4.21509616],
       [ 9.75532293]])
```

Let's plot this model's predictions (Figure 4-2):

```
plt.plot(X_new, y_predict, "r-")
plt.plot(X, y, "b.")
```

```
plt.axis([0, 2, 0, 15])
plt.show()
```

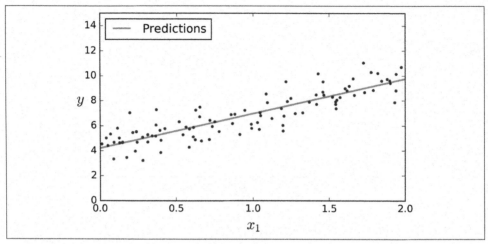

Figure 4-2. Linear Regression model predictions

Performing linear regression using Scikit-Learn is quite simple:[3]

```
>>> from sklearn.linear_model import LinearRegression
>>> lin_reg = LinearRegression()
>>> lin_reg.fit(X, y)
>>> lin_reg.intercept_, lin_reg.coef_
(array([ 4.21509616]), array([[ 2.77011339]]))
>>> lin_reg.predict(X_new)
array([[ 4.21509616],
       [ 9.75532293]])
```

The LinearRegression class is based on the scipy.linalg.lstsq() function (the name stands for "least squares"), which you could call directly:

```
>>> theta_best_svd, residuals, rank,, s = np.linalg.lstsq(X_b, y, rcond=1e-6)
>>> theta_best_svd
array([[4.21509616],
       [2.77011339]])
```

This function computes $\hat{\theta} = \mathbf{X}^{+}\mathbf{y}$, where $\mathbf{X}^{+}$ is the *pseudoinverse* of $\mathbf{X}$ (specifically the Moore-Penrose inverse). You can use np.linalg.pinv() to compute the pseudoinverse directly:

```
>>> np.linalg.pinv(X_b).dot(y)
array([[4.21509616],
       [2.77011339]])
```

---

3 Note that Scikit-Learn separates the bias term (intercept_) from the feature weights (coef_).

The pseudoinverse itself is computed using a standard matrix factorization technique called *Singular Value Decomposition* (SVD) that can decompose the training set matrix $\mathbf{X}$ into the matrix multiplication of three matrices $\mathbf{U}$ $\mathbf{\Sigma}$ $\mathbf{V}^T$ (see `numpy.linalg.svd()`). The pseudoinverse is computed as $\mathbf{X}^+ = \mathbf{V}\mathbf{\Sigma}^+\mathbf{U}^T$. To compute the matrix $\mathbf{\Sigma}^+$, the algorithm takes $\mathbf{\Sigma}$ and sets to zero all values smaller than a tiny threshold value, then it replaces all the non-zero values with their inverse, and finally it transposes the resulting matrix. This approach is more efficient than computing the Normal Equation, plus it handles edge cases nicely: indeed, the Normal Equation may not work if the matrix $\mathbf{X}^T\mathbf{X}$ is not invertible (i.e., singular), such as if $m < n$ or if some features are redundant, but the pseudoinverse is always defined.

Computational Complexity

The Normal Equation computes the inverse of $\mathbf{X}^T\,\mathbf{X}$, which is an $(n + 1) \times (n + 1)$ matrix (where n is the number of features). The *computational complexity* of inverting such a matrix is typically about $O(n^{2.4})$ to $O(n^3)$ (depending on the implementation). In other words, if you double the number of features, you multiply the computation time by roughly $2^{2.4} = 5.3$ to $2^3 = 8$.

The SVD approach used by Scikit-Learn's `LinearRegression` class is about $O(n^2)$. If you double the number of features, you multiply the computation time by roughly 4.

> Both the Normal Equation and the SVD approach get very slow when the number of features grows large (e.g., 100,000). On the positive side, both are linear with regards to the number of instances in the training set (they are $O(m)$), so they handle large training sets efficiently, provided they can fit in memory.

Also, once you have trained your Linear Regression model (using the Normal Equation or any other algorithm), predictions are very fast: the computational complexity is linear with regards to both the number of instances you want to make predictions on and the number of features. In other words, making predictions on twice as many instances (or twice as many features) will just take roughly twice as much time.

Now we will look at very different ways to train a Linear Regression model, better suited for cases where there are a large number of features, or too many training instances to fit in memory.

Gradient Descent

Gradient Descent is a very generic optimization algorithm capable of finding optimal solutions to a wide range of problems. The general idea of Gradient Descent is to tweak parameters iteratively in order to minimize a cost function.

Suppose you are lost in the mountains in a dense fog; you can only feel the slope of the ground below your feet. A good strategy to get to the bottom of the valley quickly is to go downhill in the direction of the steepest slope. This is exactly what Gradient Descent does: it measures the local gradient of the error function with regards to the parameter vector θ, and it goes in the direction of descending gradient. Once the gradient is zero, you have reached a minimum!

Concretely, you start by filling θ with random values (this is called *random initialization*), and then you improve it gradually, taking one baby step at a time, each step attempting to decrease the cost function (e.g., the MSE), until the algorithm *converges* to a minimum (see Figure 4-3).

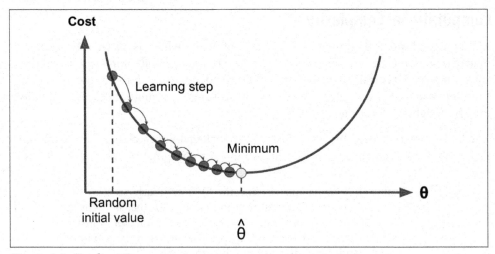

Figure 4-3. Gradient Descent

An important parameter in Gradient Descent is the size of the steps, determined by the *learning rate* hyperparameter. If the learning rate is too small, then the algorithm will have to go through many iterations to converge, which will take a long time (see Figure 4-4).

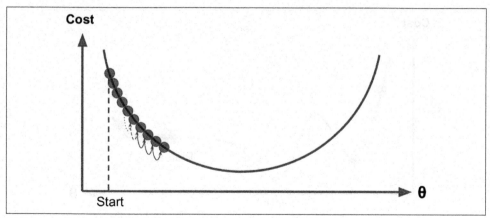

Figure 4-4. Learning rate too small

On the other hand, if the learning rate is too high, you might jump across the valley and end up on the other side, possibly even higher up than you were before. This might make the algorithm diverge, with larger and larger values, failing to find a good solution (see Figure 4-5).

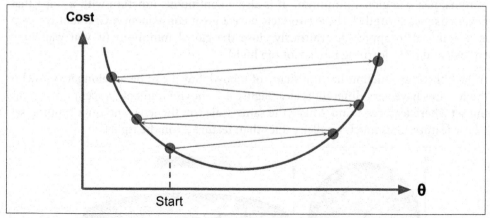

Figure 4-5. Learning rate too large

Finally, not all cost functions look like nice regular bowls. There may be holes, ridges, plateaus, and all sorts of irregular terrains, making convergence to the minimum very difficult. Figure 4-6 shows the two main challenges with Gradient Descent: if the random initialization starts the algorithm on the left, then it will converge to a *local minimum*, which is not as good as the *global minimum*. If it starts on the right, then it will take a very long time to cross the plateau, and if you stop too early you will never reach the global minimum.

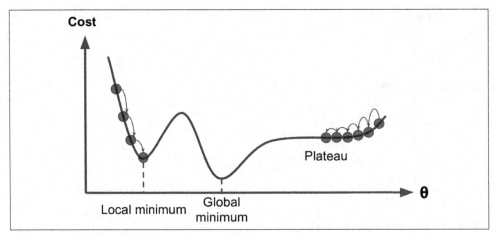

Figure 4-6. Gradient Descent pitfalls

Fortunately, the MSE cost function for a Linear Regression model happens to be a *convex function*, which means that if you pick any two points on the curve, the line segment joining them never crosses the curve. This implies that there are no local minima, just one global minimum. It is also a continuous function with a slope that never changes abruptly.[4] These two facts have a great consequence: Gradient Descent is guaranteed to approach arbitrarily close the global minimum (if you wait long enough and if the learning rate is not too high).

In fact, the cost function has the shape of a bowl, but it can be an elongated bowl if the features have very different scales. Figure 4-7 shows Gradient Descent on a training set where features 1 and 2 have the same scale (on the left), and on a training set where feature 1 has much smaller values than feature 2 (on the right).[5]

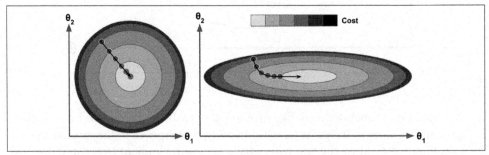

Figure 4-7. Gradient Descent with and without feature scaling

---

4 Technically speaking, its derivative is *Lipschitz continuous*.

5 Since feature 1 is smaller, it takes a larger change in θ_1 to affect the cost function, which is why the bowl is elongated along the θ_1 axis.

As you can see, on the left the Gradient Descent algorithm goes straight toward the minimum, thereby reaching it quickly, whereas on the right it first goes in a direction almost orthogonal to the direction of the global minimum, and it ends with a long march down an almost flat valley. It will eventually reach the minimum, but it will take a long time.

When using Gradient Descent, you should ensure that all features have a similar scale (e.g., using Scikit-Learn's `StandardScaler` class), or else it will take much longer to converge.

This diagram also illustrates the fact that training a model means searching for a combination of model parameters that minimizes a cost function (over the training set). It is a search in the model's *parameter space*: the more parameters a model has, the more dimensions this space has, and the harder the search is: searching for a needle in a 300-dimensional haystack is much trickier than in three dimensions. Fortunately, since the cost function is convex in the case of Linear Regression, the needle is simply at the bottom of the bowl.

Batch Gradient Descent

To implement Gradient Descent, you need to compute the gradient of the cost function with regards to each model parameter θ_j. In other words, you need to calculate how much the cost function will change if you change θ_j just a little bit. This is called a *partial derivative*. It is like asking "what is the slope of the mountain under my feet if I face east?" and then asking the same question facing north (and so on for all other dimensions, if you can imagine a universe with more than three dimensions). Equation 4-5 computes the partial derivative of the cost function with regards to parameter θ_j, noted $\frac{\partial}{\partial \theta_j}$ MSE(θ).

Equation 4-5. Partial derivatives of the cost function

$$\frac{\partial}{\partial \theta_j} \text{MSE}(\theta) = \frac{2}{m} \sum_{i=1}^{m} \left(\theta^T \mathbf{x}^{(i)} - y^{(i)} \right) x_j^{(i)}$$

Instead of computing these partial derivatives individually, you can use Equation 4-6 to compute them all in one go. The gradient vector, noted $\nabla_\theta \text{MSE}(\theta)$, contains all the partial derivatives of the cost function (one for each model parameter).

Equation 4-6. Gradient vector of the cost function

$$\nabla_{\boldsymbol{\theta}} \, \text{MSE}(\boldsymbol{\theta}) = \begin{pmatrix} \frac{\partial}{\partial \theta_0} \text{MSE}(\boldsymbol{\theta}) \\ \frac{\partial}{\partial \theta_1} \text{MSE}(\boldsymbol{\theta}) \\ \vdots \\ \frac{\partial}{\partial \theta_n} \text{MSE}(\boldsymbol{\theta}) \end{pmatrix} = \frac{2}{m} \mathbf{X}^T (\mathbf{X}\boldsymbol{\theta} - \mathbf{y})$$

 Notice that this formula involves calculations over the full training set **X**, at each Gradient Descent step! This is why the algorithm is called *Batch Gradient Descent*: it uses the whole batch of training data at every step. As a result it is terribly slow on very large training sets (but we will see much faster Gradient Descent algorithms shortly). However, Gradient Descent scales well with the number of features; training a Linear Regression model when there are hundreds of thousands of features is much faster using Gradient Descent than using the Normal Equation or SVD decomposition.

Once you have the gradient vector, which points uphill, just go in the opposite direction to go downhill. This means subtracting $\nabla_{\boldsymbol{\theta}}\text{MSE}(\boldsymbol{\theta})$ from $\boldsymbol{\theta}$. This is where the learning rate η comes into play:[6] multiply the gradient vector by η to determine the size of the downhill step (Equation 4-7).

Equation 4-7. Gradient Descent step

$$\boldsymbol{\theta}^{(\text{next step})} = \boldsymbol{\theta} - \eta \, \nabla_{\boldsymbol{\theta}} \, \text{MSE}\left(\boldsymbol{\theta}\right)$$

Let's look at a quick implementation of this algorithm:

```
eta = 0.1  # learning rate
n_iterations = 1000
m = 100

theta = np.random.randn(2,1)  # random initialization

for iteration in range(n_iterations):
    gradients = 2/m * X_b.T.dot(X_b.dot(theta) - y)
    theta = theta - eta * gradients
```

---

6 Eta (η) is the 7th letter of the Greek alphabet.

That wasn't too hard! Let's look at the resulting theta:

```
>>> theta
array([[ 4.21509616],
       [ 2.77011339]])
```

Hey, that's exactly what the Normal Equation found! Gradient Descent worked perfectly. But what if you had used a different learning rate eta? Figure 4-8 shows the first 10 steps of Gradient Descent using three different learning rates (the dashed line represents the starting point).

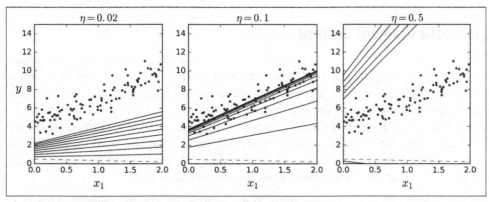

Figure 4-8. Gradient Descent with various learning rates

On the left, the learning rate is too low: the algorithm will eventually reach the solution, but it will take a long time. In the middle, the learning rate looks pretty good: in just a few iterations, it has already converged to the solution. On the right, the learning rate is too high: the algorithm diverges, jumping all over the place and actually getting further and further away from the solution at every step.

To find a good learning rate, you can use grid search (see Chapter 2). However, you may want to limit the number of iterations so that grid search can eliminate models that take too long to converge.

You may wonder how to set the number of iterations. If it is too low, you will still be far away from the optimal solution when the algorithm stops, but if it is too high, you will waste time while the model parameters do not change anymore. A simple solution is to set a very large number of iterations but to interrupt the algorithm when the gradient vector becomes tiny—that is, when its norm becomes smaller than a tiny number ϵ (called the *tolerance*)—because this happens when Gradient Descent has (almost) reached the minimum.

Convergence Rate

When the cost function is convex and its slope does not change abruptly (as is the case for the MSE cost function), Batch Gradient Descent with a fixed learning rate will eventually converge to the optimal solution, but you may have to wait a while: it can take $O(1/\epsilon)$ iterations to reach the optimum within a range of ϵ depending on the shape of the cost function. If you divide the tolerance by 10 to have a more precise solution, then the algorithm may have to run about 10 times longer.

Stochastic Gradient Descent

The main problem with Batch Gradient Descent is the fact that it uses the whole training set to compute the gradients at every step, which makes it very slow when the training set is large. At the opposite extreme, *Stochastic Gradient Descent* just picks a random instance in the training set at every step and computes the gradients based only on that single instance. Obviously this makes the algorithm much faster since it has very little data to manipulate at every iteration. It also makes it possible to train on huge training sets, since only one instance needs to be in memory at each iteration (SGD can be implemented as an out-of-core algorithm.[7])

On the other hand, due to its stochastic (i.e., random) nature, this algorithm is much less regular than Batch Gradient Descent: instead of gently decreasing until it reaches the minimum, the cost function will bounce up and down, decreasing only on average. Over time it will end up very close to the minimum, but once it gets there it will continue to bounce around, never settling down (see Figure 4-9). So once the algorithm stops, the final parameter values are good, but not optimal.

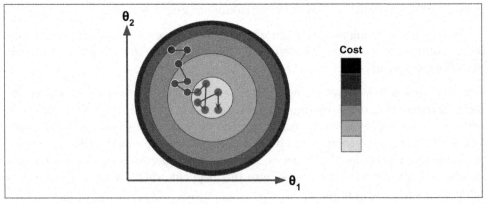

Figure 4-9. Stochastic Gradient Descent

---

7 Out-of-core algorithms are discussed in Chapter 1.

When the cost function is very irregular (as in Figure 4-6), this can actually help the algorithm jump out of local minima, so Stochastic Gradient Descent has a better chance of finding the global minimum than Batch Gradient Descent does.

Therefore randomness is good to escape from local optima, but bad because it means that the algorithm can never settle at the minimum. One solution to this dilemma is to gradually reduce the learning rate. The steps start out large (which helps make quick progress and escape local minima), then get smaller and smaller, allowing the algorithm to settle at the global minimum. This process is akin to *simulated annealing*, an algorithm inspired from the process of annealing in metallurgy where molten metal is slowly cooled down. The function that determines the learning rate at each iteration is called the *learning schedule*. If the learning rate is reduced too quickly, you may get stuck in a local minimum, or even end up frozen halfway to the minimum. If the learning rate is reduced too slowly, you may jump around the minimum for a long time and end up with a suboptimal solution if you halt training too early.

This code implements Stochastic Gradient Descent using a simple learning schedule:

```
n_epochs = 50
t0, t1 = 5, 50  # learning schedule hyperparameters

def learning_schedule(t):
    return t0 / (t + t1)

theta = np.random.randn(2,1)  # random initialization

for epoch in range(n_epochs):
    for i in range(m):
        random_index = np.random.randint(m)
        xi = X_b[random_index:random_index+1]
        yi = y[random_index:random_index+1]
        gradients = 2 * xi.T.dot(xi.dot(theta) - yi)
        eta = learning_schedule(epoch * m + i)
        theta = theta - eta * gradients
```

By convention we iterate by rounds of *m* iterations; each round is called an *epoch*. While the Batch Gradient Descent code iterated 1,000 times through the whole training set, this code goes through the training set only 50 times and reaches a fairly good solution:

```
>>> theta
array([[ 4.21076011],
       [ 2.74856079]])
```

Figure 4-10 shows the first 20 steps of training (notice how irregular the steps are).

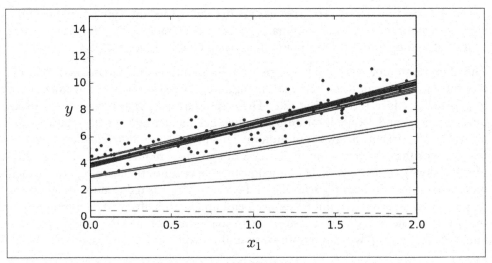

Figure 4-10. Stochastic Gradient Descent first 20 steps

Note that since instances are picked randomly, some instances may be picked several times per epoch while others may not be picked at all. If you want to be sure that the algorithm goes through every instance at each epoch, another approach is to shuffle the training set, then go through it instance by instance, then shuffle it again, and so on. However, this generally converges more slowly.

To perform Linear Regression using SGD with Scikit-Learn, you can use the `SGDRegressor` class, which defaults to optimizing the squared error cost function. The following code runs 50 epochs, starting with a learning rate of 0.1 (`eta0=0.1`), using the default learning schedule (different from the preceding one), and it does not use any regularization (`penalty=None`; more details on this shortly):

```
from sklearn.linear_model import SGDRegressor
sgd_reg = SGDRegressor(n_iter=50, penalty=None, eta0=0.1)
sgd_reg.fit(X, y.ravel())
```

Once again, you find a solution very close to the one returned by the Normal Equation:

```
>>> sgd_reg.intercept_, sgd_reg.coef_
(array([ 4.16782089]), array([ 2.72603052]))
```

Mini-batch Gradient Descent

The last Gradient Descent algorithm we will look at is called *Mini-batch Gradient Descent*. It is quite simple to understand once you know Batch and Stochastic Gradient Descent: at each step, instead of computing the gradients based on the full training set (as in Batch GD) or based on just one instance (as in Stochastic GD), Mini-batch GD computes the gradients on small random sets of instances called *mini-batches*. The main advantage of Mini-batch GD over Stochastic GD is that you can get a performance boost from hardware optimization of matrix operations, especially when using GPUs.

The algorithm's progress in parameter space is less erratic than with SGD, especially with fairly large mini-batches. As a result, Mini-batch GD will end up walking around a bit closer to the minimum than SGD. But, on the other hand, it may be harder for it to escape from local minima (in the case of problems that suffer from local minima, unlike Linear Regression as we saw earlier). Figure 4-11 shows the paths taken by the three Gradient Descent algorithms in parameter space during training. They all end up near the minimum, but Batch GD's path actually stops at the minimum, while both Stochastic GD and Mini-batch GD continue to walk around. However, don't forget that Batch GD takes a lot of time to take each step, and Stochastic GD and Mini-batch GD would also reach the minimum if you used a good learning schedule.

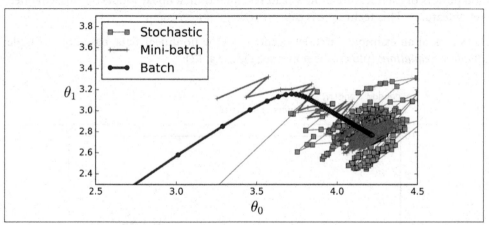

Figure 4-11. Gradient Descent paths in parameter space

Let's compare the algorithms we've discussed so far for Linear Regression[8] (recall that *m* is the number of training instances and *n* is the number of features); see Table 4-1.

Table 4-1. Comparison of algorithms for Linear Regression

Algorithm	Large *m*	Out-of-core support	Large *n*	Hyperparams	Scaling required	Scikit-Learn
Normal Equation	Fast	No	Slow	0	No	n/a
SVD	Fast	No	Slow	0	No	LinearRegression

---

8 While the Normal Equation can only perform Linear Regression, the Gradient Descent algorithms can be used to train many other models, as we will see.

Algorithm	Large m	Out-of-core support	Large n	Hyperparams	Scaling required	Scikit-Learn
Batch GD	Slow	No	Fast	2	Yes	SGDRegressor
Stochastic GD	Fast	Yes	Fast	≥ 2	Yes	SGDRegressor
Mini-batch GD	Fast	Yes	Fast	≥ 2	Yes	SGDRegressor

There is almost no difference after training: all these algorithms end up with very similar models and make predictions in exactly the same way.

Polynomial Regression

What if your data is actually more complex than a simple straight line? Surprisingly, you can actually use a linear model to fit nonlinear data. A simple way to do this is to add powers of each feature as new features, then train a linear model on this extended set of features. This technique is called *Polynomial Regression*.

Let's look at an example. First, let's generate some nonlinear data, based on a simple *quadratic equation*[9] (plus some noise; see Figure 4-12):

```
m = 100
X = 6 * np.random.rand(m, 1) - 3
y = 0.5 * X**2 + X + 2 + np.random.randn(m, 1)
```

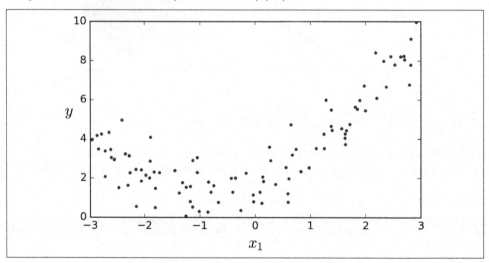

Figure 4-12. Generated nonlinear and noisy dataset

---

9 A quadratic equation is of the form $y = ax^2 + bx + c$.

Clearly, a straight line will never fit this data properly. So let's use Scikit-Learn's `Poly nomialFeatures` class to transform our training data, adding the square (2nd-degree polynomial) of each feature in the training set as new features (in this case there is just one feature):

```
>>> from sklearn.preprocessing import PolynomialFeatures
>>> poly_features = PolynomialFeatures(degree=2, include_bias=False)
>>> X_poly = poly_features.fit_transform(X)
>>> X[0]
array([-0.75275929])
>>> X_poly[0]
array([-0.75275929,  0.56664654])
```

`X_poly` now contains the original feature of X plus the square of this feature. Now you can fit a `LinearRegression` model to this extended training data (Figure 4-13):

```
>>> lin_reg = LinearRegression()
>>> lin_reg.fit(X_poly, y)
>>> lin_reg.intercept_, lin_reg.coef_
(array([ 1.78134581]), array([[ 0.93366893,  0.56456263]]))
```

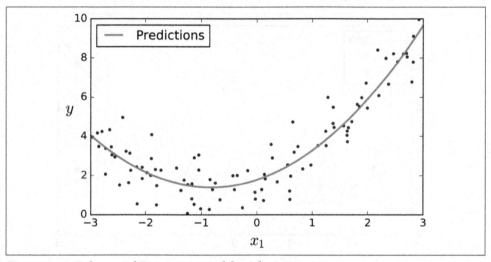

Figure 4-13. Polynomial Regression model predictions

Not bad: the model estimates $\hat{y} = 0.56x_1^2 + 0.93x_1 + 1.78$ when in fact the original function was $y = 0.5x_1^2 + 1.0x_1 + 2.0 +$ Gaussian noise.

Note that when there are multiple features, Polynomial Regression is capable of finding relationships between features (which is something a plain Linear Regression model cannot do). This is made possible by the fact that `PolynomialFeatures` also adds all combinations of features up to the given degree. For example, if there were two features a and b, `PolynomialFeatures` with `degree=3` would not only add the features a^2, a^3, b^2, and b^3, but also the combinations ab, a^2b, and ab^2.

 `PolynomialFeatures(degree=d)` transforms an array containing n features into an array containing $\dfrac{(n+d)!}{d!\,n!}$ features, where $n!$ is the *factorial* of n, equal to $1 \times 2 \times 3 \times \cdots \times n$. Beware of the combinatorial explosion of the number of features!

Learning Curves

If you perform high-degree Polynomial Regression, you will likely fit the training data much better than with plain Linear Regression. For example, Figure 4-14 applies a 300-degree polynomial model to the preceding training data, and compares the result with a pure linear model and a quadratic model (2nd-degree polynomial). Notice how the 300-degree polynomial model wiggles around to get as close as possible to the training instances.

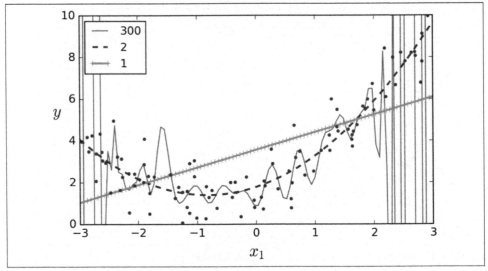

Figure 4-14. High-degree Polynomial Regression

Of course, this high-degree Polynomial Regression model is severely overfitting the training data, while the linear model is underfitting it. The model that will generalize best in this case is the quadratic model. It makes sense since the data was generated using a quadratic model, but in general you won't know what function generated the data, so how can you decide how complex your model should be? How can you tell that your model is overfitting or underfitting the data?

In Chapter 2 you used cross-validation to get an estimate of a model's generalization performance. If a model performs well on the training data but generalizes poorly according to the cross-validation metrics, then your model is overfitting. If it performs poorly on both, then it is underfitting. This is one way to tell when a model is too simple or too complex.

Another way is to look at the *learning curves*: these are plots of the model's performance on the training set and the validation set as a function of the training set size (or the training iteration). To generate the plots, simply train the model several times on different sized subsets of the training set. The following code defines a function that plots the learning curves of a model given some training data:

```python
from sklearn.metrics import mean_squared_error
from sklearn.model_selection import train_test_split

def plot_learning_curves(model, X, y):
    X_train, X_val, y_train, y_val = train_test_split(X, y, test_size=0.2)
    train_errors, val_errors = [], []
    for m in range(1, len(X_train)):
        model.fit(X_train[:m], y_train[:m])
        y_train_predict = model.predict(X_train[:m])
        y_val_predict = model.predict(X_val)
        train_errors.append(mean_squared_error(y_train[:m], y_train_predict))
        val_errors.append(mean_squared_error(y_val, y_val_predict))
    plt.plot(np.sqrt(train_errors), "r-+", linewidth=2, label="train")
    plt.plot(np.sqrt(val_errors), "b-", linewidth=3, label="val")
```

Let's look at the learning curves of the plain Linear Regression model (a straight line; Figure 4-15):

```python
lin_reg = LinearRegression()
plot_learning_curves(lin_reg, X, y)
```

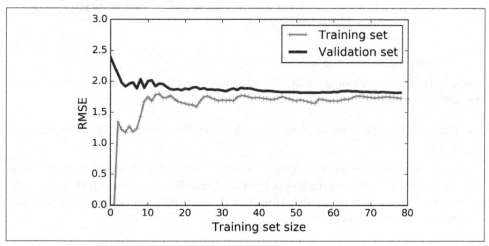

Figure 4-15. Learning curves

This deserves a bit of explanation. First, let's look at the performance on the training data: when there are just one or two instances in the training set, the model can fit them perfectly, which is why the curve starts at zero. But as new instances are added to the training set, it becomes impossible for the model to fit the training data perfectly, both because the data is noisy and because it is not linear at all. So the error on the training data goes up until it reaches a plateau, at which point adding new instances to the training set doesn't make the average error much better or worse. Now let's look at the performance of the model on the validation data. When the model is trained on very few training instances, it is incapable of generalizing properly, which is why the validation error is initially quite big. Then as the model is shown more training examples, it learns and thus the validation error slowly goes down. However, once again a straight line cannot do a good job modeling the data, so the error ends up at a plateau, very close to the other curve.

These learning curves are typical of an underfitting model. Both curves have reached a plateau; they are close and fairly high.

> If your model is underfitting the training data, adding more training examples will not help. You need to use a more complex model or come up with better features.

Now let's look at the learning curves of a 10th-degree polynomial model on the same data (Figure 4-16):

```
from sklearn.pipeline import Pipeline

polynomial_regression = Pipeline([
        ("poly_features", PolynomialFeatures(degree=10, include_bias=False)),
        ("lin_reg", LinearRegression()),
    ])

plot_learning_curves(polynomial_regression, X, y)
```

These learning curves look a bit like the previous ones, but there are two very important differences:

- The error on the training data is much lower than with the Linear Regression model.
- There is a gap between the curves. This means that the model performs significantly better on the training data than on the validation data, which is the hallmark of an overfitting model. However, if you used a much larger training set, the two curves would continue to get closer.

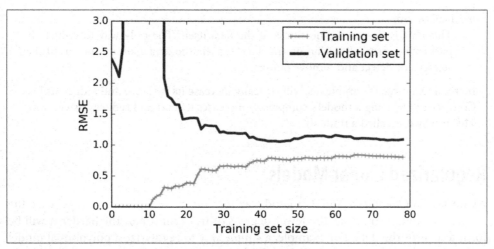

Figure 4-16. Learning curves for the polynomial model

One way to improve an overfitting model is to feed it more training
data until the validation error reaches the training error.

The Bias/Variance Tradeoff

An important theoretical result of statistics and Machine Learning is the fact that a
model's generalization error can be expressed as the sum of three very different
errors:

Bias

This part of the generalization error is due to wrong assumptions, such as assuming that the data is linear when it is actually quadratic. A high-bias model is most
likely to underfit the training data.[10]

Variance

This part is due to the model's excessive sensitivity to small variations in the
training data. A model with many degrees of freedom (such as a high-degree polynomial model) is likely to have high variance, and thus to overfit the training
data.

---

10 This notion of bias is not to be confused with the bias term of linear models.

Irreducible error

This part is due to the noisiness of the data itself. The only way to reduce this part of the error is to clean up the data (e.g., fix the data sources, such as broken sensors, or detect and remove outliers).

Increasing a model's complexity will typically increase its variance and reduce its bias. Conversely, reducing a model's complexity increases its bias and reduces its variance. This is why it is called a tradeoff.

Regularized Linear Models

As we saw in Chapters 1 and 2, a good way to reduce overfitting is to regularize the model (i.e., to constrain it): the fewer degrees of freedom it has, the harder it will be for it to overfit the data. For example, a simple way to regularize a polynomial model is to reduce the number of polynomial degrees.

For a linear model, regularization is typically achieved by constraining the weights of the model. We will now look at Ridge Regression, Lasso Regression, and Elastic Net, which implement three different ways to constrain the weights.

Ridge Regression

Ridge Regression (also called *Tikhonov regularization*) is a regularized version of Linear Regression: a *regularization term* equal to $\alpha \sum_{i=1}^{n} \theta_i^2$ is added to the cost function. This forces the learning algorithm to not only fit the data but also keep the model weights as small as possible. Note that the regularization term should only be added to the cost function during training. Once the model is trained, you want to evaluate the model's performance using the unregularized performance measure.

It is quite common for the cost function used during training to be different from the performance measure used for testing. Apart from regularization, another reason why they might be different is that a good training cost function should have optimization-friendly derivatives, while the performance measure used for testing should be as close as possible to the final objective. A good example of this is a classifier trained using a cost function such as the log loss (discussed in a moment) but evaluated using precision/recall.

The hyperparameter α controls how much you want to regularize the model. If $\alpha = 0$ then Ridge Regression is just Linear Regression. If α is very large, then all weights end up very close to zero and the result is a flat line going through the data's mean. Equation 4-8 presents the Ridge Regression cost function.[11]

Equation 4-8. Ridge Regression cost function

$$J(\boldsymbol{\theta}) = \text{MSE}(\boldsymbol{\theta}) + \alpha \frac{1}{2} \sum_{i=1}^{n} \theta_i^2$$

Note that the bias term θ_0 is not regularized (the sum starts at $i = 1$, not 0). If we define **w** as the vector of feature weights (θ_1 to θ_n), then the regularization term is simply equal to $\frac{1}{2}(\| \mathbf{w} \|_2)^2$, where $\| \mathbf{w} \|_2$ represents the ℓ_2 norm of the weight vector.[12] For Gradient Descent, just add $\alpha\mathbf{w}$ to the MSE gradient vector (Equation 4-6).

> It is important to scale the data (e.g., using a `StandardScaler`) before performing Ridge Regression, as it is sensitive to the scale of the input features. This is true of most regularized models.

Figure 4-17 shows several Ridge models trained on some linear data using different α value. On the left, plain Ridge models are used, leading to linear predictions. On the right, the data is first expanded using `PolynomialFeatures(degree=10)`, then it is scaled using a `StandardScaler`, and finally the Ridge models are applied to the resulting features: this is Polynomial Regression with Ridge regularization. Note how increasing α leads to flatter (i.e., less extreme, more reasonable) predictions; this reduces the model's variance but increases its bias.

As with Linear Regression, we can perform Ridge Regression either by computing a closed-form equation or by performing Gradient Descent. The pros and cons are the same. Equation 4-9 shows the closed-form solution (where **A** is the $(n + 1) \times (n + 1)$ *identity matrix*[13] except with a 0 in the top-left cell, corresponding to the bias term).

---

11 It is common to use the notation $J(\boldsymbol{\theta})$ for cost functions that don't have a short name; we will often use this notation throughout the rest of this book. The context will make it clear which cost function is being discussed.

12 Norms are discussed in Chapter 2.

13 A square matrix full of 0s except for 1s on the main diagonal (top-left to bottom-right).

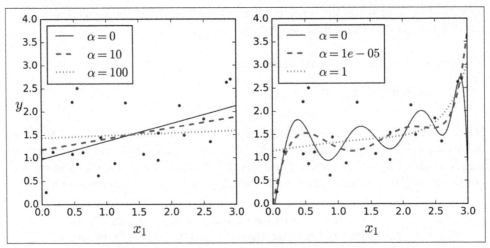

Figure 4-17. Ridge Regression

Equation 4-9. Ridge Regression closed-form solution

$$\hat{\theta} = \left(\mathbf{X}^T \mathbf{X} + \alpha \mathbf{A}\right)^{-1} \mathbf{X}^T \ \mathbf{y}$$

Here is how to perform Ridge Regression with Scikit-Learn using a closed-form solution (a variant of Equation 4-9 using a matrix factorization technique by André-Louis Cholesky):

```
>>> from sklearn.linear_model import Ridge
>>> ridge_reg = Ridge(alpha=1, solver="cholesky")
>>> ridge_reg.fit(X, y)
>>> ridge_reg.predict([[1.5]])
array([[ 1.55071465]])
```

And using Stochastic Gradient Descent:[14]

```
>>> sgd_reg = SGDRegressor(penalty="l2")
>>> sgd_reg.fit(X, y.ravel())
>>> sgd_reg.predict([[1.5]])
array([ 1.13500145])
```

The penalty hyperparameter sets the type of regularization term to use. Specifying "l2" indicates that you want SGD to add a regularization term to the cost function equal to half the square of the ℓ_2 norm of the weight vector: this is simply Ridge Regression.

---

[14] Alternatively you can use the Ridge class with the "sag" solver. Stochastic Average GD is a variant of SGD. For more details, see the presentation "Minimizing Finite Sums with the Stochastic Average Gradient Algorithm" (*http://homl.info/12*) by Mark Schmidt et al. from the University of British Columbia.

Lasso Regression

Least Absolute Shrinkage and Selection Operator Regression (simply called *Lasso Regression*) is another regularized version of Linear Regression: just like Ridge Regression, it adds a regularization term to the cost function, but it uses the ℓ_1 norm of the weight vector instead of half the square of the ℓ_2 norm (see Equation 4-10).

Equation 4-10. Lasso Regression cost function

$$J(\boldsymbol{\theta}) = \text{MSE}(\boldsymbol{\theta}) + \alpha \sum_{i=1}^{n} |\theta_i|$$

Figure 4-18 shows the same thing as Figure 4-17 but replaces Ridge models with Lasso models and uses smaller α values.

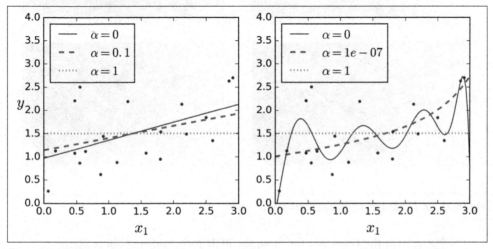

Figure 4-18. Lasso Regression

An important characteristic of Lasso Regression is that it tends to completely eliminate the weights of the least important features (i.e., set them to zero). For example, the dashed line in the right plot on Figure 4-18 (with $\alpha = 10^{-7}$) looks quadratic, almost linear: all the weights for the high-degree polynomial features are equal to zero. In other words, Lasso Regression automatically performs feature selection and outputs a *sparse model* (i.e., with few nonzero feature weights).

You can get a sense of why this is the case by looking at Figure 4-19: on the top-left plot, the background contours (ellipses) represent an unregularized MSE cost function ($\alpha = 0$), and the white circles show the Batch Gradient Descent path with that cost function. The foreground contours (diamonds) represent the ℓ_1 penalty, and the triangles show the BGD path for this penalty only ($\alpha \to \infty$). Notice how the path first reaches $\theta_1 = 0$, then rolls down a gutter until it reaches $\theta_2 = 0$. On the top-right plot, the contours represent the same cost function plus an ℓ_1 penalty with $\alpha = 0.5$. The global minimum is on the $\theta_2 = 0$ axis. BGD first reaches $\theta_2 = 0$, then rolls down the gutter until it reaches the global minimum. The two bottom plots show the same thing but uses an ℓ_2 penalty instead. The regularized minimum is closer to $\boldsymbol{\theta} = \mathbf{0}$ than the unregularized minimum, but the weights do not get fully eliminated.

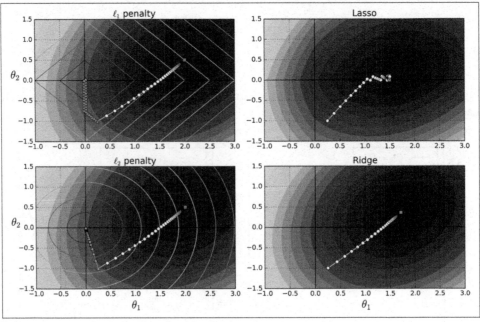

Figure 4-19. Lasso versus Ridge regularization

On the Lasso cost function, the BGD path tends to bounce across the gutter toward the end. This is because the slope changes abruptly at $\theta_2 = 0$. You need to gradually reduce the learning rate in order to actually converge to the global minimum.

The Lasso cost function is not differentiable at $\theta_i = 0$ (for $i = 1, 2, \cdots, n$), but Gradient Descent still works fine if you use a *subgradient vector* $\mathbf{g}$[15] instead when any $\theta_i = 0$.

---

15 You can think of a subgradient vector at a nondifferentiable point as an intermediate vector between the gradient vectors around that point.

Equation 4-11 shows a subgradient vector equation you can use for Gradient Descent with the Lasso cost function.

Equation 4-11. Lasso Regression subgradient vector

$$g(\theta, J) = \nabla_\theta \text{MSE}(\theta) + \alpha \begin{pmatrix} \text{sign}(\theta_1) \\ \text{sign}(\theta_2) \\ \vdots \\ \text{sign}(\theta_n) \end{pmatrix} \quad \text{where } \text{sign}(\theta_i) = \begin{cases} -1 & \text{if } \theta_i < 0 \\ 0 & \text{if } \theta_i = 0 \\ +1 & \text{if } \theta_i > 0 \end{cases}$$

Here is a small Scikit-Learn example using the `Lasso` class. Note that you could instead use an `SGDRegressor(penalty="l1")`.

```
>>> from sklearn.linear_model import Lasso
>>> lasso_reg = Lasso(alpha=0.1)
>>> lasso_reg.fit(X, y)
>>> lasso_reg.predict([[1.5]])
array([ 1.53788174])
```

Elastic Net

Elastic Net is a middle ground between Ridge Regression and Lasso Regression. The regularization term is a simple mix of both Ridge and Lasso's regularization terms, and you can control the mix ratio r. When $r = 0$, Elastic Net is equivalent to Ridge Regression, and when $r = 1$, it is equivalent to Lasso Regression (see Equation 4-12).

Equation 4-12. Elastic Net cost function

$$J(\theta) = \text{MSE}(\theta) + r\alpha \sum_{i=1}^{n} |\theta_i| + \frac{1-r}{2}\alpha \sum_{i=1}^{n} \theta_i^2$$

So when should you use plain Linear Regression (i.e., without any regularization), Ridge, Lasso, or Elastic Net? It is almost always preferable to have at least a little bit of regularization, so generally you should avoid plain Linear Regression. Ridge is a good default, but if you suspect that only a few features are actually useful, you should prefer Lasso or Elastic Net since they tend to reduce the useless features' weights down to zero as we have discussed. In general, Elastic Net is preferred over Lasso since Lasso may behave erratically when the number of features is greater than the number of training instances or when several features are strongly correlated.

Here is a short example using Scikit-Learn's `ElasticNet` (`l1_ratio` corresponds to the mix ratio r):

```
>>> from sklearn.linear_model import ElasticNet
>>> elastic_net = ElasticNet(alpha=0.1, l1_ratio=0.5)
```

```
>>> elastic_net.fit(X, y)
>>> elastic_net.predict([[1.5]])
array([ 1.54333232])
```

Early Stopping

A very different way to regularize iterative learning algorithms such as Gradient Descent is to stop training as soon as the validation error reaches a minimum. This is called *early stopping*. Figure 4-20 shows a complex model (in this case a high-degree Polynomial Regression model) being trained using Batch Gradient Descent. As the epochs go by, the algorithm learns and its prediction error (RMSE) on the training set naturally goes down, and so does its prediction error on the validation set. However, after a while the validation error stops decreasing and actually starts to go back up. This indicates that the model has started to overfit the training data. With early stopping you just stop training as soon as the validation error reaches the minimum. It is such a simple and efficient regularization technique that Geoffrey Hinton called it a "beautiful free lunch."

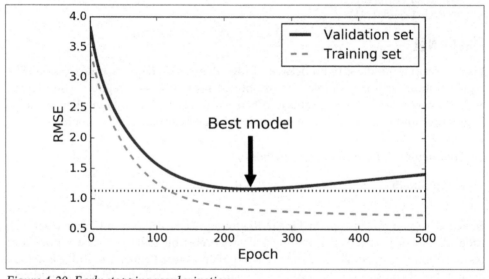

Figure 4-20. Early stopping regularization

With Stochastic and Mini-batch Gradient Descent, the curves are not so smooth, and it may be hard to know whether you have reached the minimum or not. One solution is to stop only after the validation error has been above the minimum for some time (when you are confident that the model will not do any better), then roll back the model parameters to the point where the validation error was at a minimum.

Here is a basic implementation of early stopping:

```python
from sklearn.base import clone

# prepare the data
poly_scaler = Pipeline([
        ("poly_features", PolynomialFeatures(degree=90, include_bias=False)),
        ("std_scaler", StandardScaler()) ])
X_train_poly_scaled = poly_scaler.fit_transform(X_train)
X_val_poly_scaled = poly_scaler.transform(X_val)

sgd_reg = SGDRegressor(n_iter=1, warm_start=True, penalty=None,
                       learning_rate="constant", eta0=0.0005)

minimum_val_error = float("inf")
best_epoch = None
best_model = None
for epoch in range(1000):
    sgd_reg.fit(X_train_poly_scaled, y_train)  # continues where it left off
    y_val_predict = sgd_reg.predict(X_val_poly_scaled)
    val_error = mean_squared_error(y_val, y_val_predict)
    if val_error < minimum_val_error:
        minimum_val_error = val_error
        best_epoch = epoch
        best_model = clone(sgd_reg)
```

Note that with `warm_start=True`, when the `fit()` method is called, it just continues training where it left off instead of restarting from scratch.

Logistic Regression

As we discussed in Chapter 1, some regression algorithms can be used for classification as well (and vice versa). *Logistic Regression* (also called *Logit Regression*) is commonly used to estimate the probability that an instance belongs to a particular class (e.g., what is the probability that this email is spam?). If the estimated probability is greater than 50%, then the model predicts that the instance belongs to that class (called the positive class, labeled "1"), or else it predicts that it does not (i.e., it belongs to the negative class, labeled "0"). This makes it a binary classifier.

Estimating Probabilities

So how does it work? Just like a Linear Regression model, a Logistic Regression model computes a weighted sum of the input features (plus a bias term), but instead of outputting the result directly like the Linear Regression model does, it outputs the *logistic* of this result (see Equation 4-13).

Equation 4-13. Logistic Regression model estimated probability (vectorized form)

$$\hat{p} = h_{\theta}(\mathbf{x}) = \sigma\left(\theta^T \mathbf{x}\right)$$

The logistic—noted $\sigma(\cdot)$—is a *sigmoid function* (i.e., S-shaped) that outputs a number between 0 and 1. It is defined as shown in Equation 4-14 and Figure 4-21.

Equation 4-14. Logistic function

$$\sigma(t) = \frac{1}{1 + \exp(-t)}$$

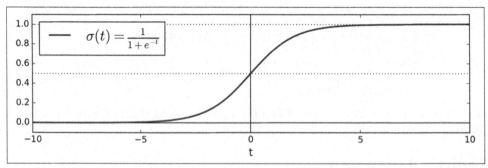

Figure 4-21. Logistic function

Once the Logistic Regression model has estimated the probability $\hat{p} = h_{\theta}(\mathbf{x})$ that an instance $\mathbf{x}$ belongs to the positive class, it can make its prediction $\hat{y}$ easily (see Equation 4-15).

Equation 4-15. Logistic Regression model prediction

$$\hat{y} = \begin{cases} 0 & \text{if } \hat{p} < 0.5 \\ 1 & \text{if } \hat{p} \geq 0.5 \end{cases}$$

Notice that $\sigma(t) < 0.5$ when $t < 0$, and $\sigma(t) \geq 0.5$ when $t \geq 0$, so a Logistic Regression model predicts 1 if $\theta^T \mathbf{x}$ is positive, and 0 if it is negative.

Training and Cost Function

Good, now you know how a Logistic Regression model estimates probabilities and makes predictions. But how is it trained? The objective of training is to set the parameter vector θ so that the model estimates high probabilities for positive instances ($y =$

1) and low probabilities for negative instances ($y = 0$). This idea is captured by the cost function shown in Equation 4-16 for a single training instance **x**.

Equation 4-16. Cost function of a single training instance

$$c(\theta) = \begin{cases} -\log(\hat{p}) & \text{if } y = 1 \\ -\log(1 - \hat{p}) & \text{if } y = 0 \end{cases}$$

This cost function makes sense because $- \log(t)$ grows very large when t approaches 0, so the cost will be large if the model estimates a probability close to 0 for a positive instance, and it will also be very large if the model estimates a probability close to 1 for a negative instance. On the other hand, $- \log(t)$ is close to 0 when t is close to 1, so the cost will be close to 0 if the estimated probability is close to 0 for a negative instance or close to 1 for a positive instance, which is precisely what we want.

The cost function over the whole training set is simply the average cost over all training instances. It can be written in a single expression (as you can verify easily), called the *log loss*, shown in Equation 4-17.

Equation 4-17. Logistic Regression cost function (log loss)

$$J(\theta) = -\frac{1}{m}\sum_{i=1}^{m}\left[y^{(i)}\log\left(\hat{p}^{(i)}\right) + \left(1 - y^{(i)}\right)\log\left(1 - \hat{p}^{(i)}\right)\right]$$

The bad news is that there is no known closed-form equation to compute the value of θ that minimizes this cost function (there is no equivalent of the Normal Equation). But the good news is that this cost function is convex, so Gradient Descent (or any other optimization algorithm) is guaranteed to find the global minimum (if the learning rate is not too large and you wait long enough). The partial derivatives of the cost function with regards to the jth model parameter θ_j is given by Equation 4-18.

Equation 4-18. Logistic cost function partial derivatives

$$\frac{\partial}{\partial\theta_j}J(\theta) = \frac{1}{m}\sum_{i=1}^{m}\left(\sigma\left(\theta^T\mathbf{x}^{(i)}\right) - y^{(i)}\right)x_j^{(i)}$$

This equation looks very much like Equation 4-5: for each instance it computes the prediction error and multiplies it by the jth feature value, and then it computes the average over all training instances. Once you have the gradient vector containing all the partial derivatives you can use it in the Batch Gradient Descent algorithm. That's it: you now know how to train a Logistic Regression model. For Stochastic GD you would of course just take one instance at a time, and for Mini-batch GD you would use a mini-batch at a time.

Decision Boundaries

Let's use the iris dataset to illustrate Logistic Regression. This is a famous dataset that contains the sepal and petal length and width of 150 iris flowers of three different species: Iris-Setosa, Iris-Versicolor, and Iris-Virginica (see Figure 4-22).

Figure 4-22. Flowers of three iris plant species[16]

Let's try to build a classifier to detect the Iris-Virginica type based only on the petal width feature. First let's load the data:

```
>>> from sklearn import datasets
>>> iris = datasets.load_iris()
>>> list(iris.keys())
['data', 'target_names', 'feature_names', 'target', 'DESCR']
>>> X = iris["data"][:, 3:]  # petal width
>>> y = (iris["target"] == 2).astype(np.int)  # 1 if Iris-Virginica, else 0
```

Now let's train a Logistic Regression model:

```
from sklearn.linear_model import LogisticRegression

log_reg = LogisticRegression()
log_reg.fit(X, y)
```

---

16 Photos reproduced from the corresponding Wikipedia pages. Iris-Virginica photo by Frank Mayfield (Creative Commons BY-SA 2.0 (*https://creativecommons.org/licenses/by-sa/2.0/*)), Iris-Versicolor photo by D. Gordon E. Robertson (Creative Commons BY-SA 3.0 (*https://creativecommons.org/licenses/by-sa/3.0/*)), and Iris-Setosa photo is public domain.

Let's look at the model's estimated probabilities for flowers with petal widths varying from 0 to 3 cm (Figure 4-23):

```
X_new = np.linspace(0, 3, 1000).reshape(-1, 1)
y_proba = log_reg.predict_proba(X_new)
plt.plot(X_new, y_proba[:, 1], "g-", label="Iris-Virginica")
plt.plot(X_new, y_proba[:, 0], "b--", label="Not Iris-Virginica")
# + more Matplotlib code to make the image look pretty
```

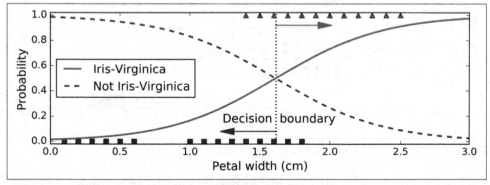

Figure 4-23. Estimated probabilities and decision boundary

The petal width of Iris-Virginica flowers (represented by triangles) ranges from 1.4 cm to 2.5 cm, while the other iris flowers (represented by squares) generally have a smaller petal width, ranging from 0.1 cm to 1.8 cm. Notice that there is a bit of overlap. Above about 2 cm the classifier is highly confident that the flower is an Iris-Virginica (it outputs a high probability to that class), while below 1 cm it is highly confident that it is not an Iris-Virginica (high probability for the "Not Iris-Virginica" class). In between these extremes, the classifier is unsure. However, if you ask it to predict the class (using the `predict()` method rather than the `predict_proba()` method), it will return whichever class is the most likely. Therefore, there is a *decision boundary* at around 1.6 cm where both probabilities are equal to 50%: if the petal width is higher than 1.6 cm, the classifier will predict that the flower is an Iris-Virginica, or else it will predict that it is not (even if it is not very confident):

```
>>> log_reg.predict([[1.7], [1.5]])
array([1, 0])
```

Figure 4-24 shows the same dataset but this time displaying two features: petal width and length. Once trained, the Logistic Regression classifier can estimate the probability that a new flower is an Iris-Virginica based on these two features. The dashed line represents the points where the model estimates a 50% probability: this is the model's decision boundary. Note that it is a linear boundary.[17] Each parallel line represents the

---

17 It is the the set of points **x** such that $\theta_0 + \theta_1 x_1 + \theta_2 x_2 = 0$, which defines a straight line.

points where the model outputs a specific probability, from 15% (bottom left) to 90% (top right). All the flowers beyond the top-right line have an over 90% chance of being Iris-Virginica according to the model.

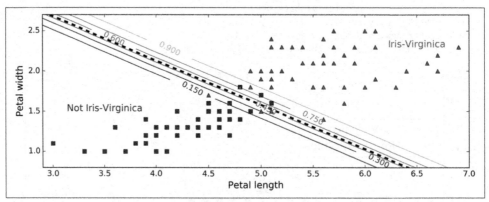

Figure 4-24. Linear decision boundary

Just like the other linear models, Logistic Regression models can be regularized using ℓ_1 or ℓ_2 penalties. Scitkit-Learn actually adds an ℓ_2 penalty by default.

 The hyperparameter controlling the regularization strength of a Scikit-Learn `LogisticRegression` model is not `alpha` (as in other linear models), but its inverse: `C`. The higher the value of `C`, the *less* the model is regularized.

Softmax Regression

The Logistic Regression model can be generalized to support multiple classes directly, without having to train and combine multiple binary classifiers (as discussed in Chapter 3). This is called *Softmax Regression*, or *Multinomial Logistic Regression*.

The idea is quite simple: when given an instance **x**, the Softmax Regression model first computes a score $s_k(\mathbf{x})$ for each class k, then estimates the probability of each class by applying the *softmax function* (also called the *normalized exponential*) to the scores. The equation to compute $s_k(\mathbf{x})$ should look familiar, as it is just like the equation for Linear Regression prediction (see Equation 4-19).

Equation 4-19. Softmax score for class k

$$s_k(\mathbf{x}) = \left(\mathbf{\theta}^{(k)}\right)^T \mathbf{x}$$

Note that each class has its own dedicated parameter vector $\theta^{(k)}$. All these vectors are typically stored as rows in a *parameter matrix* Θ.

Once you have computed the score of every class for the instance **x**, you can estimate the probability $\hat{p}_k$ that the instance belongs to class k by running the scores through the softmax function (Equation 4-20): it computes the exponential of every score, then normalizes them (dividing by the sum of all the exponentials).

Equation 4-20. Softmax function

$$\hat{p}_k = \sigma(\mathbf{s}(\mathbf{x}))_k = \frac{\exp\left(s_k(\mathbf{x})\right)}{\sum_{j=1}^{K} \exp\left(s_j(\mathbf{x})\right)}$$

- K is the number of classes.
- $\mathbf{s}(\mathbf{x})$ is a vector containing the scores of each class for the instance **x**.
- $\sigma(\mathbf{s}(\mathbf{x}))_k$ is the estimated probability that the instance **x** belongs to class k given the scores of each class for that instance.

Just like the Logistic Regression classifier, the Softmax Regression classifier predicts the class with the highest estimated probability (which is simply the class with the highest score), as shown in Equation 4-21.

Equation 4-21. Softmax Regression classifier prediction

$$\hat{y} = \underset{k}{\mathrm{argmax}} \ \sigma(\mathbf{s}(\mathbf{x}))_k = \underset{k}{\mathrm{argmax}} \ s_k(\mathbf{x}) = \underset{k}{\mathrm{argmax}} \left(\left(\theta^{(k)}\right)^{T} \mathbf{x}\right)$$

- The *argmax* operator returns the value of a variable that maximizes a function. In this equation, it returns the value of k that maximizes the estimated probability $\sigma(\mathbf{s}(\mathbf{x}))_k$.

> The Softmax Regression classifier predicts only one class at a time (i.e., it is multiclass, not multioutput) so it should be used only with mutually exclusive classes such as different types of plants. You cannot use it to recognize multiple people in one picture.

Now that you know how the model estimates probabilities and makes predictions, let's take a look at training. The objective is to have a model that estimates a high probability for the target class (and consequently a low probability for the other classes). Minimizing the cost function shown in Equation 4-22, called the *cross entropy*, should lead to this objective because it penalizes the model when it estimates a low probability for a target class. Cross entropy is frequently used to measure how well a set of estimated class probabilities match the target classes (we will use it again several times in the following chapters).

Equation 4-22. Cross entropy cost function

$$J(\Theta) = -\frac{1}{m}\sum_{i=1}^{m}\sum_{k=1}^{K}y_k^{(i)}\log\left(\hat{p}_k^{(i)}\right)$$

- $y_k^{(i)}$ is the target probability that the ith instance belongs to class k. In general, it is either equal to 1 or 0, depending on whether the instance belongs to the class or not.

Notice that when there are just two classes ($K = 2$), this cost function is equivalent to the Logistic Regression's cost function (log loss; see Equation 4-17).

Cross Entropy

Cross entropy originated from information theory. Suppose you want to efficiently transmit information about the weather every day. If there are eight options (sunny, rainy, etc.), you could encode each option using 3 bits since $2^3 = 8$. However, if you think it will be sunny almost every day, it would be much more efficient to code "sunny" on just one bit (0) and the other seven options on 4 bits (starting with a 1). Cross entropy measures the average number of bits you actually send per option. If your assumption about the weather is perfect, cross entropy will just be equal to the entropy of the weather itself (i.e., its intrinsic unpredictability). But if your assumptions are wrong (e.g., if it rains often), cross entropy will be greater by an amount called the *Kullback–Leibler divergence*.

The cross entropy between two probability distributions p and q is defined as $H(p, q) = -\sum_x p(x) \log q(x)$ (at least when the distributions are discrete).

The gradient vector of this cost function with regards to $\theta^{(k)}$ is given by Equation 4-23:

Equation 4-23. Cross entropy gradient vector for class k

$$\nabla_{\theta^{(k)}} J(\Theta) = \frac{1}{m}\sum_{i=1}^{m}\left(\hat{p}_k^{(i)} - y_k^{(i)}\right)\mathbf{x}^{(i)}$$

Now you can compute the gradient vector for every class, then use Gradient Descent (or any other optimization algorithm) to find the parameter matrix Θ that minimizes the cost function.

Let's use Softmax Regression to classify the iris flowers into all three classes. Scikit-Learn's `LogisticRegression` uses one-versus-all by default when you train it on more than two classes, but you can set the `multi_class` hyperparameter to `"multinomial"` to switch it to Softmax Regression instead. You must also specify a solver that supports Softmax Regression, such as the `"lbfgs"` solver (see Scikit-Learn's documentation for more details). It also applies ℓ_2 regularization by default, which you can control using the hyperparameter `C`.

```
X = iris["data"][:, (2, 3)]  # petal length, petal width
y = iris["target"]

softmax_reg = LogisticRegression(multi_class="multinomial",solver="lbfgs", C=10)
softmax_reg.fit(X, y)
```

So the next time you find an iris with 5 cm long and 2 cm wide petals, you can ask your model to tell you what type of iris it is, and it will answer Iris-Virginica (class 2) with 94.2% probability (or Iris-Versicolor with 5.8% probability):

```
>>> softmax_reg.predict([[5, 2]])
array([2])
>>> softmax_reg.predict_proba([[5, 2]])
array([[  6.33134078e-07,   5.75276067e-02,   9.42471760e-01]])
```

Figure 4-25 shows the resulting decision boundaries, represented by the background colors. Notice that the decision boundaries between any two classes are linear. The figure also shows the probabilities for the Iris-Versicolor class, represented by the curved lines (e.g., the line labeled with 0.450 represents the 45% probability boundary). Notice that the model can predict a class that has an estimated probability below 50%. For example, at the point where all decision boundaries meet, all classes have an equal estimated probability of 33%.

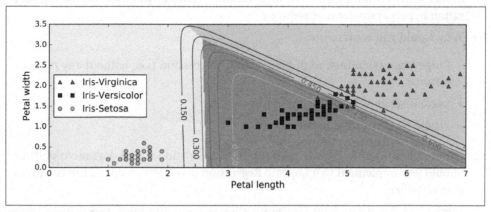

Figure 4-25. Softmax Regression decision boundaries

Exercises

1. What Linear Regression training algorithm can you use if you have a training set with millions of features?

2. Suppose the features in your training set have very different scales. What algorithms might suffer from this, and how? What can you do about it?

3. Can Gradient Descent get stuck in a local minimum when training a Logistic Regression model?

4. Do all Gradient Descent algorithms lead to the same model provided you let them run long enough?

5. Suppose you use Batch Gradient Descent and you plot the validation error at every epoch. If you notice that the validation error consistently goes up, what is likely going on? How can you fix this?

6. Is it a good idea to stop Mini-batch Gradient Descent immediately when the validation error goes up?

7. Which Gradient Descent algorithm (among those we discussed) will reach the vicinity of the optimal solution the fastest? Which will actually converge? How can you make the others converge as well?

8. Suppose you are using Polynomial Regression. You plot the learning curves and you notice that there is a large gap between the training error and the validation error. What is happening? What are three ways to solve this?

9. Suppose you are using Ridge Regression and you notice that the training error and the validation error are almost equal and fairly high. Would you say that the model suffers from high bias or high variance? Should you increase the regularization hyperparameter α or reduce it?

10. Why would you want to use:

    - Ridge Regression instead of plain Linear Regression (i.e., without any regularization)?
    - Lasso instead of Ridge Regression?
    - Elastic Net instead of Lasso?

11. Suppose you want to classify pictures as outdoor/indoor and daytime/nighttime. Should you implement two Logistic Regression classifiers or one Softmax Regression classifier?

12. Implement Batch Gradient Descent with early stopping for Softmax Regression (without using Scikit-Learn).

Solutions to these exercises are available in Appendix A.

## CHAPTER 5

Support Vector Machines

A *Support Vector Machine* (SVM) is a very powerful and versatile Machine Learning model, capable of performing linear or nonlinear classification, regression, and even outlier detection. It is one of the most popular models in Machine Learning, and anyone interested in Machine Learning should have it in their toolbox. SVMs are particularly well suited for classification of complex but small- or medium-sized datasets.

This chapter will explain the core concepts of SVMs, how to use them, and how they work.

Linear SVM Classification

The fundamental idea behind SVMs is best explained with some pictures. Figure 5-1 shows part of the iris dataset that was introduced at the end of Chapter 4. The two classes can clearly be separated easily with a straight line (they are *linearly separable*). The left plot shows the decision boundaries of three possible linear classifiers. The model whose decision boundary is represented by the dashed line is so bad that it does not even separate the classes properly. The other two models work perfectly on this training set, but their decision boundaries come so close to the instances that these models will probably not perform as well on new instances. In contrast, the solid line in the plot on the right represents the decision boundary of an SVM classifier; this line not only separates the two classes but also stays as far away from the closest training instances as possible. You can think of an SVM classifier as fitting the widest possible street (represented by the parallel dashed lines) between the classes. This is called *large margin classification*.

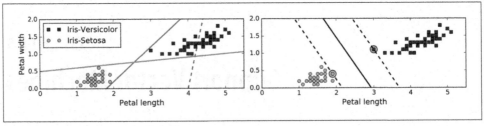

Figure 5-1. Large margin classification

Notice that adding more training instances "off the street" will not affect the decision boundary at all: it is fully determined (or "supported") by the instances located on the edge of the street. These instances are called the *support vectors* (they are circled in Figure 5-1).

 SVMs are sensitive to the feature scales, as you can see in Figure 5-2: on the left plot, the vertical scale is much larger than the horizontal scale, so the widest possible street is close to horizontal. After feature scaling (e.g., using Scikit-Learn's `StandardScaler`), the decision boundary looks much better (on the right plot).

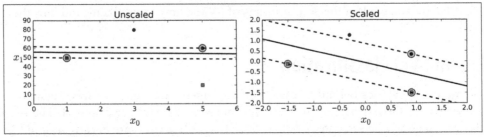

Figure 5-2. Sensitivity to feature scales

Soft Margin Classification

If we strictly impose that all instances be off the street and on the right side, this is called *hard margin classification*. There are two main issues with hard margin classification. First, it only works if the data is linearly separable, and second it is quite sensitive to outliers. Figure 5-3 shows the iris dataset with just one additional outlier: on the left, it is impossible to find a hard margin, and on the right the decision boundary ends up very different from the one we saw in Figure 5-1 without the outlier, and it will probably not generalize as well.

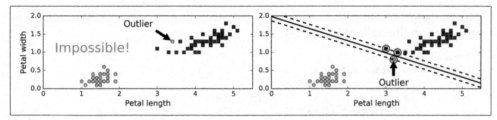

Figure 5-3. Hard margin sensitivity to outliers

To avoid these issues it is preferable to use a more flexible model. The objective is to find a good balance between keeping the street as large as possible and limiting the *margin violations* (i.e., instances that end up in the middle of the street or even on the wrong side). This is called *soft margin classification*.

In Scikit-Learn's SVM classes, you can control this balance using the C hyperparameter: a smaller C value leads to a wider street but more margin violations. Figure 5-4 shows the decision boundaries and margins of two soft margin SVM classifiers on a nonlinearly separable dataset. On the left, using a high C value the classifier makes fewer margin violations but ends up with a smaller margin. On the right, using a low C value the margin is much larger, but many instances end up on the street. However, it seems likely that the second classifier will generalize better: in fact even on this training set it makes fewer prediction errors, since most of the margin violations are actually on the correct side of the decision boundary.

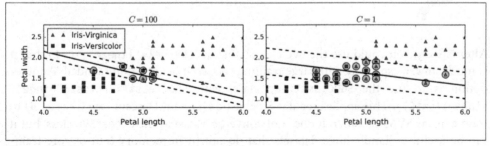

Figure 5-4. Fewer margin violations versus large margin

> If your SVM model is overfitting, you can try regularizing it by reducing C.

The following Scikit-Learn code loads the iris dataset, scales the features, and then trains a linear SVM model (using the LinearSVC class with $C = 1$ and the *hinge loss* function, described shortly) to detect Iris-Virginica flowers. The resulting model is represented on the right of Figure 5-4.

```
import numpy as np
from sklearn import datasets
from sklearn.pipeline import Pipeline
from sklearn.preprocessing import StandardScaler
from sklearn.svm import LinearSVC

iris = datasets.load_iris()
X = iris["data"][:, (2, 3)]  # petal length, petal width
y = (iris["target"] == 2).astype(np.float64)  # Iris-Virginica

svm_clf = Pipeline([
        ("scaler", StandardScaler()),
        ("linear_svc", LinearSVC(C=1, loss="hinge")),
    ])

svm_clf.fit(X, y)
```

Then, as usual, you can use the model to make predictions:

```
>>> svm_clf.predict([[5.5, 1.7]])
array([ 1.])
```

Unlike Logistic Regression classifiers, SVM classifiers do not output probabilities for each class.

Alternatively, you could use the SVC class, using SVC(kernel="linear", C=1), but it is much slower, especially with large training sets, so it is not recommended. Another option is to use the SGDClassifier class, with SGDClassifier(loss="hinge", alpha=1/(m*C)). This applies regular Stochastic Gradient Descent (see Chapter 4) to train a linear SVM classifier. It does not converge as fast as the LinearSVC class, but it can be useful to handle huge datasets that do not fit in memory (out-of-core training), or to handle online classification tasks.

The LinearSVC class regularizes the bias term, so you should center the training set first by subtracting its mean. This is automatic if you scale the data using the StandardScaler. Moreover, make sure you set the loss hyperparameter to "hinge", as it is not the default value. Finally, for better performance you should set the dual hyperparameter to False, unless there are more features than training instances (we will discuss duality later in the chapter).

Nonlinear SVM Classification

Although linear SVM classifiers are efficient and work surprisingly well in many cases, many datasets are not even close to being linearly separable. One approach to handling nonlinear datasets is to add more features, such as polynomial features (as you did in Chapter 4); in some cases this can result in a linearly separable dataset. Consider the left plot in Figure 5-5: it represents a simple dataset with just one feature x_1. This dataset is not linearly separable, as you can see. But if you add a second feature $x_2 = (x_1)^2$, the resulting 2D dataset is perfectly linearly separable.

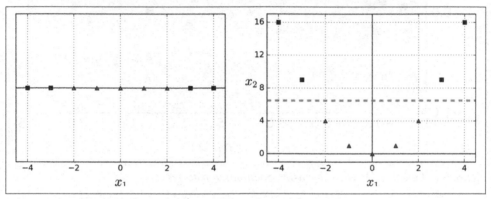

Figure 5-5. Adding features to make a dataset linearly separable

To implement this idea using Scikit-Learn, you can create a `Pipeline` containing a `PolynomialFeatures` transformer (discussed in "Polynomial Regression" on page 124), followed by a `StandardScaler` and a `LinearSVC`. Let's test this on the moons dataset: this is a toy dataset for binary classification in which the data points are shaped as two interleaving half circles (see Figure 5-6). You can generate this dataset using the `make_moons()` function:

```
from sklearn.datasets import make_moons
from sklearn.pipeline import Pipeline
from sklearn.preprocessing import PolynomialFeatures

polynomial_svm_clf = Pipeline([
        ("poly_features", PolynomialFeatures(degree=3)),
        ("scaler", StandardScaler()),
        ("svm_clf", LinearSVC(C=10, loss="hinge"))
    ])

polynomial_svm_clf.fit(X, y)
```

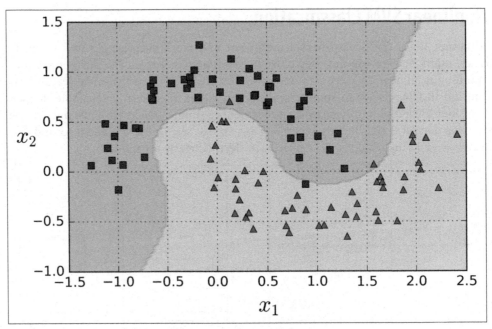

Figure 5-6. Linear SVM classifier using polynomial features

Polynomial Kernel

Adding polynomial features is simple to implement and can work great with all sorts of Machine Learning algorithms (not just SVMs), but at a low polynomial degree it cannot deal with very complex datasets, and with a high polynomial degree it creates a huge number of features, making the model too slow.

Fortunately, when using SVMs you can apply an almost miraculous mathematical technique called the *kernel trick* (it is explained in a moment). It makes it possible to get the same result as if you added many polynomial features, even with very high-degree polynomials, without actually having to add them. So there is no combinatorial explosion of the number of features since you don't actually add any features. This trick is implemented by the SVC class. Let's test it on the moons dataset:

```python
from sklearn.svm import SVC
poly_kernel_svm_clf = Pipeline([
        ("scaler", StandardScaler()),
        ("svm_clf", SVC(kernel="poly", degree=3, coef0=1, C=5))
    ])
poly_kernel_svm_clf.fit(X, y)
```

This code trains an SVM classifier using a 3rd-degree polynomial kernel. It is represented on the left of Figure 5-7. On the right is another SVM classifier using a 10th-degree polynomial kernel. Obviously, if your model is overfitting, you might want to reduce the polynomial degree. Conversely, if it is underfitting, you can try increasing it. The hyperparameter `coef0` controls how much the model is influenced by high-degree polynomials versus low-degree polynomials.

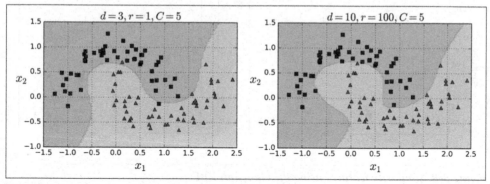

Figure 5-7. SVM classifiers with a polynomial kernel

A common approach to find the right hyperparameter values is to use grid search (see Chapter 2). It is often faster to first do a very coarse grid search, then a finer grid search around the best values found. Having a good sense of what each hyperparameter actually does can also help you search in the right part of the hyperparameter space.

Adding Similarity Features

Another technique to tackle nonlinear problems is to add features computed using a *similarity function* that measures how much each instance resembles a particular *landmark*. For example, let's take the one-dimensional dataset discussed earlier and add two landmarks to it at $x_1 = -2$ and $x_1 = 1$ (see the left plot in Figure 5-8). Next, let's define the similarity function to be the Gaussian *Radial Basis Function* (RBF) with $\gamma = 0.3$ (see Equation 5-1).

Equation 5-1. Gaussian RBF

$$\phi_\gamma(\mathbf{x}, \ell) = \exp\left(-\gamma\| \mathbf{x} - \ell \|^2\right)$$

It is a bell-shaped function varying from 0 (very far away from the landmark) to 1 (at the landmark). Now we are ready to compute the new features. For example, let's look at the instance $x_1 = -1$: it is located at a distance of 1 from the first landmark, and 2 from the second landmark. Therefore its new features are $x_2 = \exp(-0.3 \times 1^2) \approx 0.74$ and $x_3 = \exp(-0.3 \times 2^2) \approx 0.30$. The plot on the right of Figure 5-8 shows the transformed dataset (dropping the original features). As you can see, it is now linearly separable.

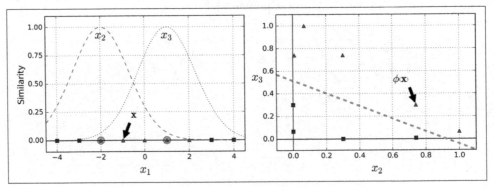

Figure 5-8. Similarity features using the Gaussian RBF

You may wonder how to select the landmarks. The simplest approach is to create a landmark at the location of each and every instance in the dataset. This creates many dimensions and thus increases the chances that the transformed training set will be linearly separable. The downside is that a training set with *m* instances and *n* features gets transformed into a training set with *m* instances and *m* features (assuming you drop the original features). If your training set is very large, you end up with an equally large number of features.

Gaussian RBF Kernel

Just like the polynomial features method, the similarity features method can be useful with any Machine Learning algorithm, but it may be computationally expensive to compute all the additional features, especially on large training sets. However, once again the kernel trick does its SVM magic: it makes it possible to obtain a similar result as if you had added many similarity features, without actually having to add them. Let's try the Gaussian RBF kernel using the SVC class:

```
rbf_kernel_svm_clf = Pipeline([
        ("scaler", StandardScaler()),
        ("svm_clf", SVC(kernel="rbf", gamma=5, C=0.001))
    ])
rbf_kernel_svm_clf.fit(X, y)
```

This model is represented on the bottom left of Figure 5-9. The other plots show models trained with different values of hyperparameters gamma (γ) and C. Increasing gamma makes the bell-shape curve narrower (see the left plot of Figure 5-8), and as a result each instance's range of influence is smaller: the decision boundary ends up being more irregular, wiggling around individual instances. Conversely, a small gamma value makes the bell-shaped curve wider, so instances have a larger range of influence, and the decision boundary ends up smoother. So γ acts like a regularization hyperparameter: if your model is overfitting, you should reduce it, and if it is underfitting, you should increase it (similar to the C hyperparameter).

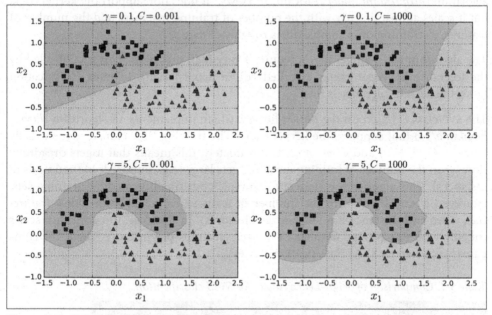

Figure 5-9. SVM classifiers using an RBF kernel

Other kernels exist but are used much more rarely. For example, some kernels are specialized for specific data structures. *String kernels* are sometimes used when classifying text documents or DNA sequences (e.g., using the *string subsequence kernel* or kernels based on the *Levenshtein distance*).

> With so many kernels to choose from, how can you decide which one to use? As a rule of thumb, you should always try the linear kernel first (remember that LinearSVC is much faster than SVC(kernel="linear")), especially if the training set is very large or if it has plenty of features. If the training set is not too large, you should try the Gaussian RBF kernel as well; it works well in most cases. Then if you have spare time and computing power, you can also experiment with a few other kernels using cross-validation and grid search, especially if there are kernels specialized for your training set's data structure.

Computational Complexity

The LinearSVC class is based on the *liblinear* library, which implements an optimized algorithm (*http://homl.info/13*) for linear SVMs.[1] It does not support the kernel trick, but it scales almost linearly with the number of training instances and the number of features: its training time complexity is roughly $O(m \times n)$.

The algorithm takes longer if you require a very high precision. This is controlled by the tolerance hyperparameter ϵ (called tol in Scikit-Learn). In most classification tasks, the default tolerance is fine.

The SVC class is based on the *libsvm* library, which implements an algorithm (*http://homl.info/14*) that supports the kernel trick.[2] The training time complexity is usually between $O(m^2 \times n)$ and $O(m^3 \times n)$. Unfortunately, this means that it gets dreadfully slow when the number of training instances gets large (e.g., hundreds of thousands of instances). This algorithm is perfect for complex but small or medium training sets. However, it scales well with the number of features, especially with *sparse features* (i.e., when each instance has few nonzero features). In this case, the algorithm scales roughly with the average number of nonzero features per instance. Table 5-1 compares Scikit-Learn's SVM classification classes.

Table 5-1. Comparison of Scikit-Learn classes for SVM classification

Class	Time complexity	Out-of-core support	Scaling required	Kernel trick
LinearSVC	$O(m \times n)$	No	Yes	No
SGDClassifier	$O(m \times n)$	Yes	Yes	No
SVC	$O(m^2 \times n)$ to $O(m^3 \times n)$	No	Yes	Yes

SVM Regression

As we mentioned earlier, the SVM algorithm is quite versatile: not only does it support linear and nonlinear classification, but it also supports linear and nonlinear regression. The trick is to reverse the objective: instead of trying to fit the largest possible street between two classes while limiting margin violations, SVM Regression tries to fit as many instances as possible *on* the street while limiting margin violations (i.e., instances *off* the street). The width of the street is controlled by a hyperparameter ϵ. Figure 5-10 shows two linear SVM Regression models trained on some random linear data, one with a large margin ($\epsilon = 1.5$) and the other with a small margin ($\epsilon = 0.5$).

---

1 "A Dual Coordinate Descent Method for Large-scale Linear SVM," Lin et al. (2008).

2 "Sequential Minimal Optimization (SMO)," J. Platt (1998).

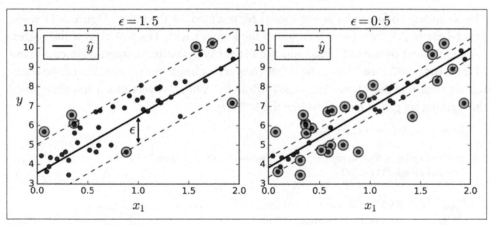

Figure 5-10. SVM Regression

Adding more training instances within the margin does not affect the model's predictions; thus, the model is said to be ε-*insensitive*.

You can use Scikit-Learn's `LinearSVR` class to perform linear SVM Regression. The following code produces the model represented on the left of Figure 5-10 (the training data should be scaled and centered first):

```
from sklearn.svm import LinearSVR

svm_reg = LinearSVR(epsilon=1.5)
svm_reg.fit(X, y)
```

To tackle nonlinear regression tasks, you can use a kernelized SVM model. For example, Figure 5-11 shows SVM Regression on a random quadratic training set, using a 2nd-degree polynomial kernel. There is little regularization on the left plot (i.e., a large C value), and much more regularization on the right plot (i.e., a small C value).

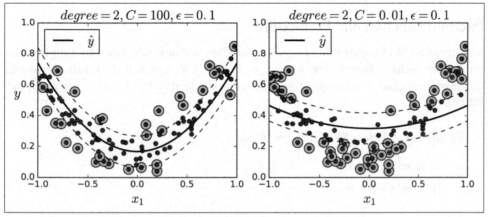

Figure 5-11. SVM regression using a 2nd-degree polynomial kernel

The following code produces the model represented on the left of Figure 5-11 using Scikit-Learn's SVR class (which supports the kernel trick). The SVR class is the regression equivalent of the SVC class, and the LinearSVR class is the regression equivalent of the LinearSVC class. The LinearSVR class scales linearly with the size of the training set (just like the LinearSVC class), while the SVR class gets much too slow when the training set grows large (just like the SVC class).

```
from sklearn.svm import SVR

svm_poly_reg = SVR(kernel="poly", degree=2, C=100, epsilon=0.1)
svm_poly_reg.fit(X, y)
```

 SVMs can also be used for outlier detection; see Scikit-Learn's documentation for more details.

Under the Hood

This section explains how SVMs make predictions and how their training algorithms work, starting with linear SVM classifiers. You can safely skip it and go straight to the exercises at the end of this chapter if you are just getting started with Machine Learning, and come back later when you want to get a deeper understanding of SVMs.

First, a word about notations: in Chapter 4 we used the convention of putting all the model parameters in one vector θ, including the bias term θ_0 and the input feature weights θ_1 to θ_n, and adding a bias input $x_0 = 1$ to all instances. In this chapter, we will use a different convention, which is more convenient (and more common) when you are dealing with SVMs: the bias term will be called b and the feature weights vector will be called **w**. No bias feature will be added to the input feature vectors.

Decision Function and Predictions

The linear SVM classifier model predicts the class of a new instance **x** by simply computing the decision function $\mathbf{w}^T \mathbf{x} + b = w_1 x_1 + \cdots + w_n x_n + b$: if the result is positive, the predicted class $\hat{y}$ is the positive class (1), or else it is the negative class (0); see Equation 5-2.

Equation 5-2. Linear SVM classifier prediction

$$\hat{y} = \begin{cases} 0 \text{ if } \mathbf{w}^T \mathbf{x} + b < 0, \\ 1 \text{ if } \mathbf{w}^T \mathbf{x} + b \geq 0 \end{cases}$$

Figure 5-12 shows the decision function that corresponds to the model on the right of Figure 5-4: it is a two-dimensional plane since this dataset has two features (petal width and petal length). The decision boundary is the set of points where the decision function is equal to 0: it is the intersection of two planes, which is a straight line (represented by the thick solid line).[3]

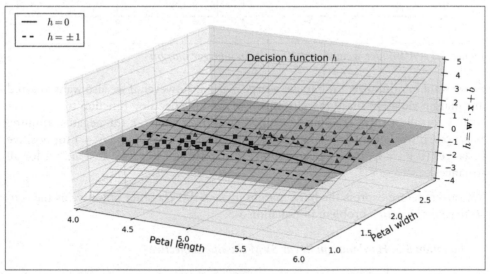

Figure 5-12. Decision function for the iris dataset

The dashed lines represent the points where the decision function is equal to 1 or −1: they are parallel and at equal distance to the decision boundary, forming a margin around it. Training a linear SVM classifier means finding the value of **w** and b that make this margin as wide as possible while avoiding margin violations (hard margin) or limiting them (soft margin).

Training Objective

Consider the slope of the decision function: it is equal to the norm of the weight vector, $\| \mathbf{w} \|$. If we divide this slope by 2, the points where the decision function is equal to ±1 are going to be twice as far away from the decision boundary. In other words, dividing the slope by 2 will multiply the margin by 2. Perhaps this is easier to visualize in 2D in Figure 5-13. The smaller the weight vector **w**, the larger the margin.

---

3 More generally, when there are n features, the decision function is an n-dimensional *hyperplane*, and the decision boundary is an $(n − 1)$-dimensional hyperplane.

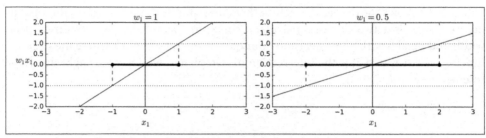

Figure 5-13. A smaller weight vector results in a larger margin

So we want to minimize $\| \mathbf{w} \|$ to get a large margin. However, if we also want to avoid any margin violation (hard margin), then we need the decision function to be greater than 1 for all positive training instances, and lower than –1 for negative training instances. If we define $t^{(i)} = -1$ for negative instances (if $y^{(i)} = 0$) and $t^{(i)} = 1$ for positive instances (if $y^{(i)} = 1$), then we can express this constraint as $t^{(i)}(\mathbf{w}^T \mathbf{x}^{(i)} + b) \geq 1$ for all instances.

We can therefore express the hard margin linear SVM classifier objective as the *constrained optimization* problem in Equation 5-3.

Equation 5-3. Hard margin linear SVM classifier objective

$$\underset{\mathbf{w},\, b}{\text{minimize}} \quad \frac{1}{2}\mathbf{w}^T \mathbf{w}$$

$$\text{subject to} \quad t^{(i)}\left(\mathbf{w}^T \mathbf{x}^{(i)} + b\right) \geq 1 \quad \text{for } i = 1, 2, \cdots, m$$

We are minimizing $\frac{1}{2}\mathbf{w}^T \mathbf{w}$, which is equal to $\frac{1}{2}\| \mathbf{w} \|^2$, rather than minimizing $\| \mathbf{w} \|$. Indeed, $\frac{1}{2}\| \mathbf{w} \|^2$ has a nice and simple derivative (it is just $\mathbf{w}$) while $\| \mathbf{w} \|$ is not differentiable at $\mathbf{w} = \mathbf{0}$. Optimization algorithms work much better on differentiable functions.

To get the soft margin objective, we need to introduce a *slack variable* $\zeta^{(i)} \geq 0$ for each instance:[4] $\zeta^{(i)}$ measures how much the ith instance is allowed to violate the margin. We now have two conflicting objectives: making the slack variables as small as possible to reduce the margin violations, and making $\frac{1}{2}\mathbf{w}^T \mathbf{w}$ as small as possible to increase the margin. This is where the C hyperparameter comes in: it allows us to define the trade-

---

4 Zeta (ζ) is the 6th letter of the Greek alphabet.

off between these two objectives. This gives us the constrained optimization problem in Equation 5-4.

Equation 5-4. Soft margin linear SVM classifier objective

$$\underset{\mathbf{w}, b, \zeta}{\text{minimize}} \quad \frac{1}{2}\mathbf{w}^T\mathbf{w} + C\sum_{i=1}^{m} \zeta^{(i)}$$

$$\text{subject to} \quad t^{(i)}\left(\mathbf{w}^T\mathbf{x}^{(i)} + b\right) \geq 1 - \zeta^{(i)} \quad \text{and} \quad \zeta^{(i)} \geq 0 \quad \text{for } i = 1, 2, \cdots, m$$

Quadratic Programming

The hard margin and soft margin problems are both convex quadratic optimization problems with linear constraints. Such problems are known as *Quadratic Programming* (QP) problems. Many off-the-shelf solvers are available to solve QP problems using a variety of techniques that are outside the scope of this book.[5] The general problem formulation is given by Equation 5-5.

Equation 5-5. Quadratic Programming problem

$$\underset{\mathbf{p}}{\text{Minimize}} \quad \frac{1}{2}\mathbf{p}^T\mathbf{H}\mathbf{p} \quad + \quad \mathbf{f}^T\mathbf{p}$$

$$\text{subject to} \quad \mathbf{A}\mathbf{p} \leq \mathbf{b}$$

$$\text{where} \quad \begin{cases} \mathbf{p} & \text{is an } n_p\text{-dimensional vector } (n_p = \text{number of parameters}), \\ \mathbf{H} & \text{is an } n_p \times n_p \text{ matrix}, \\ \mathbf{f} & \text{is an } n_p\text{-dimensional vector}, \\ \mathbf{A} & \text{is an } n_c \times n_p \text{ matrix } (n_c = \text{number of constraints}), \\ \mathbf{b} & \text{is an } n_c\text{-dimensional vector}. \end{cases}$$

Note that the expression $\mathbf{A}\,\mathbf{p} \leq \mathbf{b}$ actually defines n_c constraints: $\mathbf{p}^T\,\mathbf{a}^{(i)} \leq b^{(i)}$ for $i = 1$, $2, \cdots, n_c$, where $\mathbf{a}^{(i)}$ is the vector containing the elements of the ith row of $\mathbf{A}$ and $b^{(i)}$ is the ith element of $\mathbf{b}$.

You can easily verify that if you set the QP parameters in the following way, you get the hard margin linear SVM classifier objective:

- $n_p = n + 1$, where n is the number of features (the +1 is for the bias term).

---

[5] To learn more about Quadratic Programming, you can start by reading Stephen Boyd and Lieven Vandenberghe, *Convex Optimization* (*http://homl.info/15*) (Cambridge, UK: Cambridge University Press, 2004) or watch Richard Brown's series of video lectures (*http://homl.info/16*).

- $n_c = m$, where m is the number of training instances.
- **H** is the $n_p \times n_p$ identity matrix, except with a zero in the top-left cell (to ignore the bias term).
- **f** = **0**, an n_p-dimensional vector full of 0s.
- **b** = **–1**, an n_c-dimensional vector full of –1s.
- $\mathbf{a}^{(i)} = -t^{(i)} \dot{\mathbf{x}}^{(i)}$, where $\dot{\mathbf{x}}^{(i)}$ is equal to $\mathbf{x}^{(i)}$ with an extra bias feature $\dot{\mathbf{x}}_0 = 1$.

So one way to train a hard margin linear SVM classifier is just to use an off-the-shelf QP solver by passing it the preceding parameters. The resulting vector **p** will contain the bias term $b = p_0$ and the feature weights $w_i = p_i$ for $i = 1, 2, \cdots, n$. Similarly, you can use a QP solver to solve the soft margin problem (see the exercises at the end of the chapter).

However, to use the kernel trick we are going to look at a different constrained optimization problem.

The Dual Problem

Given a constrained optimization problem, known as the *primal problem*, it is possible to express a different but closely related problem, called its *dual problem*. The solution to the dual problem typically gives a lower bound to the solution of the primal problem, but under some conditions it can even have the same solutions as the primal problem. Luckily, the SVM problem happens to meet these conditions,[6] so you can choose to solve the primal problem or the dual problem; both will have the same solution. Equation 5-6 shows the dual form of the linear SVM objective (if you are interested in knowing how to derive the dual problem from the primal problem, see Appendix C).

Equation 5-6. Dual form of the linear SVM objective

$$\underset{\alpha}{\text{minimize}} \quad \frac{1}{2} \sum_{i=1}^{m} \sum_{j=1}^{m} \alpha^{(i)} \alpha^{(j)} t^{(i)} t^{(j)} \mathbf{x}^{(i)T} \mathbf{x}^{(j)} \quad - \quad \sum_{i=1}^{m} \alpha^{(i)}$$

$$\text{subject to} \quad \alpha^{(i)} \geq 0 \quad \text{for } i = 1, 2, \cdots, m$$

---

6 The objective function is convex, and the inequality constraints are continuously differentiable and convex functions.

Once you find the vector $\hat{\alpha}$ that minimizes this equation (using a QP solver), you can compute $\hat{\mathbf{w}}$ and $\hat{b}$ that minimize the primal problem by using Equation 5-7.

Equation 5-7. From the dual solution to the primal solution

$$\hat{\mathbf{w}} = \sum_{i=1}^{m} \hat{\alpha}^{(i)} t^{(i)} \mathbf{x}^{(i)}$$

$$\hat{b} = \frac{1}{n_s} \sum_{\substack{i=1 \\ \hat{\alpha}^{(i)} > 0}}^{m} \left(t^{(i)} - \hat{\mathbf{w}}^T \mathbf{x}^{(i)} \right)$$

The dual problem is faster to solve than the primal when the number of training instances is smaller than the number of features. More importantly, it makes the kernel trick possible, while the primal does not. So what is this kernel trick anyway?

Kernelized SVM

Suppose you want to apply a 2nd-degree polynomial transformation to a two-dimensional training set (such as the moons training set), then train a linear SVM classifier on the transformed training set. Equation 5-8 shows the 2nd-degree polynomial mapping function ϕ that you want to apply.

Equation 5-8. Second-degree polynomial mapping

$$\phi(\mathbf{x}) = \phi\left(\begin{pmatrix} x_1 \\ x_2 \end{pmatrix} \right) = \begin{pmatrix} x_1^2 \\ \sqrt{2}\,x_1 x_2 \\ x_2^2 \end{pmatrix}$$

Notice that the transformed vector is three-dimensional instead of two-dimensional. Now let's look at what happens to a couple of two-dimensional vectors, **a** and **b**, if we apply this 2nd-degree polynomial mapping and then compute the dot product[7] of the transformed vectors (See Equation 5-9).

---

[7] As explained in Chapter 4, the dot product of two vectors **a** and **b** is normally noted **a** · **b**. However, in Machine Learning, vectors are frequently represented as column vectors (i.e., single-column matrices), so the dot product is achieved by computing $\mathbf{a}^T\mathbf{b}$. To remain consistent with the rest of the book, we will use this notation here, ignoring the fact that this technically results in a single-cell matrix rather than a scalar value.

Equation 5-9. Kernel trick for a 2nd-degree polynomial mapping

$$\phi(\mathbf{a})^T \phi(\mathbf{b}) \quad = \begin{pmatrix} a_1^2 \\ \sqrt{2}\,a_1 a_2 \\ a_2^2 \end{pmatrix}^T \begin{pmatrix} b_1^2 \\ \sqrt{2}\,b_1 b_2 \\ b_2^2 \end{pmatrix} = a_1^2 b_1^2 + 2 a_1 b_1 a_2 b_2 + a_2^2 b_2^2$$

$$= \left(a_1 b_1 + a_2 b_2\right)^2 = \left(\begin{pmatrix} a_1 \\ a_2 \end{pmatrix}^T \begin{pmatrix} b_1 \\ b_2 \end{pmatrix} \right)^2 = \left(\mathbf{a}^T \mathbf{b} \right)^2$$

How about that? The dot product of the transformed vectors is equal to the square of the dot product of the original vectors: $\phi(\mathbf{a})^T \phi(\mathbf{b}) = (\mathbf{a}^T \mathbf{b})^2$.

Now here is the key insight: if you apply the transformation ϕ to all training instances, then the dual problem (see Equation 5-6) will contain the dot product $\phi(\mathbf{x}^{(i)})^T \phi(\mathbf{x}^{(j)})$. But if ϕ is the 2nd-degree polynomial transformation defined in Equation 5-8, then you can replace this dot product of transformed vectors simply by $\left(\mathbf{x}^{(i)T} \mathbf{x}^{(j)} \right)^2$. So you don't actually need to transform the training instances at all: just replace the dot product by its square in Equation 5-6. The result will be strictly the same as if you went through the trouble of actually transforming the training set then fitting a linear SVM algorithm, but this trick makes the whole process much more computationally efficient. This is the essence of the kernel trick.

The function $K(\mathbf{a}, \mathbf{b}) = (\mathbf{a}^T \mathbf{b})^2$ is called a 2nd-degree *polynomial kernel*. In Machine Learning, a *kernel* is a function capable of computing the dot product $\phi(\mathbf{a})^T \phi(\mathbf{b})$ based only on the original vectors $\mathbf{a}$ and $\mathbf{b}$, without having to compute (or even to know about) the transformation ϕ. Equation 5-10 lists some of the most commonly used kernels.

Equation 5-10. Common kernels

Linear: $\quad K(\mathbf{a}, \mathbf{b}) = \mathbf{a}^T \mathbf{b}$

Polynomial: $\quad K(\mathbf{a}, \mathbf{b}) = \left(\gamma \mathbf{a}^T \mathbf{b} + r \right)^d$

Gaussian RBF: $\quad K(\mathbf{a}, \mathbf{b}) = \exp\left(-\gamma \| \mathbf{a} - \mathbf{b} \|^2 \right)$

Sigmoid: $\quad K(\mathbf{a}, \mathbf{b}) = \tanh\left(\gamma \mathbf{a}^T \mathbf{b} + r \right)$

Mercer's Theorem

According to *Mercer's theorem*, if a function $K(\mathbf{a}, \mathbf{b})$ respects a few mathematical conditions called *Mercer's conditions* (K must be continuous, symmetric in its arguments so $K(\mathbf{a}, \mathbf{b}) = K(\mathbf{b}, \mathbf{a})$, etc.), then there exists a function ϕ that maps $\mathbf{a}$ and $\mathbf{b}$ into another space (possibly with much higher dimensions) such that $K(\mathbf{a}, \mathbf{b}) = \phi(\mathbf{a})^T \phi(\mathbf{b})$. So you can use K as a kernel since you know ϕ exists, even if you don't know what ϕ is. In the case of the Gaussian RBF kernel, it can be shown that ϕ actually maps each training instance to an infinite-dimensional space, so it's a good thing you don't need to actually perform the mapping!

Note that some frequently used kernels (such as the Sigmoid kernel) don't respect all of Mercer's conditions, yet they generally work well in practice.

There is still one loose end we must tie. Equation 5-7 shows how to go from the dual solution to the primal solution in the case of a linear SVM classifier, but if you apply the kernel trick you end up with equations that include $\phi(x^{(i)})$. In fact, $\hat{\mathbf{w}}$ must have the same number of dimensions as $\phi(x^{(i)})$, which may be huge or even infinite, so you can't compute it. But how can you make predictions without knowing $\hat{\mathbf{w}}$? Well, the good news is that you can plug in the formula for $\hat{\mathbf{w}}$ from Equation 5-7 into the decision function for a new instance $\mathbf{x}^{(n)}$, and you get an equation with only dot products between input vectors. This makes it possible to use the kernel trick, once again (Equation 5-11).

Equation 5-11. Making predictions with a kernelized SVM

$$
\begin{aligned}
h_{\hat{\mathbf{w}}, \hat{b}}\left(\phi\left(\mathbf{x}^{(n)}\right)\right) &= \hat{\mathbf{w}}^T \phi\left(\mathbf{x}^{(n)}\right) + \hat{b} = \left(\sum_{i=1}^{m} \hat{\alpha}^{(i)} t^{(i)} \phi\left(\mathbf{x}^{(i)}\right) \right)^T \phi\left(\mathbf{x}^{(n)}\right) + \hat{b} \\
&= \sum_{i=1}^{m} \hat{\alpha}^{(i)} t^{(i)} \left(\phi\left(\mathbf{x}^{(i)}\right)^T \phi\left(\mathbf{x}^{(n)}\right) \right) + \hat{b} \\
&= \sum_{\substack{i=1 \\ \hat{\alpha}^{(i)} > 0}}^{m} \hat{\alpha}^{(i)} t^{(i)} K\left(\mathbf{x}^{(i)}, \mathbf{x}^{(n)}\right) + \hat{b}
\end{aligned}
$$

Note that since $\alpha^{(i)} \neq 0$ only for support vectors, making predictions involves computing the dot product of the new input vector $\mathbf{x}^{(n)}$ with only the support vectors, not all the training instances. Of course, you also need to compute the bias term $\hat{b}$, using the same trick (Equation 5-12).

Equation 5-12. Computing the bias term using the kernel trick

$$\hat{b} = \frac{1}{n_s} \sum_{\substack{i=1 \\ \hat{\alpha}^{(i)} > 0}}^{m} \left(t^{(i)} - \hat{\mathbf{w}}^T \phi\left(\mathbf{x}^{(i)}\right) \right) = \frac{1}{n_s} \sum_{\substack{i=1 \\ \hat{\alpha}^{(i)} > 0}}^{m} \left(t^{(i)} - \left(\sum_{j=1}^{m} \hat{\alpha}^{(j)} t^{(j)} \phi\left(\mathbf{x}^{(j)}\right) \right)^T \phi\left(\mathbf{x}^{(i)}\right) \right)$$

$$= \frac{1}{n_s} \sum_{\substack{i=1 \\ \hat{\alpha}^{(i)} > 0}}^{m} \left(t^{(i)} - \sum_{\substack{j=1 \\ \hat{\alpha}^{(j)} > 0}}^{m} \hat{\alpha}^{(j)} t^{(j)} K\left(\mathbf{x}^{(i)}, \mathbf{x}^{(j)}\right) \right)$$

If you are starting to get a headache, it's perfectly normal: it's an unfortunate side effect of the kernel trick.

Online SVMs

Before concluding this chapter, let's take a quick look at online SVM classifiers (recall that online learning means learning incrementally, typically as new instances arrive).

For linear SVM classifiers, one method is to use Gradient Descent (e.g., using SGDClassifier) to minimize the cost function in Equation 5-13, which is derived from the primal problem. Unfortunately it converges much more slowly than the methods based on QP.

Equation 5-13. Linear SVM classifier cost function

$$J(\mathbf{w}, b) = \frac{1}{2}\mathbf{w}^T\mathbf{w} \; + \; C \sum_{i=1}^{m} max\left(0, 1 - t^{(i)}\left(\mathbf{w}^T\mathbf{x}^{(i)} + b\right)\right)$$

The first sum in the cost function will push the model to have a small weight vector **w**, leading to a larger margin. The second sum computes the total of all margin violations. An instance's margin violation is equal to 0 if it is located off the street and on the correct side, or else it is proportional to the distance to the correct side of the street. Minimizing this term ensures that the model makes the margin violations as small and as few as possible

---

Hinge Loss

The function $max(0, 1 - t)$ is called the *hinge loss* function (represented below). It is equal to 0 when $t \geq 1$. Its derivative (slope) is equal to -1 if $t < 1$ and 0 if $t > 1$. It is not differentiable at $t = 1$, but just like for Lasso Regression (see "Lasso Regression" on page 133) you can still use Gradient Descent using any *subderivative* at $t = 1$ (i.e., any value between -1 and 0).

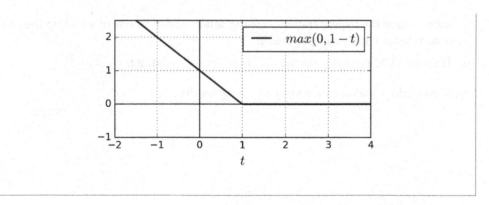

It is also possible to implement online kernelized SVMs—for example, using "Incremental and Decremental SVM Learning" (*http://homl.info/17*)[8] or "Fast Kernel Classifiers with Online and Active Learning." (*http://homl.info/18*)[9] However, these are implemented in Matlab and C++. For large-scale nonlinear problems, you may want to consider using neural networks instead (see Part II).

Exercises

1. What is the fundamental idea behind Support Vector Machines?

2. What is a support vector?

3. Why is it important to scale the inputs when using SVMs?

4. Can an SVM classifier output a confidence score when it classifies an instance? What about a probability?

5. Should you use the primal or the dual form of the SVM problem to train a model on a training set with millions of instances and hundreds of features?

6. Say you trained an SVM classifier with an RBF kernel. It seems to underfit the training set: should you increase or decrease γ (gamma)? What about C?

7. How should you set the QP parameters (**H**, **f**, **A**, and **b**) to solve the soft margin linear SVM classifier problem using an off-the-shelf QP solver?

8. Train a LinearSVC on a linearly separable dataset. Then train an SVC and a SGDClassifier on the same dataset. See if you can get them to produce roughly the same model.

9. Train an SVM classifier on the MNIST dataset. Since SVM classifiers are binary classifiers, you will need to use one-versus-all to classify all 10 digits. You may

---

8 "Incremental and Decremental Support Vector Machine Learning," G. Cauwenberghs, T. Poggio (2001).

9 "Fast Kernel Classifiers with Online and Active Learning," A. Bordes, S. Ertekin, J. Weston, L. Bottou (2005).

want to tune the hyperparameters using small validation sets to speed up the process. What accuracy can you reach?

10. Train an SVM regressor on the California housing dataset.

Solutions to these exercises are available in Appendix A.

## CHAPTER 6

Decision Trees

Like SVMs, *Decision Trees* are versatile Machine Learning algorithms that can perform both classification and regression tasks, and even multioutput tasks. They are very powerful algorithms, capable of fitting complex datasets. For example, in Chapter 2 you trained a `DecisionTreeRegressor` model on the California housing dataset, fitting it perfectly (actually overfitting it).

Decision Trees are also the fundamental components of Random Forests (see Chapter 7), which are among the most powerful Machine Learning algorithms available today.

In this chapter we will start by discussing how to train, visualize, and make predictions with Decision Trees. Then we will go through the CART training algorithm used by Scikit-Learn, and we will discuss how to regularize trees and use them for regression tasks. Finally, we will discuss some of the limitations of Decision Trees.

Training and Visualizing a Decision Tree

To understand Decision Trees, let's just build one and take a look at how it makes predictions. The following code trains a `DecisionTreeClassifier` on the iris dataset (see Chapter 4):

```
from sklearn.datasets import load_iris
from sklearn.tree import DecisionTreeClassifier

iris = load_iris()
X = iris.data[:, 2:] # petal length and width
y = iris.target

tree_clf = DecisionTreeClassifier(max_depth=2)
tree_clf.fit(X, y)
```

You can visualize the trained Decision Tree by first using the export_graphviz() method to output a graph definition file called *iris_tree.dot*:

```
from sklearn.tree import export_graphviz

export_graphviz(
        tree_clf,
        out_file=image_path("iris_tree.dot"),
        feature_names=iris.feature_names[2:],
        class_names=iris.target_names,
        rounded=True,
        filled=True
    )
```

Then you can convert this *.dot* file to a variety of formats such as PDF or PNG using the dot command-line tool from the *graphviz* package.[1] This command line converts the *.dot* file to a *.png* image file:

```
$ dot -Tpng iris_tree.dot -o iris_tree.png
```

Your first decision tree looks like Figure 6-1.

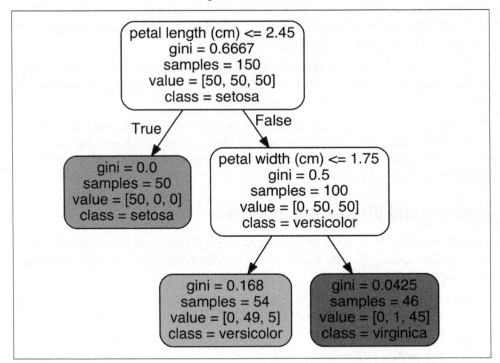

Figure 6-1. Iris Decision Tree

---

1 Graphviz is an open source graph visualization software package, available at *http://www.graphviz.org/*.

Making Predictions

Let's see how the tree represented in Figure 6-1 makes predictions. Suppose you find an iris flower and you want to classify it. You start at the *root node* (depth 0, at the top): this node asks whether the flower's petal length is smaller than 2.45 cm. If it is, then you move down to the root's left child node (depth 1, left). In this case, it is a *leaf node* (i.e., it does not have any children nodes), so it does not ask any questions: you can simply look at the predicted class for that node and the Decision Tree predicts that your flower is an Iris-Setosa (class=setosa).

Now suppose you find another flower, but this time the petal length is greater than 2.45 cm. You must move down to the root's right child node (depth 1, right), which is not a leaf node, so it asks another question: is the petal width smaller than 1.75 cm? If it is, then your flower is most likely an Iris-Versicolor (depth 2, left). If not, it is likely an Iris-Virginica (depth 2, right). It's really that simple.

> One of the many qualities of Decision Trees is that they require very little data preparation. In particular, they don't require feature scaling or centering at all.

A node's samples attribute counts how many training instances it applies to. For example, 100 training instances have a petal length greater than 2.45 cm (depth 1, right), among which 54 have a petal width smaller than 1.75 cm (depth 2, left). A node's value attribute tells you how many training instances of each class this node applies to: for example, the bottom-right node applies to 0 Iris-Setosa, 1 Iris-Versicolor, and 45 Iris-Virginica. Finally, a node's gini attribute measures its *impurity*: a node is "pure" (gini=0) if all training instances it applies to belong to the same class. For example, since the depth-1 left node applies only to Iris-Setosa training instances, it is pure and its gini score is 0. Equation 6-1 shows how the training algorithm computes the gini score G_i of the ith node. For example, the depth-2 left node has a gini score equal to $1 - (0/54)^2 - (49/54)^2 - (5/54)^2 \approx 0.168$. Another *impurity measure* is discussed shortly.

Equation 6-1. Gini impurity

$$G_i = 1 - \sum_{k=1}^{n} p_{i,k}^{\,2}$$

- $p_{i,k}$ is the ratio of class k instances among the training instances in the ith node.

Scikit-Learn uses the CART algorithm, which produces only *binary trees*: nonleaf nodes always have two children (i.e., questions only have yes/no answers). However, other algorithms such as ID3 can produce Decision Trees with nodes that have more than two children.

Figure 6-2 shows this Decision Tree's decision boundaries. The thick vertical line represents the decision boundary of the root node (depth 0): petal length = 2.45 cm. Since the left area is pure (only Iris-Setosa), it cannot be split any further. However, the right area is impure, so the depth-1 right node splits it at petal width = 1.75 cm (represented by the dashed line). Since `max_depth` was set to 2, the Decision Tree stops right there. However, if you set `max_depth` to 3, then the two depth-2 nodes would each add another decision boundary (represented by the dotted lines).

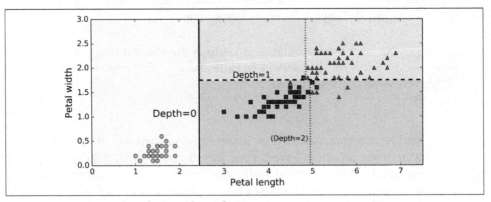

Figure 6-2. Decision Tree decision boundaries

Model Interpretation: White Box Versus Black Box

As you can see Decision Trees are fairly intuitive and their decisions are easy to interpret. Such models are often called *white box models*. In contrast, as we will see, Random Forests or neural networks are generally considered *black box models*. They make great predictions, and you can easily check the calculations that they performed to make these predictions; nevertheless, it is usually hard to explain in simple terms why the predictions were made. For example, if a neural network says that a particular person appears on a picture, it is hard to know what actually contributed to this prediction: did the model recognize that person's eyes? Her mouth? Her nose? Her shoes? Or even the couch that she was sitting on? Conversely, Decision Trees provide nice and simple classification rules that can even be applied manually if need be (e.g., for flower classification).

Estimating Class Probabilities

A Decision Tree can also estimate the probability that an instance belongs to a particular class k: first it traverses the tree to find the leaf node for this instance, and then it
returns the ratio of training instances of class k in this node. For example, suppose
you have found a flower whose petals are 5 cm long and 1.5 cm wide. The corresponding leaf node is the depth-2 left node, so the Decision Tree should output the
following probabilities: 0% for Iris-Setosa (0/54), 90.7% for Iris-Versicolor (49/54),
and 9.3% for Iris-Virginica (5/54). And of course if you ask it to predict the class, it
should output Iris-Versicolor (class 1) since it has the highest probability. Let's check
this:

```
>>> tree_clf.predict_proba([[5, 1.5]])
array([[ 0. ,  0.90740741,  0.09259259]])
>>> tree_clf.predict([[5, 1.5]])
array([1])
```

Perfect! Notice that the estimated probabilities would be identical anywhere else in
the bottom-right rectangle of Figure 6-2—for example, if the petals were 6 cm long
and 1.5 cm wide (even though it seems obvious that it would most likely be an Iris-
Virginica in this case).

The CART Training Algorithm

Scikit-Learn uses the *Classification And Regression Tree* (CART) algorithm to train
Decision Trees (also called "growing" trees). The idea is really quite simple: the algorithm first splits the training set in two subsets using a single feature k and a threshold t_k (e.g., "petal length ≤ 2.45 cm"). How does it choose k and t_k? It searches for the
pair (k, t_k) that produces the purest subsets (weighted by their size). The cost function
that the algorithm tries to minimize is given by Equation 6-2.

Equation 6-2. CART cost function for classification

$$J(k, t_k) = \frac{m_{\text{left}}}{m} G_{\text{left}} + \frac{m_{\text{right}}}{m} G_{\text{right}}$$

where $\begin{cases} G_{\text{left/right}} & \text{measures the impurity of the left/right subset,} \\ m_{\text{left/right}} & \text{is the number of instances in the left/right subset.} \end{cases}$

Once it has successfully split the training set in two, it splits the subsets using the
same logic, then the sub-subsets and so on, recursively. It stops recursing once it reaches the maximum depth (defined by the max_depth hyperparameter), or if it cannot
find a split that will reduce impurity. A few other hyperparameters (described in a

moment) control additional stopping conditions (`min_samples_split`, `min_sam`
`ples_leaf`, `min_weight_fraction_leaf`, and `max_leaf_nodes`).

 As you can see, the CART algorithm is a *greedy algorithm*: it greedily searches for an optimum split at the top level, then repeats the
process at each level. It does not check whether or not the split will
lead to the lowest possible impurity several levels down. A greedy
algorithm often produces a reasonably good solution, but it is not
guaranteed to be the optimal solution.

Unfortunately, finding the optimal tree is known to be an *NP-
Complete* problem:[2] it requires $O(\exp(m))$ time, making the problem intractable even for fairly small training sets. This is why we
must settle for a "reasonably good" solution.

Computational Complexity

Making predictions requires traversing the Decision Tree from the root to a leaf.
Decision Trees are generally approximately balanced, so traversing the Decision Tree
requires going through roughly $O(log_2(m))$ nodes.[3] Since each node only requires
checking the value of one feature, the overall prediction complexity is just $O(log_2(m))$,
independent of the number of features. So predictions are very fast, even when dealing with large training sets.

However, the training algorithm compares all features (or less if `max_features` is set)
on all samples at each node. This results in a training complexity of $O(n \times m\, log(m))$.
For small training sets (less than a few thousand instances), Scikit-Learn can speed up
training by presorting the data (set `presort=True`), but this slows down training considerably for larger training sets.

Gini Impurity or Entropy?

By default, the Gini impurity measure is used, but you can select the *entropy* impurity
measure instead by setting the `criterion` hyperparameter to `"entropy"`. The concept
of entropy originated in thermodynamics as a measure of molecular disorder:
entropy approaches zero when molecules are still and well ordered. It later spread to a
wide variety of domains, including Shannon's *information theory*, where it measures

---

2 P is the set of problems that can be solved in polynomial time. NP is the set of problems whose solutions can
be verified in polynomial time. An NP-Hard problem is a problem to which any NP problem can be reduced
in polynomial time. An NP-Complete problem is both NP and NP-Hard. A major open mathematical question is whether or not P = NP. If P ≠ NP (which seems likely), then no polynomial algorithm will ever be
found for any NP-Complete problem (except perhaps on a quantum computer).

3 log_2 is the binary logarithm. It is equal to $log_2(m) = log(m) / log(2)$.

the average information content of a message:[4] entropy is zero when all messages are identical. In Machine Learning, it is frequently used as an impurity measure: a set's entropy is zero when it contains instances of only one class. Equation 6-3 shows the definition of the entropy of the ith node, where $\log_2(p)$ is the binary log of p, equal to $\log(p)/\log(2)$. For example, the depth-2 left node in Figure 6-1 has an entropy equal to $-\frac{49}{54} \log_2\left(\frac{49}{54}\right) - \frac{5}{54} \log_2\left(\frac{5}{54}\right) \approx 0.445$.

Equation 6-3. Entropy

$$H_i = -\sum_{\substack{k=1 \\ p_{i,k} \neq 0}}^{n} p_{i,k} \log_2\left(p_{i,k}\right)$$

So should you use Gini impurity or entropy? The truth is, most of the time it does not make a big difference: they lead to similar trees. Gini impurity is slightly faster to compute, so it is a good default. However, when they differ, Gini impurity tends to isolate the most frequent class in its own branch of the tree, while entropy tends to produce slightly more balanced trees.[5]

Regularization Hyperparameters

Decision Trees make very few assumptions about the training data (as opposed to linear models, which obviously assume that the data is linear, for example). If left unconstrained, the tree structure will adapt itself to the training data, fitting it very closely, and most likely overfitting it. Such a model is often called a *nonparametric model*, not because it does not have any parameters (it often has a lot) but because the number of parameters is not determined prior to training, so the model structure is free to stick closely to the data. In contrast, a *parametric model* such as a linear model has a predetermined number of parameters, so its degree of freedom is limited, reducing the risk of overfitting (but increasing the risk of underfitting).

To avoid overfitting the training data, you need to restrict the Decision Tree's freedom during training. As you know by now, this is called regularization. The regularization hyperparameters depend on the algorithm used, but generally you can at least restrict the maximum depth of the Decision Tree. In Scikit-Learn, this is controlled by the `max_depth` hyperparameter (the default value is `None`, which means unlimited). Reducing `max_depth` will regularize the model and thus reduce the risk of overfitting.

---

4 A reduction of entropy is often called an *information gain*.

5 See Sebastian Raschka's interesting analysis for more details (*http://homl.info/19*).

The `DecisionTreeClassifier` class has a few other parameters that similarly restrict the shape of the Decision Tree: `min_samples_split` (the minimum number of samples a node must have before it can be split), `min_samples_leaf` (the minimum number of samples a leaf node must have), `min_weight_fraction_leaf` (same as `min_samples_leaf` but expressed as a fraction of the total number of weighted instances), `max_leaf_nodes` (maximum number of leaf nodes), and `max_features` (maximum number of features that are evaluated for splitting at each node). Increasing `min_*` hyperparameters or reducing `max_*` hyperparameters will regularize the model.

 Other algorithms work by first training the Decision Tree without restrictions, then *pruning* (deleting) unnecessary nodes. A node whose children are all leaf nodes is considered unnecessary if the purity improvement it provides is not *statistically significant*. Standard statistical tests, such as the χ^2 *test*, are used to estimate the probability that the improvement is purely the result of chance (which is called the *null hypothesis*). If this probability, called the *p-value*, is higher than a given threshold (typically 5%, controlled by a hyperparameter), then the node is considered unnecessary and its children are deleted. The pruning continues until all unnecessary nodes have been pruned.

Figure 6-3 shows two Decision Trees trained on the moons dataset (introduced in Chapter 5). On the left, the Decision Tree is trained with the default hyperparameters (i.e., no restrictions), and on the right the Decision Tree is trained with `min_sam ples_leaf=4`. It is quite obvious that the model on the left is overfitting, and the model on the right will probably generalize better.

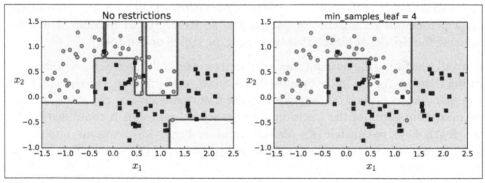

Figure 6-3. Regularization using min_samples_leaf

Regression

Decision Trees are also capable of performing regression tasks. Let's build a regression tree using Scikit-Learn's `DecisionTreeRegressor` class, training it on a noisy quadratic dataset with `max_depth=2`:

```
from sklearn.tree import DecisionTreeRegressor

tree_reg = DecisionTreeRegressor(max_depth=2)
tree_reg.fit(X, y)
```

The resulting tree is represented on Figure 6-4.

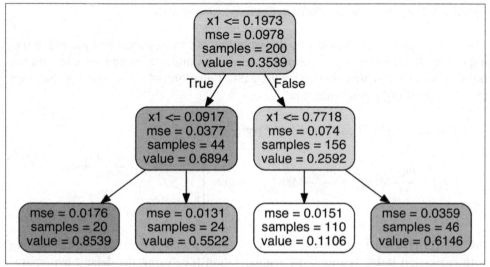

Figure 6-4. A Decision Tree for regression

This tree looks very similar to the classification tree you built earlier. The main difference is that instead of predicting a class in each node, it predicts a value. For example, suppose you want to make a prediction for a new instance with $x_1 = 0.6$. You traverse the tree starting at the root, and you eventually reach the leaf node that predicts `value=0.1106`. This prediction is simply the average target value of the 110 training instances associated to this leaf node. This prediction results in a Mean Squared Error (MSE) equal to 0.0151 over these 110 instances.

This model's predictions are represented on the left of Figure 6-5. If you set `max_depth=3`, you get the predictions represented on the right. Notice how the predicted value for each region is always the average target value of the instances in that region. The algorithm splits each region in a way that makes most training instances as close as possible to that predicted value.

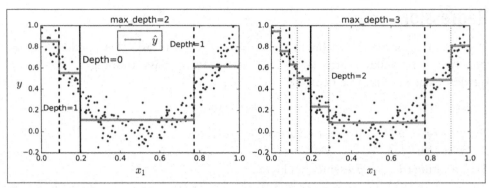

Figure 6-5. Predictions of two Decision Tree regression models

The CART algorithm works mostly the same way as earlier, except that instead of trying to split the training set in a way that minimizes impurity, it now tries to split the training set in a way that minimizes the MSE. Equation 6-4 shows the cost function that the algorithm tries to minimize.

Equation 6-4. CART cost function for regression

$$J(k, t_k) = \frac{m_{\text{left}}}{m}\text{MSE}_{\text{left}} + \frac{m_{\text{right}}}{m}\text{MSE}_{\text{right}} \quad \text{where} \begin{cases} \text{MSE}_{\text{node}} = \sum_{i \in \text{node}} \left(\hat{y}_{\text{node}} - y^{(i)}\right)^2 \\ \hat{y}_{\text{node}} = \frac{1}{m_{\text{node}}} \sum_{i \in \text{node}} y^{(i)} \end{cases}$$

Just like for classification tasks, Decision Trees are prone to overfitting when dealing with regression tasks. Without any regularization (i.e., using the default hyperparameters), you get the predictions on the left of Figure 6-6. It is obviously overfitting the training set very badly. Just setting `min_samples_leaf=10` results in a much more reasonable model, represented on the right of Figure 6-6.

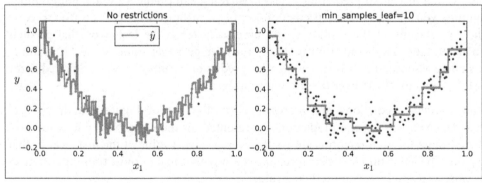

Figure 6-6. Regularizing a Decision Tree regressor

Instability

Hopefully by now you are convinced that Decision Trees have a lot going for them: they are simple to understand and interpret, easy to use, versatile, and powerful. However they do have a few limitations. First, as you may have noticed, Decision Trees love orthogonal decision boundaries (all splits are perpendicular to an axis), which makes them sensitive to training set rotation. For example, Figure 6-7 shows a simple linearly separable dataset: on the left, a Decision Tree can split it easily, while on the right, after the dataset is rotated by 45°, the decision boundary looks unnecessarily convoluted. Although both Decision Trees fit the training set perfectly, it is very likely that the model on the right will not generalize well. One way to limit this problem is to use PCA (see Chapter 8), which often results in a better orientation of the training data.

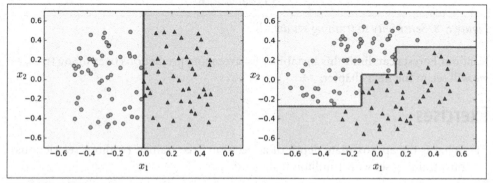

Figure 6-7. Sensitivity to training set rotation

More generally, the main issue with Decision Trees is that they are very sensitive to small variations in the training data. For example, if you just remove the widest Iris-Versicolor from the iris training set (the one with petals 4.8 cm long and 1.8 cm wide) and train a new Decision Tree, you may get the model represented in Figure 6-8. As you can see, it looks very different from the previous Decision Tree (Figure 6-2). Actually, since the training algorithm used by Scikit-Learn is stochastic[6] you may get very different models even on the same training data (unless you set the random_state hyperparameter).

---

6 It randomly selects the set of features to evaluate at each node.

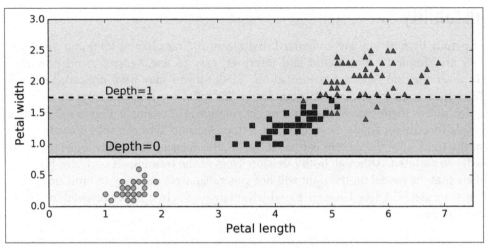

Figure 6-8. Sensitivity to training set details

Random Forests can limit this instability by averaging predictions over many trees, as we will see in the next chapter.

Exercises

1. What is the approximate depth of a Decision Tree trained (without restrictions) on a training set with 1 million instances?

2. Is a node's Gini impurity generally lower or greater than its parent's? Is it *generally* lower/greater, or *always* lower/greater?

3. If a Decision Tree is overfitting the training set, is it a good idea to try decreasing `max_depth`?

4. If a Decision Tree is underfitting the training set, is it a good idea to try scaling the input features?

5. If it takes one hour to train a Decision Tree on a training set containing 1 million instances, roughly how much time will it take to train another Decision Tree on a training set containing 10 million instances?

6. If your training set contains 100,000 instances, will setting `presort=True` speed up training?

7. Train and fine-tune a Decision Tree for the moons dataset.

   a. Generate a moons dataset using `make_moons(n_samples=10000, noise=0.4)`.

   b. Split it into a training set and a test set using `train_test_split()`.

c. Use grid search with cross-validation (with the help of the `GridSearchCV` class) to find good hyperparameter values for a `DecisionTreeClassifier`. Hint: try various values for `max_leaf_nodes`.

d. Train it on the full training set using these hyperparameters, and measure your model's performance on the test set. You should get roughly 85% to 87% accuracy.

8. Grow a forest.

a. Continuing the previous exercise, generate 1,000 subsets of the training set, each containing 100 instances selected randomly. Hint: you can use Scikit-Learn's `ShuffleSplit` class for this.

b. Train one Decision Tree on each subset, using the best hyperparameter values found above. Evaluate these 1,000 Decision Trees on the test set. Since they were trained on smaller sets, these Decision Trees will likely perform worse than the first Decision Tree, achieving only about 80% accuracy.

c. Now comes the magic. For each test set instance, generate the predictions of the 1,000 Decision Trees, and keep only the most frequent prediction (you can use SciPy's `mode()` function for this). This gives you *majority-vote predictions* over the test set.

d. Evaluate these predictions on the test set: you should obtain a slightly higher accuracy than your first model (about 0.5 to 1.5% higher). Congratulations, you have trained a Random Forest classifier!

Solutions to these exercises are available in Appendix A.

## CHAPTER 7

Ensemble Learning and Random Forests

Suppose you ask a complex question to thousands of random people, then aggregate their answers. In many cases you will find that this aggregated answer is better than an expert's answer. This is called the *wisdom of the crowd*. Similarly, if you aggregate the predictions of a group of predictors (such as classifiers or regressors), you will often get better predictions than with the best individual predictor. A group of predictors is called an *ensemble*; thus, this technique is called *Ensemble Learning*, and an Ensemble Learning algorithm is called an *Ensemble method*.

For example, you can train a group of Decision Tree classifiers, each on a different random subset of the training set. To make predictions, you just obtain the predictions of all individual trees, then predict the class that gets the most votes (see the last exercise in Chapter 6). Such an ensemble of Decision Trees is called a *Random Forest*, and despite its simplicity, this is one of the most powerful Machine Learning algorithms available today.

Moreover, as we discussed in Chapter 2, you will often use Ensemble methods near the end of a project, once you have already built a few good predictors, to combine them into an even better predictor. In fact, the winning solutions in Machine Learning competitions often involve several Ensemble methods (most famously in the Netflix Prize competition (*http://netflixprize.com/*)).

In this chapter we will discuss the most popular Ensemble methods, including *bagging*, *boosting*, *stacking*, and a few others. We will also explore Random Forests.

Voting Classifiers

Suppose you have trained a few classifiers, each one achieving about 80% accuracy. You may have a Logistic Regression classifier, an SVM classifier, a Random Forest classifier, a K-Nearest Neighbors classifier, and perhaps a few more (see Figure 7-1).

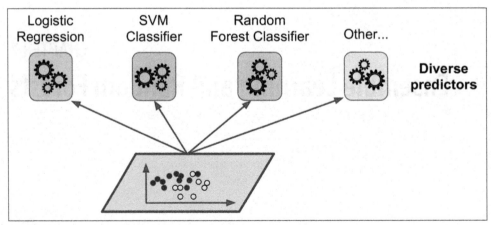

Figure 7-1. Training diverse classifiers

A very simple way to create an even better classifier is to aggregate the predictions of each classifier and predict the class that gets the most votes. This majority-vote classifier is called a *hard voting* classifier (see Figure 7-2).

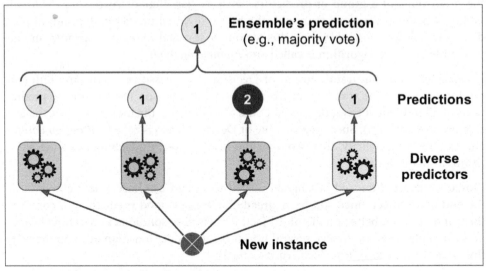

Figure 7-2. Hard voting classifier predictions

Somewhat surprisingly, this voting classifier often achieves a higher accuracy than the best classifier in the ensemble. In fact, even if each classifier is a *weak learner* (meaning it does only slightly better than random guessing), the ensemble can still be a *strong learner* (achieving high accuracy), provided there are a sufficient number of weak learners and they are sufficiently diverse.

How is this possible? The following analogy can help shed some light on this mystery. Suppose you have a slightly biased coin that has a 51% chance of coming up heads, and 49% chance of coming up tails. If you toss it 1,000 times, you will generally get more or less 510 heads and 490 tails, and hence a majority of heads. If you do the math, you will find that the probability of obtaining a majority of heads after 1,000 tosses is close to 75%. The more you toss the coin, the higher the probability (e.g., with 10,000 tosses, the probability climbs over 97%). This is due to the *law of large numbers*: as you keep tossing the coin, the ratio of heads gets closer and closer to the probability of heads (51%). Figure 7-3 shows 10 series of biased coin tosses. You can see that as the number of tosses increases, the ratio of heads approaches 51%. Eventually all 10 series end up so close to 51% that they are consistently above 50%.

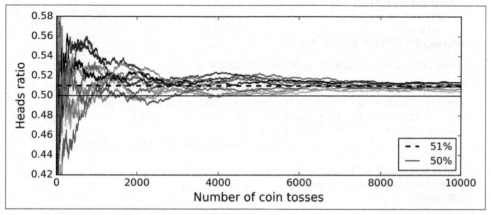

Figure 7-3. The law of large numbers

Similarly, suppose you build an ensemble containing 1,000 classifiers that are individually correct only 51% of the time (barely better than random guessing). If you predict the majority voted class, you can hope for up to 75% accuracy! However, this is only true if all classifiers are perfectly independent, making uncorrelated errors, which is clearly not the case since they are trained on the same data. They are likely to make the same types of errors, so there will be many majority votes for the wrong class, reducing the ensemble's accuracy.

> Ensemble methods work best when the predictors are as independent from one another as possible. One way to get diverse classifiers is to train them using very different algorithms. This increases the chance that they will make very different types of errors, improving the ensemble's accuracy.

The following code creates and trains a voting classifier in Scikit-Learn, composed of three diverse classifiers (the training set is the moons dataset, introduced in Chapter 5):

```
from sklearn.ensemble import RandomForestClassifier
from sklearn.ensemble import VotingClassifier
from sklearn.linear_model import LogisticRegression
from sklearn.svm import SVC

log_clf = LogisticRegression()
rnd_clf = RandomForestClassifier()
svm_clf = SVC()

voting_clf = VotingClassifier(
    estimators=[('lr', log_clf), ('rf', rnd_clf), ('svc', svm_clf)],
    voting='hard')
voting_clf.fit(X_train, y_train)
```

Let's look at each classifier's accuracy on the test set:

```
>>> from sklearn.metrics import accuracy_score
>>> for clf in (log_clf, rnd_clf, svm_clf, voting_clf):
...     clf.fit(X_train, y_train)
...     y_pred = clf.predict(X_test)
...     print(clf.__class__.__name__, accuracy_score(y_test, y_pred))
...
LogisticRegression 0.864
RandomForestClassifier 0.872
SVC 0.888
VotingClassifier 0.896
```

There you have it! The voting classifier slightly outperforms all the individual classifiers.

If all classifiers are able to estimate class probabilities (i.e., they have a `pre dict_proba()` method), then you can tell Scikit-Learn to predict the class with the highest class probability, averaged over all the individual classifiers. This is called *soft voting*. It often achieves higher performance than hard voting because it gives more weight to highly confident votes. All you need to do is replace `voting="hard"` with `voting="soft"` and ensure that all classifiers can estimate class probabilities. This is not the case of the SVC class by default, so you need to set its `probability` hyperparameter to `True` (this will make the SVC class use cross-validation to estimate class probabilities, slowing down training, and it will add a `predict_proba()` method). If you modify the preceding code to use soft voting, you will find that the voting classifier achieves over 91% accuracy!

Bagging and Pasting

One way to get a diverse set of classifiers is to use very different training algorithms, as just discussed. Another approach is to use the same training algorithm for every predictor, but to train them on different random subsets of the training set. When sampling is performed *with* replacement, this method is called *bagging* (*http://homl.info/20*)[1] (short for *bootstrap aggregating*[2]). When sampling is performed *without* replacement, it is called *pasting* (*http://homl.info/21*).[3]

In other words, both bagging and pasting allow training instances to be sampled several times across multiple predictors, but only bagging allows training instances to be sampled several times for the same predictor. This sampling and training process is represented in Figure 7-4.

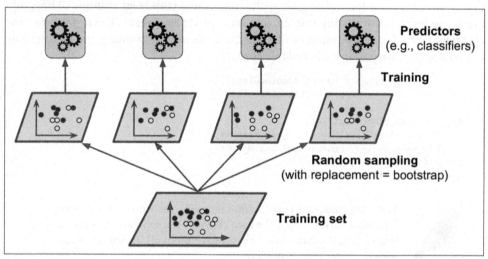

Figure 7-4. Pasting/bagging training set sampling and training

Once all predictors are trained, the ensemble can make a prediction for a new instance by simply aggregating the predictions of all predictors. The aggregation function is typically the *statistical mode* (i.e., the most frequent prediction, just like a hard voting classifier) for classification, or the average for regression. Each individual predictor has a higher bias than if it were trained on the original training set, but aggregation reduces both bias and variance.[4] Generally, the net result is that the

---

1 "Bagging Predictors," L. Breiman (1996).

2 In statistics, resampling with replacement is called *bootstrapping*.

3 "Pasting small votes for classification in large databases and on-line," L. Breiman (1999).

4 Bias and variance were introduced in Chapter 4.

ensemble has a similar bias but a lower variance than a single predictor trained on the original training set.

As you can see in Figure 7-4, predictors can all be trained in parallel, via different CPU cores or even different servers. Similarly, predictions can be made in parallel. This is one of the reasons why bagging and pasting are such popular methods: they scale very well.

Bagging and Pasting in Scikit-Learn

Scikit-Learn offers a simple API for both bagging and pasting with the `BaggingClassifier` class (or `BaggingRegressor` for regression). The following code trains an ensemble of 500 Decision Tree classifiers,[5] each trained on 100 training instances randomly sampled from the training set with replacement (this is an example of bagging, but if you want to use pasting instead, just set `bootstrap=False`). The `n_jobs` parameter tells Scikit-Learn the number of CPU cores to use for training and predictions (–1 tells Scikit-Learn to use all available cores):

```
from sklearn.ensemble import BaggingClassifier
from sklearn.tree import DecisionTreeClassifier

bag_clf = BaggingClassifier(
    DecisionTreeClassifier(), n_estimators=500,
    max_samples=100, bootstrap=True, n_jobs=-1)
bag_clf.fit(X_train, y_train)
y_pred = bag_clf.predict(X_test)
```

 The `BaggingClassifier` automatically performs soft voting instead of hard voting if the base classifier can estimate class probabilities (i.e., if it has a `predict_proba()` method), which is the case with Decision Trees classifiers.

Figure 7-5 compares the decision boundary of a single Decision Tree with the decision boundary of a bagging ensemble of 500 trees (from the preceding code), both trained on the moons dataset. As you can see, the ensemble's predictions will likely generalize much better than the single Decision Tree's predictions: the ensemble has a comparable bias but a smaller variance (it makes roughly the same number of errors on the training set, but the decision boundary is less irregular).

---

5 `max_samples` can alternatively be set to a float between 0.0 and 1.0, in which case the max number of instances to sample is equal to the size of the training set times `max_samples`.

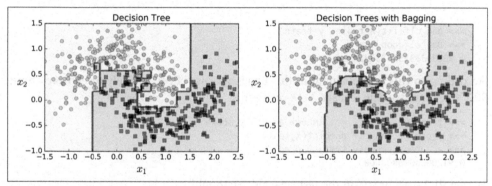

Figure 7-5. A single Decision Tree versus a bagging ensemble of 500 trees

Bootstrapping introduces a bit more diversity in the subsets that each predictor is trained on, so bagging ends up with a slightly higher bias than pasting, but this also means that predictors end up being less correlated so the ensemble's variance is reduced. Overall, bagging often results in better models, which explains why it is generally preferred. However, if you have spare time and CPU power you can use cross-validation to evaluate both bagging and pasting and select the one that works best.

Out-of-Bag Evaluation

With bagging, some instances may be sampled several times for any given predictor, while others may not be sampled at all. By default a `BaggingClassifier` samples m training instances with replacement (`bootstrap=True`), where m is the size of the training set. This means that only about 63% of the training instances are sampled on average for each predictor.[6] The remaining 37% of the training instances that are not sampled are called *out-of-bag* (oob) instances. Note that they are not the same 37% for all predictors.

Since a predictor never sees the oob instances during training, it can be evaluated on these instances, without the need for a separate validation set or cross-validation. You can evaluate the ensemble itself by averaging out the oob evaluations of each predictor.

In Scikit-Learn, you can set `oob_score=True` when creating a `BaggingClassifier` to request an automatic oob evaluation after training. The following code demonstrates this. The resulting evaluation score is available through the `oob_score_` variable:

```
>>> bag_clf = BaggingClassifier(
...     DecisionTreeClassifier(), n_estimators=500,
...     bootstrap=True, n_jobs=-1, oob_score=True)
```

---

6 As m grows, this ratio approaches $1 - \exp(-1) \approx 63.212\%$.

```
...
>>> bag_clf.fit(X_train, y_train)
>>> bag_clf.oob_score_
0.90133333333333332
```

According to this oob evaluation, this `BaggingClassifier` is likely to achieve about 90.1% accuracy on the test set. Let's verify this:

```
>>> from sklearn.metrics import accuracy_score
>>> y_pred = bag_clf.predict(X_test)
>>> accuracy_score(y_test, y_pred)
0.91200000000000003
```

We get 91.2% accuracy on the test set—close enough!

The oob decision function for each training instance is also available through the `oob_decision_function_` variable. In this case (since the base estimator has a `predict_proba()` method) the decision function returns the class probabilities for each training instance. For example, the oob evaluation estimates that the first training instance has a 68.25% probability of belonging to the positive class (and 31.75% of belonging to the negative class):

```
>>> bag_clf.oob_decision_function_
array([[ 0.31746032,  0.68253968],
       [ 0.34117647,  0.65882353],
       [ 1.        ,  0.        ],
       ...
       [ 1.        ,  0.        ],
       [ 0.03108808,  0.96891192],
       [ 0.57291667,  0.42708333]])
```

Random Patches and Random Subspaces

The `BaggingClassifier` class supports sampling the features as well. This is controlled by two hyperparameters: `max_features` and `bootstrap_features`. They work the same way as `max_samples` and `bootstrap`, but for feature sampling instead of instance sampling. Thus, each predictor will be trained on a random subset of the input features.

This is particularly useful when you are dealing with high-dimensional inputs (such as images). Sampling both training instances and features is called the *Random Patches* method (*http://homl.info/22*).[7] Keeping all training instances (i.e., boot strap=False and max_samples=1.0) but sampling features (i.e., bootstrap_fea

---

7 "Ensembles on Random Patches," G. Louppe and P. Geurts (2012).

tures=True and/or `max_features` smaller than 1.0) is called the *Random Subspaces* method (*http://homl.info/23*).[8]

Sampling features results in even more predictor diversity, trading a bit more bias for a lower variance.

Random Forests

As we have discussed, a Random Forest (*http://homl.info/24*)[9] is an ensemble of Decision Trees, generally trained via the bagging method (or sometimes pasting), typically with `max_samples` set to the size of the training set. Instead of building a `BaggingClas sifier` and passing it a `DecisionTreeClassifier`, you can instead use the `RandomFor estClassifier` class, which is more convenient and optimized for Decision Trees[10] (similarly, there is a `RandomForestRegressor` class for regression tasks). The following code trains a Random Forest classifier with 500 trees (each limited to maximum 16 nodes), using all available CPU cores:

```
from sklearn.ensemble import RandomForestClassifier

rnd_clf = RandomForestClassifier(n_estimators=500, max_leaf_nodes=16, n_jobs=-1)
rnd_clf.fit(X_train, y_train)

y_pred_rf = rnd_clf.predict(X_test)
```

With a few exceptions, a `RandomForestClassifier` has all the hyperparameters of a `DecisionTreeClassifier` (to control how trees are grown), plus all the hyperparameters of a `BaggingClassifier` to control the ensemble itself.[11]

The Random Forest algorithm introduces extra randomness when growing trees; instead of searching for the very best feature when splitting a node (see Chapter 6), it searches for the best feature among a random subset of features. This results in a greater tree diversity, which (once again) trades a higher bias for a lower variance, generally yielding an overall better model. The following `BaggingClassifier` is roughly equivalent to the previous `RandomForestClassifier`:

```
bag_clf = BaggingClassifier(
    DecisionTreeClassifier(splitter="random", max_leaf_nodes=16),
    n_estimators=500, max_samples=1.0, bootstrap=True, n_jobs=-1)
```

---

8 "The random subspace method for constructing decision forests," Tin Kam Ho (1998).

9 "Random Decision Forests," T. Ho (1995).

10 The `BaggingClassifier` class remains useful if you want a bag of something other than Decision Trees.

11 There are a few notable exceptions: `splitter` is absent (forced to `"random"`), `presort` is absent (forced to `False`), `max_samples` is absent (forced to `1.0`), and `base_estimator` is absent (forced to `DecisionTreeClassi fier` with the provided hyperparameters).

Extra-Trees

When you are growing a tree in a Random Forest, at each node only a random subset of the features is considered for splitting (as discussed earlier). It is possible to make trees even more random by also using random thresholds for each feature rather than searching for the best possible thresholds (like regular Decision Trees do).

A forest of such extremely random trees is simply called an *Extremely Randomized Trees* (*http://homl.info/25*) ensemble[12] (or *Extra-Trees* for short). Once again, this trades more bias for a lower variance. It also makes Extra-Trees much faster to train than regular Random Forests since finding the best possible threshold for each feature at every node is one of the most time-consuming tasks of growing a tree.

You can create an Extra-Trees classifier using Scikit-Learn's `ExtraTreesClassifier` class. Its API is identical to the `RandomForestClassifier` class. Similarly, the `Extra TreesRegressor` class has the same API as the `RandomForestRegressor` class.

 It is hard to tell in advance whether a `RandomForestClassifier` will perform better or worse than an `ExtraTreesClassifier`. Generally, the only way to know is to try both and compare them using cross-validation (and tuning the hyperparameters using grid search).

Feature Importance

Yet another great quality of Random Forests is that they make it easy to measure the relative importance of each feature. Scikit-Learn measures a feature's importance by looking at how much the tree nodes that use that feature reduce impurity on average (across all trees in the forest). More precisely, it is a weighted average, where each node's weight is equal to the number of training samples that are associated with it (see Chapter 6).

Scikit-Learn computes this score automatically for each feature after training, then it scales the results so that the sum of all importances is equal to 1. You can access the result using the `feature_importances_` variable. For example, the following code trains a `RandomForestClassifier` on the iris dataset (introduced in Chapter 4) and outputs each feature's importance. It seems that the most important features are the petal length (44%) and width (42%), while sepal length and width are rather unimportant in comparison (11% and 2%, respectively).

---

12 "Extremely randomized trees," P. Geurts, D. Ernst, L. Wehenkel (2005).

```
>>> from sklearn.datasets import load_iris
>>> iris = load_iris()
>>> rnd_clf = RandomForestClassifier(n_estimators=500, n_jobs=-1)
>>> rnd_clf.fit(iris["data"], iris["target"])
>>> for name, score in zip(iris["feature_names"], rnd_clf.feature_importances_):
...     print(name, score)
...
sepal length (cm) 0.112492250999
sepal width (cm) 0.0231192882825
petal length (cm) 0.441030464364
petal width (cm) 0.423357996355
```

Similarly, if you train a Random Forest classifier on the MNIST dataset (introduced in Chapter 3) and plot each pixel's importance, you get the image represented in Figure 7-6.

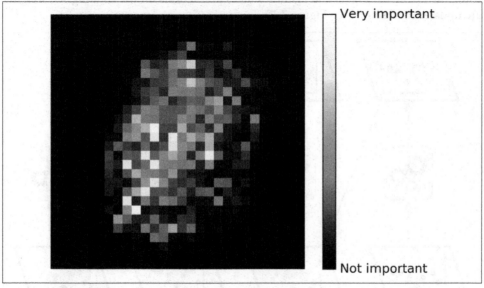

Figure 7-6. MNIST pixel importance (according to a Random Forest classifier)

Random Forests are very handy to get a quick understanding of what features actually matter, in particular if you need to perform feature selection.

Boosting

Boosting (originally called *hypothesis boosting*) refers to any Ensemble method that can combine several weak learners into a strong learner. The general idea of most boosting methods is to train predictors sequentially, each trying to correct its predecessor. There are many boosting methods available, but by far the most popular are

AdaBoost (*http://homl.info/26*)[13] (short for *Adaptive Boosting*) and *Gradient Boosting*. Let's start with AdaBoost.

AdaBoost

One way for a new predictor to correct its predecessor is to pay a bit more attention to the training instances that the predecessor underfitted. This results in new predictors focusing more and more on the hard cases. This is the technique used by AdaBoost.

For example, to build an AdaBoost classifier, a first base classifier (such as a Decision Tree) is trained and used to make predictions on the training set. The relative weight of misclassified training instances is then increased. A second classifier is trained using the updated weights and again it makes predictions on the training set, weights are updated, and so on (see Figure 7-7).

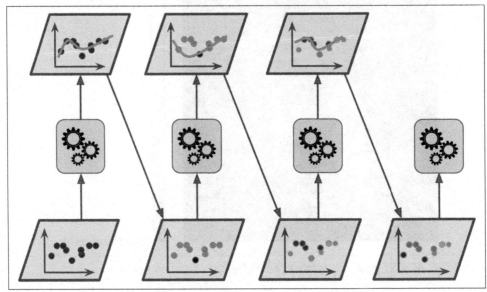

Figure 7-7. AdaBoost sequential training with instance weight updates

Figure 7-8 shows the decision boundaries of five consecutive predictors on the moons dataset (in this example, each predictor is a highly regularized SVM classifier with an RBF kernel[14]). The first classifier gets many instances wrong, so their weights

---

13 "A Decision-Theoretic Generalization of On-Line Learning and an Application to Boosting," Yoav Freund, Robert E. Schapire (1997).

14 This is just for illustrative purposes. SVMs are generally not good base predictors for AdaBoost, because they are slow and tend to be unstable with AdaBoost.

get boosted. The second classifier therefore does a better job on these instances, and so on. The plot on the right represents the same sequence of predictors except that the learning rate is halved (i.e., the misclassified instance weights are boosted half as much at every iteration). As you can see, this sequential learning technique has some similarities with Gradient Descent, except that instead of tweaking a single predictor's parameters to minimize a cost function, AdaBoost adds predictors to the ensemble, gradually making it better.

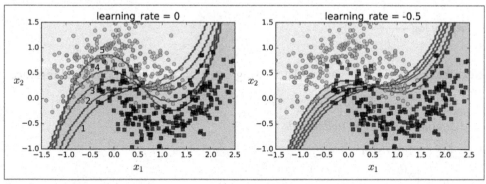

Figure 7-8. Decision boundaries of consecutive predictors

Once all predictors are trained, the ensemble makes predictions very much like bagging or pasting, except that predictors have different weights depending on their overall accuracy on the weighted training set.

 There is one important drawback to this sequential learning technique: it cannot be parallelized (or only partially), since each predictor can only be trained after the previous predictor has been trained and evaluated. As a result, it does not scale as well as bagging or pasting.

Let's take a closer look at the AdaBoost algorithm. Each instance weight $w^{(i)}$ is initially set to $\frac{1}{m}$. A first predictor is trained and its weighted error rate r_1 is computed on the training set; see Equation 7-1.

Equation 7-1. Weighted error rate of the jth predictor

$$r_j = \frac{\displaystyle\sum_{\substack{i=1 \\ \hat{y}_j^{(i)} \neq y^{(i)}}}^{m} w^{(i)}}{\displaystyle\sum_{i=1}^{m} w^{(i)}} \quad \text{where } \hat{y}_j^{(i)} \text{ is the } j^{th} \text{ predictor's prediction for the } i^{th} \text{ instance.}$$

The predictor's weight α_j is then computed using Equation 7-2, where η is the learning rate hyperparameter (defaults to 1).[15] The more accurate the predictor is, the higher its weight will be. If it is just guessing randomly, then its weight will be close to zero. However, if it is most often wrong (i.e., less accurate than random guessing), then its weight will be negative.

Equation 7-2. Predictor weight

$$\alpha_j = \eta \log \frac{1 - r_j}{r_j}$$

Next the instance weights are updated using Equation 7-3: the misclassified instances are boosted.

Equation 7-3. Weight update rule

for $i = 1, 2, \cdots, m$

$$w^{(i)} \leftarrow \begin{cases} w^{(i)} & \text{if } \widehat{y}_j^{(i)} = y^{(i)} \\ w^{(i)} \exp\left(\alpha_j\right) & \text{if } \widehat{y}_j^{(i)} \neq y^{(i)} \end{cases}$$

Then all the instance weights are normalized (i.e., divided by $\sum_{i=1}^{m} w^{(i)}$).

Finally, a new predictor is trained using the updated weights, and the whole process is repeated (the new predictor's weight is computed, the instance weights are updated, then another predictor is trained, and so on). The algorithm stops when the desired number of predictors is reached, or when a perfect predictor is found.

To make predictions, AdaBoost simply computes the predictions of all the predictors and weighs them using the predictor weights α_j. The predicted class is the one that receives the majority of weighted votes (see Equation 7-4).

Equation 7-4. AdaBoost predictions

$$\widehat{y}(\mathbf{x}) = \underset{k}{\text{argmax}} \sum_{\substack{j = 1 \\ \widehat{y}_j(\mathbf{x}) = k}}^{N} \alpha_j \quad \text{where } N \text{ is the number of predictors.}$$

---

15 The original AdaBoost algorithm does not use a learning rate hyperparameter.

Scikit-Learn actually uses a multiclass version of AdaBoost called *SAMME* (*http://homl.info/27*)[16] (which stands for *Stagewise Additive Modeling using a Multiclass Exponential loss function*). When there are just two classes, SAMME is equivalent to Ada-Boost. Moreover, if the predictors can estimate class probabilities (i.e., if they have a `predict_proba()` method), Scikit-Learn can use a variant of SAMME called *SAMME.R* (the *R* stands for "Real"), which relies on class probabilities rather than predictions and generally performs better.

The following code trains an AdaBoost classifier based on 200 *Decision Stumps* using Scikit-Learn's `AdaBoostClassifier` class (as you might expect, there is also an `Ada BoostRegressor` class). A Decision Stump is a Decision Tree with `max_depth=1`—in other words, a tree composed of a single decision node plus two leaf nodes. This is the default base estimator for the `AdaBoostClassifier` class:

```
from sklearn.ensemble import AdaBoostClassifier

ada_clf = AdaBoostClassifier(
    DecisionTreeClassifier(max_depth=1), n_estimators=200,
    algorithm="SAMME.R", learning_rate=0.5)
ada_clf.fit(X_train, y_train)
```

 If your AdaBoost ensemble is overfitting the training set, you can try reducing the number of estimators or more strongly regularizing the base estimator.

Gradient Boosting

Another very popular Boosting algorithm is *Gradient Boosting* (*http://homl.info/28*).[17] Just like AdaBoost, Gradient Boosting works by sequentially adding predictors to an ensemble, each one correcting its predecessor. However, instead of tweaking the instance weights at every iteration like AdaBoost does, this method tries to fit the new predictor to the *residual errors* made by the previous predictor.

Let's go through a simple regression example using Decision Trees as the base predictors (of course Gradient Boosting also works great with regression tasks). This is called *Gradient Tree Boosting*, or *Gradient Boosted Regression Trees* (*GBRT*). First, let's fit a `DecisionTreeRegressor` to the training set (for example, a noisy quadratic training set):

---

16 For more details, see "Multi-Class AdaBoost," J. Zhu et al. (2006).

17 First introduced in "Arcing the Edge," L. Breiman (1997).

```
from sklearn.tree import DecisionTreeRegressor

tree_reg1 = DecisionTreeRegressor(max_depth=2)
tree_reg1.fit(X, y)
```

Now train a second `DecisionTreeRegressor` on the residual errors made by the first predictor:

```
y2 = y - tree_reg1.predict(X)
tree_reg2 = DecisionTreeRegressor(max_depth=2)
tree_reg2.fit(X, y2)
```

Then we train a third regressor on the residual errors made by the second predictor:

```
y3 = y2 - tree_reg2.predict(X)
tree_reg3 = DecisionTreeRegressor(max_depth=2)
tree_reg3.fit(X, y3)
```

Now we have an ensemble containing three trees. It can make predictions on a new instance simply by adding up the predictions of all the trees:

```
y_pred = sum(tree.predict(X_new) for tree in (tree_reg1, tree_reg2, tree_reg3))
```

Figure 7-9 represents the predictions of these three trees in the left column, and the ensemble's predictions in the right column. In the first row, the ensemble has just one tree, so its predictions are exactly the same as the first tree's predictions. In the second row, a new tree is trained on the residual errors of the first tree. On the right you can see that the ensemble's predictions are equal to the sum of the predictions of the first two trees. Similarly, in the third row another tree is trained on the residual errors of the second tree. You can see that the ensemble's predictions gradually get better as trees are added to the ensemble.

A simpler way to train GBRT ensembles is to use Scikit-Learn's `GradientBoostingRegressor` class. Much like the `RandomForestRegressor` class, it has hyperparameters to control the growth of Decision Trees (e.g., `max_depth`, `min_samples_leaf`, and so on), as well as hyperparameters to control the ensemble training, such as the number of trees (`n_estimators`). The following code creates the same ensemble as the previous one:

```
from sklearn.ensemble import GradientBoostingRegressor

gbrt = GradientBoostingRegressor(max_depth=2, n_estimators=3, learning_rate=1.0)
gbrt.fit(X, y)
```

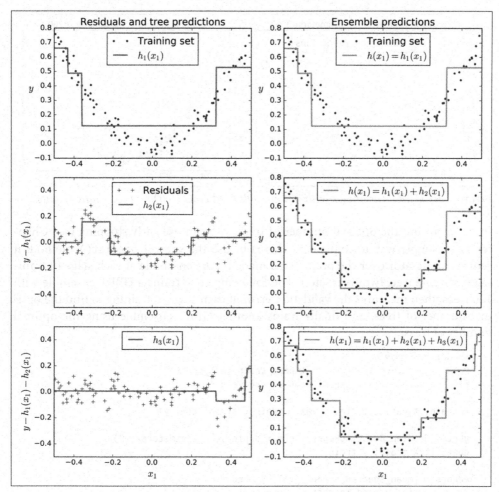

Figure 7-9. Gradient Boosting

The `learning_rate` hyperparameter scales the contribution of each tree. If you set it to a low value, such as 0.1, you will need more trees in the ensemble to fit the training set, but the predictions will usually generalize better. This is a regularization technique called *shrinkage*. Figure 7-10 shows two GBRT ensembles trained with a low learning rate: the one on the left does not have enough trees to fit the training set, while the one on the right has too many trees and overfits the training set.

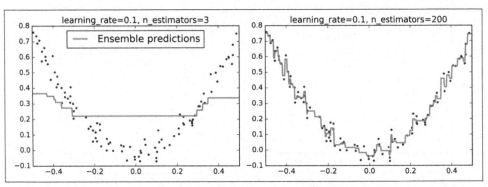

Figure 7-10. GBRT ensembles with not enough predictors (left) and too many (right)

In order to find the optimal number of trees, you can use early stopping (see Chapter 4). A simple way to implement this is to use the `staged_predict()` method: it returns an iterator over the predictions made by the ensemble at each stage of training (with one tree, two trees, etc.). The following code trains a GBRT ensemble with 120 trees, then measures the validation error at each stage of training to find the optimal number of trees, and finally trains another GBRT ensemble using the optimal number of trees:

```
import numpy as np
from sklearn.model_selection import train_test_split
from sklearn.metrics import mean_squared_error

X_train, X_val, y_train, y_val = train_test_split(X, y)

gbrt = GradientBoostingRegressor(max_depth=2, n_estimators=120)
gbrt.fit(X_train, y_train)

errors = [mean_squared_error(y_val, y_pred)
          for y_pred in gbrt.staged_predict(X_val)]
bst_n_estimators = np.argmin(errors)

gbrt_best = GradientBoostingRegressor(max_depth=2,n_estimators=bst_n_estimators)
gbrt_best.fit(X_train, y_train)
```

The validation errors are represented on the left of Figure 7-11, and the best model's predictions are represented on the right.

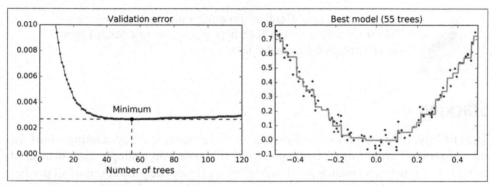

Figure 7-11. Tuning the number of trees using early stopping

It is also possible to implement early stopping by actually stopping training early (instead of training a large number of trees first and then looking back to find the optimal number). You can do so by setting warm_start=True, which makes Scikit-Learn keep existing trees when the fit() method is called, allowing incremental training. The following code stops training when the validation error does not improve for five iterations in a row:

```
gbrt = GradientBoostingRegressor(max_depth=2, warm_start=True)

min_val_error = float("inf")
error_going_up = 0
for n_estimators in range(1, 120):
    gbrt.n_estimators = n_estimators
    gbrt.fit(X_train, y_train)
    y_pred = gbrt.predict(X_val)
    val_error = mean_squared_error(y_val, y_pred)
    if val_error < min_val_error:
        min_val_error = val_error
        error_going_up = 0
    else:
        error_going_up += 1
        if error_going_up == 5:
            break  # early stopping
```

The GradientBoostingRegressor class also supports a subsample hyperparameter, which specifies the fraction of training instances to be used for training each tree. For example, if subsample=0.25, then each tree is trained on 25% of the training instances, selected randomly. As you can probably guess by now, this trades a higher bias for a lower variance. It also speeds up training considerably. This technique is called *Stochastic Gradient Boosting*.

It is possible to use Gradient Boosting with other cost functions. This is controlled by the `loss` hyperparameter (see Scikit-Learn's documentation for more details).

Stacking

The last Ensemble method we will discuss in this chapter is called *stacking* (short for *stacked generalization* (*http://homl.info/29*)).[18] It is based on a simple idea: instead of using trivial functions (such as hard voting) to aggregate the predictions of all predictors in an ensemble, why don't we train a model to perform this aggregation? Figure 7-12 shows such an ensemble performing a regression task on a new instance. Each of the bottom three predictors predicts a different value (3.1, 2.7, and 2.9), and then the final predictor (called a *blender*, or a *meta learner*) takes these predictions as inputs and makes the final prediction (3.0).

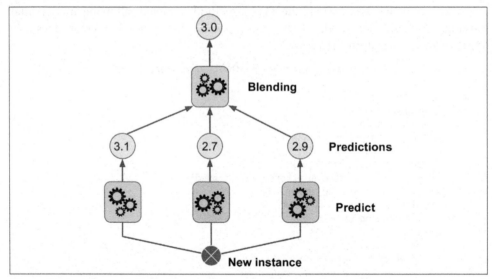

Figure 7-12. Aggregating predictions using a blending predictor

To train the blender, a common approach is to use a hold-out set.[19] Let's see how it works. First, the training set is split in two subsets. The first subset is used to train the predictors in the first layer (see Figure 7-13).

---

18 "Stacked Generalization," D. Wolpert (1992).

19 Alternatively, it is possible to use out-of-fold predictions. In some contexts this is called *stacking*, while using a hold-out set is called *blending*. However, for many people these terms are synonymous.

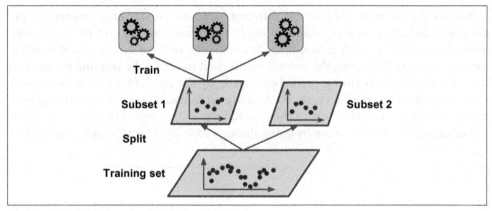

Figure 7-13. Training the first layer

Next, the first layer predictors are used to make predictions on the second (held-out) set (see Figure 7-14). This ensures that the predictions are "clean," since the predictors never saw these instances during training. Now for each instance in the hold-out set there are three predicted values. We can create a new training set using these predicted values as input features (which makes this new training set three-dimensional), and keeping the target values. The blender is trained on this new training set, so it learns to predict the target value given the first layer's predictions.

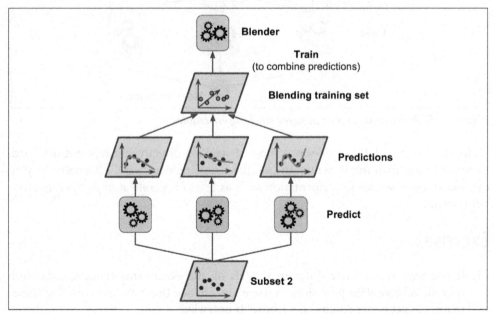

Figure 7-14. Training the blender

It is actually possible to train several different blenders this way (e.g., one using Linear Regression, another using Random Forest Regression, and so on): we get a whole layer of blenders. The trick is to split the training set into three subsets: the first one is used to train the first layer, the second one is used to create the training set used to train the second layer (using predictions made by the predictors of the first layer), and the third one is used to create the training set to train the third layer (using predictions made by the predictors of the second layer). Once this is done, we can make a prediction for a new instance by going through each layer sequentially, as shown in Figure 7-15.

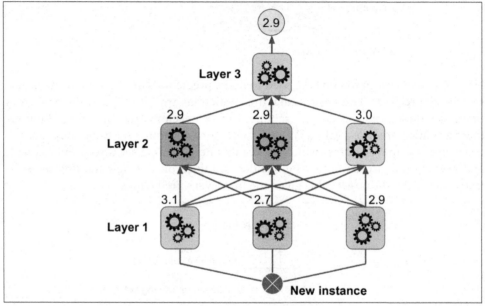

Figure 7-15. Predictions in a multilayer stacking ensemble

Unfortunately, Scikit-Learn does not support stacking directly, but it is not too hard to roll out your own implementation (see the following exercises). Alternatively, you can use an open source implementation such as brew (available at *https://github.com/ viisar/brew*).

Exercises

1. If you have trained five different models on the exact same training data, and they all achieve 95% precision, is there any chance that you can combine these models to get better results? If so, how? If not, why?
2. What is the difference between hard and soft voting classifiers?

3. Is it possible to speed up training of a bagging ensemble by distributing it across multiple servers? What about pasting ensembles, boosting ensembles, random forests, or stacking ensembles?

4. What is the benefit of out-of-bag evaluation?

5. What makes Extra-Trees more random than regular Random Forests? How can this extra randomness help? Are Extra-Trees slower or faster than regular Random Forests?

6. If your AdaBoost ensemble underfits the training data, what hyperparameters should you tweak and how?

7. If your Gradient Boosting ensemble overfits the training set, should you increase or decrease the learning rate?

8. Load the MNIST data (introduced in Chapter 3), and split it into a training set, a validation set, and a test set (e.g., use 50,000 instances for training, 10,000 for validation, and 10,000 for testing). Then train various classifiers, such as a Random Forest classifier, an Extra-Trees classifier, and an SVM. Next, try to combine them into an ensemble that outperforms them all on the validation set, using a soft or hard voting classifier. Once you have found one, try it on the test set. How much better does it perform compared to the individual classifiers?

9. Run the individual classifiers from the previous exercise to make predictions on the validation set, and create a new training set with the resulting predictions: each training instance is a vector containing the set of predictions from all your classifiers for an image, and the target is the image's class. Train a classifier on this new training set. Congratulations, you have just trained a blender, and together with the classifiers they form a stacking ensemble! Now let's evaluate the ensemble on the test set. For each image in the test set, make predictions with all your classifiers, then feed the predictions to the blender to get the ensemble's predictions. How does it compare to the voting classifier you trained earlier?

Solutions to these exercises are available in Appendix A.

## CHAPTER 8

Dimensionality Reduction

Many Machine Learning problems involve thousands or even millions of features for each training instance. Not only does this make training extremely slow, it can also make it much harder to find a good solution, as we will see. This problem is often referred to as the *curse of dimensionality*.

Fortunately, in real-world problems, it is often possible to reduce the number of features considerably, turning an intractable problem into a tractable one. For example, consider the MNIST images (introduced in Chapter 3): the pixels on the image borders are almost always white, so you could completely drop these pixels from the training set without losing much information. Figure 7-6 confirms that these pixels are utterly unimportant for the classification task. Moreover, two neighboring pixels are often highly correlated: if you merge them into a single pixel (e.g., by taking the mean of the two pixel intensities), you will not lose much information.

 Reducing dimensionality does lose some information (just like compressing an image to JPEG can degrade its quality), so even though it will speed up training, it may also make your system perform slightly worse. It also makes your pipelines a bit more complex and thus harder to maintain. So you should first try to train your system with the original data before considering using dimensionality reduction if training is too slow. In some cases, however, reducing the dimensionality of the training data may filter out some noise and unnecessary details and thus result in higher performance (but in general it won't; it will just speed up training).

Apart from speeding up training, dimensionality reduction is also extremely useful for data visualization (or *DataViz*). Reducing the number of dimensions down to two (or three) makes it possible to plot a high-dimensional training set on a graph and often gain some important insights by visually detecting patterns, such as clusters.

In this chapter we will discuss the curse of dimensionality and get a sense of what goes on in high-dimensional space. Then, we will present the two main approaches to dimensionality reduction (projection and Manifold Learning), and we will go through three of the most popular dimensionality reduction techniques: PCA, Kernel PCA, and LLE.

The Curse of Dimensionality

We are so used to living in three dimensions[1] that our intuition fails us when we try to imagine a high-dimensional space. Even a basic 4D hypercube is incredibly hard to picture in our mind (see Figure 8-1), let alone a 200-dimensional ellipsoid bent in a 1,000-dimensional space.

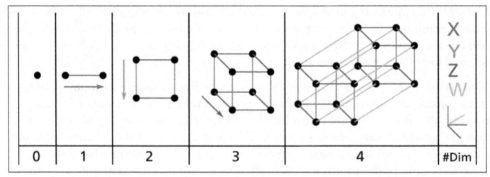

Figure 8-1. Point, segment, square, cube, and tesseract (0D to 4D hypercubes)[2]

It turns out that many things behave very differently in high-dimensional space. For example, if you pick a random point in a unit square (a 1×1 square), it will have only about a 0.4% chance of being located less than 0.001 from a border (in other words, it is very unlikely that a random point will be "extreme" along any dimension). But in a 10,000-dimensional unit hypercube (a $1 \times 1 \times \cdots \times 1$ cube, with ten thousand 1s), this probability is greater than 99.999999%. Most points in a high-dimensional hypercube are very close to the border.[3]

---

1 Well, four dimensions if you count time, and a few more if you are a string theorist.

2 Watch a rotating tesseract projected into 3D space at *http://homl.info/30*. Image by Wikipedia user Nerd-Boy1392 (Creative Commons BY-SA 3.0 (*https://creativecommons.org/licenses/by-sa/3.0/*)). Reproduced from *https://en.wikipedia.org/wiki/Tesseract*.

3 Fun fact: anyone you know is probably an extremist in at least one dimension (e.g., how much sugar they put in their coffee), if you consider enough dimensions.

Here is a more troublesome difference: if you pick two points randomly in a unit square, the distance between these two points will be, on average, roughly 0.52. If you pick two random points in a unit 3D cube, the average distance will be roughly 0.66. But what about two points picked randomly in a 1,000,000-dimensional hypercube? Well, the average distance, believe it or not, will be about 408.25 (roughly $\sqrt{1,000,000/6}$)! This is quite counterintuitive: how can two points be so far apart when they both lie within the same unit hypercube? This fact implies that high-dimensional datasets are at risk of being very sparse: most training instances are likely to be far away from each other. Of course, this also means that a new instance will likely be far away from any training instance, making predictions much less reliable than in lower dimensions, since they will be based on much larger extrapolations. In short, the more dimensions the training set has, the greater the risk of overfitting it.

In theory, one solution to the curse of dimensionality could be to increase the size of the training set to reach a sufficient density of training instances. Unfortunately, in practice, the number of training instances required to reach a given density grows exponentially with the number of dimensions. With just 100 features (much less than in the MNIST problem), you would need more training instances than atoms in the observable universe in order for training instances to be within 0.1 of each other on average, assuming they were spread out uniformly across all dimensions.

Main Approaches for Dimensionality Reduction

Before we dive into specific dimensionality reduction algorithms, let's take a look at the two main approaches to reducing dimensionality: projection and Manifold Learning.

Projection

In most real-world problems, training instances are *not* spread out uniformly across all dimensions. Many features are almost constant, while others are highly correlated (as discussed earlier for MNIST). As a result, all training instances actually lie within (or close to) a much lower-dimensional *subspace* of the high-dimensional space. This sounds very abstract, so let's look at an example. In Figure 8-2 you can see a 3D dataset represented by the circles.

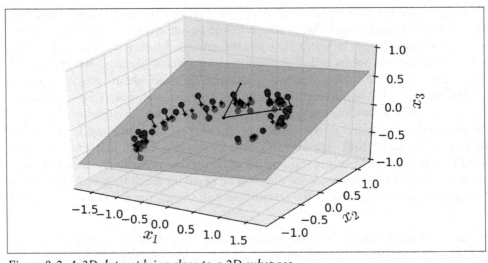

Figure 8-2. A 3D dataset lying close to a 2D subspace

Notice that all training instances lie close to a plane: this is a lower-dimensional (2D) subspace of the high-dimensional (3D) space. Now if we project every training instance perpendicularly onto this subspace (as represented by the short lines connecting the instances to the plane), we get the new 2D dataset shown in Figure 8-3. Ta-da! We have just reduced the dataset's dimensionality from 3D to 2D. Note that the axes correspond to new features z_1 and z_2 (the coordinates of the projections on the plane).

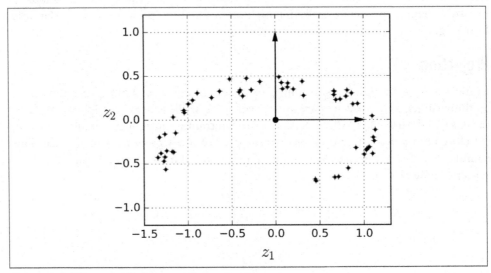

Figure 8-3. The new 2D dataset after projection

However, projection is not always the best approach to dimensionality reduction. In many cases the subspace may twist and turn, such as in the famous *Swiss roll* toy dataset represented in Figure 8-4.

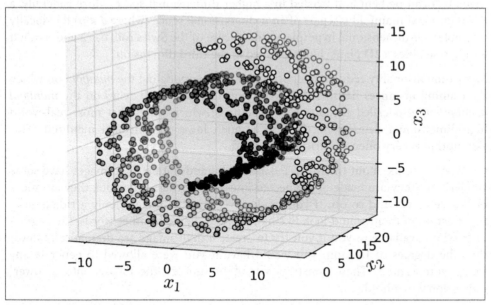

Figure 8-4. Swiss roll dataset

Simply projecting onto a plane (e.g., by dropping x_3) would squash different layers of the Swiss roll together, as shown on the left of Figure 8-5. However, what you really want is to unroll the Swiss roll to obtain the 2D dataset on the right of Figure 8-5.

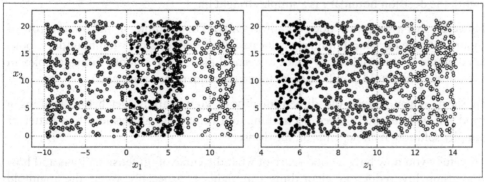

Figure 8-5. Squashing by projecting onto a plane (left) versus unrolling the Swiss roll (right)

Manifold Learning

The Swiss roll is an example of a 2D *manifold*. Put simply, a 2D manifold is a 2D shape that can be bent and twisted in a higher-dimensional space. More generally, a *d*-dimensional manifold is a part of an *n*-dimensional space (where $d < n$) that locally resembles a *d*-dimensional hyperplane. In the case of the Swiss roll, $d = 2$ and $n = 3$: it locally resembles a 2D plane, but it is rolled in the third dimension.

Many dimensionality reduction algorithms work by modeling the *manifold* on which the training instances lie; this is called *Manifold Learning*. It relies on the *manifold assumption*, also called the *manifold hypothesis*, which holds that most real-world high-dimensional datasets lie close to a much lower-dimensional manifold. This assumption is very often empirically observed.

Once again, think about the MNIST dataset: all handwritten digit images have some similarities. They are made of connected lines, the borders are white, they are more or less centered, and so on. If you randomly generated images, only a ridiculously tiny fraction of them would look like handwritten digits. In other words, the degrees of freedom available to you if you try to create a digit image are dramatically lower than the degrees of freedom you would have if you were allowed to generate any image you wanted. These constraints tend to squeeze the dataset into a lower-dimensional manifold.

The manifold assumption is often accompanied by another implicit assumption: that the task at hand (e.g., classification or regression) will be simpler if expressed in the lower-dimensional space of the manifold. For example, in the top row of Figure 8-6 the Swiss roll is split into two classes: in the 3D space (on the left), the decision boundary would be fairly complex, but in the 2D unrolled manifold space (on the right), the decision boundary is a simple straight line.

However, this assumption does not always hold. For example, in the bottom row of Figure 8-6, the decision boundary is located at $x_1 = 5$. This decision boundary looks very simple in the original 3D space (a vertical plane), but it looks more complex in the unrolled manifold (a collection of four independent line segments).

In short, if you reduce the dimensionality of your training set before training a model, it will definitely speed up training, but it may not always lead to a better or simpler solution; it all depends on the dataset.

Hopefully you now have a good sense of what the curse of dimensionality is and how dimensionality reduction algorithms can fight it, especially when the manifold assumption holds. The rest of this chapter will go through some of the most popular algorithms.

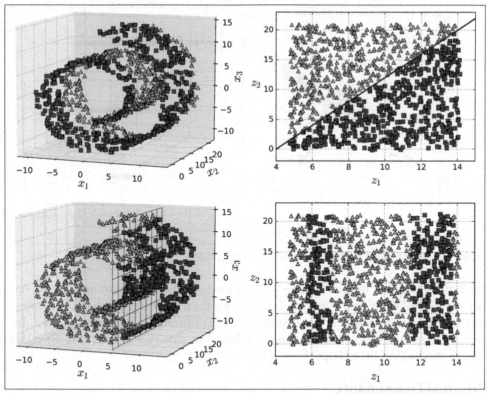

Figure 8-6. The decision boundary may not always be simpler with lower dimensions

PCA

Principal Component Analysis (PCA) is by far the most popular dimensionality reduction algorithm. First it identifies the hyperplane that lies closest to the data, and then it projects the data onto it.

Preserving the Variance

Before you can project the training set onto a lower-dimensional hyperplane, you first need to choose the right hyperplane. For example, a simple 2D dataset is represented on the left of Figure 8-7, along with three different axes (i.e., one-dimensional hyperplanes). On the right is the result of the projection of the dataset onto each of these axes. As you can see, the projection onto the solid line preserves the maximum variance, while the projection onto the dotted line preserves very little variance, and the projection onto the dashed line preserves an intermediate amount of variance.

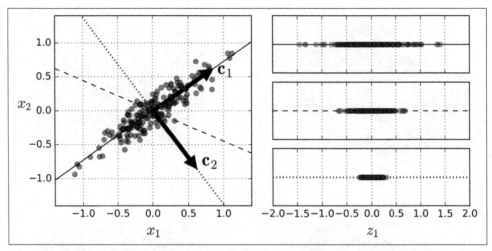

Figure 8-7. Selecting the subspace onto which to project

It seems reasonable to select the axis that preserves the maximum amount of variance, as it will most likely lose less information than the other projections. Another way to justify this choice is that it is the axis that minimizes the mean squared distance between the original dataset and its projection onto that axis. This is the rather simple idea behind PCA (*http://homl.info/31*).[4]

Principal Components

PCA identifies the axis that accounts for the largest amount of variance in the training set. In Figure 8-7, it is the solid line. It also finds a second axis, orthogonal to the first one, that accounts for the largest amount of remaining variance. In this 2D example there is no choice: it is the dotted line. If it were a higher-dimensional dataset, PCA would also find a third axis, orthogonal to both previous axes, and a fourth, a fifth, and so on—as many axes as the number of dimensions in the dataset.

The unit vector that defines the ith axis is called the ith *principal component* (PC). In Figure 8-7, the 1st PC is c_1 and the 2nd PC is c_2. In Figure 8-2 the first two PCs are represented by the orthogonal arrows in the plane, and the third PC would be orthogonal to the plane (pointing up or down).

---

4 "On Lines and Planes of Closest Fit to Systems of Points in Space," K. Pearson (1901).

The direction of the principal components is not stable: if you perturb the training set slightly and run PCA again, some of the new PCs may point in the opposite direction of the original PCs. However, they will generally still lie on the same axes. In some cases, a pair of PCs may even rotate or swap, but the plane they define will generally remain the same.

So how can you find the principal components of a training set? Luckily, there is a standard matrix factorization technique called *Singular Value Decomposition* (SVD) that can decompose the training set matrix $\mathbf{X}$ into the matrix multiplication of three matrices $\mathbf{U} \, \Sigma \, \mathbf{V}^T$, where $\mathbf{V}$ contains all the principal components that we are looking for, as shown in Equation 8-1.

Equation 8-1. Principal components matrix

$$\mathbf{V} = \begin{pmatrix} | & | & & | \\ c_1 & c_2 & \cdots & c_n \\ | & | & & | \end{pmatrix}$$

The following Python code uses NumPy's svd() function to obtain all the principal components of the training set, then extracts the first two PCs:

```
X_centered = X - X.mean(axis=0)
U, s, Vt = np.linalg.svd(X_centered)
c1 = Vt.T[:, 0]
c2 = Vt.T[:, 1]
```

PCA assumes that the dataset is centered around the origin. As we will see, Scikit-Learn's PCA classes take care of centering the data for you. However, if you implement PCA yourself (as in the preceding example), or if you use other libraries, don't forget to center the data first.

Projecting Down to d Dimensions

Once you have identified all the principal components, you can reduce the dimensionality of the dataset down to d dimensions by projecting it onto the hyperplane defined by the first d principal components. Selecting this hyperplane ensures that the projection will preserve as much variance as possible. For example, in Figure 8-2 the 3D dataset is projected down to the 2D plane defined by the first two principal components, preserving a large part of the dataset's variance. As a result, the 2D projection looks very much like the original 3D dataset.

To project the training set onto the hyperplane, you can simply compute the matrix multiplication of the training set matrix $\mathbf{X}$ by the matrix $\mathbf{W}_d$, defined as the matrix containing the first d principal components (i.e., the matrix composed of the first d columns of **V**), as shown in Equation 8-2.

Equation 8-2. Projecting the training set down to d dimensions

$$\mathbf{X}_{d\text{-proj}} = \mathbf{XW}_d$$

The following Python code projects the training set onto the plane defined by the first two principal components:

```
W2 = Vt.T[:, :2]
X2D = X_centered.dot(W2)
```

There you have it! You now know how to reduce the dimensionality of any dataset down to any number of dimensions, while preserving as much variance as possible.

Using Scikit-Learn

Scikit-Learn's PCA class implements PCA using SVD decomposition just like we did before. The following code applies PCA to reduce the dimensionality of the dataset down to two dimensions (note that it automatically takes care of centering the data):

```
from sklearn.decomposition import PCA

pca = PCA(n_components = 2)
X2D = pca.fit_transform(X)
```

After fitting the PCA transformer to the dataset, you can access the principal components using the components_ variable (note that it contains the PCs as horizontal vectors, so, for example, the first principal component is equal to pca.components_.T[:, 0]).

Explained Variance Ratio

Another very useful piece of information is the *explained variance ratio* of each principal component, available via the explained_variance_ratio_ variable. It indicates the proportion of the dataset's variance that lies along the axis of each principal component. For example, let's look at the explained variance ratios of the first two components of the 3D dataset represented in Figure 8-2:

```
>>> pca.explained_variance_ratio_
array([ 0.84248607,  0.14631839])
```

This tells you that 84.2% of the dataset's variance lies along the first axis, and 14.6% lies along the second axis. This leaves less than 1.2% for the third axis, so it is reasonable to assume that it probably carries little information.

Choosing the Right Number of Dimensions

Instead of arbitrarily choosing the number of dimensions to reduce down to, it is generally preferable to choose the number of dimensions that add up to a sufficiently large portion of the variance (e.g., 95%). Unless, of course, you are reducing dimensionality for data visualization—in that case you will generally want to reduce the dimensionality down to 2 or 3.

The following code computes PCA without reducing dimensionality, then computes the minimum number of dimensions required to preserve 95% of the training set's variance:

```
pca = PCA()
pca.fit(X_train)
cumsum = np.cumsum(pca.explained_variance_ratio_)
d = np.argmax(cumsum >= 0.95) + 1
```

You could then set n_components=d and run PCA again. However, there is a much better option: instead of specifying the number of principal components you want to preserve, you can set n_components to be a float between 0.0 and 1.0, indicating the ratio of variance you wish to preserve:

```
pca = PCA(n_components=0.95)
X_reduced = pca.fit_transform(X_train)
```

Yet another option is to plot the explained variance as a function of the number of dimensions (simply plot cumsum; see Figure 8-8). There will usually be an elbow in the curve, where the explained variance stops growing fast. You can think of this as the intrinsic dimensionality of the dataset. In this case, you can see that reducing the dimensionality down to about 100 dimensions wouldn't lose too much explained variance.

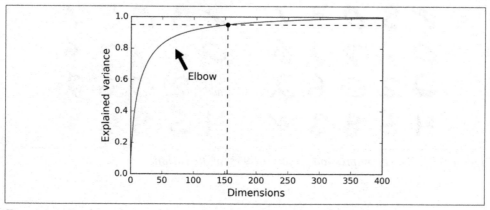

Figure 8-8. Explained variance as a function of the number of dimensions

PCA for Compression

Obviously after dimensionality reduction, the training set takes up much less space. For example, try applying PCA to the MNIST dataset while preserving 95% of its variance. You should find that each instance will have just over 150 features, instead of the original 784 features. So while most of the variance is preserved, the dataset is now less than 20% of its original size! This is a reasonable compression ratio, and you can see how this can speed up a classification algorithm (such as an SVM classifier) tremendously.

It is also possible to decompress the reduced dataset back to 784 dimensions by applying the inverse transformation of the PCA projection. Of course this won't give you back the original data, since the projection lost a bit of information (within the 5% variance that was dropped), but it will likely be quite close to the original data. The mean squared distance between the original data and the reconstructed data (compressed and then decompressed) is called the *reconstruction error*. For example, the following code compresses the MNIST dataset down to 154 dimensions, then uses the `inverse_transform()` method to decompress it back to 784 dimensions. Figure 8-9 shows a few digits from the original training set (on the left), and the corresponding digits after compression and decompression. You can see that there is a slight image quality loss, but the digits are still mostly intact.

```
pca = PCA(n_components = 154)
X_reduced = pca.fit_transform(X_train)
X_recovered = pca.inverse_transform(X_reduced)
```

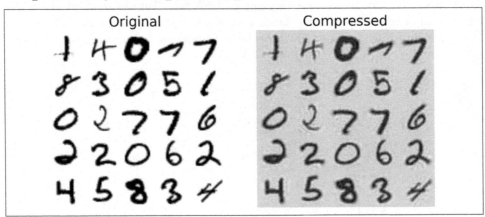

Figure 8-9. MNIST compression preserving 95% of the variance

The equation of the inverse transformation is shown in Equation 8-3.

Equation 8-3. PCA inverse transformation, back to the original number of dimensions

$$\mathbf{X}_{recovered} = \mathbf{X}_{d\text{-proj}} \mathbf{W}_d{}^T$$

Incremental PCA

One problem with the preceding implementation of PCA is that it requires the whole training set to fit in memory in order for the SVD algorithm to run. Fortunately, *Incremental PCA* (IPCA) algorithms have been developed: you can split the training set into mini-batches and feed an IPCA algorithm one mini-batch at a time. This is useful for large training sets, and also to apply PCA online (i.e., on the fly, as new instances arrive).

The following code splits the MNIST dataset into 100 mini-batches (using NumPy's `array_split()` function) and feeds them to Scikit-Learn's `IncrementalPCA` class (*http://homl.info/32*)[5] to reduce the dimensionality of the MNIST dataset down to 154 dimensions (just like before). Note that you must call the `partial_fit()` method with each mini-batch rather than the `fit()` method with the whole training set:

```
from sklearn.decomposition import IncrementalPCA

n_batches = 100
inc_pca = IncrementalPCA(n_components=154)
for X_batch in np.array_split(X_train, n_batches):
    inc_pca.partial_fit(X_batch)

X_reduced = inc_pca.transform(X_train)
```

Alternatively, you can use NumPy's `memmap` class, which allows you to manipulate a large array stored in a binary file on disk as if it were entirely in memory; the class loads only the data it needs in memory, when it needs it. Since the `IncrementalPCA` class uses only a small part of the array at any given time, the memory usage remains under control. This makes it possible to call the usual `fit()` method, as you can see in the following code:

```
X_mm = np.memmap(filename, dtype="float32", mode="readonly", shape=(m, n))

batch_size = m // n_batches
inc_pca = IncrementalPCA(n_components=154, batch_size=batch_size)
inc_pca.fit(X_mm)
```

---

5 Scikit-Learn uses the algorithm described in "Incremental Learning for Robust Visual Tracking," D. Ross et al. (2007).

Randomized PCA

Scikit-Learn offers yet another option to perform PCA, called *Randomized PCA*. This is a stochastic algorithm that quickly finds an approximation of the first d principal components. Its computational complexity is $O(m \times d^2) + O(d^3)$, instead of $O(m \times n^2) + O(n^3)$, so it is dramatically faster than the previous algorithms when d is much smaller than n.

```
rnd_pca = PCA(n_components=154, svd_solver="randomized")
X_reduced = rnd_pca.fit_transform(X_train)
```

Kernel PCA

In Chapter 5 we discussed the kernel trick, a mathematical technique that implicitly maps instances into a very high-dimensional space (called the *feature space*), enabling nonlinear classification and regression with Support Vector Machines. Recall that a linear decision boundary in the high-dimensional feature space corresponds to a complex nonlinear decision boundary in the *original space*.

It turns out that the same trick can be applied to PCA, making it possible to perform complex nonlinear projections for dimensionality reduction. This is called *Kernel PCA* (kPCA) (*http://homl.info/33*).[6] It is often good at preserving clusters of instances after projection, or sometimes even unrolling datasets that lie close to a twisted manifold.

For example, the following code uses Scikit-Learn's `KernelPCA` class to perform kPCA with an RBF kernel (see Chapter 5 for more details about the RBF kernel and the other kernels):

```
from sklearn.decomposition import KernelPCA

rbf_pca = KernelPCA(n_components = 2, kernel="rbf", gamma=0.04)
X_reduced = rbf_pca.fit_transform(X)
```

Figure 8-10 shows the Swiss roll, reduced to two dimensions using a linear kernel (equivalent to simply using the `PCA` class), an RBF kernel, and a sigmoid kernel (Logistic).

---

6 "Kernel Principal Component Analysis," B. Schölkopf, A. Smola, K. Müller (1999).

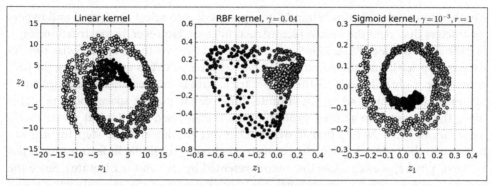

Figure 8-10. Swiss roll reduced to 2D using kPCA with various kernels

Selecting a Kernel and Tuning Hyperparameters

As kPCA is an unsupervised learning algorithm, there is no obvious performance measure to help you select the best kernel and hyperparameter values. However, dimensionality reduction is often a preparation step for a supervised learning task (e.g., classification), so you can simply use grid search to select the kernel and hyperparameters that lead to the best performance on that task. For example, the following code creates a two-step pipeline, first reducing dimensionality to two dimensions using kPCA, then applying Logistic Regression for classification. Then it uses Grid SearchCV to find the best kernel and gamma value for kPCA in order to get the best classification accuracy at the end of the pipeline:

```
from sklearn.model_selection import GridSearchCV
from sklearn.linear_model import LogisticRegression
from sklearn.pipeline import Pipeline

clf = Pipeline([
        ("kpca", KernelPCA(n_components=2)),
        ("log_reg", LogisticRegression())
    ])

param_grid = [{
        "kpca__gamma": np.linspace(0.03, 0.05, 10),
        "kpca__kernel": ["rbf", "sigmoid"]
    }]

grid_search = GridSearchCV(clf, param_grid, cv=3)
grid_search.fit(X, y)
```

The best kernel and hyperparameters are then available through the `best_params_` variable:

```
>>> print(grid_search.best_params_)
{'kpca__gamma': 0.043333333333333335, 'kpca__kernel': 'rbf'}
```

Another approach, this time entirely unsupervised, is to select the kernel and hyper-parameters that yield the lowest reconstruction error. However, reconstruction is not as easy as with linear PCA. Here's why. Figure 8-11 shows the original Swiss roll 3D dataset (top left), and the resulting 2D dataset after kPCA is applied using an RBF kernel (top right). Thanks to the kernel trick, this is mathematically equivalent to mapping the training set to an infinite-dimensional feature space (bottom right) using the *feature map* φ, then projecting the transformed training set down to 2D using linear PCA. Notice that if we could invert the linear PCA step for a given instance in the reduced space, the reconstructed point would lie in feature space, not in the original space (e.g., like the one represented by an x in the diagram). Since the feature space is infinite-dimensional, we cannot compute the reconstructed point, and therefore we cannot compute the true reconstruction error. Fortunately, it is possible to find a point in the original space that would map close to the reconstructed point. This is called the reconstruction *pre-image*. Once you have this pre-image, you can measure its squared distance to the original instance. You can then select the kernel and hyperparameters that minimize this reconstruction pre-image error.

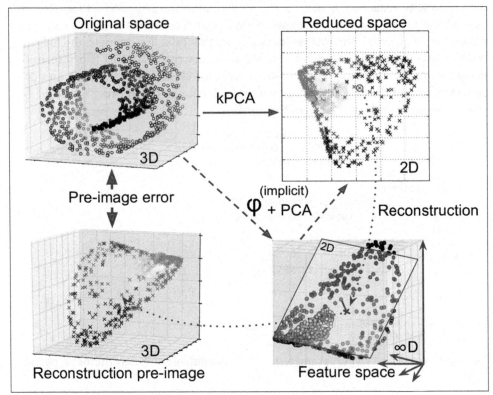

Figure 8-11. Kernel PCA and the reconstruction pre-image error

You may be wondering how to perform this reconstruction. One solution is to train a supervised regression model, with the projected instances as the training set and the original instances as the targets. Scikit-Learn will do this automatically if you set `fit_inverse_transform=True`, as shown in the following code:[7]

```
rbf_pca = KernelPCA(n_components = 2, kernel="rbf", gamma=0.0433,
                    fit_inverse_transform=True)
X_reduced = rbf_pca.fit_transform(X)
X_preimage = rbf_pca.inverse_transform(X_reduced)
```

By default, `fit_inverse_transform=False` and `KernelPCA` has no `inverse_transform()` method. This method only gets created when you set `fit_inverse_transform=True`.

You can then compute the reconstruction pre-image error:

```
>>> from sklearn.metrics import mean_squared_error
>>> mean_squared_error(X, X_preimage)
32.786308795766132
```

Now you can use grid search with cross-validation to find the kernel and hyperparameters that minimize this pre-image reconstruction error.

LLE

Locally Linear Embedding (*http://homl.info/35*) (LLE)[8] is another very powerful *nonlinear dimensionality reduction* (NLDR) technique. It is a Manifold Learning technique that does not rely on projections like the previous algorithms. In a nutshell, LLE works by first measuring how each training instance linearly relates to its closest neighbors (c.n.), and then looking for a low-dimensional representation of the training set where these local relationships are best preserved (more details shortly). This makes it particularly good at unrolling twisted manifolds, especially when there is not too much noise.

For example, the following code uses Scikit-Learn's `LocallyLinearEmbedding` class to unroll the Swiss roll. The resulting 2D dataset is shown in Figure 8-12. As you can see, the Swiss roll is completely unrolled and the distances between instances are locally well preserved. However, distances are not preserved on a larger scale: the left

---

7 Scikit-Learn uses the algorithm based on Kernel Ridge Regression described in Gokhan H. Bakır, Jason Weston, and Bernhard Scholkopf, "Learning to Find Pre-images" (*http://homl.info/34*) (Tubingen, Germany: Max Planck Institute for Biological Cybernetics, 2004).

8 "Nonlinear Dimensionality Reduction by Locally Linear Embedding," S. Roweis, L. Saul (2000).

part of the unrolled Swiss roll is squeezed, while the right part is stretched. Nevertheless, LLE did a pretty good job at modeling the manifold.

```python
from sklearn.manifold import LocallyLinearEmbedding

lle = LocallyLinearEmbedding(n_components=2, n_neighbors=10)
X_reduced = lle.fit_transform(X)
```

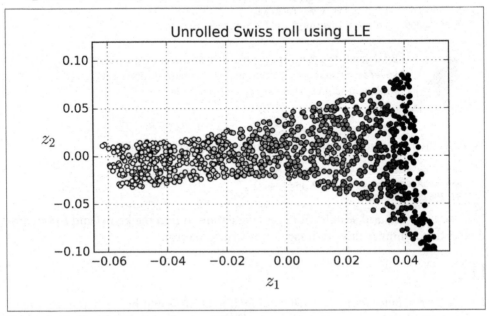

Figure 8-12. Unrolled Swiss roll using LLE

Here's how LLE works: first, for each training instance $\mathbf{x}^{(i)}$, the algorithm identifies its
k closest neighbors (in the preceding code $k = 10$), then tries to reconstruct $\mathbf{x}^{(i)}$ as a
linear function of these neighbors. More specifically, it finds the weights $w_{i,j}$ such that
the squared distance between $\mathbf{x}^{(i)}$ and $\sum_{j=1}^{m} w_{i,j} \mathbf{x}^{(j)}$ is as small as possible, assuming $w_{i,j}$
$= 0$ if $\mathbf{x}^{(j)}$ is not one of the k closest neighbors of $\mathbf{x}^{(i)}$. Thus the first step of LLE is the
constrained optimization problem described in Equation 8-4, where $\mathbf{W}$ is the weight
matrix containing all the weights $w_{i,j}$. The second constraint simply normalizes the
weights for each training instance $\mathbf{x}^{(i)}$.

Equation 8-4. LLE step 1: linearly modeling local relationships

$$\widehat{\mathbf{W}} = \underset{\mathbf{W}}{\mathrm{argmin}} \sum_{i=1}^{m} \left(\mathbf{x}^{(i)} - \sum_{j=1}^{m} w_{i,j} \mathbf{x}^{(j)} \right)^2$$

$$\text{subject to} \begin{cases} w_{i,j} = 0 & \text{if } \mathbf{x}^{(j)} \text{ is not one of the } k \text{ c.n. of } \mathbf{x}^{(i)} \\ \sum_{j=1}^{m} w_{i,j} = 1 & \text{for } i = 1, 2, \cdots, m \end{cases}$$

After this step, the weight matrix $\widehat{\mathbf{W}}$ (containing the weights $\hat{w}_{i,j}$) encodes the local linear relationships between the training instances. Now the second step is to map the training instances into a d-dimensional space (where $d < n$) while preserving these local relationships as much as possible. If $\mathbf{z}^{(i)}$ is the image of $\mathbf{x}^{(i)}$ in this d-dimensional space, then we want the squared distance between $\mathbf{z}^{(i)}$ and $\sum_{j=1}^{m} \hat{w}_{i,j} \mathbf{z}^{(j)}$ to be as small as possible. This idea leads to the unconstrained optimization problem described in Equation 8-5. It looks very similar to the first step, but instead of keeping the instances fixed and finding the optimal weights, we are doing the reverse: keeping the weights fixed and finding the optimal position of the instances' images in the low-dimensional space. Note that $\mathbf{Z}$ is the matrix containing all $\mathbf{z}^{(i)}$.

Equation 8-5. LLE step 2: reducing dimensionality while preserving relationships

$$\widehat{\mathbf{Z}} = \underset{\mathbf{Z}}{\mathrm{argmin}} \sum_{i=1}^{m} \left(\mathbf{z}^{(i)} - \sum_{j=1}^{m} \hat{w}_{i,j} \mathbf{z}^{(j)} \right)^2$$

Scikit-Learn's LLE implementation has the following computational complexity: $O(m \log(m)n \log(k))$ for finding the k nearest neighbors, $O(mnk^3)$ for optimizing the weights, and $O(dm^2)$ for constructing the low-dimensional representations. Unfortunately, the m^2 in the last term makes this algorithm scale poorly to very large datasets.

Other Dimensionality Reduction Techniques

There are many other dimensionality reduction techniques, several of which are available in Scikit-Learn. Here are some of the most popular:

- *Multidimensional Scaling* (MDS) reduces dimensionality while trying to preserve the distances between the instances (see Figure 8-13).

- *Isomap* creates a graph by connecting each instance to its nearest neighbors, then reduces dimensionality while trying to preserve the *geodesic distances*[9] between the instances.

- *t-Distributed Stochastic Neighbor Embedding* (t-SNE) reduces dimensionality while trying to keep similar instances close and dissimilar instances apart. It is mostly used for visualization, in particular to visualize clusters of instances in high-dimensional space (e.g., to visualize the MNIST images in 2D).

- *Linear Discriminant Analysis* (LDA) is actually a classification algorithm, but during training it learns the most discriminative axes between the classes, and these axes can then be used to define a hyperplane onto which to project the data. The benefit is that the projection will keep classes as far apart as possible, so LDA is a good technique to reduce dimensionality before running another classification algorithm such as an SVM classifier.

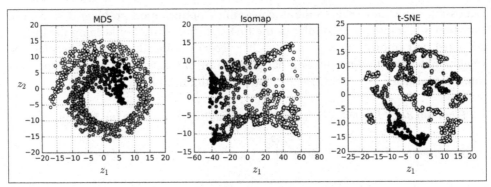

Figure 8-13. Reducing the Swiss roll to 2D using various techniques

Exercises

1. What are the main motivations for reducing a dataset's dimensionality? What are the main drawbacks?

2. What is the curse of dimensionality?

3. Once a dataset's dimensionality has been reduced, is it possible to reverse the operation? If so, how? If not, why?

4. Can PCA be used to reduce the dimensionality of a highly nonlinear dataset?

5. Suppose you perform PCA on a 1,000-dimensional dataset, setting the explained variance ratio to 95%. How many dimensions will the resulting dataset have?

---

9 The geodesic distance between two nodes in a graph is the number of nodes on the shortest path between these nodes.

6. In what cases would you use vanilla PCA, Incremental PCA, Randomized PCA, or Kernel PCA?

7. How can you evaluate the performance of a dimensionality reduction algorithm on your dataset?

8. Does it make any sense to chain two different dimensionality reduction algorithms?

9. Load the MNIST dataset (introduced in Chapter 3) and split it into a training set and a test set (take the first 60,000 instances for training, and the remaining 10,000 for testing). Train a Random Forest classifier on the dataset and time how long it takes, then evaluate the resulting model on the test set. Next, use PCA to reduce the dataset's dimensionality, with an explained variance ratio of 95%. Train a new Random Forest classifier on the reduced dataset and see how long it takes. Was training much faster? Next evaluate the classifier on the test set: how does it compare to the previous classifier?

10. Use t-SNE to reduce the MNIST dataset down to two dimensions and plot the result using Matplotlib. You can use a scatterplot using 10 different colors to represent each image's target class. Alternatively, you can write colored digits at the location of each instance, or even plot scaled-down versions of the digit images themselves (if you plot all digits, the visualization will be too cluttered, so you should either draw a random sample or plot an instance only if no other instance has already been plotted at a close distance). You should get a nice visualization with well-separated clusters of digits. Try using other dimensionality reduction algorithms such as PCA, LLE, or MDS and compare the resulting visualizations.

Solutions to these exercises are available in Appendix A.

## PART II

Neural Networks and Deep Learning

PART III

Neural Networks and Deep Learning

## CHAPTER 9

Up and Running with TensorFlow

TensorFlow is a powerful open source software library for numerical computation, particularly well suited and fine-tuned for large-scale Machine Learning. Its basic principle is simple: you first define in Python a graph of computations to perform (for example, the one in Figure 9-1), and then TensorFlow takes that graph and runs it efficiently using optimized C++ code.

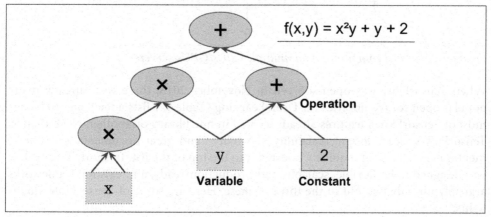

Figure 9-1. A simple computation graph

Most importantly, it is possible to break up the graph into several chunks and run them in parallel across multiple CPUs or GPUs (as shown in Figure 9-2). TensorFlow also supports distributed computing, so you can train colossal neural networks on humongous training sets in a reasonable amount of time by splitting the computations across hundreds of servers (see Chapter 12). TensorFlow can train a network with millions of parameters on a training set composed of billions of instances with millions of features each. This should come as no surprise, since TensorFlow was developed by the Google Brain team and it powers many of Google's large-scale services, such as Google Cloud Speech, Google Photos, and Google Search.

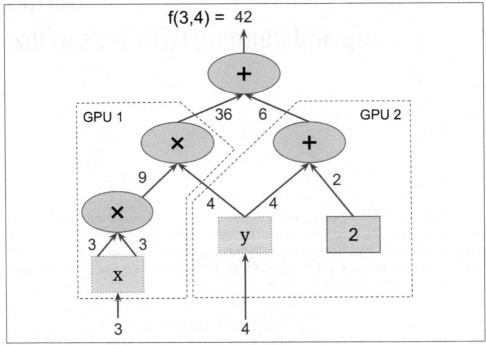

Figure 9-2. Parallel computation on multiple CPUs/GPUs/servers

When TensorFlow was open-sourced in November 2015, there were already many popular open source libraries for Deep Learning (Table 9-1 lists a few), and to be fair most of TensorFlow's features already existed in one library or another. Nevertheless, TensorFlow's clean design, scalability, flexibility,[1] and great documentation (not to mention Google's name) quickly boosted it to the top of the list. In short, TensorFlow was designed to be flexible, scalable, and production-ready, and existing frameworks arguably hit only two out of the three of these. Here are some of TensorFlow's highlights:

- It runs not only on Windows, Linux, and macOS, but also on mobile devices, including both iOS and Android.

---

1 TensorFlow is not limited to neural networks or even Machine Learning; you could run quantum physics simulations if you wanted.

- It provides a very simple Python API called *TF.Learn*[2] (`tensorflow.con trib.learn`), compatible with Scikit-Learn. As you will see, you can use it to train various types of neural networks in just a few lines of code. It was previously an independent project called *Scikit Flow* (or *skflow*).

- It also provides another simple API called *TF-slim* (`tensorflow.contrib.slim`) to simplify building, training, and evaluating neural networks.

- Several other high-level APIs have been built independently on top of Tensor-Flow, such as Keras (*http://keras.io*) (now available in `tensorflow.con trib.keras`) or Pretty Tensor (*https://github.com/google/prettytensor/*).

- Its main Python API offers much more flexibility (at the cost of higher complexity) to create all sorts of computations, including any neural network architecture you can think of.

- It includes highly efficient C++ implementations of many ML operations, particularly those needed to build neural networks. There is also a C++ API to define your own high-performance operations.

- It provides several advanced optimization nodes to search for the parameters that minimize a cost function. These are very easy to use since TensorFlow automatically takes care of computing the gradients of the functions you define. This is called *automatic differentiating* (or *autodiff*).

- It also comes with a great visualization tool called *TensorBoard* that allows you to browse through the computation graph, view learning curves, and more.

- Google also launched a cloud service to run TensorFlow graphs (*https://cloud.google.com/ml-engine/*).

- Last but not least, it has a dedicated team of passionate and helpful developers, and a growing community contributing to improving it. It is one of the most popular open source projects on GitHub, and more and more great projects are being built on top of it (for examples, check out the resources page on *https://www.tensorflow.org/*, or *https://github.com/jtoy/awesome-tensorflow*). To ask technical questions, you should use *http://stackoverflow.com/* and tag your question with `"tensorflow"`. You can file bugs and feature requests through GitHub. For general discussions, join the Google group (*http://homl.info/41*).

In this chapter, we will go through the basics of TensorFlow, from installation to creating, running, saving, and visualizing simple computational graphs. Mastering these basics is important before you build your first neural network (which we will do in the next chapter).

---

2 Not to be confused with the TFLearn library, which is an independent project.

Table 9-1. Open source Deep Learning libraries (not an exhaustive list)

Library	API	Platforms	Started by	Year
Caffe	Python, C++, Matlab	Linux, macOS, Windows	Y. Jia, UC Berkeley (BVLC)	2013
Deeplearning4j	Java, Scala, Clojure	Linux, macOS, Windows, Android	A. Gibson, J.Patterson	2014
H20	Python, R	Linux, macOS, Windows	H20.ai	2014
MXNet	Python, C++, others	Linux, macOS, Windows, iOS, Android	DMLC	2015
TensorFlow	Python, C++	Linux, macOS, Windows, iOS, Android	Google	2015
Theano	Python	Linux, macOS, iOS	University of Montreal	2010
Torch	C++, Lua	Linux, macOS, iOS, Android	R. Collobert, K. Kavukcuoglu, C. Farabet	2002

Installation

Let's get started! Assuming you installed Jupyter and Scikit-Learn by following the installation instructions in Chapter 2, you can simply use pip to install TensorFlow. If you created an isolated environment using virtualenv, you first need to activate it:

```
$ cd $ML_PATH                # Your ML working directory (e.g., $HOME/ml)
$ source env/bin/activate
```

Next, install TensorFlow (if you are not using a virtualenv, you will need administrator rights, or to add the --user option):

```
$ pip3 install --upgrade tensorflow
```

For GPU support, you need to install tensorflow-gpu instead of tensorflow. See Chapter 12 for more details.

To test your installation, type the following command. It should output the version of TensorFlow you installed.

```
$ python3 -c 'import tensorflow; print(tensorflow.__version__)'
1.3.0
```

Creating Your First Graph and Running It in a Session

The following code creates the graph represented in Figure 9-1:

```
import tensorflow as tf

x = tf.Variable(3, name="x")
y = tf.Variable(4, name="y")
f = x*x*y + y + 2
```

That's all there is to it! The most important thing to understand is that this code does not actually perform any computation, even though it looks like it does (especially the last line). It just creates a computation graph. In fact, even the variables are not initialized yet. To evaluate this graph, you need to open a TensorFlow *session* and use it to initialize the variables and evaluate f. A TensorFlow session takes care of placing the operations onto *devices* such as CPUs and GPUs and running them, and it holds all the variable values.[3] The following code creates a session, initializes the variables, and evaluates, and f then closes the session (which frees up resources):

```
>>> sess = tf.Session()
>>> sess.run(x.initializer)
>>> sess.run(y.initializer)
>>> result = sess.run(f)
>>> print(result)
42
>>> sess.close()
```

Having to repeat sess.run() all the time is a bit cumbersome, but fortunately there is a better way:

```
with tf.Session() as sess:
    x.initializer.run()
    y.initializer.run()
    result = f.eval()
```

Inside the with block, the session is set as the default session. Calling x.initial izer.run() is equivalent to calling tf.get_default_session().run(x.initial izer), and similarly f.eval() is equivalent to calling tf.get_default_session().run(f). This makes the code easier to read. Moreover, the session is automatically closed at the end of the block.

Instead of manually running the initializer for every single variable, you can use the global_variables_initializer() function. Note that it does not actually perform the initialization immediately, but rather creates a node in the graph that will initialize all variables when it is run:

```
init = tf.global_variables_initializer()  # prepare an init node

with tf.Session() as sess:
    init.run()  # actually initialize all the variables
    result = f.eval()
```

Inside Jupyter or within a Python shell you may prefer to create an InteractiveSes sion. The only difference from a regular Session is that when an InteractiveSes sion is created it automatically sets itself as the default session, so you don't need a

---

3 In distributed TensorFlow, variable values are stored on the servers instead of the session, as we will see in Chapter 12.

with block (but you do need to close the session manually when you are done with it):

```
>>> sess = tf.InteractiveSession()
>>> init.run()
>>> result = f.eval()
>>> print(result)
42
>>> sess.close()
```

A TensorFlow program is typically split into two parts: the first part builds a computation graph (this is called the *construction phase*), and the second part runs it (this is the *execution phase*). The construction phase typically builds a computation graph representing the ML model and the computations required to train it. The execution phase generally runs a loop that evaluates a training step repeatedly (for example, one step per mini-batch), gradually improving the model parameters. We will go through an example shortly.

Managing Graphs

Any node you create is automatically added to the default graph:

```
>>> x1 = tf.Variable(1)
>>> x1.graph is tf.get_default_graph()
True
```

In most cases this is fine, but sometimes you may want to manage multiple independent graphs. You can do this by creating a new Graph and temporarily making it the default graph inside a with block, like so:

```
>>> graph = tf.Graph()
>>> with graph.as_default():
...     x2 = tf.Variable(2)
...
>>> x2.graph is graph
True
>>> x2.graph is tf.get_default_graph()
False
```

 In Jupyter (or in a Python shell), it is common to run the same commands more than once while you are experimenting. As a result, you may end up with a default graph containing many duplicate nodes. One solution is to restart the Jupyter kernel (or the Python shell), but a more convenient solution is to just reset the default graph by running tf.reset_default_graph().

Lifecycle of a Node Value

When you evaluate a node, TensorFlow automatically determines the set of nodes that it depends on and it evaluates these nodes first. For example, consider the following code:

```
w = tf.constant(3)
x = w + 2
y = x + 5
z = x * 3

with tf.Session() as sess:
    print(y.eval())  # 10
    print(z.eval())  # 15
```

First, this code defines a very simple graph. Then it starts a session and runs the graph to evaluate y: TensorFlow automatically detects that y depends on x, which depends on w, so it first evaluates w, then x, then y, and returns the value of y. Finally, the code runs the graph to evaluate z. Once again, TensorFlow detects that it must first evaluate w and x. It is important to note that it will *not* reuse the result of the previous evaluation of w and x. In short, the preceding code evaluates w and x twice.

All node values are dropped between graph runs, except variable values, which are maintained by the session across graph runs (queues and readers also maintain some state, as we will see in Chapter 12). A variable starts its life when its initializer is run, and it ends when the session is closed.

If you want to evaluate y and z efficiently, without evaluating w and x twice as in the previous code, you must ask TensorFlow to evaluate both y and z in just one graph run, as shown in the following code:

```
with tf.Session() as sess:
    y_val, z_val = sess.run([y, z])
    print(y_val)  # 10
    print(z_val)  # 15
```

> In single-process TensorFlow, multiple sessions do not share any state, even if they reuse the same graph (each session would have its own copy of every variable). In distributed TensorFlow (see Chapter 12), variable state is stored on the servers, not in the sessions, so multiple sessions can share the same variables.

Linear Regression with TensorFlow

TensorFlow operations (also called *ops* for short) can take any number of inputs and produce any number of outputs. For example, the addition and multiplication ops each take two inputs and produce one output. Constants and variables take no input (they are called *source ops*). The inputs and outputs are multidimensional arrays, called *tensors* (hence the name "tensor flow"). Just like NumPy arrays, tensors have a type and a shape. In fact, in the Python API tensors are simply represented by NumPy ndarrays. They typically contain floats, but you can also use them to carry strings (arbitrary byte arrays).

In the examples so far, the tensors just contained a single scalar value, but you can of course perform computations on arrays of any shape. For example, the following code manipulates 2D arrays to perform Linear Regression on the California housing dataset (introduced in Chapter 2). It starts by fetching the dataset; then it adds an extra bias input feature ($x_0 = 1$) to all training instances (it does so using NumPy so it runs immediately); then it creates two TensorFlow constant nodes, X and y, to hold this data and the targets,[4] and it uses some of the matrix operations provided by Tensor-Flow to define theta. These matrix functions—transpose(), matmul(), and matrix_inverse()—are self-explanatory, but as usual they do not perform any computations immediately; instead, they create nodes in the graph that will perform them when the graph is run. You may recognize that the definition of theta corresponds to the Normal Equation ($\theta = (\mathbf{X}^T \mathbf{X})^{-1} \mathbf{X}^T \mathbf{y}$; see Chapter 4). Finally, the code creates a session and uses it to evaluate theta.

```
import numpy as np
from sklearn.datasets import fetch_california_housing

housing = fetch_california_housing()
m, n = housing.data.shape
housing_data_plus_bias = np.c_[np.ones((m, 1)), housing.data]

X = tf.constant(housing_data_plus_bias, dtype=tf.float32, name="X")
y = tf.constant(housing.target.reshape(-1, 1), dtype=tf.float32, name="y")
XT = tf.transpose(X)
theta = tf.matmul(tf.matmul(tf.matrix_inverse(tf.matmul(XT, X)), XT), y)

with tf.Session() as sess:
    theta_value = theta.eval()
```

The main benefit of this code versus computing the Normal Equation directly using NumPy is that TensorFlow will automatically run this on your GPU card if you have one (provided you installed TensorFlow with GPU support, of course; see Chapter 12 for more details).

---

4 Note that housing.target is a 1D array, but we need to reshape it to a column vector to compute theta. Recall that NumPy's reshape() function accepts –1 (meaning "unspecified") for one of the dimensions: that dimension will be computed based on the array's length and the remaining dimensions.

Implementing Gradient Descent

Let's try using Batch Gradient Descent (introduced in Chapter 4) instead of the Normal Equation. First we will do this by manually computing the gradients, then we will use TensorFlow's autodiff feature to let TensorFlow compute the gradients automatically, and finally we will use a couple of TensorFlow's out-of-the-box optimizers.

 When using Gradient Descent, remember that it is important to first normalize the input feature vectors, or else training may be much slower. You can do this using TensorFlow, NumPy, Scikit-Learn's StandardScaler, or any other solution you prefer. The following code assumes that this normalization has already been done.

Manually Computing the Gradients

The following code should be fairly self-explanatory, except for a few new elements:

- The random_uniform() function creates a node in the graph that will generate a tensor containing random values, given its shape and value range, much like NumPy's rand() function.

- The reduce_mean() function creates a node in the graph that will compute the mean of its input tensor, just like NumPy's mean() function.

- The assign() function creates a node that will assign a new value to a variable. In this case, it implements the Batch Gradient Descent step $\theta^{(next\ step)} = \theta - \eta \nabla_{\theta} MSE(\theta)$.

- The main loop executes the training step over and over again (n_epochs times), and every 100 iterations it prints out the current Mean Squared Error (mse). You should see the MSE go down at every iteration.

```
n_epochs = 1000
learning_rate = 0.01

X = tf.constant(scaled_housing_data_plus_bias, dtype=tf.float32, name="X")
y = tf.constant(housing.target.reshape(-1, 1), dtype=tf.float32, name="y")
theta = tf.Variable(tf.random_uniform([n + 1, 1], -1.0, 1.0), name="theta")
y_pred = tf.matmul(X, theta, name="predictions")
error = y_pred - y
mse = tf.reduce_mean(tf.square(error), name="mse")
gradients = 2/m * tf.matmul(tf.transpose(X), error)
training_op = tf.assign(theta, theta - learning_rate * gradients)

init = tf.global_variables_initializer()

with tf.Session() as sess:
```

```
sess.run(init)

for epoch in range(n_epochs):
    if epoch % 100 == 0:
        print("Epoch", epoch, "MSE =", mse.eval())
    sess.run(training_op)

best_theta = theta.eval()
```

Using autodiff

The preceding code works fine, but it requires mathematically deriving the gradients from the cost function (MSE). In the case of Linear Regression, it is reasonably easy, but if you had to do this with deep neural networks you would get quite a headache: it would be tedious and error-prone. You could use *symbolic differentiation* to automatically find the equations for the partial derivatives for you, but the resulting code would not necessarily be very efficient.

To understand why, consider the function $f(x)= \exp(\exp(\exp(x)))$. If you know calculus, you can figure out its derivative $f'(x) = \exp(x) \times \exp(\exp(x)) \times \exp(\exp(\exp(x)))$. If you code $f(x)$ and $f'(x)$ separately and exactly as they appear, your code will not be as efficient as it could be. A more efficient solution would be to write a function that first computes $\exp(x)$, then $\exp(\exp(x))$, then $\exp(\exp(\exp(x)))$, and returns all three. This gives you $f(x)$ directly (the third term), and if you need the derivative you can just multiply all three terms and you are done. With the naïve approach you would have had to call the exp function nine times to compute both $f(x)$ and $f'(x)$. With this approach you just need to call it three times.

It gets worse when your function is defined by some arbitrary code. Can you find the equation (or the code) to compute the partial derivatives of the following function? Hint: don't even try.

```
def my_func(a, b):
    z = 0
    for i in range(100):
        z = a * np.cos(z + i) + z * np.sin(b - i)
    return z
```

Fortunately, TensorFlow's autodiff feature comes to the rescue: it can automatically and efficiently compute the gradients for you. Simply replace the gradients = ... line in the Gradient Descent code in the previous section with the following line, and the code will continue to work just fine:

```
gradients = tf.gradients(mse, [theta])[0]
```

The gradients() function takes an op (in this case mse) and a list of variables (in this case just theta), and it creates a list of ops (one per variable) to compute the gradients of the op with regards to each variable. So the `gradients` node will compute the gradient vector of the MSE with regards to `theta`.

There are four main approaches to computing gradients automatically. They are summarized in Table 9-2. TensorFlow uses *reverse-mode autodiff*, which is perfect (efficient and accurate) when there are many inputs and few outputs, as is often the case in neural networks. It computes all the partial derivatives of the outputs with regards to all the inputs in just $n_{outputs} + 1$ graph traversals.

Table 9-2. Main solutions to compute gradients automatically

Technique	Nb of graph traversals to compute all gradients	Accuracy	Supports arbitrary code	Comment
Numerical differentiation	$n_{inputs} + 1$	Low	Yes	Trivial to implement
Symbolic differentiation	N/A	High	No	Builds a very different graph
Forward-mode autodiff	n_{inputs}	High	Yes	Uses *dual numbers*
Reverse-mode autodiff	$n_{outputs} + 1$	High	Yes	Implemented by TensorFlow

If you are interested in how this magic works, check out Appendix D.

Using an Optimizer

So TensorFlow computes the gradients for you. But it gets even easier: it also provides a number of optimizers out of the box, including a Gradient Descent optimizer. You can simply replace the preceding `gradients = ...` and `training_op = ...` lines with the following code, and once again everything will just work fine:

```
optimizer = tf.train.GradientDescentOptimizer(learning_rate=learning_rate)
training_op = optimizer.minimize(mse)
```

If you want to use a different type of optimizer, you just need to change one line. For example, you can use a momentum optimizer (which often converges much faster than Gradient Descent; see Chapter 11) by defining the optimizer like this:

```
optimizer = tf.train.MomentumOptimizer(learning_rate=learning_rate,
                                       momentum=0.9)
```

Feeding Data to the Training Algorithm

Let's try to modify the previous code to implement Mini-batch Gradient Descent. For this, we need a way to replace X and y at every iteration with the next mini-batch. The simplest way to do this is to use placeholder nodes. These nodes are special because they don't actually perform any computation, they just output the data you tell them to output at runtime. They are typically used to pass the training data to TensorFlow during training. If you don't specify a value at runtime for a placeholder, you get an exception.

To create a placeholder node, you must call the `placeholder()` function and specify the output tensor's data type. Optionally, you can also specify its shape, if you want to enforce it. If you specify `None` for a dimension, it means "any size." For example, the following code creates a placeholder node A, and also a node B = A + 5. When we evaluate B, we pass a `feed_dict` to the `eval()` method that specifies the value of A. Note that A must have rank 2 (i.e., it must be two-dimensional) and there must be three columns (or else an exception is raised), but it can have any number of rows.

```
>>> A = tf.placeholder(tf.float32, shape=(None, 3))
>>> B = A + 5
>>> with tf.Session() as sess:
...     B_val_1 = B.eval(feed_dict={A: [[1, 2, 3]]})
...     B_val_2 = B.eval(feed_dict={A: [[4, 5, 6], [7, 8, 9]]})
...
>>> print(B_val_1)
[[ 6.   7.   8.]]
>>> print(B_val_2)
[[  9.  10.  11.]
 [ 12.  13.  14.]]
```

You can actually feed the output of *any* operations, not just placeholders. In this case TensorFlow does not try to evaluate these operations; it uses the values you feed it.

To implement Mini-batch Gradient Descent, we only need to tweak the existing code slightly. First change the definition of X and y in the construction phase to make them placeholder nodes:

```
X = tf.placeholder(tf.float32, shape=(None, n + 1), name="X")
y = tf.placeholder(tf.float32, shape=(None, 1), name="y")
```

Then define the batch size and compute the total number of batches:

```
batch_size = 100
n_batches = int(np.ceil(m / batch_size))
```

Finally, in the execution phase, fetch the mini-batches one by one, then provide the value of X and y via the `feed_dict` parameter when evaluating a node that depends on either of them.

```
def fetch_batch(epoch, batch_index, batch_size):
    [...] # load the data from disk
    return X_batch, y_batch

with tf.Session() as sess:
    sess.run(init)

    for epoch in range(n_epochs):
```

```
    for batch_index in range(n_batches):
        X_batch, y_batch = fetch_batch(epoch, batch_index, batch_size)
        sess.run(training_op, feed_dict={X: X_batch, y: y_batch})

best_theta = theta.eval()
```

 We don't need to pass the value of X and y when evaluating theta since it does not depend on either of them.

Saving and Restoring Models

Once you have trained your model, you should save its parameters to disk so you can come back to it whenever you want, use it in another program, compare it to other models, and so on. Moreover, you probably want to save checkpoints at regular intervals during training so that if your computer crashes during training you can continue from the last checkpoint rather than start over from scratch.

TensorFlow makes saving and restoring a model very easy. Just create a Saver node at the end of the construction phase (after all variable nodes are created); then, in the execution phase, just call its save() method whenever you want to save the model, passing it the session and path of the checkpoint file:

```
[...]
theta = tf.Variable(tf.random_uniform([n + 1, 1], -1.0, 1.0), name="theta")
[...]
init = tf.global_variables_initializer()
saver = tf.train.Saver()

with tf.Session() as sess:
    sess.run(init)

    for epoch in range(n_epochs):
        if epoch % 100 == 0:  # checkpoint every 100 epochs
            save_path = saver.save(sess, "/tmp/my_model.ckpt")

        sess.run(training_op)

    best_theta = theta.eval()
    save_path = saver.save(sess, "/tmp/my_model_final.ckpt")
```

Restoring a model is just as easy: you create a Saver at the end of the construction phase just like before, but then at the beginning of the execution phase, instead of initializing the variables using the init node, you call the restore() method of the Saver object:

```
with tf.Session() as sess:
    saver.restore(sess, "/tmp/my_model_final.ckpt")
    [...]
```

By default a Saver saves and restores all variables under their own name, but if you
need more control, you can specify which variables to save or restore, and what
names to use. For example, the following Saver will save or restore only the theta
variable under the name weights:

```
saver = tf.train.Saver({"weights": theta})
```

By default, the save() method also saves the structure of the graph in a second file
with the same name plus a .meta extension. You can load this graph structure using
tf.train.import_meta_graph(). This adds the graph to the default graph, and
returns a Saver instance that you can then use to restore the graph's state (i.e., the
variable values):

```
saver = tf.train.import_meta_graph("/tmp/my_model_final.ckpt.meta")

with tf.Session() as sess:
    saver.restore(sess, "/tmp/my_model_final.ckpt")
    [...]
```

This allows you to fully restore a saved model, including both the graph structure and
the variable values, without having to search for the code that built it.

Visualizing the Graph and Training Curves Using TensorBoard

So now we have a computation graph that trains a Linear Regression model using
Mini-batch Gradient Descent, and we are saving checkpoints at regular intervals.
Sounds sophisticated, doesn't it? However, we are still relying on the print() function to visualize progress during training. There is a better way: enter TensorBoard. If
you feed it some training stats, it will display nice interactive visualizations of these
stats in your web browser (e.g., learning curves). You can also provide it the graph's
definition and it will give you a great interface to browse through it. This is very useful to identify errors in the graph, to find bottlenecks, and so on.

The first step is to tweak your program a bit so it writes the graph definition and
some training stats—for example, the training error (MSE)—to a log directory that
TensorBoard will read from. You need to use a different log directory every time you
run your program, or else TensorBoard will merge stats from different runs, which
will mess up the visualizations. The simplest solution for this is to include a time-
stamp in the log directory name. Add the following code at the beginning of the program:

```
from datetime import datetime

now = datetime.utcnow().strftime("%Y%m%d%H%M%S")
root_logdir = "tf_logs"
logdir = "{}/run-{}/".format(root_logdir, now)
```

Next, add the following code at the very end of the construction phase:

```
mse_summary = tf.summary.scalar('MSE', mse)
file_writer = tf.summary.FileWriter(logdir, tf.get_default_graph())
```

The first line creates a node in the graph that will evaluate the MSE value and write it to a TensorBoard-compatible binary log string called a *summary*. The second line creates a FileWriter that you will use to write summaries to logfiles in the log directory. The first parameter indicates the path of the log directory (in this case something like *tf_logs/run-20160906091959/*, relative to the current directory). The second (optional) parameter is the graph you want to visualize. Upon creation, the File Writer creates the log directory if it does not already exist (and its parent directories if needed), and writes the graph definition in a binary logfile called an *events file*.

Next you need to update the execution phase to evaluate the mse_summary node regularly during training (e.g., every 10 mini-batches). This will output a summary that you can then write to the events file using the file_writer. Here is the updated code:

```
[...]
for batch_index in range(n_batches):
    X_batch, y_batch = fetch_batch(epoch, batch_index, batch_size)
    if batch_index % 10 == 0:
        summary_str = mse_summary.eval(feed_dict={X: X_batch, y: y_batch})
        step = epoch * n_batches + batch_index
        file_writer.add_summary(summary_str, step)
    sess.run(training_op, feed_dict={X: X_batch, y: y_batch})
[...]
```

 Avoid logging training stats at every single training step, as this would significantly slow down training.

Finally, you want to close the FileWriter at the end of the program:

```
file_writer.close()
```

Now run this program: it will create the log directory and write an events file in this directory, containing both the graph definition and the MSE values. Open up a shell and go to your working directory, then type **ls -l tf_logs/run*** to list the contents of the log directory:

```
$ cd $ML_PATH                    # Your ML working directory (e.g., $HOME/ml)
$ ls -l tf_logs/run*
total 40
-rw-r--r-- 1 ageron staff 18620 Sep 6 11:10 events.out.tfevents.1472553182.mymac
```

If you run the program a second time, you should see a second directory in the *tf_logs/* directory:

```
$ ls -l tf_logs/
total 0
drwxr-xr-x  3 ageron  staff  102 Sep  6 10:07 run-20160906091959
drwxr-xr-x  3 ageron  staff  102 Sep  6 10:22 run-20160906092202
```

Great! Now it's time to fire up the TensorBoard server. You need to activate your vir‐
tualenv environment if you created one, then start the server by running the `tensor
board` command, pointing it to the root log directory. This starts the TensorBoard
web server, listening on port 6006 (which is "goog" written upside down):

```
$ source env/bin/activate
$ tensorboard --logdir tf_logs/
Starting TensorBoard  on port 6006
(You can navigate to http://0.0.0.0:6006)
```

Next open a browser and go to *http://0.0.0.0:6006/* (or *http://localhost:6006/*). Wel‐
come to TensorBoard! In the Events tab you should see MSE on the right. If you click
on it, you will see a plot of the MSE during training, for both runs (Figure 9-3). You
can check or uncheck the runs you want to see, zoom in or out, hover over the curve
to get details, and so on.

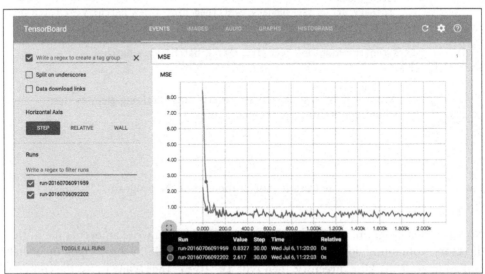

Figure 9-3. Visualizing training stats using TensorBoard

Now click on the Graphs tab. You should see the graph shown in Figure 9-4.

To reduce clutter, the nodes that have many *edges* (i.e., connections to other nodes) are separated out to an auxiliary area on the right (you can move a node back and forth between the main graph and the auxiliary area by right-clicking on it). Some parts of the graph are also collapsed by default. For example, try hovering over the gradients node, then click on the ⊕ icon to expand this subgraph. Next, in this subgraph, try expanding the mse_grad subgraph.

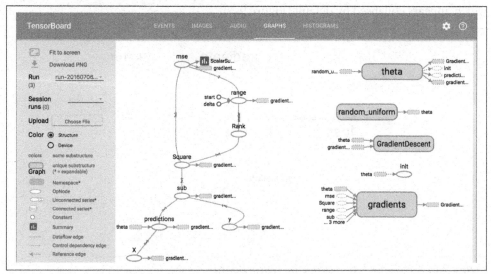

Figure 9-4. Visualizing the graph using TensorBoard

 If you want to take a peek at the graph directly within Jupyter, you can use the show_graph() function available in the notebook for this chapter. It was originally written by A. Mordvintsev in his great deepdream tutorial notebook (*http://homl.info/42*). Another option is to install E. Jang's TensorFlow debugger tool (*https://github.com/ericjang/tdb*) which includes a Jupyter extension for graph visualization (and more).

Name Scopes

When dealing with more complex models such as neural networks, the graph can easily become cluttered with thousands of nodes. To avoid this, you can create *name scopes* to group related nodes. For example, let's modify the previous code to define the error and mse ops within a name scope called "loss":

```
with tf.name_scope("loss") as scope:
    error = y_pred - y
    mse = tf.reduce_mean(tf.square(error), name="mse")
```

The name of each op defined within the scope is now prefixed with "loss/":

```
>>> print(error.op.name)
loss/sub
>>> print(mse.op.name)
loss/mse
```

In TensorBoard, the mse and error nodes now appear inside the loss namescope, which appears collapsed by default (Figure 9-5).

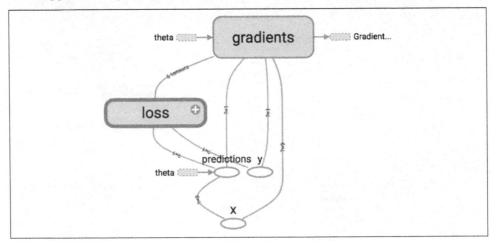

Figure 9-5. A collapsed namescope in TensorBoard

Modularity

Suppose you want to create a graph that adds the output of two *rectified linear units* (ReLU). A ReLU computes a linear function of the inputs, and outputs the result if it is positive, and 0 otherwise, as shown in Equation 9-1.

Equation 9-1. Rectified linear unit

$$h_{\mathbf{w},b}(\mathbf{X}) = \max(\mathbf{Xw} + b, 0)$$

The following code does the job, but it's quite repetitive:

```
n_features = 3
X = tf.placeholder(tf.float32, shape=(None, n_features), name="X")

w1 = tf.Variable(tf.random_normal((n_features, 1)), name="weights1")
w2 = tf.Variable(tf.random_normal((n_features, 1)), name="weights2")
b1 = tf.Variable(0.0, name="bias1")
b2 = tf.Variable(0.0, name="bias2")

z1 = tf.add(tf.matmul(X, w1), b1, name="z1")
```

```
z2 = tf.add(tf.matmul(X, w2), b2, name="z2")

relu1 = tf.maximum(z1, 0., name="relu1")
relu2 = tf.maximum(z1, 0., name="relu2")

output = tf.add(relu1, relu2, name="output")
```

Such repetitive code is hard to maintain and error-prone (in fact, this code contains a cut-and-paste error; did you spot it?). It would become even worse if you wanted to add a few more ReLUs. Fortunately, TensorFlow lets you stay DRY (Don't Repeat Yourself): simply create a function to build a ReLU. The following code creates five ReLUs and outputs their sum (note that add_n() creates an operation that will compute the sum of a list of tensors):

```
def relu(X):
    w_shape = (int(X.get_shape()[1]), 1)
    w = tf.Variable(tf.random_normal(w_shape), name="weights")
    b = tf.Variable(0.0, name="bias")
    z = tf.add(tf.matmul(X, w), b, name="z")
    return tf.maximum(z, 0., name="relu")

n_features = 3
X = tf.placeholder(tf.float32, shape=(None, n_features), name="X")
relus = [relu(X) for i in range(5)]
output = tf.add_n(relus, name="output")
```

Note that when you create a node, TensorFlow checks whether its name already exists, and if it does it appends an underscore followed by an index to make the name unique. So the first ReLU contains nodes named "weights", "bias", "z", and "relu" (plus many more nodes with their default name, such as "MatMul"); the second ReLU contains nodes named "weights_1", "bias_1", and so on; the third ReLU contains nodes named "weights_2", "bias_2", and so on. TensorBoard identifies such series and collapses them together to reduce clutter (as you can see in Figure 9-6).

Using name scopes, you can make the graph much clearer. Simply move all the content of the relu() function inside a name scope. Figure 9-7 shows the resulting graph. Notice that TensorFlow also gives the name scopes unique names by appending _1, _2, and so on.

```
def relu(X):
    with tf.name_scope("relu"):
        [...]
```

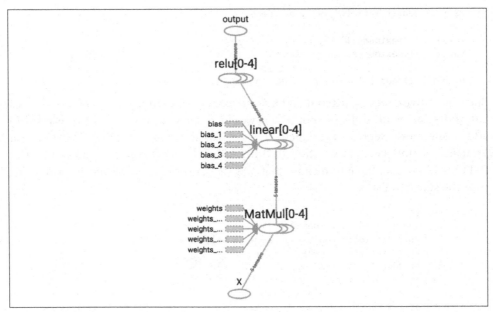

Figure 9-6. Collapsed node series

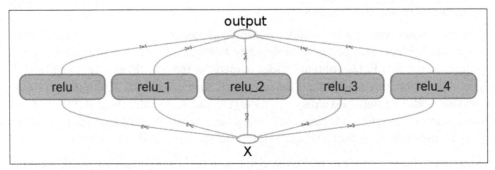

Figure 9-7. A clearer graph using name-scoped units

Sharing Variables

If you want to share a variable between various components of your graph, one simple option is to create it first, then pass it as a parameter to the functions that need it. For example, suppose you want to control the ReLU threshold (currently hardcoded to 0) using a shared `threshold` variable for all ReLUs. You could just create that variable first, and then pass it to the `relu()` function:

```
def relu(X, threshold):
    with tf.name_scope("relu"):
        [...]
        return tf.maximum(z, threshold, name="max")
```

```
threshold = tf.Variable(0.0, name="threshold")
X = tf.placeholder(tf.float32, shape=(None, n_features), name="X")
relus = [relu(X, threshold) for i in range(5)]
output = tf.add_n(relus, name="output")
```

This works fine: now you can control the threshold for all ReLUs using the threshold variable. However, if there are many shared parameters such as this one, it will be painful to have to pass them around as parameters all the time. Many people create a Python dictionary containing all the variables in their model, and pass it around to every function. Others create a class for each module (e.g., a ReLU class using class variables to handle the shared parameter). Yet another option is to set the shared variable as an attribute of the relu() function upon the first call, like so:

```
def relu(X):
    with tf.name_scope("relu"):
        if not hasattr(relu, "threshold"):
            relu.threshold = tf.Variable(0.0, name="threshold")
        [...]
        return tf.maximum(z, relu.threshold, name="max")
```

TensorFlow offers another option, which may lead to slightly cleaner and more modular code than the previous solutions.[5] This solution is a bit tricky to understand at first, but since it is used a lot in TensorFlow it is worth going into a bit of detail. The idea is to use the get_variable() function to create the shared variable if it does not exist yet, or reuse it if it already exists. The desired behavior (creating or reusing) is controlled by an attribute of the current variable_scope(). For example, the following code will create a variable named "relu/threshold" (as a scalar, since shape=(), and using 0.0 as the initial value):

```
with tf.variable_scope("relu"):
    threshold = tf.get_variable("threshold", shape=(),
                        initializer=tf.constant_initializer(0.0))
```

Note that if the variable has already been created by an earlier call to get_variable(), this code will raise an exception. This behavior prevents reusing variables by mistake. If you want to reuse a variable, you need to explicitly say so by setting the variable scope's reuse attribute to True (in which case you don't have to specify the shape or the initializer):

```
with tf.variable_scope("relu", reuse=True):
    threshold = tf.get_variable("threshold")
```

This code will fetch the existing "relu/threshold" variable, or raise an exception if it does not exist or if it was not created using get_variable(). Alternatively, you can

---

5 Creating a ReLU class is arguably the cleanest option, but it is rather heavyweight.

set the `reuse` attribute to `True` inside the block by calling the scope's `reuse_vari` `ables()` method:

```
with tf.variable_scope("relu") as scope:
    scope.reuse_variables()
    threshold = tf.get_variable("threshold")
```

 Once `reuse` is set to `True`, it cannot be set back to `False` within the block. Moreover, if you define other variable scopes inside this one, they will automatically inherit `reuse=True`. Lastly, only variables created by `get_variable()` can be reused this way.

Now you have all the pieces you need to make the `relu()` function access the `thres` `hold` variable without having to pass it as a parameter:

```
def relu(X):
    with tf.variable_scope("relu", reuse=True):
        threshold = tf.get_variable("threshold")    # reuse existing variable
        [...]
        return tf.maximum(z, threshold, name="max")

X = tf.placeholder(tf.float32, shape=(None, n_features), name="X")
with tf.variable_scope("relu"):    # create the variable
    threshold = tf.get_variable("threshold", shape=(),
                                initializer=tf.constant_initializer(0.0))
relus = [relu(X) for relu_index in range(5)]
output = tf.add_n(relus, name="output")
```

This code first defines the `relu()` function, then creates the `relu/threshold` variable (as a scalar that will later be initialized to `0.0`) and builds five ReLUs by calling the `relu()` function. The `relu()` function reuses the `relu/threshold` variable, and creates the other ReLU nodes.

 Variables created using `get_variable()` are always named using the name of their `variable_scope` as a prefix (e.g., `"relu/thres` `hold"`), but for all other nodes (including variables created with `tf.Variable()`) the variable scope acts like a new name scope. In particular, if a name scope with an identical name was already created, then a suffix is added to make the name unique. For example, all nodes created in the preceding code (except the `threshold` variable) have a name prefixed with `"relu_1/"` to `"relu_5/"`, as shown in Figure 9-8.

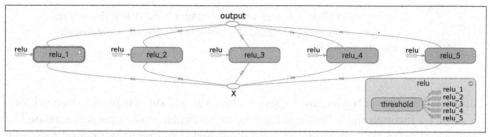

Figure 9-8. Five ReLUs sharing the threshold variable

It is somewhat unfortunate that the `threshold` variable must be defined outside the `relu()` function, where all the rest of the ReLU code resides. To fix this, the following code creates the `threshold` variable within the `relu()` function upon the first call, then reuses it in subsequent calls. Now the `relu()` function does not have to worry about name scopes or variable sharing: it just calls `get_variable()`, which will create or reuse the `threshold` variable (it does not need to know which is the case). The rest of the code calls `relu()` five times, making sure to set `reuse=None` on the first call, and `reuse=True` for the other calls.

```python
def relu(X):
    threshold = tf.get_variable("threshold", shape=(),
                                initializer=tf.constant_initializer(0.0))
    [...]
    return tf.maximum(z, threshold, name="max")

X = tf.placeholder(tf.float32, shape=(None, n_features), name="X")
relus = []
for relu_index in range(5):
    with tf.variable_scope("relu", reuse=(relu_index >= 1 or None)) as scope:
        relus.append(relu(X))
output = tf.add_n(relus, name="output")
```

The resulting graph is slightly different than before, since the shared variable lives within the first ReLU (see Figure 9-9).

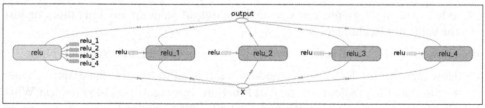

Figure 9-9. Five ReLUs sharing the threshold variable

Since TensorFlow 1.4, you can set reuse=tf.AUTO_REUSE—in this case get_variable() returns the variable if it already exists; otherwise, it creates it.

This concludes this introduction to TensorFlow. We will discuss more advanced topics as we go through the following chapters, in particular many operations related to deep neural networks, convolutional neural networks, and recurrent neural networks as well as how to scale up with TensorFlow using multithreading, queues, multiple GPUs, and multiple servers.

Exercises

1. What are the main benefits of creating a computation graph rather than directly executing the computations? What are the main drawbacks?

2. Is the statement a_val = a.eval(session=sess) equivalent to a_val = sess.run(a)?

3. Is the statement a_val, b_val = a.eval(session=sess), b.eval(session=sess) equivalent to a_val, b_val = sess.run([a, b])?

4. Can you run two graphs in the same session?

5. If you create a graph g containing a variable w, then start two threads and open a session in each thread, both using the same graph g, will each session have its own copy of the variable w or will it be shared?

6. When is a variable initialized? When is it destroyed?

7. What is the difference between a placeholder and a variable?

8. What happens when you run the graph to evaluate an operation that depends on a placeholder but you don't feed its value? What happens if the operation does not depend on the placeholder?

9. When you run a graph, can you feed the output value of any operation, or just the value of placeholders?

10. How can you set a variable to any value you want (during the execution phase)?

11. How many times does reverse-mode autodiff need to traverse the graph in order to compute the gradients of the cost function with regards to 10 variables? What about forward-mode autodiff? And symbolic differentiation?

12. Implement Logistic Regression with Mini-batch Gradient Descent using TensorFlow. Train it and evaluate it on the moons dataset (introduced in Chapter 5). Try adding all the bells and whistles:

- Define the graph within a `logistic_regression()` function that can be reused easily.

- Save checkpoints using a `Saver` at regular intervals during training, and save the final model at the end of training.

- Restore the last checkpoint upon startup if training was interrupted.

- Define the graph using name scopes so the graph looks good in TensorBoard.

- Add summaries to visualize the learning curves in TensorBoard.

- Try tweaking some hyperparameters such as the learning rate or the mini-batch size and look at the shape of the learning curve.

Solutions to these exercises are available in Appendix A.

## CHAPTER 10

Introduction to Artificial Neural Networks

Birds inspired us to fly, burdock plants inspired velcro, and nature has inspired many other inventions. It seems only logical, then, to look at the brain's architecture for inspiration on how to build an intelligent machine. This is the key idea that inspired *artificial neural networks* (ANNs). However, although planes were inspired by birds, they don't have to flap their wings. Similarly, ANNs have gradually become quite different from their biological cousins. Some researchers even argue that we should drop the biological analogy altogether (e.g., by saying "units" rather than "neurons"), lest we restrict our creativity to biologically plausible systems.[1]

ANNs are at the very core of Deep Learning. They are versatile, powerful, and scalable, making them ideal to tackle large and highly complex Machine Learning tasks, such as classifying billions of images (e.g., Google Images), powering speech recognition services (e.g., Apple's Siri), recommending the best videos to watch to hundreds of millions of users every day (e.g., YouTube), or learning to beat the world champion at the game of *Go* by examining millions of past games and then playing against itself (DeepMind's AlphaGo).

In this chapter, we will introduce artificial neural networks, starting with a quick tour of the very first ANN architectures. Then we will present *Multi-Layer Perceptrons* (MLPs) and implement one using TensorFlow to tackle the MNIST digit classification problem (introduced in Chapter 3).

---

1 You can get the best of both worlds by being open to biological inspirations without being afraid to create biologically unrealistic models, as long as they work well.

From Biological to Artificial Neurons

Surprisingly, ANNs have been around for quite a while: they were first introduced back in 1943 by the neurophysiologist Warren McCulloch and the mathematician Walter Pitts. In their landmark paper (*http://homl.info/43*),[2] "A Logical Calculus of Ideas Immanent in Nervous Activity," McCulloch and Pitts presented a simplified computational model of how biological neurons might work together in animal brains to perform complex computations using *propositional logic*. This was the first artificial neural network architecture. Since then many other architectures have been invented, as we will see.

The early successes of ANNs until the 1960s led to the widespread belief that we would soon be conversing with truly intelligent machines. When it became clear that this promise would go unfulfilled (at least for quite a while), funding flew elsewhere and ANNs entered a long dark era. In the early 1980s there was a revival of interest in ANNs as new network architectures were invented and better training techniques were developed. But by the 1990s, powerful alternative Machine Learning techniques such as Support Vector Machines (see Chapter 5) were favored by most researchers, as they seemed to offer better results and stronger theoretical foundations. Finally, we are now witnessing yet another wave of interest in ANNs. Will this wave die out like the previous ones did? There are a few good reasons to believe that this one is different and will have a much more profound impact on our lives:

- There is now a huge quantity of data available to train neural networks, and ANNs frequently outperform other ML techniques on very large and complex problems.

- The tremendous increase in computing power since the 1990s now makes it possible to train large neural networks in a reasonable amount of time. This is in part due to Moore's Law, but also thanks to the gaming industry, which has produced powerful GPU cards by the millions.

- The training algorithms have been improved. To be fair they are only slightly different from the ones used in the 1990s, but these relatively small tweaks have a huge positive impact.

- Some theoretical limitations of ANNs have turned out to be benign in practice. For example, many people thought that ANN training algorithms were doomed because they were likely to get stuck in local optima, but it turns out that this is rather rare in practice (or when it is the case, they are usually fairly close to the global optimum).

---

2 "A Logical Calculus of Ideas Immanent in Nervous Activity," W. McCulloch and W. Pitts (1943).

- ANNs seem to have entered a virtuous circle of funding and progress. Amazing products based on ANNs regularly make the headline news, which pulls more and more attention and funding toward them, resulting in more and more progress, and even more amazing products.

Biological Neurons

Before we discuss artificial neurons, let's take a quick look at a biological neuron (represented in Figure 10-1). It is an unusual-looking cell mostly found in animal cerebral cortexes (e.g., your brain), composed of a *cell body* containing the nucleus and most of the cell's complex components, and many branching extensions called *dendrites*, plus one very long extension called the *axon*. The axon's length may be just a few times longer than the cell body, or up to tens of thousands of times longer. Near its extremity the axon splits off into many branches called *telodendria*, and at the tip of these branches are minuscule structures called *synaptic terminals* (or simply *synapses*), which are connected to the dendrites (or directly to the cell body) of other neurons. Biological neurons receive short electrical impulses called *signals* from other neurons via these synapses. When a neuron receives a sufficient number of signals from other neurons within a few milliseconds, it fires its own signals.

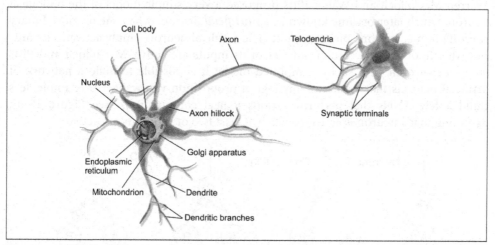

Figure 10-1. Biological neuron[3]

Thus, individual biological neurons seem to behave in a rather simple way, but they are organized in a vast network of billions of neurons, each neuron typically connected to thousands of other neurons. Highly complex computations can be performed

---

3 Image by Bruce Blaus (Creative Commons 3.0 (*https://creativecommons.org/licenses/by/3.0/*)). Reproduced from *https://en.wikipedia.org/wiki/Neuron*.

by a vast network of fairly simple neurons, much like a complex anthill can emerge from the combined efforts of simple ants. The architecture of biological neural networks (BNN)[4] is still the subject of active research, but some parts of the brain have been mapped, and it seems that neurons are often organized in consecutive layers, as shown in Figure 10-2.

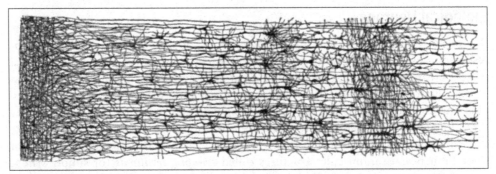

Figure 10-2. Multiple layers in a biological neural network (human cortex)[5]

Logical Computations with Neurons

Warren McCulloch and Walter Pitts proposed a very simple model of the biological neuron, which later became known as an *artificial neuron*: it has one or more binary (on/off) inputs and one binary output. The artificial neuron simply activates its output when more than a certain number of its inputs are active. McCulloch and Pitts showed that even with such a simplified model it is possible to build a network of artificial neurons that computes any logical proposition you want. For example, let's build a few ANNs that perform various logical computations (see Figure 10-3), assuming that a neuron is activated when at least two of its inputs are active.

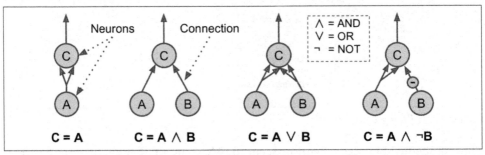

Figure 10-3. ANNs performing simple logical computations

---

4 In the context of Machine Learning, the phrase "neural networks" generally refers to ANNs, not BNNs.

5 Drawing of a cortical lamination by S. Ramon y Cajal (public domain). Reproduced from *https://en.wikipe dia.org/wiki/Cerebral_cortex*.

- The first network on the left is simply the identity function: if neuron A is activated, then neuron C gets activated as well (since it receives two input signals from neuron A), but if neuron A is off, then neuron C is off as well.

- The second network performs a logical AND: neuron C is activated only when both neurons A and B are activated (a single input signal is not enough to activate neuron C).

- The third network performs a logical OR: neuron C gets activated if either neuron A or neuron B is activated (or both).

- Finally, if we suppose that an input connection can inhibit the neuron's activity (which is the case with biological neurons), then the fourth network computes a slightly more complex logical proposition: neuron C is activated only if neuron A is active and if neuron B is off. If neuron A is active all the time, then you get a logical NOT: neuron C is active when neuron B is off, and vice versa.

You can easily imagine how these networks can be combined to compute complex logical expressions (see the exercises at the end of the chapter).

The Perceptron

The *Perceptron* is one of the simplest ANN architectures, invented in 1957 by Frank Rosenblatt. It is based on a slightly different artificial neuron (see Figure 10-4) called a *threshold logic unit* (TLU), or sometimes a *linear threshold unit* (LTU): the inputs and output are now numbers (instead of binary on/off values) and each input connection is associated with a weight. The TLU computes a weighted sum of its inputs ($z = w_1 x_1 + w_2 x_2 + \cdots + w_n x_n = \mathbf{w}^T \mathbf{x}$), then applies a *step function* to that sum and outputs the result: $h_{\mathbf{w}}(\mathbf{x}) = \text{step}(z) = \text{step}(\mathbf{w}^T \mathbf{x})$.

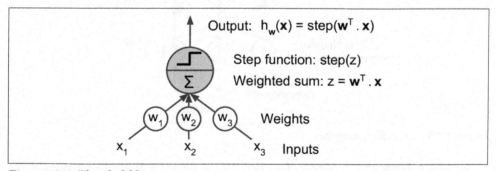

Figure 10-4. Threshold logic unit

The most common step function used in Perceptrons is the *Heaviside step function* (see Equation 10-1). Sometimes the sign function is used instead.

Equation 10-1. Common step functions used in Perceptrons

$$\text{heaviside } (z) = \begin{cases} 0 & \text{if } z < 0 \\ 1 & \text{if } z \geq 0 \end{cases} \qquad \text{sgn } (z) = \begin{cases} -1 & \text{if } z < 0 \\ 0 & \text{if } z = 0 \\ +1 & \text{if } z > 0 \end{cases}$$

A single TLU can be used for simple linear binary classification. It computes a linear combination of the inputs and if the result exceeds a threshold, it outputs the positive class or else outputs the negative class (just like a Logistic Regression classifier or a linear SVM). For example, you could use a single TLU to classify iris flowers based on the petal length and width (also adding an extra bias feature $x_0 = 1$, just like we did in previous chapters). Training a TLU means finding the right values for w_0, w_1, and w_2 (the training algorithm is discussed shortly).

A Perceptron is simply composed of a single layer of TLUs,[6] with each neuron connected to all the inputs. These connections are often represented using special pass-through neurons called *input neurons*: they just output whatever input they are fed. Moreover, an extra bias feature is generally added ($x_0 = 1$). This bias feature is typically represented using a special type of neuron called a *bias neuron*, which just outputs 1 all the time.

A Perceptron with two inputs and three outputs is represented in Figure 10-5. This Perceptron can classify instances simultaneously into three different binary classes, which makes it a multioutput classifier.

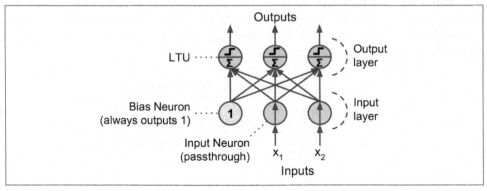

Figure 10-5. Perceptron diagram

So how is a Perceptron trained? The Perceptron training algorithm proposed by Frank Rosenblatt was largely inspired by *Hebb's rule*. In his book *The Organization of Behavior*, published in 1949, Donald Hebb suggested that when a biological neuron

---

6 The name *Perceptron* is sometimes used to mean a tiny network with a single TLU.

often triggers another neuron, the connection between these two neurons grows stronger. This idea was later summarized by Siegrid Löwel in this catchy phrase: "Cells that fire together, wire together." This rule later became known as Hebb's rule (or *Hebbian learning*); that is, the connection weight between two neurons is increased whenever they have the same output. Perceptrons are trained using a variant of this rule that takes into account the error made by the network; it does not reinforce connections that lead to the wrong output. More specifically, the Perceptron is fed one training instance at a time, and for each instance it makes its predictions. For every output neuron that produced a wrong prediction, it reinforces the connection weights from the inputs that would have contributed to the correct prediction. The rule is shown in Equation 10-2.

Equation 10-2. Perceptron learning rule (weight update)

$$w_{i,j}^{(\text{next step})} = w_{i,j} + \eta\left(y_j - \hat{y}_j\right)x_i$$

- $w_{i,j}$ is the connection weight between the ith input neuron and the jth output neuron.
- x_i is the ith input value of the current training instance.
- $\hat{y}_j$ is the output of the jth output neuron for the current training instance.
- y_j is the target output of the jth output neuron for the current training instance.
- η is the learning rate.

The decision boundary of each output neuron is linear, so Perceptrons are incapable of learning complex patterns (just like Logistic Regression classifiers). However, if the training instances are linearly separable, Rosenblatt demonstrated that this algorithm would converge to a solution.[7] This is called the *Perceptron convergence theorem*.

Scikit-Learn provides a `Perceptron` class that implements a single TLU network. It can be used pretty much as you would expect—for example, on the iris dataset (introduced in Chapter 4):

```
import numpy as np
from sklearn.datasets import load_iris
from sklearn.linear_model import Perceptron

iris = load_iris()
X = iris.data[:, (2, 3)]  # petal length, petal width
y = (iris.target == 0).astype(np.int)  # Iris Setosa?
```

---

7 Note that this solution is generally not unique: in general when the data are linearly separable, there is an infinity of hyperplanes that can separate them.

```
per_clf = Perceptron(random_state=42)
per_clf.fit(X, y)

y_pred = per_clf.predict([[2, 0.5]])
```

You may have recognized that the Perceptron learning algorithm strongly resembles Stochastic Gradient Descent. In fact, Scikit-Learn's `Perceptron` class is equivalent to using an `SGDClassifier` with the following hyperparameters: `loss="perceptron"`, `learning_rate="constant"`, `eta0=1` (the learning rate), and `penalty=None` (no regularization).

Note that contrary to Logistic Regression classifiers, Perceptrons do not output a class probability; rather, they just make predictions based on a hard threshold. This is one of the good reasons to prefer Logistic Regression over Perceptrons.

In their 1969 monograph titled *Perceptrons*, Marvin Minsky and Seymour Papert highlighted a number of serious weaknesses of Perceptrons, in particular the fact that they are incapable of solving some trivial problems (e.g., the *Exclusive OR* (XOR) classification problem; see the left side of Figure 10-6). Of course this is true of any other linear classification model as well (such as Logistic Regression classifiers), but researchers had expected much more from Perceptrons, and their disappointment was great: as a result, many researchers dropped *connectionism* altogether (i.e., the study of neural networks) in favor of higher-level problems such as logic, problem solving, and search.

However, it turns out that some of the limitations of Perceptrons can be eliminated by stacking multiple Perceptrons. The resulting ANN is called a *Multi-Layer Perceptron* (MLP). In particular, an MLP can solve the XOR problem, as you can verify by computing the output of the MLP represented on the right of Figure 10-6, for each combination of inputs: with inputs (0, 0) or (1, 1) the network outputs 0, and with inputs (0, 1) or (1, 0) it outputs 1. The numbers on the right part of the figure represent the connection weights (when a connection's weight is not shown, it is equal to 1).

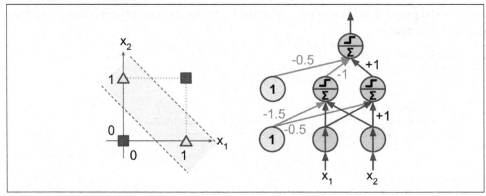

Figure 10-6. XOR classification problem and an MLP that solves it

Multi-Layer Perceptron and Backpropagation

An MLP is composed of one (passthrough) input layer, one or more layers of TLUs, called *hidden layers*, and one final layer of TLUs called the *output layer* (see Figure 10-7). Every layer except the output layer includes a bias neuron and is fully connected to the next layer. When an ANN has two or more hidden layers, it is called a *deep neural network* (DNN).

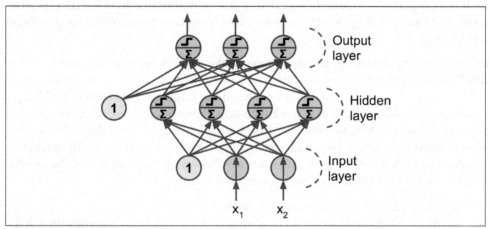

Figure 10-7. Multi-Layer Perceptron

For many years researchers struggled to find a way to train MLPs, without success. But in 1986, D. E. Rumelhart et al. published a groundbreaking article (*http://homl.info/44*)[8] introducing the *backpropagation* training algorithm.[9] Today we would describe it as Gradient Descent using reverse-mode autodiff (Gradient Descent was introduced in Chapter 4, and autodiff was discussed in Chapter 9).

For each training instance, the algorithm feeds it to the network and computes the output of every neuron in each consecutive layer (this is the forward pass, just like when making predictions). Then it measures the network's output error (i.e., the difference between the desired output and the actual output of the network), and it computes how much each neuron in the last hidden layer contributed to each output neuron's error. It then proceeds to measure how much of these error contributions came from each neuron in the previous hidden layer—and so on until the algorithm reaches the input layer. This reverse pass efficiently measures the error gradient across all the connection weights in the network by propagating the error gradient backward in the network (hence the name of the algorithm). If you check out the

---

8 "Learning Internal Representations by Error Propagation," D. Rumelhart, G. Hinton, R. Williams (1986).

9 This algorithm was actually invented several times by various researchers in different fields, starting with P. Werbos in 1974.

reverse-mode autodiff algorithm in Appendix D, you will find that the forward and reverse passes of backpropagation simply perform reverse-mode autodiff. The last step of the backpropagation algorithm is a Gradient Descent step on all the connection weights in the network, using the error gradients measured earlier.

Let's make this even shorter: for each training instance the backpropagation algorithm first makes a prediction (forward pass), measures the error, then goes through each layer in reverse to measure the error contribution from each connection (reverse pass), and finally slightly tweaks the connection weights to reduce the error (Gradient Descent step).

In order for this algorithm to work properly, the authors made a key change to the MLP's architecture: they replaced the step function with the logistic function, $\sigma(z) = 1 / (1 + \exp(-z))$. This was essential because the step function contains only flat segments, so there is no gradient to work with (Gradient Descent cannot move on a flat surface), while the logistic function has a well-defined nonzero derivative everywhere, allowing Gradient Descent to make some progress at every step. The backpropagation algorithm may be used with other *activation functions*, instead of the logistic function. Two other popular activation functions are:

The hyperbolic tangent function tanh (z) = 2σ(2z) – 1
> Just like the logistic function it is S-shaped, continuous, and differentiable, but its output value ranges from –1 to 1 (instead of 0 to 1 in the case of the logistic function), which tends to make each layer's output more or less normalized (i.e., centered around 0) at the beginning of training. This often helps speed up convergence.

The ReLU function (introduced in Chapter 9)
> ReLU (z) = max $(0, z)$. It is continuous but unfortunately not differentiable at $z = 0$ (the slope changes abruptly, which can make Gradient Descent bounce around). However, in practice it works very well and has the advantage of being fast to compute. Most importantly, the fact that it does not have a maximum output value also helps reduce some issues during Gradient Descent (we will come back to this in Chapter 11).

These popular activation functions and their derivatives are represented in Figure 10-8.

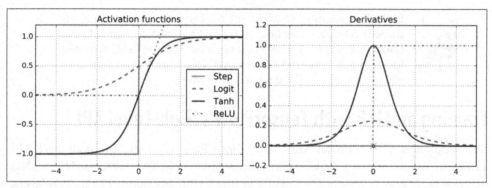

Figure 10-8. Activation functions and their derivatives

An MLP is often used for classification, with each output corresponding to a different binary class (e.g., spam/ham, urgent/not-urgent, and so on). When the classes are exclusive (e.g., classes 0 through 9 for digit image classification), the output layer is typically modified by replacing the individual activation functions by a shared *softmax* function (see Figure 10-9). The softmax function was introduced in Chapter 4. The output of each neuron corresponds to the estimated probability of the corresponding class. Note that the signal flows only in one direction (from the inputs to the outputs), so this architecture is an example of a *feedforward neural network* (FNN).

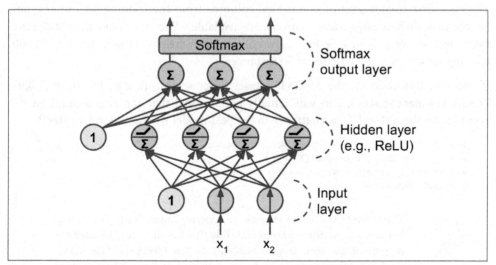

Figure 10-9. A modern MLP (including ReLU and softmax) for classification

Biological neurons seem to implement a roughly sigmoid (S-shaped) activation function, so researchers stuck to sigmoid functions for a very long time. But it turns out that the ReLU activation function generally works better in ANNs. This is one of the cases where the biological analogy was misleading.

Training an MLP with TensorFlow's High-Level API

The simplest way to train an MLP with TensorFlow is to use the high-level API TF.Learn, which offers a Scikit-Learn–compatible API. The DNNClassifier class makes it fairly easy to train a deep neural network with any number of hidden layers, and a softmax output layer to output estimated class probabilities. For example, the following code trains a DNN for classification with two hidden layers (one with 300 neurons, and the other with 100 neurons) and a softmax output layer with 10 neurons:

```
import tensorflow as tf

feature_cols = tf.contrib.learn.infer_real_valued_columns_from_input(X_train)
dnn_clf = tf.contrib.learn.DNNClassifier(hidden_units=[300,100], n_classes=10,
                                         feature_columns=feature_cols)
dnn_clf = tf.contrib.learn.SKCompat(dnn_clf)  # if TensorFlow >= 1.1
dnn_clf.fit(X_train, y_train, batch_size=50, steps=40000)
```

The code first creates a set of real valued columns from the training set (other types of columns, such as categorical columns, are available). Then we create the DNNClassifier, and we wrap it in a Scikit-Learn compatibility helper. Finally, we run 40,000 training iterations using batches of 50 instances.

If you run this code on the MNIST dataset (after scaling it, e.g., by using Scikit-Learn's StandardScaler), you will actually get a model that achieves around 98.2% accuracy on the test set! That's better than the best model we trained in Chapter 3:

```
>>> from sklearn.metrics import accuracy_score
>>> y_pred = dnn_clf.predict(X_test)
>>> accuracy_score(y_test, y_pred['classes'])
0.98250000000000004
```

The tensorflow.contrib package contains many useful functions, but it is a place for experimental code that has not yet graduated to be part of the core TensorFlow API. So the DNNClassifier class (and any other contrib code) may change without notice in the future.

Under the hood, the DNNClassifier class creates all the neuron layers, based on the ReLU activation function (we can change this by setting the activation_fn hyper-

---

parameter). The output layer relies on the softmax function, and the cost function is cross entropy (introduced in Chapter 4).

Training a DNN Using Plain TensorFlow

If you want more control over the architecture of the network, you may prefer to use TensorFlow's lower-level Python API (introduced in Chapter 9). In this section we will build the same model as before using this API, and we will implement Mini-batch Gradient Descent to train it on the MNIST dataset. The first step is the construction phase, building the TensorFlow graph. The second step is the execution phase, where you actually run the graph to train the model.

Construction Phase

Let's start. First we need to import the tensorflow library. Then we must specify the number of inputs and outputs, and set the number of hidden neurons in each layer:

```python
import tensorflow as tf

n_inputs = 28*28  # MNIST
n_hidden1 = 300
n_hidden2 = 100
n_outputs = 10
```

Next, just like you did in Chapter 9, you can use placeholder nodes to represent the training data and targets. The shape of X is only partially defined. We know that it will be a 2D tensor (i.e., a matrix), with instances along the first dimension and features along the second dimension, and we know that the number of features is going to be 28 x 28 (one feature per pixel), but we don't know yet how many instances each training batch will contain. So the shape of X is (None, n_inputs). Similarly, we know that y will be a 1D tensor with one entry per instance, but again we don't know the size of the training batch at this point, so the shape is (None).

```python
X = tf.placeholder(tf.float32, shape=(None, n_inputs), name="X")
y = tf.placeholder(tf.int64, shape=(None), name="y")
```

Now let's create the actual neural network. The placeholder X will act as the input layer; during the execution phase, it will be replaced with one training batch at a time (note that all the instances in a training batch will be processed simultaneously by the neural network). Now you need to create the two hidden layers and the output layer. The two hidden layers are almost identical: they differ only by the inputs they are connected to and by the number of neurons they contain. The output layer is also very similar, but it uses a softmax activation function instead of a ReLU activation function. So let's create a neuron_layer() function that we will use to create one layer at a time. It will need parameters to specify the inputs, the number of neurons, the activation function, and the name of the layer:

```
def neuron_layer(X, n_neurons, name, activation=None):
    with tf.name_scope(name):
        n_inputs = int(X.get_shape()[1])
        stddev = 2 / np.sqrt(n_inputs + n_neurons)
        init = tf.truncated_normal((n_inputs, n_neurons), stddev=stddev)
        W = tf.Variable(init, name="kernel")
        b = tf.Variable(tf.zeros([n_neurons]), name="bias")
        Z = tf.matmul(X, W) + b
        if activation is not None:
            return activation(Z)
        else:
            return Z
```

Let's go through this code line by line:

1. First we create a name scope using the name of the layer: it will contain all the computation nodes for this neuron layer. This is optional, but the graph will look much nicer in TensorBoard if its nodes are well organized.

2. Next, we get the number of inputs by looking up the input matrix's shape and getting the size of the second dimension (the first dimension is for instances).

3. The next three lines create a W variable that will hold the weights matrix (often called the layer's *kernel*). It will be a 2D tensor containing all the connection weights between each input and each neuron; hence, its shape will be (n_inputs, n_neurons). It will be initialized randomly, using a truncated[10] normal (Gaussian) distribution with a standard deviation of $2/\sqrt{n_{inputs} + n_{neurons}}$. Using this specific standard deviation helps the algorithm converge much faster (we will discuss this further in Chapter 11; it is one of those small tweaks to neural networks that have had a tremendous impact on their efficiency). It is important to initialize connection weights randomly for all hidden layers to avoid any symmetries that the Gradient Descent algorithm would be unable to break.[11]

4. The next line creates a b variable for biases, initialized to 0 (no symmetry issue in this case), with one bias parameter per neuron.

5. Then we create a subgraph to compute $\mathbf{Z} = \mathbf{X} \mathbf{W} + \mathbf{b}$. This vectorized implementation will efficiently compute the weighted sums of the inputs plus the bias term for each and every neuron in the layer, for all the instances in the batch in just one shot. Note that adding a 1D array (**b**) to a 2D matrix with the same number

---

10 Using a truncated normal distribution rather than a regular normal distribution ensures that there won't be any large weights, which could slow down training.

11 For example, if you set all the weights to 0, then all neurons will output 0, and the error gradient will be the same for all neurons in a given hidden layer. The Gradient Descent step will then update all the weights in exactly the same way in each layer, so they will all remain equal. In other words, despite having hundreds of neurons per layer, your model will act as if there were only one neuron per layer. It is not going to fly.

of columns (**X** . **W**) results in adding the 1D array to every row in the matrix: this is called *broadcasting*.

6. Finally, if an `activation` parameter is provided, such as `tf.nn.relu` (i.e., max (0, **Z**)), then the code returns `activation(Z)`, or else it just returns **Z**.

Okay, so now you have a nice function to create a neuron layer. Let's use it to create the deep neural network! The first hidden layer takes X as its input. The second takes the output of the first hidden layer as its input. And finally, the output layer takes the output of the second hidden layer as its input.

```
with tf.name_scope("dnn"):
    hidden1 = neuron_layer(X, n_hidden1, name="hidden1",
                           activation=tf.nn.relu)
    hidden2 = neuron_layer(hidden1, n_hidden2, name="hidden2",
                           activation=tf.nn.relu)
    logits = neuron_layer(hidden2, n_outputs, name="outputs")
```

Notice that once again we used a name scope for clarity. Also note that `logits` is the output of the neural network *before* going through the softmax activation function: for optimization reasons, we will handle the softmax computation later.

As you might expect, TensorFlow comes with many handy functions to create standard neural network layers, so there's often no need to define your own `neuron_layer()` function like we just did. For example, TensorFlow's `tf.lay ers.dense()` function (previously called `tf.contrib.layers.fully_connected()`) creates a fully connected layer, where all the inputs are connected to all the neurons in the layer. It takes care of creating the weights and biases variables, named `kernel` and `bias` respectively, using the appropriate initialization strategy, and you can set the activation function using the `activation` argument. As we will see in Chapter 11, it also supports regularization parameters. Let's tweak the preceding code to use the `dense()` function instead of our `neuron_layer()` function. Simply replace the dnn construction section with the following code:

```
with tf.name_scope("dnn"):
    hidden1 = tf.layers.dense(X, n_hidden1, name="hidden1",
                              activation=tf.nn.relu)
    hidden2 = tf.layers.dense(hidden1, n_hidden2, name="hidden2",
                              activation=tf.nn.relu)
    logits = tf.layers.dense(hidden2, n_outputs, name="outputs")
```

Now that we have the neural network model ready to go, we need to define the cost function that we will use to train it. Just as we did for Softmax Regression in Chapter 4, we will use cross entropy. As we discussed earlier, cross entropy will penalize models that estimate a low probability for the target class. TensorFlow provides several functions to compute cross entropy. We will use `sparse_soft max_cross_entropy_with_logits()`: it computes the cross entropy based on the "logits" (i.e., the output of the network *before* going through the softmax activation function), and it expects labels in the form of integers ranging from 0 to the number of classes minus 1 (in our case, from 0 to 9). This will give us a 1D tensor containing the cross entropy for each instance. We can then use TensorFlow's reduce_mean() function to compute the mean cross entropy over all instances.

```
with tf.name_scope("loss"):
    xentropy = tf.nn.sparse_softmax_cross_entropy_with_logits(labels=y,
                                                          logits=logits)
    loss = tf.reduce_mean(xentropy, name="loss")
```

The sparse_softmax_cross_entropy_with_logits() function is equivalent to applying the softmax activation function and then computing the cross entropy, but it is more efficient, and it properly takes care of corner cases: when logits are large, floating-point rounding errors may cause the softmax output to be exactly equal to 0 or 1, and in this case the cross entropy equation would contain a log(0) term, equal to negative infinity. The sparse_soft max_cross_entropy_with_logits() function solves this problem by computing log(ε) instead, where ε is a tiny positive number. This is why we did not apply the softmax activation function earlier. There is also another function called softmax_cross_entropy_with_logits(), which takes labels in the form of one-hot vectors (instead of ints from 0 to the number of classes minus 1).

We have the neural network model, we have the cost function, and now we need to define a GradientDescentOptimizer that will tweak the model parameters to minimize the cost function. Nothing new; it's just like we did in Chapter 9:

```
learning_rate = 0.01

with tf.name_scope("train"):
    optimizer = tf.train.GradientDescentOptimizer(learning_rate)
    training_op = optimizer.minimize(loss)
```

The last important step in the construction phase is to specify how to evaluate the model. We will simply use accuracy as our performance measure. First, for each instance, determine if the neural network's prediction is correct by checking whether or not the highest logit corresponds to the target class. For this you can use the in_top_k() function. This returns a 1D tensor full of boolean values, so we need to cast these booleans to floats and then compute the average. This will give us the network's overall accuracy.

```
with tf.name_scope("eval"):
    correct = tf.nn.in_top_k(logits, y, 1)
    accuracy = tf.reduce_mean(tf.cast(correct, tf.float32))
```

And, as usual, we need to create a node to initialize all variables, and we will also create a Saver to save our trained model parameters to disk:

```
init = tf.global_variables_initializer()
saver = tf.train.Saver()
```

Phew! This concludes the construction phase. This was fewer than 40 lines of code, but it was pretty intense: we created placeholders for the inputs and the targets, we created a function to build a neuron layer, we used it to create the DNN, we defined the cost function, we created an optimizer, and finally we defined the performance measure. Now on to the execution phase.

Execution Phase

This part is much shorter and simpler. First, let's load MNIST. We could use Scikit-Learn for that as we did in previous chapters, but TensorFlow offers its own helper that fetches the data, scales it (between 0 and 1), shuffles it, and provides a simple function to load one mini-batch a time. Moreover, the data is already split into a training set (55,000 instances), a validation set (5,000 instances), and a test set (10,000 instances). So let's use this helper:

```
from tensorflow.examples.tutorials.mnist import input_data
mnist = input_data.read_data_sets("/tmp/data/")
```

Now we define the number of epochs that we want to run, as well as the size of the mini-batches:

```
n_epochs = 40
batch_size = 50
```

And now we can train the model:

```
with tf.Session() as sess:
    init.run()
    for epoch in range(n_epochs):
        for iteration in range(mnist.train.num_examples // batch_size):
            X_batch, y_batch = mnist.train.next_batch(batch_size)
            sess.run(training_op, feed_dict={X: X_batch, y: y_batch})
        acc_train = accuracy.eval(feed_dict={X: X_batch, y: y_batch})
        acc_val = accuracy.eval(feed_dict={X: mnist.validation.images,
                                           y: mnist.validation.labels})
        print(epoch, "Train accuracy:", acc_train, "Val accuracy:", acc_val)

    save_path = saver.save(sess, "./my_model_final.ckpt")
```

This code opens a TensorFlow session, and it runs the init node that initializes all the variables. Then it runs the main training loop: at each epoch, the code iterates through a number of mini-batches that corresponds to the training set size. Each mini-batch is fetched via the next_batch() method, and then the code simply runs the training operation, feeding it the current mini-batch input data and targets. Next, at the end of each epoch, the code evaluates the model on the last mini-batch and on the full validation set, and it prints out the result. Finally, the model parameters are saved to disk.

Using the Neural Network

Now that the neural network is trained, you can use it to make predictions. To do that, you can reuse the same construction phase, but change the execution phase like this:

```
with tf.Session() as sess:
    saver.restore(sess, "./my_model_final.ckpt")
    X_new_scaled = [...]  # some new images (scaled from 0 to 1)
    Z = logits.eval(feed_dict={X: X_new_scaled})
    y_pred = np.argmax(Z, axis=1)
```

First the code loads the model parameters from disk. Then it loads some new images that you want to classify. Remember to apply the same feature scaling as for the training data (in this case, scale it from 0 to 1). Then the code evaluates the logits node. If you wanted to know all the estimated class probabilities, you would need to apply the softmax() function to the logits, but if you just want to predict a class, you can simply pick the class that has the highest logit value (using the argmax() function does the trick).

Fine-Tuning Neural Network Hyperparameters

The flexibility of neural networks is also one of their main drawbacks: there are many hyperparameters to tweak. Not only can you use any imaginable *network topology* (how neurons are interconnected), but even in a simple MLP you can change the number of layers, the number of neurons per layer, the type of activation function to use in each layer, the weight initialization logic, and much more. How do you know what combination of hyperparameters is the best for your task?

Of course, you can use grid search with cross-validation to find the right hyperparameters, like you did in previous chapters, but since there are many hyperparameters to tune, and since training a neural network on a large dataset takes a lot of time, you will only be able to explore a tiny part of the hyperparameter space in a reasonable amount of time. It is much better to use randomized search (*http://homl.info/45*), as we discussed in Chapter 2. Another option is to use a tool such as Oscar (*http://oscar.calldesk.ai/*), which implements more complex algorithms to help you find a good set of hyperparameters quickly.

It helps to have an idea of what values are reasonable for each hyperparameter, so you can restrict the search space. Let's start with the number of hidden layers.

Number of Hidden Layers

For many problems, you can just begin with a single hidden layer and you will get reasonable results. It has actually been shown that an MLP with just one hidden layer can model even the most complex functions provided it has enough neurons. For a long time, these facts convinced researchers that there was no need to investigate any deeper neural networks. But they overlooked the fact that deep networks have a much higher *parameter efficiency* than shallow ones: they can model complex functions using exponentially fewer neurons than shallow nets, making them much faster to train.

To understand why, suppose you are asked to draw a forest using some drawing software, but you are forbidden to use copy/paste. You would have to draw each tree individually, branch per branch, leaf per leaf. If you could instead draw one leaf, copy/paste it to draw a branch, then copy/paste that branch to create a tree, and finally copy/paste this tree to make a forest, you would be finished in no time. Real-world data is often structured in such a hierarchical way and DNNs automatically take advantage of this fact: lower hidden layers model low-level structures (e.g., line segments of various shapes and orientations), intermediate hidden layers combine these low-level structures to model intermediate-level structures (e.g., squares, circles), and the highest hidden layers and the output layer combine these intermediate structures to model high-level structures (e.g., faces).

Not only does this hierarchical architecture help DNNs converge faster to a good solution, it also improves their ability to generalize to new datasets. For example, if you have already trained a model to recognize faces in pictures, and you now want to train a new neural network to recognize hairstyles, then you can kickstart training by reusing the lower layers of the first network. Instead of randomly initializing the weights and biases of the first few layers of the new neural network, you can initialize them to the value of the weights and biases of the lower layers of the first network. This way the network will not have to learn from scratch all the low-level structures that occur in most pictures; it will only have to learn the higher-level structures (e.g., hairstyles).

In summary, for many problems you can start with just one or two hidden layers and it will work just fine (e.g., you can easily reach above 97% accuracy on the MNIST dataset using just one hidden layer with a few hundred neurons, and above 98% accuracy using two hidden layers with the same total amount of neurons, in roughly the same amount of training time). For more complex problems, you can gradually ramp up the number of hidden layers, until you start overfitting the training set. Very complex tasks, such as large image classification or speech recognition, typically require networks with dozens of layers (or even hundreds, but not fully connected ones, as we will see in Chapter 13), and they need a huge amount of training data. However, you will rarely have to train such networks from scratch: it is much more common to reuse parts of a pretrained state-of-the-art network that performs a similar task. Training will be a lot faster and require much less data (we will discuss this in Chapter 11).

Number of Neurons per Hidden Layer

Obviously the number of neurons in the input and output layers is determined by the type of input and output your task requires. For example, the MNIST task requires 28 x 28 = 784 input neurons and 10 output neurons. As for the hidden layers, a common practice is to size them to form a funnel, with fewer and fewer neurons at each layer— the rationale being that many low-level features can coalesce into far fewer high-level features. For example, a typical neural network for MNIST may have two hidden layers, the first with 300 neurons and the second with 100. However, this practice is not as common now, and you may simply use the same size for all hidden layers—for example, all hidden layers with 150 neurons: that's just one hyperparameter to tune instead of one per layer. Just like for the number of layers, you can try increasing the number of neurons gradually until the network starts overfitting. In general you will get more bang for the buck by increasing the number of layers than the number of neurons per layer. Unfortunately, as you can see, finding the perfect amount of neurons is still somewhat of a black art.

A simpler approach is to pick a model with more layers and neurons than you actually need, then use early stopping to prevent it from overfitting (and other regularization techniques, especially *dropout*, as we will see in Chapter 11). This has been dubbed the "stretch pants" approach:[12] instead of wasting time looking for pants that perfectly match your size, just use large stretch pants that will shrink down to the right size.

Activation Functions

In most cases you can use the ReLU activation function in the hidden layers (or one of its variants, as we will see in Chapter 11). It is a bit faster to compute than other activation functions, and Gradient Descent does not get stuck as much on plateaus, thanks to the fact that it does not saturate for large input values (as opposed to the logistic function or the hyperbolic tangent function, which saturate at 1).

For the output layer, the softmax activation function is generally a good choice for classification tasks when the classes are mutually exclusive. When they are not mutually exclusive (or when there are just two classes), you generally want to use the logistic function. For regression tasks, you can simply use no activation function at all for the output layer.

---

12 By Vincent Vanhoucke in his Deep Learning class (*http://homl.info/46*) on Udacity.com.

This concludes this introduction to artificial neural networks. In the following chapters, we will discuss techniques to train very deep nets, and distribute training across multiple servers and GPUs. Then we will explore a few other popular neural network architectures: convolutional neural networks, recurrent neural networks, and autoencoders.[13]

Exercises

1. Draw an ANN using the original artificial neurons (like the ones in Figure 10-3) that computes $A \oplus B$ (where $\oplus$ represents the XOR operation). Hint: $A \oplus B = (A \wedge \neg B) \vee (\neg A \wedge B)$.

2. Why is it generally preferable to use a Logistic Regression classifier rather than a classical Perceptron (i.e., a single layer of threshold logic units trained using the Perceptron training algorithm)? How can you tweak a Perceptron to make it equivalent to a Logistic Regression classifier?

3. Why was the logistic activation function a key ingredient in training the first MLPs?

4. Name three popular activation functions. Can you draw them?

5. Suppose you have an MLP composed of one input layer with 10 passthrough neurons, followed by one hidden layer with 50 artificial neurons, and finally one output layer with 3 artificial neurons. All artificial neurons use the ReLU activation function.

   - What is the shape of the input matrix $\mathbf{X}$?
   - What about the shape of the hidden layer's weight vector $\mathbf{W}_h$, and the shape of its bias vector $\mathbf{b}_h$?
   - What is the shape of the output layer's weight vector $\mathbf{W}_o$, and its bias vector $\mathbf{b}_o$?
   - What is the shape of the network's output matrix $\mathbf{Y}$?
   - Write the equation that computes the network's output matrix $\mathbf{Y}$ as a function of $\mathbf{X}$, $\mathbf{W}_h$, $\mathbf{b}_h$, $\mathbf{W}_o$ and $\mathbf{b}_o$.

6. How many neurons do you need in the output layer if you want to classify email into spam or ham? What activation function should you use in the output layer? If instead you want to tackle MNIST, how many neurons do you need in the output layer, using what activation function? Answer the same questions for getting your network to predict housing prices as in Chapter 2.

---

13 A few extra ANN architectures are presented in Appendix E.

7. What is backpropagation and how does it work? What is the difference between backpropagation and reverse-mode autodiff?

8. Can you list all the hyperparameters you can tweak in an MLP? If the MLP overfits the training data, how could you tweak these hyperparameters to try to solve the problem?

9. Train a deep MLP on the MNIST dataset and see if you can get over 98% precision. Just like in the last exercise of Chapter 9, try adding all the bells and whistles (i.e., save checkpoints, restore the last checkpoint in case of an interruption, add summaries, plot learning curves using TensorBoard, and so on).

Solutions to these exercises are available in Appendix A.

## CHAPTER 11

Training Deep Neural Nets

In Chapter 10 we introduced artificial neural networks and trained our first deep neural network. But it was a very shallow DNN, with only two hidden layers. What if you need to tackle a very complex problem, such as detecting hundreds of types of objects in high-resolution images? You may need to train a much deeper DNN, perhaps with (say) 10 layers, each containing hundreds of neurons, connected by hundreds of thousands of connections. This would not be a walk in the park:

- First, you would be faced with the tricky *vanishing gradients* problem (or the related *exploding gradients* problem) that affects deep neural networks and makes lower layers very hard to train.

- Second, with such a large network, training would be extremely slow.

- Third, a model with millions of parameters would severely risk overfitting the training set.

In this chapter, we will go through each of these problems in turn and present techniques to solve them. We will start by explaining the vanishing gradients problem and exploring some of the most popular solutions to this problem. Next we will look at various optimizers that can speed up training large models tremendously compared to plain Gradient Descent. Finally, we will go through a few popular regularization techniques for large neural networks.

With these tools, you will be able to train very deep nets: welcome to Deep Learning!

Vanishing/Exploding Gradients Problems

As we discussed in Chapter 10, the backpropagation algorithm works by going from the output layer to the input layer, propagating the error gradient on the way. Once the algorithm has computed the gradient of the cost function with regards to each parameter in the network, it uses these gradients to update each parameter with a Gradient Descent step.

Unfortunately, gradients often get smaller and smaller as the algorithm progresses down to the lower layers. As a result, the Gradient Descent update leaves the lower layer connection weights virtually unchanged, and training never converges to a good solution. This is called the *vanishing gradients* problem. In some cases, the opposite can happen: the gradients can grow bigger and bigger, so many layers get insanely large weight updates and the algorithm diverges. This is the *exploding gradients* problem, which is mostly encountered in recurrent neural networks (see Chapter 14). More generally, deep neural networks suffer from unstable gradients; different layers may learn at widely different speeds.

Although this unfortunate behavior has been empirically observed for quite a while (it was one of the reasons why deep neural networks were mostly abandoned for a long time), it is only around 2010 that significant progress was made in understanding it. A paper titled "Understanding the Difficulty of Training Deep Feedforward Neural Networks" (*http://homl.info/47*) by Xavier Glorot and Yoshua Bengio[1] found a few suspects, including the combination of the popular logistic sigmoid activation function and the weight initialization technique that was most popular at the time, namely random initialization using a normal distribution with a mean of 0 and a standard deviation of 1. In short, they showed that with this activation function and this initialization scheme, the variance of the outputs of each layer is much greater than the variance of its inputs. Going forward in the network, the variance keeps increasing after each layer until the activation function saturates at the top layers. This is actually made worse by the fact that the logistic function has a mean of 0.5, not 0 (the hyperbolic tangent function has a mean of 0 and behaves slightly better than the logistic function in deep networks).

Looking at the logistic activation function (see Figure 11-1), you can see that when inputs become large (negative or positive), the function saturates at 0 or 1, with a derivative extremely close to 0. Thus when backpropagation kicks in, it has virtually no gradient to propagate back through the network, and what little gradient exists keeps getting diluted as backpropagation progresses down through the top layers, so there is really nothing left for the lower layers.

---

1 "Understanding the Difficulty of Training Deep Feedforward Neural Networks," X. Glorot, Y Bengio (2010).

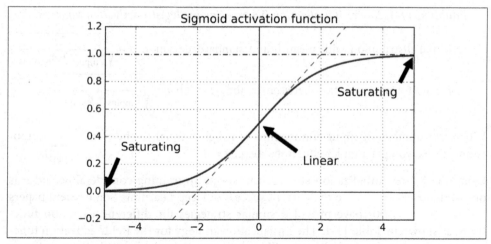

Figure 11-1. Logistic activation function saturation

Xavier and He Initialization

In their paper, Glorot and Bengio propose a way to significantly alleviate this problem. We need the signal to flow properly in both directions: in the forward direction
when making predictions, and in the reverse direction when backpropagating gradients. We don't want the signal to die out, nor do we want it to explode and saturate.
For the signal to flow properly, the authors argue that we need the variance of the
outputs of each layer to be equal to the variance of its inputs,[2] and we also need the
gradients to have equal variance before and after flowing through a layer in the
reverse direction (please check out the paper if you are interested in the mathematical
details). It is actually not possible to guarantee both unless the layer has an equal
number of input and output connections, but they proposed a good compromise that
has proven to work very well in practice: the connection weights must be initialized
randomly as described in Equation 11-1, where n_{inputs} and $n_{outputs}$ are the number of
input and output connections for the layer whose weights are being initialized (also
called *fan-in* and *fan-out*). This initialization strategy is often called *Xavier initialization* (after the author's first name), or sometimes *Glorot initialization*.

---

2 Here's an analogy: if you set a microphone amplifier's knob too close to zero, people won't hear your voice, but
  if you set it too close to the max, your voice will be saturated and people won't understand what you are saying. Now imagine a chain of such amplifiers: they all need to be set properly in order for your voice to come
  out loud and clear at the end of the chain. Your voice has to come out of each amplifier at the same amplitude
  as it came in.

Equation 11-1. Xavier initialization (when using the logistic activation function)

Normal distribution with mean 0 and standard deviation $\sigma = \sqrt{\dfrac{2}{n_{\text{inputs}} + n_{\text{outputs}}}}$

Or a uniform distribution between -r and +r, with $r = \sqrt{\dfrac{6}{n_{\text{inputs}} + n_{\text{outputs}}}}$

When the number of input connections is roughly equal to the number of output connections, you get simpler equations[3] (e.g., $\sigma = 1/\sqrt{n_{\text{inputs}}}$ or $r = \sqrt{3}/\sqrt{n_{\text{inputs}}}$).

Using the Xavier initialization strategy can speed up training considerably, and it is one of the tricks that led to the current success of Deep Learning. Some recent papers (*http://homl.info/48*)[4] have provided similar strategies for different activation functions, as shown in Table 11-1. The initialization strategy for the ReLU activation function (and its variants, including the ELU activation described shortly) is sometimes called *He initialization* (after the last name of its author). This is the strategy we used in Chapter 10.

Table 11-1. Initialization parameters for each type of activation function

Activation function	Uniform distribution [−r, r]	Normal distribution
Logistic	$r = \sqrt{\dfrac{6}{n_{\text{inputs}} + n_{\text{outputs}}}}$	$\sigma = \sqrt{\dfrac{2}{n_{\text{inputs}} + n_{\text{outputs}}}}$
Hyperbolic tangent	$r = 4\sqrt{\dfrac{6}{n_{\text{inputs}} + n_{\text{outputs}}}}$	$\sigma = 4\sqrt{\dfrac{2}{n_{\text{inputs}} + n_{\text{outputs}}}}$
ReLU (and its variants)	$r = \sqrt{2}\sqrt{\dfrac{6}{n_{\text{inputs}} + n_{\text{outputs}}}}$	$\sigma = \sqrt{2}\sqrt{\dfrac{2}{n_{\text{inputs}} + n_{\text{outputs}}}}$

By default, the `tf.layers.dense()` function (introduced in Chapter 10) uses Xavier initialization (with a uniform distribution). You can change this to He initialization by using the `variance_scaling_initializer()` function like this:

```
he_init = tf.contrib.layers.variance_scaling_initializer()
hidden1 = tf.layers.dense(X, n_hidden1, activation=tf.nn.relu,
                          kernel_initializer=he_init, name="hidden1")
```

---

3 This simplified strategy was actually already proposed much earlier—for example, in the 1998 book *Neural Networks: Tricks of the Trade* by Genevieve Orr and Klaus-Robert Müller (Springer).

4 Such as "Delving Deep into Rectifiers: Surpassing Human-Level Performance on ImageNet Classification," K. He et al. (2015).

He initialization considers only the fan-in, not the average between fan-in and fan-out like in Xavier initialization. This is also the default for the `variance_scaling_initializer()` function, but you can change this by setting the argument `mode="FAN_AVG"`.

Nonsaturating Activation Functions

One of the insights in the 2010 paper by Glorot and Bengio was that the vanishing/exploding gradients problems were in part due to a poor choice of activation function. Until then most people had assumed that if Mother Nature had chosen to use roughly sigmoid activation functions in biological neurons, they must be an excellent choice. But it turns out that other activation functions behave much better in deep neural networks, in particular the ReLU activation function, mostly because it does not saturate for positive values (and also because it is quite fast to compute).

Unfortunately, the ReLU activation function is not perfect. It suffers from a problem known as the *dying ReLUs*: during training, some neurons effectively die, meaning they stop outputting anything other than 0. In some cases, you may find that half of your network's neurons are dead, especially if you used a large learning rate. During training, if a neuron's weights get updated such that the weighted sum of the neuron's inputs is negative, it will start outputting 0. When this happens, the neuron is unlikely to come back to life since the gradient of the ReLU function is 0 when its input is negative.

To solve this problem, you may want to use a variant of the ReLU function, such as the *leaky ReLU*. This function is defined as $\text{LeakyReLU}_\alpha(z) = \max(\alpha z, z)$ (see Figure 11-2). The hyperparameter α defines how much the function "leaks": it is the slope of the function for $z < 0$, and is typically set to 0.01. This small slope ensures that leaky ReLUs never die; they can go into a long coma, but they have a chance to eventually wake up. A recent paper (*http://homl.info/49*)[5] compared several variants of the ReLU activation function and one of its conclusions was that the leaky variants always outperformed the strict ReLU activation function. In fact, setting $\alpha = 0.2$ (huge leak) seemed to result in better performance than $\alpha = 0.01$ (small leak). They also evaluated the *randomized leaky ReLU* (RReLU), where α is picked randomly in a given range during training, and it is fixed to an average value during testing. It also performed fairly well and seemed to act as a regularizer (reducing the risk of overfitting the training set). Finally, they also evaluated the *parametric leaky ReLU* (PReLU), where α is authorized to be learned during training (instead of being a hyperparameter, it becomes a parameter that can be modified by backpropagation like any other

---

5 "Empirical Evaluation of Rectified Activations in Convolution Network," B. Xu et al. (2015).

parameter). This was reported to strongly outperform ReLU on large image datasets, but on smaller datasets it runs the risk of overfitting the training set.

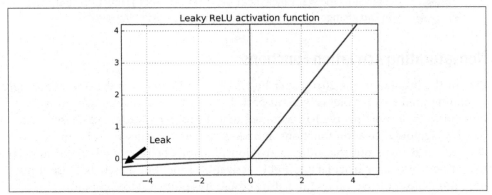

Figure 11-2. Leaky ReLU

Last but not least, a 2015 paper (*http://homl.info/50*) by Djork-Arné Clevert et al.[6] proposed a new activation function called the *exponential linear unit* (ELU) that outperformed all the ReLU variants in their experiments: training time was reduced and the neural network performed better on the test set. It is represented in Figure 11-3, and Equation 11-2 shows its definition.

Equation 11-2. ELU activation function

$$\text{ELU}_\alpha (z) = \begin{cases} \alpha(\exp (z) - 1) & \text{if } z < 0 \\ z & \text{if } z \ge 0 \end{cases}$$

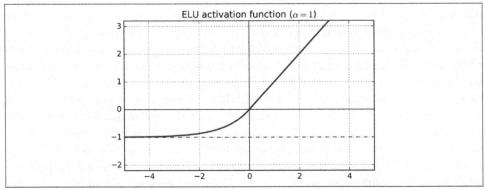

Figure 11-3. ELU activation function

---

6 "Fast and Accurate Deep Network Learning by Exponential Linear Units (ELUs)," D. Clevert, T. Unterthiner, S. Hochreiter (2015).

It looks a lot like the ReLU function, with a few major differences:

- First it takes on negative values when $z < 0$, which allows the unit to have an average output closer to 0. This helps alleviate the vanishing gradients problem, as discussed earlier. The hyperparameter α defines the value that the ELU function approaches when z is a large negative number. It is usually set to 1, but you can tweak it like any other hyperparameter if you want.
- Second, it has a nonzero gradient for $z < 0$, which avoids the dying units issue.
- Third, if α is equal to 1 then the function is smooth everywhere, including around $z = 0$, which helps speed up Gradient Descent, since it does not bounce as much left and right of $z = 0$.

The main drawback of the ELU activation function is that it is slower to compute than the ReLU and its variants (due to the use of the exponential function), but during training this is compensated by the faster convergence rate. However, at test time an ELU network will be slower than a ReLU network.

> So which activation function should you use for the hidden layers of your deep neural networks? Although your mileage will vary, in general ELU > leaky ReLU (and its variants) > ReLU > tanh > logistic. If you care a lot about runtime performance, then you may prefer leaky ReLUs over ELUs. If you don't want to tweak yet another hyperparameter, you may just use the default α values suggested earlier (0.01 for the leaky ReLU, and 1 for ELU). If you have spare time and computing power, you can use cross-validation to evaluate other activation functions, in particular RReLU if your network is overfitting, or PReLU if you have a huge training set.

TensorFlow offers an `elu()` function that you can use to build your neural network. Simply set the `activation` argument when calling the `dense()` function, like this:

```
hidden1 = tf.layers.dense(X, n_hidden1, activation=tf.nn.elu, name="hidden1")
```

TensorFlow does not have a predefined function for leaky ReLUs, but it is easy enough to define:

```
def leaky_relu(z, name=None):
    return tf.maximum(0.01 * z, z, name=name)

hidden1 = tf.layers.dense(X, n_hidden1, activation=leaky_relu, name="hidden1")
```

Batch Normalization

Although using He initialization along with ELU (or any variant of ReLU) can significantly reduce the vanishing/exploding gradients problems at the beginning of training, it doesn't guarantee that they won't come back during training.

In a 2015 paper (*http://homl.info/51*),[7] Sergey Ioffe and Christian Szegedy proposed a technique called *Batch Normalization* (BN) to address the vanishing/exploding gradients problems, and more generally the problem that the distribution of each layer's inputs changes during training, as the parameters of the previous layers change (which they call the *Internal Covariate Shift* problem).

The technique consists of adding an operation in the model just before the activation function of each layer, simply zero-centering and normalizing the inputs, then scaling and shifting the result using two new parameters per layer (one for scaling, the other for shifting). In other words, this operation lets the model learn the optimal scale and mean of the inputs for each layer.

In order to zero-center and normalize the inputs, the algorithm needs to estimate the inputs' mean and standard deviation. It does so by evaluating the mean and standard deviation of the inputs over the current mini-batch (hence the name "Batch Normalization"). The whole operation is summarized in Equation 11-3.

Equation 11-3. Batch Normalization algorithm

1. $\displaystyle \mu_B = \frac{1}{m_B} \sum_{i=1}^{m_B} \mathbf{x}^{(i)}$

2. $\displaystyle \sigma_B^2 = \frac{1}{m_B} \sum_{i=1}^{m_B} \left(\mathbf{x}^{(i)} - \mu_B \right)^2$

3. $\displaystyle \widehat{\mathbf{x}}^{(i)} = \frac{\mathbf{x}^{(i)} - \mu_B}{\sqrt{\sigma_B^2 + \epsilon}}$

4. $\mathbf{z}^{(i)} = \gamma \widehat{\mathbf{x}}^{(i)} + \beta$

- μ_B is the empirical mean, evaluated over the whole mini-batch B.
- σ_B is the empirical standard deviation, also evaluated over the whole mini-batch.
- m_B is the number of instances in the mini-batch.

---

[7] "Batch Normalization: Accelerating Deep Network Training by Reducing Internal Covariate Shift," S. Ioffe and C. Szegedy (2015).

- $\hat{\mathbf{x}}^{(i)}$ is the zero-centered and normalized input.
- γ is the scaling parameter for the layer.
- β is the shifting parameter (offset) for the layer.
- ϵ is a tiny number to avoid division by zero (typically 10^{-5}). This is called a *smoothing term*.
- $\mathbf{z}^{(i)}$ is the output of the BN operation: it is a scaled and shifted version of the inputs.

At test time, there is no mini-batch to compute the empirical mean and standard deviation, so instead you simply use the whole training set's mean and standard deviation. These are typically efficiently computed during training using a moving average. So, in total, four parameters are learned for each batch-normalized layer: γ (scale), β (offset), μ (mean), and σ (standard deviation).

The authors demonstrated that this technique considerably improved all the deep neural networks they experimented with. The vanishing gradients problem was strongly reduced, to the point that they could use saturating activation functions such as the tanh and even the logistic activation function. The networks were also much less sensitive to the weight initialization. They were able to use much larger learning rates, significantly speeding up the learning process. Specifically, they note that "Applied to a state-of-the-art image classification model, Batch Normalization achieves the same accuracy with 14 times fewer training steps, and beats the original model by a significant margin. [...] Using an ensemble of batch-normalized networks, we improve upon the best published result on ImageNet classification: reaching 4.9% top-5 validation error (and 4.8% test error), exceeding the accuracy of human raters." Finally, like a gift that keeps on giving, Batch Normalization also acts like a regularizer, reducing the need for other regularization techniques (such as dropout, described later in the chapter).

Batch Normalization does, however, add some complexity to the model (although it removes the need for normalizing the input data since the first hidden layer will take care of that, provided it is batch-normalized). Moreover, there is a runtime penalty: the neural network makes slower predictions due to the extra computations required at each layer. So if you need predictions to be lightning-fast, you may want to check how well plain ELU + He initialization perform before playing with Batch Normalization.

You may find that training is rather slow at first while Gradient Descent is searching for the optimal scales and offsets for each layer, but it accelerates once it has found reasonably good values.

Implementing Batch Normalization with TensorFlow

TensorFlow provides a `tf.nn.batch_normalization()` function that simply centers and normalizes the inputs, but you must compute the mean and standard deviation yourself (based on the mini-batch data during training or on the full dataset during testing, as just discussed) and pass them as parameters to this function, and you must also handle the creation of the scaling and offset parameters (and pass them to this function). It is doable, but not the most convenient approach. Instead, you should use the `tf.layers.batch_normalization()` function, which handles all this for you, as in the following code:

```
import tensorflow as tf

n_inputs = 28 * 28
n_hidden1 = 300
n_hidden2 = 100
n_outputs = 10

X = tf.placeholder(tf.float32, shape=(None, n_inputs), name="X")

training = tf.placeholder_with_default(False, shape=(), name='training')

hidden1 = tf.layers.dense(X, n_hidden1, name="hidden1")
bn1 = tf.layers.batch_normalization(hidden1, training=training, momentum=0.9)
bn1_act = tf.nn.elu(bn1)
hidden2 = tf.layers.dense(bn1_act, n_hidden2, name="hidden2")
bn2 = tf.layers.batch_normalization(hidden2, training=training, momentum=0.9)
bn2_act = tf.nn.elu(bn2)
logits_before_bn = tf.layers.dense(bn2_act, n_outputs, name="outputs")
logits = tf.layers.batch_normalization(logits_before_bn, training=training,
                                       momentum=0.9)
```

Let's walk through this code. The first lines are fairly self-explanatory, until we define the `training` placeholder: we will set it to `True` during training, but otherwise it will default to `False`. This will be used to tell the `tf.layers.batch_normalization()` function whether it should use the current mini-batch's mean and standard deviation (during training) or the whole training set's mean and standard deviation (during testing).

Then, we alternate fully connected layers and batch normalization layers: the fully connected layers are created using the `tf.layers.dense()` function, just like we did in Chapter 10. Note that we don't specify any activation function for the fully connected layers because we want to apply the activation function after each batch normalization layer.[8] We create the batch normalization layers using the

---

8 Many researchers argue that it is just as good, or even better, to place the batch normalization layers after (rather than before) the activations.

`tf.layers.batch_normalization()` function, setting its `training` and `momentum` parameters. The BN algorithm uses *exponential decay* to compute the running averages, which is why it requires the `momentum` parameter: given a new value v, the running average $\hat{v}$ is updated through the equation:

$$\hat{v} \leftarrow \hat{v} \times \text{momentum} + v \times (1 - \text{momentum})$$

A good momentum value is typically close to 1—for example, 0.9, 0.99, or 0.999 (you want more 9s for larger datasets and smaller mini-batches).

You may have noticed that the code is quite repetitive, with the same batch normalization parameters appearing over and over again. To avoid this repetition, you can use the `partial()` function from the `functools` module (part of Python's standard library). It creates a thin wrapper around a function and allows you to define default values for some parameters. The creation of the network layers in the preceding code can be modified like so:

```
from functools import partial

my_batch_norm_layer = partial(tf.layers.batch_normalization,
                              training=training, momentum=0.9)

hidden1 = tf.layers.dense(X, n_hidden1, name="hidden1")
bn1 = my_batch_norm_layer(hidden1)
bn1_act = tf.nn.elu(bn1)
hidden2 = tf.layers.dense(bn1_act, n_hidden2, name="hidden2")
bn2 = my_batch_norm_layer(hidden2)
bn2_act = tf.nn.elu(bn2)
logits_before_bn = tf.layers.dense(bn2_act, n_outputs, name="outputs")
logits = my_batch_norm_layer(logits_before_bn)
```

It may not look much better than before in this small example, but if you have 10 layers and want to use the same activation function, initializer, regularizer, and so on, in all layers, this trick will make your code much more readable.

The rest of the construction phase is the same as in Chapter 10: define the cost function, create an optimizer, tell it to minimize the cost function, define the evaluation operations, create a variable initializer, create a `Saver`, and so on.

The execution phase is also pretty much the same, with two exceptions. First, during training, whenever you run an operation that depends on the `batch_normaliza tion()` layer, you need to set the `training` placeholder to `True`. Second, the `batch_normalization()` function creates a few operations that must be evaluated at each step during training in order to update the moving averages (recall that these moving averages are needed to evaluate the training set's mean and standard deviation). These operations are automatically added to the `UPDATE_OPS` collection, so all we need to do is get the list of operations in that collection and run them at each training iteration:

```
extra_update_ops = tf.get_collection(tf.GraphKeys.UPDATE_OPS)

with tf.Session() as sess:
    init.run()
    for epoch in range(n_epochs):
        for iteration in range(mnist.train.num_examples // batch_size):
            X_batch, y_batch = mnist.train.next_batch(batch_size)
            sess.run([training_op, extra_update_ops],
                     feed_dict={training: True, X: X_batch, y: y_batch})
        accuracy_val = accuracy.eval(feed_dict={X: mnist.test.images,
                                                y: mnist.test.labels})
        print(epoch, "Test accuracy:", accuracy_val)

    save_path = saver.save(sess, "./my_model_final.ckpt")
```

That's all! In this tiny example with just two layers, it's unlikely that Batch Normalization will have a very positive impact, but for deeper networks it can make a tremendous difference.

Gradient Clipping

A popular technique to lessen the exploding gradients problem is to simply clip the gradients during backpropagation so that they never exceed some threshold (this is mostly useful for recurrent neural networks; see Chapter 14). This is called *Gradient Clipping* (*http://homl.info/52*).[9] In general people now prefer Batch Normalization, but it's still useful to know about Gradient Clipping and how to implement it.

In TensorFlow, the optimizer's `minimize()` function takes care of both computing the gradients and applying them, so you must instead call the optimizer's `compute_gradi ents()` method first, then create an operation to clip the gradients using the `clip_by_value()` function, and finally create an operation to apply the clipped gradients using the optimizer's `apply_gradients()` method:

```
threshold = 1.0
optimizer = tf.train.GradientDescentOptimizer(learning_rate)
grads_and_vars = optimizer.compute_gradients(loss)
capped_gvs = [(tf.clip_by_value(grad, -threshold, threshold), var)
              for grad, var in grads_and_vars]
training_op = optimizer.apply_gradients(capped_gvs)
```

You would then run this `training_op` at every training step, as usual. It will compute the gradients, clip them between –1.0 and 1.0, and apply them. The threshold is a hyperparameter you can tune.

---

9 "On the difficulty of training recurrent neural networks," R. Pascanu et al. (2013).

Reusing Pretrained Layers

It is generally not a good idea to train a very large DNN from scratch: instead, you should always try to find an existing neural network that accomplishes a similar task to the one you are trying to tackle, then just reuse the lower layers of this network: this is called *transfer learning*. It will not only speed up training considerably, but will also require much less training data.

For example, suppose that you have access to a DNN that was trained to classify pictures into 100 different categories, including animals, plants, vehicles, and everyday objects. You now want to train a DNN to classify specific types of vehicles. These tasks are very similar, so you should try to reuse parts of the first network (see Figure 11-4).

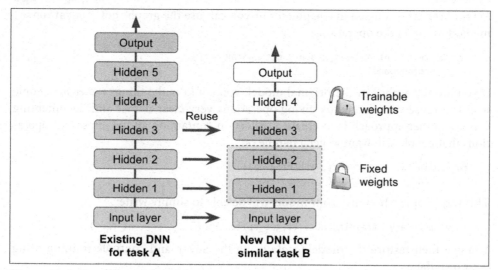

Figure 11-4. Reusing pretrained layers

> If the input pictures of your new task don't have the same size as the ones used in the original task, you will have to add a preprocessing step to resize them to the size expected by the original model. More generally, transfer learning will only work well if the inputs have similar low-level features.

Reusing a TensorFlow Model

If the original model was trained using TensorFlow, you can simply restore it and train it on the new task. As we discussed in Chapter 9, you can use the `import_meta_graph()` function to import the operations into the default graph. This returns a `Saver` that you can later use to load the model's state:

```
saver = tf.train.import_meta_graph("./my_model_final.ckpt.meta")
```

You must then get a handle on the operations and tensors you will need for training. For this, you can use the graph's `get_operation_by_name()` and `get_ten sor_by_name()` methods. The name of a tensor is the name of the operation that outputs it followed by :0 (or :1 if it is the second output, :2 if it is the third, and so on):

```
X = tf.get_default_graph().get_tensor_by_name("X:0")
y = tf.get_default_graph().get_tensor_by_name("y:0")
accuracy = tf.get_default_graph().get_tensor_by_name("eval/accuracy:0")
training_op = tf.get_default_graph().get_operation_by_name("GradientDescent")
```

If the pretrained model is not well documented, then you will have to explore the graph to find the names of the operations you will need. In this case, you can either explore the graph using TensorBoard (for this you must first export the graph using a `FileWriter`, as discussed in Chapter 9), or you can use the graph's `get_operations()` method to list all the operations:

```
for op in tf.get_default_graph().get_operations():
    print(op.name)
```

If you are the author of the original model, you could make things easier for people who will reuse your model by giving operations very clear names and documenting them. Another approach is to create a collection containing all the important operations that people will want to get a handle on:

```
for op in (X, y, accuracy, training_op):
    tf.add_to_collection("my_important_ops", op)
```

This way people who reuse your model will be able to simply write:

```
X, y, accuracy, training_op = tf.get_collection("my_important_ops")
```

You can then restore the model's state using the `Saver` and continue training using your own data:

```
with tf.Session() as sess:
    saver.restore(sess, "./my_model_final.ckpt")
    [...] # train the model on your own data
```

Alternatively, if you have access to the Python code that built the original graph, you can use it instead of `import_meta_graph()`.

In general, you will want to reuse only part of the original model, typically the lower layers. If you use `import_meta_graph()` to restore the graph, it will load the entire original graph, but nothing prevents you from just ignoring the layers you do not care about. For example, as shown in Figure 11-4, you could build new layers (e.g., one hidden layer and one output layer) on top of a pretrained layer (e.g., pretrained hidden layer 3). You would also need to compute the loss for this new output, and create an optimizer to minimize that loss.

If you have access to the pretrained graph's Python code, you can just reuse the parts you need and chop out the rest. However, in this case you need a `Saver` to restore the pretrained model (specifying which variables you want to restore; otherwise, Tensor-Flow will complain that the graphs do not match), and another `Saver` to save the new model. For example, the following code restores only hidden layers 1, 2, and 3:

```
[...] # build the new model with the same hidden layers 1-3 as before

reuse_vars = tf.get_collection(tf.GraphKeys.GLOBAL_VARIABLES,
                               scope="hidden[123]") # regular expression
restore_saver = tf.train.Saver(reuse_vars) # to restore layers 1-3

init = tf.global_variables_initializer() # to init all variables, old and new
saver = tf.train.Saver() # to save the new model

with tf.Session() as sess:
    init.run()
    restore_saver.restore(sess, "./my_model_final.ckpt")
    [...] # train the model
    save_path = saver.save(sess, "./my_new_model_final.ckpt")
```

First we build the new model, making sure to copy the original model's hidden layers 1 to 3. Then we get the list of all variables in hidden layers 1 to 3, using the regular expression `"hidden[123]"`. Next, we create a dictionary that maps the name of each variable in the original model to its name in the new model (generally you want to keep the exact same names). Then we create a `Saver` that will restore only these variables. We also create an operation to initialize all the variables (old and new) and a second `Saver` to save the entire new model, not just layers 1 to 3. We then start a session and initialize all variables in the model, then restore the variable values from the original model's layers 1 to 3. Finally, we train the model on the new task and save it.

> The more similar the tasks are, the more layers you want to reuse (starting with the lower layers). For very similar tasks, you can try keeping all the hidden layers and just replace the output layer.

Reusing Models from Other Frameworks

If the model was trained using another framework, you will need to load the model parameters manually (e.g., using Theano code if it was trained with Theano), then assign them to the appropriate variables. This can be quite tedious. For example, the following code shows how you would copy the weight and biases from the first hidden layer of a model trained using another framework:

```
original_w = [...] # Load the weights from the other framework
original_b = [...] # Load the biases from the other framework
```

```
X = tf.placeholder(tf.float32, shape=(None, n_inputs), name="X")
hidden1 = tf.layers.dense(X, n_hidden1, activation=tf.nn.relu, name="hidden1")
[...] # Build the rest of the model

# Get a handle on the assignment nodes for the hidden1 variables
graph = tf.get_default_graph()
assign_kernel = graph.get_operation_by_name("hidden1/kernel/Assign")
assign_bias = graph.get_operation_by_name("hidden1/bias/Assign")
init_kernel = assign_kernel.inputs[1]
init_bias = assign_bias.inputs[1]

init = tf.global_variables_initializer()

with tf.Session() as sess:
    sess.run(init, feed_dict={init_kernel: original_w, init_bias: original_b})
    # [...] Train the model on your new task
```

In this implementation, we first load the pretrained model using the other framework (not shown here), and we extract from it the model parameters we want to reuse. Next, we build our TensorFlow model as usual. Then comes the tricky part: every TensorFlow variable has an associated assignment operation that is used to initialize it. We start by getting a handle on these assignment operations (they have the same name as the variable, plus "/Assign"). We also get a handle on each assignment operation's second input: in the case of an assignment operation, the second input corresponds to the value that will be assigned to the variable, so in this case it is the variable's initialization value. Once we start the session, we run the usual initialization operation, but this time we feed it the values we want for the variables we want to reuse. Alternatively, we could have created new assignment operations and placeholders, and used them to set the values of the variables after initialization. But why create new nodes in the graph when everything we need is already there?

Freezing the Lower Layers

It is likely that the lower layers of the first DNN have learned to detect low-level features in pictures that will be useful across both image classification tasks, so you can just reuse these layers as they are. It is generally a good idea to "freeze" their weights when training the new DNN: if the lower-layer weights are fixed, then the higher-layer weights will be easier to train (because they won't have to learn a moving target). To freeze the lower layers during training, one solution is to give the optimizer the list of variables to train, excluding the variables from the lower layers:

```
train_vars = tf.get_collection(tf.GraphKeys.TRAINABLE_VARIABLES,
                               scope="hidden[34]|outputs")
training_op = optimizer.minimize(loss, var_list=train_vars)
```

The first line gets the list of all trainable variables in hidden layers 3 and 4 and in the output layer. This leaves out the variables in the hidden layers 1 and 2. Next we provide this restricted list of trainable variables to the optimizer's minimize() function.

Ta-da! Layers 1 and 2 are now frozen: they will not budge during training (these are often called *frozen layers*).

Another option is to add a `stop_gradient()` layer in the graph. Any layer below it will be frozen:

```
with tf.name_scope("dnn"):
    hidden1 = tf.layers.dense(X, n_hidden1, activation=tf.nn.relu,
                              name="hidden1") # reused frozen
    hidden2 = tf.layers.dense(hidden1, n_hidden2, activation=tf.nn.relu,
                              name="hidden2") # reused frozen
    hidden2_stop = tf.stop_gradient(hidden2)
    hidden3 = tf.layers.dense(hidden2_stop, n_hidden3, activation=tf.nn.relu,
                              name="hidden3") # reused, not frozen
    hidden4 = tf.layers.dense(hidden3, n_hidden4, activation=tf.nn.relu,
                              name="hidden4") # new!
    logits = tf.layers.dense(hidden4, n_outputs, name="outputs") # new!
```

Caching the Frozen Layers

Since the frozen layers won't change, it is possible to cache the output of the topmost frozen layer for each training instance. Since training goes through the whole dataset many times, this will give you a huge speed boost as you will only need to go through the frozen layers once per training instance (instead of once per epoch). For example, you could first run the whole training set through the lower layers (assuming you have enough RAM), then during training, instead of building batches of training instances, you would build batches of outputs from hidden layer 2 and feed them to the training operation:

```
import numpy as np

n_batches = mnist.train.num_examples // batch_size

with tf.Session() as sess:
    init.run()
    restore_saver.restore(sess, "./my_model_final.ckpt")

    h2_cache = sess.run(hidden2, feed_dict={X: mnist.train.images})

    for epoch in range(n_epochs):
        shuffled_idx = np.random.permutation(mnist.train.num_examples)
        hidden2_batches = np.array_split(h2_cache[shuffled_idx], n_batches)
        y_batches = np.array_split(mnist.train.labels[shuffled_idx], n_batches)
        for hidden2_batch, y_batch in zip(hidden2_batches, y_batches):
            sess.run(training_op, feed_dict={hidden2:hidden2_batch, y:y_batch})

    save_path = saver.save(sess, "./my_new_model_final.ckpt")
```

The last line of the training loop runs the training operation defined earlier (which does not touch layers 1 and 2), and feeds it a batch of outputs from the second hidden layer (as well as the targets for that batch). Since we give TensorFlow the output of hidden layer 2, it does not try to evaluate it (or any node it depends on).

Tweaking, Dropping, or Replacing the Upper Layers

The output layer of the original model should usually be replaced since it is most likely not useful at all for the new task, and it may not even have the right number of outputs for the new task.

Similarly, the upper hidden layers of the original model are less likely to be as useful as the lower layers, since the high-level features that are most useful for the new task may differ significantly from the ones that were most useful for the original task. You want to find the right number of layers to reuse.

Try freezing all the copied layers first, then train your model and see how it performs. Then try unfreezing one or two of the top hidden layers to let backpropagation tweak them and see if performance improves. The more training data you have, the more layers you can unfreeze.

If you still cannot get good performance, and you have little training data, try dropping the top hidden layer(s) and freeze all remaining hidden layers again. You can iterate until you find the right number of layers to reuse. If you have plenty of training data, you may try replacing the top hidden layers instead of dropping them, and even add more hidden layers.

Model Zoos

Where can you find a neural network trained for a task similar to the one you want to tackle? The first place to look is obviously in your own catalog of models. This is one good reason to save all your models and organize them so you can retrieve them later easily. Another option is to search in a *model zoo*. Many people train Machine Learning models for various tasks and kindly release their pretrained models to the public.

TensorFlow has its own model zoo available at *https://github.com/tensorflow/models*. In particular, it contains most of the state-of-the-art image classification nets such as VGG, Inception, and ResNet (see Chapter 13, and check out the *models/slim* directory), including the code, the pretrained models, and tools to download popular image datasets.

Another popular model zoo is Caffe's Model Zoo (*http://homl.info/53*). It also contains many computer vision models (e.g., LeNet, AlexNet, ZFNet, GoogLeNet, VGGNet, inception) trained on various datasets (e.g., ImageNet, Places Database, CIFAR10, etc.). Saumitro Dasgupta wrote a converter, which is available at *https://github.com/ethereon/caffe-tensorflow*.

Unsupervised Pretraining

Suppose you want to tackle a complex task for which you don't have much labeled training data, but unfortunately you cannot find a model trained on a similar task. Don't lose all hope! First, you should of course try to gather more labeled training data, but if this is too hard or too expensive, you may still be able to perform *unsupervised pretraining* (see Figure 11-5). That is, if you have plenty of unlabeled training data, you can try to train the layers one by one, starting with the lowest layer and then going up, using an unsupervised feature detector algorithm such as *Restricted Boltzmann Machines* (RBMs; see Appendix E) or autoencoders (see Chapter 15). Each layer is trained on the output of the previously trained layers (all layers except the one being trained are frozen). Once all layers have been trained this way, you can fine-tune the network using supervised learning (i.e., with backpropagation).

This is a rather long and tedious process, but it often works well; in fact, it is this technique that Geoffrey Hinton and his team used in 2006 and which led to the revival of neural networks and the success of Deep Learning. Until 2010, unsupervised pretraining (typically using RBMs) was the norm for deep nets, and it was only after the vanishing gradients problem was alleviated that it became much more common to train DNNs purely using backpropagation. However, unsupervised pretraining (today typically using autoencoders rather than RBMs) is still a good option when you have a complex task to solve, no similar model you can reuse, and little labeled training data but plenty of unlabeled training data.

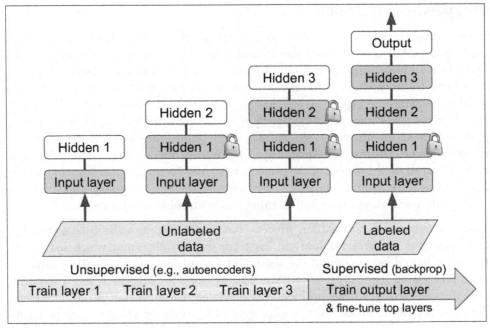

Figure 11-5. Unsupervised pretraining

Pretraining on an Auxiliary Task

One last option is to train a first neural network on an auxiliary task for which you can easily obtain or generate labeled training data, then reuse the lower layers of that network for your actual task. The first neural network's lower layers will learn feature detectors that will likely be reusable by the second neural network.

For example, if you want to build a system to recognize faces, you may only have a few pictures of each individual—clearly not enough to train a good classifier. Gathering hundreds of pictures of each person would not be practical. However, you could gather a lot of pictures of random people on the internet and train a first neural network to detect whether or not two different pictures feature the same person. Such a network would learn good feature detectors for faces, so reusing its lower layers would allow you to train a good face classifier using little training data.

It is often rather cheap to gather unlabeled training examples, but quite expensive to label them. In this situation, a common technique is to label all your training examples as "good," then generate many new training instances by corrupting the good ones, and label these corrupted instances as "bad." Then you can train a first neural network to classify instances as good or bad. For example, you could download millions of sentences, label them as "good," then randomly change a word in each sentence and label the resulting sentences as "bad." If a neural network can tell that "The dog sleeps" is a good sentence but "The dog they" is bad, it probably knows quite a lot about language. Reusing its lower layers will likely help in many language processing tasks.

Another approach is to train a first network to output a score for each training instance, and use a cost function that ensures that a good instance's score is greater than a bad instance's score by at least some margin. This is called *max margin learning*.

Faster Optimizers

Training a very large deep neural network can be painfully slow. So far we have seen four ways to speed up training (and reach a better solution): applying a good initialization strategy for the connection weights, using a good activation function, using Batch Normalization, and reusing parts of a pretrained network. Another huge speed boost comes from using a faster optimizer than the regular Gradient Descent optimizer. In this section we will present the most popular ones: Momentum optimization, Nesterov Accelerated Gradient, AdaGrad, RMSProp, and finally Adam optimization.

Momentum Optimization

Imagine a bowling ball rolling down a gentle slope on a smooth surface: it will start out slowly, but it will quickly pick up momentum until it eventually reaches terminal velocity (if there is some friction or air resistance). This is the very simple idea behind *Momentum optimization*, proposed by Boris Polyak in 1964 (*http://homl.info/54*).[10] In contrast, regular Gradient Descent will simply take small regular steps down the slope, so it will take much more time to reach the bottom.

Recall that Gradient Descent simply updates the weights θ by directly subtracting the gradient of the cost function $J(\theta)$ with regards to the weights ($\nabla_\theta J(\theta)$) multiplied by the learning rate η. The equation is: $\theta \leftarrow \theta - \eta \nabla_\theta J(\theta)$. It does not care about what the earlier gradients were. If the local gradient is tiny, it goes very slowly.

Momentum optimization cares a great deal about what previous gradients were: at each iteration, it subtracts the local gradient from the *momentum vector* **m** (multiplied by the learning rate η), and it updates the weights by simply adding this momentum vector (see Equation 11-4). In other words, the gradient is used as an acceleration, not as a speed. To simulate some sort of friction mechanism and prevent the momentum from growing too large, the algorithm introduces a new hyperpara-

---

10 "Some methods of speeding up the convergence of iteration methods," B. Polyak (1964).

meter β, simply called the *momentum*, which must be set between 0 (high friction) and 1 (no friction). A typical momentum value is 0.9.

Equation 11-4. Momentum algorithm

1. $\mathbf{m} \leftarrow \beta\mathbf{m} - \eta\nabla_\theta J(\theta)$

2. $\theta \leftarrow \theta + \mathbf{m}$

You can easily verify that if the gradient remains constant, the terminal velocity (i.e., the maximum size of the weight updates) is equal to that gradient multiplied by the learning rate η multiplied by $\frac{1}{1-\beta}$ (ignoring the sign). For example, if $\beta = 0.9$, then the terminal velocity is equal to 10 times the gradient times the learning rate, so Momentum optimization ends up going 10 times faster than Gradient Descent! This allows Momentum optimization to escape from plateaus much faster than Gradient Descent. In particular, we saw in Chapter 4 that when the inputs have very different scales the cost function will look like an elongated bowl (see Figure 4-7). Gradient Descent goes down the steep slope quite fast, but then it takes a very long time to go down the valley. In contrast, Momentum optimization will roll down the bottom of the valley faster and faster until it reaches the bottom (the optimum). In deep neural networks that don't use Batch Normalization, the upper layers will often end up having inputs with very different scales, so using Momentum optimization helps a lot. It can also help roll past local optima.

 Due to the momentum, the optimizer may overshoot a bit, then come back, overshoot again, and oscillate like this many times before stabilizing at the minimum. This is one of the reasons why it is good to have a bit of friction in the system: it gets rid of these oscillations and thus speeds up convergence.

Implementing Momentum optimization in TensorFlow is a no-brainer: just replace the `GradientDescentOptimizer` with the `MomentumOptimizer`, then lie back and profit!

```
optimizer = tf.train.MomentumOptimizer(learning_rate=learning_rate,
                                       momentum=0.9)
```

The one drawback of Momentum optimization is that it adds yet another hyperparameter to tune. However, the momentum value of 0.9 usually works well in practice and almost always goes faster than Gradient Descent.

Nesterov Accelerated Gradient

One small variant to Momentum optimization, proposed by Yurii Nesterov in 1983 (*http://homl.info/55*),[11] is almost always faster than vanilla Momentum optimization. The idea of *Nesterov Momentum optimization,* or *Nesterov Accelerated Gradient* (NAG), is to measure the gradient of the cost function not at the local position but slightly ahead in the direction of the momentum (see Equation 11-5). The only difference from vanilla Momentum optimization is that the gradient is measured at $\theta + \beta\mathbf{m}$ rather than at θ.

Equation 11-5. Nesterov Accelerated Gradient algorithm

1. $\mathbf{m} \leftarrow \beta\mathbf{m} - \eta\nabla_\theta J(\theta + \beta\mathbf{m})$

2. $\theta \leftarrow \theta + \mathbf{m}$

This small tweak works because in general the momentum vector will be pointing in the right direction (i.e., toward the optimum), so it will be slightly more accurate to use the gradient measured a bit farther in that direction rather than using the gradient at the original position, as you can see in Figure 11-6 (where ∇_1 represents the gradient of the cost function measured at the starting point θ, and ∇_2 represents the gradient at the point located at $\theta + \beta\mathbf{m}$). As you can see, the Nesterov update ends up slightly closer to the optimum. After a while, these small improvements add up and NAG ends up being significantly faster than regular Momentum optimization. Moreover, note that when the momentum pushes the weights across a valley, ∇_1 continues to push further across the valley, while ∇_2 pushes back toward the bottom of the valley. This helps reduce oscillations and thus converges faster.

NAG will almost always speed up training compared to regular Momentum optimization. To use it, simply set `use_nesterov=True` when creating the `MomentumOptim izer`:

```
optimizer = tf.train.MomentumOptimizer(learning_rate=learning_rate,
                                       momentum=0.9, use_nesterov=True)
```

---

[11] "A Method for Unconstrained Convex Minimization Problem with the Rate of Convergence $O(1/k^2)$," Yurii Nesterov (1983).

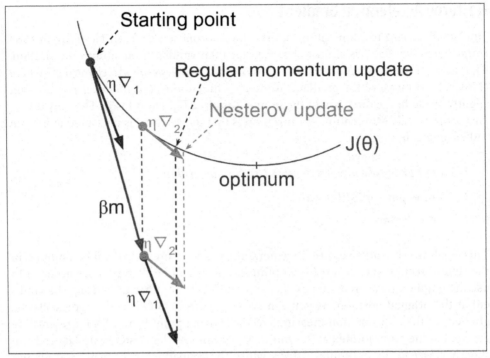

Figure 11-6. Regular versus Nesterov Momentum optimization

AdaGrad

Consider the elongated bowl problem again: Gradient Descent starts by quickly going down the steepest slope, then slowly goes down the bottom of the valley. It would be nice if the algorithm could detect this early on and correct its direction to point a bit more toward the global optimum.

The *AdaGrad* algorithm (*http://homl.info/56*)[12] achieves this by scaling down the gradient vector along the steepest dimensions (see Equation 11-6):

Equation 11-6. AdaGrad algorithm

1. $\mathbf{s} \leftarrow \mathbf{s} + \nabla_{\theta} J(\theta) \otimes \nabla_{\theta} J(\theta)$

2. $\theta \leftarrow \theta - \eta \nabla_{\theta} J(\theta) \oslash \sqrt{\mathbf{s} + \epsilon}$

The first step accumulates the square of the gradients into the vector $\mathbf{s}$ (the $\otimes$ symbol represents the element-wise multiplication). This vectorized form is equivalent to

---

12 "Adaptive Subgradient Methods for Online Learning and Stochastic Optimization," J. Duchi et al. (2011).

computing $s_i \leftarrow s_i + (\partial\,J(\theta) \,/\, \partial\,\theta_i)^2$ for each element s_i of the vector $\mathbf{s}$; in other words, each s_i accumulates the squares of the partial derivative of the cost function with regards to parameter θ_i. If the cost function is steep along the ith dimension, then s_i will get larger and larger at each iteration.

The second step is almost identical to Gradient Descent, but with one big difference: the gradient vector is scaled down by a factor of $\sqrt{\mathbf{s} + \epsilon}$ (the $\oslash$ symbol represents the element-wise division, and ϵ is a smoothing term to avoid division by zero, typically set to 10^{-10}). This vectorized form is equivalent to computing $\theta_i \leftarrow \theta_i - \eta\,\partial J(\theta) / \partial\theta_i / \sqrt{s_i + \epsilon}$ for all parameters θ_i (simultaneously).

In short, this algorithm decays the learning rate, but it does so faster for steep dimensions than for dimensions with gentler slopes. This is called an *adaptive learning rate*. It helps point the resulting updates more directly toward the global optimum (see Figure 11-7). One additional benefit is that it requires much less tuning of the learning rate hyperparameter η.

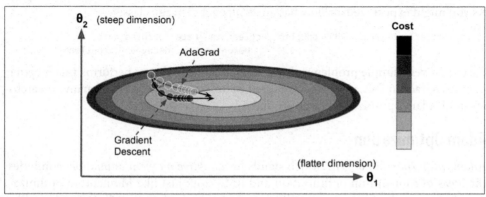

Figure 11-7. AdaGrad versus Gradient Descent

AdaGrad often performs well for simple quadratic problems, but unfortunately it often stops too early when training neural networks. The learning rate gets scaled down so much that the algorithm ends up stopping entirely before reaching the global optimum. So even though TensorFlow has an AdagradOptimizer, you should not use it to train deep neural networks (it may be efficient for simpler tasks such as Linear Regression, though).

RMSProp

Although AdaGrad slows down a bit too fast and ends up never converging to the global optimum, the *RMSProp* algorithm[13] fixes this by accumulating only the gradients from the most recent iterations (as opposed to all the gradients since the beginning of training). It does so by using exponential decay in the first step (see Equation 11-7).

Equation 11-7. RMSProp algorithm

1. $\mathbf{s} \leftarrow \beta \mathbf{s} + (1 - \beta) \nabla_\theta J(\theta) \otimes \nabla_\theta J(\theta)$

2. $\theta \leftarrow \theta - \eta \nabla_\theta J(\theta) \oslash \sqrt{\mathbf{s} + \epsilon}$

The decay rate β is typically set to 0.9. Yes, it is once again a new hyperparameter, but this default value often works well, so you may not need to tune it at all.

As you might expect, TensorFlow has an `RMSPropOptimizer` class:[14]

```
optimizer = tf.train.RMSPropOptimizer(learning_rate=learning_rate,
                                      momentum=0.9, decay=0.9, epsilon=1e-10)
```

Except on very simple problems, this optimizer almost always performs much better than AdaGrad. In fact, it was the preferred optimization algorithm of many researchers until Adam optimization came around.

Adam Optimization

Adam (*http://homl.info/59*),[15] which stands for *adaptive moment estimation*, combines the ideas of Momentum optimization and RMSProp: just like Momentum optimization it keeps track of an exponentially decaying average of past gradients, and just like RMSProp it keeps track of an exponentially decaying average of past squared gradients (see Equation 11-8).[16]

---

13 This algorithm was created by Tijmen Tieleman and Geoffrey Hinton in 2012, and presented by Geoffrey Hinton in his Coursera class on neural networks (slides: *http://homl.info/57*; video: *http://homl.info/58*). Amusingly, since the authors have not written a paper to describe it, researchers often cite "slide 29 in lecture 6" in their papers.

14 Note that TensorFlow's implementation of RMSProp combines the original RMSProp algorithm with Momentum optimization (regular, not Nesterov), which is why there is a `momentum` hyperparameter.

15 "Adam: A Method for Stochastic Optimization," D. Kingma, J. Ba (2015).

16 These are estimations of the mean and (uncentered) variance of the gradients. The mean is often called the *first moment*, while the variance is often called the *second moment*, hence the name of the algorithm.

Equation 11-8. Adam algorithm

1. $\quad \mathbf{m} \leftarrow \beta_1 \mathbf{m} - (1 - \beta_1) \nabla_\theta J(\theta)$

2. $\quad \mathbf{s} \leftarrow \beta_2 \mathbf{s} + (1 - \beta_2) \nabla_\theta J(\theta) \otimes \nabla_\theta J(\theta)$

3. $\quad \widehat{\mathbf{m}} \leftarrow \dfrac{\mathbf{m}}{1 - \beta_1{}^t}$

4. $\quad \widehat{\mathbf{s}} \leftarrow \dfrac{\mathbf{s}}{1 - \beta_2{}^t}$

5. $\quad \theta \leftarrow \theta + \eta\, \widehat{\mathbf{m}} \oslash \sqrt{\widehat{\mathbf{s}} + \epsilon}$

- t represents the iteration number (starting at 1).

If you just look at steps 1, 2, and 5, you will notice Adam's close similarity to both Momentum optimization and RMSProp. The only difference is that step 1 computes an exponentially decaying average rather than an exponentially decaying sum, but these are actually equivalent except for a constant factor (the decaying average is just $1 - \beta_1$ times the decaying sum). Steps 3 and 4 are somewhat of a technical detail: since $\mathbf{m}$ and $\mathbf{s}$ are initialized at 0, they will be biased toward 0 at the beginning of training, so these two steps will help boost $\mathbf{m}$ and $\mathbf{s}$ at the beginning of training.

The momentum decay hyperparameter β_1 is typically initialized to 0.9, while the scaling decay hyperparameter β_2 is often initialized to 0.999. As earlier, the smoothing term ϵ is usually initialized to a tiny number such as 10^{-8}. These are the default values for TensorFlow's AdamOptimizer class, so you can simply use:

```
optimizer = tf.train.AdamOptimizer(learning_rate=learning_rate)
```

In fact, since Adam is an adaptive learning rate algorithm (like AdaGrad and RMSProp), it requires less tuning of the learning rate hyperparameter η. You can often use the default value $\eta = 0.001$, making Adam even easier to use than Gradient Descent.

This book initially recommended using Adam optimization, because it was generally considered faster and better than other methods. However, a 2017 paper (*http://homl.info/60*)[17] by Ashia C. Wilson et al. showed that adaptive optimization methods (i.e., Ada-Grad, RMSProp and Adam optimization) can lead to solutions that generalize poorly on some datasets. So you may want to stick to Momentum optimization or Nesterov Accelerated Gradient for now, until researchers have a better understanding of this issue.

All the optimization techniques discussed so far only rely on the *first-order partial derivatives* (*Jacobians*). The optimization literature contains amazing algorithms based on the *second-order partial derivatives* (the *Hessians*). Unfortunately, these algorithms are very hard to apply to deep neural networks because there are n^2 Hessians per output (where n is the number of parameters), as opposed to just n Jacobians per output. Since DNNs typically have tens of thousands of parameters, the second-order optimization algorithms often don't even fit in memory, and even when they do, computing the Hessians is just too slow.

Training Sparse Models

All the optimization algorithms just presented produce dense models, meaning that most parameters will be nonzero. If you need a blazingly fast model at runtime, or if you need it to take up less memory, you may prefer to end up with a sparse model instead.

One trivial way to achieve this is to train the model as usual, then get rid of the tiny weights (set them to 0).

Another option is to apply strong ℓ_1 regularization during training, as it pushes the optimizer to zero out as many weights as it can (as discussed in Chapter 4 about Lasso Regression).

However, in some cases these techniques may remain insufficient. One last option is to apply *Dual Averaging*, often called *Follow The Regularized Leader* (FTRL), a technique proposed by Yurii Nesterov (*http://homl.info/61*).[18] When used with ℓ_1 regularization, this technique often leads to very sparse models. TensorFlow implements a variant of FTRL called *FTRL-Proximal* (*http://homl.info/62*)[19] in the `FTRLOptimizer` class.

---

17 "The Marginal Value of Adaptive Gradient Methods in Machine Learning," A. C. Wilson et al. (2017).

18 "Primal-Dual Subgradient Methods for Convex Problems," Yurii Nesterov (2005).

19 "Ad Click Prediction: a View from the Trenches," H. McMahan et al. (2013).

Learning Rate Scheduling

Finding a good learning rate can be tricky. If you set it way too high, training may actually diverge (as we discussed in Chapter 4). If you set it too low, training will eventually converge to the optimum, but it will take a very long time. If you set it slightly too high, it will make progress very quickly at first, but it will end up dancing around the optimum, never settling down (unless you use an adaptive learning rate optimization algorithm such as AdaGrad, RMSProp, or Adam, but even then it may take time to settle). If you have a limited computing budget, you may have to interrupt training before it has converged properly, yielding a suboptimal solution (see Figure 11-8).

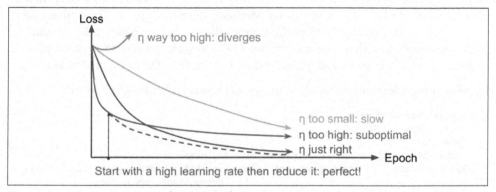

Figure 11-8. Learning curves for various learning rates η

You may be able to find a fairly good learning rate by training your network several times during just a few epochs using various learning rates and comparing the learning curves. The ideal learning rate will learn quickly and converge to good solution.

However, you can do better than a constant learning rate: if you start with a high learning rate and then reduce it once it stops making fast progress, you can reach a good solution faster than with the optimal constant learning rate. There are many different strategies to reduce the learning rate during training. These strategies are called *learning schedules* (we briefly introduced this concept in Chapter 4), the most common of which are:

Predetermined piecewise constant learning rate
> For example, set the learning rate to $\eta_0 = 0.1$ at first, then to $\eta_1 = 0.001$ after 50 epochs. Although this solution can work very well, it often requires fiddling around to figure out the right learning rates and when to use them.

Performance scheduling
> Measure the validation error every N steps (just like for early stopping) and reduce the learning rate by a factor of λ when the error stops dropping.

Exponential scheduling

Set the learning rate to a function of the iteration number t: $\eta(t) = \eta_0 \, 10^{-t/r}$. This works great, but it requires tuning η_0 and r. The learning rate will drop by a factor of 10 every r steps.

Power scheduling

Set the learning rate to $\eta(t) = \eta_0 \, (1 + t/r)^{-c}$. The hyperparameter c is typically set to 1. This is similar to exponential scheduling, but the learning rate drops much more slowly.

A 2013 paper (*http://homl.info/63*)[20] by Andrew Senior et al. compared the performance of some of the most popular learning schedules when training deep neural networks for speech recognition using Momentum optimization. The authors concluded that, in this setting, both performance scheduling and exponential scheduling performed well, but they favored exponential scheduling because it is simpler to implement, is easy to tune, and converged slightly faster to the optimal solution.

Implementing a learning schedule with TensorFlow is fairly straightforward:

```
initial_learning_rate = 0.1
decay_steps = 10000
decay_rate = 1/10
global_step = tf.Variable(0, trainable=False, name="global_step")
learning_rate = tf.train.exponential_decay(initial_learning_rate, global_step,
                                           decay_steps, decay_rate)
optimizer = tf.train.MomentumOptimizer(learning_rate, momentum=0.9)
training_op = optimizer.minimize(loss, global_step=global_step)
```

After setting the hyperparameter values, we create a nontrainable variable `global_step` (initialized to 0) to keep track of the current training iteration number. Then we define an exponentially decaying learning rate (with $\eta_0 = 0.1$ and $r = 10,000$) using TensorFlow's `exponential_decay()` function. Next, we create an optimizer (in this example, a `MomentumOptimizer`) using this decaying learning rate. Finally, we create the training operation by calling the optimizer's `minimize()` method; since we pass it the `global_step` variable, it will kindly take care of incrementing it. That's it!

Since AdaGrad, RMSProp, and Adam optimization automatically reduce the learning rate during training, it is not necessary to add an extra learning schedule. For other optimization algorithms, using exponential decay or performance scheduling can considerably speed up convergence.

---

[20] "An Empirical Study of Learning Rates in Deep Neural Networks for Speech Recognition," A. Senior et al. (2013).

Avoiding Overfitting Through Regularization

> With four parameters I can fit an elephant and with five I can make him wiggle his trunk.
>
> —John von Neumann, *cited by Enrico Fermi in Nature 427*

Deep neural networks typically have tens of thousands of parameters, sometimes even millions. With so many parameters, the network has an incredible amount of freedom and can fit a huge variety of complex datasets. But this great flexibility also means that it is prone to overfitting the training set.

With millions of parameters you can fit the whole zoo. In this section we will present some of the most popular regularization techniques for neural networks, and how to implement them with TensorFlow: early stopping, ℓ_1 and ℓ_2 regularization, dropout, max-norm regularization, and data augmentation.

Early Stopping

To avoid overfitting the training set, a great solution is early stopping (introduced in Chapter 4): just interrupt training when its performance on the validation set starts dropping.

One way to implement this with TensorFlow is to evaluate the model on a validation set at regular intervals (e.g., every 50 steps), and save a "winner" snapshot if it outperforms previous "winner" snapshots. Count the number of steps since the last "winner" snapshot was saved, and interrupt training when this number reaches some limit (e.g., 2,000 steps). Then restore the last "winner" snapshot.

Although early stopping works very well in practice, you can usually get much higher performance out of your network by combining it with other regularization techniques.

ℓ_1 and ℓ_2 Regularization

Just like you did in Chapter 4 for simple linear models, you can use ℓ_1 and ℓ_2 regularization to constrain a neural network's connection weights (but typically not its biases).

One way to do this using TensorFlow is to simply add the appropriate regularization terms to your cost function. For example, assuming you have just one hidden layer with weights W1 and one output layer with weights W2, then you can apply ℓ_1 regularization like this:

```
[...] # construct the neural network
W1 = tf.get_default_graph().get_tensor_by_name("hidden1/kernel:0")
W2 = tf.get_default_graph().get_tensor_by_name("outputs/kernel:0")

scale = 0.001 # l1 regularization hyperparameter

with tf.name_scope("loss"):
    xentropy = tf.nn.sparse_softmax_cross_entropy_with_logits(labels=y,
                                                              logits=logits)
    base_loss = tf.reduce_mean(xentropy, name="avg_xentropy")
    reg_losses = tf.reduce_sum(tf.abs(W1)) + tf.reduce_sum(tf.abs(W2))
    loss = tf.add(base_loss, scale * reg_losses, name="loss")
```

However, if there are many layers, this approach is not very convenient. Fortunately, TensorFlow provides a better option. Many functions that create variables (such as get_variable() or tf.layers.dense()) accept a *_regularizer argument for each created variable (e.g., kernel_regularizer). You can pass any function that takes weights as an argument and returns the corresponding regularization loss. The l1_regularizer(), l2_regularizer(), and l1_l2_regularizer() functions return such functions. The following code puts all this together:

```
my_dense_layer = partial(
    tf.layers.dense, activation=tf.nn.relu,
    kernel_regularizer=tf.contrib.layers.l1_regularizer(scale))

with tf.name_scope("dnn"):
    hidden1 = my_dense_layer(X, n_hidden1, name="hidden1")
    hidden2 = my_dense_layer(hidden1, n_hidden2, name="hidden2")
    logits = my_dense_layer(hidden2, n_outputs, activation=None,
                            name="outputs")
```

This code creates a neural network with two hidden layers and one output layer, and it also creates nodes in the graph to compute the ℓ_1 regularization loss corresponding to each layer's weights. TensorFlow automatically adds these nodes to a special collection containing all the regularization losses. You just need to add these regularization losses to your overall loss, like this:

```
reg_losses = tf.get_collection(tf.GraphKeys.REGULARIZATION_LOSSES)
loss = tf.add_n([base_loss] + reg_losses, name="loss")
```

> Don't forget to add the regularization losses to your overall loss, or else they will simply be ignored.

Dropout

The most popular regularization technique for deep neural networks is arguably *dropout*. It was proposed (*http://homl.info/64*)[21] by G. E. Hinton in 2012 and further detailed in a paper (*http://homl.info/65*)[22] by Nitish Srivastava et al., and it has proven to be highly successful: even the state-of-the-art neural networks got a 1–2% accuracy boost simply by adding dropout. This may not sound like a lot, but when a model already has 95% accuracy, getting a 2% accuracy boost means dropping the error rate by almost 40% (going from 5% error to roughly 3%).

It is a fairly simple algorithm: at every training step, every neuron (including the input neurons but excluding the output neurons) has a probability p of being temporarily "dropped out," meaning it will be entirely ignored during this training step, but it may be active during the next step (see Figure 11-9). The hyperparameter p is called the *dropout rate*, and it is typically set to 50%. After training, neurons don't get dropped anymore. And that's all (except for a technical detail we will discuss momentarily).

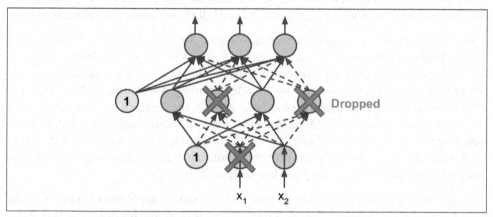

Figure 11-9. Dropout regularization

It is quite surprising at first that this rather brutal technique works at all. Would a company perform better if its employees were told to toss a coin every morning to decide whether or not to go to work? Well, who knows; perhaps it would! The company would obviously be forced to adapt its organization; it could not rely on any single person to fill in the coffee machine or perform any other critical tasks, so this expertise would have to be spread across several people. Employees would have to learn to cooperate with many of their coworkers, not just a handful of them. The

---

21 "Improving neural networks by preventing co-adaptation of feature detectors," G. Hinton et al. (2012).

22 "Dropout: A Simple Way to Prevent Neural Networks from Overfitting," N. Srivastava et al. (2014).

company would become much more resilient. If one person quit, it wouldn't make much of a difference. It's unclear whether this idea would actually work for companies, but it certainly does for neural networks. Neurons trained with dropout cannot co-adapt with their neighboring neurons; they have to be as useful as possible on their own. They also cannot rely excessively on just a few input neurons; they must pay attention to each of their input neurons. They end up being less sensitive to slight changes in the inputs. In the end you get a more robust network that generalizes better.

Another way to understand the power of dropout is to realize that a unique neural network is generated at each training step. Since each neuron can be either present or absent, there is a total of 2^N possible networks (where N is the total number of droppable neurons). This is such a huge number that it is virtually impossible for the same neural network to be sampled twice. Once you have run a 10,000 training steps, you have essentially trained 10,000 different neural networks (each with just one training instance). These neural networks are obviously not independent since they share many of their weights, but they are nevertheless all different. The resulting neural network can be seen as an averaging ensemble of all these smaller neural networks.

There is one small but important technical detail. Suppose p = 50%, in which case during testing a neuron will be connected to twice as many input neurons as it was (on average) during training. To compensate for this fact, we need to multiply each neuron's input connection weights by 0.5 after training. If we don't, each neuron will get a total input signal roughly twice as large as what the network was trained on, and it is unlikely to perform well. More generally, we need to multiply each input connection weight by the *keep probability* $(1 - p)$ after training. Alternatively, we can divide each neuron's output by the keep probability during training (these alternatives are not perfectly equivalent, but they work equally well).

To implement dropout using TensorFlow, you can simply apply the `tf.layers.drop out()` function to the input layer and/or to the output of any hidden layer you want. During training, this function randomly drops some items (setting them to 0) and divides the remaining items by the keep probability. After training, this function does nothing at all. The following code applies dropout regularization to our three-layer neural network:

```
[...]
training = tf.placeholder_with_default(False, shape=(), name='training')

dropout_rate = 0.5  # == 1 - keep_prob
X_drop = tf.layers.dropout(X, dropout_rate, training=training)

with tf.name_scope("dnn"):
    hidden1 = tf.layers.dense(X_drop, n_hidden1, activation=tf.nn.relu,
                              name="hidden1")
    hidden1_drop = tf.layers.dropout(hidden1, dropout_rate, training=training)
```

```
hidden2 = tf.layers.dense(hidden1_drop, n_hidden2, activation=tf.nn.relu,
                          name="hidden2")
hidden2_drop = tf.layers.dropout(hidden2, dropout_rate, training=training)
logits = tf.layers.dense(hidden2_drop, n_outputs, name="outputs")
```

You want to use the `tf.layers.dropout()` function, not `tf.nn.dropout()`. The first one turns off (no-op) when not training, which is what you want, while the second one does not.

Of course, just like you did earlier for Batch Normalization, you need to set `training` to `True` when training, and leave the default `False` value when testing.

If you observe that the model is overfitting, you can increase the dropout rate. Conversely, you should try decreasing the dropout rate if the model underfits the training set. It can also help to increase the dropout rate for large layers, and reduce it for small ones.

Dropout does tend to significantly slow down convergence, but it usually results in a much better model when tuned properly. So, it is generally well worth the extra time and effort.

Dropconnect is a variant of dropout where individual connections are dropped randomly rather than whole neurons. In general dropout performs better.

Max-Norm Regularization

Another regularization technique that is quite popular for neural networks is called *max-norm regularization*: for each neuron, it constrains the weights **w** of the incoming connections such that $\| \mathbf{w} \|_2 \le r$, where r is the max-norm hyperparameter and $\| \cdot \|_2$ is the ℓ_2 norm.

We typically implement this constraint by computing $\|\mathbf{w}\|_2$ after each training step and clipping **w** if needed ($\mathbf{w} \leftarrow \mathbf{w} \frac{r}{\| \mathbf{w} \|_2}$).

Reducing r increases the amount of regularization and helps reduce overfitting. Max-norm regularization can also help alleviate the vanishing/exploding gradients problems (if you are not using Batch Normalization).

TensorFlow does not provide an off-the-shelf max-norm regularizer, but it is not too hard to implement. The following code gets a handle on the weights of the first hidden layer, then it uses the `clip_by_norm()` function to create an operation that will clip the weights along the second axis so that each row vector ends up with a maximum norm of 1.0. The last line creates an assignment operation that will assign the clipped weights to the weights variable:

```
threshold = 1.0
weights = tf.get_default_graph().get_tensor_by_name("hidden1/kernel:0")
clipped_weights = tf.clip_by_norm(weights, clip_norm=threshold, axes=1)
clip_weights = tf.assign(weights, clipped_weights)
```

Then you just apply this operation after each training step, like so:

```
sess.run(training_op, feed_dict={X: X_batch, y: y_batch})
clip_weights.eval()
```

In general, you would do this for every hidden layer. Although this solution should work fine, it is a bit messy. A cleaner solution is to create a max_norm_regularizer() function and use it just like the earlier l1_regularizer() function:

```
def max_norm_regularizer(threshold, axes=1, name="max_norm",
                         collection="max_norm"):
    def max_norm(weights):
        clipped = tf.clip_by_norm(weights, clip_norm=threshold, axes=axes)
        clip_weights = tf.assign(weights, clipped, name=name)
        tf.add_to_collection(collection, clip_weights)
        return None    # there is no regularization loss term
    return max_norm
```

This function returns a parametrized max_norm() function that you can use like any other regularizer:

```
max_norm_reg = max_norm_regularizer(threshold=1.0)

with tf.name_scope("dnn"):
    hidden1 = tf.layers.dense(X, n_hidden1, activation=tf.nn.relu,
                              kernel_regularizer=max_norm_reg, name="hidden1")
    hidden2 = tf.layers.dense(hidden1, n_hidden2, activation=tf.nn.relu,
                              kernel_regularizer=max_norm_reg, name="hidden2")
    logits = tf.layers.dense(hidden2, n_outputs, name="outputs")
```

Note that max-norm regularization does not require adding a regularization loss term to your overall loss function, which is why the max_norm() function returns None. But you still need to be able to run the clip_weights operations after each training step, so you need to be able to get a handle on them. This is why the max_norm() function adds the clip_weights operation to a collection of max-norm clipping operations. You need to fetch these clipping operations and run them after each training step:

```
clip_all_weights = tf.get_collection("max_norm")

with tf.Session() as sess:
    init.run()
    for epoch in range(n_epochs):
        for iteration in range(mnist.train.num_examples // batch_size):
```

```
        X_batch, y_batch = mnist.train.next_batch(batch_size)
        sess.run(training_op, feed_dict={X: X_batch, y: y_batch})
        sess.run(clip_all_weights)
```

Much cleaner code, isn't it?

Data Augmentation

One last regularization technique, data augmentation, consists of generating new training instances from existing ones, artificially boosting the size of the training set. This will reduce overfitting, making this a regularization technique. The trick is to generate realistic training instances; ideally, a human should not be able to tell which instances were generated and which ones were not. Moreover, simply adding white noise will not help; the modifications you apply should be learnable (white noise is not).

For example, if your model is meant to classify pictures of mushrooms, you can slightly shift, rotate, and resize every picture in the training set by various amounts and add the resulting pictures to the training set (see Figure 11-10). This forces the model to be more tolerant to the position, orientation, and size of the mushrooms in the picture. If you want the model to be more tolerant to lighting conditions, you can similarly generate many images with various contrasts. Assuming the mushrooms are symmetrical, you can also flip the pictures horizontally. By combining these transformations you can greatly increase the size of your training set.

Figure 11-10. Generating new training instances from existing ones

It is often preferable to generate training instances on the fly during training rather than wasting storage space and network bandwidth. TensorFlow offers several image manipulation operations such as transposing (shifting), rotating, resizing, flipping, and cropping, as well as adjusting the brightness, contrast, saturation, and hue (see the API documentation for more details). This makes it easy to implement data augmentation for image datasets.

 Another powerful technique to train very deep neural networks is to add *skip connections* (a skip connection is when you add the input of a layer to the output of a higher layer). We will explore this idea in Chapter 13 when we talk about deep residual networks.

Practical Guidelines

In this chapter, we have covered a wide range of techniques and you may be wondering which ones you should use. The configuration in Table 11-2 will work fine in most cases.

Table 11-2. Default DNN configuration

Initialization	He initialization
Activation function	ELU
Normalization	Batch Normalization
Regularization	Dropout
Optimizer	Nesterov Accelerated Gradient
Learning rate schedule	None

Of course, you should try to reuse parts of a pretrained neural network if you can find one that solves a similar problem.

This default configuration may need to be tweaked:

- If you can't find a good learning rate (convergence was too slow, so you increased the training rate, and now convergence is fast but the network's accuracy is suboptimal), then you can try adding a learning schedule such as exponential decay.
- If your training set is a bit too small, you can implement data augmentation.
- If you need a sparse model, you can add some ℓ_1 regularization to the mix (and optionally zero out the tiny weights after training). If you need an even sparser model, you can try using FTRL instead of Adam optimization, along with ℓ_1 regularization.

- If you need a lightning-fast model at runtime, you may want to drop Batch Normalization, and possibly replace the ELU activation function with the leaky ReLU. Having a sparse model will also help.

With these guidelines, you are now ready to train very deep nets—well, if you are very patient, that is! If you use a single machine, you may have to wait for days or even months for training to complete. In the next chapter we will discuss how to use distributed TensorFlow to train and run models across many servers and GPUs.

Exercises

1. Is it okay to initialize all the weights to the same value as long as that value is selected randomly using He initialization?

2. Is it okay to initialize the bias terms to 0?

3. Name three advantages of the ELU activation function over ReLU.

4. In which cases would you want to use each of the following activation functions: ELU, leaky ReLU (and its variants), ReLU, tanh, logistic, and softmax?

5. What may happen if you set the momentum hyperparameter too close to 1 (e.g., 0.99999) when using a MomentumOptimizer?

6. Name three ways you can produce a sparse model.

7. Does dropout slow down training? Does it slow down inference (i.e., making predictions on new instances)?

8. Deep Learning.

   a. Build a DNN with five hidden layers of 100 neurons each, He initialization, and the ELU activation function.

   b. Using Adam optimization and early stopping, try training it on MNIST but only on digits 0 to 4, as we will use transfer learning for digits 5 to 9 in the next exercise. You will need a softmax output layer with five neurons, and as always make sure to save checkpoints at regular intervals and save the final model so you can reuse it later.

   c. Tune the hyperparameters using cross-validation and see what precision you can achieve.

   d. Now try adding Batch Normalization and compare the learning curves: is it converging faster than before? Does it produce a better model?

   e. Is the model overfitting the training set? Try adding dropout to every layer and try again. Does it help?

9. Transfer learning.

a. Create a new DNN that reuses all the pretrained hidden layers of the previous model, freezes them, and replaces the softmax output layer with a new one.

b. Train this new DNN on digits 5 to 9, using only 100 images per digit, and time how long it takes. Despite this small number of examples, can you achieve high precision?

c. Try caching the frozen layers, and train the model again: how much faster is it now?

d. Try again reusing just four hidden layers instead of five. Can you achieve a higher precision?

e. Now unfreeze the top two hidden layers and continue training: can you get the model to perform even better?

10. Pretraining on an auxiliary task.

a. In this exercise you will build a DNN that compares two MNIST digit images and predicts whether they represent the same digit or not. Then you will reuse the lower layers of this network to train an MNIST classifier using very little training data. Start by building two DNNs (let's call them DNN A and B), both similar to the one you built earlier but without the output layer: each DNN should have five hidden layers of 100 neurons each, He initialization, and ELU activation. Next, add one more hidden layer with 10 units on top of both DNNs. To do this, you should use TensorFlow's concat() function with axis=1 to concatenate the outputs of both DNNs for each instance, then feed the result to the hidden layer. Finally, add an output layer with a single neuron using the logistic activation function.

b. Split the MNIST training set in two sets: split #1 should containing 55,000 images, and split #2 should contain contain 5,000 images. Create a function that generates a training batch where each instance is a pair of MNIST images picked from split #1. Half of the training instances should be pairs of images that belong to the same class, while the other half should be images from different classes. For each pair, the training label should be 0 if the images are from the same class, or 1 if they are from different classes.

c. Train the DNN on this training set. For each image pair, you can simultaneously feed the first image to DNN A and the second image to DNN B. The whole network will gradually learn to tell whether two images belong to the same class or not.

d. Now create a new DNN by reusing and freezing the hidden layers of DNN A and adding a softmax output layer on top with 10 neurons. Train this network on split #2 and see if you can achieve high performance despite having only 500 images per class.

Solutions to these exercises are available in Appendix A.

## CHAPTER 12

Distributing TensorFlow Across Devices and Servers

In Chapter 11 we discussed several techniques that can considerably speed up training: better weight initialization, Batch Normalization, sophisticated optimizers, and so on. However, even with all of these techniques, training a large neural network on a single machine with a single CPU can take days or even weeks.

In this chapter we will see how to use TensorFlow to distribute computations across multiple devices (CPUs and GPUs) and run them in parallel (see Figure 12-1). First we will distribute computations across multiple devices on just one machine, then on multiple devices across multiple machines.

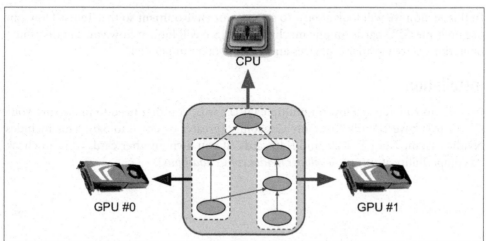

Figure 12-1. Executing a TensorFlow graph across multiple devices in parallel

TensorFlow's support of distributed computing is one of its main highlights compared to other neural network frameworks. It gives you full control over how to split (or replicate) your computation graph across devices and servers, and it lets you parallelize and synchronize operations in flexible ways so you can choose between all sorts of parallelization approaches.

We will look at some of the most popular approaches to parallelizing the execution and training of a neural network. Instead of waiting for weeks for a training algorithm to complete, you may end up waiting for just a few hours. Not only does this save an enormous amount of time, it also means that you can experiment with various models much more easily, and frequently retrain your models on fresh data.

Other great use cases of parallelization include exploring a much larger hyperparameter space when fine-tuning your model, and running large ensembles of neural networks efficiently.

But we must learn to walk before we can run. Let's start by parallelizing simple graphs across several GPUs on a single machine.

Multiple Devices on a Single Machine

You can often get a major performance boost simply by adding GPU cards to a single machine. In fact, in many cases this will suffice; you won't need to use multiple machines at all. For example, you can typically train a neural network just as fast using 8 GPUs on a single machine rather than 16 GPUs across multiple machines (due to the extra delay imposed by network communications in a multimachine setup).

In this section we will look at how to set up your environment so that TensorFlow can use multiple GPU cards on one machine. Then we will look at how you can distribute operations across available devices and execute them in parallel.

Installation

In order to run TensorFlow on multiple GPU cards, you first need to make sure your GPU cards have NVidia Compute Capability (greater or equal to 3.0). This includes Nvidia's Titan, Titan X, K20, and K40 cards (if you own another card, you can check its compatibility at *https://developer.nvidia.com/cuda-gpus*).

If you don't own any GPU cards, you can use a hosting service with GPU capability such as Amazon AWS (e.g., check out AWS Sage-Maker) or *Google Cloud Machine Learning Engine* (*https:// cloud.google.com/ml-engine/*) to train and/or run TensorFlow graphs. In May 2016, they announced that their platform now includes servers equipped with *tensor processing units* (TPUs), processors specialized for Machine Learning that are much faster than GPUs for many ML tasks. Of course, another option is simply to buy your own GPU card. Tim Dettmers wrote a great blog post (*http://homl.info/66*) to help you choose, and he updates it fairly regularly.

You must then download and install the appropriate version of the CUDA and cuDNN libraries (CUDA 8.0 and cuDNN v6 if you are using the binary installation of TensorFlow 1.3), and set a few environment variables so TensorFlow knows where to find CUDA and cuDNN. The detailed installation instructions are likely to change fairly quickly, so it is best that you follow the instructions on TensorFlow's website.

Nvidia's *Compute Unified Device Architecture* library (CUDA) allows developers to use CUDA-enabled GPUs for all sorts of computations (not just graphics acceleration). Nvidia's *CUDA Deep Neural Network* library (cuDNN) is a GPU-accelerated library of primitives for DNNs. It provides optimized implementations of common DNN computations such as activation layers, normalization, forward and backward convolutions, and pooling (see Chapter 13). It is part of Nvidia's Deep Learning SDK (note that it requires creating an Nvidia developer account in order to download it). TensorFlow uses CUDA and cuDNN to control the GPU cards and accelerate computations (see Figure 12-2).

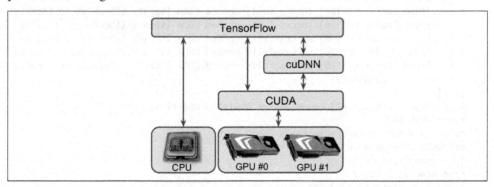

Figure 12-2. TensorFlow uses CUDA and cuDNN to control GPUs and boost DNNs

You can use the `nvidia-smi` command to check that CUDA is properly installed. It lists the available GPU cards, as well as processes running on each card:

```
$ nvidia-smi
Wed Sep 16 09:50:03 2016
+------------------------------------------------------+
| NVIDIA-SMI 352.63     Driver Version: 352.63         |
|-------------------------------+----------------------+----------------------+
| GPU  Name        Persistence-M| Bus-Id        Disp.A | Volatile Uncorr. ECC |
| Fan  Temp  Perf  Pwr:Usage/Cap|         Memory-Usage | GPU-Util  Compute M. |
|===============================+======================+======================|
|   0  GRID K520           Off  | 0000:00:03.0     Off |                  N/A |
| N/A   27C    P8    17W / 125W |     11MiB / 4095MiB  |      0%      Default |
+-------------------------------+----------------------+----------------------+

+-----------------------------------------------------------------------------+
| Processes:                                                       GPU Memory |
|  GPU       PID   Type   Process name                             Usage      |
|=============================================================================|
|  No running processes found                                                 |
+-----------------------------------------------------------------------------+
```

Finally, you must install TensorFlow with GPU support. If you created an isolated environment using virtualenv, you first need to activate it:

```
$ cd $ML_PATH              # Your ML working directory (e.g., $HOME/ml)
$ source env/bin/activate
```

Then install the appropriate GPU-enabled version of TensorFlow:

```
$ pip3 install --upgrade tensorflow-gpu
```

Now you can open up a Python shell and check that TensorFlow detects and uses CUDA and cuDNN properly by importing TensorFlow and creating a session:

```
>>> import tensorflow as tf
I [...]/dso_loader.cc:108] successfully opened CUDA library libcublas.so locally
I [...]/dso_loader.cc:108] successfully opened CUDA library libcudnn.so locally
I [...]/dso_loader.cc:108] successfully opened CUDA library libcufft.so locally
I [...]/dso_loader.cc:108] successfully opened CUDA library libcuda.so.1 locally
I [...]/dso_loader.cc:108] successfully opened CUDA library libcurand.so locally
>>> sess = tf.Session()
[...]
I [...]/gpu_init.cc:102] Found device 0 with properties:
name: GRID K520
major: 3 minor: 0 memoryClockRate (GHz) 0.797
pciBusID 0000:00:03.0
Total memory: 4.00GiB
Free memory: 3.95GiB
I [...]/gpu_init.cc:126] DMA: 0
I [...]/gpu_init.cc:136] 0:   Y
I [...]/gpu_device.cc:839] Creating TensorFlow device
(/gpu:0) -> (device: 0, name: GRID K520, pci bus id: 0000:00:03.0)
```

Looks good! TensorFlow detected the CUDA and cuDNN libraries, and it used the CUDA library to detect the GPU card (in this case an Nvidia Grid K520 card).

Managing the GPU RAM

By default TensorFlow automatically grabs all the RAM in all available GPUs the first time you run a graph, so you will not be able to start a second TensorFlow program while the first one is still running. If you try, you will get the following error:

```
E [...]/cuda_driver.cc:965] failed to allocate 3.66G (3928915968 bytes) from
device: CUDA_ERROR_OUT_OF_MEMORY
```

One solution is to run each process on different GPU cards. To do this, the simplest option is to set the CUDA_VISIBLE_DEVICES environment variable so that each process only sees the appropriate GPU cards. For example, you could start two programs like this:

```
$ CUDA_VISIBLE_DEVICES=0,1 python3 program_1.py
# and in another terminal:
$ CUDA_VISIBLE_DEVICES=3,2 python3 program_2.py
```

Program #1 will only see GPU cards 0 and 1 (numbered 0 and 1, respectively), and program #2 will only see GPU cards 2 and 3 (numbered 1 and 0, respectively). Everything will work fine (see Figure 12-3).

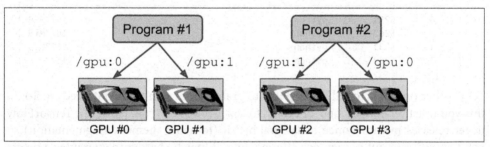

Figure 12-3. Each program gets two GPUs for itself

Another option is to tell TensorFlow to grab only a fraction of the memory. For example, to make TensorFlow grab only 40% of each GPU's memory, you must create a ConfigProto object, set its gpu_options.per_process_gpu_memory_fraction option to 0.4, and create the session using this configuration:

```
config = tf.ConfigProto()
config.gpu_options.per_process_gpu_memory_fraction = 0.4
session = tf.Session(config=config)
```

Now two programs like this one can run in parallel using the same GPU cards (but not three, since $3 \times 0.4 > 1$). See Figure 12-4.

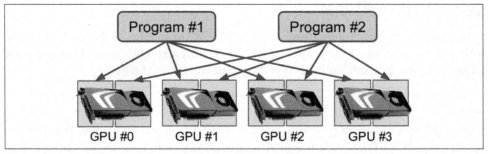

Figure 12-4. Each program gets all four GPUs, but with only 40% of the RAM each

If you run the `nvidia-smi` command while both programs are running, you should see that each process holds roughly 40% of the total RAM of each card:

```
$ nvidia-smi
[...]
+-----------------------------------------------------------------------------+
| Processes:                                                       GPU Memory |
|  GPU       PID  Type  Process name                               Usage      |
|=============================================================================|
|    0      5231    C   python                                       1677MiB  |
|    0      5262    C   python                                       1677MiB  |
|    1      5231    C   python                                       1677MiB  |
|    1      5262    C   python                                       1677MiB  |
[...]
```

Yet another option is to tell TensorFlow to grab memory only when it needs it. To do this you must set `config.gpu_options.allow_growth` to `True`. However, TensorFlow never releases memory once it has grabbed it (to avoid memory fragmentation) so you may still run out of memory after a while. It may be harder to guarantee a deterministic behavior using this option, so in general you probably want to stick with one of the previous options.

Okay, now you have a working GPU-enabled TensorFlow installation. Let's see how to use it!

Placing Operations on Devices

The TensorFlow whitepaper (*http://homl.info/67*)[1] presents a friendly *dynamic placer* algorithm that automagically distributes operations across all available devices, taking into account things like the measured computation time in previous runs of the graph, estimations of the size of the input and output tensors to each operation, the amount of RAM available in each device, communication delay when transferring

---

1 "TensorFlow: Large-Scale Machine Learning on Heterogeneous Distributed Systems," Google Research (2015).

data in and out of devices, hints and constraints from the user, and more. Unfortunately, this sophisticated algorithm is internal to Google; it was not released in the open source version of TensorFlow. The reason it was left out seems to be that in practice a small set of placement rules specified by the user actually results in more efficient placement than what the dynamic placer is capable of. However, the TensorFlow team is working on improving the dynamic placer, and perhaps it will eventually be good enough to be released.

Until then TensorFlow relies on the *simple placer*, which (as its name suggests) is very basic.

Simple placement

Whenever you run a graph, if TensorFlow needs to evaluate a node that is not placed on a device yet, it uses the simple placer to place it, along with all other nodes that are not placed yet. The simple placer respects the following rules:

- If a node was already placed on a device in a previous run of the graph, it is left on that device.
- Else, if the user *pinned* a node to a device (described next), the placer places it on that device.
- Else, it defaults to GPU #0, or the CPU if there is no GPU.

As you can see, placing operations on the appropriate device is mostly up to you. If you don't do anything, the whole graph will be placed on the default device. To pin nodes onto a device, you must create a device block using the `device()` function. For example, the following code pins the variable a and the constant b on the CPU, but the multiplication node c is not pinned on any device, so it will be placed on the default device:

```
with tf.device("/cpu:0"):
    a = tf.Variable(3.0)
    b = tf.constant(4.0)

c = a * b
```

The "/cpu:0" device aggregates all CPUs on a multi-CPU system. There is currently no way to pin nodes on specific CPUs or to use just a subset of all CPUs.

Logging placements

Let's check that the simple placer respects the placement constraints we have just defined. For this you can set the `log_device_placement` option to `True`; this tells the placer to log a message whenever it places a node. For example:

```
>>> config = tf.ConfigProto()
>>> config.log_device_placement = True
>>> sess = tf.Session(config=config)
I [...] Creating TensorFlow device (/gpu:0) -> (device: 0, name: GRID K520,
pci bus id: 0000:00:03.0)
[...]
>>> a.initializer.run(session=sess)
I [...] a: /job:localhost/replica:0/task:0/cpu:0
I [...] a/read: /job:localhost/replica:0/task:0/cpu:0
I [...] mul: /job:localhost/replica:0/task:0/gpu:0
I [...] a/Assign: /job:localhost/replica:0/task:0/cpu:0
I [...] b: /job:localhost/replica:0/task:0/cpu:0
I [...] a/initial_value: /job:localhost/replica:0/task:0/cpu:0
>>> sess.run(c)
12
```

The lines starting with `"I"` for Info are the log messages. When we create a session, TensorFlow logs a message to tell us that it has found a GPU card (in this case the Grid K520 card). Then the first time we run the graph (in this case when initializing the variable a), the simple placer is run and places each node on the device it was assigned to. As expected, the log messages show that all nodes are placed on `"/cpu:0"` except the multiplication node, which ends up on the default device `"/gpu:0"` (you can safely ignore the prefix `/job:localhost/replica:0/task:0` for now; we will talk about it in a moment). Notice that the second time we run the graph (to compute c), the placer is not used since all the nodes TensorFlow needs to compute c are already placed.

Dynamic placement function

When you create a device block, you can specify a function instead of a device name. TensorFlow will call this function for each operation it needs to place in the device block, and the function must return the name of the device to pin the operation on. For example, the following code pins all the variable nodes to `"/cpu:0"` (in this case just the variable a) and all other nodes to `"/gpu:0"`:

```
def variables_on_cpu(op):
    if op.type == "Variable":
        return "/cpu:0"
    else:
        return "/gpu:0"

with tf.device(variables_on_cpu):
    a = tf.Variable(3.0)
```

```
b = tf.constant(4.0)
c = a * b
```

You can easily implement more complex algorithms, such as pinning variables across GPUs in a round-robin fashion.

Operations and kernels

For a TensorFlow operation to run on a device, it needs to have an implementation for that device; this is called a *kernel*. Many operations have kernels for both CPUs and GPUs, but not all of them. For example, TensorFlow does not have a GPU kernel for integer variables, so the following code will fail when TensorFlow tries to place the variable i on GPU #0:

```
>>> with tf.device("/gpu:0"):
...         i = tf.Variable(3)
[...]
>>> sess.run(i.initializer)
Traceback (most recent call last):
[...]
tensorflow.python.framework.errors.InvalidArgumentError: Cannot assign a device
to node 'Variable': Could not satisfy explicit device specification
```

Note that TensorFlow infers that the variable must be of type int32 since the initialization value is an integer. If you change the initialization value to 3.0 instead of 3, or if you explicitly set dtype=tf.float32 when creating the variable, everything will work fine.

Soft placement

By default, if you try to pin an operation on a device for which the operation has no kernel, you get the exception shown earlier when TensorFlow tries to place the operation on the device. If you prefer TensorFlow to fall back to the CPU instead, you can set the allow_soft_placement configuration option to True:

```
with tf.device("/gpu:0"):
    i = tf.Variable(3)

config = tf.ConfigProto()
config.allow_soft_placement = True
sess = tf.Session(config=config)
sess.run(i.initializer)  # the placer runs and falls back to /cpu:0
```

So far we have discussed how to place nodes on different devices. Now let's see how TensorFlow will run these nodes in parallel.

Parallel Execution

When TensorFlow runs a graph, it starts by finding out the list of operations that need to be evaluated, and it counts how many dependencies each of them has. TensorFlow then adds each operation with zero dependencies (i.e., each source operation) to the evaluation queue of this operation's device (see Figure 12-5). Once an operation has been evaluated, the dependency counter of each operation that depends on it is decremented. Once an operation's dependency counter reaches zero, it is pushed to the evaluation queue of its device. And once all the nodes that TensorFlow needs have been evaluated, it returns their outputs.

Operations in the CPU's evaluation queue are dispatched to a thread pool called the *inter-op thread pool*. If the CPU has multiple cores, then these operations will effectively be evaluated in parallel. Some operations have multithreaded CPU kernels: these kernels split their task into multiple sub-operations which are placed in another evaluation queue and dispatched to a second thread pool called the *intra-op thread pool* (shared by all multithreaded CPU kernels). In short, multiple operations and sub-operations may be evaluated in parallel on different CPU cores.

For the GPU, things are a bit simpler: operations in a GPU's evaluation queue are just evaluated sequentially. However, many operations have multithreaded GPU kernels, typically implemented by libraries that TensorFlow depends on, such as CUDA and cuDNN. These implementations have their own thread pools, and they typically exploit as many GPU threads as they can (which is probably the reason why there is no need for an inter-op thread pool in GPUs, since each operation already uses up most GPU threads).

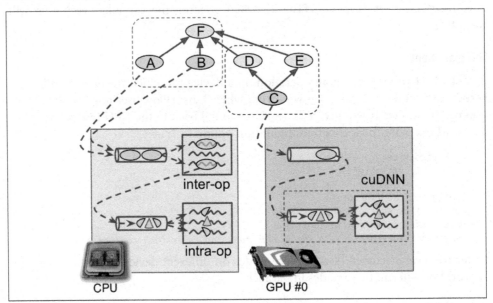

Figure 12-5. Parallelized execution of a TensorFlow graph

For example, in Figure 12-5, operations A, B, and C are source ops, so they can immediately be evaluated. Operations A and B are placed on the CPU, so they are sent to the CPU's evaluation queue, then they are dispatched to the inter-op thread pool, and immediately evaluated in parallel. Operation A happens to have a multi-threaded kernel; its computations are split into three parts, which are executed in parallel by the intra-op thread pool. Operation C goes to GPU #0's evaluation queue, and in this example its GPU kernel happens to use cuDNN, which manages its own intra-op thread pool and runs the operation across many GPU threads in parallel. Suppose C finishes first, the dependency counter of D and E are decremented, and they reach zero, so both operations are pushed to GPU #0's evaluation queue, and they are executed sequentially. Note that C only gets evaluated once, even though both D and E depend on it. Suppose B finishes next, then F's dependency counter is decremented from 4 to 3, and since that's not 0, it does not run yet. Once A, D and E are finished, then F's dependency counter reaches 0, and it is pushed to the CPU's evaluation queue, and evaluated. Finally, TensorFlow returns the requested outputs.

> You can control the number of threads in the inter-op pool by setting the `inter_op_parallelism_threads` option. Note that the first session you start creates the inter-op thread pool. All other sessions will just reuse it unless you set the `use_per_session_threads` option to `True`. You can control the number of threads in the intra-op pool by setting the `intra_op_parallelism_threads` option.

Control Dependencies

In some cases, it may be wise to postpone the evaluation of an operation even though all the operations it depends on have been executed. For example, if it uses a lot of memory but its value is needed only much further in the graph, it would be best to evaluate it at the last moment to avoid needlessly occupying RAM that other operations may need. Another example is a set of operations that depend on data located outside of the device. If they all run at the same time, they may saturate the device's communication bandwidth, and they will end up all waiting on I/O. Other operations that need to communicate data will also be blocked. It would be preferable to execute these communication-heavy operations sequentially, allowing the device to perform other operations in parallel.

To postpone evaluation of some nodes, a simple solution is to add *control dependencies*. For example, the following code tells TensorFlow to evaluate x and y only after a and b have been evaluated:

```
a = tf.constant(1.0)
b = a + 2.0

with tf.control_dependencies([a, b]):
```

```
x = tf.constant(3.0)
y = tf.constant(4.0)
```

```
z = x + y
```

Obviously, since z depends on x and y, evaluating z also implies waiting for a and b to be evaluated, even though it is not explicitly in the control_dependencies() block. Also, since b depends on a, we could simplify the preceding code by just creating a control dependency on [b] instead of [a, b], but in some cases "explicit is better than implicit."

Great! Now you know:

- How to place operations on multiple devices in any way you please
- How these operations get executed in parallel
- How to create control dependencies to optimize parallel execution

It's time to distribute computations across multiple servers!

Multiple Devices Across Multiple Servers

To run a graph across multiple servers, you first need to define a *cluster*. A cluster is composed of one or more TensorFlow servers, called *tasks*, typically spread across several machines (see Figure 12-6). Each task belongs to a *job*. A job is just a named group of tasks that typically have a common role, such as keeping track of the model parameters (such a job is usually named "ps" for *parameter server*), or performing computations (such a job is usually named "worker").

The following *cluster specification* defines two jobs, "ps" and "worker", containing one task and two tasks, respectively. In this example, machine A hosts two Tensor-Flow servers (i.e., tasks), listening on different ports: one is part of the "ps" job, and the other is part of the "worker" job. Machine B just hosts one TensorFlow server, part of the "worker" job.

```
cluster_spec = tf.train.ClusterSpec({
    "ps": [
        "machine-a.example.com:2221",   # /job:ps/task:0
    ],
    "worker": [
        "machine-a.example.com:2222",   # /job:worker/task:0
        "machine-b.example.com:2222",   # /job:worker/task:1
    ]})
```

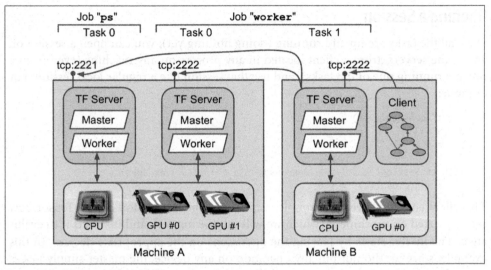

Figure 12-6. TensorFlow cluster

To start a TensorFlow server, you must create a Server object, passing it the cluster specification (so it can communicate with other servers) and its own job name and task number. For example, to start the first worker task, you would run the following code on machine A:

```
server = tf.train.Server(cluster_spec, job_name="worker", task_index=0)
```

It is usually simpler to just run one task per machine, but the previous example demonstrates that TensorFlow allows you to run multiple tasks on the same machine if you want.[2] If you have several servers on one machine, you will need to ensure that they don't all try to grab all the RAM of every GPU, as explained earlier. For example, in Figure 12-6 the "ps" task does not see the GPU devices, since presumably its process was launched with CUDA_VISIBLE_DEVICES="". Note that the CPU is shared by all tasks located on the same machine.

If you want the process to do nothing other than run the TensorFlow server, you can block the main thread by telling it to wait for the server to finish using the join() method (otherwise the server will be killed as soon as your main thread exits). Since there is currently no way to stop the server, this will actually block forever:

```
server.join()  # blocks until the server stops (i.e., never)
```

---

2 You can even start multiple tasks in the same process. It may be useful for tests, but it is not recommended in production.

Opening a Session

Once all the tasks are up and running (doing nothing yet), you can open a session on any of the servers, from a client located in any process on any machine (even from a process running one of the tasks), and use that session like a regular local session. For example:

```
a = tf.constant(1.0)
b = a + 2
c = a * 3

with tf.Session("grpc://machine-b.example.com:2222") as sess:
    print(c.eval())  # 9.0
```

This client code first creates a simple graph, then opens a session on the TensorFlow server located on machine B (which we will call the *master*), and instructs it to evaluate c. The master starts by placing the operations on the appropriate devices. In this example, since we did not pin any operation on any device, the master simply places them all on its own default device—in this case, machine B's GPU device. Then it just evaluates c as instructed by the client, and it returns the result.

The Master and Worker Services

The client uses the *gRPC* protocol (*Google Remote Procedure Call*) to communicate with the server. This is an efficient open source framework to call remote functions and get their outputs across a variety of platforms and languages.[3] It is based on HTTP2, which opens a connection and leaves it open during the whole session, allowing efficient bidirectional communication once the connection is established. Data is transmitted in the form of *protocol buffers*, another open source Google technology. This is a lightweight binary data interchange format.

 All servers in a TensorFlow cluster may communicate with any other server in the cluster, so make sure to open the appropriate ports on your firewall.

Every TensorFlow server provides two services: the *master service* and the *worker service*. The master service allows clients to open sessions and use them to run graphs. It coordinates the computations across tasks, relying on the worker service to actually execute computations on other tasks and get their results.

---

3 It is the next version of Google's internal *Stubby* service, which Google has used successfully for over a decade. See *http://grpc.io/* for more details.

This architecture gives you a lot of flexibility. One client can connect to multiple servers by opening multiple sessions in different threads. One server can handle multiple sessions simultaneously from one or more clients. You can run one client per task (typically within the same process), or just one client to control all tasks. All options are open.

Pinning Operations Across Tasks

You can use device blocks to pin operations on any device managed by any task, by specifying the job name, task index, device type, and device index. For example, the following code pins a to the CPU of the first task in the "ps" job (that's the CPU on machine A), and it pins b to the second GPU managed by the first task of the "worker" job (that's GPU #1 on machine A). Finally, c is not pinned to any device, so the master places it on its own default device (machine B's GPU #0 device).

```
with tf.device("/job:ps/task:0/cpu:0"):
    a = tf.constant(1.0)

with tf.device("/job:worker/task:0/gpu:1"):
    b = a + 2

c = a + b
```

As earlier, if you omit the device type and index, TensorFlow will default to the task's default device; for example, pinning an operation to "/job:ps/task:0" will place it on the default device of the first task of the "ps" job (machine A's CPU). If you also omit the task index (e.g., "/job:ps"), TensorFlow defaults to "/task:0". If you omit the job name and the task index, TensorFlow defaults to the session's master task.

Sharding Variables Across Multiple Parameter Servers

As we will see shortly, a common pattern when training a neural network on a distributed setup is to store the model parameters on a set of parameter servers (i.e., the tasks in the "ps" job) while other tasks focus on computations (i.e., the tasks in the "worker" job). For large models with millions of parameters, it is useful to shard these parameters across multiple parameter servers, to reduce the risk of saturating a single parameter server's network card. If you were to manually pin every variable to a different parameter server, it would be quite tedious. Fortunately, TensorFlow provides the replica_device_setter() function, which distributes variables across all the "ps" tasks in a round-robin fashion. For example, the following code pins five variables to two parameter servers:

```
with tf.device(tf.train.replica_device_setter(ps_tasks=2)):
    v1 = tf.Variable(1.0)  # pinned to /job:ps/task:0
    v2 = tf.Variable(2.0)  # pinned to /job:ps/task:1
    v3 = tf.Variable(3.0)  # pinned to /job:ps/task:0
```

```
v4 = tf.Variable(4.0)  # pinned to /job:ps/task:1
v5 = tf.Variable(5.0)  # pinned to /job:ps/task:0
```

Instead of passing the number of ps_tasks, you can pass the cluster spec clus
ter=cluster_spec and TensorFlow will simply count the number of tasks in the "ps"
job.

If you create other operations in the block, beyond just variables, TensorFlow automatically pins them to "/job:worker", which will default to the first device managed
by the first task in the "worker" job. You can pin them to another device by setting
the worker_device parameter, but a better approach is to use embedded device
blocks. An inner device block can override the job, task, or device defined in an outer
block. For example:

```
with tf.device(tf.train.replica_device_setter(ps_tasks=2)):
    v1 = tf.Variable(1.0)  # pinned to /job:ps/task:0 (+ defaults to /cpu:0)
    v2 = tf.Variable(2.0)  # pinned to /job:ps/task:1 (+ defaults to /cpu:0)
    v3 = tf.Variable(3.0)  # pinned to /job:ps/task:0 (+ defaults to /cpu:0)
    [...]
    s = v1 + v2            # pinned to /job:worker (+ defaults to task:0/gpu:0)
    with tf.device("/gpu:1"):
        p1 = 2 * s         # pinned to /job:worker/gpu:1 (+ defaults to /task:0)
        with tf.device("/task:1"):
            p2 = 3 * s     # pinned to /job:worker/task:1/gpu:1
```

 This example assumes that the parameter servers are CPU-only,
which is typically the case since they only need to store and communicate parameters, not perform intensive computations.

Sharing State Across Sessions Using Resource Containers

When you are using a plain *local session* (not the distributed kind), each variable's
state is managed by the session itself; as soon as it ends, all variable values are lost.
Moreover, multiple local sessions cannot share any state, even if they both run the
same graph; each session has its own copy of every variable (as we discussed in Chapter 9). In contrast, when you are using *distributed sessions*, variable state is managed
by *resource containers* located on the cluster itself, not by the sessions. So if you create
a variable named x using one client session, it will automatically be available to any
other session on the same cluster (even if both sessions are connected to a different
server). For example, consider the following client code:

```
# simple_client.py
import tensorflow as tf
import sys

x = tf.Variable(0.0, name="x")
```

```
increment_x = tf.assign(x, x + 1)

with tf.Session(sys.argv[1]) as sess:
    if sys.argv[2:]==["init"]:
        sess.run(x.initializer)
    sess.run(increment_x)
    print(x.eval())
```

Let's suppose you have a TensorFlow cluster up and running on machines A and B, port 2222. You could launch the client, have it open a session with the server on machine A, and tell it to initialize the variable, increment it, and print its value by launching the following command:

```
$ python3 simple_client.py grpc://machine-a.example.com:2222 init
1.0
```

Now if you launch the client with the following command, it will connect to the server on machine B and magically reuse the same variable x (this time we don't ask the server to initialize the variable):

```
$ python3 simple_client.py grpc://machine-b.example.com:2222
2.0
```

This feature cuts both ways: it's great if you want to share variables across multiple sessions, but if you want to run completely independent computations on the same cluster you will have to be careful not to use the same variable names by accident. One way to ensure that you won't have name clashes is to wrap all of your construction phase inside a variable scope with a unique name for each computation, for example:

```
with tf.variable_scope("my_problem_1"):
    [...] # Construction phase of problem 1
```

A better option is to use a container block:

```
with tf.container("my_problem_1"):
    [...] # Construction phase of problem 1
```

This will use a container dedicated to problem #1, instead of the default one (whose name is an empty string ""). One advantage is that variable names remain nice and short. Another advantage is that you can easily reset a named container. For example, the following command will connect to the server on machine A and ask it to reset the container named "my_problem_1", which will free all the resources this container used (and also close all sessions open on the server). Any variable managed by this container must be initialized before you can use it again:

```
tf.Session.reset("grpc://machine-a.example.com:2222", ["my_problem_1"])
```

Resource containers make it easy to share variables across sessions in flexible ways. For example, Figure 12-7 shows four clients running different graphs on the same cluster, but sharing some variables. Clients A and B share the same variable x managed by the default container, while clients C and D share another variable named x managed by the container named "my_problem_1". Note that client C even uses variables from both containers.

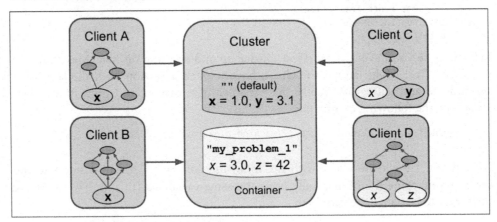

Figure 12-7. Resource containers

Resource containers also take care of preserving the state of other stateful operations, namely queues and readers. Let's take a look at queues first.

Asynchronous Communication Using TensorFlow Queues

Queues are another great way to exchange data between multiple sessions; for example, one common use case is to have a client create a graph that loads the training data and pushes it into a queue, while another client creates a graph that pulls the data from the queue and trains a model (see Figure 12-8). This can speed up training considerably because the training operations don't have to wait for the next mini-batch at every step.

TensorFlow provides various kinds of queues. The simplest kind is the *first-in first-out (FIFO)* queue. For example, the following code creates a FIFO queue that can store up to 10 tensors containing two float values each:

```
q = tf.FIFOQueue(capacity=10, dtypes=[tf.float32], shapes=[[2]],
                 name="q", shared_name="shared_q")
```

 To share variables across sessions, all you had to do was to specify the same name and container on both ends. With queues Tensor-Flow does not use the name attribute but instead uses shared_name, so it is important to specify it (even if it is the same as the name). And, of course, use the same container.

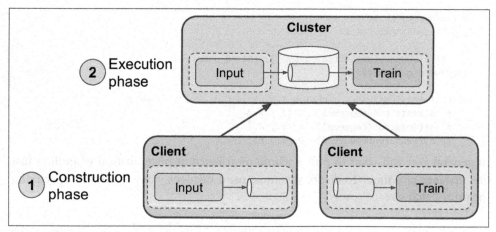

Figure 12-8. Using queues to load the training data asynchronously

Enqueuing data

To push data to a queue, you must create an enqueue operation. For example, the following code pushes three training instances to the queue:

```python
# training_data_loader.py
import tensorflow as tf

q = tf.FIFOQueue(capacity=10, [...], shared_name="shared_q")
training_instance = tf.placeholder(tf.float32, shape=[2])
enqueue = q.enqueue([training_instance])

with tf.Session("grpc://machine-a.example.com:2222") as sess:
    sess.run(enqueue, feed_dict={training_instance: [1., 2.]})
    sess.run(enqueue, feed_dict={training_instance: [3., 4.]})
    sess.run(enqueue, feed_dict={training_instance: [5., 6.]})
```

Instead of enqueuing instances one by one, you can enqueue several at a time using an enqueue_many operation:

```python
[...]
training_instances = tf.placeholder(tf.float32, shape=(None, 2))
enqueue_many = q.enqueue_many([training_instances])

with tf.Session("grpc://machine-a.example.com:2222") as sess:
    sess.run(enqueue_many,
            feed_dict={training_instances: [[1., 2.], [3., 4.], [5., 6.]]})
```

Both examples enqueue the same three tensors to the queue.

Dequeuing data

To pull the instances out of the queue, on the other end, you need to use a dequeue operation:

```
# trainer.py
import tensorflow as tf

q = tf.FIFOQueue(capacity=10, [...], shared_name="shared_q")
dequeue = q.dequeue()

with tf.Session("grpc://machine-a.example.com:2222") as sess:
    print(sess.run(dequeue))   # [1., 2.]
    print(sess.run(dequeue))   # [3., 4.]
    print(sess.run(dequeue))   # [5., 6.]
```

In general you will want to pull a whole mini-batch at once, instead of pulling just one instance at a time. To do so, you must use a dequeue_many operation, specifying the mini-batch size:

```
[...]
batch_size = 2
dequeue_mini_batch = q.dequeue_many(batch_size)

with tf.Session("grpc://machine-a.example.com:2222") as sess:
    print(sess.run(dequeue_mini_batch))   # [[1., 2.], [4., 5.]]
    print(sess.run(dequeue_mini_batch))   # blocked waiting for another instance
```

When a queue is full, the enqueue operation will block until items are pulled out by a dequeue operation. Similarly, when a queue is empty (or you are using dequeue_many() and there are fewer items than the mini-batch size), the dequeue operation will block until enough items are pushed into the queue using an enqueue operation.

Queues of tuples

Each item in a queue can be a tuple of tensors (of various types and shapes) instead of just a single tensor. For example, the following queue stores pairs of tensors, one of type int32 and shape (), and the other of type float32 and shape [3,2]:

```
q = tf.FIFOQueue(capacity=10, dtypes=[tf.int32, tf.float32], shapes=[[],[3,2]],
                 name="q", shared_name="shared_q")
```

The enqueue operation must be given pairs of tensors (note that each pair represents only one item in the queue):

```
a = tf.placeholder(tf.int32, shape=())
b = tf.placeholder(tf.float32, shape=(3, 2))
enqueue = q.enqueue((a, b))

with tf.Session([...]) as sess:
    sess.run(enqueue, feed_dict={a: 10, b:[[1., 2.], [3., 4.], [5., 6.]]})
    sess.run(enqueue, feed_dict={a: 11, b:[[2., 4.], [6., 8.], [0., 2.]]})
    sess.run(enqueue, feed_dict={a: 12, b:[[3., 6.], [9., 2.], [5., 8.]]})
```

On the other end, the dequeue() function now creates a pair of dequeue operations:

```
dequeue_a, dequeue_b = q.dequeue()
```

In general, you should run these operations together:

```
with tf.Session([...]) as sess:
    a_val, b_val = sess.run([dequeue_a, dequeue_b])
    print(a_val) # 10
    print(b_val) # [[1., 2.], [3., 4.], [5., 6.]]
```

 If you run dequeue_a on its own, it will dequeue a pair and return only the first element; the second element will be lost (and similarly, if you run dequeue_b on its own, the first element will be lost).

The dequeue_many() function also returns a pair of operations:

```
batch_size = 2
dequeue_as, dequeue_bs = q.dequeue_many(batch_size)
```

You can use it as you would expect:

```
with tf.Session([...]) as sess:
    a, b = sess.run([dequeue_as, dequeue_bs])
    print(a) # [10, 11]
    print(b) # [[[1., 2.], [3., 4.], [5., 6.]], [[2., 4.], [6., 8.], [0., 2.]]]
    a, b = sess.run([dequeue_as,dequeue_bs]) # blocked waiting for another pair
```

Closing a queue

It is possible to close a queue to signal to the other sessions that no more data will be enqueued:

```
close_q = q.close()

with tf.Session([...]) as sess:
    [...]
    sess.run(close_q)
```

Subsequent executions of enqueue or enqueue_many operations will raise an exception. By default, any pending enqueue request will be honored, unless you call q.close(cancel_pending_enqueues=True).

Subsequent executions of dequeue or dequeue_many operations will continue to succeed as long as there are items in the queue, but they will fail when there are not enough items left in the queue. If you are using a dequeue_many operation and there are a few instances left in the queue, but fewer than the mini-batch size, they will be lost. You may prefer to use a dequeue_up_to operation instead; it behaves exactly like dequeue_many except when a queue is closed and there are fewer than batch_size instances left in the queue, in which case it just returns them.

RandomShuffleQueue

TensorFlow also supports a couple more types of queues, including `RandomShuffle Queue`, which can be used just like a `FIFOQueue` except that items are dequeued in a random order. This can be useful to shuffle training instances at each epoch during training. First, let's create the queue:

```
q = tf.RandomShuffleQueue(capacity=50, min_after_dequeue=10,
                          dtypes=[tf.float32], shapes=[()],
                          name="q", shared_name="shared_q")
```

The `min_after_dequeue` specifies the minimum number of items that must remain in the queue after a dequeue operation. This ensures that there will be enough instances in the queue to have enough randomness (once the queue is closed, the `min_after_dequeue` limit is ignored). Now suppose that you enqueued 22 items in this queue (floats 1. to 22.). Here is how you could dequeue them:

```
dequeue = q.dequeue_many(5)

with tf.Session([...]) as sess:
    print(sess.run(dequeue)) # [ 20.  15.  11.  12.   4.]  (17 items left)
    print(sess.run(dequeue)) # [  5.  13.   6.   0.  17.]  (12 items left)
    print(sess.run(dequeue)) # 12 - 5 < 10: blocked waiting for 3 more instances
```

PaddingFifoQueue

A `PaddingFIFOQueue` can also be used just like a `FIFOQueue` except that it accepts tensors of variable sizes along any dimension (but with a fixed rank). When you are dequeuing them with a `dequeue_many` or `dequeue_up_to` operation, each tensor is padded with zeros along every variable dimension to make it the same size as the largest tensor in the mini-batch. For example, you could enqueue 2D tensors (matrices) of arbitrary sizes:

```
q = tf.PaddingFIFOQueue(capacity=50,
                        dtypes=[tf.float32], shapes=[(None, None)],
                        name="q", shared_name="shared_q")
v = tf.placeholder(tf.float32, shape=(None, None))
enqueue = q.enqueue([v])

with tf.Session([...]) as sess:
    sess.run(enqueue, feed_dict={v: [[1., 2.], [3., 4.], [5., 6.]]})      # 3x2
    sess.run(enqueue, feed_dict={v: [[1.]]})                               # 1x1
    sess.run(enqueue, feed_dict={v: [[7., 8., 9., 5.], [6., 7., 8., 9.]]}) # 2x4
```

If we just dequeue one item at a time, we get the exact same tensors that were enqueued. But if we dequeue several items at a time (using `dequeue_many()` or `dequeue_up_to()`), the queue automatically pads the tensors appropriately. For example, if we dequeue all three items at once, all tensors will be padded with zeros to become 3×4 tensors, since the maximum size for the first dimension is 3 (first item) and the maximum size for the second dimension is 4 (third item):

```
>>> q = [...]
>>> dequeue = q.dequeue_many(3)
>>> with tf.Session([...]) as sess:
...     print(sess.run(dequeue))
...
[[[ 1.  2.  0.  0.]
  [ 3.  4.  0.  0.]
  [ 5.  6.  0.  0.]]

 [[ 1.  0.  0.  0.]
  [ 0.  0.  0.  0.]
  [ 0.  0.  0.  0.]]

 [[ 7.  8.  9.  5.]
  [ 6.  7.  8.  9.]
  [ 0.  0.  0.  0.]]]
```

This type of queue can be useful when you are dealing with variable length inputs, such as sequences of words (see Chapter 14).

Okay, now let's pause for a second: so far you have learned to distribute computations across multiple devices and servers, share variables across sessions, and communicate asynchronously using queues. Before you start training neural networks, though, there's one last topic we need to discuss: how to efficiently load training data.

Loading Data Directly from the Graph

So far we have assumed that the clients would load the training data and feed it to the cluster using placeholders. This is simple and works quite well for simple setups, but it is rather inefficient since it transfers the training data several times:

1. From the filesystem to the client

2. From the client to the master task

3. Possibly from the master task to other tasks where the data is needed

It gets worse if you have several clients training various neural networks using the same training data (for example, for hyperparameter tuning): if every client loads the data simultaneously, you may end up even saturating your file server or the network's bandwidth.

Preload the data into a variable

For datasets that can fit in memory, a better option is to load the training data once and assign it to a variable, then just use that variable in your graph. This is called *preloading* the training set. This way the data will be transferred only once from the client to the cluster (but it may still need to be moved around from task to task depending on which operations need it). The following code shows how to load the full training set into a variable:

```
training_set_init = tf.placeholder(tf.float32, shape=(None, n_features))
training_set = tf.Variable(training_set_init, trainable=False, collections=[],
                           name="training_set")

with tf.Session([...]) as sess:
    data = [...]  # load the training data from the datastore
    sess.run(training_set.initializer, feed_dict={training_set_init: data})
```

You must set `trainable=False` so the optimizers don't try to tweak this variable. You should also set `collections=[]` to ensure that this variable won't get added to the `GraphKeys.GLOBAL_VARIABLES` collection, which is used for saving and restoring checkpoints.

 This example assumes that all of your training set (including the labels) consists only of `float32` values. If that's not the case, you will need one variable per type.

Reading the training data directly from the graph

If the training set does not fit in memory, a good solution is to use *reader operations*: these are operations capable of reading data directly from the filesystem. This way the training data never needs to flow through the clients at all. TensorFlow provides readers for various file formats:

- CSV
- Fixed-length binary records
- TensorFlow's own `TFRecords` format, based on protocol buffers

Let's look at a simple example reading from a CSV file (for other formats, please check out the API documentation). Suppose you have file named *my_test.csv* that contains training instances, and you want to create operations to read it. Suppose it has the following content, with two float features x1 and x2 and one integer `target` representing a binary class:

```
x1, x2, target
1. , 2. , 0
4. , 5 , 1
7. ,   , 0
```

First, let's create a `TextLineReader` to read this file. A `TextLineReader` opens a file (once we tell it which one to open) and reads lines one by one. It is a stateful operation, like variables and queues: it preserves its state across multiple runs of the graph, keeping track of which file it is currently reading and what its current position is in this file.

```
reader = tf.TextLineReader(skip_header_lines=1)
```

Next, we create a queue that the reader will pull from to know which file to read next. We also create an enqueue operation and a placeholder to push any filename we want to the queue, and we create an operation to close the queue once we have no more files to read:

```
filename_queue = tf.FIFOQueue(capacity=10, dtypes=[tf.string], shapes=[()])
filename = tf.placeholder(tf.string)
enqueue_filename = filename_queue.enqueue([filename])
close_filename_queue = filename_queue.close()
```

Now we are ready to create a read operation that will read one record (i.e., a line) at a time and return a key/value pair. The key is the record's unique identifier—a string composed of the filename, a colon (:), and the line number—and the value is simply a string containing the content of the line:

```
key, value = reader.read(filename_queue)
```

We have all we need to read the file line by line! But we are not quite done yet—we need to parse this string to get the features and target:

```
x1, x2, target = tf.decode_csv(value, record_defaults=[[-1.], [-1.], [-1]])
features = tf.stack([x1, x2])
```

The first line uses TensorFlow's CSV parser to extract the values from the current line. The default values are used when a field is missing (in this example the third training instance's x2 feature), and they are also used to determine the type of each field (in this case two floats and one integer).

Finally, we can push this training instance and its target to a RandomShuffleQueue that we will share with the training graph (so it can pull mini-batches from it), and we create an operation to close that queue when we are done pushing instances to it:

```
instance_queue = tf.RandomShuffleQueue(
    capacity=10, min_after_dequeue=2,
    dtypes=[tf.float32, tf.int32], shapes=[[2],[]],
    name="instance_q", shared_name="shared_instance_q")
enqueue_instance = instance_queue.enqueue([features, target])
close_instance_queue = instance_queue.close()
```

Wow! That was a lot of work just to read a file. Plus we only created the graph, so now we need to run it:

```
with tf.Session([...]) as sess:
    sess.run(enqueue_filename, feed_dict={filename: "my_test.csv"})
    sess.run(close_filename_queue)
    try:
```

```
    while True:
        sess.run(enqueue_instance)
except tf.errors.OutOfRangeError as ex:
    pass # no more records in the current file and no more files to read
sess.run(close_instance_queue)
```

First we open the session, and then we enqueue the filename "my_test.csv" and immediately close that queue since we will not enqueue any more filenames. Then we run an infinite loop to enqueue instances one by one. The enqueue_instance depends on the reader reading the next line, so at every iteration a new record is read until it reaches the end of the file. At that point it tries to read the filename queue to know which file to read next, and since the queue is closed it throws an OutOfRan geError exception (if we did not close the queue, it would just remain blocked until we pushed another filename or closed the queue). Lastly, we close the instance queue so that the training operations pulling from it won't get blocked forever. Figure 12-9 summarizes what we have learned; it represents a typical graph for reading training instances from a set of CSV files.

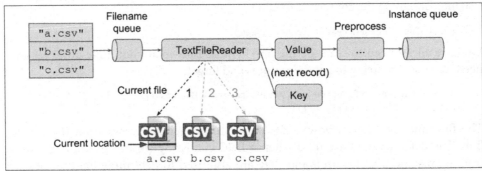

Figure 12-9. A graph dedicated to reading training instances from CSV files

In the training graph, you need to create the shared instance queue and simply dequeue mini-batches from it:

```
instance_queue = tf.RandomShuffleQueue([...], shared_name="shared_instance_q")
mini_batch_instances, mini_batch_targets = instance_queue.dequeue_up_to(2)
[...] # use the mini_batch instances and targets to build the training graph
training_op = [...]

with tf.Session([...]) as sess:
    try:
        for step in range(max_steps):
            sess.run(training_op)
    except tf.errors.OutOfRangeError as ex:
        pass # no more training instances
```

In this example, the first mini-batch will contain the first two instances of the CSV file, and the second mini-batch will contain the last instance.

TensorFlow queues don't handle sparse tensors well, so if your training instances are sparse you should parse the records after the instance queue.

This architecture will only use one thread to read records and push them to the instance queue. You can get a much higher throughput by having multiple threads read simultaneously from multiple files using multiple readers. Let's see how.

Multithreaded readers using a Coordinator and a QueueRunner

To have multiple threads read instances simultaneously, you could create Python threads (using the `threading` module) and manage them yourself. However, Tensor-Flow provides some tools to make this simpler: the `Coordinator` class and the `QueueR unner` class.

A `Coordinator` is a very simple object whose sole purpose is to coordinate stopping multiple threads. First you create a `Coordinator`:

```
coord = tf.train.Coordinator()
```

Then you give it to all threads that need to stop jointly, and their main loop looks like this:

```
while not coord.should_stop():
    [...] # do something
```

Any thread can request that every thread stop by calling the Coordinator's `request_stop()` method:

```
coord.request_stop()
```

Every thread will stop as soon as it finishes its current iteration. You can wait for all of the threads to finish by calling the Coordinator's `join()` method, passing it the list of threads:

```
coord.join(list_of_threads)
```

A `QueueRunner` runs multiple threads that each run an enqueue operation repeatedly, filling up a queue as fast as possible. As soon as the queue is closed, the next thread that tries to push an item to the queue will get an `OutOfRangeError`; this thread catches the error and immediately tells other threads to stop using a `Coordinator`. The following code shows how you can use a `QueueRunner` to have five threads reading instances simultaneously and pushing them to an instance queue:

```
[...] # same construction phase as earlier
queue_runner = tf.train.QueueRunner(instance_queue, [enqueue_instance] * 5)

with tf.Session() as sess:
```

```
sess.run(enqueue_filename, feed_dict={filename: "my_test.csv"})
sess.run(close_filename_queue)
coord = tf.train.Coordinator()
enqueue_threads = queue_runner.create_threads(sess, coord=coord, start=True)
```

The first line creates the `QueueRunner` and tells it to run five threads, all running the same `enqueue_instance` operation repeatedly. Then we start a session and we enqueue the name of the files to read (in this case just `"my_test.csv"`). Next we create a `Coordinator` that the `QueueRunner` will use to stop gracefully, as just explained. Finally, we tell the `QueueRunner` to create the threads and start them. The threads will read all training instances and push them to the instance queue, and then they will all stop gracefully.

This will be a bit more efficient than earlier, but we can do better. Currently all threads are reading from the same file. We can make them read simultaneously from separate files instead (assuming the training data is sharded across multiple CSV files) by creating multiple readers (see Figure 12-10).

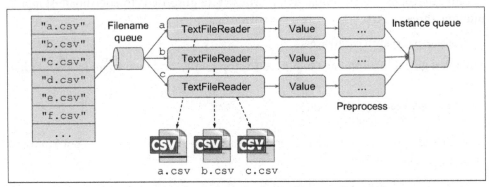

Figure 12-10. Reading simultaneously from multiple files

For this we need to write a small function to create a reader and the nodes that will read and push one instance to the instance queue:

```
def read_and_push_instance(filename_queue, instance_queue):
    reader = tf.TextLineReader(skip_header_lines=1)
    key, value = reader.read(filename_queue)
    x1, x2, target = tf.decode_csv(value, record_defaults=[[-1.], [-1.], [-1]])
    features = tf.stack([x1, x2])
    enqueue_instance = instance_queue.enqueue([features, target])
    return enqueue_instance
```

Next we define the queues:

```
filename_queue = tf.FIFOQueue(capacity=10, dtypes=[tf.string], shapes=[()])
filename = tf.placeholder(tf.string)
enqueue_filename = filename_queue.enqueue([filename])
close_filename_queue = filename_queue.close()
```

```
instance_queue = tf.RandomShuffleQueue([...])
```

And finally we create the `QueueRunner`, but this time we give it a list of different enqueue operations. Each operation will use a different reader, so the threads will simultaneously read from different files:

```
read_and_enqueue_ops = [
    read_and_push_instance(filename_queue, instance_queue)
    for i in range(5)]
queue_runner = tf.train.QueueRunner(instance_queue, read_and_enqueue_ops)
```

The execution phase is then the same as before: first push the names of the files to read, then create a `Coordinator` and create and start the `QueueRunner` threads. This time all threads will read from different files simultaneously until all files are read entirely, and then the `QueueRunner` will close the instance queue so that other ops pulling from it don't get blocked.

Other convenience functions

TensorFlow also offers a few convenience functions to simplify some common tasks when reading training instances. We will go over just a few (see the API documentation for the full list).

The `string_input_producer()` takes a 1D tensor containing a list of filenames, creates a thread that pushes one filename at a time to the filename queue, and then closes the queue. If you specify a number of epochs, it will cycle through the filenames once per epoch before closing the queue. By default, it shuffles the filenames at each epoch. It creates a `QueueRunner` to manage its thread, and adds it to the `Graph Keys.QUEUE_RUNNERS` collection. To start every `QueueRunner` in that collection, you can call the `tf.train.start_queue_runners()` function. Note that if you forget to start the `QueueRunner`, the filename queue will be open and empty, and your readers will be blocked forever.

There are a few other *producer* functions that similarly create a queue and a corresponding `QueueRunner` for running an enqueue operation (e.g., `input_producer()`, `range_input_producer()`, and `slice_input_producer()`).

The `shuffle_batch()` function takes a list of tensors (e.g., `[features, target]`) and creates:

- A `RandomShuffleQueue`
- A `QueueRunner` to enqueue the tensors to the queue (added to the `Graph Keys.QUEUE_RUNNERS` collection)
- A `dequeue_many` operation to extract a mini-batch from the queue

This makes it easy to manage in a single process a multithreaded input pipeline feeding a queue and a training pipeline reading mini-batches from that queue. Also check out the batch(), batch_join(), and shuffle_batch_join() functions that provide similar functionality.

Okay! You now have all the tools you need to start training and running neural networks efficiently across multiple devices and servers on a TensorFlow cluster. Let's review what you have learned:

- Using multiple GPU devices
- Setting up and starting a TensorFlow cluster
- Distributing computations across multiple devices and servers
- Sharing variables (and other stateful ops such as queues and readers) across sessions using containers
- Coordinating multiple graphs working asynchronously using queues
- Reading inputs efficiently using readers, queue runners, and coordinators

Now let's use all of this to parallelize neural networks!

Parallelizing Neural Networks on a TensorFlow Cluster

In this section, first we will look at how to parallelize several neural networks by simply placing each one on a different device. Then we will look at the much trickier problem of training a single neural network across multiple devices and servers.

One Neural Network per Device

The most trivial way to train and run neural networks on a TensorFlow cluster is to take the exact same code you would use for a single device on a single machine, and specify the master server's address when creating the session. That's it—you're done! Your code will be running on the server's default device. You can change the device that will run your graph simply by putting your code's construction phase within a device block.

By running several client sessions in parallel (in different threads or different processes), connecting them to different servers, and configuring them to use different devices, you can quite easily train or run many neural networks in parallel, across all devices and all machines in your cluster (see Figure 12-11). The speedup is almost linear.[4]

---

[4] Not 100% linear if you wait for all devices to finish, since the total time will be the time taken by the slowest device.

Training 100 neural networks across 50 servers with 2 GPUs each will not take much longer than training just 1 neural network on 1 GPU.

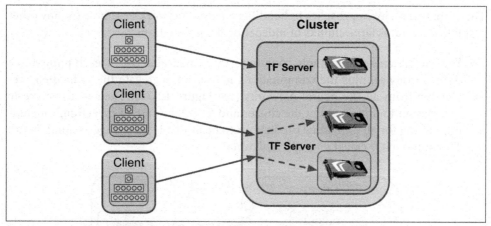

Figure 12-11. Training one neural network per device

This solution is perfect for hyperparameter tuning: each device in the cluster will train a different model with its own set of hyperparameters. The more computing power you have, the larger the hyperparameter space you can explore.

It also works perfectly if you host a web service that receives a large number of *queries per second* (QPS) and you need your neural network to make a prediction for each query. Simply replicate the neural network across all devices on the cluster and dispatch queries across all devices. By adding more servers you can handle an unlimited number of QPS (however, this will not reduce the time it takes to process a single request since it will still have to wait for a neural network to make a prediction).

> Another option is to serve your neural networks using *TensorFlow Serving*. It is an open source system, released by Google in February 2016, designed to serve a high volume of queries to Machine Learning models (typically built with TensorFlow). It handles model versioning, so you can easily deploy a new version of your network to production, or experiment with various algorithms without interrupting your service, and it can sustain a heavy load by adding more servers. For more details, check out *https://www.tensorflow.org/serving/*.

In-Graph Versus Between-Graph Replication

You can also parallelize the training of a large ensemble of neural networks by simply placing every neural network on a different device (ensembles were introduced in Chapter 7). However, once you want to *run* the ensemble, you will need to aggregate the individual predictions made by each neural network to produce the ensemble's prediction, and this requires a bit of coordination.

There are two major approaches to handling a neural network ensemble (or any other graph that contains large chunks of independent computations):

- You can create one big graph, containing every neural network, each pinned to a different device, plus the computations needed to aggregate the individual predictions from all the neural networks (see Figure 12-12). Then you just create one session to any server in the cluster and let it take care of everything (including waiting for all individual predictions to be available before aggregating them). This approach is called *in-graph replication*.

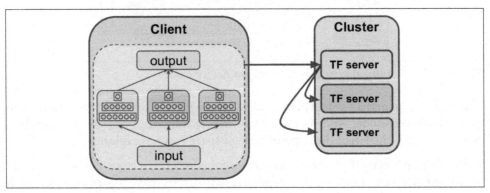

Figure 12-12. In-graph replication

- Alternatively, you can create one separate graph for each neural network and handle synchronization between these graphs yourself. This approach is called *between-graph replication*. One typical implementation is to coordinate the execution of these graphs using queues (see Figure 12-13). A set of clients handles one neural network each, reading from its dedicated input queue, and writing to its dedicated prediction queue. Another client is in charge of reading the inputs and pushing them to all the input queues (copying all inputs to every queue). Finally, one last client is in charge of reading one prediction from each prediction queue and aggregating them to produce the ensemble's prediction.

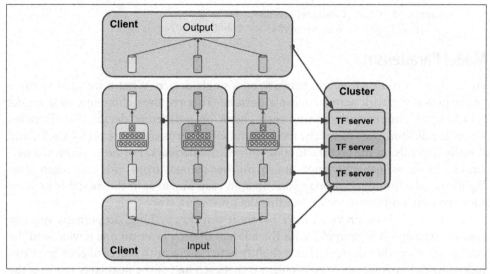

Figure 12-13. Between-graph replication

These solutions have their pros and cons. In-graph replication is somewhat simpler to implement since you don't have to manage multiple clients and multiple queues. However, between-graph replication is a bit easier to organize into well-bounded and easy-to-test modules. Moreover, it gives you more flexibility. For example, you could add a dequeue timeout in the aggregator client so that the ensemble would not fail even if one of the neural network clients crashes or if one neural network takes too long to produce its prediction. TensorFlow lets you specify a timeout when calling the run() function by passing a RunOptions with timeout_in_ms:

```
with tf.Session([...]) as sess:
    [...]
    run_options = tf.RunOptions()
    run_options.timeout_in_ms = 1000  # 1s timeout
    try:
        pred = sess.run(dequeue_prediction, options=run_options)
    except tf.errors.DeadlineExceededError as ex:
        [...] # the dequeue operation timed out after 1s
```

Another way you can specify a timeout is to set the session's operation_time out_in_ms configuration option, but in this case the run() function times out if *any* operation takes longer than the timeout delay:

```
config = tf.ConfigProto()
config.operation_timeout_in_ms = 1000  # 1s timeout for every operation

with tf.Session([...], config=config) as sess:
    [...]
    try:
        pred = sess.run(dequeue_prediction)
```

```
except tf.errors.DeadlineExceededError as ex:
    [...]  # the dequeue operation timed out after 1s
```

Model Parallelism

So far we have run each neural network on a single device. What if we want to run a single neural network across multiple devices? This requires chopping your model into separate chunks and running each chunk on a different device. This is called *model parallelism*. Unfortunately, model parallelism turns out to be pretty tricky, and it really depends on the architecture of your neural network. For fully connected networks, there is generally not much to be gained from this approach (see Figure 12-14). Intuitively, it may seem that an easy way to split the model is to place each layer on a different device, but this does not work since each layer needs to wait for the output of the previous layer before it can do anything. So perhaps you can slice it vertically—for example, with the left half of each layer on one device, and the right part on another device? This is slightly better, since both halves of each layer can indeed work in parallel, but the problem is that each half of the next layer requires the output of both halves, so there will be a lot of cross-device communication (represented by the dashed arrows). This is likely to completely cancel out the benefit of the parallel computation, since cross-device communication is slow (especially if it is across separate machines).

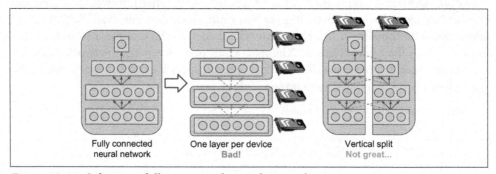

Figure 12-14. Splitting a fully connected neural network

However, as we will see in Chapter 13, some neural network architectures, such as convolutional neural networks, contain layers that are only partially connected to the lower layers, so it is much easier to distribute chunks across devices in an efficient way.

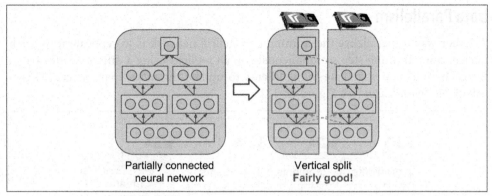

Partially connected
neural network

Vertical split
Fairly good!

Figure 12-15. Splitting a partially connected neural network

Moreover, as we will see in Chapter 14, some deep recurrent neural networks are composed of several layers of *memory cells* (see the left side of Figure 12-16). A cell's output at time t is fed back to its input at time $t + 1$ (as you can see more clearly on the right side of Figure 12-16). If you split such a network horizontally, placing each layer on a different device, then at the first step only one device will be active, at the second step two will be active, and by the time the signal propagates to the output layer all devices will be active simultaneously. There is still a lot of cross-device communication going on, but since each cell may be fairly complex, the benefit of running multiple cells in parallel often outweighs the communication penalty.

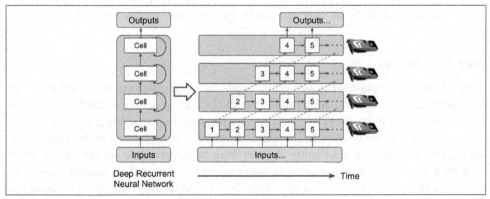

Figure 12-16. Splitting a deep recurrent neural network

In short, model parallelism can speed up running or training some types of neural networks, but not all, and it requires special care and tuning, such as making sure that devices that need to communicate the most run on the same machine.

Data Parallelism

Another way to parallelize the training of a neural network is to replicate it on each device, run a training step simultaneously on all replicas using a different mini-batch for each, and then aggregate the gradients to update the model parameters. This is called *data parallelism* (see Figure 12-17).

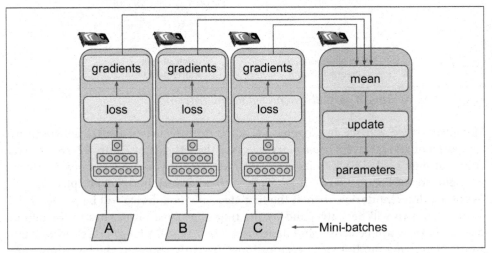

Figure 12-17. Data parallelism

There are two variants of this approach: *synchronous updates* and *asynchronous updates*.

Synchronous updates

With *synchronous updates*, the aggregator waits for all gradients to be available before computing the average and applying the result (i.e., using the aggregated gradients to update the model parameters). Once a replica has finished computing its gradients, it must wait for the parameters to be updated before it can proceed to the next mini-batch. The downside is that some devices may be slower than others, so all other devices will have to wait for them at every step. Moreover, the parameters will be copied to every device almost at the same time (immediately after the gradients are applied), which may saturate the parameter servers' bandwidth.

To reduce the waiting time at each step, you could ignore the gradients from the slowest few replicas (typically ~10%). For example, you could run 20 replicas, but only aggregate the gradients from the fastest 18 replicas at each step, and just ignore the gradients from the last 2. As soon as the parameters are updated, the first 18 replicas can start working again immediately, without having to wait for the 2 slowest replicas. This setup is generally described as having 18 replicas plus 2 *spare replicas*.[5]

Asynchronous updates

With asynchronous updates, whenever a replica has finished computing the gradients, it immediately uses them to update the model parameters. There is no aggregation (remove the "mean" step in Figure 12-17), and no synchronization. Replicas just work independently of the other replicas. Since there is no waiting for the other replicas, this approach runs more training steps per minute. Moreover, although the parameters still need to be copied to every device at every step, this happens at different times for each replica so the risk of bandwidth saturation is reduced.

Data parallelism with asynchronous updates is an attractive choice, because of its simplicity, the absence of synchronization delay, and a better use of the bandwidth. However, although it works reasonably well in practice, it is almost surprising that it works at all! Indeed, by the time a replica has finished computing the gradients based on some parameter values, these parameters will have been updated several times by other replicas (on average $N - 1$ times if there are N replicas) and there is no guarantee that the computed gradients will still be pointing in the right direction (see Figure 12-18). When gradients are severely out-of-date, they are called *stale gradients*: they can slow down convergence, introducing noise and wobble effects (the learning curve may contain temporary oscillations), or they can even make the training algorithm diverge.

---

5 This name is slightly confusing since it sounds like some replicas are special, doing nothing. In reality, all replicas are equivalent: they all work hard to be among the fastest at each training step, and the losers vary at every step (unless some devices are really slower than others).

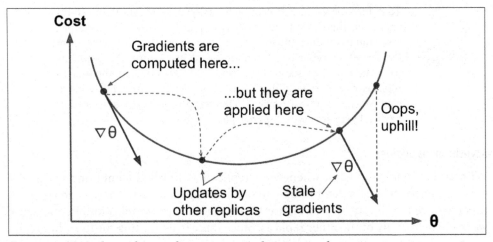

Figure 12-18. Stale gradients when using asynchronous updates

There are a few ways to reduce the effect of stale gradients:

- Reduce the learning rate.
- Drop stale gradients or scale them down.
- Adjust the mini-batch size.
- Start the first few epochs using just one replica (this is called the *warmup phase*). Stale gradients tend to be more damaging at the beginning of training, when gradients are typically large and the parameters have not settled into a valley of the cost function yet, so different replicas may push the parameters in quite different directions.

A paper published by the Google Brain team in April 2016 (*http://homl.info/68*) benchmarked various approaches and found that data parallelism with synchronous updates using a few spare replicas was the most efficient, not only converging faster but also producing a better model. However, this is still an active area of research, so you should not rule out asynchronous updates quite yet.

Bandwidth saturation

Whether you use synchronous or asynchronous updates, data parallelism still requires communicating the model parameters from the parameter servers to every replica at the beginning of every training step, and the gradients in the other direction at the end of each training step. Unfortunately, this means that there always comes a point where adding an extra GPU will not improve performance at all because the time spent moving the data in and out of GPU RAM (and possibly across the network) will outweigh the speedup obtained by splitting the computation load. At that point, adding more GPUs will just increase saturation and slow down training.

For some models, typically relatively small and trained on a very large training set, you are often better off training the model on a single machine with a single GPU.

Saturation is more severe for large dense models, since they have a lot of parameters and gradients to transfer. It is less severe for small models (but the parallelization gain is small) and also for large sparse models since the gradients are typically mostly zeros, so they can be communicated efficiently. Jeff Dean, initiator and lead of the Google Brain project, reported (*http://homl.info/69*) typical speedups of 25–40x when distributing computations across 50 GPUs for dense models, and 300x speedup for sparser models trained across 500 GPUs. As you can see, sparse models really do scale better. Here are a few concrete examples:

- Neural Machine Translation: 6x speedup on 8 GPUs
- Inception/ImageNet: 32x speedup on 50 GPUs
- RankBrain: 300x speedup on 500 GPUs

These numbers represent the state of the art in Q1 2016. Beyond a few dozen GPUs for a dense model or few hundred GPUs for a sparse model, saturation kicks in and performance degrades. There is plenty of research going on to solve this problem (exploring peer-to-peer architectures rather than centralized parameter servers, using lossy model compression, optimizing when and what the replicas need to communicate, and so on), so there will likely be a lot of progress in parallelizing neural networks in the next few years.

In the meantime, here are a few simple steps you can take to reduce the saturation problem:

- Group your GPUs on a few servers rather than scattering them across many servers. This will avoid unnecessary network hops.
- Shard the parameters across multiple parameter servers (as discussed earlier).
- Drop the model parameters' float precision from 32 bits (tf.float32) to 16 bits (tf.bfloat16). This will cut in half the amount of data to transfer, without much impact on the convergence rate or the model's performance.

Although 16-bit precision is the minimum for training neural network, you can actually drop down to 8-bit precision after training to reduce the size of the model and speed up computations. This is called *quantizing* the neural network. It is particularly useful for deploying and running pretrained models on mobile phones. See Pete Warden's great post (*http://homl.info/70*) on the subject.

TensorFlow implementation

To implement data parallelism using TensorFlow, you first need to choose whether you want in-graph replication or between-graph replication, and whether you want synchronous updates or asynchronous updates. Let's look at how you would implement each combination (see the exercises and the Jupyter notebooks for complete code examples).

With in-graph replication + synchronous updates, you build one big graph containing all the model replicas (placed on different devices), and a few nodes to aggregate all their gradients and feed them to an optimizer. Your code opens a session to the cluster and simply runs the training operation repeatedly.

With in-graph replication + asynchronous updates, you also create one big graph, but with one optimizer per replica, and you run one thread per replica, repeatedly running the replica's optimizer.

With between-graph replication + asynchronous updates, you run multiple independent clients (typically in separate processes), each training the model replica as if it were alone in the world, but the parameters are actually shared with other replicas (using a resource container).

With between-graph replication + synchronous updates, once again you run multiple clients, each training a model replica based on shared parameters, but this time you wrap the optimizer (e.g., a `MomentumOptimizer`) within a `SyncReplicasOptimizer`. Each replica uses this optimizer as it would use any other optimizer, but under the hood this optimizer sends the gradients to a set of queues (one per variable), which is read by one of the replica's `SyncReplicasOptimizer`, called the *chief*. The chief aggregates the gradients and applies them, then writes a token to a *token queue* for each replica, signaling it that it can go ahead and compute the next gradients. This approach supports having *spare replicas*.

If you go through the exercises, you will implement each of these four solutions. You will easily be able to apply what you have learned to train large deep neural networks across dozens of servers and GPUs! In the following chapters we will go through a few more important neural network architectures before we tackle Reinforcement Learning.

Exercises

1. If you get a `CUDA_ERROR_OUT_OF_MEMORY` when starting your TensorFlow program, what is probably going on? What can you do about it?

2. What is the difference between pinning an operation on a device and placing an operation on a device?

3. If you are running on a GPU-enabled TensorFlow installation, and you just use the default placement, will all operations be placed on the first GPU?

4. If you pin a variable to `"/gpu:0"`, can it be used by operations placed on `/gpu:1`? Or by operations placed on `"/cpu:0"`? Or by operations pinned to devices located on other servers?

5. Can two operations placed on the same device run in parallel?

6. What is a control dependency and when would you want to use one?

7. Suppose you train a DNN for days on a TensorFlow cluster, and immediately after your training program ends you realize that you forgot to save the model using a `Saver`. Is your trained model lost?

8. Train several DNNs in parallel on a TensorFlow cluster, using different hyperparameter values. This could be DNNs for MNIST classification or any other task you are interested in. The simplest option is to write a single client program that trains only one DNN, then run this program in multiple processes in parallel, with different hyperparameter values for each client. The program should have command-line options to control what server and device the DNN should be placed on, and what resource container and hyperparameter values to use (make sure to use a different resource container for each DNN). Use a validation set or cross-validation to select the top three models.

9. Create an ensemble using the top three models from the previous exercise. Define it in a single graph, ensuring that each DNN runs on a different device. Evaluate it on the validation set: does the ensemble perform better than the individual DNNs?

10. Train a DNN using between-graph replication and data parallelism with asynchronous updates, timing how long it takes to reach a satisfying performance. Next, try again using synchronous updates. Do synchronous updates produce a better model? Is training faster? Split the DNN vertically and place each vertical slice on a different device, and train the model again. Is training any faster? Is the performance any different?

Solutions to these exercises are available in Appendix A.

## CHAPTER 13

Convolutional Neural Networks

Although IBM's Deep Blue supercomputer beat the chess world champion Garry Kasparov back in 1996, until quite recently computers were unable to reliably perform seemingly trivial tasks such as detecting a puppy in a picture or recognizing spoken words. Why are these tasks so effortless to us humans? The answer lies in the fact that perception largely takes place outside the realm of our consciousness, within specialized visual, auditory, and other sensory modules in our brains. By the time sensory information reaches our consciousness, it is already adorned with high-level features; for example, when you look at a picture of a cute puppy, you cannot choose *not* to see the puppy, or *not* to notice its cuteness. Nor can you explain *how* you recognize a cute puppy; it's just obvious to you. Thus, we cannot trust our subjective experience: perception is not trivial at all, and to understand it we must look at how the sensory modules work.

Convolutional neural networks (CNNs) emerged from the study of the brain's visual cortex, and they have been used in image recognition since the 1980s. In the last few years, thanks to the increase in computational power, the amount of available training data, and the tricks presented in Chapter 11 for training deep nets, CNNs have managed to achieve superhuman performance on some complex visual tasks. They power image search services, self-driving cars, automatic video classification systems, and more. Moreover, CNNs are not restricted to visual perception: they are also successful at other tasks, such as *voice recognition* or *natural language processing* (NLP); however, we will focus on visual applications for now.

In this chapter we will present where CNNs came from, what their building blocks look like, and how to implement them using TensorFlow. Then we will present some of the best CNN architectures.

The Architecture of the Visual Cortex

David H. Hubel and Torsten Wiesel performed a series of experiments on cats in 1958 (*http://homl.info/71*)[1] and 1959 (*http://homl.info/72*)[2] (and a few years later on monkeys (*http://homl.info/73*)[3]), giving crucial insights on the structure of the visual cortex (the authors received the Nobel Prize in Physiology or Medicine in 1981 for their work). In particular, they showed that many neurons in the visual cortex have a small *local receptive field*, meaning they react only to visual stimuli located in a limited region of the visual field (see Figure 13-1, in which the local receptive fields of five neurons are represented by dashed circles). The receptive fields of different neurons may overlap, and together they tile the whole visual field. Moreover, the authors showed that some neurons react only to images of horizontal lines, while others react only to lines with different orientations (two neurons may have the same receptive field but react to different line orientations). They also noticed that some neurons have larger receptive fields, and they react to more complex patterns that are combinations of the lower-level patterns. These observations led to the idea that the higher-level neurons are based on the outputs of neighboring lower-level neurons (in Figure 13-1, notice that each neuron is connected only to a few neurons from the previous layer). This powerful architecture is able to detect all sorts of complex patterns in any area of the visual field.

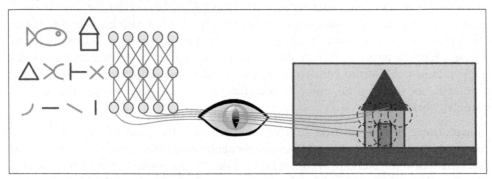

Figure 13-1. Local receptive fields in the visual cortex

These studies of the visual cortex inspired the neocognitron, introduced in 1980 (*http://homl.info/74*),[4] which gradually evolved into what we now call *convolutional*

---

1 "Single Unit Activity in Striate Cortex of Unrestrained Cats," D. Hubel and T. Wiesel (1958).

2 "Receptive Fields of Single Neurones in the Cat's Striate Cortex," D. Hubel and T. Wiesel (1959).

3 "Receptive Fields and Functional Architecture of Monkey Striate Cortex," D. Hubel and T. Wiesel (1968).

4 "Neocognitron: A Self-organizing Neural Network Model for a Mechanism of Pattern Recognition Unaffected by Shift in Position," K. Fukushima (1980).

neural networks. An important milestone was a 1998 paper (*http://homl.info/75*)[5] by Yann LeCun, Léon Bottou, Yoshua Bengio, and Patrick Haffner, which introduced the famous *LeNet-5* architecture, widely used to recognize handwritten check numbers. This architecture has some building blocks that you already know, such as fully connected layers and sigmoid activation functions, but it also introduces two new building blocks: *convolutional layers* and *pooling layers*. Let's look at them now.

 Why not simply use a regular deep neural network with fully connected layers for image recognition tasks? Unfortunately, although this works fine for small images (e.g., MNIST), it breaks down for larger images because of the huge number of parameters it requires. For example, a 100 × 100 image has 10,000 pixels, and if the first layer has just 1,000 neurons (which already severely restricts the amount of information transmitted to the next layer), this means a total of 10 million connections. And that's just the first layer. CNNs solve this problem using partially connected layers.

Convolutional Layer

The most important building block of a CNN is the *convolutional layer*:[6] neurons in the first convolutional layer are not connected to every single pixel in the input image (like they were in previous chapters), but only to pixels in their receptive fields (see Figure 13-2). In turn, each neuron in the second convolutional layer is connected only to neurons located within a small rectangle in the first layer. This architecture allows the network to concentrate on low-level features in the first hidden layer, then assemble them into higher-level features in the next hidden layer, and so on. This hierarchical structure is common in real-world images, which is one of the reasons why CNNs work so well for image recognition.

---

5 "Gradient-Based Learning Applied to Document Recognition," Y. LeCun et al. (1998).

6 A convolution is a mathematical operation that slides one function over another and measures the integral of their pointwise multiplication. It has deep connections with the Fourier transform and the Laplace transform, and is heavily used in signal processing. Convolutional layers actually use cross-correlations, which are very similar to convolutions (see *http://homl.info/76* for more details).

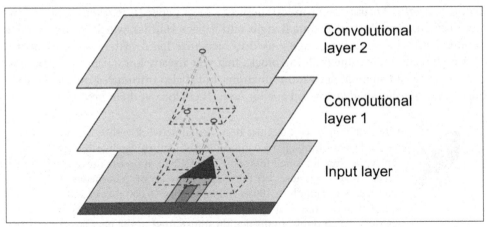

Figure 13-2. CNN layers with rectangular local receptive fields

 Until now, all multilayer neural networks we looked at had layers composed of a long line of neurons, and we had to flatten input images to 1D before feeding them to the neural network. Now each layer is represented in 2D, which makes it easier to match neurons with their corresponding inputs.

A neuron located in row i, column j of a given layer is connected to the outputs of the neurons in the previous layer located in rows i to $i + f_h - 1$, columns j to $j + f_w - 1$, where f_h and f_w are the height and width of the receptive field (see Figure 13-3). In order for a layer to have the same height and width as the previous layer, it is common to add zeros around the inputs, as shown in the diagram. This is called *zero padding*.

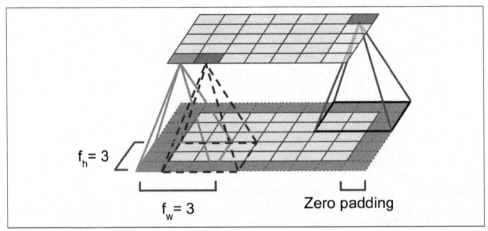

Figure 13-3. Connections between layers and zero padding

It is also possible to connect a large input layer to a much smaller layer by spacing out the receptive fields, as shown in Figure 13-4. The distance between two consecutive receptive fields is called the *stride*. In the diagram, a 5 × 7 input layer (plus zero padding) is connected to a 3 × 4 layer, using 3 × 3 receptive fields and a stride of 2 (in this example the stride is the same in both directions, but it does not have to be so). A neuron located in row i, column j in the upper layer is connected to the outputs of the neurons in the previous layer located in rows $i \times s_h$ to $i \times s_h + f_h - 1$, columns $j \times s_w$ to $j \times s_w + f_w - 1$, where s_h and s_w are the vertical and horizontal strides.

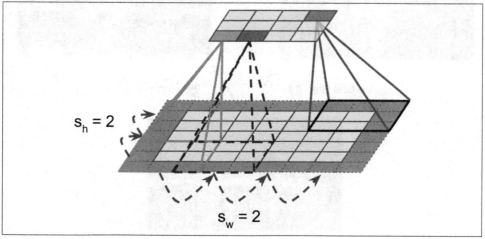

Figure 13-4. Reducing dimensionality using a stride of 2

Filters

A neuron's weights can be represented as a small image the size of the receptive field. For example, Figure 13-5 shows two possible sets of weights, called *filters* (or *convolution kernels*). The first one is represented as a black square with a vertical white line in the middle (it is a 7 × 7 matrix full of 0s except for the central column, which is full of 1s); neurons using these weights will ignore everything in their receptive field except for the central vertical line (since all inputs will get multiplied by 0, except for the ones located in the central vertical line). The second filter is a black square with a horizontal white line in the middle. Once again, neurons using these weights will ignore everything in their receptive field except for the central horizontal line.

Now if all neurons in a layer use the same vertical line filter (and the same bias term), and you feed the network the input image shown in Figure 13-5 (bottom image), the layer will output the top-left image. Notice that the vertical white lines get enhanced while the rest gets blurred. Similarly, the upper-right image is what you get if all neurons use the horizontal line filter; notice that the horizontal white lines get enhanced while the rest is blurred out. Thus, a layer full of neurons using the same filter gives you a *feature map*, which highlights the areas in an image that are most similar to the filter. During training, a CNN finds the most useful filters for its task, and it learns to combine them into more complex patterns (e.g., a cross is an area in an image where both the vertical filter and the horizontal filter are active).

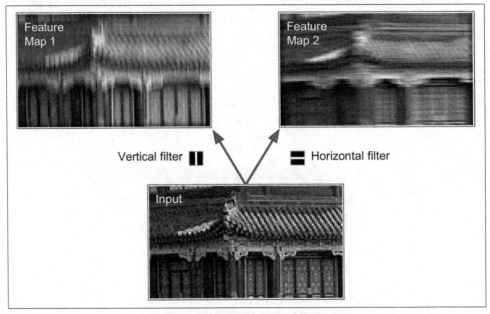

Figure 13-5. Applying two different filters to get two feature maps

Stacking Multiple Feature Maps

Up to now, for simplicity, we have represented each convolutional layer as a thin 2D layer, but in reality it is composed of several feature maps of equal sizes, so it is more accurately represented in 3D (see Figure 13-6). Within one feature map, all neurons share the same parameters (weights and bias term), but different feature maps may have different parameters. A neuron's receptive field is the same as described earlier, but it extends across all the previous layers' feature maps. In short, a convolutional layer simultaneously applies multiple filters to its inputs, making it capable of detecting multiple features anywhere in its inputs.

 The fact that all neurons in a feature map share the same parameters dramatically reduces the number of parameters in the model, but most importantly it means that once the CNN has learned to recognize a pattern in one location, it can recognize it in any other location. In contrast, once a regular DNN has learned to recognize a pattern in one location, it can recognize it only in that particular location.

Moreover, input images are also composed of multiple sublayers: one per *color channel*. There are typically three: red, green, and blue (RGB). Grayscale images have just one channel, but some images may have much more—for example, satellite images that capture extra light frequencies (such as infrared).

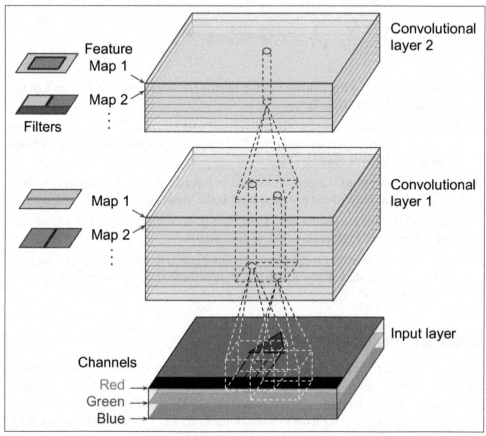

Figure 13-6. Convolution layers with multiple feature maps, and images with three channels

Specifically, a neuron located in row i, column j of the feature map k in a given convolutional layer l is connected to the outputs of the neurons in the previous layer $l - 1$, located in rows $i \times s_h$ to $i \times s_h + f_h - 1$ and columns $j \times s_w$ to $j \times s_w + f_w - 1$, across all feature maps (in layer $l - 1$). Note that all neurons located in the same row i and column j but in different feature maps are connected to the outputs of the exact same neurons in the previous layer.

Equation 13-1 summarizes the preceding explanations in one big mathematical equation: it shows how to compute the output of a given neuron in a convolutional layer.

It is a bit ugly due to all the different indices, but all it does is calculate the weighted sum of all the inputs, plus the bias term.

Equation 13-1. Computing the output of a neuron in a convolutional layer

$$z_{i,j,k} = b_k + \sum_{u=0}^{f_h - 1} \sum_{v=0}^{f_w - 1} \sum_{k'=0}^{f_{n'} - 1} x_{i',j',k'} \cdot w_{u,v,k',k} \quad \text{with} \quad \begin{cases} i' = i \times s_h + u \\ j' = j \times s_w + v \end{cases}$$

- $z_{i,j,k}$ is the output of the neuron located in row i, column j in feature map k of the convolutional layer (layer l).
- As explained earlier, s_h and s_w are the vertical and horizontal strides, f_h and f_w are the height and width of the receptive field, and $f_{n'}$ is the number of feature maps in the previous layer (layer $l - 1$).
- $x_{i',j',k'}$ is the output of the neuron located in layer $l - 1$, row i', column j', feature map k' (or channel k' if the previous layer is the input layer).
- b_k is the bias term for feature map k (in layer l). You can think of it as a knob that tweaks the overall brightness of the feature map k.
- $w_{u,v,k',k}$ is the connection weight between any neuron in feature map k of the layer l and its input located at row u, column v (relative to the neuron's receptive field), and feature map k'.

TensorFlow Implementation

In TensorFlow, each input image is typically represented as a 3D tensor of shape [height, width, channels]. A mini-batch is represented as a 4D tensor of shape [mini-batch size, height, width, channels]. The weights of a convolutional layer are represented as a 4D tensor of shape $[f_h, f_w, f_{n'}, f_n]$. The bias terms of a convolutional layer are simply represented as a 1D tensor of shape $[f_n]$.

Let's look at a simple example. The following code loads two sample images, using Scikit-Learn's load_sample_images() (which loads two color images, one of a Chinese temple, and the other of a flower). Then it creates two 7 × 7 filters (one with a vertical white line in the middle, and the other with a horizontal white line in the middle), and applies them to both images using a convolutional layer built using TensorFlow's tf.nn.conv2d() function (with zero padding and a stride of 2). Finally, it plots one of the resulting feature maps (similar to the top-right image in Figure 13-5).

```
import numpy as np
from sklearn.datasets import load_sample_images

# Load sample images
china = load_sample_image("china.jpg")
flower = load_sample_image("flower.jpg")
dataset = np.array([china, flower], dtype=np.float32)
batch_size, height, width, channels = dataset.shape

# Create 2 filters
filters = np.zeros(shape=(7, 7, channels, 2), dtype=np.float32)
filters[:, 3, :, 0] = 1  # vertical line
filters[3, :, :, 1] = 1  # horizontal line

# Create a graph with input X plus a convolutional layer applying the 2 filters
X = tf.placeholder(tf.float32, shape=(None, height, width, channels))
convolution = tf.nn.conv2d(X, filters, strides=[1,2,2,1], padding="SAME")

with tf.Session() as sess:
    output = sess.run(convolution, feed_dict={X: dataset})

plt.imshow(output[0, :, :, 1], cmap="gray") # plot 1st image's 2nd feature map
plt.show()
```

Most of this code is self-explanatory, but the `tf.nn.conv2d()` line deserves a bit of explanation:

- X is the input mini-batch (a 4D tensor, as explained earlier).

- filters is the set of filters to apply (also a 4D tensor, as explained earlier).

- strides is a four-element 1D array, where the two central elements are the vertical and horizontal strides (s_h and s_w). The first and last elements must currently be equal to 1. They may one day be used to specify a batch stride (to skip some instances) and a channel stride (to skip some of the previous layer's feature maps or channels).

- padding must be either "VALID" or "SAME":

  — If set to "VALID", the convolutional layer does *not* use zero padding, and may ignore some rows and columns at the bottom and right of the input image, depending on the stride, as shown in Figure 13-7 (for simplicity, only the horizontal dimension is shown here, but of course the same logic applies to the vertical dimension).

  — If set to "SAME", the convolutional layer uses zero padding if necessary. In this case, the number of output neurons is equal to the number of input neurons divided by the stride, rounded up (in this example, ceil (13 / 5) = 3). Then zeros are added as evenly as possible around the inputs.

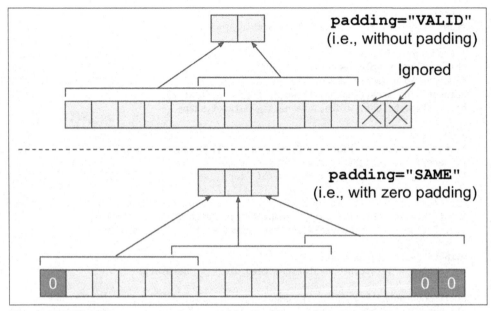

Figure 13-7. Padding options—input width: 13, filter width: 6, stride: 5

In this simple example, we manually created the filters, but in a real CNN you would let the training algorithm discover the best filters automatically. TensorFlow has a `tf.layers.conv2d()` function which creates the filters variable for you (named `kernel`), and initializes it randomly. It also creates the bias variable (named `bias`) and initializes it with zeros. For example, the following code creates an input placeholder followed by a convolutional layer with two 7 × 7 feature maps, using 2 × 2 strides (note that this function only expects the vertical and horizontal strides), and "SAME" padding:

```
X = tf.placeholder(shape=(None, height, width, channels), dtype=tf.float32)
conv = tf.layers.conv2d(X, filters=2, kernel_size=7, strides=[2,2],
                        padding="SAME")
```

Unfortunately, convolutional layers have quite a few hyperparameters: you must choose the number of filters, their height and width, the strides, and the padding type. As always, you can use cross-validation to find the right hyperparameter values, but this is very time-consuming. We will discuss common CNN architectures later, to give you some idea of what hyperparameter values work best in practice.

Memory Requirements

Another problem with CNNs is that the convolutional layers require a huge amount of RAM, especially during training, because the reverse pass of backpropagation requires all the intermediate values computed during the forward pass.

For example, consider a convolutional layer with 5 × 5 filters, outputting 200 feature maps of size 150 × 100, with stride 1 and SAME padding. If the input is a 150 × 100 RGB image (three channels), then the number of parameters is (5 × 5 × 3 + 1) × 200 = 15,200 (the +1 corresponds to the bias terms), which is fairly small compared to a fully connected layer.[7] However, each of the 200 feature maps contains 150 × 100 neurons, and each of these neurons needs to compute a weighted sum of its 5 × 5 × 3 = 75 inputs: that's a total of 225 million float multiplications. Not as bad as a fully connected layer, but still quite computationally intensive. Moreover, if the feature maps are represented using 32-bit floats, then the convolutional layer's output will occupy 200 × 150 × 100 × 32 = 96 million bits (about 11.4 MB) of RAM.[8] And that's just for one instance! If a training batch contains 100 instances, then this layer will use up over 1 GB of RAM!

During inference (i.e., when making a prediction for a new instance) the RAM occupied by one layer can be released as soon as the next layer has been computed, so you only need as much RAM as required by two consecutive layers. But during training everything computed during the forward pass needs to be preserved for the reverse pass, so the amount of RAM needed is (at least) the total amount of RAM required by all layers.

If training crashes because of an out-of-memory error, you can try reducing the mini-batch size. Alternatively, you can try reducing dimensionality using a stride, or removing a few layers. Or you can try using 16-bit floats instead of 32-bit floats. Or you could distribute the CNN across multiple devices.

Now let's look at the second common building block of CNNs: the *pooling layer*.

Pooling Layer

Once you understand how convolutional layers work, the pooling layers are quite easy to grasp. Their goal is to *subsample* (i.e., shrink) the input image in order to reduce the computational load, the memory usage, and the number of parameters (thereby limiting the risk of overfitting).

Just like in convolutional layers, each neuron in a pooling layer is connected to the outputs of a limited number of neurons in the previous layer, located within a small rectangular receptive field. You must define its size, the stride, and the padding type, just like before. However, a pooling neuron has no weights; all it does is aggregate the

---

7 A fully connected layer with 150 × 100 neurons, each connected to all 150 × 100 × 3 inputs, would have $150^2 \times 100^2 \times 3$ = 675 million parameters!

8 1 MB = 1,024 kB = 1,024 × 1,024 bytes = 1,024 × 1,024 × 8 bits.

inputs using an aggregation function such as the max or mean. Figure 13-8 shows a *max pooling layer*, which is the most common type of pooling layer. In this example, we use a 2 × 2 *pooling kernel*, a stride of 2, and no padding. Note that only the max input value in each kernel makes it to the next layer. The other inputs are dropped.

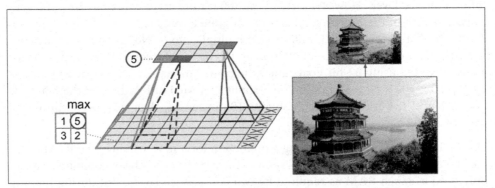

Figure 13-8. Max pooling layer (2 × 2 pooling kernel, stride 2, no padding)

This is obviously a very destructive kind of layer: even with a tiny 2 × 2 kernel and a stride of 2, the output will be two times smaller in both directions (so its area will be four times smaller), simply dropping 75% of the input values.

A pooling layer typically works on every input channel independently, so the output depth is the same as the input depth. You may alternatively pool over the depth dimension, as we will see next, in which case the image's spatial dimensions (height and width) remain unchanged, but the number of channels is reduced.

Implementing a max pooling layer in TensorFlow is quite easy. The following code creates a max pooling layer using a 2 × 2 kernel, stride 2, and no padding, then applies it to all the images in the dataset:

```
[...] # load the image dataset, just like above

# Create a graph with input X plus a max pooling layer
X = tf.placeholder(tf.float32, shape=(None, height, width, channels))
max_pool = tf.nn.max_pool(X, ksize=[1,2,2,1], strides=[1,2,2,1],padding="VALID")

with tf.Session() as sess:
    output = sess.run(max_pool, feed_dict={X: dataset})

plt.imshow(output[0].astype(np.uint8))  # plot the output for the 1st image
plt.show()
```

The `ksize` argument contains the kernel shape along all four dimensions of the input tensor: [`batch size, height, width, channels`]. TensorFlow currently does not support pooling over multiple instances, so the first element of `ksize` must be equal to 1. Moreover, it does not support pooling over both the spatial dimensions (height and width) and the depth dimension, so either `ksize[1]` and `ksize[2]` must both be equal to 1, or `ksize[3]` must be equal to 1.

To create an *average pooling layer*, just use the `avg_pool()` function instead of `max_pool()`.

Now you know all the building blocks to create a convolutional neural network. Let's see how to assemble them.

CNN Architectures

Typical CNN architectures stack a few convolutional layers (each one generally followed by a ReLU layer), then a pooling layer, then another few convolutional layers (+ReLU), then another pooling layer, and so on. The image gets smaller and smaller as it progresses through the network, but it also typically gets deeper and deeper (i.e., with more feature maps) thanks to the convolutional layers (see Figure 13-9). At the top of the stack, a regular feedforward neural network is added, composed of a few fully connected layers (+ReLUs), and the final layer outputs the prediction (e.g., a softmax layer that outputs estimated class probabilities).

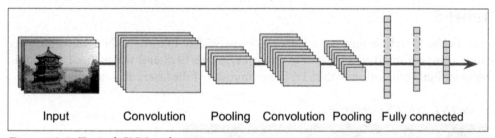

Input   Convolution   Pooling   Convolution   Pooling   Fully connected

Figure 13-9. Typical CNN architecture

> A common mistake is to use convolution kernels that are too large. You can often get the same effect as one convolutional layer with a 9 × 9 kernel by stacking two layers with 3 × 3 kernels, for a lot less compute and parameters.

Over the years, variants of this fundamental architecture have been developed, leading to amazing advances in the field. A good measure of this progress is the error rate in competitions such as the ILSVRC ImageNet challenge (*http://image-net.org/*). In this competition the top-5 error rate for image classification fell from over 26% to less than 3% in just six years. The top-five error rate is the number of test images for which the system's top 5 predictions did not include the correct answer. The images are large (256 pixels high) and there are 1,000 classes, some of which are really subtle (try distinguishing 120 dog breeds). Looking at the evolution of the winning entries is a good way to understand how CNNs work.

We will first look at the classical LeNet-5 architecture (1998), then three of the winners of the ILSVRC challenge: AlexNet (2012), GoogLeNet (2014), and ResNet (2015).

Other Visual Tasks

There was stunning progress as well in other visual tasks such as object detection and localization, and image segmentation. In object detection and localization, the neural network typically outputs a sequence of bounding boxes around various objects in the image. For example, see Maxine Oquab et al.'s 2015 paper (*http://homl.info/77*) that outputs a heat map for each object class, or Russell Stewart et al.'s 2015 paper (*http://homl.info/78*) that uses a combination of a CNN to detect faces and a recurrent neural network to output a sequence of bounding boxes around them. In image segmentation, the net outputs an image (usually of the same size as the input) where each pixel indicates the class of the object to which the corresponding input pixel belongs. For example, check out Evan Shelhamer et al.'s 2016 paper (*http://homl.info/79*).

LeNet-5

The LeNet-5 architecture is perhaps the most widely known CNN architecture. As mentioned earlier, it was created by Yann LeCun in 1998 and widely used for handwritten digit recognition (MNIST). It is composed of the layers shown in Table 13-1.

Table 13-1. LeNet-5 architecture

Layer	Type	Maps	Size	Kernel size	Stride	Activation
Out	Fully Connected	–	10	–	–	RBF
F6	Fully Connected	–	84	–	–	tanh
C5	Convolution	120	1×1	5×5	1	tanh
S4	Avg Pooling	16	5×5	2×2	2	tanh
C3	Convolution	16	10×10	5×5	1	tanh
S2	Avg Pooling	6	14×14	2×2	2	tanh
C1	Convolution	6	28×28	5×5	1	tanh
In	Input	1	32×32	–	–	–

There are a few extra details to be noted:

- MNIST images are 28 × 28 pixels, but they are zero-padded to 32 × 32 pixels and normalized before being fed to the network. The rest of the network does not use any padding, which is why the size keeps shrinking as the image progresses through the network.

- The average pooling layers are slightly more complex than usual: each neuron computes the mean of its inputs, then multiplies the result by a learnable coefficient (one per map) and adds a learnable bias term (again, one per map), then finally applies the activation function.
- Most neurons in C3 maps are connected to neurons in only three or four S2 maps (instead of all six S2 maps). See table 1 in the original paper for details.
- The output layer is a bit special: instead of computing the matrix multiplication of the inputs and the weight vector, each neuron outputs the square of the Euclidian distance between its input vector and its weight vector. Each output measures how much the image belongs to a particular digit class. The cross entropy cost function is now preferred, as it penalizes bad predictions much more, producing larger gradients and thus converging faster.

Yann LeCun's website (*http://yann.lecun.com/*) ("LENET" section) features great demos of LeNet-5 classifying digits.

AlexNet

The *AlexNet* CNN architecture (*http://homl.info/80*)[9] won the 2012 ImageNet ILSVRC challenge by a large margin: it achieved 17% top-5 error rate while the second best achieved only 26%! It was developed by Alex Krizhevsky (hence the name), Ilya Sutskever, and Geoffrey Hinton. It is quite similar to LeNet-5, only much larger and deeper, and it was the first to stack convolutional layers directly on top of each other, instead of stacking a pooling layer on top of each convolutional layer. Table 13-2 presents this architecture.

Table 13-2. AlexNet architecture

Layer	Type	Maps	Size	Kernel size	Stride	Padding	Activation
Out	Fully Connected	–	1,000	–	–	–	Softmax
F9	Fully Connected	–	4,096	–	–	–	ReLU
F8	Fully Connected	–	4,096	–	–	–	ReLU
C7	Convolution	256	13×13	3×3	1	SAME	ReLU
C6	Convolution	384	13×13	3×3	1	SAME	ReLU
C5	Convolution	384	13×13	3×3	1	SAME	ReLU
S4	Max Pooling	256	13×13	3×3	2	VALID	–
C3	Convolution	256	27×27	5×5	1	SAME	ReLU
S2	Max Pooling	96	27×27	3×3	2	VALID	–
C1	Convolution	96	55×55	11×11	4	VALID	ReLU

---

9 "ImageNet Classification with Deep Convolutional Neural Networks," A. Krizhevsky et al. (2012).

Layer	Type	Maps	Size	Kernel size	Stride	Padding	Activation
In	Input	3 (RGB)	227 × 227	–	–	–	–

To reduce overfitting, the authors used two regularization techniques we discussed in previous chapters: first they applied dropout (with a 50% dropout rate) during training to the outputs of layers F8 and F9. Second, they performed data augmentation by randomly shifting the training images by various offsets, flipping them horizontally, and changing the lighting conditions.

AlexNet also uses a competitive normalization step immediately after the ReLU step of layers C1 and C3, called *local response normalization*. This form of normalization makes the neurons that most strongly activate inhibit neurons at the same location but in neighboring feature maps (such competitive activation has been observed in biological neurons). This encourages different feature maps to specialize, pushing them apart and forcing them to explore a wider range of features, ultimately improving generalization. Equation 13-2 shows how to apply LRN.

Equation 13-2. Local response normalization

$$b_i = a_i \left(k + \alpha \sum_{j = j_{\text{low}}}^{j_{\text{high}}} a_j^2 \right)^{-\beta} \quad \text{with} \quad \begin{cases} j_{\text{high}} = \min\left(i + \frac{r}{2}, f_n - 1\right) \\ j_{\text{low}} = \max\left(0, i - \frac{r}{2}\right) \end{cases}$$

- b_i is the normalized output of the neuron located in feature map i, at some row u and column v (note that in this equation we consider only neurons located at this row and column, so u and v are not shown).
- a_i is the activation of that neuron after the ReLU step, but before normalization.
- k, α, β, and r are hyperparameters. k is called the *bias*, and r is called the *depth radius*.
- f_n is the number of feature maps.

For example, if $r = 2$ and a neuron has a strong activation, it will inhibit the activation of the neurons located in the feature maps immediately above and below its own.

In AlexNet, the hyperparameters are set as follows: $r = 2$, $\alpha = 0.00002$, $\beta = 0.75$, and $k = 1$. This step can be implemented using TensorFlow's `tf.nn.local_response_nor malization()` operation.

A variant of AlexNet called *ZF Net* was developed by Matthew Zeiler and Rob Fergus and won the 2013 ILSVRC challenge. It is essentially AlexNet with a few tweaked hyperparameters (number of feature maps, kernel size, stride, etc.).

GoogLeNet

The GoogLeNet architecture (*http://homl.info/81*) was developed by Christian Szegedy et al. from Google Research,[10] and it won the ILSVRC 2014 challenge by pushing the top-5 error rate below 7%. This great performance came in large part from the fact that the network was much deeper than previous CNNs (see Figure 13-11). This was made possible by sub-networks called *inception modules*,[11] which allow GoogLeNet to use parameters much more efficiently than previous architectures: GoogLeNet actually has 10 times fewer parameters than AlexNet (roughly 6 million instead of 60 million).

Figure 13-10 shows the architecture of an inception module. The notation "3 × 3 + 2(S)" means that the layer uses a 3 × 3 kernel, stride 2, and SAME padding. The input signal is first copied and fed to four different layers. All convolutional layers use the ReLU activation function. Note that the second set of convolutional layers uses different kernel sizes (1 × 1, 3 × 3, and 5 × 5), allowing them to capture patterns at different scales. Also note that every single layer uses a stride of 1 and SAME padding (even the max pooling layer), so their outputs all have the same height and width as their inputs. This makes it possible to concatenate all the outputs along the depth dimension in the final *depth concat layer* (i.e., stack the feature maps from all four top convolutional layers). This concatenation layer can be implemented in TensorFlow using the `tf.concat()` operation, with `axis=3` (axis 3 is the depth).

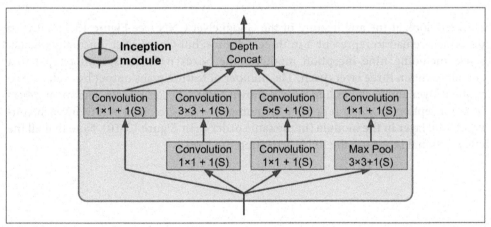

Figure 13-10. Inception module

---

10 "Going Deeper with Convolutions," C. Szegedy et al. (2015).

11 In the 2010 movie *Inception*, the characters keep going deeper and deeper into multiple layers of dreams, hence the name of these modules.

You may wonder why inception modules have convolutional layers with 1×1 kernels. Surely these layers cannot capture any features since they look at only one pixel at a time? In fact, these layers serve two purposes:

- First, they are configured to output many fewer feature maps than their inputs, so they serve as *bottleneck layers*, meaning they reduce dimensionality. This is particularly useful before the 3×3 and 5×5 convolutions, since these are very computationally expensive layers.

- Second, each pair of convolutional layers ([1×1, 3×3] and [1×1, 5×5]) acts like a single, powerful convolutional layer, capable of capturing more complex patterns. Indeed, instead of sweeping a simple linear classifier across the image (as a single convolutional layer does), this pair of convolutional layers sweeps a two-layer neural network across the image.

In short, you can think of the whole inception module as a convolutional layer on steroids, able to output feature maps that capture complex patterns at various scales.

> The number of convolutional kernels for each convolutional layer is a hyperparameter. Unfortunately, this means that you have six more hyperparameters to tweak for every inception layer you add.

Now let's look at the architecture of the GoogLeNet CNN (see Figure 13-11). It is so deep that we had to represent it in three columns, but GoogLeNet is actually one tall stack, including nine inception modules (the boxes with the spinning tops) that actually contain three layers each. The number of feature maps output by each convolutional layer and each pooling layer is shown before the kernel size. The six numbers in the inception modules represent the number of feature maps output by each convolutional layer in the module (in the same order as in Figure 13-10). Note that all the convolutional layers use the ReLU activation function.

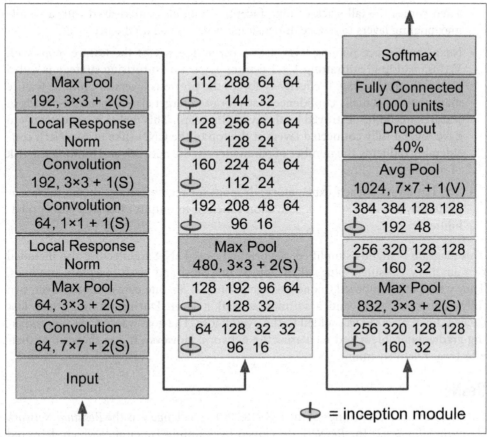

Figure 13-11. GoogLeNet architecture

Let's go through this network:

- The first two layers divide the image's height and width by 4 (so its area is divided by 16), to reduce the computational load.

- Then the local response normalization layer ensures that the previous layers learn a wide variety of features (as discussed earlier).

- Two convolutional layers follow, where the first acts like a *bottleneck layer*. As explained earlier, you can think of this pair as a single smarter convolutional layer.

- Again, a local response normalization layer ensures that the previous layers capture a wide variety of patterns.

- Next a max pooling layer reduces the image height and width by 2, again to speed up computations.

- Then comes the tall stack of nine inception modules, interleaved with a couple max pooling layers to reduce dimensionality and speed up the net.

- Next, the average pooling layer uses a kernel the size of the feature maps with VALID padding, outputting 1×1 feature maps: this surprising strategy is called *global average pooling*. It effectively forces the previous layers to produce feature maps that are actually confidence maps for each target class (since other kinds of features would be destroyed by the averaging step). This makes it unnecessary to have several fully connected layers at the top of the CNN (like in AlexNet), considerably reducing the number of parameters in the network and limiting the risk of overfitting.

- The last layers are self-explanatory: dropout for regularization, then a fully connected layer with a softmax activation function to output estimated class probabilities.

This diagram is slightly simplified: the original GoogLeNet architecture also included two auxiliary classifiers plugged on top of the third and sixth inception modules. They were both composed of one average pooling layer, one convolutional layer, two fully connected layers, and a softmax activation layer. During training, their loss (scaled down by 70%) was added to the overall loss. The goal was to fight the vanishing gradients problem and regularize the network. However, it was shown that their effect was relatively minor.

ResNet

Last but not least, the winner of the ILSVRC 2015 challenge was the *Residual Network* (*http://homl.info/82*) (or *ResNet*), developed by Kaiming He et al.,[12] which delivered an astounding top-5 error rate under 3.6%, using an extremely deep CNN composed of 152 layers. The key to being able to train such a deep network is to use *skip connections* (also called *shortcut connections*): the signal feeding into a layer is also added to the output of a layer located a bit higher up the stack. Let's see why this is useful.

When training a neural network, the goal is to make it model a target function $h(\mathbf{x})$. If you add the input $\mathbf{x}$ to the output of the network (i.e., you add a skip connection), then the network will be forced to model $f(\mathbf{x}) = h(\mathbf{x}) - \mathbf{x}$ rather than $h(\mathbf{x})$. This is called *residual learning* (see Figure 13-12).

---

12 "Deep Residual Learning for Image Recognition," K. He (2015).

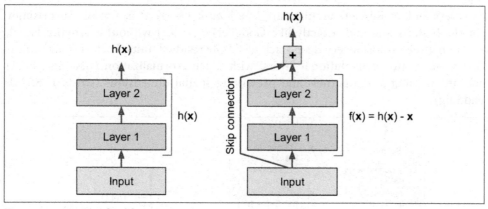

Figure 13-12. Residual learning

When you initialize a regular neural network, its weights are close to zero, so the network just outputs values close to zero. If you add a skip connection, the resulting network just outputs a copy of its inputs; in other words, it initially models the identity function. If the target function is fairly close to the identity function (which is often the case), this will speed up training considerably.

Moreover, if you add many skip connections, the network can start making progress even if several layers have not started learning yet (see Figure 13-13). Thanks to skip connections, the signal can easily make its way across the whole network. The deep residual network can be seen as a stack of *residual units*, where each residual unit is a small neural network with a skip connection.

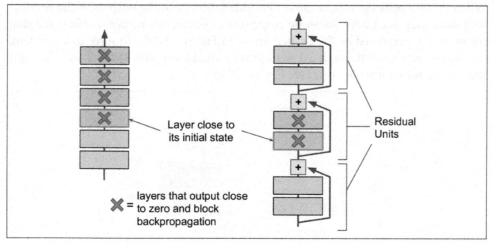

Figure 13-13. Regular deep neural network (left) and deep residual network (right)

Now let's look at ResNet's architecture (see Figure 13-14). It is actually surprisingly simple. It starts and ends exactly like GoogLeNet (except without a dropout layer), and in between is just a very deep stack of simple residual units. Each residual unit is composed of two convolutional layers, with Batch Normalization (BN) and ReLU activation, using 3 × 3 kernels and preserving spatial dimensions (stride 1, SAME padding).

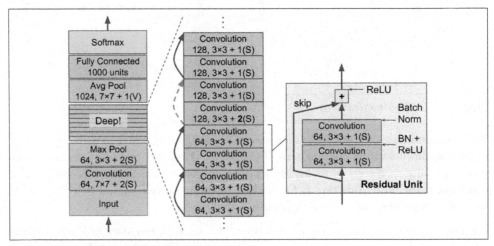

Figure 13-14. ResNet architecture

Note that the number of feature maps is doubled every few residual units, at the same time as their height and width are halved (using a convolutional layer with stride 2). When this happens the inputs cannot be added directly to the outputs of the residual unit since they don't have the same shape (for example, this problem affects the skip connection represented by the dashed arrow in Figure 13-14). To solve this problem, the inputs are passed through a 1 × 1 convolutional layer with stride 2 and the right number of output feature maps (see Figure 13-15).

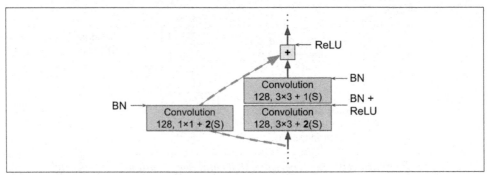

Figure 13-15. Skip connection when changing feature map size and depth

ResNet-34 is the ResNet with 34 layers (only counting the convolutional layers and the fully connected layer) containing three residual units that output 64 feature maps, 4 RUs with 128 maps, 6 RUs with 256 maps, and 3 RUs with 512 maps.

ResNets deeper than that, such as ResNet-152, use slightly different residual units. Instead of two 3 × 3 convolutional layers with (say) 256 feature maps, they use three convolutional layers: first a 1 × 1 convolutional layer with just 64 feature maps (4 times less), which acts a a bottleneck layer (as discussed already), then a 3 × 3 layer with 64 feature maps, and finally another 1 × 1 convolutional layer with 256 feature maps (4 times 64) that restores the original depth. ResNet-152 contains three such RUs that output 256 maps, then 8 RUs with 512 maps, a whopping 36 RUs with 1,024 maps, and finally 3 RUs with 2,048 maps.

As you can see, the field is moving rapidly, with all sorts of architectures popping out every year. One clear trend is that CNNs keep getting deeper and deeper. They are also getting lighter, requiring fewer and fewer parameters. At present, the ResNet architecture is both the most powerful and arguably the simplest, so it is really the one you should probably use for now, but keep looking at the ILSVRC challenge every year. The 2016 winners were the Trimps-Soushen team from China with an astounding 2.99% error rate. To achieve this they trained combinations of the previous models and joined them into an ensemble. Depending on the task, the reduced error rate may or may not be worth the extra complexity.

There are a few other architectures that you may want to look at, in particular VGGNet (*http://homl.info/83*)[13] (runner-up of the ILSVRC 2014 challenge) and Inception-v4 (*http://homl.info/84*)[14] (which merges the ideas of GoogLeNet and ResNet and achieves close to 3% top-5 error rate on ImageNet classification).

There is really nothing special about implementing the various CNN architectures we just discussed. We saw earlier how to build all the individual building blocks, so now all you need is to assemble them to create the desired architecture. We will build a complete CNN in the upcoming exercises and you will find full working code in the Jupyter notebooks.

---

13 "Very Deep Convolutional Networks for Large-Scale Image Recognition," K. Simonyan and A. Zisserman (2015).

14 "Inception-v4, Inception-ResNet and the Impact of Residual Connections on Learning," C. Szegedy et al. (2016).

TensorFlow Convolution Operations

TensorFlow also offers a few other kinds of convolutional layers:

- `tf.layers.conv1d()` creates a convolutional layer for 1D inputs. This is useful, for example, in natural language processing, where a sentence may be represented as a 1D array of words, and the receptive field covers a few neighboring words.

- `tf.layers.conv3d()` creates a convolutional layer for 3D inputs, such as 3D PET scan.

- `tf.nn.atrous_conv2d()` creates an *atrous convolutional layer* ("à trous" is French for "with holes"). This is equivalent to using a regular convolutional layer with a filter dilated by inserting rows and columns of zeros (i.e., holes). For example, a 1 × 3 filter equal to `[[1,2,3]]` may be dilated with a *dilation rate* of 4, resulting in a *dilated filter* `[[1, 0, 0, 0, 2, 0, 0, 0, 3]]`. This allows the convolutional layer to have a larger receptive field at no computational price and using no extra parameters.

- `tf.layers.conv2d_transpose()` creates a *transpose convolutional layer,*[15] sometimes called a *deconvolutional layer,* which *upsamples* an image. It does so by inserting zeros between the inputs, so you can think of this as a regular convolutional layer using a fractional stride. Upsampling is useful, for example, in image segmentation: in a typical CNN, feature maps get smaller and smaller as you progress through the network, so if you want to output an image of the same size as the input, you need an upsampling layer.

- `tf.nn.depthwise_conv2d()` creates a *depthwise convolutional layer* that applies every filter to every individual input channel independently. Thus, if there are f_n filters and $f_{n'}$ input channels, then this will output $f_n \times f_{n'}$ feature maps.

- `tf.layers.separable_conv2d()` creates a *separable convolutional layer* that first acts like a depthwise convolutional layer, then applies a 1 × 1 convolutional layer to the resulting feature maps. This makes it possible to apply filters to arbitrary sets of inputs channels.

Exercises

1. What are the advantages of a CNN over a fully connected DNN for image classification?

---

15 This name is quite misleading since this layer does *not* perform a deconvolution, which is a well-defined mathematical operation (the inverse of a convolution).

2. Consider a CNN composed of three convolutional layers, each with 3×3 kernels, a stride of 2, and SAME padding. The lowest layer outputs 100 feature maps, the middle one outputs 200, and the top one outputs 400. The input images are RGB images of 200×300 pixels. What is the total number of parameters in the CNN? If we are using 32-bit floats, at least how much RAM will this network require when making a prediction for a single instance? What about when training on a mini-batch of 50 images?

3. If your GPU runs out of memory while training a CNN, what are five things you could try to solve the problem?

4. Why would you want to add a max pooling layer rather than a convolutional layer with the same stride?

5. When would you want to add a *local response normalization* layer?

6. Can you name the main innovations in AlexNet, compared to LeNet-5? What about the main innovations in GoogLeNet and ResNet?

7. Build your own CNN and try to achieve the highest possible accuracy on MNIST.

8. Classifying large images using Inception v3.

   a. Download some images of various animals. Load them in Python, for example using the `matplotlib.image.mpimg.imread()` function or the `imageio.imread()` function. Resize and/or crop them to 299×299 pixels, and ensure that they have just three channels (RGB), with no transparency channel. The images that the Inception model was trained on were preprocessed so that their values range from -1.0 to 1.0, so you must ensure that your images do too.

   b. Download the latest pretrained Inception v3 model: the checkpoint is available at *http://homl.info/85*. The list of class names is available at *http://homl.info/86*, but you must insert a "background" class at the beginning.

   c. Create the Inception v3 model by calling the `inception_v3()` function, as shown below. This must be done within an argument scope created by the `inception_v3_arg_scope()` function. Also, you must set `is_training=False` and `num_classes=1001` like so:

```
from tensorflow.contrib.slim.nets import inception
import tensorflow.contrib.slim as slim

X = tf.placeholder(tf.float32, shape=[None, 299, 299, 3], name="X")
with slim.arg_scope(inception.inception_v3_arg_scope()):
    logits, end_points = inception.inception_v3(
        X, num_classes=1001, is_training=False)
predictions = end_points["Predictions"]
saver = tf.train.Saver()
```

d. Open a session and use the `Saver` to restore the pretrained model checkpoint you downloaded earlier.

e. Run the model to classify the images you prepared. Display the top five predictions for each image, along with the estimated probability. How accurate is the model?

9. Transfer learning for large image classification.

a. Create a training set containing at least 100 images per class. For example, you could classify your own pictures based on the location (beach, mountain, city, etc.), or alternatively you can just use an existing dataset, such as the flowers dataset (*http://homl.info/87*) or MIT's places dataset (*http://places.csail.mit.edu/*) (requires registration, and it is huge).

b. Write a preprocessing step that will resize and crop the image to 299 × 299, with some randomness for data augmentation.

c. Using the pretrained Inception v3 model from the previous exercise, freeze all layers up to the bottleneck layer (i.e., the last layer before the output layer), and replace the output layer with the appropriate number of outputs for your new classification task (e.g., the flowers dataset has five mutually exclusive classes so the output layer must have five neurons and use the softmax activation function).

d. Split your dataset into a training set and a test set. Train the model on the training set and evaluate it on the test set.

10. Go through TensorFlow's DeepDream tutorial (*http://homl.info/42*). It is a fun way to familiarize yourself with various ways of visualizing the patterns learned by a CNN, and to generate art using Deep Learning.

Solutions to these exercises are available in Appendix A.

## CHAPTER 14

Recurrent Neural Networks

The batter hits the ball. You immediately start running, anticipating the ball's trajectory. You track it and adapt your movements, and finally catch it (under a thunder of applause). Predicting the future is what you do all the time, whether you are finishing a friend's sentence or anticipating the smell of coffee at breakfast. In this chapter, we are going to discuss *recurrent neural networks* (RNN), a class of nets that can predict the future (well, up to a point, of course). They can analyze *time series* data such as stock prices, and tell you when to buy or sell. In autonomous driving systems, they can anticipate car trajectories and help avoid accidents. More generally, they can work on *sequences* of arbitrary lengths, rather than on fixed-sized inputs like all the nets we have discussed so far. For example, they can take sentences, documents, or audio samples as input, making them extremely useful for natural language processing (NLP) systems such as automatic translation, speech-to-text, or *sentiment analysis* (e.g., reading movie reviews and extracting the rater's feeling about the movie).

Moreover, RNNs' ability to anticipate also makes them capable of surprising creativity. You can ask them to predict which are the most likely next notes in a melody, then randomly pick one of these notes and play it. Then ask the net for the next most likely notes, play it, and repeat the process again and again. Before you know it, your net will compose a melody such as the one (*http://homl.info/88*) produced by Google's Magenta project (*https://magenta.tensorflow.org/*). Similarly, RNNs can generate sentences (*http://homl.info/89*), image captions (*http://homl.info/90*), and much more. The result is not exactly Shakespeare or Mozart yet, but who knows what they will produce a few years from now?

In this chapter, we will look at the fundamental concepts underlying RNNs, the main problem they face (namely, vanishing/exploding gradients, discussed in Chapter 11), and the solutions widely used to fight it: LSTM and GRU cells. Along the way, as always, we will show how to implement RNNs using TensorFlow. Finally, we will take a look at the architecture of a machine translation system.

Recurrent Neurons

Up to now we have mostly looked at feedforward neural networks, where the activations flow only in one direction, from the input layer to the output layer (except for a few networks in Appendix E). A recurrent neural network looks very much like a feedforward neural network, except it also has connections pointing backward. Let's look at the simplest possible RNN, composed of just one neuron receiving inputs, producing an output, and sending that output back to itself, as shown in Figure 14-1 (left). At each *time step* t (also called a *frame*), this *recurrent neuron* receives the inputs $\mathbf{x}_{(t)}$ as well as its own output from the previous time step, $y_{(t-1)}$. We can represent this tiny network against the time axis, as shown in Figure 14-1 (right). This is called *unrolling the network through time*.

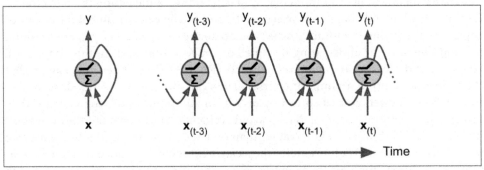

Figure 14-1. A recurrent neuron (left), unrolled through time (right)

You can easily create a layer of recurrent neurons. At each time step t, every neuron receives both the input vector $\mathbf{x}_{(t)}$ and the output vector from the previous time step $\mathbf{y}_{(t-1)}$, as shown in Figure 14-2. Note that both the inputs and outputs are vectors now (when there was just a single neuron, the output was a scalar).

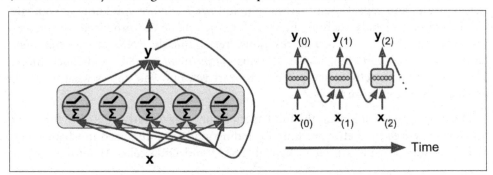

Figure 14-2. A layer of recurrent neurons (left), unrolled through time (right)

Each recurrent neuron has two sets of weights: one for the inputs $\mathbf{x}_{(t)}$ and the other for the outputs of the previous time step, $\mathbf{y}_{(t-1)}$. Let's call these weight vectors $\mathbf{w}_x$ and $\mathbf{w}_y$. If we consider the whole recurrent layer instead of just one recurrent neuron, we can place all the weight vectors in two weight matrices, $\mathbf{W}_x$ and $\mathbf{W}_y$. The output vector of the whole recurrent layer can then be computed pretty much as you might expect, as shown in Equation 14-1 (**b** is the bias vector and $\phi(\cdot)$ is the activation function, e.g., ReLU[1]).

Equation 14-1. Output of a recurrent layer for a single instance

$$\mathbf{y}_{(t)} = \phi\left(\mathbf{W}_x^T \mathbf{x}_{(t)} + \mathbf{W}_y^T \mathbf{y}_{(t-1)} + \mathbf{b}\right)$$

Just like for feedforward neural networks, we can compute a recurrent layer's output in one shot for a whole mini-batch by placing all the inputs at time step t in an input matrix $\mathbf{X}_{(t)}$ (see Equation 14-2).

Equation 14-2. Outputs of a layer of recurrent neurons for all instances in a mini-batch

$$\mathbf{Y}_{(t)} = \phi\left(\mathbf{X}_{(t)}\mathbf{W}_x + \mathbf{Y}_{(t-1)}\mathbf{W}_y + \mathbf{b}\right)$$
$$= \phi\left(\left[\mathbf{X}_{(t)} \quad \mathbf{Y}_{(t-1)}\right]\mathbf{W} + \mathbf{b}\right) \text{ with } \mathbf{W} = \begin{bmatrix} \mathbf{W}_x \\ \mathbf{W}_y \end{bmatrix}$$

- $\mathbf{Y}_{(t)}$ is an $m \times n_{\text{neurons}}$ matrix containing the layer's outputs at time step t for each instance in the mini-batch (m is the number of instances in the mini-batch and n_{neurons} is the number of neurons).

- $\mathbf{X}_{(t)}$ is an $m \times n_{\text{inputs}}$ matrix containing the inputs for all instances (n_{inputs} is the number of input features).

- $\mathbf{W}_x$ is an $n_{\text{inputs}} \times n_{\text{neurons}}$ matrix containing the connection weights for the inputs of the current time step.

- $\mathbf{W}_y$ is an $n_{\text{neurons}} \times n_{\text{neurons}}$ matrix containing the connection weights for the outputs of the previous time step.

- **b** is a vector of size n_{neurons} containing each neuron's bias term.

---

[1] Note that many researchers prefer to use the hyperbolic tangent (tanh) activation function in RNNs rather than the ReLU activation function. For example, take a look at by Vu Pham et al.'s paper "Dropout Improves Recurrent Neural Networks for Handwriting Recognition" (*http://homl.info/91*). However, ReLU-based RNNs are also possible, as shown in Quoc V. Le et al.'s paper "A Simple Way to Initialize Recurrent Networks of Rectified Linear Units" (*http://homl.info/92*).

- The weight matrices $\mathbf{W}_x$ and $\mathbf{W}_y$ are often concatenated vertically into a single weight matrix $\mathbf{W}$ of shape $(n_{\text{inputs}} + n_{\text{neurons}}) \times n_{\text{neurons}}$ (see the second line of Equation 14-2).

- The notation $[\mathbf{X}_{(t)}\ \mathbf{Y}_{(t-1)}]$ represents the horizontal concatenation of the matrices $\mathbf{X}_{(t)}$ and $\mathbf{Y}_{(t-1)}$.

Notice that $\mathbf{Y}_{(t)}$ is a function of $\mathbf{X}_{(t)}$ and $\mathbf{Y}_{(t-1)}$, which is a function of $\mathbf{X}_{(t-1)}$ and $\mathbf{Y}_{(t-2)}$, which is a function of $\mathbf{X}_{(t-2)}$ and $\mathbf{Y}_{(t-3)}$, and so on. This makes $\mathbf{Y}_{(t)}$ a function of all the inputs since time $t = 0$ (that is, $\mathbf{X}_{(0)}, \mathbf{X}_{(1)}, \ldots, \mathbf{X}_{(t)}$). At the first time step, $t = 0$, there are no previous outputs, so they are typically assumed to be all zeros.

Memory Cells

Since the output of a recurrent neuron at time step t is a function of all the inputs from previous time steps, you could say it has a form of *memory*. A part of a neural network that preserves some state across time steps is called a *memory cell* (or simply a *cell*). A single recurrent neuron, or a layer of recurrent neurons, is a very *basic cell*, but later in this chapter we will look at some more complex and powerful types of cells.

In general a cell's state at time step t, denoted $\mathbf{h}_{(t)}$ (the "h" stands for "hidden"), is a function of some inputs at that time step and its state at the previous time step: $\mathbf{h}_{(t)} = f(\mathbf{h}_{(t-1)}, \mathbf{x}_{(t)})$. Its output at time step t, denoted $\mathbf{y}_{(t)}$, is also a function of the previous state and the current inputs. In the case of the basic cells we have discussed so far, the output is simply equal to the state, but in more complex cells this is not always the case, as shown in Figure 14-3.

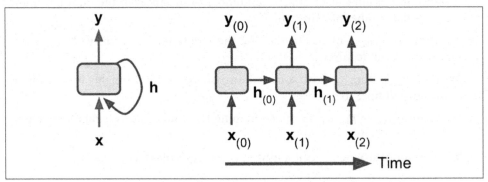

Figure 14-3. A cell's hidden state and its output may be different

Input and Output Sequences

An RNN can simultaneously take a sequence of inputs and produce a sequence of outputs (see Figure 14-4, top-left network). For example, this type of network is useful for predicting time series such as stock prices: you feed it the prices over the last N days, and it must output the prices shifted by one day into the future (i.e., from $N - 1$ days ago to tomorrow).

Alternatively, you could feed the network a sequence of inputs, and ignore all outputs except for the last one (see the top-right network). In other words, this is a sequence-to-vector network. For example, you could feed the network a sequence of words corresponding to a movie review, and the network would output a sentiment score (e.g., from –1 [hate] to +1 [love]).

Conversely, you could feed the network a single input at the first time step (and zeros for all other time steps), and let it output a sequence (see the bottom-left network). This is a vector-to-sequence network. For example, the input could be an image, and the output could be a caption for that image.

Lastly, you could have a sequence-to-vector network, called an *encoder*, followed by a vector-to-sequence network, called a *decoder* (see the bottom-right network). For example, this can be used for translating a sentence from one language to another. You would feed the network a sentence in one language, the encoder would convert this sentence into a single vector representation, and then the decoder would decode this vector into a sentence in another language. This two-step model, called an Encoder–Decoder, works much better than trying to translate on the fly with a single sequence-to-sequence RNN (like the one represented on the top left), since the last words of a sentence can affect the first words of the translation, so you need to wait until you have heard the whole sentence before translating it.

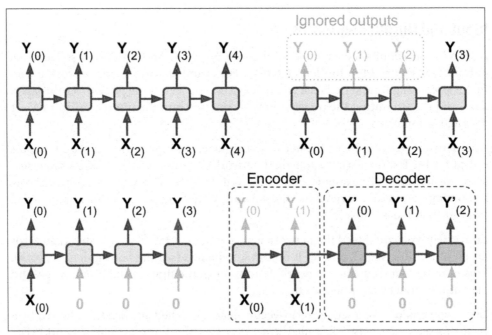

Figure 14-4. Seq to seq (top left), seq to vector (top right), vector to seq (bottom left), delayed seq to seq (bottom right)

Sounds promising, so let's start coding!

Basic RNNs in TensorFlow

First, let's implement a very simple RNN model, without using any of TensorFlow's RNN operations, to better understand what goes on under the hood. We will create an RNN composed of a layer of five recurrent neurons (like the RNN represented in Figure 14-2), using the tanh activation function. We will assume that the RNN runs over only two time steps, taking input vectors of size 3 at each time step. The following code builds this RNN, unrolled through two time steps:

```
n_inputs = 3
n_neurons = 5

X0 = tf.placeholder(tf.float32, [None, n_inputs])
X1 = tf.placeholder(tf.float32, [None, n_inputs])

Wx = tf.Variable(tf.random_normal(shape=[n_inputs, n_neurons],dtype=tf.float32))
Wy = tf.Variable(tf.random_normal(shape=[n_neurons,n_neurons],dtype=tf.float32))
b = tf.Variable(tf.zeros([1, n_neurons], dtype=tf.float32))

Y0 = tf.tanh(tf.matmul(X0, Wx) + b)
Y1 = tf.tanh(tf.matmul(Y0, Wy) + tf.matmul(X1, Wx) + b)
```

```
init = tf.global_variables_initializer()
```

This network looks much like a two-layer feedforward neural network, with a few twists: first, the same weights and bias terms are shared by both layers, and second, we feed inputs at each layer, and we get outputs from each layer. To run the model, we need to feed it the inputs at both time steps, like so:

```
import numpy as np

# Mini-batch:        instance 0, instance 1, instance 2, instance 3
X0_batch = np.array([[0, 1, 2], [3, 4, 5], [6, 7, 8], [9, 0, 1]]) # t = 0
X1_batch = np.array([[9, 8, 7], [0, 0, 0], [6, 5, 4], [3, 2, 1]]) # t = 1

with tf.Session() as sess:
    init.run()
    Y0_val, Y1_val = sess.run([Y0, Y1], feed_dict={X0: X0_batch, X1: X1_batch})
```

This mini-batch contains four instances, each with an input sequence composed of exactly two inputs. At the end, Y0_val and Y1_val contain the outputs of the network at both time steps for all neurons and all instances in the mini-batch:

```
>>> print(Y0_val)  # output at t = 0
[[-0.0664006   0.96257669  0.68105787  0.70918542 -0.89821595]  # instance 0
 [ 0.9977755  -0.71978885 -0.99657625  0.9673925  -0.99989718]  # instance 1
 [ 0.99999774 -0.99898815 -0.99999893  0.99677622 -0.99999988]  # instance 2
 [ 1.         -1.         -1.         -0.99818915  0.99950868]]  # instance 3
>>> print(Y1_val)  # output at t = 1
[[ 1.         -1.         -1.          0.40200216 -1.        ]  # instance 0
 [-0.12210433  0.62805319  0.96718419 -0.99371207 -0.25839335]  # instance 1
 [ 0.99999827 -0.9999994  -0.9999975  -0.85943311 -0.9999879 ]  # instance 2
 [ 0.99928284 -0.99999815 -0.99990582  0.98579615 -0.92205751]]  # instance 3
```

That wasn't too hard, but of course if you want to be able to run an RNN over 100 time steps, the graph is going to be pretty big. Now let's look at how to create the same model using TensorFlow's RNN operations.

Static Unrolling Through Time

The static_rnn() function creates an unrolled RNN network by chaining cells. The following code creates the exact same model as the previous one:

```
X0 = tf.placeholder(tf.float32, [None, n_inputs])
X1 = tf.placeholder(tf.float32, [None, n_inputs])

basic_cell = tf.contrib.rnn.BasicRNNCell(num_units=n_neurons)
output_seqs, states = tf.contrib.rnn.static_rnn(basic_cell, [X0, X1],
                                                dtype=tf.float32)
Y0, Y1 = output_seqs
```

First we create the input placeholders, as before. Then we create a BasicRNNCell, which you can think of as a factory that creates copies of the cell to build the unrolled

RNN (one for each time step). Then we call `static_rnn()`, giving it the cell factory and the input tensors, and telling it the data type of the inputs (this is used to create the initial state matrix, which by default is full of zeros). The `static_rnn()` function calls the cell factory's `__call__()` function once per input, creating two copies of the cell (each containing a layer of five recurrent neurons), with shared weights and bias terms, and it chains them just like we did earlier. The `static_rnn()` function returns two objects. The first is a Python list containing the output tensors for each time step. The second is a tensor containing the final states of the network. When you are using basic cells, the final state is simply equal to the last output.

If there were 50 time steps, it would not be very convenient to have to define 50 input placeholders and 50 output tensors. Moreover, at execution time you would have to feed each of the 50 placeholders and manipulate the 50 outputs. Let's simplify this. The following code builds the same RNN again, but this time it takes a single input placeholder of shape `[None, n_steps, n_inputs]` where the first dimension is the mini-batch size. Then it extracts the list of input sequences for each time step. `X_seqs` is a Python list of `n_steps` tensors of shape `[None, n_inputs]`, where once again the first dimension is the mini-batch size. To do this, we first swap the first two dimensions using the `transpose()` function, so that the time steps are now the first dimension. Then we extract a Python list of tensors along the first dimension (i.e., one tensor per time step) using the `unstack()` function. The next two lines are the same as before. Finally, we merge all the output tensors into a single tensor using the `stack()` function, and we swap the first two dimensions to get a final `outputs` tensor of shape `[None, n_steps, n_neurons]` (again the first dimension is the mini-batch size).

```
X = tf.placeholder(tf.float32, [None, n_steps, n_inputs])
X_seqs = tf.unstack(tf.transpose(X, perm=[1, 0, 2]))
basic_cell = tf.contrib.rnn.BasicRNNCell(num_units=n_neurons)
output_seqs, states = tf.contrib.rnn.static_rnn(basic_cell, X_seqs,
                                                dtype=tf.float32)
outputs = tf.transpose(tf.stack(output_seqs), perm=[1, 0, 2])
```

Now we can run the network by feeding it a single tensor that contains all the mini-batch sequences:

```
X_batch = np.array([
        # t = 0      t = 1
        [[0, 1, 2], [9, 8, 7]], # instance 0
        [[3, 4, 5], [0, 0, 0]], # instance 1
        [[6, 7, 8], [6, 5, 4]], # instance 2
        [[9, 0, 1], [3, 2, 1]], # instance 3
    ])

with tf.Session() as sess:
    init.run()
    outputs_val = outputs.eval(feed_dict={X: X_batch})
```

And we get a single `outputs_val` tensor for all instances, all time steps, and all neurons:

```
>>> print(outputs_val)
[[[-0.91279727  0.83698678 -0.89277941  0.80308062 -0.5283336 ]
  [-1.          1.         -0.99794829  0.99985468 -0.99273592]]

 [[-0.99994391  0.99951613 -0.9946925   0.99030769 -0.94413054]
  [ 0.48733309  0.93389565 -0.31362072  0.88573611  0.2424476 ]]

 [[-1.          0.99999875 -0.99975014  0.99956584 -0.99466234]
  [-0.99994856  0.99999434 -0.96058172  0.99784708 -0.9099462 ]]

 [[-0.95972425  0.99951482  0.96938795 -0.969908   -0.67668229]
  [-0.84596014  0.96288228  0.96856463 -0.14777924 -0.9119423 ]]]
```

However, this approach still builds a graph containing one cell per time step. If there were 50 time steps, the graph would look pretty ugly. It is a bit like writing a program without ever using loops (e.g., `Y0=f(0, X0); Y1=f(Y0, X1); Y2=f(Y1, X2); ...; Y50=f(Y49, X50)`). With such as large graph, you may even get out-of-memory (OOM) errors during backpropagation (especially with the limited memory of GPU cards), since it must store all tensor values during the forward pass so it can use them to compute gradients during the reverse pass.

Fortunately, there is a better solution: the `dynamic_rnn()` function.

Dynamic Unrolling Through Time

The `dynamic_rnn()` function uses a `while_loop()` operation to run over the cell the appropriate number of times, and you can set `swap_memory=True` if you want it to swap the GPU's memory to the CPU's memory during backpropagation to avoid OOM errors. Conveniently, it also accepts a single tensor for all inputs at every time step (shape `[None, n_steps, n_inputs]`) and it outputs a single tensor for all outputs at every time step (shape `[None, n_steps, n_neurons]`); there is no need to stack, unstack, or transpose. The following code creates the same RNN as earlier using the `dynamic_rnn()` function. It's so much nicer!

```
X = tf.placeholder(tf.float32, [None, n_steps, n_inputs])

basic_cell = tf.contrib.rnn.BasicRNNCell(num_units=n_neurons)
outputs, states = tf.nn.dynamic_rnn(basic_cell, X, dtype=tf.float32)
```

During backpropagation, the `while_loop()` operation does the appropriate magic: it stores the tensor values for each iteration during the forward pass so it can use them to compute gradients during the reverse pass.

Handling Variable Length Input Sequences

So far we have used only fixed-size input sequences (all exactly two steps long). What if the input sequences have variable lengths (e.g., like sentences)? In this case you should set the sequence_length argument when calling the dynamic_rnn() (or static_rnn()) function; it must be a 1D tensor indicating the length of the input sequence for each instance. For example:

```
seq_length = tf.placeholder(tf.int32, [None])

[...]
outputs, states = tf.nn.dynamic_rnn(basic_cell, X, dtype=tf.float32,
                                    sequence_length=seq_length)
```

For example, suppose the second input sequence contains only one input instead of two. It must be padded with a zero vector in order to fit in the input tensor X (because the input tensor's second dimension is the size of the longest sequence—i.e., 2).

```
X_batch = np.array([
        # step 0      step 1
        [[0, 1, 2], [9, 8, 7]], # instance 0
        [[3, 4, 5], [0, 0, 0]], # instance 1 (padded with a zero vector)
        [[6, 7, 8], [6, 5, 4]], # instance 2
        [[9, 0, 1], [3, 2, 1]], # instance 3
    ])
seq_length_batch = np.array([2, 1, 2, 2])
```

Of course, you now need to feed values for both placeholders X and seq_length:

```
with tf.Session() as sess:
    init.run()
    outputs_val, states_val = sess.run(
        [outputs, states], feed_dict={X: X_batch, seq_length: seq_length_batch})
```

Now the RNN outputs zero vectors for every time step past the input sequence length (look at the second instance's output for the second time step):

```
>>> print(outputs_val)
[[[-0.68579948 -0.25901747 -0.80249101 -0.18141513 -0.37491536]
  [-0.99996698 -0.94501185  0.98072106 -0.9689762   0.99966913]] # final state

 [[-0.99099374 -0.64768541 -0.67801034 -0.7415446   0.7719509 ]  # final state
  [ 0.          0.          0.          0.          0.        ]] # zero vector

 [[-0.99978048 -0.85583007 -0.49696958 -0.93838578  0.98505187]
  [-0.99951065 -0.89148796  0.94170523 -0.38407657  0.97499216]] # final state

 [[-0.02052618 -0.94588047  0.99935204  0.37283331  0.9998163 ]
  [-0.91052347  0.05769409  0.47446665 -0.44611037  0.89394671]]] # final state
```

Moreover, the states tensor contains the final state of each cell (excluding the zero vectors):

```
>>> print(states_val)
[[-0.99996698 -0.94501185  0.98072106 -0.9689762   0.99966913]  # t = 1
 [-0.99099374 -0.64768541 -0.67801034 -0.7415446   0.7719509 ]  # t = 0 !!!
 [-0.99951065 -0.89148796  0.94170523 -0.38407657  0.97499216]  # t = 1
 [-0.91052347  0.05769409  0.47446665 -0.44611037  0.89394671]] # t = 1
```

Handling Variable-Length Output Sequences

What if the output sequences have variable lengths as well? If you know in advance what length each sequence will have (for example if you know that it will be the same length as the input sequence), then you can set the `sequence_length` parameter as described above. Unfortunately, in general this will not be possible: for example, the length of a translated sentence is generally different from the length of the input sentence. In this case, the most common solution is to define a special output called an *end-of-sequence token* (EOS token). Any output past the EOS should be ignored (we will discuss this later in this chapter).

Okay, now you know how to build an RNN network (or more precisely an RNN network unrolled through time). But how do you train it?

Training RNNs

To train an RNN, the trick is to unroll it through time (like we just did) and then simply use regular backpropagation (see Figure 14-5). This strategy is called *backpropagation through time* (BPTT).

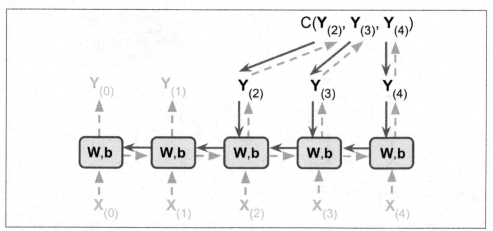

Figure 14-5. Backpropagation through time

Just like in regular backpropagation, there is a first forward pass through the unrolled network (represented by the dashed arrows); then the output sequence is evaluated using a cost function $C\left(\mathbf{Y}_{(t_{min})}, \mathbf{Y}_{(t_{min}+1)}, \cdots, \mathbf{Y}_{(t_{max})}\right)$ (where t_{min} and t_{max} are the first and last output time steps, not counting the ignored outputs), and the gradients of that cost function are propagated backward through the unrolled network (represented by the solid arrows); and finally the model parameters are updated using the gradients computed during BPTT. Note that the gradients flow backward through all the outputs used by the cost function, not just through the final output (for example, in Figure 14-5 the cost function is computed using the last three outputs of the network, $\mathbf{Y}_{(2)}$, $\mathbf{Y}_{(3)}$, and $\mathbf{Y}_{(4)}$, so gradients flow through these three outputs, but not through $\mathbf{Y}_{(0)}$ and $\mathbf{Y}_{(1)}$). Moreover, since the same parameters $\mathbf{W}$ and $\mathbf{b}$ are used at each time step, backpropagation will do the right thing and sum over all time steps.

Training a Sequence Classifier

Let's train an RNN to classify MNIST images. A convolutional neural network would be better suited for image classification (see Chapter 13), but this makes for a simple example that you are already familiar with. We will treat each image as a sequence of 28 rows of 28 pixels each (since each MNIST image is 28 × 28 pixels). We will use cells of 150 recurrent neurons, plus a fully connected layer containing 10 neurons (one per class) connected to the output of the last time step, followed by a softmax layer (see Figure 14-6).

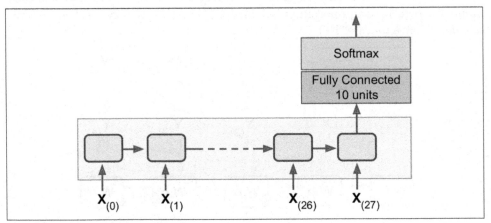

Figure 14-6. Sequence classifier

The construction phase is quite straightforward; it's pretty much the same as the MNIST classifier we built in Chapter 10 except that an unrolled RNN replaces the hidden layers. Note that the fully connected layer is connected to the states tensor, which contains only the final state of the RNN (i.e., the 28th output). Also note that y is a placeholder for the target classes.

```
n_steps = 28
n_inputs = 28
n_neurons = 150
n_outputs = 10

learning_rate = 0.001

X = tf.placeholder(tf.float32, [None, n_steps, n_inputs])
y = tf.placeholder(tf.int32, [None])

basic_cell = tf.contrib.rnn.BasicRNNCell(num_units=n_neurons)
outputs, states = tf.nn.dynamic_rnn(basic_cell, X, dtype=tf.float32)

logits = tf.layers.dense(states, n_outputs)
xentropy = tf.nn.sparse_softmax_cross_entropy_with_logits(labels=y,
                                                          logits=logits)
loss = tf.reduce_mean(xentropy)
optimizer = tf.train.AdamOptimizer(learning_rate=learning_rate)
training_op = optimizer.minimize(loss)
correct = tf.nn.in_top_k(logits, y, 1)
accuracy = tf.reduce_mean(tf.cast(correct, tf.float32))

init = tf.global_variables_initializer()
```

Now let's load the MNIST data and reshape the test data to [batch_size, n_steps, n_inputs] as is expected by the network. We will take care of reshaping the training data in a moment.

```
from tensorflow.examples.tutorials.mnist import input_data

mnist = input_data.read_data_sets("/tmp/data/")
X_test = mnist.test.images.reshape((-1, n_steps, n_inputs))
y_test = mnist.test.labels
```

Now we are ready to train the RNN. The execution phase is exactly the same as for the MNIST classifier in Chapter 10, except that we reshape each training batch before feeding it to the network.

```
n_epochs = 100
batch_size = 150

with tf.Session() as sess:
    init.run()
    for epoch in range(n_epochs):
        for iteration in range(mnist.train.num_examples // batch_size):
            X_batch, y_batch = mnist.train.next_batch(batch_size)
            X_batch = X_batch.reshape((-1, n_steps, n_inputs))
            sess.run(training_op, feed_dict={X: X_batch, y: y_batch})
        acc_train = accuracy.eval(feed_dict={X: X_batch, y: y_batch})
        acc_test = accuracy.eval(feed_dict={X: X_test, y: y_test})
        print(epoch, "Train accuracy:", acc_train, "Test accuracy:", acc_test)
```

The output should look like this:

```
0 Train accuracy: 0.94 Test accuracy: 0.9308
1 Train accuracy: 0.933333 Test accuracy: 0.9431
[...]
98 Train accuracy: 0.98 Test accuracy: 0.9794
99 Train accuracy: 1.0 Test accuracy: 0.9804
```

We get over 98% accuracy—not bad! Plus you would certainly get a better result by tuning the hyperparameters, initializing the RNN weights using He initialization, training longer, or adding a bit of regularization (e.g., dropout).

> You can specify an initializer for the RNN by wrapping its construction code in a variable scope (e.g., use `variable_scope("rnn", initializer=variance_scaling_ini tializer())` to use He initialization).

Training to Predict Time Series

Now let's take a look at how to handle time series, such as stock prices, air temperature, brain wave patterns, and so on. In this section we will train an RNN to predict the next value in a generated time series. Each training instance is a randomly selected sequence of 20 consecutive values from the time series, and the target sequence is the same as the input sequence, except it is shifted by one time step into the future (see Figure 14-7).

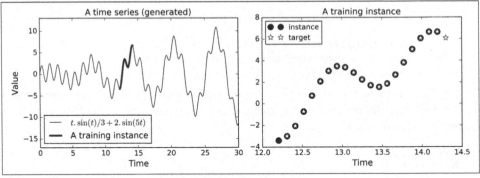

Figure 14-7. Time series (left), and a training instance from that series (right)

First, let's create the RNN. It will contain 100 recurrent neurons and we will unroll it over 20 time steps since each training instance will be 20 inputs long. Each input will contain only one feature (the value at that time). The targets are also sequences of 20 inputs, each containing a single value. The code is almost the same as earlier:

```
n_steps = 20
n_inputs = 1
n_neurons = 100
n_outputs = 1
```

```
X = tf.placeholder(tf.float32, [None, n_steps, n_inputs])
y = tf.placeholder(tf.float32, [None, n_steps, n_outputs])
cell = tf.contrib.rnn.BasicRNNCell(num_units=n_neurons, activation=tf.nn.relu)
outputs, states = tf.nn.dynamic_rnn(cell, X, dtype=tf.float32)
```

 In general you would have more than just one input feature. For example, if you were trying to predict stock prices, you would likely have many other input features at each time step, such as prices of competing stocks, ratings from analysts, or any other feature that might help the system make its predictions.

At each time step we now have an output vector of size 100. But what we actually want is a single output value at each time step. The simplest solution is to wrap the cell in an `OutputProjectionWrapper`. A cell wrapper acts like a normal cell, proxying every method call to an underlying cell, but it also adds some functionality. The `Out putProjectionWrapper` adds a fully connected layer of linear neurons (i.e., without any activation function) on top of each output (but it does not affect the cell state). All these fully connected layers share the same (trainable) weights and bias terms. The resulting RNN is represented in Figure 14-8.

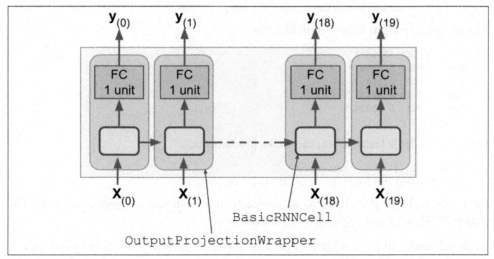

Figure 14-8. RNN cells using output projections

Wrapping a cell is quite easy. Let's tweak the preceding code by wrapping the `BasicRNNCell` into an `OutputProjectionWrapper`:

```
cell = tf.contrib.rnn.OutputProjectionWrapper(
    tf.contrib.rnn.BasicRNNCell(num_units=n_neurons, activation=tf.nn.relu),
    output_size=n_outputs)
```

So far, so good. Now we need to define the cost function. We will use the Mean Squared Error (MSE), as we did in previous regression tasks. Next we will create an Adam optimizer, the training op, and the variable initialization op, as usual:

```
learning_rate = 0.001

loss = tf.reduce_mean(tf.square(outputs - y))
optimizer = tf.train.AdamOptimizer(learning_rate=learning_rate)
training_op = optimizer.minimize(loss)

init = tf.global_variables_initializer()
```

Now on to the execution phase:

```
n_iterations = 1500
batch_size = 50

with tf.Session() as sess:
    init.run()
    for iteration in range(n_iterations):
        X_batch, y_batch = [...]  # fetch the next training batch
        sess.run(training_op, feed_dict={X: X_batch, y: y_batch})
        if iteration % 100 == 0:
            mse = loss.eval(feed_dict={X: X_batch, y: y_batch})
            print(iteration, "\tMSE:", mse)
```

The program's output should look like this:

```
0       MSE: 13.6543
100     MSE: 0.538476
200     MSE: 0.168532
300     MSE: 0.0879579
400     MSE: 0.0633425
[...]
```

Once the model is trained, you can make predictions:

```
X_new = [...]  # New sequences
y_pred = sess.run(outputs, feed_dict={X: X_new})
```

Figure 14-9 shows the predicted sequence for the instance we looked at earlier (in Figure 14-7), after just 1,000 training iterations.

Although using an OutputProjectionWrapper is the simplest solution to reduce the dimensionality of the RNN's output sequences down to just one value per time step (per instance), it is not the most efficient. There is a trickier but more efficient solution: you can reshape the RNN outputs from [batch_size, n_steps, n_neurons] to [batch_size * n_steps, n_neurons], then apply a single fully connected layer with the appropriate output size (in our case just 1), which will result in an output tensor of shape [batch_size * n_steps, n_outputs], and then reshape this tensor to [batch_size, n_steps, n_outputs]. These operations are represented in Figure 14-10.

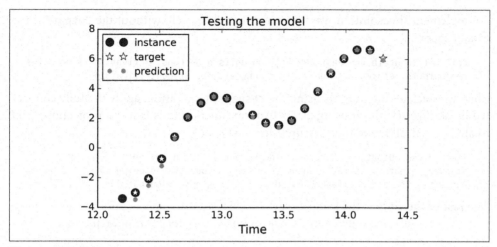

Figure 14-9. Time series prediction

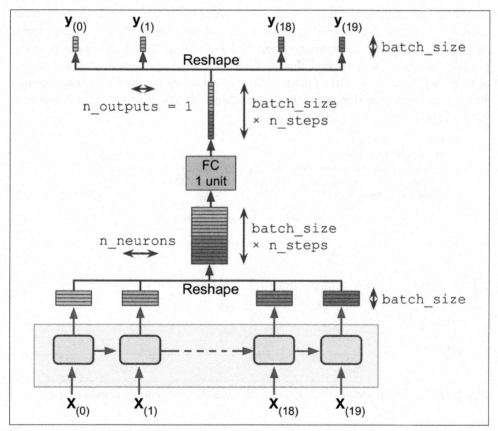

Figure 14-10. Stack all the outputs, apply the projection, then unstack the result

To implement this solution, we first revert to a basic cell, without the OutputProjec tionWrapper:

```
cell = tf.contrib.rnn.BasicRNNCell(num_units=n_neurons, activation=tf.nn.relu)
rnn_outputs, states = tf.nn.dynamic_rnn(cell, X, dtype=tf.float32)
```

Then we stack all the outputs using the reshape() operation, apply the fully connected linear layer (without using any activation function; this is just a projection), and finally unstack all the outputs, again using reshape():

```
stacked_rnn_outputs = tf.reshape(rnn_outputs, [-1, n_neurons])
stacked_outputs = tf.layers.dense(stacked_rnn_outputs, n_outputs)
outputs = tf.reshape(stacked_outputs, [-1, n_steps, n_outputs])
```

The rest of the code is the same as earlier. This can provide a significant speed boost since there is just one fully connected layer instead of one per time step.

Creative RNN

Now that we have a model that can predict the future, we can use it to generate some creative sequences, as explained at the beginning of the chapter. All we need is to provide it a seed sequence containing n_steps values (e.g., full of zeros), use the model to predict the next value, append this predicted value to the sequence, feed the last n_steps values to the model to predict the next value, and so on. This process generates a new sequence that has some resemblance to the original time series (see Figure 14-11).

```
sequence = [0.] * n_steps
for iteration in range(300):
    X_batch = np.array(sequence[-n_steps:]).reshape(1, n_steps, 1)
    y_pred = sess.run(outputs, feed_dict={X: X_batch})
    sequence.append(y_pred[0, -1, 0])
```

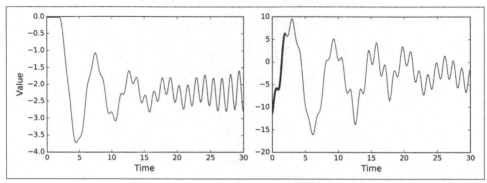

Figure 14-11. Creative sequences, seeded with zeros (left) or with an instance (right)

Now you can try to feed all your John Lennon albums to an RNN and see if it can generate the next "Imagine." However, you will probably need a much more powerful RNN, with more neurons, and also much deeper. Let's look at deep RNNs now.

Deep RNNs

It is quite common to stack multiple layers of cells, as shown in Figure 14-12. This gives you a *deep RNN*.

To implement a deep RNN in TensorFlow, you can create several cells and stack them into a `MultiRNNCell`. In the following code we stack three identical cells (but you could very well use various kinds of cells with a different number of neurons):

```
n_neurons = 100
n_layers = 3

layers = [tf.contrib.rnn.BasicRNNCell(num_units=n_neurons,
                                      activation=tf.nn.relu)
          for layer in range(n_layers)]
multi_layer_cell = tf.contrib.rnn.MultiRNNCell(layers)
outputs, states = tf.nn.dynamic_rnn(multi_layer_cell, X, dtype=tf.float32)
```

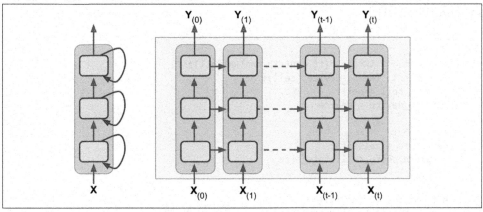

Figure 14-12. Deep RNN (left), unrolled through time (right)

That's all there is to it! The `states` variable is a tuple containing one tensor per layer, each representing the final state of that layer's cell (with shape [`batch_size`, `n_neurons`]). If you set `state_is_tuple=False` when creating the `MultiRNNCell`, then `states` becomes a single tensor containing the states from every layer, concatenated along the column axis (i.e., its shape is [`batch_size`, `n_layers * n_neurons`]). Note that before TensorFlow 0.11.0, this behavior was the default.

Distributing a Deep RNN Across Multiple GPUs

Chapter 12 pointed out that we can efficiently distribute deep RNNs across multiple GPUs by pinning each layer to a different GPU (see Figure 12-16). However, if you try to create each cell in a different `device()` block, it will not work:

```python
with tf.device("/gpu:0"):  # BAD! This is ignored.
    layer1 = tf.contrib.rnn.BasicRNNCell(num_units=n_neurons)

with tf.device("/gpu:1"):  # BAD! Ignored again.
    layer2 = tf.contrib.rnn.BasicRNNCell(num_units=n_neurons)
```

This fails because a `BasicRNNCell` is a cell factory, not a cell *per se* (as mentioned earlier); no cells get created when you create the factory, and thus no variables do either. The device block is simply ignored. The cells actually get created later. When you call `dynamic_rnn()`, it calls the `MultiRNNCell`, which calls each individual `BasicRNNCell`, which create the actual cells (including their variables). Unfortunately, none of these classes provide any way to control the devices on which the variables get created. If you try to put the `dynamic_rnn()` call within a device block, the whole RNN gets pinned to a single device. So are you stuck? Fortunately not! The trick is to create your own cell wrapper (or use the `tf.contrib.rnn.DeviceWrapper` class, which was added in TensorFlow 1.1):

```python
import tensorflow as tf

class DeviceCellWrapper(tf.contrib.rnn.RNNCell):
    def __init__(self, device, cell):
        self._cell = cell
        self._device = device

    @property
    def state_size(self):
        return self._cell.state_size

    @property
    def output_size(self):
        return self._cell.output_size

    def __call__(self, inputs, state, scope=None):
        with tf.device(self._device):
            return self._cell(inputs, state, scope)
```

This wrapper simply proxies every method call to another cell, except it wraps the `__call__()` function within a device block.[2] Now you can distribute each layer on a different GPU:

---

2 This uses the *decorator* design pattern.

```
devices = ["/gpu:0", "/gpu:1", "/gpu:2"]
cells = [DeviceCellWrapper(dev,tf.contrib.rnn.BasicRNNCell(num_units=n_neurons))
         for dev in devices]
multi_layer_cell = tf.contrib.rnn.MultiRNNCell(cells)
outputs, states = tf.nn.dynamic_rnn(multi_layer_cell, X, dtype=tf.float32)
```

 Do not set `state_is_tuple=False`, or the `MultiRNNCell` will concatenate all the cell states into a single tensor, on a single GPU.

Applying Dropout

If you build a very deep RNN, it may end up overfitting the training set. To prevent that, a common technique is to apply dropout (introduced in Chapter 11). You can simply add a dropout layer before or after the RNN as usual, but if you also want to apply dropout between the RNN layers, you need to use a `DropoutWrapper`. The following code applies dropout to the inputs of each layer in the RNN:

```
keep_prob = tf.placeholder_with_default(1.0, shape=())

cells = [tf.contrib.rnn.BasicRNNCell(num_units=n_neurons)
         for layer in range(n_layers)]
cells_drop = [tf.contrib.rnn.DropoutWrapper(cell, input_keep_prob=keep_prob)
              for cell in cells]
multi_layer_cell = tf.contrib.rnn.MultiRNNCell(cells_drop)
rnn_outputs, states = tf.nn.dynamic_rnn(multi_layer_cell, X, dtype=tf.float32)
# The rest of the construction phase is just like earlier.
```

During training, you can feed any value you want to the `keep_prob` placeholder (typically, 0.5):

```
n_iterations = 1500
batch_size = 50
train_keep_prob = 0.5

with tf.Session() as sess:
    init.run()
    for iteration in range(n_iterations):
        X_batch, y_batch = next_batch(batch_size, n_steps)
        _, mse = sess.run([training_op, loss],
                          feed_dict={X: X_batch, y: y_batch,
                                     keep_prob: train_keep_prob})
    saver.save(sess, "./my_dropout_time_series_model")
```

During testing, you should let `keep_prob` default to 1.0, effectively turning dropout off (remember that it should only be active during training):

```
with tf.Session() as sess:
    saver.restore(sess, "./my_dropout_time_series_model")
```

```
X_new = [...] # some test data
y_pred = sess.run(outputs, feed_dict={X: X_new})
```

Note that it is also possible to apply dropout to the outputs by setting out
put_keep_prob, and since TensorFlow 1.1, it is also possible to apply dropout to the
cell's state using state_keep_prob.

With that you should be able to train all sorts of RNNs! Unfortunately, if you want to
train an RNN on long sequences, things will get a bit harder. Let's see why and what
you can do about it.

The Difficulty of Training over Many Time Steps

To train an RNN on long sequences, you will need to run it over many time steps,
making the unrolled RNN a very deep network. Just like any deep neural network it
may suffer from the vanishing/exploding gradients problem (discussed in Chap‐
ter 11) and take forever to train. Many of the tricks we discussed to alleviate this
problem can be used for deep unrolled RNNs as well: good parameter initialization,
nonsaturating activation functions (e.g., ReLU), Batch Normalization, Gradient Clip‐
ping, and faster optimizers. However, if the RNN needs to handle even moderately
long sequences (e.g., 100 inputs), then training will still be very slow.

The simplest and most common solution to this problem is to unroll the RNN only
over a limited number of time steps during training. This is called *truncated backpro‐
pagation through time*. In TensorFlow you can implement it simply by truncating the
input sequences. For example, in the time series prediction problem, you would sim‐
ply reduce n_steps during training. The problem, of course, is that the model will
not be able to learn long-term patterns. One workaround could be to make sure that
these shortened sequences contain both old and recent data, so that the model can
learn to use both (e.g., the sequence could contain monthly data for the last five
months, then weekly data for the last five weeks, then daily data over the last five
days). But this workaround has its limits: what if fine-grained data from last year is
actually useful? What if there was a brief but significant event that absolutely must be
taken into account, even years later (e.g., the result of an election)?

Besides the long training time, a second problem faced by long-running RNNs is the
fact that the memory of the first inputs gradually fades away. Indeed, due to the trans‐
formations that the data goes through when traversing an RNN, some information is
lost after each time step. After a while, the RNN's state contains virtually no trace of
the first inputs. This can be a showstopper. For example, say you want to perform
sentiment analysis on a long review that starts with the four words "I loved this
movie," but the rest of the review lists the many things that could have made the
movie even better. If the RNN gradually forgets the first four words, it will completely
misinterpret the review. To solve this problem, various types of cells with long-term

memory have been introduced. They have proved so successful that the basic cells are not much used anymore. Let's first look at the most popular of these long memory cells: the LSTM cell.

LSTM Cell

The *Long Short-Term Memory* (LSTM) cell was proposed in 1997 (*http://homl.info/93*)[3] by Sepp Hochreiter and Jürgen Schmidhuber, and it was gradually improved over the years by several researchers, such as Alex Graves, Haşim Sak (*http://homl.info/94*),[4] Wojciech Zaremba (*http://homl.info/95*),[5] and many more. If you consider the LSTM cell as a black box, it can be used very much like a basic cell, except it will perform much better; training will converge faster and it will detect long-term dependencies in the data. In TensorFlow, you can simply use a `BasicLSTM Cell` instead of a `BasicRNNCell`:

```
lstm_cell = tf.contrib.rnn.BasicLSTMCell(num_units=n_neurons)
```

LSTM cells manage two state vectors, and for performance reasons they are kept separate by default. You can change this default behavior by setting `state_is_tuple=False` when creating the `BasicLSTMCell`.

So how does an LSTM cell work? The architecture of a basic LSTM cell is shown in Figure 14-13.

---

3 "Long Short-Term Memory," S. Hochreiter and J. Schmidhuber (1997).

4 "Long Short-Term Memory Recurrent Neural Network Architectures for Large Scale Acoustic Modeling," H. Sak et al. (2014).

5 "Recurrent Neural Network Regularization," W. Zaremba et al. (2015).

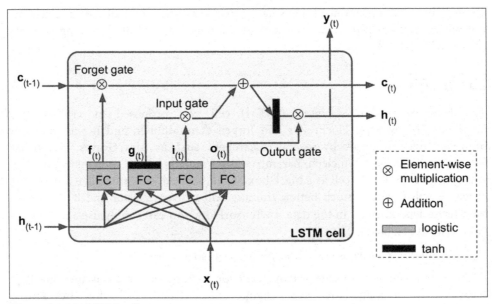

Figure 14-13. LSTM cell

If you don't look at what's inside the box, the LSTM cell looks exactly like a regular cell, except that its state is split in two vectors: $\mathbf{h}_{(t)}$ and $\mathbf{c}_{(t)}$ ("c" stands for "cell"). You can think of $\mathbf{h}_{(t)}$ as the short-term state and $\mathbf{c}_{(t)}$ as the long-term state.

Now let's open the box! The key idea is that the network can learn what to store in the long-term state, what to throw away, and what to read from it. As the long-term state $\mathbf{c}_{(t-1)}$ traverses the network from left to right, you can see that it first goes through a *forget gate*, dropping some memories, and then it adds some new memories via the addition operation (which adds the memories that were selected by an *input gate*). The result $\mathbf{c}_{(t)}$ is sent straight out, without any further transformation. So, at each time step, some memories are dropped and some memories are added. Moreover, after the addition operation, the long-term state is copied and passed through the tanh function, and then the result is filtered by the *output gate*. This produces the short-term state $\mathbf{h}_{(t)}$ (which is equal to the cell's output for this time step $\mathbf{y}_{(t)}$). Now let's look at where new memories come from and how the gates work.

First, the current input vector $\mathbf{x}_{(t)}$ and the previous short-term state $\mathbf{h}_{(t-1)}$ are fed to four different fully connected layers. They all serve a different purpose:

- The main layer is the one that outputs $\mathbf{g}_{(t)}$. It has the usual role of analyzing the current inputs $\mathbf{x}_{(t)}$ and the previous (short-term) state $\mathbf{h}_{(t-1)}$. In a basic cell, there is nothing else than this layer, and its output goes straight out to $\mathbf{y}_{(t)}$ and $\mathbf{h}_{(t)}$. In contrast, in an LSTM cell this layer's output does not go straight out, but instead it is partially stored in the long-term state.

- The three other layers are *gate controllers*. Since they use the logistic activation function, their outputs range from 0 to 1. As you can see, their outputs are fed to element-wise multiplication operations, so if they output 0s, they close the gate, and if they output 1s, they open it. Specifically:
  - The *forget gate* (controlled by $\mathbf{f}_{(t)}$) controls which parts of the long-term state should be erased.
  - The *input gate* (controlled by $\mathbf{i}_{(t)}$) controls which parts of $\mathbf{g}_{(t)}$ should be added to the long-term state (this is why we said it was only "partially stored").
  - Finally, the *output gate* (controlled by $\mathbf{o}_{(t)}$) controls which parts of the long-term state should be read and output at this time step (both to $\mathbf{h}_{(t)}$) and $\mathbf{y}_{(t)}$.

In short, an LSTM cell can learn to recognize an important input (that's the role of the input gate), store it in the long-term state, learn to preserve it for as long as it is needed (that's the role of the forget gate), and learn to extract it whenever it is needed. This explains why they have been amazingly successful at capturing long-term patterns in time series, long texts, audio recordings, and more.

Equation 14-3 summarizes how to compute the cell's long-term state, its short-term state, and its output at each time step for a single instance (the equations for a whole mini-batch are very similar).

Equation 14-3. LSTM computations

$$\mathbf{i}_{(t)} = \sigma\left(\mathbf{W}_{xi}^{T}\mathbf{x}_{(t)} + \mathbf{W}_{hi}^{T}\mathbf{h}_{(t-1)} + \mathbf{b}_{i}\right)$$

$$\mathbf{f}_{(t)} = \sigma\left(\mathbf{W}_{xf}^{T}\mathbf{x}_{(t)} + \mathbf{W}_{hf}^{T}\mathbf{h}_{(t-1)} + \mathbf{b}_{f}\right)$$

$$\mathbf{o}_{(t)} = \sigma\left(\mathbf{W}_{xo}^{T}\mathbf{x}_{(t)} + \mathbf{W}_{ho}^{T}\mathbf{h}_{(t-1)} + \mathbf{b}_{o}\right)$$

$$\mathbf{g}_{(t)} = \tanh\left(\mathbf{W}_{xg}^{T}\mathbf{x}_{(t)} + \mathbf{W}_{hg}^{T}\mathbf{h}_{(t-1)} + \mathbf{b}_{g}\right)$$

$$\mathbf{c}_{(t)} = \mathbf{f}_{(t)} \otimes \mathbf{c}_{(t-1)} + \mathbf{i}_{(t)} \otimes \mathbf{g}_{(t)}$$

$$\mathbf{y}_{(t)} = \mathbf{h}_{(t)} = \mathbf{o}_{(t)} \otimes \tanh\left(\mathbf{c}_{(t)}\right)$$

- $\mathbf{W}_{xi}$, $\mathbf{W}_{xf}$, $\mathbf{W}_{xo}$, $\mathbf{W}_{xg}$ are the weight matrices of each of the four layers for their connection to the input vector $\mathbf{x}_{(t)}$.
- $\mathbf{W}_{hi}$, $\mathbf{W}_{hf}$, $\mathbf{W}_{ho}$, and $\mathbf{W}_{hg}$ are the weight matrices of each of the four layers for their connection to the previous short-term state $\mathbf{h}_{(t-1)}$.
- $\mathbf{b}_{i}$, $\mathbf{b}_{f}$, $\mathbf{b}_{o}$, and $\mathbf{b}_{g}$ are the bias terms for each of the four layers. Note that TensorFlow initializes $\mathbf{b}_{f}$ to a vector full of 1s instead of 0s. This prevents forgetting everything at the beginning of training.

Peephole Connections

In a basic LSTM cell, the gate controllers can look only at the input $x_{(t)}$ and the previous short-term state $h_{(t-1)}$. It may be a good idea to give them a bit more context by letting them peek at the long-term state as well. This idea was proposed by Felix Gers and Jürgen Schmidhuber in 2000 (*http://homl.info/96*).[6] They proposed an LSTM variant with extra connections called *peephole connections*: the previous long-term state $c_{(t-1)}$ is added as an input to the controllers of the forget gate and the input gate, and the current long-term state $c_{(t)}$ is added as input to the controller of the output gate.

To implement peephole connections in TensorFlow, you must use the `LSTMCell` instead of the `BasicLSTMCell` and set `use_peepholes=True`:

```
lstm_cell = tf.contrib.rnn.LSTMCell(num_units=n_neurons, use_peepholes=True)
```

There are many other variants of the LSTM cell. One particularly popular variant is the GRU cell, which we will look at now.

GRU Cell

The *Gated Recurrent Unit* (GRU) cell (see Figure 14-14) was proposed by Kyunghyun Cho et al. in a 2014 paper (*http://homl.info/97*)[7] that also introduced the Encoder–Decoder network we mentioned earlier.

---

6 "Recurrent Nets that Time and Count," F. Gers and J. Schmidhuber (2000).

7 "Learning Phrase Representations using RNN Encoder–Decoder for Statistical Machine Translation," K. Cho et al. (2014).

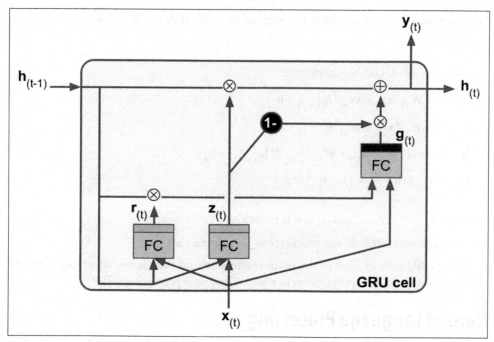

Figure 14-14. GRU cell

The GRU cell is a simplified version of the LSTM cell, and it seems to perform just as well[8] (which explains its growing popularity). The main simplifications are:

- Both state vectors are merged into a single vector $h_{(t)}$.

- A single gate controller controls both the forget gate and the input gate. If the gate controller outputs a 1, the forget gate is open and the input gate is closed. If it outputs a 0, the opposite happens. In other words, whenever a memory must be stored, the location where it will be stored is erased first. This is actually a frequent variant to the LSTM cell in and of itself.

- There is no output gate; the full state vector is output at every time step. However, there is a new gate controller that controls which part of the previous state will be shown to the main layer.

---

8 A 2015 paper by Klaus Greff et al., "LSTM: A Search Space Odyssey," (*http://homl.info/98*) seems to show that all LSTM variants perform roughly the same.

Equation 14-4 summarizes how to compute the cell's state at each time step for a single instance.

Equation 14-4. GRU computations

$$\mathbf{z}_{(t)} = \sigma\left(\mathbf{W}_{xz}{}^T\mathbf{x}_{(t)} + \mathbf{W}_{hz}{}^T\mathbf{h}_{(t-1)} + \mathbf{b}_z\right)$$

$$\mathbf{r}_{(t)} = \sigma\left(\mathbf{W}_{xr}{}^T\mathbf{x}_{(t)} + \mathbf{W}_{hr}{}^T\mathbf{h}_{(t-1)} + \mathbf{b}_r\right)$$

$$\mathbf{g}_{(t)} = \tanh\left(\mathbf{W}_{xg}{}^T\mathbf{x}_{(t)} + \mathbf{W}_{hg}{}^T\left(\mathbf{r}_{(t)} \otimes \mathbf{h}_{(t-1)}\right) + \mathbf{b}_g\right)$$

$$\mathbf{h}_{(t)} = \mathbf{z}_{(t)} \otimes \mathbf{h}_{(t-1)} + \left(1 - \mathbf{z}_{(t)}\right) \otimes \mathbf{g}_{(t)}$$

Creating a GRU cell in TensorFlow is trivial:

```
gru_cell = tf.contrib.rnn.GRUCell(num_units=n_neurons)
```

LSTM or GRU cells are one of the main reasons behind the success of RNNs in recent years, in particular for applications in *natural language processing* (NLP).

Natural Language Processing

Most of the state-of-the-art NLP applications, such as machine translation, automatic summarization, parsing, sentiment analysis, and more, are now based (at least in part) on RNNs. In this last section, we will take a quick look at what a machine translation model looks like. This topic is very well covered by TensorFlow's awesome Word2Vec (*http://homl.info/99*) and Seq2Seq (*http://homl.info/100*) tutorials, so you should definitely check them out.

Word Embeddings

Before we start, we need to choose a word representation. One option could be to represent each word using a one-hot vector. Suppose your vocabulary contains 50,000 words, then the nth word would be represented as a 50,000-dimensional vector, full of 0s except for a 1 at the nth position. However, with such a large vocabulary, this sparse representation would not be efficient at all. Ideally, you want similar words to have similar representations, making it easy for the model to generalize what it learns about a word to all similar words. For example, if the model is told that "I drink milk" is a valid sentence, and if it knows that "milk" is close to "water" but far from "shoes," then it will know that "I drink water" is probably a valid sentence as well, while "I drink shoes" is probably not. But how can you come up with such a meaningful representation?

The most common solution is to represent each word in the vocabulary using a fairly small and dense vector (e.g., 150 dimensions), called an *embedding*, and just let the neural network learn a good embedding for each word during training. At the beginning of training, embeddings are simply chosen randomly, but during training, back-propagation automatically moves the embeddings around in a way that helps the neural network perform its task. Typically this means that similar words will gradually cluster close to one another, and even end up organized in a rather meaningful way. For example, embeddings may end up placed along various axes that represent gender, singular/plural, adjective/noun, and so on. The result can be truly amazing.[9]

In TensorFlow, you first need to create the variable representing the embeddings for every word in your vocabulary (initialized randomly):

```
vocabulary_size = 50000
embedding_size = 150

init_embeds = tf.random_uniform([vocabulary_size, embedding_size], -1.0, 1.0)
embeddings = tf.Variable(init_embeds)
```

Now suppose you want to feed the sentence "I drink milk" to your neural network. You should first preprocess the sentence and break it into a list of known words. For example you may remove unnecessary characters, replace unknown words by a predefined token word such as "[UNK]", replace numerical values by "[NUM]", replace URLs by "[URL]", and so on. Once you have a list of known words, you can look up each word's integer identifier (from 0 to 49999) in a dictionary, for example [72, 3335, 288]. At that point, you are ready to feed these word identifiers to TensorFlow using a placeholder, and apply the embedding_lookup() function to get the corresponding embeddings:

```
train_inputs = tf.placeholder(tf.int32, shape=[None])  # from ids...
embed = tf.nn.embedding_lookup(embeddings, train_inputs)  # ...to embeddings
```

Once your model has learned good word embeddings, they can actually be reused fairly efficiently in any NLP application: after all, "milk" is still close to "water" and far from "shoes" no matter what your application is. In fact, instead of training your own word embeddings, you may want to download pretrained word embeddings. Just like when reusing pretrained layers (see Chapter 11), you can choose to freeze the pretrained embeddings (e.g., creating the embeddings variable using trainable=False) or let backpropagation tweak them for your application. The first option will speed up training, but the second may lead to slightly higher performance.

Embeddings are also useful for representing categorical attributes that can take on a large number of different values, especially when there are complex similarities between values. For example, consider professions, hobbies, dishes, species, brands, and so on.

---

9 For more details, check out Christopher Olah's great post (*http://homl.info/101*), or Sebastian Ruder's series of posts (*http://homl.info/102*).

You now have almost all the tools you need to implement a machine translation system. Let's look at this now.

An Encoder–Decoder Network for Machine Translation

Let's take a look at a simple machine translation model (*http://homl.info/103*)[10] that will translate English sentences to French (see Figure 14-15).

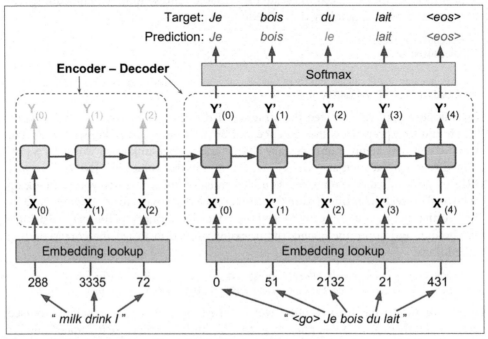

Figure 14-15. A simple machine translation model

The English sentences are fed to the encoder, and the decoder outputs the French translations. Note that the French translations are also used as inputs to the decoder, but pushed back by one step. In other words, the decoder is given as input the word that it *should* have output at the previous step (regardless of what it actually output). For the very first word, it is given a token that represents the beginning of the sentence (e.g., "<go>"). The decoder is expected to end the sentence with an end-of-sequence (EOS) token (e.g., "<eos>").

Note that the English sentences are reversed before they are fed to the encoder. For example "I drink milk" is reversed to "milk drink I." This ensures that the beginning

---

10 "Sequence to Sequence learning with Neural Networks," I. Sutskever et al. (2014).

of the English sentence will be fed last to the encoder, which is useful because that's generally the first thing that the decoder needs to translate.

Each word is initially represented by a simple integer identifier (e.g., 288 for the word "milk"). Next, an embedding lookup returns the word embedding (as explained earlier, this is a dense, fairly low-dimensional vector). These word embeddings are what is actually fed to the encoder and the decoder.

At each step, the decoder outputs a score for each word in the output vocabulary (i.e., French), and then the Softmax layer turns these scores into probabilities. For example, at the first step the word "Je" may have a probability of 20%, "Tu" may have a probability of 1%, and so on. The word with the highest probability is output. This is very much like a regular classification task, so you can train the model using the `soft max_cross_entropy_with_logits()` function.

Note that at inference time (after training), you will not have the target sentence to feed to the decoder. Instead, simply feed the decoder the word that it output at the previous step, as shown in Figure 14-16 (this will require an embedding lookup that is not shown on the diagram).

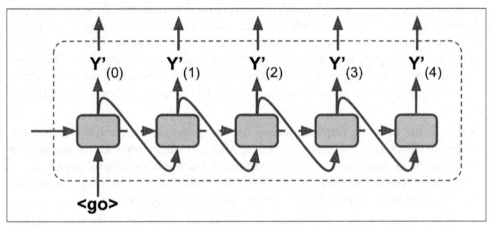

Figure 14-16. Feeding the previous output word as input at inference time

Okay, now you have the big picture. However, if you go through TensorFlow's sequence-to-sequence tutorial and you look at the code in *rnn/translate/seq2seq_model.py* (in the TensorFlow models (*https://github.com/tensorflow/models*)), you will notice a few important differences:

- First, so far we have assumed that all input sequences (to the encoder and to the decoder) have a constant length. But obviously sentence lengths may vary. There are several ways that this can be handled—for example, using the `sequence_length` argument to the `static_rnn()` or `dynamic_rnn()` functions to specify each sentence's length (as discussed earlier). However, another approach is used in the tutorial (presumably for performance reasons): sentences are grouped into buckets of similar lengths (e.g., a bucket for the 1- to 6-word sentences, another for the 7- to 12-word sentences, and so on[11]), and the shorter sentences are padded using a special padding token (e.g., "<pad>"). For example "I drink milk" becomes "<pad> <pad> <pad> milk drink I", and its translation becomes "Je bois du lait <eos> <pad>". Of course, we want to ignore any output past the EOS token. For this, the tutorial's implementation uses a `target_weights` vector. For example, for the target sentence "Je bois du lait <eos> <pad>", the weights would be set to [1.0, 1.0, 1.0, 1.0, 1.0, 0.0] (notice the weight 0.0 that corresponds to the padding token in the target sentence). Simply multiplying the losses by the target weights will zero out the losses that correspond to words past EOS tokens.

- Second, when the output vocabulary is large (which is the case here), outputting a probability for each and every possible word would be terribly slow. If the target vocabulary contains, say, 50,000 French words, then the decoder would output 50,000-dimensional vectors, and then computing the softmax function over such a large vector would be very computationally intensive. To avoid this, one solution is to let the decoder output much smaller vectors, such as 1,000-dimensional vectors, then use a sampling technique to estimate the loss without having to compute it over every single word in the target vocabulary. This *Sampled Softmax* technique was introduced in 2015 by Sébastien Jean et al (*http://homl.info/104*).[12] In TensorFlow you can use the `sampled_softmax_loss()` function.

- Third, the tutorial's implementation uses an *attention mechanism* that lets the decoder peek into the input sequence. Attention augmented RNNs are beyond the scope of this book, but if you are interested there are helpful papers about machine translation (*http://homl.info/105*),[13] machine reading (*http://homl.info/106*),[14] and image captions (*http://homl.info/107*)[15] using attention.

- Finally, the tutorial's implementation makes use of the `tf.nn.legacy_seq2seq` module, which provides tools to build various Encoder–Decoder models easily. For example, the `embedding_rnn_seq2seq()` function creates a simple Encoder–Decoder model that automatically takes care of word embeddings for you, just

---

11 The bucket sizes used in the tutorial are different.

12 "On Using Very Large Target Vocabulary for Neural Machine Translation," S. Jean et al. (2015).

13 "Neural Machine Translation by Jointly Learning to Align and Translate," D. Bahdanau et al. (2014).

14 "Long Short-Term Memory-Networks for Machine Reading," J. Cheng (2016).

15 "Show, Attend and Tell: Neural Image Caption Generation with Visual Attention," K. Xu et al. (2015).

like the one represented in Figure 14-15. This code will likely be updated quickly to use the new `tf.nn.seq2seq` module.

You now have all the tools you need to understand the sequence-to-sequence tutorial's implementation. Check it out and train your own English-to-French translator!

Exercises

1. Can you think of a few applications for a sequence-to-sequence RNN? What about a sequence-to-vector RNN? And a vector-to-sequence RNN?

2. Why do people use encoder–decoder RNNs rather than plain sequence-to-sequence RNNs for automatic translation?

3. How could you combine a convolutional neural network with an RNN to classify videos?

4. What are the advantages of building an RNN using `dynamic_rnn()` rather than `static_rnn()`?

5. How can you deal with variable-length input sequences? What about variable-length output sequences?

6. What is a common way to distribute training and execution of a deep RNN across multiple GPUs?

7. *Embedded Reber grammars* were used by Hochreiter and Schmidhuber in their paper about LSTMs. They are artificial grammars that produce strings such as "BPBTSXXVPSEPE." Check out Jenny Orr's nice introduction (*http://homl.info/108*) to this topic. Choose a particular embedded Reber grammar (such as the one represented on Jenny Orr's page), then train an RNN to identify whether a string respects that grammar or not. You will first need to write a function capable of generating a training batch containing about 50% strings that respect the grammar, and 50% that don't.

8. Tackle the "How much did it rain? II" Kaggle competition (*http://homl.info/109*). This is a time series prediction task: you are given snapshots of polarimetric radar values and asked to predict the hourly rain gauge total. Luis Andre Dutra e Silva's interview (*http://homl.info/110*) gives some interesting insights into the techniques he used to reach second place in the competition. In particular, he used an RNN composed of two LSTM layers.

9. Go through TensorFlow's Word2Vec (*http://homl.info/99*) tutorial to create word embeddings, and then go through the Seq2Seq (*http://homl.info/100*) tutorial to train an English-to-French translation system.

Solutions to these exercises are available in Appendix A.

## CHAPTER 15

Autoencoders

Autoencoders are artificial neural networks capable of learning efficient representations of the input data, called *codings*, without any supervision (i.e., the training set is unlabeled). These codings typically have a much lower dimensionality than the input data, making autoencoders useful for dimensionality reduction (see Chapter 8). More importantly, autoencoders act as powerful feature detectors, and they can be used for unsupervised pretraining of deep neural networks (as we discussed in Chapter 11). Lastly, they are capable of randomly generating new data that looks very similar to the training data; this is called a *generative model*. For example, you could train an autoencoder on pictures of faces, and it would then be able to generate new faces.

Surprisingly, autoencoders work by simply learning to copy their inputs to their outputs. This may sound like a trivial task, but we will see that constraining the network in various ways can make it rather difficult. For example, you can limit the size of the internal representation, or you can add noise to the inputs and train the network to recover the original inputs. These constraints prevent the autoencoder from trivially copying the inputs directly to the outputs, which forces it to learn efficient ways of representing the data. In short, the codings are byproducts of the autoencoder's attempt to learn the identity function under some constraints.

In this chapter we will explain in more depth how autoencoders work, what types of constraints can be imposed, and how to implement them using TensorFlow, whether it is for dimensionality reduction, feature extraction, unsupervised pretraining, or as generative models.

Efficient Data Representations

Which of the following number sequences do you find the easiest to memorize?

- 40, 27, 25, 36, 81, 57, 10, 73, 19, 68
- 50, 25, 76, 38, 19, 58, 29, 88, 44, 22, 11, 34, 17, 52, 26, 13, 40, 20

At first glance, it would seem that the first sequence should be easier, since it is much shorter. However, if you look carefully at the second sequence, you may notice that it follows two simple rules: even numbers are followed by their half, and odd numbers are followed by their triple plus one (this is a famous sequence known as the *hailstone sequence*). Once you notice this pattern, the second sequence becomes much easier to memorize than the first because you only need to memorize the two rules, the first number, and the length of the sequence. Note that if you could quickly and easily memorize very long sequences, you would not care much about the existence of a pattern in the second sequence. You would just learn every number by heart, and that would be that. It is the fact that it is hard to memorize long sequences that makes it useful to recognize patterns, and hopefully this clarifies why constraining an autoencoder during training pushes it to discover and exploit patterns in the data.

The relationship between memory, perception, and pattern matching was famously studied by William Chase and Herbert Simon in the early 1970s (*http://homl.info/111*).[1] They observed that expert chess players were able to memorize the positions of all the pieces in a game by looking at the board for just 5 seconds, a task that most people would find impossible. However, this was only the case when the pieces were placed in realistic positions (from actual games), not when the pieces were placed randomly. Chess experts don't have a much better memory than you and I, they just see chess patterns more easily thanks to their experience with the game. Noticing patterns helps them store information efficiently.

Just like the chess players in this memory experiment, an autoencoder looks at the inputs, converts them to an efficient internal representation, and then spits out something that (hopefully) looks very close to the inputs. An autoencoder is always composed of two parts: an *encoder* (or *recognition network*) that converts the inputs to an internal representation, followed by a *decoder* (or *generative network*) that converts the internal representation to the outputs (see Figure 15-1).

As you can see, an autoencoder typically has the same architecture as a Multi-Layer Perceptron (MLP; see Chapter 10), except that the number of neurons in the output layer must be equal to the number of inputs. In this example, there is just one hidden

---

1 "Perception in chess," W. Chase and H. Simon (1973).

layer composed of two neurons (the encoder), and one output layer composed of three neurons (the decoder). The outputs are often called the *reconstructions* since the autoencoder tries to reconstruct the inputs, and the cost function contains a *reconstruction loss* that penalizes the model when the reconstructions are different from the inputs.

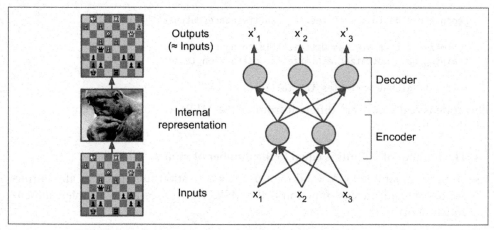

Figure 15-1. The chess memory experiment (left) and a simple autoencoder (right)

Because the internal representation has a lower dimensionality than the input data (it is 2D instead of 3D), the autoencoder is said to be *undercomplete*. An undercomplete autoencoder cannot trivially copy its inputs to the codings, yet it must find a way to output a copy of its inputs. It is forced to learn the most important features in the input data (and drop the unimportant ones).

Let's see how to implement a very simple undercomplete autoencoder for dimensionality reduction.

Performing PCA with an Undercomplete Linear Autoencoder

If the autoencoder uses only linear activations and the cost function is the Mean Squared Error (MSE), then it can be shown that it ends up performing Principal Component Analysis (see Chapter 8).

The following code builds a simple linear autoencoder to perform PCA on a 3D dataset, projecting it to 2D:

```
import tensorflow as tf

n_inputs = 3  # 3D inputs
n_hidden = 2  # 2D codings
n_outputs = n_inputs
```

```
learning_rate = 0.01

X = tf.placeholder(tf.float32, shape=[None, n_inputs])
hidden = tf.layers.dense(X, n_hidden)
outputs = tf.layers.dense(hidden, n_outputs)

reconstruction_loss = tf.reduce_mean(tf.square(outputs - X))  # MSE

optimizer = tf.train.AdamOptimizer(learning_rate)
training_op = optimizer.minimize(reconstruction_loss)

init = tf.global_variables_initializer()
```

This code is really not very different from all the MLPs we built in past chapters. The two things to note are:

- The number of outputs is equal to the number of inputs.
- To perform simple PCA, we do not use any activation function (i.e., all neurons are linear) and the cost function is the MSE. We will see more complex autoencoders shortly.

Now let's load the dataset, train the model on the training set, and use it to encode the test set (i.e., project it to 2D):

```
X_train, X_test = [...] # load the dataset

n_iterations = 1000
codings = hidden  # the output of the hidden layer provides the codings

with tf.Session() as sess:
    init.run()
    for iteration in range(n_iterations):
        training_op.run(feed_dict={X: X_train})  # no labels (unsupervised)
    codings_val = codings.eval(feed_dict={X: X_test})
```

Figure 15-2 shows the original 3D dataset (at the left) and the output of the autoencoder's hidden layer (i.e., the coding layer, at the right). As you can see, the autoencoder found the best 2D plane to project the data onto, preserving as much variance in the data as it could (just like PCA).

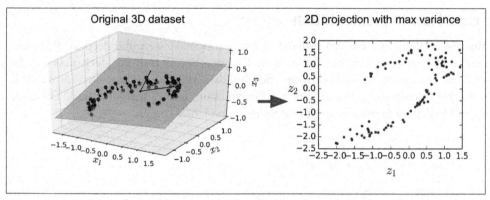

Figure 15-2. PCA performed by an undercomplete linear autoencoder

Stacked Autoencoders

Just like other neural networks we have discussed, autoencoders can have multiple hidden layers. In this case they are called *stacked autoencoders* (or *deep autoencoders*). Adding more layers helps the autoencoder learn more complex codings. However, one must be careful not to make the autoencoder too powerful. Imagine an encoder so powerful that it just learns to map each input to a single arbitrary number (and the decoder learns the reverse mapping). Obviously such an autoencoder will reconstruct the training data perfectly, but it will not have learned any useful data representation in the process (and it is unlikely to generalize well to new instances).

The architecture of a stacked autoencoder is typically symmetrical with regards to the central hidden layer (the coding layer). To put it simply, it looks like a sandwich. For example, an autoencoder for MNIST (introduced in Chapter 3) may have 784 inputs, followed by a hidden layer with 300 neurons, then a central hidden layer of 150 neurons, then another hidden layer with 300 neurons, and an output layer with 784 neurons. This stacked autoencoder is represented in Figure 15-3.

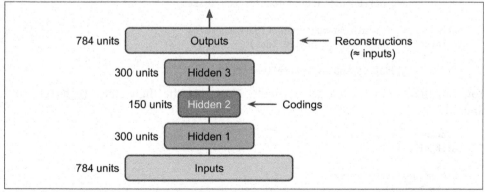

Figure 15-3. Stacked autoencoder

TensorFlow Implementation

You can implement a stacked autoencoder very much like a regular deep MLP. In particular, the same techniques we used in Chapter 11 for training deep nets can be applied. For example, the following code builds a stacked autoencoder for MNIST, using He initialization, the ELU activation function, and ℓ_2 regularization. The code should look very familiar, except that there are no labels (no y):

```python
from functools import partial

n_inputs = 28 * 28   # for MNIST
n_hidden1 = 300
n_hidden2 = 150   # codings
n_hidden3 = n_hidden1
n_outputs = n_inputs

learning_rate = 0.01
l2_reg = 0.0001

X = tf.placeholder(tf.float32, shape=[None, n_inputs])

he_init = tf.contrib.layers.variance_scaling_initializer()
l2_regularizer = tf.contrib.layers.l2_regularizer(l2_reg)
my_dense_layer = partial(tf.layers.dense,
                         activation=tf.nn.elu,
                         kernel_initializer=he_init,
                         kernel_regularizer=l2_regularizer)

hidden1 = my_dense_layer(X, n_hidden1)
hidden2 = my_dense_layer(hidden1, n_hidden2)   # codings
hidden3 = my_dense_layer(hidden2, n_hidden3)
outputs = my_dense_layer(hidden3, n_outputs, activation=None)

reconstruction_loss = tf.reduce_mean(tf.square(outputs - X))   # MSE

reg_losses = tf.get_collection(tf.GraphKeys.REGULARIZATION_LOSSES)
loss = tf.add_n([reconstruction_loss] + reg_losses)

optimizer = tf.train.AdamOptimizer(learning_rate)
training_op = optimizer.minimize(loss)

init = tf.global_variables_initializer()
```

You can then train the model normally. Note that the digit labels (y_batch) are unused:

```python
n_epochs = 5
batch_size = 150

with tf.Session() as sess:
    init.run()
    for epoch in range(n_epochs):
```

```
n_batches = mnist.train.num_examples // batch_size
for iteration in range(n_batches):
    X_batch, y_batch = mnist.train.next_batch(batch_size)
    sess.run(training_op, feed_dict={X: X_batch})
```

Tying Weights

When an autoencoder is neatly symmetrical, like the one we just built, a common technique is to *tie the weights* of the decoder layers to the weights of the encoder layers. This halves the number of weights in the model, speeding up training and limiting the risk of overfitting. Specifically, if the autoencoder has a total of N layers (not counting the input layer), and $\mathbf{W}_L$ represents the connection weights of the Lth layer (e.g., layer 1 is the first hidden layer, layer $\frac{N}{2}$ is the coding layer, and layer N is the output layer), then the decoder layer weights can be defined simply as: $\mathbf{W}_{N-L+1} = \mathbf{W}_L^T$ (with $L = 1, 2, \cdots, \frac{N}{2}$).

Unfortunately, implementing tied weights in TensorFlow using the dense() function is a bit cumbersome; it's actually easier to just define the layers manually. The code ends up significantly more verbose:

```
activation = tf.nn.elu
regularizer = tf.contrib.layers.l2_regularizer(l2_reg)
initializer = tf.contrib.layers.variance_scaling_initializer()

X = tf.placeholder(tf.float32, shape=[None, n_inputs])

weights1_init = initializer([n_inputs, n_hidden1])
weights2_init = initializer([n_hidden1, n_hidden2])

weights1 = tf.Variable(weights1_init, dtype=tf.float32, name="weights1")
weights2 = tf.Variable(weights2_init, dtype=tf.float32, name="weights2")
weights3 = tf.transpose(weights2, name="weights3")  # tied weights
weights4 = tf.transpose(weights1, name="weights4")  # tied weights

biases1 = tf.Variable(tf.zeros(n_hidden1), name="biases1")
biases2 = tf.Variable(tf.zeros(n_hidden2), name="biases2")
biases3 = tf.Variable(tf.zeros(n_hidden3), name="biases3")
biases4 = tf.Variable(tf.zeros(n_outputs), name="biases4")

hidden1 = activation(tf.matmul(X, weights1) + biases1)
hidden2 = activation(tf.matmul(hidden1, weights2) + biases2)
hidden3 = activation(tf.matmul(hidden2, weights3) + biases3)
outputs = tf.matmul(hidden3, weights4) + biases4

reconstruction_loss = tf.reduce_mean(tf.square(outputs - X))
reg_loss = regularizer(weights1) + regularizer(weights2)
loss = reconstruction_loss + reg_loss

optimizer = tf.train.AdamOptimizer(learning_rate)
```

```
training_op = optimizer.minimize(loss)

init = tf.global_variables_initializer()
```

This code is fairly straightforward, but there are a few important things to note:

- First, `weights3` and `weights4` are not variables, they are respectively the transpose of `weights2` and `weights1` (they are "tied" to them).
- Second, since they are not variables, it's no use regularizing them: we only regularize `weights1` and `weights2`.
- Third, biases are never tied, and never regularized.

Training One Autoencoder at a Time

Rather than training the whole stacked autoencoder in one go like we just did, it is often much faster to train one shallow autoencoder at a time, then stack all of them into a single stacked autoencoder (hence the name), as shown on Figure 15-4. This is especially useful for very deep autoencoders.

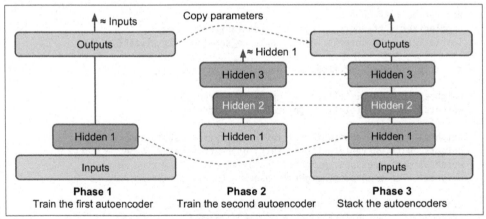

Figure 15-4. Training one autoencoder at a time

During the first phase of training, the first autoencoder learns to reconstruct the inputs. During the second phase, the second autoencoder learns to reconstruct the output of the first autoencoder's hidden layer. Finally, you just build a big sandwich using all these autoencoders, as shown in Figure 15-4 (i.e., you first stack the hidden layers of each autoencoder, then the output layers in reverse order). This gives you the final stacked autoencoder. You could easily train more autoencoders this way, building a very deep stacked autoencoder.

To implement this multiphase training algorithm, the simplest approach is to use a different TensorFlow graph for each phase. After training an autoencoder, you just run the training set through it and capture the output of the hidden layer. This output then serves as the training set for the next autoencoder. Once all autoencoders have been trained this way, you simply copy the weights and biases from each autoencoder and use them to build the stacked autoencoder. Implementing this approach is quite straightforward, so we won't detail it here, but please check out the code in the Jupyter notebooks (*https://github.com/ageron/handson-ml*) for an example.

Another approach is to use a single graph containing the whole stacked autoencoder, plus some extra operations to perform each training phase, as shown in Figure 15-5.

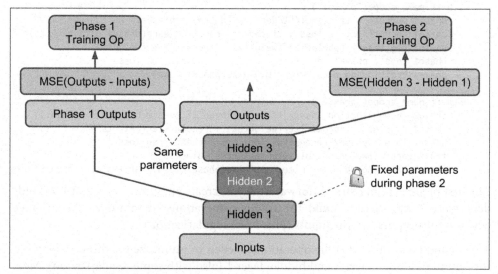

Figure 15-5. A single graph to train a stacked autoencoder

This deserves a bit of explanation:

- The central column in the graph is the full stacked autoencoder. This part can be used after training.

- The left column is the set of operations needed to run the first phase of training. It creates an output layer that bypasses hidden layers 2 and 3. This output layer shares the same weights and biases as the stacked autoencoder's output layer. On top of that are the training operations that will aim at making the output as close as possible to the inputs. Thus, this phase will train the weights and biases for the hidden layer 1 and the output layer (i.e., the first autoencoder).

- The right column in the graph is the set of operations needed to run the second phase of training. It adds the training operation that will aim at making the output of hidden layer 3 as close as possible to the output of hidden layer 1. Note that we must freeze hidden layer 1 while running phase 2. This phase will train the weights and biases for hidden layers 2 and 3 (i.e., the second autoencoder).

The TensorFlow code looks like this:

```
[...] # Build the whole stacked autoencoder normally.
      # In this example, the weights are not tied.

optimizer = tf.train.AdamOptimizer(learning_rate)

with tf.name_scope("phase1"):
    phase1_outputs = tf.matmul(hidden1, weights4) + biases4
    phase1_reconstruction_loss = tf.reduce_mean(tf.square(phase1_outputs - X))
    phase1_reg_loss = regularizer(weights1) + regularizer(weights4)
    phase1_loss = phase1_reconstruction_loss + phase1_reg_loss
    phase1_training_op = optimizer.minimize(phase1_loss)

with tf.name_scope("phase2"):
    phase2_reconstruction_loss = tf.reduce_mean(tf.square(hidden3 - hidden1))
    phase2_reg_loss = regularizer(weights2) + regularizer(weights3)
    phase2_loss = phase2_reconstruction_loss + phase2_reg_loss
    train_vars = [weights2, biases2, weights3, biases3]
    phase2_training_op = optimizer.minimize(phase2_loss, var_list=train_vars)
```

The first phase is rather straightforward: we just create an output layer that skips hidden layers 2 and 3, then build the training operations to minimize the distance between the outputs and the inputs (plus some regularization).

The second phase just adds the operations needed to minimize the distance between the output of hidden layer 3 and hidden layer 1 (also with some regularization). Most importantly, we provide the list of trainable variables to the `minimize()` method, making sure to leave out `weights1` and `biases1`; this effectively freezes hidden layer 1 during phase 2.

During the execution phase, all you need to do is run the phase 1 training op for a number of epochs, then the phase 2 training op for some more epochs.

Since hidden layer 1 is frozen during phase 2, its output will always be the same for any given training instance. To avoid having to recompute the output of hidden layer 1 at every single epoch, you can compute it for the whole training set at the end of phase 1, then directly feed the cached output of hidden layer 1 during phase 2. This can give you a nice performance boost.

Visualizing the Reconstructions

One way to ensure that an autoencoder is properly trained is to compare the inputs and the outputs. They must be fairly similar, and the differences should be unimportant details. Let's plot two random digits and their reconstructions:

```
n_test_digits = 2
X_test = mnist.test.images[:n_test_digits]

with tf.Session() as sess:
    [...] # Train the Autoencoder
    outputs_val = outputs.eval(feed_dict={X: X_test})

def plot_image(image, shape=[28, 28]):
    plt.imshow(image.reshape(shape), cmap="Greys", interpolation="nearest")
    plt.axis("off")

for digit_index in range(n_test_digits):
    plt.subplot(n_test_digits, 2, digit_index * 2 + 1)
    plot_image(X_test[digit_index])
    plt.subplot(n_test_digits, 2, digit_index * 2 + 2)
    plot_image(outputs_val[digit_index])
```

Figure 15-6 shows the resulting images.

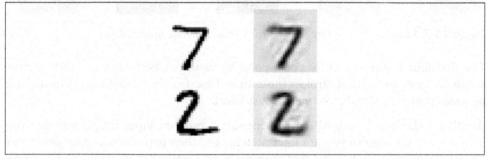

Figure 15-6. Original digits (left) and their reconstructions (right)

Looks close enough. So the autoencoder has properly learned to reproduce its inputs, but has it learned useful features? Let's take a look.

Visualizing Features

Once your autoencoder has learned some features, you may want to take a look at them. There are various techniques for this. Arguably the simplest technique is to consider each neuron in every hidden layer, and find the training instances that activate it the most. This is especially useful for the top hidden layers since they often capture relatively large features that you can easily spot in a group of training instances that contain them. For example, if a neuron strongly activates when it sees a cat in a picture, it will be pretty obvious that the pictures that activate it the most all contain cats. However, for lower layers, this technique does not work so well, as the features are smaller and more abstract, so it's often hard to understand exactly what the neuron is getting all excited about.

Let's look at another technique. For each neuron in the first hidden layer, you can create an image where a pixel's intensity corresponds to the weight of the connection to the given neuron. For example, the following code plots the features learned by five neurons in the first hidden layer:

```python
with tf.Session() as sess:
    [...] # train autoencoder
    weights1_val = weights1.eval()

for i in range(5):
    plt.subplot(1, 5, i + 1)
    plot_image(weights1_val.T[i])
```

You may get low-level features such as the ones shown in Figure 15-7.

Figure 15-7. Features learned by five neurons from the first hidden layer

The first four features seem to correspond to small patches, while the fifth feature seems to look for vertical strokes (note that these features come from the stacked denoising autoencoder that we will discuss later).

Another technique is to feed the autoencoder a random input image, measure the activation of the neuron you are interested in, and then perform backpropagation to tweak the image in such a way that the neuron will activate even more. If you iterate several times (performing gradient ascent), the image will gradually turn into the most exciting image (for the neuron). This is a useful technique to visualize the kinds of inputs that a neuron is looking for.

Finally, if you are using an autoencoder to perform unsupervised pretraining—for example, for a classification task—a simple way to verify that the features learned by the autoencoder are useful is to measure the performance of the classifier.

Unsupervised Pretraining Using Stacked Autoencoders

As we discussed in Chapter 11, if you are tackling a complex supervised task but you do not have a lot of labeled training data, one solution is to find a neural network that performs a similar task, and then reuse its lower layers. This makes it possible to train a high-performance model using only little training data because your neural network won't have to learn all the low-level features; it will just reuse the feature detectors learned by the existing net.

Similarly, if you have a large dataset but most of it is unlabeled, you can first train a stacked autoencoder using all the data, then reuse the lower layers to create a neural network for your actual task, and train it using the labeled data. For example, Figure 15-8 shows how to use a stacked autoencoder to perform unsupervised pretraining for a classification neural network. The stacked autoencoder itself is typically trained one autoencoder at a time, as discussed earlier. When training the classifier, if you really don't have much labeled training data, you may want to freeze the pretrained layers (at least the lower ones).

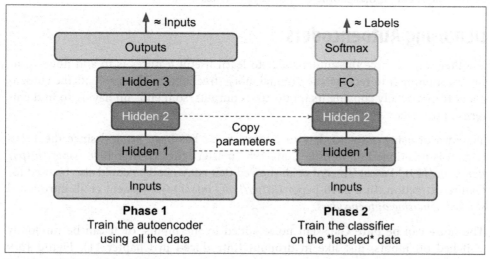

Figure 15-8. Unsupervised pretraining using autoencoders

This situation is actually quite common, because building a large unlabeled dataset is often cheap (e.g., a simple script can download millions of images off the internet), but labeling them can only be done reliably by humans (e.g., classifying images as cute or not). Labeling instances is time-consuming and costly, so it is quite common to have only a few thousand labeled instances.

As we discussed earlier, one of the triggers of the current Deep Learning tsunami is the discovery in 2006 by Geoffrey Hinton et al. that deep neural networks can be pretrained in an unsupervised fashion. They used restricted Boltzmann machines for that (see Appendix E), but in 2007 Yoshua Bengio et al. showed (*http://homl.info/112*)[2] that autoencoders worked just as well.

There is nothing special about the TensorFlow implementation: just train an autoencoder using all the training data, then reuse its encoder layers to create a new neural network (see Chapter 11 for more details on how to reuse pretrained layers, or check out the code examples in the Jupyter notebooks).

Up to now, in order to force the autoencoder to learn interesting features, we have limited the size of the coding layer, making it undercomplete. There are actually many other kinds of constraints that can be used, including ones that allow the coding layer to be just as large as the inputs, or even larger, resulting in an *overcomplete autoencoder*. Let's look at some of those approaches now.

Denoising Autoencoders

Another way to force the autoencoder to learn useful features is to add noise to its inputs, training it to recover the original, noise-free inputs. This prevents the autoencoder from trivially copying its inputs to its outputs, so it ends up having to find patterns in the data.

The idea of using autoencoders to remove noise has been around since the 1980s (e.g., it is mentioned in Yann LeCun's 1987 master's thesis). In a 2008 paper (*http://homl.info/113*),[3] Pascal Vincent et al. showed that autoencoders could also be used for feature extraction. In a 2010 paper (*http://homl.info/114*),[4] Vincent et al. introduced *stacked denoising autoencoders*.

The noise can be pure Gaussian noise added to the inputs, or it can be randomly switched off inputs, just like in dropout (introduced in Chapter 11). Figure 15-9 shows both options.

---

2 "Greedy Layer-Wise Training of Deep Networks," Y. Bengio et al. (2007).

3 "Extracting and Composing Robust Features with Denoising Autoencoders," P. Vincent et al. (2008).

4 "Stacked Denoising Autoencoders: Learning Useful Representations in a Deep Network with a Local Denoising Criterion," P. Vincent et al. (2010).

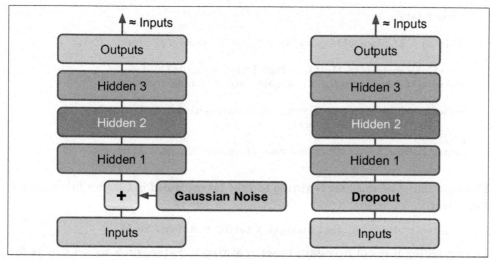

Figure 15-9. Denoising autoencoders, with Gaussian noise (left) or dropout (right)

TensorFlow Implementation

Implementing denoising autoencoders in TensorFlow is not too hard. Let's start with Gaussian noise. It's really just like training a regular autoencoder, except you add noise to the inputs, and the reconstruction loss is calculated based on the original inputs:

```
noise_level = 1.0
X = tf.placeholder(tf.float32, shape=[None, n_inputs])
X_noisy = X + noise_level * tf.random_normal(tf.shape(X))

hidden1 = tf.layers.dense(X_noisy, n_hidden1, activation=tf.nn.relu,
                          name="hidden1")
[...]
reconstruction_loss = tf.reduce_mean(tf.square(outputs - X)) # MSE
[...]
```

Since the shape of X is only partially defined during the construction phase, we cannot know in advance the shape of the noise that we must add to X. We cannot call X.get_shape() because this would just return the partially defined shape of X ([None, n_inputs]), and random_normal() expects a fully defined shape so it would raise an exception. Instead, we call tf.shape(X), which creates an operation that will return the shape of X at runtime, which will be fully defined at that point.

Implementing the dropout version, which is more common, is not much harder:

```
dropout_rate = 0.3

training = tf.placeholder_with_default(False, shape=(), name='training')

X = tf.placeholder(tf.float32, shape=[None, n_inputs])
X_drop = tf.layers.dropout(X, dropout_rate, training=training)

hidden1 = tf.layers.dense(X_drop, n_hidden1, activation=tf.nn.relu,
                          name="hidden1")
[...]
reconstruction_loss = tf.reduce_mean(tf.square(outputs - X)) # MSE
[...]
```

During training we must set `training` to `True` (as explained in Chapter 11) using the `feed_dict`:

```
sess.run(training_op, feed_dict={X: X_batch, training: True})
```

During testing it is not necessary to set `training` to `False`, since we set that as the default in the call to the `placeholder_with_default()` function.

Sparse Autoencoders

Another kind of constraint that often leads to good feature extraction is *sparsity*: by adding an appropriate term to the cost function, the autoencoder is pushed to reduce the number of active neurons in the coding layer. For example, it may be pushed to have on average only 5% significantly active neurons in the coding layer. This forces the autoencoder to represent each input as a combination of a small number of activations. As a result, each neuron in the coding layer typically ends up representing a useful feature (if you could speak only a few words per month, you would probably try to make them worth listening to).

In order to favor sparse models, we must first measure the actual sparsity of the coding layer at each training iteration. We do so by computing the average activation of each neuron in the coding layer, over the whole training batch. The batch size must not be too small, or else the mean will not be accurate.

Once we have the mean activation per neuron, we want to penalize the neurons that are too active by adding a *sparsity loss* to the cost function. For example, if we measure that a neuron has an average activation of 0.3, but the target sparsity is 0.1, it must be penalized to activate less. One approach could be simply adding the squared error $(0.3 - 0.1)^2$ to the cost function, but in practice a better approach is to use the Kullback–Leibler divergence (briefly discussed in Chapter 4), which has much stronger gradients than the Mean Squared Error, as you can see in Figure 15-10.

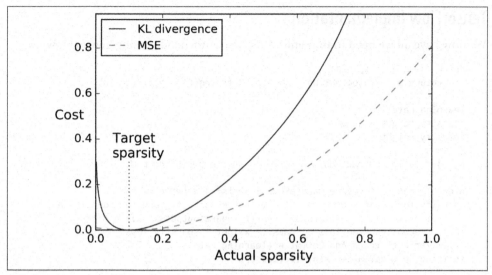

Figure 15-10. Sparsity loss

Given two discrete probability distributions P and Q, the KL divergence between these distributions, noted $D_{KL}(P \parallel Q)$, can be computed using Equation 15-1.

Equation 15-1. Kullback–Leibler divergence

$$D_{KL}(P \parallel Q) = \sum_i P(i) \log \frac{P(i)}{Q(i)}$$

In our case, we want to measure the divergence between the target probability p that a neuron in the coding layer will activate, and the actual probability q (i.e., the mean activation over the training batch). So the KL divergence simplifies to Equation 15-2.

Equation 15-2. KL divergence between the target sparsity p and the actual sparsity q

$$D_{KL}(p \parallel q) = p \log \frac{p}{q} + (1 - p) \log \frac{1 - p}{1 - q}$$

Once we have computed the sparsity loss for each neuron in the coding layer, we just sum up these losses, and add the result to the cost function. In order to control the relative importance of the sparsity loss and the reconstruction loss, we can multiply the sparsity loss by a sparsity weight hyperparameter. If this weight is too high, the model will stick closely to the target sparsity, but it may not reconstruct the inputs properly, making the model useless. Conversely, if it is too low, the model will mostly ignore the sparsity objective and it will not learn any interesting features.

TensorFlow Implementation

We now have all we need to implement a sparse autoencoder using TensorFlow:

```
def kl_divergence(p, q):
    return p * tf.log(p / q) + (1 - p) * tf.log((1 - p) / (1 - q))

learning_rate = 0.01
sparsity_target = 0.1
sparsity_weight = 0.2

[...] # Build a normal autoencoder (in this example the coding layer is hidden1)

hidden1_mean = tf.reduce_mean(hidden1, axis=0) # batch mean
sparsity_loss = tf.reduce_sum(kl_divergence(sparsity_target, hidden1_mean))
reconstruction_loss = tf.reduce_mean(tf.square(outputs - X)) # MSE
loss = reconstruction_loss + sparsity_weight * sparsity_loss
optimizer = tf.train.AdamOptimizer(learning_rate)
training_op = optimizer.minimize(loss)
```

An important detail is the fact that the activations of the coding layer must be between 0 and 1 (but not equal to 0 or 1), or else the KL divergence will return NaN (Not a Number). A simple solution is to use the logistic activation function for the coding layer:

```
hidden1 = tf.layers.dense(X, n_hidden1, activation=tf.nn.sigmoid)
```

One simple trick can speed up convergence: instead of using the MSE, we can choose a reconstruction loss that will have larger gradients. Cross entropy is often a good choice. To use it, we must normalize the inputs to make them take on values from 0 to 1, and use the logistic activation function in the output layer so the outputs also take on values from 0 to 1. TensorFlow's sigmoid_cross_entropy_with_logits() function takes care of efficiently applying the logistic (sigmoid) activation function to the logits and computing the cross entropy:

```
[...]
logits = tf.layers.dense(hidden1, n_outputs)
outputs = tf.nn.sigmoid(logits)

xentropy = tf.nn.sigmoid_cross_entropy_with_logits(labels=X, logits=logits)
reconstruction_loss = tf.reduce_sum(xentropy)
```

Note that the outputs operation is not needed during training (we use it only when we want to look at the reconstructions).

Variational Autoencoders

Another important category of autoencoders was introduced in 2014 (*http://homl.info/115*) by Diederik Kingma and Max Welling,[5] and has quickly become one of the most popular types of autoencoders: *variational autoencoders*.

They are quite different from all the autoencoders we have discussed so far, in particular:

- They are *probabilistic autoencoders*, meaning that their outputs are partly determined by chance, even after training (as opposed to denoising autoencoders, which use randomness only during training).

- Most importantly, they are *generative autoencoders*, meaning that they can generate new instances that look like they were sampled from the training set.

Both these properties make them rather similar to RBMs (see Appendix E), but they are easier to train and the sampling process is much faster (with RBMs you need to wait for the network to stabilize into a "thermal equilibrium" before you can sample a new instance).

Let's take a look at how they work. Figure 15-11 (left) shows a variational autoencoder. You can recognize, of course, the basic structure of all autoencoders, with an encoder followed by a decoder (in this example, they both have two hidden layers), but there is a twist: instead of directly producing a coding for a given input, the encoder produces a *mean coding* μ and a standard deviation σ. The actual coding is then sampled randomly from a Gaussian distribution with mean μ and standard deviation σ. After that the decoder just decodes the sampled coding normally. The right part of the diagram shows a training instance going through this autoencoder. First, the encoder produces μ and σ, then a coding is sampled randomly (notice that it is not exactly located at μ), and finally this coding is decoded, and the final output resembles the training instance.

---

5 "Auto-Encoding Variational Bayes," D. Kingma and M. Welling (2014).

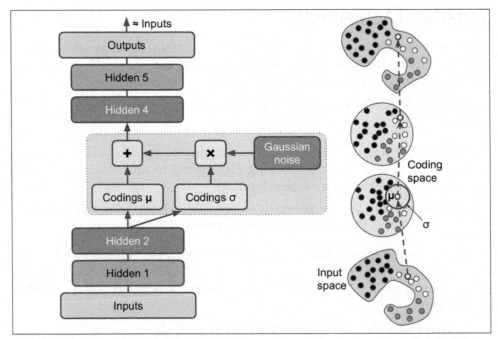

Figure 15-11. Variational autoencoder (left), and an instance going through it (right)

As you can see on the diagram, although the inputs may have a very convoluted distribution, a variational autoencoder tends to produce codings that look as though they were sampled from a simple Gaussian distribution:[6] during training, the cost function (discussed next) pushes the codings to gradually migrate within the coding space (also called the *latent space*) to occupy a roughly (hyper)spherical region that looks like a cloud of Gaussian points. One great consequence is that after training a variational autoencoder, you can very easily generate a new instance: just sample a random coding from the Gaussian distribution, decode it, and voilà!

So let's look at the cost function. It is composed of two parts. The first is the usual reconstruction loss that pushes the autoencoder to reproduce its inputs (we can use cross entropy for this, as discussed earlier). The second is the *latent loss* that pushes the autoencoder to have codings that look as though they were sampled from a simple Gaussian distribution, for which we use the KL divergence between the target distribution (the Gaussian distribution) and the actual distribution of the codings. The math is a bit more complex than earlier, in particular because of the Gaussian noise, which limits the amount of information that can be transmitted to the coding layer

---

6 Variational autoencoders are actually more general; the codings are not limited to Gaussian distributions.

(thus pushing the autoencoder to learn useful features). Luckily, the equations simplify to the following code for the latent loss:[7]

```
eps = 1e-10  # smoothing term to avoid computing log(0) which is NaN
latent_loss = 0.5 * tf.reduce_sum(
    tf.square(hidden3_sigma) + tf.square(hidden3_mean)
    - 1 - tf.log(eps + tf.square(hidden3_sigma)))
```

One common variant is to train the encoder to output $\gamma = \log(\sigma^2)$ rather than σ. Wherever we need σ we can just compute $\sigma = \exp\left(\frac{\gamma}{2}\right)$. This makes it a bit easier for the encoder to capture sigmas of different scales, and thus it helps speed up convergence. The latent loss ends up a bit simpler:

```
latent_loss = 0.5 * tf.reduce_sum(
    tf.exp(hidden3_gamma) + tf.square(hidden3_mean) - 1 - hidden3_gamma)
```

The following code builds the variational autoencoder shown in Figure 15-11 (left), using the $\log(\sigma^2)$ variant:

```
from functools import partial

n_inputs = 28 * 28
n_hidden1 = 500
n_hidden2 = 500
n_hidden3 = 20  # codings
n_hidden4 = n_hidden2
n_hidden5 = n_hidden1
n_outputs = n_inputs
learning_rate = 0.001

initializer = tf.contrib.layers.variance_scaling_initializer()
my_dense_layer = partial(
    tf.layers.dense,
    activation=tf.nn.elu,
    kernel_initializer=initializer)

X = tf.placeholder(tf.float32, [None, n_inputs])
hidden1 = my_dense_layer(X, n_hidden1)
hidden2 = my_dense_layer(hidden1, n_hidden2)
hidden3_mean = my_dense_layer(hidden2, n_hidden3, activation=None)
hidden3_gamma = my_dense_layer(hidden2, n_hidden3, activation=None)
noise = tf.random_normal(tf.shape(hidden3_gamma), dtype=tf.float32)
hidden3 = hidden3_mean + tf.exp(0.5 * hidden3_gamma) * noise
hidden4 = my_dense_layer(hidden3, n_hidden4)
hidden5 = my_dense_layer(hidden4, n_hidden5)
logits = my_dense_layer(hidden5, n_outputs, activation=None)
outputs = tf.sigmoid(logits)
```

---

[7] For more mathematical details, check out the original paper on variational autoencoders, or Carl Doersch's great tutorial (*http://homl.info/116*) (2016).

```
xentropy = tf.nn.sigmoid_cross_entropy_with_logits(labels=X, logits=logits)
reconstruction_loss = tf.reduce_sum(xentropy)
latent_loss = 0.5 * tf.reduce_sum(
    tf.exp(hidden3_gamma) + tf.square(hidden3_mean) - 1 - hidden3_gamma)
loss = reconstruction_loss + latent_loss

optimizer = tf.train.AdamOptimizer(learning_rate=learning_rate)
training_op = optimizer.minimize(loss)

init = tf.global_variables_initializer()
saver = tf.train.Saver()
```

Generating Digits

Now let's use this variational autoencoder to generate images that look like handwritten digits. All we need to do is train the model, then sample random codings from a Gaussian distribution and decode them.

```
import numpy as np

n_digits = 60
n_epochs = 50
batch_size = 150

with tf.Session() as sess:
    init.run()
    for epoch in range(n_epochs):
        n_batches = mnist.train.num_examples // batch_size
        for iteration in range(n_batches):
            X_batch, y_batch = mnist.train.next_batch(batch_size)
            sess.run(training_op, feed_dict={X: X_batch})

    codings_rnd = np.random.normal(size=[n_digits, n_hidden3])
    outputs_val = outputs.eval(feed_dict={hidden3: codings_rnd})
```

That's it. Now we can see what the "handwritten" digits produced by the autoencoder look like (see Figure 15-12):

```
for iteration in range(n_digits):
    plt.subplot(n_digits, 10, iteration + 1)
    plot_image(outputs_val[iteration])
```

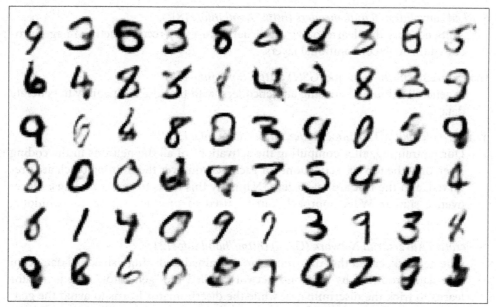

Figure 15-12. Images of handwritten digits generated by the variational autoencoder

A majority of these digits look pretty convincing, while a few are rather "creative." But don't be too harsh on the autoencoder—it only started learning less than an hour ago. Give it a bit more training time, and those digits will look better and better.

Other Autoencoders

The amazing successes of supervised learning in image recognition, speech recognition, text translation, and more have somewhat overshadowed unsupervised learning, but it is actually booming. New architectures for autoencoders and other unsupervised learning algorithms are invented regularly, so much so that we cannot cover them all in this book. Here is a brief (by no means exhaustive) overview of a few more types of autoencoders that you may want to check out:

Contractive autoencoder (CAE) (http://homl.info/117)[8]
    The autoencoder is constrained during training so that the derivatives of the codings with regards to the inputs are small. In other words, two similar inputs must have similar codings.

---

8 "Contractive Auto-Encoders: Explicit Invariance During Feature Extraction," S. Rifai et al. (2011).

Stacked convolutional autoencoders (http://homl.info/118)[9]

Autoencoders that learn to extract visual features by reconstructing images processed through convolutional layers.

Generative stochastic network (GSN) (http://homl.info/119)[10]

A generalization of denoising autoencoders, with the added capability to generate data.

Winner-take-all (WTA) autoencoder (http://homl.info/120)[11]

During training, after computing the activations of all the neurons in the coding layer, only the top k% activations for each neuron over the training batch are preserved, and the rest are set to zero. Naturally this leads to sparse codings. Moreover, a similar WTA approach can be used to produce sparse convolutional autoencoders.

Generative Adversarial Network (GAN) (http://homl.info/121)[12]

One network, called the "discriminator," is trained to distinguish actual data from fake data produced by a second network, called the "generator." The generator learns to trick the discriminator, while the discriminator learns to avoid the generator's tricks. This competition leads to increasingly realistic fake data, and quite robust codings. Adversarial training is a very powerful idea, currently gaining a lot of momentum. Yann Lecun even called it "the coolest thing since sliced bread."

Exercises

1. What are the main tasks that autoencoders are used for?

2. Suppose you want to train a classifier and you have plenty of unlabeled training data, but only a few thousand labeled instances. How can autoencoders help? How would you proceed?

3. If an autoencoder perfectly reconstructs the inputs, is it necessarily a good autoencoder? How can you evaluate the performance of an autoencoder?

4. What are undercomplete and overcomplete autoencoders? What is the main risk of an excessively undercomplete autoencoder? What about the main risk of an overcomplete autoencoder?

5. How do you tie weights in a stacked autoencoder? What is the point of doing so?

---

9 "Stacked Convolutional Auto-Encoders for Hierarchical Feature Extraction," J. Masci et al. (2011).

10 "GSNs: Generative Stochastic Networks," G. Alain et al. (2015).

11 "Winner-Take-All Autoencoders," A. Makhzani and B. Frey (2015).

12 "Generative Adversarial Networks," I. Goodfellow et al. (2014).

6. What is a common technique to visualize features learned by the lower layer of a stacked autoencoder? What about higher layers?

7. What is a generative model? Can you name a type of generative autoencoder?

8. Let's use a denoising autoencoder to pretrain an image classifier:

   - You can use MNIST (simplest), or another large set of images such as CIFAR10 (*http://homl.info/122*) if you want a bigger challenge. If you choose CIFAR10, you need to write code to load batches of images for training. If you want to skip this part, TensorFlow's model zoo contains tools to do just that (*http://homl.info/123*).

   - Split the dataset into a training set and a test set. Train a deep denoising autoencoder on the full training set.

   - Check that the images are fairly well reconstructed, and visualize the low-level features. Visualize the images that most activate each neuron in the coding layer.

   - Build a classification deep neural network, reusing the lower layers of the autoencoder. Train it using only 10% of the training set. Can you get it to perform as well as the same classifier trained on the full training set?

9. *Semantic hashing*, introduced in 2008 by Ruslan Salakhutdinov and Geoffrey Hinton (*http://homl.info/124*),[13] is a technique used for efficient *information retrieval*: a document (e.g., an image) is passed through a system, typically a neural network, which outputs a fairly low-dimensional binary vector (e.g., 30 bits). Two similar documents are likely to have identical or very similar hashes. By indexing each document using its hash, it is possible to retrieve many documents similar to a particular document almost instantly, even if there are billions of documents: just compute the hash of the document and look up all documents with that same hash (or hashes differing by just one or two bits). Let's implement semantic hashing using a slightly tweaked stacked autoencoder:

   - Create a stacked autoencoder containing two hidden layers below the coding layer, and train it on the image dataset you used in the previous exercise. The coding layer should contain 30 neurons and use the logistic activation function to output values between 0 and 1. After training, to produce the hash of an image, you can simply run it through the autoencoder, take the output of the coding layer, and round every value to the closest integer (0 or 1).

   - One neat trick proposed by Salakhutdinov and Hinton is to add Gaussian noise (with zero mean) to the inputs of the coding layer, during training only.

---

13 "Semantic Hashing," R. Salakhutdinov and G. Hinton (2008).

In order to preserve a high signal-to-noise ratio, the autoencoder will learn to feed large values to the coding layer (so that the noise becomes negligible). In turn, this means that the logistic function of the coding layer will likely saturate at 0 or 1. As a result, rounding the codings to 0 or 1 won't distort them too much, and this will improve the reliability of the hashes.

- Compute the hash of every image, and see if images with identical hashes look alike. Since MNIST and CIFAR10 are labeled, a more objective way to measure the performance of the autoencoder for semantic hashing is to ensure that images with the same hash generally have the same class. One way to do this is to measure the average Gini purity (introduced in Chapter 6) of the sets of images with identical (or very similar) hashes.

- Try fine-tuning the hyperparameters using cross-validation.

- Note that with a labeled dataset, another approach is to train a convolutional neural network (see Chapter 13) for classification, then use the layer below the output layer to produce the hashes. See Jinma Guo and Jianmin Li's 2015 paper (*http://homl.info/125*).[14] See if that performs better.

10. Train a variational autoencoder on the image dataset used in the previous exercises (MNIST or CIFAR10), and make it generate images. Alternatively, you can try to find an unlabeled dataset that you are interested in and see if you can generate new samples.

Solutions to these exercises are available in Appendix A.

---

14 "CNN Based Hashing for Image Retrieval," J. Guo and J. Li (2015).

## CHAPTER 16

Reinforcement Learning

Reinforcement Learning (RL) is one of the most exciting fields of Machine Learning today, and also one of the oldest. It has been around since the 1950s, producing many interesting applications over the years,[1] in particular in games (e.g., *TD-Gammon*, a *Backgammon* playing program) and in machine control, but seldom making the headline news. But a revolution took place in 2013 when researchers from an English startup called DeepMind demonstrated a system that could learn to play just about any Atari game from scratch (*http://homl.info/128*),[2] eventually outperforming humans (*http://homl.info/129*)[3] in most of them, using only raw pixels as inputs and without any prior knowledge of the rules of the games.[4] This was the first of a series of amazing feats, culminating in May 2017 with the victory of their system AlphaGo against Ke Jie, the world champion of the game of *Go*. No program had ever come close to beating a master of this game, let alone the world champion. Today the whole field of RL is boiling with new ideas, with a wide range of applications. DeepMind was bought by Google for over 500 million dollars in 2014.

So how did they do it? With hindsight it seems rather simple: they applied the power of Deep Learning to the field of Reinforcement Learning, and it worked beyond their wildest dreams. In this chapter we will first explain what Reinforcement Learning is and what it is good at, and then we will present two of the most important techniques

---

1 For more details, be sure to check out Richard Sutton and Andrew Barto's book on RL (*http://homl.info/126*), *Reinforcement Learning: An Introduction* (MIT Press), or David Silver's free online RL course (*http://homl.info/127*) at University College London.

2 "Playing Atari with Deep Reinforcement Learning," V. Mnih et al. (2013).

3 "Human-level control through deep reinforcement learning," V. Mnih et al. (2015).

4 Check out the videos of DeepMind's system learning to play *Space Invaders*, *Breakout*, and more at *http://homl.info/130*.

in deep Reinforcement Learning: *policy gradients* and *deep Q-networks* (DQN), including a discussion of *Markov decision processes* (MDP). We will use these techniques to train a model to balance a pole on a moving cart, and another to play Atari games. The same techniques can be used for a wide variety of tasks, from walking robots to self-driving cars.

Learning to Optimize Rewards

In Reinforcement Learning, a software *agent* makes *observations* and takes *actions* within an *environment*, and in return it receives *rewards*. Its objective is to learn to act in a way that will maximize its expected long-term rewards. If you don't mind a bit of anthropomorphism, you can think of positive rewards as pleasure, and negative rewards as pain (the term "reward" is a bit misleading in this case). In short, the agent acts in the environment and learns by trial and error to maximize its pleasure and minimize its pain.

This is quite a broad setting, which can apply to a wide variety of tasks. Here are a few examples (see Figure 16-1):

a. The agent can be the program controlling a walking robot. In this case, the environment is the real world, the agent observes the environment through a set of *sensors* such as cameras and touch sensors, and its actions consist of sending signals to activate motors. It may be programmed to get positive rewards whenever it approaches the target destination, and negative rewards whenever it wastes time, goes in the wrong direction, or falls down.

b. The agent can be the program controlling Ms. Pac-Man. In this case, the environment is a simulation of the Atari game, the actions are the nine possible joystick positions (upper left, down, center, and so on), the observations are screenshots, and the rewards are just the game points.

c. Similarly, the agent can be the program playing a board game such as the game of *Go*.

d. The agent does not have to control a physically (or virtually) moving thing. For example, it can be a smart thermostat, getting rewards whenever it is close to the target temperature and saves energy, and negative rewards when humans need to tweak the temperature, so the agent must learn to anticipate human needs.

e. The agent can observe stock market prices and decide how much to buy or sell every second. Rewards are obviously the monetary gains and losses.

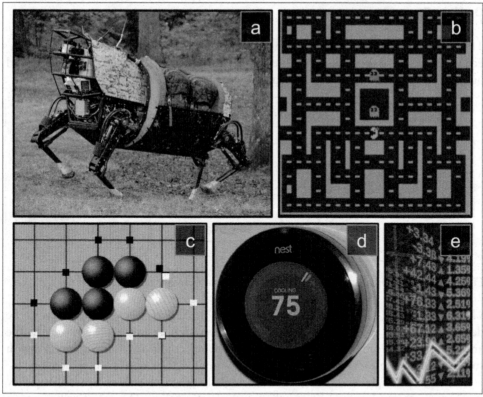

Figure 16-1. Reinforcement Learning examples: (a) walking robot, (b) Ms. Pac-Man, (c) Go player, (d) thermostat, (e) automatic trader[5]

Note that there may not be any positive rewards at all; for example, the agent may move around in a maze, getting a negative reward at every time step, so it better find the exit as quickly as possible! There are many other examples of tasks where Reinforcement Learning is well suited, such as self-driving cars, placing ads on a web page, or controlling where an image classification system should focus its attention.

---

5 Images (a), (c), and (d) are reproduced from Wikipedia. (a) and (d) are in the public domain. (c) was created by user Stevertigo and released under Creative Commons BY-SA 2.0 (*https://creativecommons.org/licenses/by-sa/2.0/*). (b) is a screenshot from the Ms. Pac-Man game, copyright Atari (the author believes it to be fair use in this chapter). (e) was reproduced from Pixabay, released under Creative Commons CC0 (*https://creativecommons.org/publicdomain/zero/1.0/*).

Policy Search

The algorithm used by the software agent to determine its actions is called its *policy*. For example, the policy could be a neural network taking observations as inputs and outputting the action to take (see Figure 16-2).

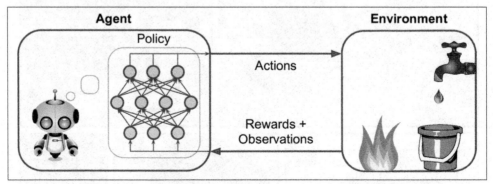

Figure 16-2. Reinforcement Learning using a neural network policy

The policy can be any algorithm you can think of, and it does not even have to be deterministic. For example, consider a robotic vacuum cleaner whose reward is the amount of dust it picks up in 30 minutes. Its policy could be to move forward with some probability p every second, or randomly rotate left or right with probability $1 - p$. The rotation angle would be a random angle between $-r$ and $+r$. Since this policy involves some randomness, it is called a *stochastic policy*. The robot will have an erratic trajectory, which guarantees that it will eventually get to any place it can reach and pick up all the dust. The question is: how much dust will it pick up in 30 minutes?

How would you train such a robot? There are just two *policy parameters* you can tweak: the probability p and the angle range r. One possible learning algorithm could be to try out many different values for these parameters, and pick the combination that performs best (see Figure 16-3). This is an example of *policy search*, in this case using a brute force approach. However, when the *policy space* is too large (which is generally the case), finding a good set of parameters this way is like searching for a needle in a gigantic haystack.

Another way to explore the policy space is to use *genetic algorithms*. For example, you could randomly create a first generation of 100 policies and try them out, then "kill" the 80 worst policies[6] and make the 20 survivors produce 4 offspring each. An off-

---

6 It is often better to give the poor performers a slight chance of survival, to preserve some diversity in the "gene pool."

spring is just a copy of its parent[7] plus some random variation. The surviving policies plus their offspring together constitute the second generation. You can continue to iterate through generations this way, until you find a good policy.

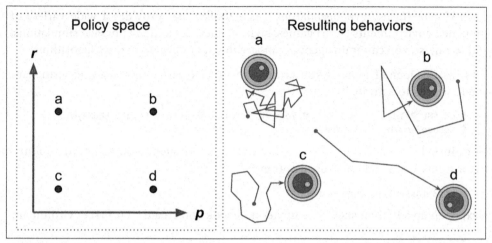

Figure 16-3. Four points in policy space and the agent's corresponding behavior

Yet another approach is to use optimization techniques, by evaluating the gradients of the rewards with regards to the policy parameters, then tweaking these parameters by following the gradient toward higher rewards (*gradient ascent*). This approach is called *policy gradients* (PG), which we will discuss in more detail later in this chapter. For example, going back to the vacuum cleaner robot, you could slightly increase *p* and evaluate whether this increases the amount of dust picked up by the robot in 30 minutes; if it does, then increase *p* some more, or else reduce *p*. We will implement a popular PG algorithm using TensorFlow, but before we do we need to create an environment for the agent to live in, so it's time to introduce OpenAI gym.

Introduction to OpenAI Gym

One of the challenges of Reinforcement Learning is that in order to train an agent, you first need to have a working environment. If you want to program an agent that will learn to play an Atari game, you will need an Atari game simulator. If you want to program a walking robot, then the environment is the real world and you can directly train your robot in that environment, but this has its limits: if the robot falls off a cliff, you can't just click "undo." You can't speed up time either; adding more computing

---

7 If there is a single parent, this is called *asexual reproduction*. With two (or more) parents, it is called *sexual reproduction*. An offspring's genome (in this case a set of policy parameters) is randomly composed of parts of its parents' genomes.

power won't make the robot move any faster. And it's generally too expensive to train 1,000 robots in parallel. In short, training is hard and slow in the real world, so you generally need a *simulated environment* at least to bootstrap training.

OpenAI gym (*https://gym.openai.com/*)[8] is a toolkit that provides a wide variety of simulated environments (Atari games, board games, 2D and 3D physical simulations, and so on), so you can train agents, compare them, or develop new RL algorithms.

Let's install OpenAI gym. If you created an isolated environment using virtualenv, you first need to activate it:

```
$ cd $ML_PATH              # Your ML working directory (e.g., $HOME/ml)
$ source env/bin/activate
```

Next, install OpenAI Gym (if you are not using a virtualenv, you will need administrator rights, or to add the --user option):

```
$ pip3 install --upgrade gym
```

Next open up a Python shell or a Jupyter notebook and create your first environment:

```
>>> import gym
>>> env = gym.make("CartPole-v0")
[2017-08-27 11:08:05,742] Making new env: CartPole-v0
>>> obs = env.reset()
>>> obs
array([-0.03799846, -0.03288115,  0.02337094,  0.00720711])
>>> env.render()
```

The make() function creates an environment, in this case a CartPole environment. This is a 2D simulation in which a cart can be accelerated left or right in order to balance a pole placed on top of it (see Figure 16-4). After the environment is created, we must initialize it using the reset() method. This returns the first observation. Observations depend on the type of environment. For the CartPole environment, each observation is a 1D NumPy array containing four floats: these floats represent the cart's horizontal position (0.0 = center), its velocity, the angle of the pole (0.0 = vertical), and its angular velocity. Finally, the render() method displays the environment as shown in Figure 16-4.

---

8 OpenAI is a nonprofit artificial intelligence research company, funded in part by Elon Musk. Its stated goal is to promote and develop friendly AIs that will benefit humanity (rather than exterminate it).

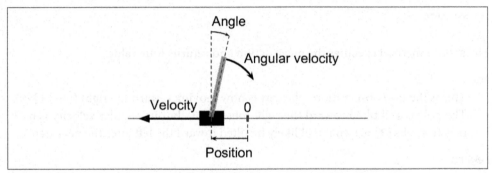

Figure 16-4. The CartPole environment

If you want `render()` to return the rendered image as a NumPy array, you can set the mode parameter to `rgb_array` (note that other environments may support different modes):

```
>>> img = env.render(mode="rgb_array")
>>> img.shape  # height, width, channels (3=RGB)
(400, 600, 3)
```

Unfortunately, the CartPole (and a few other environments) renders the image to the screen even if you set the mode to `"rgb_array"`. The only way to avoid this is to use a fake X server such as Xvfb or Xdummy. For example, you can install Xvfb and start Python using the following command: `xvfb-run -s "-screen 0 1400x900x24" python`. Or use the xvfbwrapper package (*http://homl.info/131*).

Let's ask the environment what actions are possible:

```
>>> env.action_space
Discrete(2)
```

`Discrete(2)` means that the possible actions are integers 0 and 1, which represent accelerating left (0) or right (1). Other environments may have more discrete actions, or other kinds of actions (e.g., continuous). Since the pole is leaning toward the right, let's accelerate the cart toward the right:

```
>>> action = 1  # accelerate right
>>> obs, reward, done, info = env.step(action)
>>> obs
array([-0.03865608,  0.16189797,  0.02351508, -0.27801135])
>>> reward
1.0
>>> done
False
```

```
>>> info
{}
```

The step() method executes the given action and returns four values:

obs
> This is the new observation. The cart is now moving toward the right (obs[1]>0). The pole is still tilted toward the right (obs[2]>0), but its angular velocity is now negative (obs[3]<0), so it will likely be tilted toward the left after the next step.

reward
> In this environment, you get a reward of 1.0 at every step, no matter what you do, so the goal is to keep running as long as possible.

done
> This value will be True when the *episode* is over. This will happen when the pole tilts too much. After that, the environment must be reset before it can be used again.

info
> This dictionary may provide extra debug information in other environments. This data should not be used for training (it would be cheating).

Let's hardcode a simple policy that accelerates left when the pole is leaning toward the left and accelerates right when the pole is leaning toward the right. We will run this policy to see the average rewards it gets over 500 episodes:

```python
def basic_policy(obs):
    angle = obs[2]
    return 0 if angle < 0 else 1

totals = []
for episode in range(500):
    episode_rewards = 0
    obs = env.reset()
    for step in range(1000): # 1000 steps max, we don't want to run forever
        action = basic_policy(obs)
        obs, reward, done, info = env.step(action)
        episode_rewards += reward
        if done:
            break
    totals.append(episode_rewards)
```

This code is hopefully self-explanatory. Let's look at the result:

```
>>> import numpy as np
>>> np.mean(totals), np.std(totals), np.min(totals), np.max(totals)
(42.125999999999998, 9.1237121830974033, 24.0, 68.0)
```

Even with 500 tries, this policy never managed to keep the pole upright for more than 68 consecutive steps. Not great. If you look at the simulation in the Jupyter notebooks (*https://github.com/ageron/handson-ml*), you will see that the cart oscillates left and right more and more strongly until the pole tilts too much. Let's see if a neural network can come up with a better policy.

Neural Network Policies

Let's create a neural network policy. Just like the policy we hardcoded earlier, this neural network will take an observation as input, and it will output the action to be executed. More precisely, it will estimate a probability for each action, and then we will select an action randomly according to the estimated probabilities (see Figure 16-5). In the case of the CartPole environment, there are just two possible actions (left or right), so we only need one output neuron. It will output the probability p of action 0 (left), and of course the probability of action 1 (right) will be $1 - p$. For example, if it outputs 0.7, then we will pick action 0 with 70% probability, and action 1 with 30% probability.

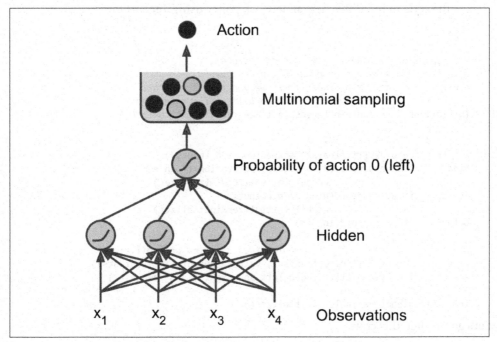

Figure 16-5. Neural network policy

You may wonder why we are picking a random action based on the probability given by the neural network, rather than just picking the action with the highest score. This approach lets the agent find the right balance between *exploring* new actions and *exploiting* the actions that are known to work well. Here's an analogy: suppose you go to a restaurant for the first time, and all the dishes look equally appealing so you randomly pick one. If it turns out to be good, you can increase the probability to order it next time, but you shouldn't increase that probability up to 100%, or else you will never try out the other dishes, some of which may be even better than the one you tried.

Also note that in this particular environment, the past actions and observations can safely be ignored, since each observation contains the environment's full state. If there were some hidden state, then you may need to consider past actions and observations as well. For example, if the environment only revealed the position of the cart but not its velocity, you would have to consider not only the current observation but also the previous observation in order to estimate the current velocity. Another example is when the observations are noisy; in that case, you generally want to use the past few observations to estimate the most likely current state. The CartPole problem is thus as simple as can be; the observations are noise-free and they contain the environment's full state.

Here is the code to build this neural network policy using TensorFlow:

```
import tensorflow as tf

# 1. Specify the neural network architecture
n_inputs = 4  # == env.observation_space.shape[0]
n_hidden = 4  # it's a simple task, we don't need more hidden neurons
n_outputs = 1 # only outputs the probability of accelerating left
initializer = tf.contrib.layers.variance_scaling_initializer()

# 2. Build the neural network
X = tf.placeholder(tf.float32, shape=[None, n_inputs])
hidden = tf.layers.dense(X, n_hidden, activation=tf.nn.elu,
                         kernel_initializer=initializer)
logits = tf.layers.dense(hidden, n_outputs,
                         kernel_initializer=initializer)
outputs = tf.nn.sigmoid(logits)

# 3. Select a random action based on the estimated probabilities
p_left_and_right = tf.concat(axis=1, values=[outputs, 1 - outputs])
action = tf.multinomial(tf.log(p_left_and_right), num_samples=1)

init = tf.global_variables_initializer()
```

Let's go through this code:

1. After the imports, we define the neural network architecture. The number of inputs is the size of the observation space (which in the case of the CartPole is four), we just have four hidden units and no need for more, and we have just one output probability (the probability of going left).

2. Next we build the neural network. In this example, it's a vanilla Multi-Layer Perceptron, with a single output. Note that the output layer uses the logistic (sig-

moid) activation function in order to output a probability from 0.0 to 1.0. If there were more than two possible actions, there would be one output neuron per action, and you would use the softmax activation function instead.

3. Lastly, we call the `multinomial()` function to pick a random action. This function independently samples one (or more) integers, given the log probability of each integer. For example, if you call it with the array [np.log(0.5), np.log(0.2), np.log(0.3)] and with num_samples=5, then it will output five integers, each of which will have a 50% probability of being 0, 20% of being 1, and 30% of being 2. In our case we just need one integer representing the action to take. Since the `outputs` tensor only contains the probability of going left, we must first concatenate `1-outputs` to it to have a tensor containing the probability of both left and right actions. Note that if there were more than two possible actions, the neural network would have to output one probability per action so you would not need the concatenation step.

Okay, we now have a neural network policy that will take observations and output actions. But how do we train it?

Evaluating Actions: The Credit Assignment Problem

If we knew what the best action was at each step, we could train the neural network as usual, by minimizing the cross entropy between the estimated probability and the target probability. It would just be regular supervised learning. However, in Reinforcement Learning the only guidance the agent gets is through rewards, and rewards are typically sparse and delayed. For example, if the agent manages to balance the pole for 100 steps, how can it know which of the 100 actions it took were good, and which of them were bad? All it knows is that the pole fell after the last action, but surely this last action is not entirely responsible. This is called the *credit assignment problem*: when the agent gets a reward, it is hard for it to know which actions should get credited (or blamed) for it. Think of a dog that gets rewarded hours after it behaved well; will it understand what it is rewarded for?

To tackle this problem, a common strategy is to evaluate an action based on the sum of all the rewards that come after it, usually applying a *discount factor* γ (gamma) at each step. For example (see Figure 16-6), if an agent decides to go right three times in a row and gets +10 reward after the first step, 0 after the second step, and finally –50 after the third step, then assuming we use a discount factor $\gamma = 0.8$, the first action will have a total score of $10 + \gamma \times 0 + \gamma^2 \times (-50) = -22$. If the discount factor is close to 0, then future rewards won't count for much compared to immediate rewards. Conversely, if the discount factor is close to 1, then rewards far into the future will count almost as much as immediate rewards. Typical discount factors are 0.95 or 0.99. With a discount factor of 0.95, rewards 13 steps into the future count roughly for half as much as immediate rewards (since $0.95^{13} \approx 0.5$), while with a discount factor of 0.99, rewards 69 steps into the future count for half as much as immediate rewards. In the CartPole environment, actions have fairly short-term effects, so choosing a discount factor of 0.95 seems reasonable.

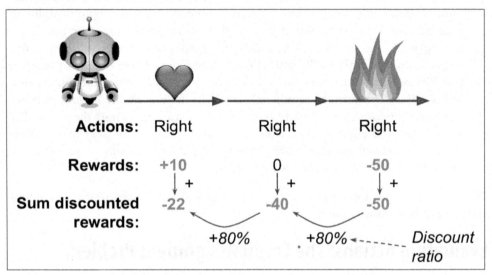

Figure 16-6. Discounted rewards

Of course, a good action may be followed by several bad actions that cause the pole to fall quickly, resulting in the good action getting a low score (similarly, a good actor may sometimes star in a terrible movie). However, if we play the game enough times, on average good actions will get a better score than bad ones. So, to get fairly reliable action scores, we must run many episodes and normalize all the action scores (by subtracting the mean and dividing by the standard deviation). After that, we can reasonably assume that actions with a negative score were bad while actions with a positive score were good. Perfect—now that we have a way to evaluate each action, we are ready to train our first agent using policy gradients. Let's see how.

Policy Gradients

As discussed earlier, PG algorithms optimize the parameters of a policy by following the gradients toward higher rewards. One popular class of PG algorithms, called *REINFORCE algorithms*, was introduced back in 1992 (*http://homl.info/132*)[9] by Ronald Williams. Here is one common variant:

---

9 "Simple Statistical Gradient-Following Algorithms for Connectionist Reinforcement Learning," R. Williams (1992).

1. First, let the neural network policy play the game several times and at each step compute the gradients that would make the chosen action even more likely, but don't apply these gradients yet.

2. Once you have run several episodes, compute each action's score (using the method described in the previous paragraph).

3. If an action's score is positive, it means that the action was good and you want to apply the gradients computed earlier to make the action even more likely to be chosen in the future. However, if the score is negative, it means the action was bad and you want to apply the opposite gradients to make this action slightly *less* likely in the future. The solution is simply to multiply each gradient vector by the corresponding action's score.

4. Finally, compute the mean of all the resulting gradient vectors, and use it to perform a Gradient Descent step.

Let's implement this algorithm using TensorFlow. We will train the neural network policy we built earlier so that it learns to balance the pole on the cart. Let's start by completing the construction phase we coded earlier to add the target probability, the cost function, and the training operation. Since we are acting as though the chosen action is the best possible action, the target probability must be 1.0 if the chosen action is action 0 (left) and 0.0 if it is action 1 (right):

```
y = 1. - tf.to_float(action)
```

Now that we have a target probability, we can define the cost function (cross entropy) and compute the gradients:

```
learning_rate = 0.01

cross_entropy = tf.nn.sigmoid_cross_entropy_with_logits(labels=y,
                                                        logits=logits)
optimizer = tf.train.AdamOptimizer(learning_rate)
grads_and_vars = optimizer.compute_gradients(cross_entropy)
```

Note that we are calling the optimizer's `compute_gradients()` method instead of the `minimize()` method. This is because we want to tweak the gradients before we apply them.[10] The `compute_gradients()` method returns a list of gradient vector/variable pairs (one pair per trainable variable). Let's put all the gradients in a list, to make it more convenient to obtain their values:

```
gradients = [grad for grad, variable in grads_and_vars]
```

---

10 We already did something similar in Chapter 11 when we discussed Gradient Clipping: we first computed the gradients, then we clipped them, and finally we applied the clipped gradients.

Okay, now comes the tricky part. During the execution phase, the algorithm will run the policy and at each step it will evaluate these gradient tensors and store their values. After a number of episodes it will tweak these gradients as explained earlier (i.e., multiply them by the action scores and normalize them) and compute the mean of the tweaked gradients. Next, it will need to feed the resulting gradients back to the optimizer so that it can perform an optimization step. This means we need one placeholder per gradient vector. Moreover, we must create the operation that will apply the updated gradients. For this we will call the optimizer's `apply_gradients()` function, which takes a list of gradient vector/variable pairs. Instead of giving it the original gradient vectors, we will give it a list containing the updated gradients (i.e., the ones fed through the gradient placeholders):

```
gradient_placeholders = []
grads_and_vars_feed = []
for grad, variable in grads_and_vars:
    gradient_placeholder = tf.placeholder(tf.float32, shape=grad.get_shape())
    gradient_placeholders.append(gradient_placeholder)
    grads_and_vars_feed.append((gradient_placeholder, variable))

training_op = optimizer.apply_gradients(grads_and_vars_feed)
```

Let's step back and take a look at the full construction phase:

```
n_inputs = 4
n_hidden = 4
n_outputs = 1
initializer = tf.contrib.layers.variance_scaling_initializer()

learning_rate = 0.01

X = tf.placeholder(tf.float32, shape=[None, n_inputs])
hidden = tf.layers.dense(X, n_hidden, activation=tf.nn.elu,
                         kernel_initializer=initializer)
logits = tf.layers.dense(hidden, n_outputs,
                         kernel_initializer=initializer)
outputs = tf.nn.sigmoid(logits)
p_left_and_right = tf.concat(axis=1, values=[outputs, 1 - outputs])
action = tf.multinomial(tf.log(p_left_and_right), num_samples=1)

y = 1. - tf.to_float(action)
cross_entropy = tf.nn.sigmoid_cross_entropy_with_logits(
                        labels=y, logits=logits)
optimizer = tf.train.AdamOptimizer(learning_rate)
grads_and_vars = optimizer.compute_gradients(cross_entropy)
gradients = [grad for grad, variable in grads_and_vars]
gradient_placeholders = []
grads_and_vars_feed = []
for grad, variable in grads_and_vars:
    gradient_placeholder = tf.placeholder(tf.float32, shape=grad.get_shape())
    gradient_placeholders.append(gradient_placeholder)
    grads_and_vars_feed.append((gradient_placeholder, variable))
```

```
    training_op = optimizer.apply_gradients(grads_and_vars_feed)

init = tf.global_variables_initializer()
saver = tf.train.Saver()
```

On to the execution phase! We will need a couple of functions to compute the total discounted rewards, given the raw rewards, and to normalize the results across multiple episodes:

```
def discount_rewards(rewards, gamma):
    discounted_rewards = np.empty(len(rewards))
    cumulative_rewards = 0
    for step in reversed(range(len(rewards))):
        cumulative_rewards = rewards[step] + cumulative_rewards * gamma
        discounted_rewards[step] = cumulative_rewards
    return discounted_rewards

def discount_and_normalize_rewards(all_rewards, gamma):
    all_discounted_rewards = [discount_rewards(rewards, gamma)
                              for rewards in all_rewards]
    flat_rewards = np.concatenate(all_discounted_rewards)
    reward_mean = flat_rewards.mean()
    reward_std = flat_rewards.std()
    return [(discounted_rewards - reward_mean)/reward_std
            for discounted_rewards in all_discounted_rewards]
```

Let's check that this works:

```
>>> discount_rewards([10, 0, -50], gamma=0.8)
array([-22., -40., -50.])
>>> discount_and_normalize_rewards([[10, 0, -50], [10, 20]], gamma=0.8)
[array([-0.28435071, -0.86597718, -1.18910299]),
 array([ 1.26665318,  1.0727777 ])]
```

The call to discount_rewards() returns exactly what we expect (see Figure 16-6). You can verify that the function discount_and_normalize_rewards() does indeed return the normalized scores for each action in both episodes. Notice that the first episode was much worse than the second, so its normalized scores are all negative; all actions from the first episode would be considered bad, and conversely all actions from the second episode would be considered good.

We now have all we need to train the policy:

```
n_iterations = 250        # number of training iterations
n_max_steps = 1000        # max steps per episode
n_games_per_update = 10   # train the policy every 10 episodes
save_iterations = 10      # save the model every 10 training iterations
gamma = 0.95              # the discount factor

with tf.Session() as sess:
    init.run()
    for iteration in range(n_iterations):
        all_rewards = []    # all sequences of raw rewards for each episode
```

```
all_gradients = []  # gradients saved at each step of each episode
for game in range(n_games_per_update):
    current_rewards = []    # all raw rewards from the current episode
    current_gradients = [] # all gradients from the current episode
    obs = env.reset()
    for step in range(n_max_steps):
        action_val, gradients_val = sess.run(
            [action, gradients],
            feed_dict={X: obs.reshape(1, n_inputs)}) # one obs
        obs, reward, done, info = env.step(action_val[0][0])
        current_rewards.append(reward)
        current_gradients.append(gradients_val)
        if done:
            break
    all_rewards.append(current_rewards)
    all_gradients.append(current_gradients)

    # At this point we have run the policy for 10 episodes, and we are
    # ready for a policy update using the algorithm described earlier.
    all_rewards = discount_and_normalize_rewards(all_rewards, gamma)
    feed_dict = {}
    for var_index, grad_placeholder in enumerate(gradient_placeholders):
        # multiply the gradients by the action scores, and compute the mean
        mean_gradients = np.mean(
            [reward * all_gradients[game_index][step][var_index]
                for game_index, rewards in enumerate(all_rewards)
                for step, reward in enumerate(rewards)],
            axis=0)
        feed_dict[grad_placeholder] = mean_gradients
    sess.run(training_op, feed_dict=feed_dict)
    if iteration % save_iterations == 0:
        saver.save(sess, "./my_policy_net_pg.ckpt")
```

Each training iteration starts by running the policy for 10 episodes (with maximum 1,000 steps per episode, to avoid running forever). At each step, we also compute the gradients, pretending that the chosen action was the best. After these 10 episodes have been run, we compute the action scores using the discount_and_normal ize_rewards() function; we go through each trainable variable, across all episodes and all steps, to multiply each gradient vector by its corresponding action score; and we compute the mean of the resulting gradients. Finally, we run the training operation, feeding it these mean gradients (one per trainable variable). We also save the model every 10 training operations.

And we're done! This code will train the neural network policy, and it will successfully learn to balance the pole on the cart (you can try it out in the Jupyter notebooks). Note that there are actually two ways the agent can lose the game: either the pole can tilt too much, or the cart can go completely off the screen. With 250 training iterations, the policy learns to balance the pole quite well, but it is not yet good enough at avoiding going off the screen. A few hundred more training iterations will fix that.

Researchers try to find algorithms that work well even when the agent initially knows nothing about the environment. However, unless you are writing a paper, you should inject as much prior knowledge as possible into the agent, as it will speed up training dramatically. For example, you could add negative rewards proportional to the distance from the center of the screen, and to the pole's angle. Also, if you already have a reasonably good policy (e.g., hardcoded), you may want to train the neural network to imitate it before using policy gradients to improve it.

Despite its relative simplicity, this algorithm is quite powerful. You can use it to tackle much harder problems than balancing a pole on a cart. In fact, AlphaGo was based on a similar PG algorithm (plus *Monte Carlo Tree Search*, which is beyond the scope of this book).

We will now look at another popular family of algorithms. Whereas PG algorithms directly try to optimize the policy to increase rewards, the algorithms we will look at now are less direct: the agent learns to estimate the expected sum of discounted future rewards for each state, or the expected sum of discounted future rewards for each action in each state, then uses this knowledge to decide how to act. To understand these algorithms, we must first introduce *Markov decision processes* (MDP).

Markov Decision Processes

In the early 20th century, the mathematician Andrey Markov studied stochastic processes with no memory, called *Markov chains*. Such a process has a fixed number of states, and it randomly evolves from one state to another at each step. The probability for it to evolve from a state s to a state s' is fixed, and it depends only on the pair (s,s'), not on past states (the system has no memory).

Figure 16-7 shows an example of a Markov chain with four states. Suppose that the process starts in state s_0, and there is a 70% chance that it will remain in that state at the next step. Eventually it is bound to leave that state and never come back since no other state points back to s_0. If it goes to state s_1, it will then most likely go to state s_2 (90% probability), then immediately back to state s_1 (with 100% probability). It may alternate a number of times between these two states, but eventually it will fall into state s_3 and remain there forever (this is a *terminal state*). Markov chains can have very different dynamics, and they are heavily used in thermodynamics, chemistry, statistics, and much more.

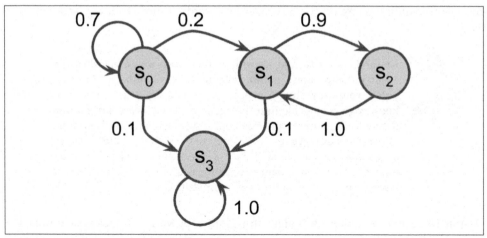

Figure 16-7. Example of a Markov chain

Markov decision processes were first described in the 1950s by Richard Bellman (*http://homl.info/133*).[11] They resemble Markov chains but with a twist: at each step, an agent can choose one of several possible actions, and the transition probabilities depend on the chosen action. Moreover, some state transitions return some reward (positive or negative), and the agent's goal is to find a policy that will maximize rewards over time.

For example, the MDP represented in Figure 16-8 has three states and up to three possible discrete actions at each step. If it starts in state s_0, the agent can choose between actions a_0, a_1, or a_2. If it chooses action a_1, it just remains in state s_0 with certainty, and without any reward. It can thus decide to stay there forever if it wants. But if it chooses action a_0, it has a 70% probability of gaining a reward of +10, and remaining in state s_0. It can then try again and again to gain as much reward as possible. But at one point it is going to end up instead in state s_1. In state s_1 it has only two possible actions: a_0 or a_2. It can choose to stay put by repeatedly choosing action a_0, or it can choose to move on to state s_2 and get a negative reward of –50 (ouch). In state s_2 it has no other choice than to take action a_1, which will most likely lead it back to state s_0, gaining a reward of +40 on the way. You get the picture. By looking at this MDP, can you guess which strategy will gain the most reward over time? In state s_0 it is clear that action a_0 is the best option, and in state s_2 the agent has no choice but to take action a_1, but in state s_1 it is not obvious whether the agent should stay put (a_0) or go through the fire (a_2).

---

11 "A Markovian Decision Process," R. Bellman (1957).

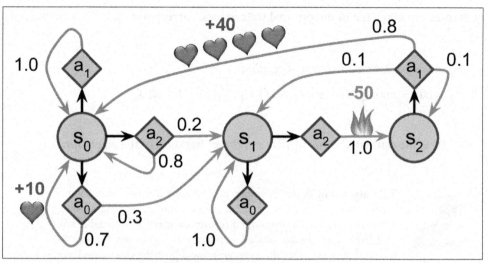

Figure 16-8. Example of a Markov decision process

Bellman found a way to estimate the *optimal state value* of any state s, noted $V^*(s)$, which is the sum of all discounted future rewards the agent can expect on average after it reaches a state s, assuming it acts optimally. He showed that if the agent acts optimally, then the *Bellman Optimality Equation* applies (see Equation 16-1). This recursive equation says that if the agent acts optimally, then the optimal value of the current state is equal to the reward it will get on average after taking one optimal action, plus the expected optimal value of all possible next states that this action can lead to.

Equation 16-1. Bellman Optimality Equation

$$V^*(s) = \max_a \sum_{s'} T(s, a, s')[R(s, a, s') + \gamma . V^*(s')] \quad \text{for all } s$$

- $T(s, a, s')$ is the transition probability from state s to state s′, given that the agent chose action a.
- $R(s, a, s')$ is the reward that the agent gets when it goes from state s to state s′, given that the agent chose action a.
- γ is the discount factor.

This equation leads directly to an algorithm that can precisely estimate the optimal state value of every possible state: you first initialize all the state value estimates to zero, and then you iteratively update them using the *Value Iteration* algorithm (see Equation 16-2). A remarkable result is that, given enough time, these estimates are guaranteed to converge to the optimal state values, corresponding to the optimal policy.

Equation 16-2. Value Iteration algorithm

$$V_{k+1}(s) \leftarrow \max_a \sum_{s'} T(s, a, s')[R(s, a, s') + \gamma \cdot V_k(s')] \quad \text{for all } s$$

- $V_k(s)$ is the estimated value of state s at the kth iteration of the algorithm.

 This algorithm is an example of *Dynamic Programming*, which breaks down a complex problem (in this case estimating a potentially infinite sum of discounted future rewards) into tractable subproblems that can be tackled iteratively (in this case finding the action that maximizes the average reward plus the discounted next state value).

Knowing the optimal state values can be useful, in particular to evaluate a policy, but it does not tell the agent explicitly what to do. Luckily, Bellman found a very similar algorithm to estimate the optimal *state-action values*, generally called *Q-Values*. The optimal Q-Value of the state-action pair (s,a), noted $Q^*(s,a)$, is the sum of discounted future rewards the agent can expect on average after it reaches the state s and chooses action a, but before it sees the outcome of this action, assuming it acts optimally after that action.

Here is how it works: once again, you start by initializing all the Q-Value estimates to zero, then you update them using the *Q-Value Iteration* algorithm (see Equation 16-3).

Equation 16-3. Q-Value Iteration algorithm

$$Q_{k+1}(s, a) \leftarrow \sum_{s'} T(s, a, s')\left[R(s, a, s') + \gamma \cdot \max_{a'} Q_k(s', a')\right] \quad \text{for all } (s, a)$$

Once you have the optimal Q-Values, defining the optimal policy, noted $\pi^*(s)$, is trivial: when the agent is in state s, it should choose the action with the highest Q-Value for that state: $\pi^*(s) = \underset{a}{\text{argmax}} \ Q^*(s, a)$.

Let's apply this algorithm to the MDP represented in Figure 16-8. First, we need to define the MDP:

```
nan = np.nan  # represents impossible actions
T = np.array([  # shape=[s, a, s']
        [[0.7, 0.3, 0.0], [1.0, 0.0, 0.0], [0.8, 0.2, 0.0]],
```

```
        [[0.0, 1.0, 0.0], [nan, nan, nan], [0.0, 0.0, 1.0]],
        [[nan, nan, nan], [0.8, 0.1, 0.1], [nan, nan, nan]],
    ])
R = np.array([  # shape=[s, a, s']
        [[10., 0.0, 0.0], [0.0, 0.0, 0.0], [0.0, 0.0, 0.0]],
        [[0.0, 0.0, 0.0], [nan, nan, nan], [0.0, 0.0, -50.]],
        [[nan, nan, nan], [40., 0.0, 0.0], [nan, nan, nan]],
    ])
possible_actions = [[0, 1, 2], [0, 2], [1]]
```

Now let's run the Q-Value Iteration algorithm:

```
Q = np.full((3, 3), -np.inf)  # -inf for impossible actions
for state, actions in enumerate(possible_actions):
    Q[state, actions] = 0.0  # Initial value = 0.0, for all possible actions

gamma = 0.95  # the discount factor
n_iterations = 100

for iteration in range(n_iterations):
    Q_prev = Q.copy()
    for s in range(3):
        for a in possible_actions[s]:
            Q[s, a] = np.sum([
                T[s, a, sp] * (R[s, a, sp] + gamma * np.max(Q_prev[sp]))
                for sp in range(3)
            ])
```

The resulting Q-Values look like this:

```
>>> Q
array([[ 21.89498982,  20.80024033,  16.86353093],
       [  1.11669335,         -inf,   1.17573546],
       [        -inf,  53.86946068,         -inf]])
>>> np.argmax(Q, axis=1)  # optimal action for each state
array([0, 2, 1])
```

This gives us the optimal policy for this MDP, when using a discount factor of 0.95: in state s_0 choose action a_0, in state s_1 choose action a_2 (go through the fire!), and in state s_2 choose action a_1 (the only possible action). Interestingly, if you reduce the discount factor to 0.9, the optimal policy changes: in state s_1 the best action becomes a_0 (stay put; don't go through the fire). It makes sense because if you value the present much more than the future, then the prospect of future rewards is not worth immediate pain.

Temporal Difference Learning and Q-Learning

Reinforcement Learning problems with discrete actions can often be modeled as Markov decision processes, but the agent initially has no idea what the transition probabilities are (it does not know $T(s, a, s')$), and it does not know what the rewards are going to be either (it does not know $R(s, a, s')$). It must experience each state and each transition at least once to know the rewards, and it must experience them multiple times if it is to have a reasonable estimate of the transition probabilities.

The *Temporal Difference Learning* (TD Learning) algorithm is very similar to the Value Iteration algorithm, but tweaked to take into account the fact that the agent has only partial knowledge of the MDP. In general we assume that the agent initially knows only the possible states and actions, and nothing more. The agent uses an *exploration policy*—for example, a purely random policy—to explore the MDP, and as it progresses the TD Learning algorithm updates the estimates of the state values based on the transitions and rewards that are actually observed (see Equation 16-4).

Equation 16-4. TD Learning algorithm

$$V_{k+1}(s) \leftarrow (1 - \alpha)V_k(s) + \alpha\big(r + \gamma . V_k(s')\big)$$

- α is the learning rate (e.g., 0.01).

 TD Learning has many similarities with Stochastic Gradient Descent, in particular the fact that it handles one sample at a time. Just like SGD, it can only truly converge if you gradually reduce the learning rate (otherwise it will keep bouncing around the optimum).

For each state s, this algorithm simply keeps track of a running average of the immediate rewards the agent gets upon leaving that state, plus the rewards it expects to get later (assuming it acts optimally).

Similarly, the Q-Learning algorithm is an adaptation of the Q-Value Iteration algorithm to the situation where the transition probabilities and the rewards are initially unknown (see Equation 16-5).

Equation 16-5. Q-Learning algorithm

$$Q_{k+1}(s, a) \leftarrow (1 - \alpha)Q_k(s, a) + \alpha\Big(r + \gamma . \max_{a'} Q_k(s', a')\Big)$$

For each state-action pair (s, a), this algorithm keeps track of a running average of the rewards r the agent gets upon leaving the state s with action a, plus the rewards it expects to get later. Since the target policy would act optimally, we take the maximum of the Q-Value estimates for the next state.

Here is how Q-Learning can be implemented:

```
learning_rate0 = 0.05
learning_rate_decay = 0.1
n_iterations = 20000

s = 0 # start in state 0

Q = np.full((3, 3), -np.inf)  # -inf for impossible actions
for state, actions in enumerate(possible_actions):
    Q[state, actions] = 0.0  # Initial value = 0.0, for all possible actions

for iteration in range(n_iterations):
    a = np.random.choice(possible_actions[s])  # choose an action (randomly)
    sp = np.random.choice(range(3), p=T[s, a]) # pick next state using T[s, a]
    reward = R[s, a, sp]
    learning_rate = learning_rate0 / (1 + iteration * learning_rate_decay)
    Q[s, a] = ((1 - learning_rate) * Q[s, a] +
               learning_rate * (reward + gamma * np.max(Q[sp])))
    s = sp # move to next state
```

Given enough iterations, this algorithm will converge to the optimal Q-Values. This is called an *off-policy* algorithm because the policy being trained is not the one being executed. It is somewhat surprising that this algorithm is capable of learning the optimal policy by just watching an agent act randomly (imagine learning to play golf when your teacher is a drunken monkey). Can we do better?

Exploration Policies

Of course Q-Learning can work only if the exploration policy explores the MDP thoroughly enough. Although a purely random policy is guaranteed to eventually visit every state and every transition many times, it may take an extremely long time to do so. Therefore, a better option is to use the *ε-greedy policy*: at each step it acts randomly with probability ε, or greedily (choosing the action with the highest Q-Value) with probability 1-ε. The advantage of the ε-greedy policy (compared to a completely random policy) is that it will spend more and more time exploring the interesting parts of the environment, as the Q-Value estimates get better and better, while still spending some time visiting unknown regions of the MDP. It is quite common to start with a high value for ε (e.g., 1.0) and then gradually reduce it (e.g., down to 0.05).

Alternatively, rather than relying on chance for exploration, another approach is to encourage the exploration policy to try actions that it has not tried much before. This can be implemented as a bonus added to the Q-Value estimates, as shown in Equation 16-6.

Equation 16-6. Q-Learning using an exploration function

$$Q(s, a) \leftarrow (1 - \alpha)Q(s, a) + \alpha\left(r + \gamma \, \max_{a'} f\big(Q(s', a'), N(s', a')\big)\right)$$

- $N(s', a')$ counts the number of times the action a' was chosen in state s'.
- $f(q, n)$ is an *exploration function*, such as $f(q, n) = q + K/(1 + n)$, where K is a curiosity hyperparameter that measures how much the agent is attracted to to the unknown.

Approximate Q-Learning and Deep Q-Learning

The main problem with Q-Learning is that it does not scale well to large (or even medium) MDPs with many states and actions. Consider trying to use Q-Learning to train an agent to play Ms. Pac-Man. There are over 250 pellets that Ms. Pac-Man can eat, each of which can be present or absent (i.e., already eaten). So the number of possible states is greater than $2^{250} \approx 10^{75}$ (and that's considering the possible states only of the pellets). This is way more than the number of atoms in our galaxy, so there's absolutely no way you can keep track of an estimate for every single Q-Value.

The solution is to find a function $Q_\theta(s, a)$ that approximates the Q-Value of any state-action pair (s,a) using a manageable number of parameters (given by the parameter vector θ). This is called *Approximate Q-Learning*. For years it was recommended to use linear combinations of hand-crafted features extracted from the state (e.g., distance of the closest ghosts, their directions, and so on) to estimate Q-Values, but DeepMind showed that using deep neural networks can work much better, especially for complex problems, and it does not require any feature engineering. A DNN used to estimate Q-Values is called a *deep Q-network* (DQN), and using a DQN for Approximate Q-Learning is called *Deep Q-Learning*.

Now how can we train a DQN? Well, consider the approximate Q-Value computed by the DQN for a given state-action pair (s,a). Thanks to Bellman, we know we want this approximate Q-Value to be as close as possible to the reward r that we actually observe after playing action a in state s, plus the discounted value of playing optimally from then on. To estimate this future discounted value, we can simply run the DQN on the next state s' and for all possible actions a'. We get an approximate future Q-Value for each possible action. We then pick the highest (since we assume we will be playing optimally), we discount it, and this gives us an estimate of the future discounted value. By summing the reward r and the future discounted value estimate, we get a target Q-Value $y(s, a)$ for the state-action pair (s, a), as shown in Equation 16-7.

Equation 16-7. Target Q-Value

$$y\left(s, a\right) = r + \gamma \cdot \max_{a'} Q_\theta\left(s', a'\right)$$

With this target Q-Value, we can run a training iteration using any Gradient Descent algorithm. Specifically, we generally try to minimize the squared error between the estimated Q-Value and the target Q-Value. And that's all for the basic Deep Q-Learning algorithm!

However, in DeepMind's DQN algorithm, two crucial modifications were introduced:

- Instead of training the DQN based on the latest experiences, DeepMind's DQN algorithm stores experiences in a large *replay memory*, and it samples a random training batch from it at each training iteration. This helps reduce the correlations between the experiences in a training batch, which tremendously helps training.

- The algorithm uses two DQNs instead of one: the first one, called the *online DQN* is the one that plays and learns at each training iteration. The second, called the *target DQN* is only used to compute the target Q-Values (Equation 16-7). At regular intervals, the weights of the online network are copied to the target network. DeepMind showed that this change dramatically improves the performance of the algorithm. Indeed, without it, there is a single network that sets its own targets and tries to reach them, a bit like a dog chasing its own tail. This can lead to feedback loops, making the network unstable (it can diverge, oscillate, freeze, and so on). Having two networks helps reduce these feedback loops, which stabilizes the training process.

In the rest of this chapter, we will use DeepMind's DQN algorithm to train an agent to play Ms. Pac-Man, much like DeepMind did in 2013. The code can easily be tweaked to learn to play the majority of Atari games quite well, provided you train it for long enough (it may take days or weeks, depending on your hardware). It can achieve superhuman skill at most action games, but it is not so good at games with long-running storylines.

Learning to Play Ms. Pac-Man Using the DQN Algorithm

Since we will be using an Atari environment, we must first install OpenAI gym's Atari dependencies. While we're at it, we will also install dependencies for other OpenAI gym environments that you may want to play with. On macOS, assuming you have installed Homebrew (*http://brew.sh/*), you need to run:

```
$ brew install cmake boost boost-python sdl2 swig wget
```

On Ubuntu, type the following command (replacing python3 with python if you are using Python 2):

```
$ apt-get install -y python3-numpy python3-dev cmake zlib1g-dev libjpeg-dev\
    xvfb libav-tools xorg-dev python3-opengl libboost-all-dev libsdl2-dev swig
```

Then install the extra Python modules (if you are using a virtualenv, make sure to activate it first):

```
$ pip3 install --upgrade 'gym[all]'
```

If everything went well, you should be able to create a Ms. Pac-Man environment:

```
>>> env = gym.make("MsPacman-v0")
>>> obs = env.reset()
>>> obs.shape   # [height, width, channels]
(210, 160, 3)
>>> env.action_space
Discrete(9)
```

As you can see, there are nine discrete actions available, which correspond to the nine possible positions of the joystick (center, up, right, left, down, upper right, and so on), and the observations are simply screenshots of the Atari screen (see Figure 16-9, left), represented as 3D NumPy arrays. These images are a bit large, so we will create a small preprocessing function that will crop the image and shrink it down to 88 × 80 pixels, convert it to grayscale, and improve the contrast of Ms. Pac-Man. This will reduce the amount of computations required by the DQN, and speed up training.

```
mspacman_color = np.array([210, 164, 74]).mean()

def preprocess_observation(obs):
    img = obs[1:176:2, ::2] # crop and downsize
    img = img.mean(axis=2) # to grayscale
    img[img==mspacman_color] = 0 # improve contrast
    img = (img - 128) / 128 - 1 # normalize from -1. to 1.
    return img.reshape(88, 80, 1)
```

The result of preprocessing is shown in Figure 16-9 (right).

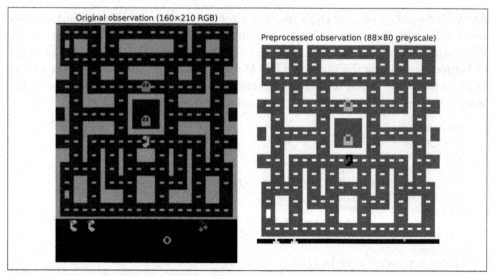

Figure 16-9. Ms. Pac-Man observation, original (left) and after preprocessing (right)

Next, let's create the DQN. It could just take a state-action pair (s,a) as input, and output an estimate of the corresponding Q-Value $Q(s,a)$, but since the actions are discrete it is more convenient and efficient to use a neural network that takes only a state s as input and outputs one Q-Value estimate per action. The DQN will be composed of three convolutional layers, followed by two fully connected layers, including the output layer (see Figure 16-10).

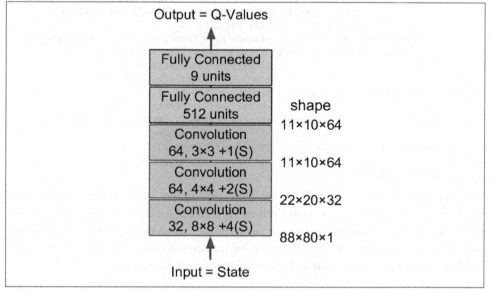

Figure 16-10. Deep Q-network to play Ms. Pac-Man

As we discussed earlier, the DQN training algorithm designed by DeepMind requires two DQNs with the same architecture (but different parameters): the online DQN will learn to drive Ms. Pac-Man, and the target DQN will be used to build the target Q-Values for training the online DQN. At regular intervals we will copy the online DQN to the target DQN, replacing its parameters. Since we need two DQNs with the same architecture, we will create a q_network() function to build them:

```python
input_height = 88
input_width = 80
input_channels = 1
conv_n_maps = [32, 64, 64]
conv_kernel_sizes = [(8,8), (4,4), (3,3)]
conv_strides = [4, 2, 1]
conv_paddings = ["SAME"] * 3
conv_activation = [tf.nn.relu] * 3
n_hidden_in = 64 * 11 * 10  # conv3 has 64 maps of 11x10 each
n_hidden = 512
hidden_activation = tf.nn.relu
n_outputs = env.action_space.n  # 9 discrete actions are available
initializer = tf.contrib.layers.variance_scaling_initializer()

def q_network(X_state, name):
    prev_layer = X_state
    with tf.variable_scope(name) as scope:
        for n_maps, kernel_size, strides, padding, activation in zip(
                conv_n_maps, conv_kernel_sizes, conv_strides,
                conv_paddings, conv_activation):
            prev_layer = tf.layers.conv2d(
                prev_layer, filters=n_maps, kernel_size=kernel_size,
                strides=strides, padding=padding, activation=activation,
                kernel_initializer=initializer)
        last_conv_layer_flat = tf.reshape(prev_layer, shape=[-1, n_hidden_in])
        hidden = tf.layers.dense(last_conv_layer_flat, n_hidden,
                                 activation=hidden_activation,
                                 kernel_initializer=initializer)
        outputs = tf.layers.dense(hidden, n_outputs,
                                  kernel_initializer=initializer)
    trainable_vars = tf.get_collection(tf.GraphKeys.TRAINABLE_VARIABLES,
                                       scope=scope.name)
    trainable_vars_by_name = {var.name[len(scope.name):]: var
                              for var in trainable_vars}
    return outputs, trainable_vars_by_name
```

The first part of this code defines the hyperparameters of the DQN architecture. Then the q_network() function is defined to create the DQNs, taking the environment's state X_state as input, and the name of the variable scope. Note that we will just use one observation to represent the environment's state since there's almost no hidden state (except for blinking objects and the ghosts' directions).

Games such as Pong or Breakout contain a moving ball whose direction and speed cannot be determined with a single observation, so they would require combining the last few observations into the environment's state. One way to do that would be to create an image with one channel for each of the last few observations. Alternatively, we could merge the last few observations into a single channel image, for example by computing the max of these observations (after diming the older observations, so that the direction of time is clear on the final image).

The `trainable_vars_by_name` dictionary gathers all the trainable variables of this DQN. It will be useful in a minute when we create operations to copy the online DQN to the target DQN. The keys of the dictionary are the names of the variables, stripping the part of the prefix that just corresponds to the scope's name. It looks like this:

```
>>> trainable_vars_by_name
{'/conv2d/bias:0': <tf.Variable... shape=(32,) dtype=float32_ref>,
 '/conv2d/kernel:0': <tf.Variable... shape=(8, 8, 1, 32) dtype=float32_ref>,
 '/conv2d_1/bias:0': <tf.Variable... shape=(64,) dtype=float32_ref>,
 '/conv2d_1/kernel:0': <tf.Variable... shape=(4, 4, 32, 64) dtype=float32_ref>,
 '/conv2d_2/bias:0': <tf.Variable... shape=(64,) dtype=float32_ref>,
 '/conv2d_2/kernel:0': <tf.Variable... shape=(3, 3, 64, 64) dtype=float32_ref>,
 '/dense/bias:0': <tf.Variable... shape=(512,) dtype=float32_ref>,
 '/dense/kernel:0': <tf.Variable... shape=(7040, 512) dtype=float32_ref>,
 '/dense_1/bias:0': <tf.Variable... shape=(9,) dtype=float32_ref>,
 '/dense_1/kernel:0': <tf.Variable... shape=(512, 9) dtype=float32_ref>}
```

Now let's create the input placeholder, the two DQNs, and the operation to copy the online DQN to the target DQN:

```
X_state = tf.placeholder(tf.float32, shape=[None, input_height, input_width,
                                            input_channels])
online_q_values, online_vars = q_network(X_state, name="q_networks/online")
target_q_values, target_vars = q_network(X_state, name="q_networks/target")

copy_ops = [target_var.assign(online_vars[var_name])
            for var_name, target_var in target_vars.items()]
copy_online_to_target = tf.group(*copy_ops)
```

Let's step back for a second: we now have two DQNs that are both capable of taking an environment state as input (in this example, a single preprocessed observation) and outputting an estimated Q-Value for each possible action in that state. Plus we have an operation called `copy_online_to_target` to copy the values of all the trainable variables of the online DQN to the corresponding target DQN variables. We use TensorFlow's `tf.group()` function to group all the assignment operations into a single convenient operation.

Now, let's add the online DQN's training operations. First, we need to be able to compute its predicted Q-Value for each state-action pair in the memory batch. Since the DQN outputs one Q-Value for every possible action, we need to keep only the Q-Value that corresponds to the action that was actually played. For this, we will convert the action to a one-hot vector (recall that this is a vector full of 0s except for a 1 at the ith index), and multiply it by the Q-Values: this will zero out all Q-Values except for the one corresponding to the memorized action. Then just sum over the first axis to obtain only the desired Q-Value prediction for each memory.

```
X_action = tf.placeholder(tf.int32, shape=[None])
q_value = tf.reduce_sum(target_q_values * tf.one_hot(X_action, n_outputs),
                        axis=1, keepdims=True)
```

Next, we create a placeholder y that we will use to provide the target Q-Values, and then we compute the loss: we use the squared error when it is smaller than 1.0, and twice the absolute error when the squared error is larger than 1.0. In other words, the loss is quadratic for small errors and linear for large errors. This reduces the effect of large errors and helps stabilize training.

```
y = tf.placeholder(tf.float32, shape=[None, 1])
error = tf.abs(y - q_value)
clipped_error = tf.clip_by_value(error, 0.0, 1.0)
linear_error = 2 * (error - clipped_error)
loss = tf.reduce_mean(tf.square(clipped_error) + linear_error)
```

Lastly, we create a Nesterov Accelerated Gradient optimizer to minimize the loss. We also create a nontrainable variable called global_step to track the training step. The training operation will take care of incrementing it. Plus we create the usual init operation and a Saver.

```
learning_rate = 0.001
momentum = 0.95

global_step = tf.Variable(0, trainable=False, name='global_step')
optimizer = tf.train.MomentumOptimizer(learning_rate, momentum, use_nesterov=True)
training_op = optimizer.minimize(loss, global_step=global_step)

init = tf.global_variables_initializer()
saver = tf.train.Saver()
```

That's it for the construction phase. Before we look at the execution phase, we will need a couple of tools. First, let's start by implementing the replay memory. We will use a deque list since it is very efficient at pushing items to the queue and popping the oldest one out when the maximum memory size is reached. We will also write a small function to randomly sample a batch of experiences from the replay memory. Each experience will be a 5-tuple (state, action, reward, next state, continue), where the "continue" item will be equal to 0.0 when the game is over, or 1.0 otherwise.

```
from collections import deque

replay_memory_size = 500000
replay_memory = deque([], maxlen=replay_memory_size)

def sample_memories(batch_size):
    indices = np.random.permutation(len(replay_memory))[:batch_size]
    cols = [[], [], [], [], []] # state, action, reward, next_state, continue
    for idx in indices:
        memory = replay_memory[idx]
        for col, value in zip(cols, memory):
            col.append(value)
    cols = [np.array(col) for col in cols]
    return (cols[0], cols[1], cols[2].reshape(-1, 1), cols[3],
            cols[4].reshape(-1, 1))
```

Next, we will need the agent to explore the game. We will use the ε-greedy policy, and gradually decrease ε from 1.0 to 0.1, in two million training steps:

```
eps_min = 0.1
eps_max = 1.0
eps_decay_steps = 2000000

def epsilon_greedy(q_values, step):
    epsilon = max(eps_min, eps_max - (eps_max-eps_min) * step/eps_decay_steps)
    if np.random.rand() < epsilon:
        return np.random.randint(n_outputs) # random action
    else:
        return np.argmax(q_values) # optimal action
```

That's it! We have all we need to start training. The execution phase does not contain anything too complex, but it is a bit long, so take a deep breath. Ready? Let's go! First, let's set a few parameters:

```
n_steps = 4000000  # total number of training steps
training_start = 10000  # start training after 10,000 game iterations
training_interval = 4 # run a training step every 4 game iterations
save_steps = 1000  # save the model every 1,000 training steps
copy_steps = 10000  # copy online DQN to target DQN every 10,000 training steps
gamma = 0.99  # the discount factor
skip_start = 90  # Skip the start of every game (it's just waiting time).
batch_size = 50
iteration = 0  # game iterations
checkpoint_path = "./my_dqn.ckpt"
done = True # env needs to be reset
```

Next, let's open the session and run the main training loop:

```
with tf.Session() as sess:
    if os.path.isfile(checkpoint_path + ".index"):
        saver.restore(sess, checkpoint_path)
    else:
        init.run()
```

```
        copy_online_to_target.run()
while True:
    step = global_step.eval()
    if step >= n_steps:
        break
    iteration += 1
    if done: # game over, start again
        obs = env.reset()
        for skip in range(skip_start): # skip the start of each game
            obs, reward, done, info = env.step(0)
        state = preprocess_observation(obs)

    # Online DQN evaluates what to do
    q_values = online_q_values.eval(feed_dict={X_state: [state]})
    action = epsilon_greedy(q_values, step)

    # Online DQN plays
    obs, reward, done, info = env.step(action)
    next_state = preprocess_observation(obs)

    # Let's memorize what just happened
    replay_memory.append((state, action, reward, next_state, 1.0 - done))
    state = next_state

    if iteration < training_start or iteration % training_interval != 0:
        continue # only train after warmup period and at regular intervals

    # Sample memories and use the target DQN to produce the target Q-Value
    X_state_val, X_action_val, rewards, X_next_state_val, continues = (
        sample_memories(batch_size))
    next_q_values = target_q_values.eval(
        feed_dict={X_state: X_next_state_val})
    max_next_q_values = np.max(next_q_values, axis=1, keepdims=True)
    y_val = rewards + continues * gamma * max_next_q_values

    # Train the online DQN
    training_op.run(feed_dict={X_state: X_state_val,
                               X_action: X_action_val, y: y_val})

    # Regularly copy the online DQN to the target DQN
    if step % copy_steps == 0:
        copy_online_to_target.run()

    # And save regularly
    if step % save_steps == 0:
        saver.save(sess, checkpoint_path)
```

We start by restoring the model if a checkpoint file exists, or else we just initialize the
variables normally, and copy the online DQN to the target DQN. Then the main loop
starts, where iteration counts the total number of game steps we have gone through
since the program started, and step counts the total number of training steps since

training started (if a checkpoint is restored, then the step is restored as well, thanks to the `global_step` variable). Then the code resets the game and skips the first boring game steps, where nothing happens. Next, the online DQN evaluates what to do, plays the game, and its experience is memorized in the replay memory. Then, at regular intervals (after a warmup period), the online DQN goes through a training step. We first sample a batch of memories and we ask the target DQN to estimate the Q-Values of all possible actions for each memory's "next state", then we apply Equation 16-7 to compute `y_val`, containing the target Q-Value for each state-action pair. The only tricky part here is that we must multiply the `max_next_q_values` vector by the `continues` vector to zero out the future values that correspond to memories where the game ended. Next we run a training operation to improve the online DQN's ability to predict Q-Values. Finally, at regular intervals we copy the online DQN to the target DQN, and we save the model.

 Unfortunately, training is very slow: if you use your laptop for training, it will take days before Ms. Pac-Man gets any good. You can plot learning curves, for example measuring the average rewards per game, or computing the max Q-Value estimated by the online DQN at every game step and tracking the mean of these max Q-Values over each game. You will notice that these curves are extremely noisy. At some points there may be no apparent progress for a very long time until suddenly the agent learns to survive a reasonable amount of time. As mentioned earlier, one solution is to inject as much prior knowledge as possible into the model (e.g., through preprocessing, rewards, and so on), and you can also try to bootstrap the model by first training it to imitate a basic strategy. In any case, RL still requires quite a lot of patience and tweaking, but the end result is very exciting.

Exercises

1. How would you define Reinforcement Learning? How is it different from regular supervised or unsupervised learning?

2. Can you think of three possible applications of RL that were not mentioned in this chapter? For each of them, what is the environment? What is the agent? What are possible actions? What are the rewards?

3. What is the discount factor? Can the optimal policy change if you modify the discount factor?

4. How do you measure the performance of a Reinforcement Learning agent?

5. What is the credit assignment problem? When does it occur? How can you alleviate it?

6. What is the point of using a replay memory?

7. What is an off-policy RL algorithm?

8. Use policy gradients to tackle OpenAI gym's "BipedalWalker-v2".

9. Use the DQN algorithm to train an agent to play *Pong*, the famous Atari game (Pong-v0 in the OpenAI gym). Beware: an individual observation is insufficient to tell the direction and speed of the ball.

10. If you have about $100 to spare, you can purchase a Raspberry Pi 3 plus some cheap robotics components, install TensorFlow on the Pi, and go wild! For an example, check out this fun post (*http://homl.info/2*) by Lukas Biewald, or take a look at GoPiGo or BrickPi. Why not try to build a real-life cartpole by training the robot using policy gradients? Or build a robotic spider that learns to walk; give it rewards any time it gets closer to some objective (you will need sensors to measure the distance to the objective). The only limit is your imagination.

Solutions to these exercises are available in Appendix A.

Thank You!

Before we close the last chapter of this book, I would like to thank you for reading it up to the last paragraph. I truly hope that you had as much pleasure reading this book as I had writing it, and that it will be useful for your projects, big or small.

If you find errors, please send feedback. More generally, I would love to know what you think, so please don't hesitate to contact me via O'Reilly, through the *ageron/handson-ml* GitHub project or on Twitter at @aureliengeron.

Going forward, my best advice to you is to practice and practice: try going through all the exercises if you have not done so already, play with the Jupyter notebooks, join Kaggle.com or some other ML community, watch ML courses, read papers, attend conferences, meet experts. You may also want to study some topics that we did not cover in this book, including recommender systems, clustering algorithms, anomaly detection algorithms, and genetic algorithms.

My greatest hope is that this book will inspire you to build a wonderful ML application that will benefit all of us! What will it be?

Aurélien Géron, November 26th, 2016

Exercise Solutions

 Solutions to the coding exercises are available in the online Jupyter notebooks at *https://github.com/ageron/handson-ml*.

Chapter 1: The Machine Learning Landscape

1. Machine Learning is about building systems that can learn from data. Learning means getting better at some task, given some performance measure.

2. Machine Learning is great for complex problems for which we have no algorithmic solution, to replace long lists of hand-tuned rules, to build systems that adapt to fluctuating environments, and finally to help humans learn (e.g., data mining).

3. A labeled training set is a training set that contains the desired solution (a.k.a. a label) for each instance.

4. The two most common supervised tasks are regression and classification.

5. Common unsupervised tasks include clustering, visualization, dimensionality reduction, and association rule learning.

6. Reinforcement Learning is likely to perform best if we want a robot to learn to walk in various unknown terrains since this is typically the type of problem that Reinforcement Learning tackles. It might be possible to express the problem as a supervised or semisupervised learning problem, but it would be less natural.

7. If you don't know how to define the groups, then you can use a clustering algorithm (unsupervised learning) to segment your customers into clusters of similar customers. However, if you know what groups you would like to have, then you

can feed many examples of each group to a classification algorithm (supervised learning), and it will classify all your customers into these groups.

8. Spam detection is a typical supervised learning problem: the algorithm is fed many emails along with their label (spam or not spam).

9. An online learning system can learn incrementally, as opposed to a batch learning system. This makes it capable of adapting rapidly to both changing data and autonomous systems, and of training on very large quantities of data.

10. Out-of-core algorithms can handle vast quantities of data that cannot fit in a computer's main memory. An out-of-core learning algorithm chops the data into mini-batches and uses online learning techniques to learn from these mini-batches.

11. An instance-based learning system learns the training data by heart; then, when given a new instance, it uses a similarity measure to find the most similar learned instances and uses them to make predictions.

12. A model has one or more model parameters that determine what it will predict given a new instance (e.g., the slope of a linear model). A learning algorithm tries to find optimal values for these parameters such that the model generalizes well to new instances. A hyperparameter is a parameter of the learning algorithm itself, not of the model (e.g., the amount of regularization to apply).

13. Model-based learning algorithms search for an optimal value for the model parameters such that the model will generalize well to new instances. We usually train such systems by minimizing a cost function that measures how bad the system is at making predictions on the training data, plus a penalty for model complexity if the model is regularized. To make predictions, we feed the new instance's features into the model's prediction function, using the parameter values found by the learning algorithm.

14. Some of the main challenges in Machine Learning are the lack of data, poor data quality, nonrepresentative data, uninformative features, excessively simple models that underfit the training data, and excessively complex models that overfit the data.

15. If a model performs great on the training data but generalizes poorly to new instances, the model is likely overfitting the training data (or we got extremely lucky on the training data). Possible solutions to overfitting are getting more data, simplifying the model (selecting a simpler algorithm, reducing the number of parameters or features used, or regularizing the model), or reducing the noise in the training data.

16. A test set is used to estimate the generalization error that a model will make on new instances, before the model is launched in production.

17. A validation set is used to compare models. It makes it possible to select the best model and tune the hyperparameters.

18. If you tune hyperparameters using the test set, you risk overfitting the test set, and the generalization error you measure will be optimistic (you may launch a model that performs worse than you expect).

19. Cross-validation is a technique that makes it possible to compare models (for model selection and hyperparameter tuning) without the need for a separate validation set. This saves precious training data.

Chapter 2: End-to-End Machine Learning Project

See the Jupyter notebooks available at *https://github.com/ageron/handson-ml*.

Chapter 3: Classification

See the Jupyter notebooks available at *https://github.com/ageron/handson-ml*.

Chapter 4: Training Models

1. If you have a training set with millions of features you can use Stochastic Gradient Descent or Mini-batch Gradient Descent, and perhaps Batch Gradient Descent if the training set fits in memory. But you cannot use the Normal Equation or the SVD approach because the computational complexity grows quickly (more than quadratically) with the number of features.

2. If the features in your training set have very different scales, the cost function will have the shape of an elongated bowl, so the Gradient Descent algorithms will take a long time to converge. To solve this you should scale the data before training the model. Note that the Normal Equation or SVD approach will work just fine without scaling. Moreover, regularized models may converge to a suboptimal solution if the features are not scaled: indeed, since regularization penalizes large weights, features with smaller values will tend to be ignored compared to features with larger values.

3. Gradient Descent cannot get stuck in a local minimum when training a Logistic Regression model because the cost function is convex.[1]

4. If the optimization problem is convex (such as Linear Regression or Logistic Regression), and assuming the learning rate is not too high, then all Gradient Descent algorithms will approach the global optimum and end up producing

---

1 If you draw a straight line between any two points on the curve, the line never crosses the curve.

fairly similar models. However, unless you gradually reduce the learning rate, Stochastic GD and Mini-batch GD will never truly converge; instead, they will keep jumping back and forth around the global optimum. This means that even if you let them run for a very long time, these Gradient Descent algorithms will produce slightly different models.

5. If the validation error consistently goes up after every epoch, then one possibility is that the learning rate is too high and the algorithm is diverging. If the training error also goes up, then this is clearly the problem and you should reduce the learning rate. However, if the training error is not going up, then your model is overfitting the training set and you should stop training.

6. Due to their random nature, neither Stochastic Gradient Descent nor Mini-batch Gradient Descent is guaranteed to make progress at every single training iteration. So if you immediately stop training when the validation error goes up, you may stop much too early, before the optimum is reached. A better option is to save the model at regular intervals, and when it has not improved for a long time (meaning it will probably never beat the record), you can revert to the best saved model.

7. Stochastic Gradient Descent has the fastest training iteration since it considers only one training instance at a time, so it is generally the first to reach the vicinity of the global optimum (or Mini-batch GD with a very small mini-batch size). However, only Batch Gradient Descent will actually converge, given enough training time. As mentioned, Stochastic GD and Mini-batch GD will bounce around the optimum, unless you gradually reduce the learning rate.

8. If the validation error is much higher than the training error, this is likely because your model is overfitting the training set. One way to try to fix this is to reduce the polynomial degree: a model with fewer degrees of freedom is less likely to overfit. Another thing you can try is to regularize the model—for example, by adding an ℓ_2 penalty (Ridge) or an ℓ_1 penalty (Lasso) to the cost function. This will also reduce the degrees of freedom of the model. Lastly, you can try to increase the size of the training set.

9. If both the training error and the validation error are almost equal and fairly high, the model is likely underfitting the training set, which means it has a high bias. You should try reducing the regularization hyperparameter α.

10. Let's see:

   • A model with some regularization typically performs better than a model without any regularization, so you should generally prefer Ridge Regression over plain Linear Regression.

   • Lasso Regression uses an ℓ_1 penalty, which tends to push the weights down to exactly zero. This leads to sparse models, where all weights are zero except for the most important weights. This is a way to perform feature selection automatically, which is good if you suspect that only a few features actually matter. When you are not sure, you should prefer Ridge Regression.

- Elastic Net is generally preferred over Lasso since Lasso may behave erratically in some cases (when several features are strongly correlated or when there are more features than training instances). However, it does add an extra hyperparameter to tune. If you just want Lasso without the erratic behavior, you can just use Elastic Net with an `l1_ratio` close to 1.

11. If you want to classify pictures as outdoor/indoor and daytime/nighttime, since these are not exclusive classes (i.e., all four combinations are possible) you should train two Logistic Regression classifiers.

12. See the Jupyter notebooks available at *https://github.com/ageron/handson-ml*.

Chapter 5: Support Vector Machines

1. The fundamental idea behind Support Vector Machines is to fit the widest possible "street" between the classes. In other words, the goal is to have the largest possible margin between the decision boundary that separates the two classes and the training instances. When performing soft margin classification, the SVM searches for a compromise between perfectly separating the two classes and having the widest possible street (i.e., a few instances may end up on the street). Another key idea is to use kernels when training on nonlinear datasets.

2. After training an SVM, a *support vector* is any instance located on the "street" (see the previous answer), including its border. The decision boundary is entirely determined by the support vectors. Any instance that is *not* a support vector (i.e., off the street) has no influence whatsoever; you could remove them, add more instances, or move them around, and as long as they stay off the street they won't affect the decision boundary. Computing the predictions only involves the support vectors, not the whole training set.

3. SVMs try to fit the largest possible "street" between the classes (see the first answer), so if the training set is not scaled, the SVM will tend to neglect small features (see Figure 5-2).

4. An SVM classifier can output the distance between the test instance and the decision boundary, and you can use this as a confidence score. However, this score cannot be directly converted into an estimation of the class probability. If you set `probability=True` when creating an SVM in Scikit-Learn, then after training it will calibrate the probabilities using Logistic Regression on the SVM's scores (trained by an additional five-fold cross-validation on the training data). This will add the `predict_proba()` and `predict_log_proba()` methods to the SVM.

5. This question applies only to linear SVMs since kernelized can only use the dual form. The computational complexity of the primal form of the SVM problem is proportional to the number of training instances m, while the computational complexity of the dual form is proportional to a number between m^2 and m^3. So if there are millions of instances, you should definitely use the primal form, because the dual form will be much too slow.

6. If an SVM classifier trained with an RBF kernel underfits the training set, there might be too much regularization. To decrease it, you need to increase gamma or C (or both).

7. Let's call the QP parameters for the hard-margin problem $\mathbf{H}'$, $\mathbf{f}'$, $\mathbf{A}'$ and $\mathbf{b}'$ (see "Quadratic Programming" on page 161). The QP parameters for the soft-margin problem have m additional parameters ($n_p = n + 1 + m$) and m additional constraints ($n_c = 2m$). They can be defined like so:

- $\mathbf{H}$ is equal to $\mathbf{H}'$, plus m columns of 0s on the right and m rows of 0s at the bottom: $\mathbf{H} = \begin{pmatrix} \mathbf{H}' & 0 & \cdots \\ 0 & 0 & \\ \vdots & & \ddots \end{pmatrix}$

- $\mathbf{f}$ is equal to $\mathbf{f}'$ with m additional elements, all equal to the value of the hyperparameter C.

- $\mathbf{b}$ is equal to $\mathbf{b}'$ with m additional elements, all equal to 0.

- $\mathbf{A}$ is equal to $\mathbf{A}'$, with an extra $m \times m$ identity matrix $\mathbf{I}_m$ appended to the right, $-\mathbf{I}_m$ just below it, and the rest filled with zeros: $\mathbf{A} = \begin{pmatrix} \mathbf{A}' & \mathbf{I}_m \\ 0 & -\mathbf{I}_m \end{pmatrix}$

For the solutions to exercises 8, 9, and 10, please see the Jupyter notebooks available at *https://github.com/ageron/handson-ml*.

Chapter 6: Decision Trees

1. The depth of a well-balanced binary tree containing m leaves is equal to $\log_2(m)^2$, rounded up. A binary Decision Tree (one that makes only binary decisions, as is the case of all trees in Scikit-Learn) will end up more or less well balanced at the end of training, with one leaf per training instance if it is trained without restrictions. Thus, if the training set contains one million instances, the Decision Tree will have a depth of $\log_2(10^6) \approx 20$ (actually a bit more since the tree will generally not be perfectly well balanced).

---

2 $\log_2$ is the binary log, $\log_2(m) = \log(m) / \log(2)$.

2. A node's Gini impurity is generally lower than its parent's. This is due to the CART training algorithm's cost function, which splits each node in a way that minimizes the weighted sum of its children's Gini impurities. However, it is possible for a node to have a higher Gini impurity than its parent, as long as this increase is more than compensated for by a decrease of the other child's impurity. For example, consider a node containing four instances of class A and 1 of class B. Its Gini impurity is $1 - \left(\frac{1}{5}\right)^2 - \left(\frac{4}{5}\right)^2 = 0.32$. Now suppose the dataset is one-dimensional and the instances are lined up in the following order: A, B, A, A, A. You can verify that the algorithm will split this node after the second instance, producing one child node with instances A, B, and the other child node with instances A, A, A. The first child node's Gini impurity is $1 - \left(\frac{1}{2}\right)^2 - \left(\frac{1}{2}\right)^2 = 0.5$, which is higher than its parent. This is compensated for by the fact that the other node is pure, so the overall weighted Gini impurity is $\frac{2}{5} \times 0.5 + \frac{3}{5} \times 0 = 0.2$, which is lower than the parent's Gini impurity.

3. If a Decision Tree is overfitting the training set, it may be a good idea to decrease `max_depth`, since this will constrain the model, regularizing it.

4. Decision Trees don't care whether or not the training data is scaled or centered; that's one of the nice things about them. So if a Decision Tree underfits the training set, scaling the input features will just be a waste of time.

5. The computational complexity of training a Decision Tree is $O(n \times m \log(m))$. So if you multiply the training set size by 10, the training time will be multiplied by $K = (n \times 10m \times \log(10m)) / (n \times m \times \log(m)) = 10 \times \log(10m) / \log(m)$. If $m = 10^6$, then $K \approx 11.7$, so you can expect the training time to be roughly 11.7 hours.

6. Presorting the training set speeds up training only if the dataset is smaller than a few thousand instances. If it contains 100,000 instances, setting `presort=True` will considerably slow down training.

For the solutions to exercises 7 and 8, please see the Jupyter notebooks available at *https://github.com/ageron/handson-ml*.

Chapter 7: Ensemble Learning and Random Forests

1. If you have trained five different models and they all achieve 95% precision, you can try combining them into a voting ensemble, which will often give you even better results. It works better if the models are very different (e.g., an SVM classifier, a Decision Tree classifier, a Logistic Regression classifier, and so on). It is even better if they are trained on different training instances (that's the whole point of bagging and pasting ensembles), but if not it will still work as long as the models are very different.

2. A hard voting classifier just counts the votes of each classifier in the ensemble and picks the class that gets the most votes. A soft voting classifier computes the average estimated class probability for each class and picks the class with the highest probability. This gives high-confidence votes more weight and often performs better, but it works only if every classifier is able to estimate class probabilities (e.g., for the SVM classifiers in Scikit-Learn you must set `probability=True`).

3. It is quite possible to speed up training of a bagging ensemble by distributing it across multiple servers, since each predictor in the ensemble is independent of the others. The same goes for pasting ensembles and Random Forests, for the same reason. However, each predictor in a boosting ensemble is built based on the previous predictor, so training is necessarily sequential, and you will not gain anything by distributing training across multiple servers. Regarding stacking ensembles, all the predictors in a given layer are independent of each other, so they can be trained in parallel on multiple servers. However, the predictors in one layer can only be trained after the predictors in the previous layer have all been trained.

4. With out-of-bag evaluation, each predictor in a bagging ensemble is evaluated using instances that it was not trained on (they were held out). This makes it possible to have a fairly unbiased evaluation of the ensemble without the need for an additional validation set. Thus, you have more instances available for training, and your ensemble can perform slightly better.

5. When you are growing a tree in a Random Forest, only a random subset of the features is considered for splitting at each node. This is true as well for Extra-Trees, but they go one step further: rather than searching for the best possible thresholds, like regular Decision Trees do, they use random thresholds for each feature. This extra randomness acts like a form of regularization: if a Random Forest overfits the training data, Extra-Trees might perform better. Moreover, since Extra-Trees don't search for the best possible thresholds, they are much faster to train than Random Forests. However, they are neither faster nor slower than Random Forests when making predictions.

6. If your AdaBoost ensemble underfits the training data, you can try increasing the number of estimators or reducing the regularization hyperparameters of the base estimator. You may also try slightly increasing the learning rate.

7. If your Gradient Boosting ensemble overfits the training set, you should try decreasing the learning rate. You could also use early stopping to find the right number of predictors (you probably have too many).

For the solutions to exercises 8 and 9, please see the Jupyter notebooks available at *https://github.com/ageron/handson-ml*.

Chapter 8: Dimensionality Reduction

1. Motivations and drawbacks:

   - The main motivations for dimensionality reduction are:
     - To speed up a subsequent training algorithm (in some cases it may even remove noise and redundant features, making the training algorithm perform better).
     - To visualize the data and gain insights on the most important features.
     - Simply to save space (compression).
   - The main drawbacks are:
     - Some information is lost, possibly degrading the performance of subsequent training algorithms.
     - It can be computationally intensive.
     - It adds some complexity to your Machine Learning pipelines.
     - Transformed features are often hard to interpret.

2. The curse of dimensionality refers to the fact that many problems that do not exist in low-dimensional space arise in high-dimensional space. In Machine Learning, one common manifestation is the fact that randomly sampled high-dimensional vectors are generally very sparse, increasing the risk of overfitting and making it very difficult to identify patterns in the data without having plenty of training data.

3. Once a dataset's dimensionality has been reduced using one of the algorithms we discussed, it is almost always impossible to perfectly reverse the operation, because some information gets lost during dimensionality reduction. Moreover, while some algorithms (such as PCA) have a simple reverse transformation procedure that can reconstruct a dataset relatively similar to the original, other algorithms (such as T-SNE) do not.

4. PCA can be used to significantly reduce the dimensionality of most datasets, even if they are highly nonlinear, because it can at least get rid of useless dimensions. However, if there are no useless dimensions—for example, the Swiss roll—then reducing dimensionality with PCA will lose too much information. You want to unroll the Swiss roll, not squash it.

5. That's a trick question: it depends on the dataset. Let's look at two extreme examples. First, suppose the dataset is composed of points that are almost perfectly aligned. In this case, PCA can reduce the dataset down to just one dimension while still preserving 95% of the variance. Now imagine that the dataset is composed of perfectly random points, scattered all around the 1,000 dimensions. In

this case roughly 950 dimensions are required to preserve 95% of the variance. So the answer is, it depends on the dataset, and it could be any number between 1 and 950. Plotting the explained variance as a function of the number of dimensions is one way to get a rough idea of the dataset's intrinsic dimensionality.

6. Regular PCA is the default, but it works only if the dataset fits in memory. Incremental PCA is useful for large datasets that don't fit in memory, but it is slower than regular PCA, so if the dataset fits in memory you should prefer regular PCA. Incremental PCA is also useful for online tasks, when you need to apply PCA on the fly, every time a new instance arrives. Randomized PCA is useful when you want to considerably reduce dimensionality and the dataset fits in memory; in this case, it is much faster than regular PCA. Finally, Kernel PCA is useful for nonlinear datasets.

7. Intuitively, a dimensionality reduction algorithm performs well if it eliminates a lot of dimensions from the dataset without losing too much information. One way to measure this is to apply the reverse transformation and measure the reconstruction error. However, not all dimensionality reduction algorithms provide a reverse transformation. Alternatively, if you are using dimensionality reduction as a preprocessing step before another Machine Learning algorithm (e.g., a Random Forest classifier), then you can simply measure the performance of that second algorithm; if dimensionality reduction did not lose too much information, then the algorithm should perform just as well as when using the original dataset.

8. It can absolutely make sense to chain two different dimensionality reduction algorithms. A common example is using PCA to quickly get rid of a large number of useless dimensions, then applying another much slower dimensionality reduction algorithm, such as LLE. This two-step approach will likely yield the same performance as using LLE only, but in a fraction of the time.

For the solutions to exercises 9 and 10, please see the Jupyter notebooks available at *https://github.com/ageron/handson-ml*.

Chapter 9: Up and Running with TensorFlow

1. Main benefits and drawbacks of creating a computation graph rather than directly executing the computations:

   - Main benefits:
     — TensorFlow can automatically compute the gradients for you (using reverse-mode autodiff).
     — TensorFlow can take care of running the operations in parallel in different threads.

— It makes it easier to run the same model across different devices.

— It simplifies introspection—for example, to view the model in TensorBoard.

- Main drawbacks:

— It makes the learning curve steeper.

— It makes step-by-step debugging harder.

2. Yes, the statement `a_val = a.eval(session=sess)` is indeed equivalent to `a_val = sess.run(a)`.

3. No, the statement `a_val, b_val = a.eval(session=sess), b.eval(session=sess)` is not equivalent to `a_val, b_val = sess.run([a, b])`. Indeed, the first statement runs the graph twice (once to compute a, once to compute b), while the second statement runs the graph only once. If any of these operations (or the ops they depend on) have side effects (e.g., a variable is modified, an item is inserted in a queue, or a reader reads a file), then the effects will be different. If they don't have side effects, both statements will return the same result, but the second statement will be faster than the first.

4. No, you cannot run two graphs in the same session. You would have to merge the graphs into a single graph first.

5. In local TensorFlow, sessions manage variable values, so if you create a graph g containing a variable w, then start two threads and open a local session in each thread, both using the same graph g, then each session will have its own copy of the variable w. However, in distributed TensorFlow, variable values are stored in containers managed by the cluster, so if both sessions connect to the same cluster and use the same container, then they will share the same variable value for w.

6. A variable is initialized when you call its initializer, and it is destroyed when the session ends. In distributed TensorFlow, variables live in containers on the cluster, so closing a session will not destroy the variable. To destroy a variable, you need to clear its container.

7. Variables and placeholders are extremely different, but beginners often confuse them:

- A variable is an operation that holds a value. If you run the variable, it returns that value. Before you can run it, you need to initialize it. You can change the variable's value (for example, by using an assignment operation). It is stateful: the variable keeps the same value upon successive runs of the graph. It is typically used to hold model parameters but also for other purposes (e.g., to count the global training step).

- Placeholders technically don't do much: they just hold information about the type and shape of the tensor they represent, but they have no value. In fact, if you try to evaluate an operation that depends on a placeholder, you must feed TensorFlow the value of the placeholder (using the `feed_dict` argument) or else you will get an exception. Placeholders are typically used to feed training or test data to TensorFlow during the execution phase. They are also useful to pass a value to an assignment node, to change the value of a variable (e.g., model weights).

8. If you run the graph to evaluate an operation that depends on a placeholder but you don't feed its value, you get an exception. If the operation does not depend on the placeholder, then no exception is raised.

9. When you run a graph, you can feed the output value of any operation, not just the value of placeholders. In practice, however, this is rather rare (it can be useful, for example, when you are caching the output of frozen layers; see Chapter 11).

10. You can specify a variable's initial value when constructing the graph, and it will be initialized later when you run the variable's initializer during the execution phase. If you want to change that variable's value to anything you want during the execution phase, then the simplest option is to create an assignment node (during the graph construction phase) using the `tf.assign()` function, passing the variable and a placeholder as parameters. During the execution phase, you can run the assignment operation and feed the variable's new value using the placeholder.

```
import tensorflow as tf

x = tf.Variable(tf.random_uniform(shape=(), minval=0.0, maxval=1.0))
x_new_val = tf.placeholder(shape=(), dtype=tf.float32)
x_assign = tf.assign(x, x_new_val)

with tf.Session():
    x.initializer.run() # random number is sampled *now*
    print(x.eval()) # 0.646157 (some random number)
    x_assign.eval(feed_dict={x_new_val: 5.0})
    print(x.eval()) # 5.0
```

11. Reverse-mode autodiff (implemented by TensorFlow) needs to traverse the graph only twice in order to compute the gradients of the cost function with regards to any number of variables. On the other hand, forward-mode autodiff would need to run once for each variable (so 10 times if we want the gradients with regards to 10 different variables). As for symbolic differentiation, it would build a different graph to compute the gradients, so it would not traverse the original graph at all (except when building the new gradients graph). A highly optimized symbolic differentiation system could potentially run the new gradients graph only once to compute the gradients with regards to all variables, but that new graph may be horribly complex and inefficient compared to the original graph.

12. See the Jupyter notebooks available at *https://github.com/ageron/handson-ml*.

Chapter 10: Introduction to Artificial Neural Networks

1. Here is a neural network based on the original artificial neurons that computes $A \oplus B$ (where $\oplus$ represents the exclusive OR), using the fact that $A \oplus B = (A \wedge \neg B) \vee (\neg A \wedge B)$. There are other solutions—for example, using the fact that $A \oplus B = (A \vee B) \wedge \neg(A \wedge B)$, or the fact that $A \oplus B = (A \vee B) \wedge (\neg A \vee \wedge B)$, and so on.

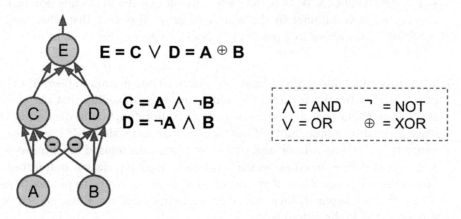

2. A classical Perceptron will converge only if the dataset is linearly separable, and it won't be able to estimate class probabilities. In contrast, a Logistic Regression classifier will converge to a good solution even if the dataset is not linearly separable, and it will output class probabilities. If you change the Perceptron's activation function to the logistic activation function (or the softmax activation function if there are multiple neurons), and if you train it using Gradient Descent (or some other optimization algorithm minimizing the cost function, typically cross entropy), then it becomes equivalent to a Logistic Regression classifier.

3. The logistic activation function was a key ingredient in training the first MLPs because its derivative is always nonzero, so Gradient Descent can always roll down the slope. When the activation function is a step function, Gradient Descent cannot move, as there is no slope at all.

4. The step function, the logistic function, the hyperbolic tangent, the rectified linear unit (see Figure 10-8). See Chapter 11 for other examples, such as ELU and variants of the ReLU.

5. Considering the MLP described in the question: suppose you have an MLP composed of one input layer with 10 passthrough neurons, followed by one hidden layer with 50 artificial neurons, and finally one output layer with 3 artificial neurons. All artificial neurons use the ReLU activation function.

- The shape of the input matrix X is $m \times 10$, where m represents the training batch size.
- The shape of the hidden layer's weight vector W_h is 10×50 and the length of its bias vector b_h is 50.
- The shape of the output layer's weight vector W_o is 50×3, and the length of its bias vector b_o is 3.
- The shape of the network's output matrix Y is $m \times 3$.
- $Y = \text{ReLU}(\text{ReLU}(X\ W_h + b_h)\ W_o + b_o)$. Recall that the ReLU function just sets every negative number in the matrix to zero. Also note that when you are adding a bias vector to a matrix, it is added to every single row in the matrix, which is called *broadcasting*.

6. To classify email into spam or ham, you just need one neuron in the output layer of a neural network—for example, indicating the probability that the email is spam. You would typically use the logistic activation function in the output layer when estimating a probability. If instead you want to tackle MNIST, you need 10 neurons in the output layer, and you must replace the logistic function with the softmax activation function, which can handle multiple classes, outputting one probability per class. Now, if you want your neural network to predict housing prices like in Chapter 2, then you need one output neuron, using no activation function at all in the output layer.[3]

7. Backpropagation is a technique used to train artificial neural networks. It first computes the gradients of the cost function with regards to every model parameter (all the weights and biases), and then it performs a Gradient Descent step using these gradients. This backpropagation step is typically performed thousands or millions of times, using many training batches, until the model parameters converge to values that (hopefully) minimize the cost function. To compute the gradients, backpropagation uses reverse-mode autodiff (although it wasn't called that when backpropagation was invented, and it has been reinvented several times). Reverse-mode autodiff performs a forward pass through a computation graph, computing every node's value for the current training batch, and then it performs a reverse pass, computing all the gradients at once (see Appendix D for more details). So what's the difference? Well, backpropagation refers to the whole process of training an artificial neural network using multiple backpropagation steps, each of which computes gradients and uses them to perform a Gra-

---

3 When the values to predict can vary by many orders of magnitude, then you may want to predict the logarithm of the target value rather than the target value directly. Simply computing the exponential of the neural network's output will give you the estimated value (since $\exp(\log v) = v$).

dient Descent step. In contrast, reverse-mode autodiff is a simply a technique to compute gradients efficiently, and it happens to be used by backpropagation.

8. Here is a list of all the hyperparameters you can tweak in a basic MLP: the number of hidden layers, the number of neurons in each hidden layer, and the activation function used in each hidden layer and in the output layer.[4] In general, the ReLU activation function (or one of its variants; see Chapter 11) is a good default for the hidden layers. For the output layer, in general you will want the logistic activation function for binary classification, the softmax activation function for multiclass classification, or no activation function for regression.

   If the MLP overfits the training data, you can try reducing the number of hidden layers and reducing the number of neurons per hidden layer.

9. See the Jupyter notebooks available at *https://github.com/ageron/handson-ml*.

Chapter 11: Training Deep Neural Nets

1. No, all weights should be sampled independently; they should not all have the same initial value. One important goal of sampling weights randomly is to break symmetries: if all the weights have the same initial value, even if that value is not zero, then symmetry is not broken (i.e., all neurons in a given layer are equivalent), and backpropagation will be unable to break it. Concretely, this means that all the neurons in any given layer will always have the same weights. It's like having just one neuron per layer, and much slower. It is virtually impossible for such a configuration to converge to a good solution.

2. It is perfectly fine to initialize the bias terms to zero. Some people like to initialize them just like weights, and that's okay too; it does not make much difference.

3. A few advantages of the ELU function over the ReLU function are:

   • It can take on negative values, so the average output of the neurons in any given layer is typically closer to 0 than when using the ReLU activation function (which never outputs negative values). This helps alleviate the vanishing gradients problem.

   • It always has a nonzero derivative, which avoids the dying units issue that can affect ReLU units.

---

4 In Chapter 11 we discuss many techniques that introduce additional hyperparameters: type of weight initialization, activation function hyperparameters (e.g., amount of leak in leaky ReLU), Gradient Clipping threshold, type of optimizer and its hyperparameters (e.g., the momentum hyperparameter when using a MomentumOptimizer), type of regularization for each layer, and the regularization hyperparameters (e.g., dropout rate when using dropout) and so on.

- It is smooth everywhere, whereas the ReLU's slope abruptly jumps from 0 to 1 at $z = 0$. Such an abrupt change can slow down Gradient Descent because it will bounce around $z = 0$.

4. The ELU activation function is a good default. If you need the neural network to be as fast as possible, you can use one of the leaky ReLU variants instead (e.g., a simple leaky ReLU using the default hyperparameter value). The simplicity of the ReLU activation function makes it many people's preferred option, despite the fact that they are generally outperformed by the ELU and leaky ReLU. However, the ReLU activation function's capability of outputting precisely zero can be useful in some cases (e.g., see Chapter 15). The hyperbolic tangent (tanh) can be useful in the output layer if you need to output a number between –1 and 1, but nowadays it is not used much in hidden layers. The logistic activation function is also useful in the output layer when you need to estimate a probability (e.g., for binary classification), but it is also rarely used in hidden layers (there are exceptions—for example, for the coding layer of variational autoencoders; see Chapter 15). Finally, the softmax activation function is useful in the output layer to output probabilities for mutually exclusive classes, but other than that it is rarely (if ever) used in hidden layers.

5. If you set the momentum hyperparameter too close to 1 (e.g., 0.99999) when using a MomentumOptimizer, then the algorithm will likely pick up a lot of speed, hopefully roughly toward the global minimum, but then it will shoot right past the minimum, due to its momentum. Then it will slow down and come back, accelerate again, overshoot again, and so on. It may oscillate this way many times before converging, so overall it will take much longer to converge than with a smaller momentum value.

6. One way to produce a sparse model (i.e., with most weights equal to zero) is to train the model normally, then zero out tiny weights. For more sparsity, you can apply ℓ_1 regularization during training, which pushes the optimizer toward sparsity. A third option is to combine ℓ_1 regularization with *dual averaging*, using TensorFlow's FTRLOptimizer class.

7. Yes, dropout does slow down training, in general roughly by a factor of two. However, it has no impact on inference since it is only turned on during training.

For the solutions to exercises 8, 9, and 10, please see the Jupyter notebooks available at *https://github.com/ageron/handson-ml*.

Chapter 12: Distributing TensorFlow Across Devices and Servers

1. When a TensorFlow process starts, it grabs all the available memory on all GPU devices that are visible to it, so if you get a CUDA_ERROR_OUT_OF_MEMORY when starting your TensorFlow program, it probably means that other processes are running that have already grabbed all the memory on at least one visible GPU device (most likely it is another TensorFlow process). To fix this problem, a trivial solution is to stop the other processes and try again. However, if you need all processes to run simultaneously, a simple option is to dedicate different devices to each process, by setting the CUDA_VISIBLE_DEVICES environment variable appropriately for each device. Another option is to configure TensorFlow to grab only part of the GPU memory, instead of all of it, by creating a ConfigProto, setting its gpu_options.per_process_gpu_memory_fraction to the proportion of the total memory that it should grab (e.g., 0.4), and using this ConfigProto when opening a session. The last option is to tell TensorFlow to grab memory only when it needs it by setting the gpu_options.allow_growth to True. However, this last option is usually not recommended because any memory that Tensor-Flow grabs is never released, and it is harder to guarantee a repeatable behavior (there may be race conditions depending on which processes start first, how much memory they need during training, and so on).

2. By pinning an operation on a device, you are telling TensorFlow that this is where you would like this operation to be placed. However, some constraints may prevent TensorFlow from honoring your request. For example, the operation may have no implementation (called a *kernel*) for that particular type of device. In this case, TensorFlow will raise an exception by default, but you can configure it to fall back to the CPU instead (this is called *soft placement*). Another example is an operation that can modify a variable; this operation and the variable need to be collocated. So the difference between pinning an operation and placing an operation is that pinning is what you ask TensorFlow ("Please place this operation on GPU #1") while placement is what TensorFlow actually ends up doing ("Sorry, falling back to the CPU").

3. If you are running on a GPU-enabled TensorFlow installation, and you just use the default placement, then if all operations have a GPU kernel (i.e., a GPU implementation), yes, they will all be placed on the first GPU. However, if one or more operations do not have a GPU kernel, then by default TensorFlow will raise an exception. If you configure TensorFlow to fall back to the CPU instead (soft placement), then all operations will be placed on the first GPU except the ones without a GPU kernel and all the operations that must be collocated with them (see the answer to the previous exercise).

4. Yes, if you pin a variable to `/gpu:0`, it can be used by operations placed on `/gpu:1`. TensorFlow will automatically take care of adding the appropriate operations to transfer the variable's value across devices. The same goes for devices located on different servers (as long as they are part of the same cluster).

5. Yes, two operations placed on the same device can run in parallel: TensorFlow automatically takes care of running operations in parallel (on different CPU cores or different GPU threads), as long as no operation depends on another operation's output. Moreover, you can start multiple sessions in parallel threads (or processes), and evaluate operations in each thread. Since sessions are independent, TensorFlow will be able to evaluate any operation from one session in parallel with any operation from another session.

6. Control dependencies are used when you want to postpone the evaluation of an operation X until after some other operations are run, even though these operations are not required to compute X. This is useful in particular when X would occupy a lot of memory and you only need it later in the computation graph, or if X uses up a lot of I/O (for example, it requires a large variable value located on a different device or server) and you don't want it to run at the same time as other I/O-hungry operations, to avoid saturating the bandwidth.

7. You're in luck! In distributed TensorFlow, the variable values live in containers managed by the cluster, so even if you close the session and exit the client program, the model parameters are still alive and well on the cluster. You simply need to open a new session to the cluster and save the model (make sure you don't call the variable initializers or restore a previous model, as this would destroy your precious new model!).

For the solutions to exercises 8, 9, and 10, please see the Jupyter notebooks available at *https://github.com/ageron/handson-ml*.

Chapter 13: Convolutional Neural Networks

1. These are the main advantages of a CNN over a fully connected DNN for image classification:

   - Because consecutive layers are only partially connected and because it heavily reuses its weights, a CNN has many fewer parameters than a fully connected DNN, which makes it much faster to train, reduces the risk of overfitting, and requires much less training data.

   - When a CNN has learned a kernel that can detect a particular feature, it can detect that feature anywhere on the image. In contrast, when a DNN learns a feature in one location, it can detect it only in that particular location. Since images typically have very repetitive features, CNNs are able to generalize much better than DNNs for image processing tasks such as classification, using fewer training examples.

- Finally, a DNN has no prior knowledge of how pixels are organized; it does not know that nearby pixels are close. A CNN's architecture embeds this prior knowledge. Lower layers typically identify features in small areas of the images, while higher layers combine the lower-level features into larger features. This works well with most natural images, giving CNNs a decisive head start compared to DNNs.

2. Let's compute how many parameters the CNN has. Since its first convolutional layer has 3×3 kernels, and the input has three channels (red, green, and blue), then each feature map has $3 \times 3 \times 3$ weights, plus a bias term. That's 28 parameters per feature map. Since this first convolutional layer has 100 feature maps, it has a total of 2,800 parameters. The second convolutional layer has 3×3 kernels, and its input is the set of 100 feature maps of the previous layer, so each feature map has $3 \times 3 \times 100 = 900$ weights, plus a bias term. Since it has 200 feature maps, this layer has $901 \times 200 = 180,200$ parameters. Finally, the third and last convolutional layer also has 3×3 kernels, and its input is the set of 200 feature maps of the previous layers, so each feature map has $3 \times 3 \times 200 = 1,800$ weights, plus a bias term. Since it has 400 feature maps, this layer has a total of $1,801 \times 400 = 720,400$ parameters. All in all, the CNN has $2,800 + 180,200 + 720,400 = 903,400$ parameters.

Now let's compute how much RAM this neural network will require (at least) when making a prediction for a single instance. First let's compute the feature map size for each layer. Since we are using a stride of 2 and SAME padding, the horizontal and vertical size of the feature maps are divided by 2 at each layer (rounding up if necessary), so as the input channels are 200×300 pixels, the first layer's feature maps are 100×150, the second layer's feature maps are 50×75, and the third layer's feature maps are 25×38. Since 32 bits is 4 bytes and the first convolutional layer has 100 feature maps, this first layer takes up $4 \times 100 \times 150 \times 100 = 6$ million bytes (about 5.7 MB, considering that 1 MB = 1,024 KB and 1 KB = 1,024 bytes). The second layer takes up $4 \times 50 \times 75 \times 200 = 3$ million bytes (about 2.9 MB). Finally, the third layer takes up $4 \times 25 \times 38 \times 400 = 1,520,000$ bytes (about 1.4 MB). However, once a layer has been computed, the memory occupied by the previous layer can be released, so if everything is well optimized, only $6 + 3 = 9$ million bytes (about 8.6 MB) of RAM will be required (when the second layer has just been computed, but the memory occupied by the first layer is not released yet). But wait, you also need to add the memory occupied by the CNN's parameters. We computed earlier that it has 903,400 parameters, each using up 4 bytes, so this adds 3,613,600 bytes (about 3.4 MB). The total RAM required is (at least) 12,613,600 bytes (about 12.0 MB).

Lastly, let's compute the minimum amount of RAM required when training the CNN on a mini-batch of 50 images. During training TensorFlow uses backpropagation, which requires keeping all values computed during the forward pass until the reverse pass begins. So we must compute the total RAM required by all layers for a single instance and multiply that by 50! At that point let's start counting in megabytes rather than bytes. We computed before that the three layers require respectively 5.7, 2.9, and 1.4 MB for each instance. That's a total of 10.0 MB per instance. So for 50 instances the total RAM is 500 MB. Add to that the RAM required by the input images, which is $50 \times 4 \times 200 \times 300 \times 3 = 36$ million bytes (about 34.3 MB), plus the RAM required for the model parameters, which is about 3.4 MB (computed earlier), plus some RAM for the gradients (we will neglect them since they can be released gradually as backpropagation goes down the layers during the reverse pass). We are up to a total of roughly 500.0 + 34.3 + 3.4 = 537.7 MB. And that's really an optimistic bare minimum.

3. If your GPU runs out of memory while training a CNN, here are five things you could try to solve the problem (other than purchasing a GPU with more RAM):

   - Reduce the mini-batch size.

   - Reduce dimensionality using a larger stride in one or more layers.

   - Remove one or more layers.

   - Use 16-bit floats instead of 32-bit floats.

   - Distribute the CNN across multiple devices.

4. A max pooling layer has no parameters at all, whereas a convolutional layer has quite a few (see the previous questions).

5. A *local response normalization* layer makes the neurons that most strongly activate inhibit neurons at the same location but in neighboring feature maps, which encourages different feature maps to specialize and pushes them apart, forcing them to explore a wider range of features. It is typically used in the lower layers to have a larger pool of low-level features that the upper layers can build upon.

6. The main innovations in AlexNet compared to LeNet-5 are (1) it is much larger and deeper, and (2) it stacks convolutional layers directly on top of each other, instead of stacking a pooling layer on top of each convolutional layer. The main innovation in GoogLeNet is the introduction of *inception modules*, which make it possible to have a much deeper net than previous CNN architectures, with fewer parameters. Finally, ResNet's main innovation is the introduction of skip connections, which make it possible to go well beyond 100 layers. Arguably, its simplicity and consistency are also rather innovative.

For the solutions to exercises 7, 8, 9, and 10, please see the Jupyter notebooks available at *https://github.com/ageron/handson-ml*.

Chapter 14: Recurrent Neural Networks

1. Here are a few RNN applications:

   - For a sequence-to-sequence RNN: predicting the weather (or any other time series), machine translation (using an encoder–decoder architecture), video captioning, speech to text, music generation (or other sequence generation), identifying the chords of a song.

   - For a sequence-to-vector RNN: classifying music samples by music genre, analyzing the sentiment of a book review, predicting what word an aphasic patient is thinking of based on readings from brain implants, predicting the probability that a user will want to watch a movie based on her watch history (this is one of many possible implementations of *collaborative filtering*).

   - For a vector-to-sequence RNN: image captioning, creating a music playlist based on an embedding of the current artist, generating a melody based on a set of parameters, locating pedestrians in a picture (e.g., a video frame from a self-driving car's camera).

2. In general, if you translate a sentence one word at a time, the result will be terrible. For example, the French sentence "Je vous en prie" means "You are welcome," but if you translate it one word at a time, you get "I you in pray." Huh? It is much better to read the whole sentence first and then translate it. A plain sequence-to-sequence RNN would start translating a sentence immediately after reading the first word, while an encoder–decoder RNN will first read the whole sentence and then translate it. That said, one could imagine a plain sequence-to-sequence RNN that would output silence whenever it is unsure about what to say next (just like human translators do when they must translate a live broadcast).

3. To classify videos based on the visual content, one possible architecture could be to take (say) one frame per second, then run each frame through a convolutional neural network, feed the output of the CNN to a sequence-to-vector RNN, and finally run its output through a softmax layer, giving you all the class probabilities. For training you would just use cross entropy as the cost function. If you wanted to use the audio for classification as well, you could convert every second of audio to a spectrograph, feed this spectrograph to a CNN, and feed the output of this CNN to the RNN (along with the corresponding output of the other CNN).

4. Building an RNN using `dynamic_rnn()` rather than `static_rnn()` offers several advantages:

   - It is based on a `while_loop()` operation that is able to swap the GPU's memory to the CPU's memory during backpropagation, avoiding out-of-memory errors.

- It is arguably easier to use, as it can directly take a single tensor as input and output (covering all time steps), rather than a list of tensors (one per time step). No need to stack, unstack, or transpose.
- It generates a smaller graph, easier to visualize in TensorBoard.

5. To handle variable length input sequences, the simplest option is to set the sequence_length parameter when calling the static_rnn() or dynamic_rnn() functions. Another option is to pad the smaller inputs (e.g., with zeros) to make them the same size as the largest input (this may be faster than the first option if the input sequences all have very similar lengths). To handle variable-length output sequences, if you know in advance the length of each output sequence, you can use the sequence_length parameter (for example, consider a sequence-to-sequence RNN that labels every frame in a video with a violence score: the output sequence will be exactly the same length as the input sequence). If you don't know in advance the length of the output sequence, you can use the padding trick: always output the same size sequence, but ignore any outputs that come after the end-of-sequence token (by ignoring them when computing the cost function).

6. To distribute training and execution of a deep RNN across multiple GPUs, a common technique is simply to place each layer on a different GPU (see Chapter 12).

For the solutions to exercises 7, 8, and 9, please see the Jupyter notebooks available at *https://github.com/ageron/handson-ml.*

Chapter 15: Autoencoders

1. Here are some of the main tasks that autoencoders are used for:

- Feature extraction
- Unsupervised pretraining
- Dimensionality reduction
- Generative models
- Anomaly detection (an autoencoder is generally bad at reconstructing outliers)

2. If you want to train a classifier and you have plenty of unlabeled training data, but only a few thousand labeled instances, then you could first train a deep autoencoder on the full dataset (labeled + unlabeled), then reuse its lower half for the classifier (i.e., reuse the layers up to the codings layer, included) and train the classifier using the labeled data. If you have little labeled data, you probably want to freeze the reused layers when training the classifier.

3. The fact that an autoencoder perfectly reconstructs its inputs does not necessarily mean that it is a good autoencoder; perhaps it is simply an overcomplete autoencoder that learned to copy its inputs to the codings layer and then to the outputs. In fact, even if the codings layer contained a single neuron, it would be possible for a very deep autoencoder to learn to map each training instance to a different coding (e.g., the first instance could be mapped to 0.001, the second to 0.002, the third to 0.003, and so on), and it could learn "by heart" to reconstruct the right training instance for each coding. It would perfectly reconstruct its inputs without really learning any useful pattern in the data. In practice such a mapping is unlikely to happen, but it illustrates the fact that perfect reconstructions are not a guarantee that the autoencoder learned anything useful. However, if it produces very bad reconstructions, then it is almost guaranteed to be a bad autoencoder. To evaluate the performance of an autoencoder, one option is to measure the reconstruction loss (e.g., compute the MSE, the mean square of the outputs minus the inputs). Again, a high reconstruction loss is a good sign that the autoencoder is bad, but a low reconstruction loss is not a guarantee that it is good. You should also evaluate the autoencoder according to what it will be used for. For example, if you are using it for unsupervised pretraining of a classifier, then you should also evaluate the classifier's performance.

4. An undercomplete autoencoder is one whose codings layer is smaller than the input and output layers. If it is larger, then it is an overcomplete autoencoder. The main risk of an excessively undercomplete autoencoder is that it may fail to reconstruct the inputs. The main risk of an overcomplete autoencoder is that it may just copy the inputs to the outputs, without learning any useful feature.

5. To tie the weights of an encoder layer and its corresponding decoder layer, you simply make the decoder weights equal to the transpose of the encoder weights. This reduces the number of parameters in the model by half, often making training converge faster with less training data, and reducing the risk of overfitting the training set.

6. To visualize the features learned by the lower layer of a stacked autoencoder, a common technique is simply to plot the weights of each neuron, by reshaping each weight vector to the size of an input image (e.g., for MNIST, reshaping a weight vector of shape [784] to [28, 28]). To visualize the features learned by higher layers, one technique is to display the training instances that most activate each neuron.

7. A generative model is a model capable of randomly generating outputs that resemble the training instances. For example, once trained successfully on the MNIST dataset, a generative model can be used to randomly generate realistic images of digits. The output distribution is typically similar to the training data. For example, since MNIST contains many images of each digit, the generative model would output roughly the same number of images of each digit. Some

generative models can be parametrized—for example, to generate only some kinds of outputs. An example of a generative autoencoder is the variational autoencoder.

For the solutions to exercises 8, 9, and 10, please see the Jupyter notebooks available at *https://github.com/ageron/handson-ml*.

Chapter 16: Reinforcement Learning

1. Reinforcement Learning is an area of Machine Learning aimed at creating agents capable of taking actions in an environment in a way that maximizes rewards over time. There are many differences between RL and regular supervised and unsupervised learning. Here are a few:

   - In supervised and unsupervised learning, the goal is generally to find patterns in the data and use them to make predictions. In Reinforcement Learning, the goal is to find a good policy.

   - Unlike in supervised learning, the agent is not explicitly given the "right" answer. It must learn by trial and error.

   - Unlike in unsupervised learning, there is a form of supervision, through rewards. We do not tell the agent how to perform the task, but we do tell it when it is making progress or when it is failing.

   - A Reinforcement Learning agent needs to find the right balance between exploring the environment, looking for new ways of getting rewards, and exploiting sources of rewards that it already knows. In contrast, supervised and unsupervised learning systems generally don't need to worry about exploration; they just feed on the training data they are given.

   - In supervised and unsupervised learning, training instances are typically independent (in fact, they are generally shuffled). In Reinforcement Learning, consecutive observations are generally *not* independent. An agent may remain in the same region of the environment for a while before it moves on, so consecutive observations will be very correlated. In some cases a replay memory is used to ensure that the training algorithm gets fairly independent observations.

2. Here are a few possible applications of Reinforcement Learning, other than those mentioned in Chapter 16:

   Music personalization
   The environment is a user's personalized web radio. The agent is the software deciding what song to play next for that user. Its possible actions are to play any song in the catalog (it must try to choose a song the user will enjoy) or to

play an advertisement (it must try to choose an ad that the user will be interested in). It gets a small reward every time the user listens to a song, a larger reward every time the user listens to an ad, a negative reward when the user skips a song or an ad, and a very negative reward if the user leaves.

Marketing

The environment is your company's marketing department. The agent is the software that defines which customers a mailing campaign should be sent to, given their profile and purchase history (for each customer it has two possible actions: send or don't send). It gets a negative reward for the cost of the mailing campaign, and a positive reward for estimated revenue generated from this campaign.

Product delivery

Let the agent control a fleet of delivery trucks, deciding what they should pick up at the depots, where they should go, what they should drop off, and so on. They would get positive rewards for each product delivered on time, and negative rewards for late deliveries.

3. When estimating the value of an action, Reinforcement Learning algorithms typically sum all the rewards that this action led to, giving more weight to immediate rewards, and less weight to later rewards (considering that an action has more influence on the near future than on the distant future). To model this, a discount factor is typically applied at each time step. For example, with a discount factor of 0.9, a reward of 100 that is received two time steps later is counted as only $0.9^2 \times 100 = 81$ when you are estimating the value of the action. You can think of the discount factor as a measure of how much the future is valued relative to the present: if it is very close to 1, then the future is valued almost as much as the present. If it is close to 0, then only immediate rewards matter. Of course, this impacts the optimal policy tremendously: if you value the future, you may be willing to put up with a lot of immediate pain for the prospect of eventual rewards, while if you don't value the future, you will just grab any immediate reward you can find, never investing in the future.

4. To measure the performance of a Reinforcement Learning agent, you can simply sum up the rewards it gets. In a simulated environment, you can run many episodes and look at the total rewards it gets on average (and possibly look at the min, max, standard deviation, and so on).

5. The credit assignment problem is the fact that when a Reinforcement Learning agent receives a reward, it has no direct way of knowing which of its previous actions contributed to this reward. It typically occurs when there is a large delay between an action and the resulting rewards (e.g., during a game of Atari's *Pong*, there may be a few dozen time steps between the moment the agent hits the ball and the moment it wins the point). One way to alleviate it is to provide the agent

with shorter-term rewards, when possible. This usually requires prior knowledge about the task. For example, if we want to build an agent that will learn to play chess, instead of giving it a reward only when it wins the game, we could give it a reward every time it captures one of the opponent's pieces.

6. An agent can often remain in the same region of its environment for a while, so all of its experiences will be very similar for that period of time. This can introduce some bias in the learning algorithm. It may tune its policy for this region of the environment, but it will not perform well as soon as it moves out of this region. To solve this problem, you can use a replay memory; instead of using only the most immediate experiences for learning, the agent will learn based on a buffer of its past experiences, recent and not so recent (perhaps this is why we dream at night: to replay our experiences of the day and better learn from them?).

7. An off-policy RL algorithm learns the value of the optimal policy (i.e., the sum of discounted rewards that can be expected for each state if the agent acts optimally) while the agent follows a different policy. Q-Learning is a good example of such an algorithm. In contrast, an on-policy algorithm learns the value of the policy that the agent actually executes, including both exploration and exploitation.

For the solutions to exercises 8, 9, and 10, please see the Jupyter notebooks available at *https://github.com/ageron/handson-ml*.

Machine Learning Project Checklist

This checklist can guide you through your Machine Learning projects. There are eight main steps:

1. Frame the problem and look at the big picture.
2. Get the data.
3. Explore the data to gain insights.
4. Prepare the data to better expose the underlying data patterns to Machine Learning algorithms.
5. Explore many different models and short-list the best ones.
6. Fine-tune your models and combine them into a great solution.
7. Present your solution.
8. Launch, monitor, and maintain your system.

Obviously, you should feel free to adapt this checklist to your needs.

Frame the Problem and Look at the Big Picture

1. Define the objective in business terms.
2. How will your solution be used?
3. What are the current solutions/workarounds (if any)?
4. How should you frame this problem (supervised/unsupervised, online/offline, etc.)?
5. How should performance be measured?
6. Is the performance measure aligned with the business objective?

7. What would be the minimum performance needed to reach the business objective?

8. What are comparable problems? Can you reuse experience or tools?

9. Is human expertise available?

10. How would you solve the problem manually?

11. List the assumptions you (or others) have made so far.

12. Verify assumptions if possible.

Get the Data

Note: automate as much as possible so you can easily get fresh data.

1. List the data you need and how much you need.

2. Find and document where you can get that data.

3. Check how much space it will take.

4. Check legal obligations, and get authorization if necessary.

5. Get access authorizations.

6. Create a workspace (with enough storage space).

7. Get the data.

8. Convert the data to a format you can easily manipulate (without changing the data itself).

9. Ensure sensitive information is deleted or protected (e.g., anonymized).

10. Check the size and type of data (time series, sample, geographical, etc.).

11. Sample a test set, put it aside, and never look at it (no data snooping!).

Explore the Data

Note: try to get insights from a field expert for these steps.

1. Create a copy of the data for exploration (sampling it down to a manageable size if necessary).

2. Create a Jupyter notebook to keep a record of your data exploration.

3. Study each attribute and its characteristics:

   • Name

   • Type (categorical, int/float, bounded/unbounded, text, structured, etc.)

- % of missing values
- Noisiness and type of noise (stochastic, outliers, rounding errors, etc.)
- Possibly useful for the task?
- Type of distribution (Gaussian, uniform, logarithmic, etc.)

4. For supervised learning tasks, identify the target attribute(s).
5. Visualize the data.
6. Study the correlations between attributes.
7. Study how you would solve the problem manually.
8. Identify the promising transformations you may want to apply.
9. Identify extra data that would be useful (go back to "Get the Data" on page 508).
10. Document what you have learned.

Prepare the Data

Notes:

- Work on copies of the data (keep the original dataset intact).
- Write functions for all data transformations you apply, for five reasons:
    — So you can easily prepare the data the next time you get a fresh dataset
    — So you can apply these transformations in future projects
    — To clean and prepare the test set
    — To clean and prepare new data instances once your solution is live
    — To make it easy to treat your preparation choices as hyperparameters

1. Data cleaning:
    - Fix or remove outliers (optional).
    - Fill in missing values (e.g., with zero, mean, median...) or drop their rows (or columns).

2. Feature selection (optional):
    - Drop the attributes that provide no useful information for the task.

3. Feature engineering, where appropriate:
    - Discretize continuous features.

- Decompose features (e.g., categorical, date/time, etc.).
- Add promising transformations of features (e.g., $\log(x)$, $\text{sqrt}(x)$, x^2, etc.).
- Aggregate features into promising new features.

4. Feature scaling: standardize or normalize features.

Short-List Promising Models

Notes:

- If the data is huge, you may want to sample smaller training sets so you can train many different models in a reasonable time (be aware that this penalizes complex models such as large neural nets or Random Forests).
- Once again, try to automate these steps as much as possible.

1. Train many quick and dirty models from different categories (e.g., linear, naive Bayes, SVM, Random Forests, neural net, etc.) using standard parameters.
2. Measure and compare their performance.

   - For each model, use N-fold cross-validation and compute the mean and standard deviation of the performance measure on the N folds.

3. Analyze the most significant variables for each algorithm.
4. Analyze the types of errors the models make.

   - What data would a human have used to avoid these errors?

5. Have a quick round of feature selection and engineering.
6. Have one or two more quick iterations of the five previous steps.
7. Short-list the top three to five most promising models, preferring models that make different types of errors.

Fine-Tune the System

Notes:

- You will want to use as much data as possible for this step, especially as you move toward the end of fine-tuning.
- As always automate what you can.

1. Fine-tune the hyperparameters using cross-validation.

   - Treat your data transformation choices as hyperparameters, especially when you are not sure about them (e.g., should I replace missing values with zero or with the median value? Or just drop the rows?).

   - Unless there are very few hyperparameter values to explore, prefer random search over grid search. If training is very long, you may prefer a Bayesian optimization approach (e.g., using Gaussian process priors, as described by Jasper Snoek, Hugo Larochelle, and Ryan Adams (*http://homl.info/134*)).[1]

2. Try Ensemble methods. Combining your best models will often perform better than running them individually.

3. Once you are confident about your final model, measure its performance on the test set to estimate the generalization error.

 Don't tweak your model after measuring the generalization error: you would just start overfitting the test set.

Present Your Solution

1. Document what you have done.

2. Create a nice presentation.

   - Make sure you highlight the big picture first.

3. Explain why your solution achieves the business objective.

4. Don't forget to present interesting points you noticed along the way.

   - Describe what worked and what did not.

   - List your assumptions and your system's limitations.

5. Ensure your key findings are communicated through beautiful visualizations or easy-to-remember statements (e.g., "the median income is the number-one predictor of housing prices").

---

1 "Practical Bayesian Optimization of Machine Learning Algorithms," J. Snoek, H. Larochelle, R. Adams (2012).

Launch!

1. Get your solution ready for production (plug into production data inputs, write unit tests, etc.).

2. Write monitoring code to check your system's live performance at regular intervals and trigger alerts when it drops.

   - Beware of slow degradation too: models tend to "rot" as data evolves.

   - Measuring performance may require a human pipeline (e.g., via a crowdsourcing service).

   - Also monitor your inputs' quality (e.g., a malfunctioning sensor sending random values, or another team's output becoming stale). This is particularly important for online learning systems.

3. Retrain your models on a regular basis on fresh data (automate as much as possible).

SVM Dual Problem

To understand *duality*, you first need to understand the *Lagrange multipliers* method. The general idea is to transform a constrained optimization objective into an unconstrained one, by moving the constraints into the objective function. Let's look at a simple example. Suppose you want to find the values of x and y that minimize the function $f(x,y) = x^2 + 2y$, subject to an *equality constraint*: $3x + 2y + 1 = 0$. Using the Lagrange multipliers method, we start by defining a new function called the *Lagrangian* (or *Lagrange function*): $g(x, y, \alpha) = f(x, y) - \alpha(3x + 2y + 1)$. Each constraint (in this case just one) is subtracted from the original objective, multiplied by a new variable called a Lagrange multiplier.

Joseph-Louis Lagrange showed that if $(\hat{x}, \hat{y})$ is a solution to the constrained optimization problem, then there must exist an $\hat{\alpha}$ such that $(\hat{x}, \hat{y}, \hat{\alpha})$ is a *stationary point* of the Lagrangian (a stationary point is a point where all partial derivatives are equal to zero). In other words, we can compute the partial derivatives of $g(x, y, \alpha)$ with regards to x, y, and α; we can find the points where these derivatives are all equal to zero; and the solutions to the constrained optimization problem (if they exist) must be among these stationary points.

In this example the partial derivatives are: $\begin{cases} \frac{\partial}{\partial x}g(x, y, \alpha) = 2x - 3\alpha \\ \frac{\partial}{\partial y}g(x, y, \alpha) = 2 - 2\alpha \\ \frac{\partial}{\partial \alpha}g(x, y, \alpha) = -3x - 2y - 1 \end{cases}$

When all these partial derivatives are equal to 0, we find that $2\hat{x} - 3\hat{\alpha} = 2 - 2\hat{\alpha} = -3\hat{x} - 2\hat{y} - 1 = 0$, from which we can easily find that $\hat{x} = \frac{3}{2}$, $\hat{y} = -\frac{11}{4}$, and $\hat{\alpha} = 1$. This is the only stationary point, and as it respects the constraint, it must be the solution to the constrained optimization problem.

However, this method applies only to equality constraints. Fortunately, under some regularity conditions (which are respected by the SVM objectives), this method can be generalized to *inequality constraints* as well (e.g., $3x + 2y + 1 \geq 0$). The *generalized Lagrangian* for the hard margin problem is given by Equation C-1, where the $\alpha^{(i)}$ variables are called the *Karush–Kuhn–Tucker* (KKT) multipliers, and they must be greater or equal to zero.

Equation C-1. Generalized Lagrangian for the hard margin problem

$$\mathcal{L}(\mathbf{w}, b, \alpha) = \frac{1}{2}\mathbf{w}^T\mathbf{w} - \sum_{i=1}^{m} \alpha^{(i)}\left(t^{(i)}\left(\mathbf{w}^T\mathbf{x}^{(i)} + b\right) - 1\right)$$

$$\text{with} \quad \alpha^{(i)} \geq 0 \quad \text{for } i = 1, 2, \cdots, m$$

Just like with the Lagrange multipliers method, you can compute the partial derivatives and locate the stationary points. If there is a solution, it will necessarily be among the stationary points $\left(\widehat{\mathbf{w}}, \hat{b}, \hat{\alpha}\right)$ that respect the *KKT conditions*:

- Respect the problem's constraints: $t^{(i)}\left(\widehat{\mathbf{w}}^T\mathbf{x}^{(i)} + \hat{b}\right) \geq 1 \quad \text{for } i = 1, 2, \ldots, m,$

- Verify $\hat{\alpha}^{(i)} \geq 0 \quad \text{for } i = 1, 2, \cdots, m,$

- Either $\hat{\alpha}^{(i)} = 0$ or the ith constraint must be an *active constraint*, meaning it must hold by equality: $t^{(i)}\left((\widehat{\mathbf{w}})^T\mathbf{x}^{(i)} + \hat{b}\right) = 1$. This condition is called the *complementary slackness* condition. It implies that either $\hat{\alpha}^{(i)} = 0$ or the ith instance lies on the boundary (it is a support vector).

Note that the KKT conditions are necessary conditions for a stationary point to be a solution of the constrained optimization problem. Under some conditions, they are also sufficient conditions. Luckily, the SVM optimization problem happens to meet these conditions, so any stationary point that meets the KKT conditions is guaranteed to be a solution to the constrained optimization problem.

We can compute the partial derivatives of the generalized Lagrangian with regards to $\mathbf{w}$ and b with Equation C-2.

Equation C-2. Partial derivatives of the generalized Lagrangian

$$\nabla_{\mathbf{w}}\mathcal{L}(\mathbf{w}, b, \alpha) = \mathbf{w} - \sum_{i=1}^{m} \alpha^{(i)}t^{(i)}\mathbf{x}^{(i)}$$

$$\frac{\partial}{\partial b}\mathcal{L}(\mathbf{w}, b, \alpha) = -\sum_{i=1}^{m} \alpha^{(i)}t^{(i)}$$

When these partial derivatives are equal to 0, we have Equation C-3.

Equation C-3. Properties of the stationary points

$$\widehat{\mathbf{w}} = \sum_{i=1}^{m} \widehat{\alpha}^{(i)} t^{(i)} \mathbf{x}^{(i)}$$

$$\sum_{i=1}^{m} \widehat{\alpha}^{(i)} t^{(i)} = 0$$

If we plug these results into the definition of the generalized Lagrangian, some terms disappear and we find Equation C-4.

Equation C-4. Dual form of the SVM problem

$$\mathscr{L}\left(\widehat{\mathbf{w}}, \widehat{b}, \alpha\right) = \frac{1}{2} \sum_{i=1}^{m} \sum_{j=1}^{m} \alpha^{(i)} \alpha^{(j)} t^{(i)} t^{(j)} \mathbf{x}^{(i)T} \mathbf{x}^{(j)} \quad - \quad \sum_{i=1}^{m} \alpha^{(i)}$$

$$\text{with} \quad \alpha^{(i)} \geq 0 \quad \text{for} \quad i = 1, 2, \cdots, m$$

The goal is now to find the vector $\widehat{\boldsymbol{\alpha}}$ that minimizes this function, with $\widehat{\alpha}^{(i)} \geq 0$ for all instances. This constrained optimization problem is the dual problem we were looking for.

Once you find the optimal $\widehat{\boldsymbol{\alpha}}$, you can compute $\widehat{\mathbf{w}}$ using the first line of Equation C-3. To compute $\widehat{b}$, you can use the fact that a support vector must verify $t^{(i)}(\widehat{\mathbf{w}}^T \mathbf{x}^{(i)} + \widehat{b}) = 1$, so if the kth instance is a support vector (i.e., $\widehat{\alpha}^{(k)} > 0$), you can use it to compute $\widehat{b} = t^{(k)} - \widehat{\mathbf{w}}^T \mathbf{x}^{(k)}$. However, it is often prefered to compute the average over all support vectors to get a more stable and precise value, as in Equation C-5.

Equation C-5. Bias term estimation using the dual form

$$\widehat{b} = \frac{1}{n_s} \sum_{\substack{i=1 \\ \widehat{\alpha}^{(i)} > 0}}^{m} \left[t^{(i)} - \widehat{\mathbf{w}}^T \mathbf{x}^{(i)} \right]$$

Autodiff

This appendix explains how TensorFlow's autodiff feature works, and how it compares to other solutions.

Suppose you define a function $f(x,y) = x^2y + y + 2$, and you need its partial derivatives $\frac{\partial f}{\partial x}$ and $\frac{\partial f}{\partial y}$, typically to perform Gradient Descent (or some other optimization algorithm). Your main options are manual differentiation, symbolic differentiation, numerical differentiation, forward-mode autodiff, and finally reverse-mode autodiff. TensorFlow implements this last option. Let's go through each of these options.

Manual Differentiation

The first approach is to pick up a pencil and a piece of paper and use your calculus knowledge to derive the partial derivatives manually. For the function $f(x,y)$ just defined, it is not too hard; you just need to use five rules:

- The derivative of a constant is 0.

- The derivative of λx is λ (where λ is a constant).

- The derivative of x^λ is $\lambda x^{\lambda-1}$, so the derivative of x^2 is $2x$.

- The derivative of a sum of functions is the sum of these functions' derivatives.

- The derivative of λ times a function is λ times its derivative.

From these rules, you can derive Equation D-1:

Equation D-1. Partial derivatives of f(x,y)

$$\frac{\partial f}{\partial x} = \frac{\partial\left(x^2 y\right)}{\partial x} + \frac{\partial y}{\partial x} + \frac{\partial 2}{\partial x} = y\frac{\partial\left(x^2\right)}{\partial x} + 0 + 0 = 2xy$$

$$\frac{\partial f}{\partial y} = \frac{\partial\left(x^2 y\right)}{\partial y} + \frac{\partial y}{\partial y} + \frac{\partial 2}{\partial y} = x^2 + 1 + 0 = x^2 + 1$$

This approach can become very tedious for more complex functions, and you run the risk of making mistakes. The good news is that deriving the mathematical equations for the partial derivatives like we just did can be automated, through a process called *symbolic differentiation*.

Symbolic Differentiation

Figure D-1 shows how symbolic differentiation works on an even simpler function, $g(x,y) = 5 + xy$. The graph for that function is represented on the left. After symbolic differentiation, we get the graph on the right, which represents the partial derivative $\frac{\partial g}{\partial x} = 0 + (0 \times x + y \times 1) = y$ (we could similarly obtain the partial derivative with regards to y).

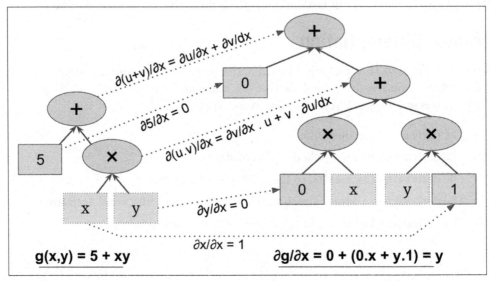

Figure D-1. Symbolic differentiation

The algorithm starts by getting the partial derivative of the leaf nodes. The constant node (5) returns the constant 0, since the derivative of a constant is always 0. The variable x returns the constant 1 since $\frac{\partial x}{\partial x} = 1$, and the variable y returns the constant 0 since $\frac{\partial y}{\partial x} = 0$ (if we were looking for the partial derivative with regards to y, it would be the reverse).

Now we have all we need to move up the graph to the multiplication node in function g. Calculus tells us that the derivative of the product of two functions u and v is $\frac{\partial(u \times v)}{\partial x} = \frac{\partial v}{\partial x} \times u + v \times \frac{\partial u}{\partial x}$. We can therefore construct a large part of the graph on the right, representing $0 \times x + y \times 1$.

Finally, we can go up to the addition node in function g. As mentioned, the derivative of a sum of functions is the sum of these functions' derivatives. So we just need to create an addition node and connect it to the parts of the graph we have already computed. We get the correct partial derivative: $\frac{\partial g}{\partial x} = 0 + (0 \times x + y \times 1)$.

However, it can be simplified (a lot). A few trivial pruning steps can be applied to this graph to get rid of all unnecessary operations, and we get a much smaller graph with just one node: $\frac{\partial g}{\partial x} = y$.

In this case, simplification is fairly easy, but for a more complex function, symbolic differentiation can produce a huge graph that may be tough to simplify and lead to suboptimal performance. Most importantly, symbolic differentiation cannot deal with functions defined with arbitrary code—for example, the following function discussed in Chapter 9:

```python
def my_func(a, b):
    z = 0
    for i in range(100):
        z = a * np.cos(z + i) + z * np.sin(b - i)
    return z
```

Numerical Differentiation

The simplest solution is to compute an approximation of the derivatives, numerically. Recall that the derivative $h'(x_0)$ of a function $h(x)$ at a point x_0 is the slope of the function at that point, or more precisely Equation D-2.

Equation D-2. Derivative of a function $h(x)$ at point x_0

$$h'(x_0) = \lim_{x \to x_0} \frac{h(x) - h(x_0)}{x - x_0}$$

$$= \lim_{\epsilon \to 0} \frac{h(x_0 + \epsilon) - h(x_0)}{\epsilon}$$

So if we want to calculate the partial derivative of $f(x,y)$ with regards to x, at $x = 3$ and $y = 4$, we can simply compute $f(3 + \epsilon, 4) - f(3, 4)$ and divide the result by ϵ, using a very small value for ϵ. That's exactly what the following code does:

```
def f(x, y):
    return x**2*y + y + 2

def derivative(f, x, y, x_eps, y_eps):
    return (f(x + x_eps, y + y_eps) - f(x, y)) / (x_eps + y_eps)

df_dx = derivative(f, 3, 4, 0.00001, 0)
df_dy = derivative(f, 3, 4, 0, 0.00001)
```

Unfortunately, the result is imprecise (and it gets worse for more complex functions). The correct results are respectively 24 and 10, but instead we get:

```
>>> print(df_dx)
24.000039999805264
>>> print(df_dy)
10.000000000331966
```

Notice that to compute both partial derivatives, we have to call `f()` at least three times (we called it four times in the preceding code, but it could be optimized). If there were 1,000 parameters, we would need to call `f()` at least 1,001 times. When you are dealing with large neural networks, this makes numerical differentiation way too inefficient.

However, numerical differentiation is so simple to implement that it is a great tool to check that the other methods are implemented correctly. For example, if it disagrees with your manually derived function, then your function probably contains a mistake.

Forward-Mode Autodiff

Forward-mode autodiff is neither numerical differentiation nor symbolic differentiation, but in some ways it is their love child. It relies on *dual numbers*, which are (weird but fascinating) numbers of the form $a + b\epsilon$ where a and b are real numbers and ϵ is an infinitesimal number such that $\epsilon^2 = 0$ (but $\epsilon \neq 0$). You can think of the dual number $42 + 24\epsilon$ as something akin to $42.0000\cdots000024$ with an infinite number of 0s (but of course this is simplified just to give you some idea of what dual numbers are). A dual number is represented in memory as a pair of floats. For example, $42 + 24\epsilon$ is represented by the pair (42.0, 24.0).

Dual numbers can be added, multiplied, and so on, as shown in Equation D-3.

Equation D-3. A few operations with dual numbers

$$\lambda(a + b\epsilon) = \lambda a + \lambda b\epsilon$$
$$(a + b\epsilon) + (c + d\epsilon) = (a + c) + (b + d)\epsilon$$
$$(a + b\epsilon) \times (c + d\epsilon) = ac + (ad + bc)\epsilon + (bd)\epsilon^2 = ac + (ad + bc)\epsilon$$

Most importantly, it can be shown that $h(a + b\epsilon) = h(a) + b \times h'(a)\epsilon$, so computing $h(a + \epsilon)$ gives you both $h(a)$ and the derivative $h'(a)$ in just one shot. Figure D-2 shows how forward-mode autodiff computes the partial derivative of $f(x,y)$ with regards to x at $x = 3$ and $y = 4$. All we need to do is compute $f(3 + \epsilon, 4)$; this will output a dual number whose first component is equal to $f(3, 4)$ and whose second component is equal to $\frac{\partial f}{\partial x}(3, 4)$.

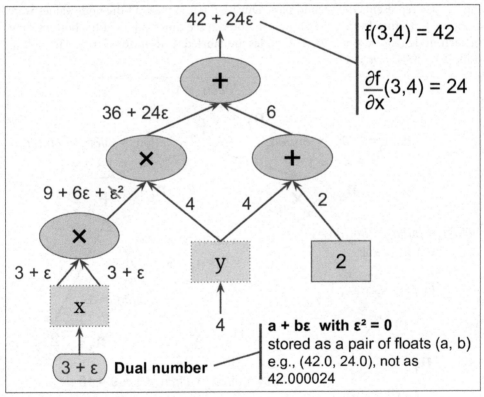

Figure D-2. Forward-mode autodiff

To compute $\frac{\partial f}{\partial y}(3, 4)$ we would have to go through the graph again, but this time with $x = 3$ and $y = 4 + \epsilon$.

So forward-mode autodiff is much more accurate than numerical differentiation, but it suffers from the same major flaw: if there were 1,000 parameters, it would require 1,000 passes through the graph to compute all the partial derivatives. This is where reverse-mode autodiff shines: it can compute all of them in just two passes through the graph.

Reverse-Mode Autodiff

Reverse-mode autodiff is the solution implemented by TensorFlow. It first goes through the graph in the forward direction (i.e., from the inputs to the output) to compute the value of each node. Then it does a second pass, this time in the reverse direction (i.e., from the output to the inputs) to compute all the partial derivatives. Figure D-3 represents the second pass. During the first pass, all the node values were computed, starting from $x = 3$ and $y = 4$. You can see those values at the bottom right of each node (e.g., $x \times x = 9$). The nodes are labeled n_1 to n_7 for clarity. The output node is n_7: $f(3,4) = n_7 = 42$.

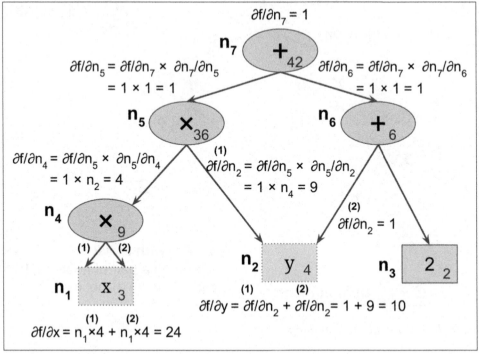

Figure D-3. Reverse-mode autodiff

The idea is to gradually go down the graph, computing the partial derivative of $f(x,y)$ with regards to each consecutive node, until we reach the variable nodes. For this, reverse-mode autodiff relies heavily on the *chain rule*, shown in Equation D-4.

Equation D-4. Chain rule

$$\frac{\partial f}{\partial x} = \frac{\partial f}{\partial n_i} \times \frac{\partial n_i}{\partial x}$$

Since n_7 is the output node, $f = n_7$ so trivially $\frac{\partial f}{\partial n_7} = 1$.

Let's continue down the graph to n_5: how much does f vary when n_5 varies? The answer is $\frac{\partial f}{\partial n_5} = \frac{\partial f}{\partial n_7} \times \frac{\partial n_7}{\partial n_5}$. We already know that $\frac{\partial f}{\partial n_7} = 1$, so all we need is $\frac{\partial n_7}{\partial n_5}$. Since n_7 simply performs the sum $n_5 + n_6$, we find that $\frac{\partial n_7}{\partial n_5} = 1$, so $\frac{\partial f}{\partial n_5} = 1 \times 1 = 1$.

Now we can proceed to node n_4: how much does f vary when n_4 varies? The answer is $\frac{\partial f}{\partial n_4} = \frac{\partial f}{\partial n_5} \times \frac{\partial n_5}{\partial n_4}$. Since $n_5 = n_4 \times n_2$, we find that $\frac{\partial n_5}{\partial n_4} = n_2$, so $\frac{\partial f}{\partial n_4} = 1 \times n_2 = 4$.

The process continues until we reach the bottom of the graph. At that point we will have calculated all the partial derivatives of $f(x,y)$ at the point $x = 3$ and $y = 4$. In this example, we find $\frac{\partial f}{\partial x} = 24$ and $\frac{\partial f}{\partial y} = 10$. Sounds about right!

Reverse-mode autodiff is a very powerful and accurate technique, especially when there are many inputs and few outputs, since it requires only one forward pass plus one reverse pass per output to compute all the partial derivatives for all outputs with regards to all the inputs. Most importantly, it can deal with functions defined by arbitrary code. It can also handle functions that are not entirely differentiable, as long as you ask it to compute the partial derivatives at points that are differentiable.

If you implement a new type of operation in TensorFlow and you want to make it compatible with autodiff, then you need to provide a function that builds a subgraph to compute its partial derivatives with regards to its inputs. For example, suppose you implement a function that computes the square of its input $f(x) = x^2$. In that case you would need to provide the corresponding derivative function $f'(x) = 2x$. Note that this function does not compute a numerical result, but instead builds a subgraph that will (later) compute the result. This is very useful because it means that you can compute gradients of gradients (to compute second-order derivatives, or even higher-order derivatives).

Other Popular ANN Architectures

In this appendix we will give a quick overview of a few historically important neural network architectures that are much less used today than deep Multi-Layer Perceptrons (Chapter 10), convolutional neural networks (Chapter 13), recurrent neural networks (Chapter 14), or autoencoders (Chapter 15). They are often mentioned in the literature, and some are still used in many applications, so it is worth knowing about them. Moreover, we will discuss *deep belief nets* (DBNs), which were the state of the art in Deep Learning until the early 2010s. They are still the subject of very active research, so they may well come back with a vengeance in the near future.

Hopfield Networks

Hopfield networks were first introduced by W. A. Little in 1974, then popularized by J. Hopfield in 1982. They are *associative memory* networks: you first teach them some patterns, and then when they see a new pattern they (hopefully) output the closest learned pattern. This has made them useful in particular for character recognition before they were outperformed by other approaches. You first train the network by showing it examples of character images (each binary pixel maps to one neuron), and then when you show it a new character image, after a few iterations it outputs the closest learned character.

They are fully connected graphs (see Figure E-1); that is, every neuron is connected to every other neuron. Note that on the diagram the images are 6 × 6 pixels, so the neural network on the left should contain 36 neurons (and 630 connections), but for visual clarity a much smaller network is represented.

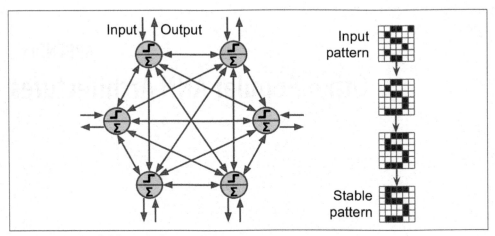

Figure E-1. Hopfield network

The training algorithm works by using Hebb's rule: for each training image, the weight between two neurons is increased if the corresponding pixels are both on or both off, but decreased if one pixel is on and the other is off.

To show a new image to the network, you just activate the neurons that correspond to active pixels. The network then computes the output of every neuron, and this gives you a new image. You can then take this new image and repeat the whole process. After a while, the network reaches a stable state. Generally, this corresponds to the training image that most resembles the input image.

A so-called *energy function* is associated with Hopfield nets. At each iteration, the energy decreases, so the network is guaranteed to eventually stabilize to a low-energy state. The training algorithm tweaks the weights in a way that decreases the energy level of the training patterns, so the network is likely to stabilize in one of these low-energy configurations. Unfortunately, some patterns that were not in the training set also end up with low energy, so the network sometimes stabilizes in a configuration that was not learned. These are called *spurious patterns*.

Another major flaw with Hopfield nets is that they don't scale very well—their memory capacity is roughly equal to 14% of the number of neurons. For example, to classify 28 × 28 images, you would need a Hopfield net with 784 fully connected neurons and 306,936 weights. Such a network would only be able to learn about 110 different characters (14% of 784). That's a lot of parameters for such a small memory.

Boltzmann Machines

Boltzmann machines were invented in 1985 by Geoffrey Hinton and Terrence Sejnowski. Just like Hopfield nets, they are fully connected ANNs, but they are based on *sto-*

chastic neurons: instead of using a deterministic step function to decide what value to output, these neurons output 1 with some probability, and 0 otherwise. The probability function that these ANNs use is based on the Boltzmann distribution (used in statistical mechanics) hence their name. Equation E-1 gives the probability that a particular neuron will output a 1.

Equation E-1. Probability that the ith neuron will output 1

$$p\left(s_i^{(\text{next step})} = 1\right) = \sigma\left(\frac{\sum_{j=1}^{N} w_{i,j} s_j + b_i}{T}\right)$$

- s_j is the jth neuron's state (0 or 1).
- $w_{i,j}$ is the connection weight between the ith and j^{th} neurons. Note that $w_{i,i} = 0$.
- b_i is the ith neuron's bias term. We can implement this term by adding a bias neuron to the network.
- N is the number of neurons in the network.
- T is a number called the network's *temperature*; the higher the temperature, the more random the output is (i.e., the more the probability approaches 50%).
- σ is the logistic function.

Neurons in Boltzmann machines are separated into two groups: *visible units* and *hidden units* (see Figure E-2). All neurons work in the same stochastic way, but the visible units are the ones that receive the inputs and from which outputs are read.

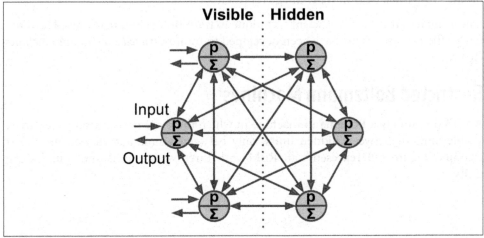

Figure E-2. Boltzmann machine

Because of its stochastic nature, a Boltzmann machine will never stabilize into a fixed configuration, but instead it will keep switching between many configurations. If it is left running for a sufficiently long time, the probability of observing a particular configuration will only be a function of the connection weights and bias terms, not of the original configuration (similarly, after you shuffle a deck of cards for long enough, the configuration of the deck does not depend on the initial state). When the network reaches this state where the original configuration is "forgotten," it is said to be in *thermal equilibrium* (although its configuration keeps changing all the time). By setting the network parameters appropriately, letting the network reach thermal equilibrium, and then observing its state, we can simulate a wide range of probability distributions. This is called a *generative model*.

Training a Boltzmann machine means finding the parameters that will make the network approximate the training set's probability distribution. For example, if there are three visible neurons and the training set contains 75% (0, 1, 1) triplets, 10% (0, 0, 1) triplets, and 15% (1, 1, 1) triplets, then after training a Boltzmann machine, you could use it to generate random binary triplets with about the same probability distribution. For example, about 75% of the time it would output the (0, 1, 1) triplet.

Such a generative model can be used in a variety of ways. For example, if it is trained on images, and you provide an incomplete or noisy image to the network, it will automatically "repair" the image in a reasonable way. You can also use a generative model for classification. Just add a few visible neurons to encode the training image's class (e.g., add 10 visible neurons and turn on only the fifth neuron when the training image represents a 5). Then, when given a new image, the network will automatically turn on the appropriate visible neurons, indicating the image's class (e.g., it will turn on the fifth visible neuron if the image represents a 5).

Unfortunately, there is no efficient technique to train Boltzmann machines. However, fairly efficient algorithms have been developed to train *restricted Boltzmann machines* (RBM).

Restricted Boltzmann Machines

An RBM is simply a Boltzmann machine in which there are no connections between visible units or between hidden units, only between visible and hidden units. For example, Figure E-3 represents an RBM with three visible units and four hidden units.

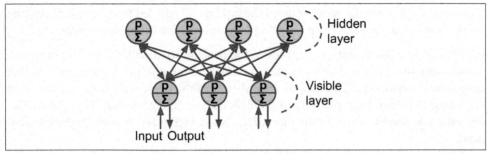

Figure E-3. Restricted Boltzmann machine

A very efficient training algorithm, called *Contrastive Divergence*, was introduced in 2005 by Miguel Á. Carreira-Perpiñán and Geoffrey Hinton (*http://homl.info/135*).[1] Here is how it works: for each training instance **x**, the algorithm starts by feeding it to the network by setting the state of the visible units to $x_1, x_2, \cdots, x_n$. Then you compute the state of the hidden units by applying the stochastic equation described before (Equation E-1). This gives you a hidden vector **h** (where h_i is equal to the state of the ith unit). Next you compute the state of the visible units, by applying the same stochastic equation. This gives you a vector **x′**. Then once again you compute the state of the hidden units, which gives you a vector **h′**. Now you can update each connection weight by applying the rule in Equation E-2, where η is the learning rate.

Equation E-2. Contrastive divergence weight update

$$w_{i,j} \leftarrow w_{i,j} + \eta\left(\mathbf{x}\mathbf{h}^T - \mathbf{x'}\mathbf{h'}^T\right)$$

The great benefit of this algorithm it that it does not require waiting for the network to reach thermal equilibrium: it just goes forward, backward, and forward again, and that's it. This makes it incomparably more efficient than previous algorithms, and it was a key ingredient to the first success of Deep Learning based on multiple stacked RBMs.

Deep Belief Nets

Several layers of RBMs can be stacked; the hidden units of the first-level RBM serves as the visible units for the second-layer RBM, and so on. Such an RBM stack is called a *deep belief net* (DBN).

Yee-Whye Teh, one of Geoffrey Hinton's students, observed that it was possible to train DBNs one layer at a time using Contrastive Divergence, starting with the lower

---

[1] "On Contrastive Divergence Learning," M. Á. Carreira-Perpiñán and G. Hinton (2005).

layers and then gradually moving up to the top layers. This led to the groundbreaking article that kickstarted the Deep Learning tsunami in 2006 (*http://homl.info/136*).[2]

Just like RBMs, DBNs learn to reproduce the probability distribution of their inputs, without any supervision. However, they are much better at it, for the same reason that deep neural networks are more powerful than shallow ones: real-world data is often organized in hierarchical patterns, and DBNs take advantage of that. Their lower layers learn low-level features in the input data, while higher layers learn high-level features.

Just like RBMs, DBNs are fundamentally unsupervised, but you can also train them in a supervised manner by adding some visible units to represent the labels. Moreover, one great feature of DBNs is that they can be trained in a semisupervised fashion. Figure E-4 represents such a DBN configured for semisupervised learning.

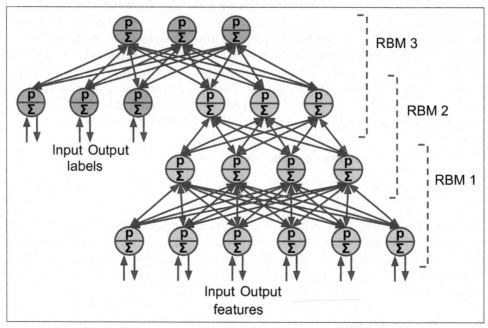

Figure E-4. A deep belief network configured for semisupervised learning

First, the RBM 1 is trained without supervision. It learns low-level features in the training data. Then RBM 2 is trained with RBM 1's hidden units as inputs, again without supervision: it learns higher-level features (note that RBM 2's hidden units include only the three rightmost units, not the label units). Several more RBMs could be stacked this way, but you get the idea. So far, training was 100% unsupervised.

---

2 "A Fast Learning Algorithm for Deep Belief Nets," G. Hinton, S. Osindero, Y. Teh (2006).

Lastly, RBM 3 is trained using both RBM 2's hidden units as inputs, as well as extra visible units used to represent the target labels (e.g., a one-hot vector representing the instance class). It learns to associate high-level features with training labels. This is the supervised step.

At the end of training, if you feed RBM 1 a new instance, the signal will propagate up to RBM 2, then up to the top of RBM 3, and then back down to the label units; hopefully, the appropriate label will light up. This is how a DBN can be used for classification.

One great benefit of this semisupervised approach is that you don't need much labeled training data. If the unsupervised RBMs do a good enough job, then only a small amount of labeled training instances per class will be necessary. Similarly, a baby learns to recognize objects without supervision, so when you point to a chair and say "chair," the baby can associate the word "chair" with the class of objects it has already learned to recognize on its own. You don't need to point to every single chair and say "chair"; only a few examples will suffice (just enough so the baby can be sure that you are indeed referring to the chair, not to its color or one of the chair's parts).

Quite amazingly, DBNs can also work in reverse. If you activate one of the label units, the signal will propagate up to the hidden units of RBM 3, then down to RBM 2, and then RBM 1, and a new instance will be output by the visible units of RBM 1. This new instance will usually look like a regular instance of the class whose label unit you activated. This generative capability of DBNs is quite powerful. For example, it has been used to automatically generate captions for images, and vice versa: first a DBN is trained (without supervision) to learn features in images, and another DBN is trained (again without supervision) to learn features in sets of captions (e.g., "car" often comes with "automobile"). Then an RBM is stacked on top of both DBNs and trained with a set of images along with their captions; it learns to associate high-level features in images with high-level features in captions. Next, if you feed the image DBN an image of a car, the signal will propagate through the network, up to the top-level RBM, and back down to the bottom of the caption DBN, producing a caption. Due to the stochastic nature of RBMs and DBNs, the caption will keep changing randomly, but it will generally be appropriate for the image. If you generate a few hundred captions, the most frequently generated ones will likely be a good description of the image.[3]

Self-Organizing Maps

Self-organizing maps (SOM) are quite different from all the other types of neural networks we have discussed so far. They are used to produce a low-dimensional repre-

---

3 See this video by Geoffrey Hinton for more details and a demo: *http://homl.info/137*.

sentation of a high-dimensional dataset, generally for visualization, clustering, or classification. The neurons are spread across a map (typically 2D for visualization, but it can be any number of dimensions you want), as shown in Figure E-5, and each neuron has a weighted connection to every input (note that the diagram shows just two inputs, but there are typically a very large number, since the whole point of SOMs is to reduce dimensionality).

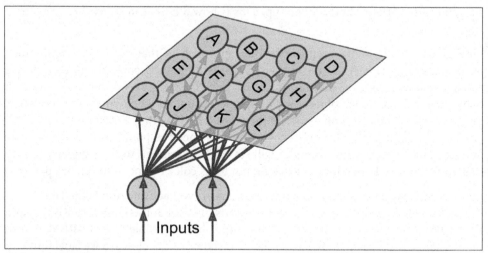

Figure E-5. Self-organizing maps

Once the network is trained, you can feed it a new instance and this will activate only one neuron (i.e., hence one point on the map): the neuron whose weight vector is closest to the input vector. In general, instances that are nearby in the original input space will activate neurons that are nearby on the map. This makes SOMs useful for visualization (in particular, you can easily identify clusters on the map), but also for applications like speech recognition. For example, if each instance represents the audio recording of a person pronouncing a vowel, then different pronunciations of the vowel "a" will activate neurons in the same area of the map, while instances of the vowel "e" will activate neurons in another area, and intermediate sounds will generally activate intermediate neurons on the map.

 One important difference with the other dimensionality reduction techniques discussed in Chapter 8 is that all instances get mapped to a discrete number of points in the low-dimensional space (one point per neuron). When there are very few neurons, this technique is better described as clustering rather than dimensionality reduction.

The training algorithm is unsupervised. It works by having all the neurons compete against each other. First, all the weights are initialized randomly. Then a training instance is picked randomly and fed to the network. All neurons compute the distance between their weight vector and the input vector (this is very different from the artificial neurons we have seen so far). The neuron that measures the smallest distance wins and tweaks its weight vector to be even slightly closer to the input vector, making it more likely to win future competitions for other inputs similar to this one. It also recruits its neighboring neurons, and they too update their weight vector to be slightly closer to the input vector (but they don't update their weights as much as the winner neuron). Then the algorithm picks another training instance and repeats the process, again and again. This algorithm tends to make nearby neurons gradually specialize in similar inputs.[4]

---

4 You can imagine a class of young children with roughly similar skills. One child happens to be slightly better at basketball. This motivates her to practice more, especially with her friends. After a while, this group of friends gets so good at basketball that other kids cannot compete. But that's okay, because the other kids specialize in other topics. After a while, the class is full of little specialized groups.

Index

VGGNet, 383
visual cortex, 362
visualization, 244-247
visualization algorithms, 11-12
voice recognition, 361
voting classifiers, 183-186

W

warmup phase, 356
weak learners, 184
weight-tying, 427
weights, 271
    freezing, 294
while_loop(), 395
white box models, 172

worker, 330
worker service, 332
worker_device, 334
workspace directory, 40-43

X

Xavier initialization, 280-283

Y

YouTube, 257

Z

zero padding, 364, 369

About the Author

Aurélien Géron is a Machine Learning consultant. A former Googler, he led the YouTube video classification team from 2013 to 2016. He was also a founder and CTO of Wifirst from 2002 to 2012, a leading Wireless ISP in France; and a founder and CTO of Polyconseil in 2001, the firm that now manages the electric car sharing service Autolib'.

Before this he worked as an engineer in a variety of domains: finance (JP Morgan and Société Générale), defense (Canada's DOD), and healthcare (blood transfusion). He published a few technical books (on C++, WiFi, and internet architectures), and was a Computer Science lecturer in a French engineering school.

A few fun facts: he taught his three children to count in binary with their fingers (up to 1023), he studied microbiology and evolutionary genetics before going into software engineering, and his parachute didn't open on the second jump.

Colophon

The animal on the cover of *Hands-On Machine Learning with Scikit-Learn and TensorFlow* is the far eastern fire salamander (*Salamandra infraimmaculata*), an amphibian found in the Middle East. They have black skin featuring large yellow spots on their back and head. These spots are a warning coloration meant to keep predators at bay. Full-grown salamanders can be over a foot in length.

Far eastern fire salamanders live in subtropical shrubland and forests near rivers or other freshwater bodies. They spend most of their life on land, but lay their eggs in the water. They subsist mostly on a diet of insects, worms, and small crustaceans, but occasionally eat other salamanders. Males of the species have been known to live up to 23 years, while females can live up to 21 years.

Although not yet endangered, the far eastern fire salamander population is in decline. Primary threats include damming of rivers (which disrupts the salamander's breeding) and pollution. They are also threatened by the recent introduction of predatory fish, such as the mosquitofish. These fish were intended to control the mosquito population, but they also feed on young salamanders.

Many of the animals on O'Reilly covers are endangered; all of them are important to the world. To learn more about how you can help, go to *animals.oreilly.com*.

The cover image is from *Wood's Illustrated Natural History*. The cover fonts are URW Typewriter and Guardian Sans. The text font is Adobe Minion Pro; the heading font is Adobe Myriad Condensed; and the code font is Dalton Maag's Ubuntu Mono.